GLOBAL BANKING, FINANCIAL MARKETS AND CRISES

INTERNATIONAL FINANCE REVIEW

Series Editor: J. Jay Choi

International Finance Review publishes theme-oriented volumes on various issues in international finance, such as international business finance, international investment and capital markets, global risk management, international corporate governance and institution, currency markets, emerging market finance, international economic integration, and related issues in international financial economics.

Volume 5:	Latin American Financial Markets: Developments in Financial Innovations, Edited by Harvey Arbeláez and Reid W. Click, 2004, Elsevier Science (ISBN 0-7623-1163-0)
Volume 6:	Emerging European Financial Markets: Independence and Integration Post-Enlargement, Edited by J. A. Batten and C. Kearney, 2006, Elsevier Science (ISBN 0-7623-1264-5)
Volume 7:	Value Creation in Multinational Enterprise, Edited by J. Jay Choi and Reid W. Click, 2007, Elsevier Science (ISBN 0-7623-1392-7)
Volume 8:	Asia-Pacific Financial Markets: Integration, Innovation and Challenges, Edited by Suk-Joong Kim and Michael McKenzie, 2008, Elsevier Science (ISBN 978-0-7623-1471-3)
Volume 9:	Institutional Approach to Global Corporate Governance: Business Systems and Beyond, Edited by J. Jay Choi and Sandra Dow, 2008, Emerald Publishing (ISBN 978-1-84855-320-0)
Volume 10:	Currency, Credit and Crisis: In Search of Financial Stability, Edited by J. Jay Choi and Michael G. Papaioannou, Emerald Publishing, 2009, Emerald Publishing (ISBN 978-1-84950-601-4)
Volume 11:	International Banking in the New Era: Post-Crisis Challenges and Opportunities, Edited by Suk-Joong Kim and Michael D. McKenzie, 2010, Emerald Publishing, 2010 (ISBN: 978-1-84950-912-1)
Volume 12:	Institutional Investors in Global Capital Markets, Edited by Narjess Boubakri and Jean-Claude Cosset, 2011, Emerald Publishing, 2011 (ISBN: 978-1-78052-242-5)
Volume 13:	Transparency and Governance in a Global World, Edited by J. Jay Choi and Heibatollah Sami, 2012, Emerald Publishing, 2012 (ISBN: 978-1-78052-764-2)

INTERNATIONAL FINANCE REVIEW VOLUME 14

GLOBAL BANKING, FINANCIAL MARKETS AND CRISES

EDITED BY

BANG NAM JEON
Drexel University, USA

MARÍA PÍA OLIVERO
Drexel University, USA

United Kingdom – North America – Japan
India – Malaysia – China

Emerald Group Publishing Limited
Howard House, Wagon Lane, Bingley BD16 1WA, UK

First edition 2013

British Library Cataloguing in Publication Data
A catalogue record for this book is available from the British Library

ISBN: 978-1-78350-170-0
ISSN: 1569-3767 (Series)

ISOQAR
REGISTERED
Certificate Number 1985
ISO 14001

ISOQAR certified Management System, awarded to Emerald for adherence to Environmental standard ISO 14001:2004.

INVESTOR IN PEOPLE

CONTENTS

LIST OF CONTRIBUTORS

Arnelyn Abdon	Asian Development Bank, Manila, Philippines
Franklin Allen	The Wharton School of the University of Pennsylvania, Philadelphia, PA, USA
Jonathan A. Batten	Department of Banking and Finance, Monash University, Victoria, Australia
Hongyi Chen	Hong Kong Institute for Monetary Research, Hong Kong, P.R. China
Qianying Chen	Hong Kong Institute for Monetary Research, Hong Kong, P.R. China
Sheng-Hung Chen	Department of Finance, Nanhua University, Taiwan
Panagiotis Dontis-Charitos	Westminster Business School, London, UK
Hae Jin Chung	College of Business, Korea Advanced Institute of Science and Technology (KAIST), Seoul, Korea
Gemma Estrada	Asian Development Bank, Manila, Philippines
Arturo J. Galindo	Inter-American Development Bank, Washington, DC, USA
Stefan Gerlach	Central Bank of Ireland and the CEPR, Dublin, Ireland
Orla Gough	Westminster Business School, London, UK
Xian Gu	The Wharton Financial Institutions Center, Philadelphia, PA, USA

Alejandro Izquierdo Inter-American Development Bank, Washington, DC, USA

Eunyoung Jang College of Business, Korea Advanced Institute of Science and Technology (KAIST), Seoul, Korea

Bang Nam Jeon Department of Economics and International Business, Bennett S. LeBow College of Business, Drexel University, Philadelphia, PA, USA

Hatice Gokce Karasoy Central Bank of the Republic of Turkey, Ankara, Turkey

Zubeyir Kilinc Central Bank of the Republic of Turkey, Ankara, Turkey

Jinyong Kim College of Business, Korea Advanced Institute of Science and Technology (KAIST), Seoul, Korea

Suk-Joong Kim University of Sydney Business School, The University of Sydney, Sydney, NSW, Australia

Yong-Cheol Kim Department of Finance, Sheldon B. Lubar School of Business, University of Wisconsin, Milwaukee, WI, USA

Oskar Kowalewski Kozminski University, Department of Banking and Insurance, Warsaw, Poland

Linda Lee School of Banking and Finance, The University of New South Wales, Kensington, NSW, Australia

Minsoo Lee Asian Development Bank, Manila, Philippines

Igor Loncarski Faculty of Economics, University of Ljubljana, Slovenia

K. Ben Nowman Westminster Business School, London, UK

María Pía Olivero	Department of Economics and International Business, Bennett S. LeBow College of Business, Drexel University, Philadelphia, PA, USA
Donghyun Park	Asian Development Bank, Manila, Philippines
Kwangwoo Park	College of Business, Korea Advanced Institute of Science and Technology (KAIST), Seoul, Korea
Jungsoo Park	School of Economics, Sogang University, Seoul, Korea
Liliana Rojas-Suarez	Center for Global Deveopment, Washington, DC, USA
Hyun-Han Shin	School of Business, Yonsei University, Seoul, Korea
Sheeja Sivaprasad	Westminster Business School, London, UK
Jeong Ho Suh	Korea Institute of Finance, Seoul, Korea
Vighneswara Swamy	IBS-Hyderabad, Hyderabad, India
Peter G. Szilagyi	Judge Business School, University of Cambridge, Cambridge, UK
Honglin Wang	Hong Kong Institute for Monetary Research, Hong Kong, P.R. China
Eliza Wu	Finance Discipline Group, UTS Business School, University of Technology Sydney, Sydney, NSW, Australia
Ji Wu	The Research Institute of Economics and Management (RIEM), Southwestern University of Finance and Economics, Sichuan, P.R. China
Aidan Yao	Hong Kong Monetary Authority, Hong Kong, P.R. China
Eray Yucel	TOBB University of Economics and Technology, Ankara, Turkey

PART I
AN OVERVIEW

AN OVERVIEW: GLOBAL BANKING AND FINANCIAL MARKETS IN CRISIS

Bang Nam Jeon and María Pía Olivero

One of the most salient features of the 2007–2009 global financial crisis was the role that multinational banks played in transmitting international financial shocks and in affecting credit stability in global banking. The literature has argued that through both cross-border lending and the use of their internal capital markets, global banks have played a central role in the 'sudden stop' or 'reversal' of global capital flows from developed countries to emerging economies, and in the transmission of the crisis effects. Moreover, arguably foreign banks have been observed to increase the volatility of credit and to raise various concerns on the effectiveness of the monetary policy transmission mechanism during crises in host emerging economies.

A better understanding of global banking and its interaction with domestic financial markets is needed for the design of optimal policy responses to control contagion of crises from abroad and for harmonizing the occasional conflict of interest between multinational banks and policy makers in the host economies. The 14th volume of "International Finance Review" which we title *Global Banking, Financial Markets and Crises* aims to meet this important need. This volume consists of five parts: An Overview (Part I), Global Banking and Crises (Part II), Financial Markets and Crises (Part III), Crisis Spillovers to Emerging Economies (Part IV), and Policy Implications and Lessons (Part V).

In Part I, we provide a summary of this volume and highlight the most important contributions in each chapter.

Part II deals with the relationship between global banking and financial crises. Within this relationship the contributors for this part take on the issues of cross-border baking, monetary policy implementation and interbank markets, the relationship between noncore liabilities in banks' balance sheets and credit growth, the role played by foreign bank penetration in the implementation of monetary policy in emerging economies, risk-taking and profitability by super-size banks, and the determinants of productivity in global banking in crises, among others.

Taking on a context in which banks are motivated to internationalize to provide better services to their customers worldwide as well as to diversify balance sheet risks and to insulate from domestic shocks, Batten, Loncarski, and Szilagyi study cross-border banking within Europe. By looking at the international exposures of assets and liabilities of BIS reporting banks during recent episodes of financial crisis, both worldwide and within Europe's core and peripheral countries, Batten et al. provide evidence of these banks responding to crises through better matching of their international assets and liabilities to reduce balance sheet risks. Their research contributes to better understanding how international banking responds to crises in the management of international balance sheet positions of banks and how international banking may contribute to domestic and international financial stability.

Chen, Chen, and Gerlach focus on the implementation of monetary policy by the People's Bank of China, which, differently from what is the case with other central banks in advanced economies, uses different instruments to influence liquidity in money markets and to intervene in the retail deposit and loan markets. For the former, Chinese monetary authorities use changes in the required reserve ratios and open market operations. For the latter, they adjust the regulated deposit and lending rates and loan targets. It is a crucial contribution to study the particularities of monetary policy in China in light of previous findings in the literature that the interest rate channel of policy transmission is at most weak in China, and that retail lending and money market rates do not exhibit a predictable relationship with loan and money growth. With this goal, Chen et al. present a model based on those of Porter and Xu (2009) and Freixas and Rochet (2008) that integrate regulated deposit and lending rates with a competitive interbank market. Specifically, Chen et al. study the effects of policy on both interbank and retail lending rates, since interbank money market rates are insufficient and even potentially misleading indicators of the stance of monetary policy. Further, they conclude that by combining alternative policy instruments simultaneously within a short period of time, the People's Bank of China was able to effectively impact both money and credit growth and to control inflation. For example, during the recent global financial crisis, the central bank of China, which faced large capital inflows and inflationary pressure, raised the required reserve ratio 12 times to unprecedentedly high 21.5%, and raised lending rates and deposit rates of banks 5 times, which were successful in bring inflation under control. The research by Chen et al. contributes to our better understanding of different options for monetary policy implementation in an emerging economy of China in crises, in particular.

The state of bank leverage, and in particular, the composition of bank liabilities, has captured a lot of attention after the global financial crisis. When households' savings rates decline and the demand for credit increases as a result of the crisis, banks tend to resort to noncore liabilities (including those held by other financial intermediaries and foreign creditors) to meet the excess demand for loans. Kilinc, Karasoy, and Yucel take on this issue for the particular case of the small open economy of Turkey. They are able to provide the following consistent evidence on the robust relationship between noncore bank liabilities and credit growth: In both the short-run and the long-run, credit growth pulls noncore liabilities.

Jeon and Wu study the role that foreign bank penetration plays in the implementation of monetary policy in Asia during periods of financial crisis, including both the Asian crisis of 1997–1999 and the global crisis of 2008–2009. They find that foreign banks are slower than domestic banks in adjusting the growth of their loans to monetary policy shocks in the host country. They provide evidence that foreign banks' different patterns of responses to crises from domestic banks were more pronounced in the recent 2008–2009 global crisis than in the 1997–1999 Asian financial crisis. Importantly, this effect is also heterogeneous across banks, depending on the state of parent banks' balance sheets, their scope of operation, and mode of entry into the host countries, among other factors. These findings can be interpreted as saying that foreign bank penetration reduces the effectiveness of domestic monetary policy, and this adverse effect of foreign banks becomes more conspicuous during the global crisis period than during the regional crisis period. In our view this provides an important contribution, due to the implications of these results, for the surveillance of foreign banks and search for the optimal monetary policy implementation in emerging economies with growing or high foreign bank penetration, in particular.

Kim and Kim study bank holding companies in the United States during the period 2000–2010, and document that a small number of big banks become super-sized and these big banks seem to take more risk evidenced by holding derivatives for trading purposes. They also present empirical evidence, however, that overall the risk-taking large banks have not experienced either higher risk-adjusted return performance or reduced risk. The study by Kim and Kim sheds some light on recently discussed issues on the too-big-to-fail proposition and increasing risk-taking behavior by the largest U.S. banks in crises.

Chen studies the determinants of productivity in the banking sector as they relate in particular to the degree of banking competition, bank regulation, and the global financial crisis. Using a cross-country bank-level dataset for 82 countries during the period 2004–2012, Chen is able to show that bank productivity is enhanced through increased market competition and foreign bank penetration, the three pillars of capital market regulations in Basel II, and tighter bank supervision (that allows private agents to overcome transaction costs and those derived from informational asymmetries). Chen identifies other factors that enhance bank productivity during the sample period, such as the imposition of restrictions of banks activities relating to securities, insurance, real estate and ownership of nonfinancial firms, better national governance, and increased financial stability. On the negative side, Chen documents the significantly negative impact that the global financial crisis had on banks' productivity performance.

Part III deals with the relationship among global stock markets, financial markets, and financial crises. The current state of the global economic system and the nature of systemic risk such that it transcends sectoral boundaries grant the importance of studying the interdependencies among economic sectors. They are of outmost importance for regulators and policymakers alike. Thus, Part III complements Part II, which focused on the banking sector, by analyzing the relationship between banking and other "actors" in the economy. One important aspect of this relationship that we selected to publish in this volume is the impact of monetary policy news on the stock market. In particular, the segment of a stock market that is likely to be most sensitive to this news is the commercial banking sector due to its role in managing balance sheet mismatches of interest rate-sensitive assets and liabilities. Another aspect is given by the return and volatility spillovers from the banking sector to the stock market. Also, in this section we publish a very relevant study that informs readers about a program that should play an important role in channeling Chinese capital to global financial markets as China becomes more integrated into the world economy.

Kim, Lee, and Wu study the effects of monetary policy news coming from the two most influential central banks in the world (the Fed and the ECB) on the two largest banking sectors in the world (those in the United States and Germany) during the period 1995–2009. Their findings suggest that monetary policy shocks in the United States have the most influence on both U.S. and German listed bank stocks, through unexpected shocks' lowering stock returns and raising their volatility. On the other hand, ECB news affects volatility in the United States but has little domestic impact. In our view, Kim et al.'s main contribution is to consider the significant information leadership of U.S. stock markets and to build on previous work by studying the effects of monetary policy news internationally, and not just domestically. They show that while the global financial crisis increased the sensitivity of all banks to monetary shocks, since the German and the U.S. banking industries respond heterogeneously to monetary shocks, the German and U.S. banking industries have largely decoupled from each other during the global financial crisis. Also, Kim et al.'s results call for greater transparency and timely communication from central banks to reduce the likelihood of disruptions in domestic as well as global financial markets.

Yao and Wang study the Qualified Domestic Institutional Investor (QDII) Scheme in China, which was instituted in 2007 to help Chinese investors participate in foreign capital markets. Since then, the fund has experienced significant losses and capital outflows. The authors conclude that the main reason behind the fund's poor performance is the lack of knowledge by the average investor to manage a global portfolio. Also, the "Hong-Kong bias" in the fund is consistent with the well-known home-bias effect in cross-border portfolio investment, and it is greatly exacerbated by the lack of global investing experience of QDII managers. Looking ahead, given the clear increasing trend in capital market openness, it is highly likely that outward portfolio investment from China will rise in the coming years (He, Cheung, Zhang, & Wu, 2012). Yao and Wang argue that to capitalize on this growth, the industry needs to first address its existing problems and to regain investors trust. They propose that Chinese authorities can play two important roles here to overcome the challenges facing the QDII industry: first, a role in increasing the size of the QDII program. Second, a role in making it more diversified by encouraging and providing tax incentives to large institutions to invest in QDII funds, raising eligibility requirements for QDII managers and investing in the financial literacy of the general public. Yao and Yang contribute to the identification of practical policy options, with specific focus on the QDII industry, for China positioned in the transition phase toward more integration into the world economy.

Dontis-Charitos, Gough, Nowman, and Sivaprasad study the return and volatility spillovers from major bank stocks to the national stock market in the United Kingdom during the period 1999–2010. In our view,

Dontis-Charitos et al.'s contribution is fundamentally important because it informs the discussion around concerns that the effects of the global financial crisis may spill over more easily across financial institutions if they are highly interconnected. Using daily, weekly, and monthly data they provide empirical estimates of both uni- and bi-directional return and volatility spillovers. The discrete time results show that volatility is indeed transmitted from large bank stocks to the national stock market, providing evidence in favor of the hypothesis that idiosyncratic shocks in one sector may easily transmit to others and cause system-wide problems. The implication is that large financial intermediaries should narrow the scale and/or scope of their operations and/or be closely monitored and regulated to avoid financial crises such as the recent one. In any case, Dontis-Charitos et al.'s results from the continuous time analysis are sensitive to the choice of the modeling approach and provide mixed evidence for these feedback effects.

Part IV is devoted to the study of how financial crises spill over from advanced economies, the origin of crises mostly in recent years, to the emerging markets including developing Asia, Latin America, and India.

In the case of Asia, the links with Europe are extremely important. Initially, the region's export-oriented industrialization policies relied heavily on the high-income economies of Western Europe as the main markets for the region's exports. Even today this is true. Despite this unarguably strong trade channel, the rapid and significant growth of the Asian major economies in the last years makes the researcher wonder whether it is time to think about a decoupling of Asia from the advanced world. The work in this volume by Lee, Park, Abdon, and Estrada on Asia and Swamy on India allows us to conclude that this is still not the case. Furthermore, Galindo, Izquierdo, and Rojas-Suarez raise important concerns on increasing crisis of contagion effects from abroad in the case of Latin America.

The economic impact of the Eurozone crisis for developing Asia is studied by Lee et al. Focusing on both the trade (the shift of Asian exports from the G3 to the developing world which peaked momentum after the crisis) and financial channels (for both bond and equity markets, through banks exposure to bonds issued by governments in the Euro zone periphery countries or through European banks cutting their lending in Asia to repair their damaged balance sheets) of transmission of the euro crisis, Lee et al. conclude that while sizable, the impact on this region is still manageable at least in the short term. This is in part due to the bold counter-cyclical fiscal stimulus packages (allowed by the region's tradition of fiscal prudence and the Asian countries' relatively low debt-to-GDP ratios) implemented in response to the negative impact of the crisis on the region's exports. It is important to keep in mind that in drawing these conclusions the authors assume the euro crisis is to be largely confined to the Eurozone and to a recession in the real economy rather than a full-blown financial crisis.

The implications of the European sovereign debt crisis for India are reviewed in the chapter by Swamy. Fiscal consolidation measures and lower consumption in Europe have resulted in first, the Euro-zone share of Indian exports to decline significantly; second, strong capital outflows by European banks in India; and third, slowing down of both equity and debt FDI flows into the Indian economy. The last two have in turn led to a sharp depreciation of the Indian rupee. Swamy documents that the direct impact of the Eurozone crisis on Indian banks is limited as foreign banks account for only less than 10 percent of assets and credit in the Indian banking sector, and domestic banks have no significant exposure to bonds issued by the affected European sovereigns. However, Swamy calls attention that an indirect impact on specialized types of financing, like structured long-term, project, and trade finance, is highly likely. In Swamy's opinion, the observations in this chapter raise concerns about India's policy of requiring banks to hold some share of public debt.

In Latin America, financial integration has also increased significantly, with some particular features that are worthy of note. First, regulatory and supervisory domestic frameworks in Latin America have improved significantly in the last two decades. Second, capital account liberalization has been steadily increasing since the 1990s. By 2006 this region was the most financially open in the developing world, second only to developed countries. Third, a larger proportion of lending by BIS reporting banks in the region is now directed to the private sector as opposed to local governments. Last, the average maturity of these loans has increased consistently.

Galindo, Izquierdo, and Rojas-Suarez use both aggregate country and detailed bank-level data on Latin American banking sectors during the period 1996–2008 to study the role that financial integration and foreign bank penetration play in the transmission of external financial shocks in this region. Galindo et al. find that financial integration in Latin America has played a positive role in the deepening of Latin American credit markets in almost all states of nature, the increased savings rates, and the lower cost of finance. However, the favorable impacts come with a significant side-effect: exacerbated contagion effects of external financial shocks. Namely, the interest rates charged and loans supplied by most foreign-owned banks (with the exception of Spanish banks) are more volatile than their domestic bank counterparts. In our view, Galindo et al. provide an important contribution by departing from the standard shocks used in this literature.

Up until now the literature has focused mostly on real shocks in the domestic economy or the home country of the foreign banks, with little regard for the role of external financial shocks related to changes in risk aversion. Rather than saying that foreign bank participation should be limited in the region, these findings should be interpreted as calling for strategies such as ring-fencing or the incorporation of agreements with foreign supervisors, that avoid the strong contagion of foreign financial shocks during financial crisis periods, in particular.

Part V covers the policy implications and lessons that can be drawn from this work. In a nutshell, the contributions in this volume call for improved governance and monitoring of globalized banks, as well as for the institution of newly redesigned regulations on banks' liability structure.

Allen, Gu, and Kowalewski study bank-holding companies in the European Union during the crisis. To do so they build a dataset of transactions between parent banks and their foreign subsidiaries. They are able to show that these transactions, both income and asset transfers, may create a serious problem for the stability of the foreign banks' subsidiaries, and even pose a threat to the financial sector in host countries. Their results are consistent with the hypothesis postulated in the theoretical model by Allen and Gale (2000), according to which when banks are hit by a negative shock, they will typically try to meet their liquidity needs by drawing on their deposits at other banks before liquidating long-term assets. Since Allen et al. partly attribute this to the effects of weak governance in foreign subsidiaries, their results call for improved governance, increased disclosure, and better monitoring of these intra-group transactions in Europe, the new EU member states, in particular, where foreign bank penetration ratio is very high. Allen et al. also discuss the European Bank Coordination "Vienna" Initiative aimed at preventing a large-scale withdrawal of cross-border bank groups from Europe. We view that this work by Allen et al. provides important contributions to better understanding of the adverse impact of internal capital markets in multinational banking on crisis contagion and how to respond to it.

Park, Shin, and Suh provide a survey of the literature that looks at the liability side of banks' balance sheets as a potential source for increased risk during liquidity crises, most importantly, Shin (2009); Suh, Park, and Shin (2010); and Hahm, Shin, and Shin (2013). From this survey they conclude that instituting redesigned regulations on liability structure, which require a larger weight of stable sources of funding, should be seriously considered to prevent undesirable systemic effects of liquidity crises. The research by Park et al. provides an important policy implication on search for optimal bank regulations on liability structure of global banks.

Chung, Jang, and Park examine the disciplining role that creditors' monitoring has on the profitability of firm acquisitions by mitigating agency problems. To do so they study the syndicated loan market in the United States, especially the shares retained by lead arrangers. Chung et al.'s results show that lead arrangers with proper responsibility of monitoring borrowers are important for successful acquisitions by acquirers in the U.S. M&A activities. This is consistent with previous results in the literature that suggest that stock markets tend to react positively to announcements of new and renewal of bank loans when they allow the shareholders of borrowing firms to gain wealth. Chung et al. end with policy suggestions for this market, concluding that policy makers should design financial covenants to improve the efficiency of monitoring activities by lead arranging banks in syndicated bank loan deals.

Academics, policy makers, and financial sector participants alike have for a long time now debated the issues related to global banking and its effects on international crisis contagion, the impact of foreign banks on host emerging economies, spillovers of international financial shocks across other financial markets, and the effectiveness of monetary policy implementation and macro-prudential regulations. This special issue of the *International Finance Review* contains quality chapters written by diverse authors with specific focus on each of these important issues. We hope that this volume will contribute significantly to address the relevant questions in this debate.

REFERENCES

Allen, F., & Gale, D. (2000). Financial contagion. *Journal of Political Economy*, *108*(1), 1–33.

Freixas, X., & Rochet, J.-C. (2008). *Microeconomics of banking*. Cambridge, MA: MIT Press.

Hahm, J. H., Shin, H. S., & Shin, K. (2013). Noncore bank liabilities and financial vulnerability. *Journal of Money, Credit, and Banking*, *45*(S1), 3–36.

He, D., Cheung, L., Zhang, W. L., & Wu, T. (2012). *How would capital account liberalization affect China's capital flows and the renminbi real exchange rate?* HKIMR Working Paper No. 09/2012.

Porter, N., & Xu, T. T. (2009). *What drives China's interbank market?* IMF Working Paper No. 09/189. International Monetary Fund, Washington, DC.

Shin, H. S. (2009). Reflections on northern rock: The bank run that heralded the global financial crisis. *Journal of Economic Perspectives*, *23*(1), 101–119.

Suh, J. H., Park, J., & Shin, H. H. (2010). The impact of depositor structure on bank risk in liquidity crisis. *Journal of Money & Finance*, *24*(1), 99–129.

PART II
GLOBAL BANKING AND CRISES

RECENT CROSS-BORDER BANKING WITHIN EUROPE: INTERNATIONAL BALANCE SHEET PERSPECTIVES

Jonathan A. Batten, Igor Loncarski and Peter G. Szilagyi

ABSTRACT

We compare the aggregated international assets and liabilities of banks that report to the Bank for International Settlements (BIS) to establish their gross and net international exposures during recent episodes of financial crisis. Initially we consider these positions worldwide and then focus on the cross-border flows within Europe, considered in terms of core and peripheral countries. These gross and net asset–liability positions are both time-varying and respond to crisis periods, through better matching of international assets and liabilities as well as the realignment of asset positions to reduce balance sheet risks. These conclusions are consistent with other studies that utilise international banking flow data, while the European experience highlights the diversity of international position taking. This is due to the complexity of managing risks within

Global Banking, Financial Markets and Crises
International Finance Review, Volume 14, 15–30

ISSN: 1569-3767/doi:10.1108/S1569-3767(2013)0000014004

the eurozone (EZ) and peripheral countries, and those emerging European countries that retain legacy currencies.

Keywords: Cross-border banking; international banking; financial crisis

JEL classifications: F34; G18; O57

INTRODUCTION

Bank lending is generally considered one key precursor to sustainable economic growth. In a globalised world, lending may be provided both domestically, or internationally. Lending institutions may in turn fund their assets through deposits, or the issuance of securities in both domestic and international markets. Banks are motivated to internationalise to provide international services to their customers as well as to diversify balance sheet risks (e.g. Domenech & Correa-Lopez, 2012). In addition, Cetorelli and Goldberg (2012) show that having international operations insulates otherwise locally focused banks from changes in monetary policy shocks. Importantly, bank internationalisation has systemic risk implications, since banks may transmit financial shocks to their subsidiaries, as many are reliant upon internal as well as external funding (e.g. Jeon, Olivero, & Wu, 2013; Pontines & Siregar, 2012). The financial markets in which these banks operate are also becoming more integrated and sensitive to international business cycles (Kalemli-Ozcan, Papaioannou, & Perri, 2013), and international banking itself is concentrated through a small number of financial centres, especially London, which may exacerbate counterparty risks (Clare, Gulamhussen, & Pinheiro, 2013).

In this chapter we survey aggregate cross-border banking positions and focus on the relationship between international bank assets and liabilities as reported by the Bank for International Settlements (BIS). International asset and liabilities refer to reporting banks' positions in any currency with non-residents (i.e. their external or cross-border business) plus their transactions in foreign (non-local) currency with residents, while 'external' positions or 'cross-border' positions are asset and liability positions vis-à-vis banks and non-banks located in a country other than the country of residence of the reporting banking office positions (BIS, 2008). Both may be received, or paid, in the form of deposits, or securities. Our findings contribute to recent studies that utilise aggregate banking data to shed insights into international banking activities in Asian and Japanese markets (Batten & Szilagyi, 2011a, 2011b), emerging markets more generally (Avdjiev, Kuti, & Takats, 2012) and international markets as a whole (McGuire & von Peter, 2012).

We contribute to this literature by taking a European perspective, which embraces the core developed countries and those on the periphery, as well as those countries that have adopted the euro and those that have not. Our coverage includes the period of the Global Financial Crisis (GFC) and how this affected the international balance sheets of European banks. While Eichengreen, Mody, Nedeljkovic, and Sarno (2012) highlight the correlation between international banking and short-term economic effects, we focus on the regional diversity that still remains within the European financial system. Others have done so for other regions, including Tille's (2012) perspective on capital flows and cross-border banking in Asia.

Better understanding of the European position is critical: bank lending undertaken domestically typically requires banks to make decisions on credit, with interest rate risk managed, or hedged. When international assets are held, credit risk remains, but so too are potential effects from exchange-rate revaluations should the asset not be denominated in the same currency as the liability. While this form of foreign-exchange risk is easily managed using cross-currency swaps, Batten and Szilagyi (2012) argue that banks may prefer to match these positions and simply take the interest rate difference between the two (the interest rate margin) as the reward for taking credit risk.

Our results show that from a worldwide perspective international assets totaled US$33.7 trillion in December 2012 and were greater than liabilities, which totaled US$32.4 trillion in December 2012. This suggests that only a very small proportion of international assets (about 4.0%) are funded domestically through domestic deposits or equity. Most international loans made are also to banks (59.4% in December, 2012), although this ratio has declined slightly in recent years.[1] This is important for economic growth since a corporation unable to attract funds domestically may not be unable to do so from an international bank, even if there are no regulatory restrictions on borrowing from non-residents.

Taken together, these findings suggest that the role of banks internationally remains that of intermediation. The high ratio of lending to other financial institutions is also consistent with various theories that suggest international banks lack lending experience in foreign markets and so are reluctant to lend directly to the corporate sector in a foreign country. This lack of experience may be overcome through foreign banks forming joint ventures with a local bank, although such relationships need to be managed carefully. For example, Amici, Fiordelisi, Masala, Ricci, and Sist (2013) show that local banks create shareholder value by forming joint ventures with non-banking financial partners, while international strategic alliances tend to destroy shareholder value.[2]

Our results for Europe highlight the complexity of these issues and how they may interact during periods of financial crisis. When international assets and liabilities are denominated in currencies different to the home currency, an international bank whose international assets are greater than their international liabilities may be forced to fund the difference in foreign currency. This makes their balance sheet position more sensitive to exchange rate movements, unless they have hedged this exposure with derivatives. Matching international assets and liabilities not only reduces internal and external funding risks of individual banks but also helps minimise the transmission of financial shocks to the financial system as a whole. For example, Jeon et al. (2013) show the importance of internal capital markets in multinational banking and how they contribute to the transmission of financial shocks from parent banks to foreign subsidiaries, or vice-versa. These shocks would be expected to be more significant if the subsidiary was reliant upon the parent for funding. Thus, it would be expected that during periods of crisis, international banks would try to reduce foreign-exchange risk and interest-rate risks associated with maturity mismatches. In the case of Europe, lending within the EZ incurs no foreign-exchange risk, and would be favoured over lending outside the EZ. The realignment of the aggregate balance sheet positions of European banks during the GFC appears consistent with this view. However, the prospect of the withdrawal by Greece, and more recently Cyprus, may have had a destabilising effect on this type of position-taking.

Overall, our findings are consistent with a number of other studies that highlight the growing importance and role of cross-border banking (e.g. Bruno & Shin, 2013), especially for European banks after the introduction of the euro (e.g. Vallascas & Keasey, 2013) and the impact of the GFC on international bank balance sheets (e.g. Avdjiev et al., 2012; Tintchev, 2013).

The chapter is set out as follows. In the next section we provide a context for this work by discussing the international positions of banks. Then attention is directed towards Europe segmented into those countries considered developed, core, peripheral and those within the EZ. The final section provides some concluding remarks and comments.

THE GLOBAL PERSPECTIVE

We initially update the international banking positions broadly discussed in BIS (2013 March, June) and also by Batten and Szilagyi (2011a, 2011b). The international positions of banks that report to the BIS comprise claims on non-residents (termed external positions) and claims on residents (termed local positions). These claims in turn are grouped into bank and non-bank claims. A bank is a deposit-taking institution typically incorporated as such under local law and differs from investment, or merchant, banks and other non-bank intermediaries. For example, a bank resident in Germany can lend to a German corporation in US dollars, in which case the loan (an asset) is treated as an international loan made locally to a non-bank. However, if this loan was made to a corporation in Japan, then it would be a loan made to a non-resident non-bank and be treated as an external asset (EA).

Summary tables of the international positions of banks reported to the BIS from December 1995 to December 2012 are provided in Table 1. This table provides the international asset and liability positions, along with a number of relevant ratios based upon these positions. Three figures are also provided to better illustrate the long-term trends: Fig. 1 plots the ratio of EA to external liabilities (EL); Fig. 2 plots the bank share; while Fig. 3 plots the non-bank share over the same period from December 1977 to December 2012.

Table 1 records that total international assets were US$33,658.66 billion in December 2012, while liabilities were US$32,417.01 billion. The difference of US$1,241.65 billion shows the amount of international assets funded through domestically sourced liabilities (either debt or equity). This difference was 3.69% of assets in December 2012 a decline from December 2009, when the ratio was 5.12%. International assets peaked earlier at US$40,521.80 billion in March 2008 and subsequently declined due to counterparty credit concerns as well as reduced loan demand by corporations. Nonetheless, the high ratio of domestic funded assets, up to December 2009, accompanied by an earlier peaking in lending, is also consistent with reduced access to foreign markets for funding following the GFC of 2007–2008. Despite these recent reductions in both lending and the sourcing of funds internationally, Table 1 highlights the rapid internationalisation of bank balance sheets especially from 2000: the growth of international assets from December 2000 to 2012 was 274% and international liabilities 273%.

Table 1. International Positions of BIS Banks (International Assets and International Liabilities 1990–2012).

	Dec.90	Dec.93	Dec.95	Dec.00	Dec.05	Dec.06	Dec.07	Dec.08	Dec.09	Dec.10	Dec.11	Dec.12
Total international assets (BIS Table 1A) US$ Billion	7694.13	7827.36	9494.64	12278.87	23911.64	29368.26	37379.02	35334.20	33830.76	34036.20	34225.25	33658.66
Total international liabilities (BIS Table 1B) US$ Billion	7633.31	7518.18	9252.74	11875.16	22824.45	28134.20	35936.72	33760.20	32098.12	32638.76	33171.64	32417.01
Total other (Table 1A–Table 1B)	60.82	309.18	241.90	403.72	1087.19	1234.06	1442.30	1574.00	1732.64	1397.44	1053.61	1241.65
Ratio total international assets/liabilities (Table 1A/Table 1B)	1.0080	1.0411	1.0261	1.0340	1.0476	1.0439	1.0401	1.0466	1.0540	1.0428	1.0318	1.0383
Ratio EA/EL (Table 1B/Table 1F)	1.0025	1.0938	1.0946	1.1273	1.1737	1.1732	1.1517	1.1627	1.1827	1.1607	1.1517	1.1733
Ratio local assets (Table 1C/Table 1B)	0.2266	0.2040	0.1805	0.1429	0.1335	0.1276	0.1199	0.1329	0.1274	0.1290	0.1309	0.1318
Ratio local liabilities (Table 1G/Table 1F)	0.1874	0.2138	0.2050	0.1703	0.1824	0.1774	0.1617	0.1827	0.1685	0.1684	0.1772	0.1815
Bank share international assets	0.7149	0.6814	0.6842	0.6547	0.6231	0.6199	0.6252	0.6298	0.6232	0.6183	0.6215	0.5935
Bank share international liabilities	0.7732	0.7648	0.7604	0.7372	0.7179	0.7098	0.7135	0.7153	0.7151	0.7039	0.7071	0.6767
Non-bank share international assets	0.2851	0.3186	0.3158	0.3453	0.3769	0.3801	0.3748	0.3702	0.3768	0.3817	0.3785	0.4065
Non-bank share international liabilities	0.2268	0.2352	0.2396	0.2628	0.2821	0.2902	0.2865	0.2847	0.2849	0.2961	0.2929	0.3233
Bank EA/ Bank EL	0.7894	0.7834	0.7842	0.8099	0.8010	0.8094	0.8194	0.8158	0.8165	0.8193	0.8055	0.8029
Non Bank EA/ Non Bank EL	1.1370	1.4378	1.4373	1.4401	1.5968	1.5577	1.5396	1.5118	1.5997	1.5265	1.5231	1.5087

Source: Table 1 BIS *Quarterly Review* (March, 2013). The term 'international' refers to 'banks' transactions in any currency with non-residents (i.e. their external or cross-border business) plus their transactions in foreign (non-local) currency with residents', and 'external' positions or 'cross-border' positions are asset and liability positions vis-à-vis banks and non-banks located in a country other than the country of residence of the reporting banking office positions (BIS 2008, 'Guidelines to the International Locational Banking Statistics', Monetary and Economic Department, November 2006 and update December 2008).

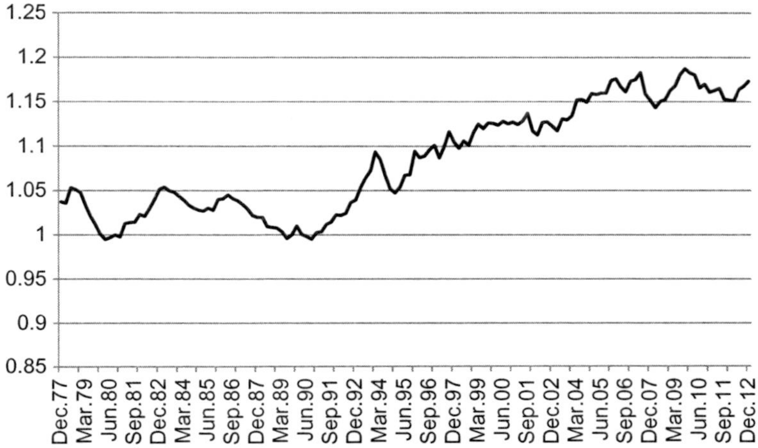

Fig. 1. Worldwide Ratio of BIS Reporting Bank EA/EL: December 1977–December 2012. *Source*: BIS (2013, Table 1B and Table 1F).

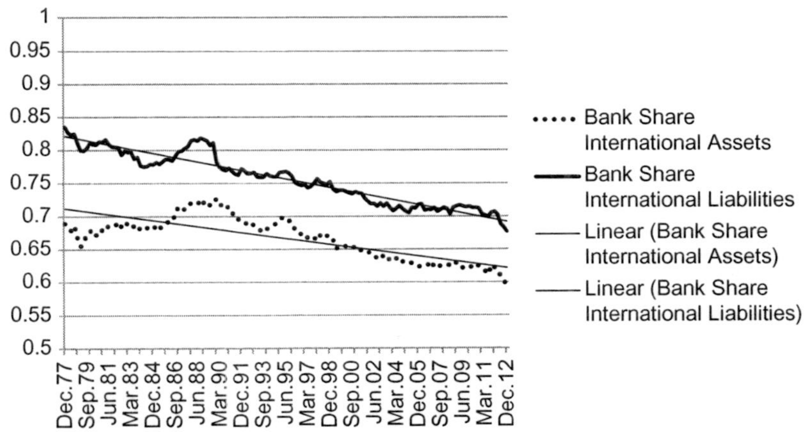

Fig. 2. Bank Share of International Assets and Liabilities: December 1977–December 2012. *Source*: BIS (2013, Table 1B and Table 1F).

Table 1 also records the ratio of international assets to liabilities, which in December 2012 was 1.0383, which is an almost exact matching in nominal terms. This suggests international banks generally fund their international assets with international liabilities, which likely minimises country's

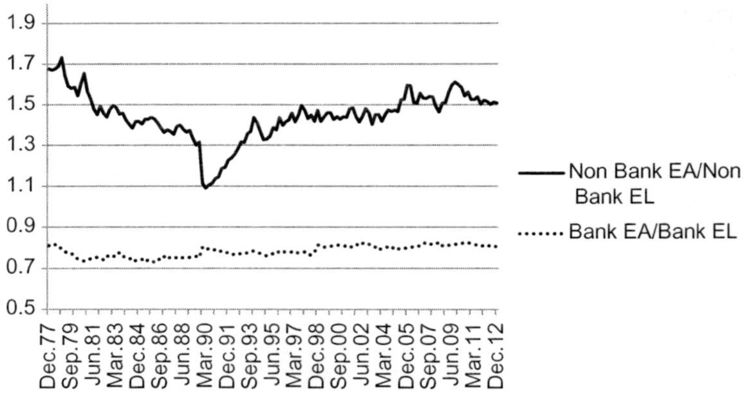

Fig. 3. Bank and Non-Bank Share of EA and EL: December 1977–December 2012. *Source*: BIS (2013, Table 1B and Table 1F).

risk exposures (e.g. assets and liabilities are in the same country) and also currency exposures (e.g. assets and liabilities are also in the same currencies). However, the EA and EL positions are a better guide to the degree of bank internationalisation since these numbers represent transactions with non-residents.

Table 1 records the EA/EL ratio (1.1733 in December 2012) with this ratio being plotted in Fig. 1 from 1977 to 2012. Notice that in the lead up to the 1988 Basel Accord, and shortly thereafter to 1990, the EA/EL ratio declined to approximately 1.000, which is consistent with an almost perfect matching of the nominal values of EA and EL. From 1991 the ratio increased to just below 1.20. Importantly, during this period there was also rapid growth in the over-the-counter (OTC) currency swap market, which enabled any foreign-exchange exposures remaining after netting asset–liability positions, to be hedged. Attention should be drawn to the peaking of the next EA/EL ratio in December 2009.

Another important feature of the international asset–liability positions concerns the role now played by non-bank intermediaries, which include various forms of investment banks and hedge funds. Table 1 shows that the bank share of international assets is just 59.40% (December 2012), whereas the bank share of liabilities is higher at 67.67% (December 2012). While these ratios highlight the overall importance of the interbank lending and borrowing market, it also highlights the importance now played by the non-bank sector as a direct source of funds. The declining role of intermediated lending (i.e. foreign bank lends to a local bank, which then lends locally) is clearer in Fig. 2, which plots the trend from 1997 to 2012.

The final figure in this section reports the different relationship between EA/EL ratio made to non-banks and to other banks. In December 2012 the EA/EL ratio for the bank sector was 0.8029, whereas it was 1.5087 for the non-bank sector. Fig. 3 also plots this ratio from 1977. The bank EA/EL ratio has been relatively stable since 1977 (it was 0.8098 in December 1977 and had a standard deviation of just 0.0270 for the period from 1977–2012), whereas the non-bank ratio has been much more volatile (it was 1.6776 in December 1977 and had a standard deviation of 0.1190). Nonetheless, the data highlight the importance BIS reporting banks place on sourcing funding, then used for lending to the non-bank sector, from other offshore or foreign banks. During periods of crisis, these relationships may become unstuck as counterparty credit concerns become more important. This is only of concern for bank assets and not for liabilities, and is very apparent when the positions of European banks are discussed in the next section.

INTERNATIONAL ASSET AND LIABILITY POSITIONS TO EUROPEAN BANKS

Initially we proceed by constructing ratios of the EA and EL positions of reporting banks with respect to individual countries in Europe, looking separately into selected EZ countries and Emerging Europe countries (as reported in the BIS locational banking statistics). The EZ countries are grouped into 'Core' and 'Periphery' countries, as popularly referred to by the media since the onset of the sovereign debt crisis in Europe. As 'core' EZ countries we consider Germany, France, the Netherlands, Finland, Belgium, Austria and Luxembourg, while as 'peripheral' EZ countries we consider Portugal, Ireland, Italy, Greece and Spain (the PIIGS), together with Cyprus and Slovenia.[3] We emphasise these external positions of reporting banks with respect to individual EZ member states in order to shed light on issues relating to the origin and consequences of the sovereign debt crisis in Europe. We use data on the external positions of reporting banks, which are reported for all sectors in Table 6A of the BIS locational banking statistics and in Table 6B for non-bank sector, and then estimate the locational banking statistics for the bank sector by subtracting the positions of the non-bank sector from those for all sectors. We then discuss the ratios of EA to EL that reporting banks hold against individual countries for the bank and non-bank sectors. We also aggregate the ratios of individual countries by grouping them into the 'core' and the 'periphery' EZ countries and then compute the weighted average of the ratios per 'group' by weighting the individual country GDP share in terms of the 'group' GDP.

Our approach is to take the GDP values from 2011 and form aggregates for each 'core' and 'periphery' group. The GDP share of individual countries in each group is then used as the basis for computing the weighted average of the EA/EL ratio. For example, the weight of Germany in the 'core' EZ group is 42.64% and the weight of Italy in the 'periphery' group is 49.06%. For simplicity we do not vary weights over time. However, we believe that the main results are not significantly affected with this simplification. The results for the banking sector are then plotted in Fig. 4.

The euro was introduced on 1 January 1999, when it replaced the European Currency Unit (ECU). It became a 'true' currency when paper notes and coins were circulated in the initial 12 EZ member states on 1 January 2002. We emphasize the importance of the introduction of euro, since it represents a break point in the process of European integration, which should weigh heavily on the external positions of reporting banks. For example, the decline in the EA/EL ratios of the bank sector for the 'core' group of EZ countries corresponds to the introduction of the euro in 1999. To the extent that European banks are lending and

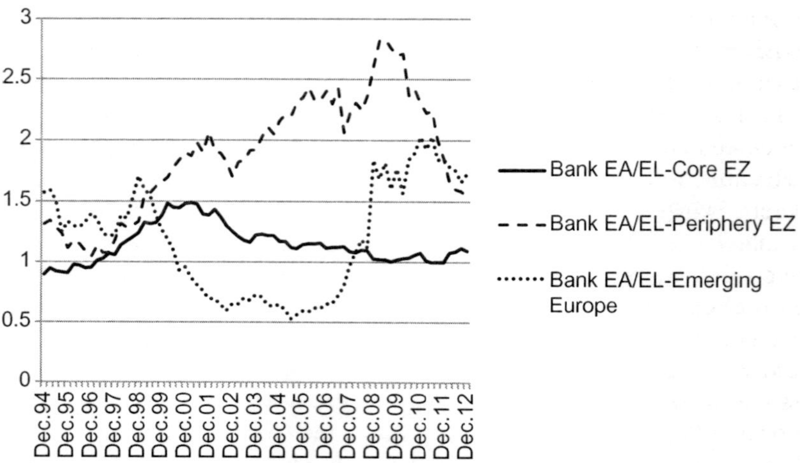

Fig. 4. Bank EA and EL in EZ (Core and Periphery) and Emerging Europe: December 1977–December 2012. *Source*: BIS (2013, Table 6A and Table 6B).

borrowing cross-border in euros there should be no effect on the EUR/USD exchange rate. However, there may be minor indirect effects arising from hedging arrangements associated with non-euro exposures.

After the introduction of the euro there was an increase in the EA/EL ratios for the banking sector of the 'periphery' group of EZ countries. This was especially so for the period from 2002 onwards, with an eventual peak in the wake of the Greek debt crisis towards the end of 2009. At this time the value of the EA/EL ratio was around 2.8. One could argue that the introduction of the euro and the corresponding decrease in interest rates in the 'peripheral' countries encouraged massive inflows of foreign borrowing. These funds were subsequently used to finance local assets, especially housing. Interestingly, prior to the introduction of the euro in 1999 the EA/EL ratios of the 'core' EZ countries was mostly around 1.0, with a persistent increase commencing in the second half of the 1990s. This ratio eventually reached 1.5 just after the introduction of the euro, although it subsequently reverted back to a value of one.

For comparison, we include a third series of data in Fig. 4, the EA/EL ratio for Emerging Europe. According to the BIS classification, Emerging Europe includes a very diverse set of countries, some being members of EU since 2004 (Hungary, Poland, Czech Republic, Latvia, Lithuania) and 2007 (Bulgaria, Romania), while others have indicated interest but so far have not been admitted (e.g. Turkey and the former Yugoslav republics). Then, there are those that have little immediate prospect of joining the EU including Albania, Belarus and Ukraine. For these emerging countries the EA/EL ratio is more volatile. One important observation that can be drawn based on the data is that the external position of the banking sector of many of these countries had been deteriorating until they joined the EU in 2004 and 2007. This simply followed as the consequence of the economic integration of these countries (and their foreign trade) in the EU (e.g. Bekaert, Harvey, Lundblad, & Siegel, 2013).

Finally, we observe a sharp decrease in the ratio for the 'periphery' group of EZ member states after the beginning of 2010, corresponding to the onset of the sovereign debt crisis in Europe. It seems that the series of sovereign bailouts and debt restructurings, as well as some newly introduced ECB mechanisms (e.g. Long Term Refinancing Operations) made it possible for reporting banks to offload their asset exposures to the banking sector in 'peripheral' EZ countries. This has essentially led to financial market segmentation in the EZ, while at the same time funnelling a large part of the exposures and risks onto the ECB and Target balances (e.g. Sinn & Wollmershäuser, 2012). As of December 2012 the EA/EL ratio for 'periphery' EZ countries was 1.58. It will be interesting to see if this ratio approaches the 'core' EZ countries ration of close to one in future years.

In addition to what we mentioned regarding the funneling of the exposures and risk, it is almost certain that part of the decrease of these external positions came at the expense of the deleveraging of banks and corporates in 'periphery' EZ countries, impeding the credit transmission channel, and hampering in large part the efforts made by the ECB in terms of loose monetary policy. Consequently, the overall impact on credit has been minimal with little impact on economic growth.

When looking into the external positions of the reporting banks regarding the non-bank sector (Fig. 5), we can see a very similar pattern to what was observed in the banking sector of individual countries. However, the magnitude of the ratios is twofold–fivefold larger. This is not surprising, since the non-bank sector is predominantly composed of corporates that by and large are net borrowers, while retail investors hardly hold any assets with foreign banks. Again, the data demonstrates the important dynamics in the external positions and highlights those economic (political) events that have impacted on economic (financial) (dis)integration.

Up until the introduction of the euro in 1999 the EA/EL ratio of the 'periphery' EU member states co-moved with those of the 'core' EU

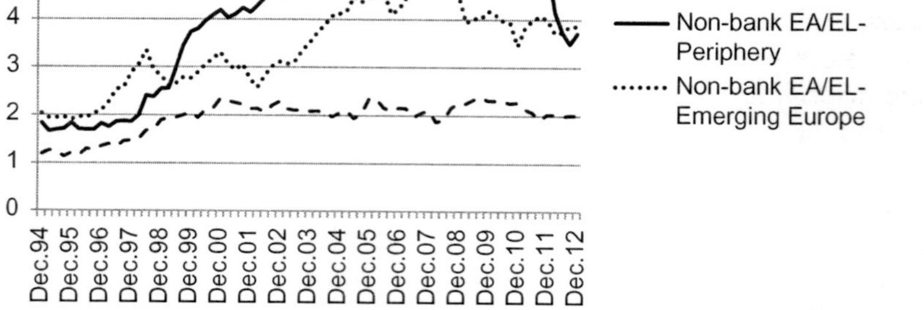

Fig. 5. Non-Bank EA and EL in EZ (Core and Periphery) and Emerging Europe: December 1977–December 2012. *Source*: BIS (2013, Table 6A and Table 6B).

countries. There is a clear sign of decoupling after the introduction of the euro in 1999 (the value of the ratio is less than 3), after which the ratio more than doubled at its peak in 2006 (the value of the ratio increased above 8). This was followed by a sharp decline in the ratio of EA to EL to around four at the end of December 2012. This decline is consistent with significant deleveraging (at least in terms of external exposures) and again, as before in the case of bank sector, provides evidence of the segmentation of financial markets in the EZ.

Of course, one could argue that the EA/EL ratios seen for 'peripheral' EZ countries (and Emerging Europe as well) were excessive in the period 2000–2009 and would have to revert to a more sustainable long-term level at par with the one we observe in the case of 'core' EZ countries. This is due in part to differences in the level of financial sector development, as well as the balance of payments positions, between the 'core' and 'periphery' EZ countries, especially due to general regulatory and market conditions that emerged with the introduction of the Euro. In developed financial markets (such as the United States) foreign banks can both lend and borrow (via securities and deposits) in the local market. Less developed countries have shallow financial markets and lower degrees of financial intermediation (lower diversity of financial intermediaries and products, lower savings rates due to lower income, etc.).

In addition, there may be capital and exchange rate controls (e.g. even in the case of monetary union such is de facto situation in Cyprus at the moment), although foreign banks are typically able to lend to local banks. The access to the corporate sector is generally more limited, in part due to information asymmetries as well (on top of regulatory controls). Therefore, in less developed financial markets one would expect the EA/EL ratio to be greater than one. Nevertheless, a large part remains unaccounted for when simply looking at conventional explanations. In this chapter, we can only discuss these issues in qualitative terms, although the authors recognise that a more in-depth econometric analysis is needed to be able to understand determinants and causality.

CONCLUSION AND IMPLICATIONS

This chapter focuses on the international balance sheet positions of banks, with a particular focus on European positions. The survey of worldwide positions suggests that only a very small proportion of international assets are funded domestically through domestic deposits or equity, while most international loans made are made to banks. Together these observations suggest that the role of banks internationally tends to be that of intermediation.

Nonetheless, the results for Europe highlight the complexity of international relationships and how they may interact during periods of financial crisis. Europe is unique in that while most countries use the euro as a common currency, others rely on legacy currencies, which ensure that international exposures carry foreign exchange as well as credit- and interest-rate risk. This makes the balance sheet position of lending countries more sensitive to exchange rate movements, unless the exposure is hedged derivatives. Thus when a bank matches its international assets and liabilities it reduces both internal and external funding risks but also helps minimise the transmission of financial shocks to the financial system as a whole.

Our findings contribute to those efforts aimed at better understanding how international banking may contribute to both domestic and international financial stability, although we do not specifically address how shocks are transmitted, the processes necessary to safeguard financial stability (e.g. Jeon et al., 2013; Vallascas & Keasey, 2013), or potential regulatory conflicts and incentive distortions that may exacerbate impacts (e.g. Cubillas, Fonseca, & Gonzalez, 2012; D'Hulster, 2012). They are also consistent with, extend or update a number of studies that use aggregate banking statistics (e.g. Avdjiev et al., 2012; Batten & Szilagyi, 2012; McGuire & von Peter, 2012). The time-varying nature of these banking flows is also consistent with the episodes of surges and stops in international capital flows, recently described by (Forbes & Warnock, 2012), movements in international asset prices and interest differentials (e.g. Aizenman & Pasricha, 2012; McKinnon, 2012) and also changes in demand for financial products, such as syndicated loans and structured securities (e.g. Giannetti & Laeven, 2012). These areas offer researchers a multitude of opportunities for extensions and further analysis.

NOTES

1. All data is sourced from the 'Locational Banking Statistics' provided by the BIS 2013: http://www.bis.org/statistics/bankstats.htm

2. Banks may also expand through mergers. However, recent evidence suggests that when banks do so they target similar banks (with similar balance sheets and business models) to those domestically (e.g. Caiazza, Clare, & Pozzolo, 2012).

3. As of June 2013 Cyprus has already been forced to ask for the financial assistance and Slovenia is, according to government bond yields and reports of scrutiny by the European Commission regarding excess budget deficits, considered by many to be next in line.

REFERENCES

Aizenman, J., & Pasricha, G. K. (2012). Determinants of financial stress and recovery during the great recession. *International Journal of Finance and Economics*, *17*(4), 347–372.

Amici, A., Fiordelisi, F., Masala, F., Ricci, O., & Sist, F. (2013). Value creation in banking through strategic alliances and joint ventures. *Journal of Banking and Finance*, *37*(5), 1386–1396.

Avdjiev, S., Kuti, Z., & Takats, E. (2012). The euro area crisis and cross-border bank lending to emerging markets. *BIS Quarterly Review*, 37–47.

Bank for International Settlements (BIS). (2008). Guidelines to the international locational banking statistics, monetary and economic department, November 2006 and update December 2008, Basel, Switzerland.

Bank for International Settlements (BIS). (2013). Highlights of the BIS international statistics. *Quarterly Review*, Basel, Switzerland, March, 15–22.

Batten, J. A., & Szilagyi, P. G. (2011a). The recent internationalization of Japanese banks. *The Japanese Economy*, *38*(1), 81–120.

Batten, J. A., & Szilagyi, P. G. (2011b). Bank internationalization during the global financial crisis: An Asia pacific perspective. *Journal of the Asia Pacific Economy*, *16*(3), 372–392.

Batten, J. A., & Szilagyi, P. G. (2012). International banking during the global financial crisis: U.K. and U.S. perspectives. *International Review of Financial Analysis*, *25*(1), 136–141.

Bekaert, G., Harvey, C. R., Lundblad, C. T., & Siegel, S. (2013). The European Union, the Euro, and equity market integration. *Journal of Financial Economics*, *109*(3), 583–603.

Bruno, V., & Shin, H. S. (2013). *Capital flows, cross-border banking and global liquidity*. Working Paper No. 19038. National Bureau of Economic Research, Inc., NBER.

Caiazza, S., Clare, A., & Pozzolo, A. F. (2012). What do bank acquirers want? Evidence from worldwide bank M&A targets. *Journal of Banking and Finance*, *36*(9), 2641–2659.

Cetorelli, N., & Goldberg, L. S. (2012). Banking globalization and monetary transmission. *Journal of Finance*, *67*(5), 1811–1843.

Clare, A., Gulamhussen, M. A., & Pinheiro, C. (2013). What factors cause foreign banks to stay in London? *Journal of International Money and Finance*, *32*(1), 739–761.

Cubillas, E., Fonseca, A. R., & Gonzalez, F. (2012). Banking crises and market discipline: International evidence. *Journal of Banking and Finance*, *36*(8), 2285–2298.

D'Hulster, K. (2012). Cross-border banking supervision: Incentive conflicts in supervisory information sharing between home and host supervisors. *Journal of Banking Regulation*, *13*(4), 300–319.

Domenech, R., & Correa-Lopez, M. (2012). *The internationalisation of Spanish firms*. Working Paper No. 1230. BBVA bank, economic research department.

Eichengreen, B., Mody, A., Nedeljkovic, M., & Sarno, L. (2012). How the subprime crisis went global: Evidence from bank credit default swap spreads. *Journal of International Money and Finance*, *31*(5), 1299–1318.

Forbes, K. J., & Warnock, F. E. (2012). Capital flow waves: Surges, stops, flight, and retrenchment. *Journal of International Economics*, *88*(2), 235–251.

Giannetti, M., & Laeven, L. (2012). The flight home effect: Evidence from the syndicated loan market during financial crises. *Journal of Financial Economics*, *104*(1), 23–43.

Jeon, B. N., Olivero, M. P., & Wu, J. (2013). Multinational banking and the international transmission of financial shocks: Evidence from foreign bank subsidiaries. *Journal of Banking and Finance*, *37*(3), 952–972.

Kalemli-Ozcan, S., Papaioannou, E., & Perri, F. (2013). Global banks and crisis transmission. *Journal of International Economics*, *89*(2), 495–510.

McGuire, P., & von Peter, G. (2012). The dollar shortage in global banking and the international policy response. *International Finance*, *15*(2), 155–178.

McKinnon, R. (2012). Carry trades, interest differentials, and international monetary reform. *Journal of Policy Modeling*, *34*(4), 549–567.

Pontines, V., & Siregar, R. (2012). *How should we bank with foreigners? An Empirical Assessment of Lending Behaviour of International Banks to Six East Asian Countries*. CAMA Working Paper No. 31/2012. Australian National University, Centre for Applied Macroeconomic Analysis, Canberra, Australia.

Sinn, H.-W., & Wollmershäuser, T. (2012). Target loans, current account balances and capital flows: The ECB's rescue facility. *International Tax and Public Finance*, *19*(4), 468–508.

Tille, C. (2012). Sailing through this storm? Capital flows in asia during the crisis. *Pacific Economic Review*, *17*(3), 467–488.

Tintchev, K. (2013). *Connected to whom? International interbank borrowing during the global crisis*. Working Papers: 13/14. International Monetary Fund, IMF.

Vallascas, F., & Keasey, K. (2013). The volatility of European banking systems: A two-decade study. *Journal of Financial Services Research*, *43*(1), 37–68.

THE IMPLEMENTATION OF MONETARY POLICY IN CHINA: THE INTERBANK MARKET AND BANK LENDING

Hongyi Chen, Qianying Chen and Stefan Gerlach

ABSTRACT

We analyze the impact of monetary policy instruments on interbank lending rates and retail bank lending in China using an extended version of the model developed by Porter and Xu (2009). Unlike the central banks of advanced economies, the People's Bank of China (PBoC) uses changes in the required reserve ratios and open market operations to influence liquidity in money markets and adjusts the regulated deposit and lending rates and loan targets to intervene in the retail deposit and lending market. These interventions prevent the interbank lending rate from signaling monetary policy stance and transmitting the effect of policy to the growth of bank loans. Since the global financial crisis, the PBoC's monetary policy has gone through a full cycle. The combining effects of using different policy instruments simultaneously within a short period of time were quite effective in bringing the credit and money growth in line with its desired level. Most recently steps have been taken

Global Banking, Financial Markets and Crises
International Finance Review, Volume 14, 31–69

ISSN: 1569-3767/doi:10.1108/S1569-3767(2013)0000014005

to speed up the interest rate liberalization. Effective July 2013, the PBoC removed the floors of the benchmark lending rates.

Keywords: Monetary policy implementation; regulated interest rates; transmission mechanism; window guidance; bank loans; China

JEL classifications: E42; E52; E58

INTRODUCTION

In normal times, when interest rates bound away from zero, central banks in advanced economies typically implement monetary policy by steering a short-term interbank rate. While the exact ways in which this is done differ among countries, the focus is squarely on the price of liquidity. Thus, given the policy interest rate, other variables contain no information about the stance of monetary policy. In the case of China, however, it is generally felt that the interbank rate is not a good measure of the stance of monetary policy.[1]

Indeed, empirical evidence suggests that the interest rate channel of monetary policy transmission is weak or non-existent in China. Geiger (2006) finds that retail lending and money market rates do not have a tight and predictable relationship with loan and money growth, and Laurens and Maino (2007) find that the GDP and price do not react to short-term interest rates, although they react significantly to M2 growth. Green and Chang (2006) show that the People's Bank of China (PBoC) controls reserve money but not M2 well, as there is no close relationship between reserve money and M2. This evidence suggests that the relationship between monetary policy instruments, short-term interest rates, loan growth, and money growth in China differs from what we observe in advanced economies.

In considering the transmission mechanism of monetary policy in China, it is useful to distinguish the link between policy instruments and interbank rates as well as between interbank rates and the cost and availability of bank loans. Explanations put forward in the literature of the ineffectiveness of the monetary policy in China have typically focused on how structural impediments in financial markets have weakened the second link (see Laurens & Maino, 2007; Liu & Zhang, 2007; Podpiera, 2006). In this chapter, by contrast, we also study the first link, as understanding it is a prerequisite for understanding the overall transmission of monetary policy to the real economy.

The PBoC conducts monetary policy using an array of instruments. These include changes in required reserve ratios (RRR), the interest rates on reserves, open market operations (OMOs), the issuance of central bank bills, and changes in regulated deposit and retail lending rates plus window guidance. Window guidance is a measure that pressures banks to follow PBoC's guidelines on retail lending, a practice also used by the Bank of Japan in the early stages of Japan's economic development. The two regulated rates and window guidance are important for the implementation of monetary policy in China, in contrast to advanced economies. As the bank lending is the main official finance channel for corporations in China, this raises the question of what the coexistence of such regulations and market forces implies for PBoC's policy to influence interbank lending rates and total lending.

To study this issue, we present a model of bank behavior in China, which is an extension of the model of Porter and Xu (2009a), which, in turn, is an extension of Freixas and Rochet (2008). The model illustrates how the interbank rate and the quantity and price of retail lending are determined when banks compete, when deposit and lending rates are regulated, and when there is credit guidance. To implement the monetary policy, the PBoC intervenes in both the wholesale money market by OMOs, adjusting RRR, and in the retail deposit and lending market by changing the ceiling for deposit rates and the floor for retail lending rates and bank loan targets. Therefore, a reverse transmission of policy from the retail interest rates to the wholesale money market occurs.

The model suggests that the effect of policy instruments on the interbank money market and bank loans depends on how the regulated interest rates deviate from their equilibrium levels, defined as the rates we would observe in the absence of regulation. In the current case of China, the PBoC's intervention in the deposit and lending market impairs the transmission of OMOs and changes in RRR to bank credit growth through interbanks, therefore sometimes rendering window guidance of credit growth necessary for the PBoC's implementation of monetary policy. The effectiveness of window guidance depends on the perceived penalty cost for not obeying the guidance.

Three implications for Chinese monetary policy transmission follow this result.

First, the interbank money market lending rates, such as Repo and SHIBOR, are insufficient and potentially misleading indicators of the central bank's monetary policy intentions. In particular, the deposit rate in

China is believed to be binding. In this case, adjusting the ceiling for the deposit rate and the floor for the lending rate distorts the effect of OMOs and changes in RRR on interbank rates. To characterize the stance of monetary policy, all policy instruments must be considered.

Second, the interbank rates do not play a role in transmitting the money market liquidity condition to retail bank lending when both the ceiling for deposit rate and the floor for retail lending rate are binding. As a consequence, a disconnect between interbank rates and the growth of bank loans exists.

Third, the uncertainty about the equilibrium deposit and lending rates in the absence of regulation complicates the conduct of monetary policy. As the equilibrium is unobservable, the central bank may not know if a change in the floor and ceiling of the retail interest rates would result in expansionary or contractionary effects on bank lending, which may make the window guidance and other administrative measures necessary to keep loan growth consistent with policy intention. Liberalizing the regulated rates eliminates this uncertainty and would facilitate the setting of policies, which would greatly improve the efficiency and effectiveness of the monetary policy implementation.

The rest of the chapter is organized as follows. The second section introduces the institutional background of monetary policy in China. The third section reviews the pattern and effectiveness of monetary policy implementation in recent years. The fourth section presents the model and its policy implications. The fifth section concludes.

INSTITUTIONAL BACKGROUND

In this section, we provide a review of the institutional arrangements that underpin the implementation of monetary policy in China. In particular, we highlight the regulation of interest rates for deposits, retail lending, and window guidance, which are not used in monetary policy operations in advanced economies. We further discuss the development of the interbank market, which has recently become more important for the monetary policy implementation in China.

The Objectives and Instruments of Monetary Policy

According to the Central Bank Law, the goal of the monetary policy in China is to maintain the stability of the value of the currency and, thereby, promote economic growth. To achieve this final objective, a group of intermediate targets is set for M2 growth, domestic loan growth, exchange rate stability, and overall banking system stability, which implies maintaining the profitability of state-owned banks. The PBoC is under the leadership of the State Council; thus, the final authority on major monetary policy decisions lies with the State Council.

The PBoC uses a range of instruments to achieve these targets. These instruments can be classified into two categories. The first category serves to influence liquidity in the interbank money market and comprises changes in the RRR, changes in interest rates for required and excess reserves, and OMOs. The second category contains instruments that directly influence retail deposit and lending, such as changes in the regulated retail deposit and lending rates, and window guidance on loan growth. This second set of instruments is generally not used by central banks in advanced economies. The use of these instruments at both the wholesale and retail levels of banking liquidity indicates that the implementation of monetary policy in China is still in transition from direct quantity control to a more market-based framework. Furthermore, adjusting regulated deposit and lending rates implies a reverse transmission of monetary policy from the retail banking to the wholesale money market, as denoted in Fig. 1. We introduce the second group of instruments in detail.

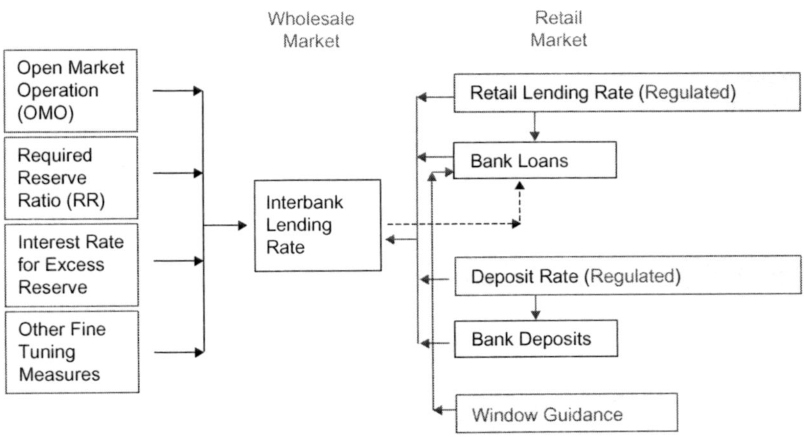

Fig. 1. The Framework of Monetary Policy Implementation in China.

Window Guidance

The use of window guidance by the PBoC has a long history. At an early stage of China's economic reform, the PBoC used credit plans to control the lending of state-owned banks. Only after the first round of banking reforms in 1995 were both the quarterly and annual targets of bank lending of state-owned banks abolished. Instead, the PBoC announced a new annual reference target in the form of growth for total bank lending, a practice that has continued until the present. Furthermore, the PBoC now annually announces an M2 growth target. These two targets play key roles in the PBoC's quantity-based monetary policy.

To achieve the lending target, the PBoC uses moral suasion in the form of window guidance as a supplementary tool. By maintaining regular communication with commercial banks, the PBoC can monitor the lending growth and, if necessary, persuade banks to maintain loan growth at a target level. In most of the cases, the PBoC was concerned about fast loan growth that exceeded the target. In some rare cases, when loan growth was far below the target, the PBoC would encourage banks to lend. This happened during the global financial crisis of 2008–2009, when the central bank encouraged more lending to mitigate the impact of the crisis. The window guidance can target over- or under-lending banks or specific overheating or underdeveloped sectors.

The effectiveness of window guidance depends on the bank's perception of the consequences of disregarding it. Together with the China Banking Regulatory Commission (CBRC), the PBoC has the authority to approve senior personnel appointments at commercial banks. This gives the PBoC influence over the lending behaviors of banks, especially state-owned banks. For those banks with excessive loan growth that disregard the PBoC's guidance, the PBoC can request that the banks make large time deposits with punishment rates into their accounts with the central bank or buy central bank bills.

Thus far, window guidance has been effective in slowing the loan growth of commercial banks in China. However, with financial liberalization, channels other than borrowing from commercial banks are available for firms to raise funds. These channels include the corporate bond market and the equity market. Therefore, the effectiveness of window guidance in achieving the final objective of controlling inflation has been eroded because firms do not have to borrow solely from commercial banks.

The role of window guidance in the interest rate transmission process is included in the model in the fourth section of this chapter.

Regulations of Retail Lending and Deposit Rates

In the era of the centrally planned economy, the PBoC established interest rates for deposits and lending in domestic and foreign currencies. From the mid-1990s onward, the deposit and retail lending markets were deregulated as part of the transition into a market-based economy. The PBoC first liberalized foreign currency interest rates before turning to domestic currency rates. It liberalized lending rates before deposit rates and rates with large, long-term deposits before those with small, short-term deposits.[2]

By October 2004, most of the interest rates were liberalized, with the exception of retail deposit rates, for which the PBoC retained a ceiling and retail lending rates for which it maintained a floor.[3] These two restrictions are likely to remain in the foreseeable future, although steps have been taken recently to speed up the interest rate liberation. The PBoC considers the two restrictions important for maintaining financial stability. In particular, removing the limits of lending and deposit rates might result in undesirable market competition (Zhou, 2005). Another reason for keeping them is to maintain a healthy profit margin and, thus, the profitability for commercial banks in China (Geiger, 2006).

Previously, during the era when central banks set deposit and lending rates, changes in the regulated rates directly influenced the retail lending market. This effect is still present, but only when the regulated (ceiling for) deposit rates or the regulated (floor for) lending rates are binding. It is generally believed that regulated deposit rates are binding, as the actual deposit rates have been clustered at the regulated level, which implies that the equilibrium deposit rates in the absence of such a restriction could be higher than the regulated rates.

By contrast, it is less clear whether regulated lending rates are binding. As the PBoC allows actual lending rates to float downward to 90% of the regulated rates, we consider this lower bound as the floor for lending rates. Table 1 shows that more than 80% of the bank's commercial loans were lent at rates higher than the floor for lending rates. The proportion of loans lent around the floor rate has decreased in recent years. This clearly showed the effects of monetary policy tightening as less liquidity drove up the effective lending rates.

The Interbank Money Market in China

From 1981 until 1996, lending and borrowing among Chinese banks was unregulated. However, the market was characterized by irregularities and

Table 1. Percentage of Commercial Loans Priced at Different Rates.

	Floating Downward [90% to 100% of benchmark]	At Regulated Level [100% benchmark]	Floating Upward [above benchmark]
2004	22.02	26.83	51.16
2005	21.67	24.99	53.34
2006	24.71	27.01	48.28
2007	27.60	27.83	44.57
2008	22.89	31.22	45.90
2009	29.53	32.32	38.15
2010	28.24	30.20	41.56
2011	10.79	28.20	61.00
2012	8.53	25.10	66.36
2013Q1	11.25	24.64	64.11

Source: PBoC Monetary Policy Report (2004–2010) and authors' calculation.

was generating excessive risk-taking by banks. Therefore, the PBoC centralized lending and borrowing through the China Foreign Exchange Trading System and created a national interbank market in 1996. This helped the PBoC monitor banks' behavior.

The interbank market[4] is composed of a money market, a bond market and a foreign exchange market. The money market is the focus of our chapter. The participants in the interbank money market include commercial banks and other financial corporations. While the market was initially intended to allow participants to trade short-term liquidity among themselves, later it became an important platform for the PBoC to conduct open-market operations. The bond market is for direct financing but it is restricted to a few financial institutions and big corporations. The PBoC regularly intervenes in the foreign exchange market to manage the fluctuation of the RMB exchange rate with US dollar. Currently, eight currency pairs are traded in the foreign exchange market.

At present, there are several instruments trading in the interbank money market in addition to uncollateralized lending and borrowing. The repo market is the most liquid, with an average daily turnover of 566.8 billion renminbi in 2012, which is three times the daily turnover of interbank lending and borrowing.[5] It is worth noting that the four largest state-owned banks are generally net lenders in the repo market, and other commercial banks, foreign banks, and other financial institutions are net borrowers in 2012.

Close to 90% of the transactions in the repo market are concentrated in agreements with maturities equal to or less than 7 days, and the 7-day repo rate is therefore the most representative short-term interbank rate. The central bank interest rate on excessive reserves serves as a floor for short-term interest rates, while the PBoC's discount rate can be considered a ceiling. The 7-day repo rate is sometimes very volatile. Large IPO activities and central bank monetary policy actions all affect the liquidity in the interbank market and therefore the short-term interest rates. Another two frequently quoted interbank rates are the Shanghai Interbank Offered Rate (SHIBOR) and the China Interbank Offered Rate (CHIBOR). In 2007, the PBoC established the SHIBOR system. The SHIBOR is not based on transaction rates in the interbank market but is a quote-based average similar to LIBOR. Currently, 16 banks provide quotes, and the rates are fixed at 11:30 a.m. every business day. The CHIBOR is a weighted average of the daily transaction rates announced at the end of every business day. The PBoC has been pushing SHIBOR as the benchmark interest rate for pricing. In the meantime, the CHIBOR is less used for the purpose of pricing. On the other hand, the 7-day SHIBOR, CHIBOR, and repo rates have followed each other closely. The wide use of the SHIBOR as the benchmark rate for pricing is yet to be achieved.

Open market operations, changes in reserve requirements and intervention in the foreign exchange market directly affect the liquidity in the interbank market. Changes in the benchmark lending and deposit rates, as well as window guidance, indirectly affect the interbank liquidity through banks' reactions to those changes. In the next section, the pattern and effectiveness of China's monetary policy implementation is analyzed, with special attention paid to the recent global financial crisis period

IMPLEMENTING MONETARY POLICY IN CHINA

General Pattern of China's Monetary Policy Implementation

As the PBoC uses a variety of policy instruments to implement monetary policy, we start by briefly reviewing the changes in these instruments over time and the relationships between the instruments and the interbank rates. Fig. 2 plots the RRR, net liquidity injection through OMOs, regulated deposit and lending rates, and remuneration rates on required and excess

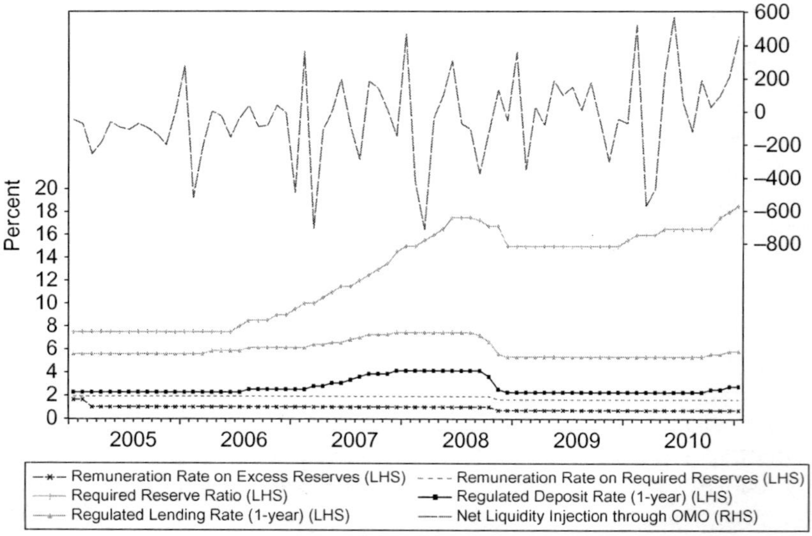

Fig. 2. Monetary Policy Instruments. *Source*: CEIC and authors' calculation.

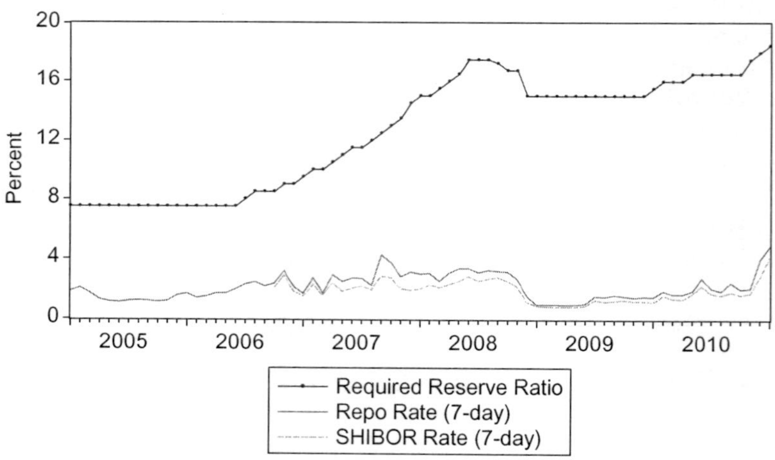

Fig. 3. RRR and Interbank Rates. *Source*: CEIC and authors' calculation.

reserves together. Figs. 3–5 plot the first four instruments against the interbank rates.

Several observations are warranted. First, changes in RRR, regulated deposit rate and lending rate, and OMO are the most frequently used

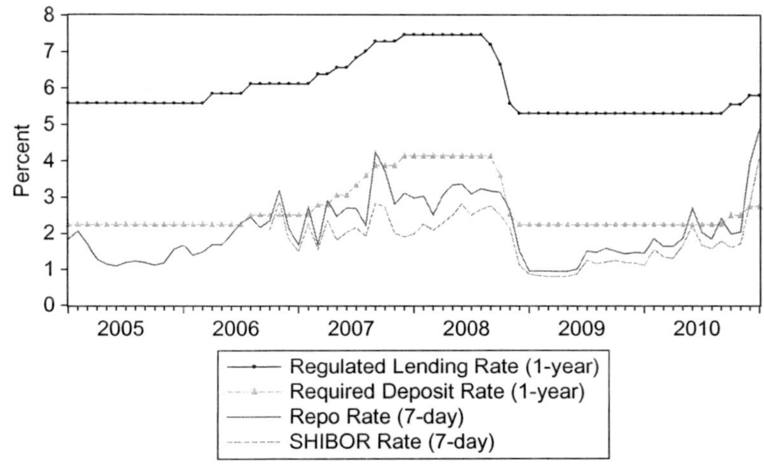

Fig. 4. Regulated Deposit, Lending Rate, and Interbank Rates. *Source*: CEIC and authors' calculation.

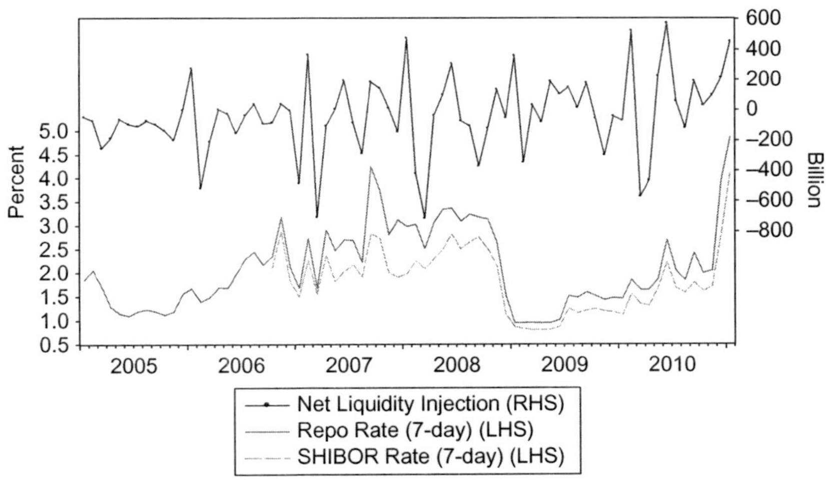

Fig. 5. Net Liquidity Injection through OMO and Interbank Rates. *Source*: WIND, CEIC, and authors' calculation.

policy tools. Other measures such as changes in the remuneration on reserves are used much less frequently. Second, the first three instruments experienced sharp increases or falls together. The net injection or withdraw of liquidity through OMOs had sharp changes during the period when the other tools were on the path of increasing or decreasing. This indicates that when the PBoC tightens or loosens the monetary policy stance, it seeks to adjust banks' costs of funds both in interbank and deposit markets and to adjust the cost of capital for firms and individuals simultaneously. One example is the progressive tightening from 2005 onwards in response to overheating in the economy, in particular to very high investment spending and a rise in inflation in 2005 and 2007. Another example is the policy loosening in the fall of 2008, aiming to mitigate the effects on the Chinese economy of the rapidly worsening global economic and financial conditions. These are compatible with a "belts and suspenders" approach to the monetary policy in which many, if not all, policy levers are pulled simultaneously to achieve the desired change in monetary conditions. Again, this approach is in contrast to the approach in advanced economies where, typically, only a short-term policy rate is changed as a result of a change in the monetary policy stance. In the case of the United States, the short-term policy rate is the federal funds rate, while in the Euro area, it is the refinancing rate. Third, changes in the regulated lending and deposit rates were the same in the past two years, showing the intention of the PBoC to maintain a stable interest rate gap for banks. Fourth, changes in the policy instruments do not have a clear relationship with the changes in the interbank rates. For example, in Fig. 3, during mid-2006 and mid-2007, the repo and SHIBOR rates, on an average, did not increase continuously following the continued rise in the RRR, although in some periods, they showed a positive relationship. Fig. 4 shows that raising the regulated deposit and lending rates tends to be associated with lower interbank rates for several months in 2006, 2007, and 2010, which seems to be inconsistent with the policy intention. The model in the next section tries to explain this point.

Furthermore, it is not possible to assess the effect of changes in the various monetary policy instruments on total bank lending. Table 2 provides an example of an episode of monetary policy changes in 2006. From August to September 2006, the PBoC tightened monetary conditions by raising regulated rates for deposits and lending, raising the RRR, and withdrawing liquidity.[6] Surprisingly, however, the interbank rate fell and new loans increased, suggesting that these measures were in fact expansionary. However, these ex-post data masked the individual effect of each policy instrument since the data reflected the combining effects of different policy instruments.

Table 2. Episode in 2006 August–October.

Period		Policy Actions		7-Day Repo Rate Change (bps)	New Loan Growth (%)
August 15–September 30	August 15 August 19	Increase in RRR by 0.5% Increase in the regulated deposit of liquidity and lending rate by 27 bps	Withdraw liquidity through OMOs of 59.2 billion	− 14.5	18
October 1–31		Withdraw liquidity through OMO of 97.25 billion		31	−90

Note: Liquidity withdrawn through OMOs is a sum of weekly net liquidity injection throughout the corresponding period. Liquidity injected during a period shorter than a working week is computed as a proportion of the weekly amount. The change in the 7-day repo rate is the difference between the rate on the last day and the first day of that period. The new loan growth from August 15 to September 30 is the growth relative to the new loans in July 1 to August 14, treated as the new loans in July plus half of the new loans in August. The same growth in October takes the new loans in September as a base month.
Source: CEIC, WIND, and author's calculation.

Implementation of Monetary Policy in China Since the Global Financial Crisis

The global financial crisis hit China in the middle of a tightening cycle of monetary policy. From 2006 onward, the PBoC increased the RRR 18 times, raising it to 17.5% in June 2008. The benchmark deposit and lending rates were raised 7 times until the one-year benchmark lending rate reached 7.47% and the one-year benchmark deposit rate reached 4.14% in September 2008. The resulting interest rate spread of 3.33% was intended to maintain a healthy profit margin for commercial banks and give them incentives to lend.

With the global financial crisis worsening after the collapse of Lehman in September 2008, the Chinese government adopted an RMB 4 trillion fiscal stimulus package in late 2008. On the monetary side, the PBoC drastically stopped the tightening cycle. Within three months after September 2008, the PBoC lowered RRR repeatedly to 15.5%. It also lowered the benchmark lending rate to 5.31% and the benchmark deposit to 2.25%, maintaining an interest rate differential of 3.06%. While window guidance traditionally had been used solely to curtail excess lending, in this period and through 2009 the PBoC used it to encourage banks to lend. As a result, new lending in 2009 reached RMB 9.6 trillion, or twice the amount in

2008. The loosening of several monetary policy instruments simultaneously and continuously in a short period of time was thus effective in achieving the PBoC's policy objectives.

With the global financial crisis deepening, policy interest rates in advanced economies were cut to almost zero and quantitative easing was adopted in the United States and the United Kingdom. With interest rates much above those in the major currencies, China faced strong appreciation pressure on its currency. Large capital inflows, irrespectively of whether they take the form of QFII, FDI, or are disguised in the form of a trade surplus, together with unprecedented fiscal and monetary stimulus drove up CPI inflation rapidly to 5.4% in 2011. With one-year deposit rates at only 2.25%, China entered into a period of negative real interest rates.

To dampen inflation, the PBoC started a new round of policy tightening in the middle of the global financial crisis. From January 2010 to July 2011, the PBoC raised RRR 12 times to 21.5% for large banks. Compared with issuing central bank bills, raising RRR is a less costly way to sterilize capital inflows and control money supply growth. In Governor Zhou Xiaochuan's words, it is a way to quarantine the base money in a pool (Zhou, 2010). During the same period, the PBoC also raised interest rates repeatedly, with the one-year benchmark lending rate reaching 6.56% and the one-year benchmark deposit rate 3.5%. As a result of this sharp policy tightening, CPI inflation was quickly brought under control and reached 2.7% in 2012.

China was among the few emerging market countries that were forced to tighten monetary policy during the financial crisis, in its case because of large capital inflows and the adoption of highly expansionary fiscal and monetary policy at the very beginning of the global financial turmoil. However, Chinese exports were hard hit by the crisis and domestic demand grew slowly, leading to a significant slowdown in economic growth. When inflation started to stabilize, the PBoC therefore began to relax monetary policy in November 2011. By the summer of 2012 the PBoC had cut its RRR three times to 20% for large banks, and cut interest rates twice, with the one year benchmark lending cut to 6% and one year deposit rate cut to 3%.

In sum, monetary policy in China has gone through a full cycle since the beginning of the global financial crisis. The PBoC drastically stopped the tightening in September 2008 after the collapse of Lehman Brothers, relaxed the policy until late 2009 when inflation picked up and started to tighten the policy again. Facing the prospect of significant economic slowdown, and with inflation pressures expected to remain moderate, the PBoC began to loosen policy yet again in November 2011. The main characteristics of the monetary policy actions of the PBoC in recent years were that several policy instruments were used simultaneously and in a series of actions within a short period of time. Adjustments of RRR were used extensively to sterilize the capital inflow. While these policy actions appear to have achieved the PBoC's objectives, with the rapid development of the capital market and shadow banking there is a risk that the ability of the PBoC to control credit and money growth is being eroded.

Recently the PBoC started a new series of reforms of its monetary policy framework (Zhou, 2012). In April 2012, it widened the band for the RMB-US dollar exchange rate around the central parity from 0.5% to 1%, which was intended to reduce the need for central bank intervention in the foreign exchange market. In June 2012, the PBoC increased the flexibility of the benchmark rates by allowing the one-year deposit rate to float up to 10% above (or 1.1 times) the benchmark deposit rate, and the one-year lending rate to float down to 30% below (or 0.7 times) the benchmark lending rate. This effectively made the benchmark deposit and lending rates less binding, which is a step towards their full liberalization. Furthermore, in July 2013 the PBOC removed the floors on the lending rates, controls on bill discount rates and lending rates of rural cooperatives.

In the next section, the effects of changes in individual policy instruments are analyzed in a model where market forces and regulation coexist.

THE MODELING FRAMEWORK

The Theoretical Model

To study the effect of monetary policy instruments on aggregate bank loans, we present a simple model that integrates regulated deposit and lending rates with a competitive interbank market. This model is based on the model developed by Porter and Xu (2009), which is, in turn, an extended version of the model developed by Freixas and Rochet (2008). We assume that each bank chooses deposits, excess reserves, central bank bills, and loans to maximize profits, given the RRR, the reserve remuneration rate, and the regulated interest rates for deposit and lending. Thus, each bank's profit maximization problem is given as

$$\pi_i = \max_{L_i, E_i, D_i, B_i} \Big\{ r_L L_i + r_E E_i + r_R \alpha D_i + r_B B_i + r M_i - r_D D_i \tag{1}$$

$$- c(D_i, L_i) - \frac{\beta}{2}\left(E_i - E^T\right)^2 - \frac{\kappa}{2}\left(L_i - L^T\right)^2 \Big\}$$

where L_i denotes the level of loans, E_i is the level of excess reserves, αD_i is the amount of required reserves (with α being the RRR and D_i the total deposits), B_i is the quantity of central bank bill holdings, which changes as a consequence of open-market operations,[7] and M_i is the net position in the interbank market. The relevant interest rates are denoted by r_L, r_E, r_R, r, r_D, and r_B.

Eq. (1) states that bank profits are the sum of revenue minus costs. Revenue comes from retail lending, $r_L L_i$; holdings of excess reserves,[8] $r_E E_i$; holdings of required reserves, $r_R \alpha D$; revenues on holdings of central bank bills, $r_B B_i$; and lending in the interbank market, $r M_i$. The costs arise from interest payments on deposits, $r_D D_i$; the management of central bank bill holdings, deposits, and loans, $c(\cdot)$;[9] and the cost of deviations of reserves from their target level E_i^T, $\frac{\beta}{2}\left(E_i - E_i^T\right)^2$, with $\beta>0$.[10] The last term captures window guidance, that is, the target loan level L^T set occasionally by the PBoC. Banks who lend more or less than the policy target level have to pay a penalty, which is the product of the quantity $\frac{1}{2}\left(L_i - L^T\right)^2$ and the unit cost κ.[11]

The net position on the interbank market is given by M_i such that

$$M_i = D_i - L_i - E_i - \alpha D_i - B_i \tag{2}$$

The management costs are given by

$$C(D_i, L_i) = \frac{c_{Di} D_i^2 + c_{Li} L_i^2}{2} \tag{3}$$

with c_{Di}, $c_{Li}>0$.

Following Bartolini, Bertola, and Prati (1999) and Campbell (1987), we assume that banks are concerned about their access to liquidity. The cost is modeled as a quadratic function of the deviation of the actual excess reserves holding from the target level. Using Eqs. (2) and (3), the profit maximization problem (1) becomes

$$\pi_i = \max_{L_i,\, E_i,\, D_i,\, B_i} \Big\{ (r_L - r)L_i + (r_E - r)E_i + [r - r_D + \alpha(r_R - r)]D_i \tag{4}$$

$$+ (r_B - r)B_i - \frac{c_{Di}D_i^2 + c_{Li}L_i^2}{2} - \frac{\beta}{2}\left(E_i - E_i^T\right)^2 - \frac{\kappa}{2}\left(L_i - L^T\right)^2 \Big\} \tag{5}$$

Rearranging the first-order conditions with respect to L_i, we obtain

$$r_L = r + c_{Li}L_i + \kappa\left(L_i - L^T\right) \tag{6}$$

Eq. (6) indicates that the optimal amount of loans is given by the point where the marginal benefit of loans equals the marginal cost of loans. The marginal benefit is the interest rate in retail lending, and the marginal cost consists of three components: the interbank rate, the cost of managing the loans, and the cost of deviating from the policy-guided level of loans.

Similarly, the first-order condition for excess reserves can be rearranged to yield

$$r_E = r + \beta[E_i - E_i^T] \tag{7}$$

Thus, the optimal level of excess reserves is selected such that remuneration equals the cost of holding them. This cost is given by the sum of the interbank rate and the cost of deviation from the target excess reserve level.

Turning to deposits, we obtain

$$\alpha r_R + (1 - \alpha)r = r_D + c_{Di}D_i \tag{8}$$

Thus, the bank should attract deposits to the point where their marginal benefit and marginal cost are equal. The benefit of holding deposits is the sum of the interest earned on required reserves, αr_R, and the return of interbank lending from the part of deposits that do not serve as required reserves, $(1 - \alpha)r$. The cost is composed of the interest rate on deposits, r_D, and management costs.

Finally, the optimal quantity of central bank bills to hold is given by the level that equates the central bank bill yield with the opportunity cost of holding central bank bills, r:

$$r_B = r \tag{9}$$

Holding central bank bills is therefore a perfect substitute for lending the same amount of funds in the interbank market.

From Eq. (6), the supply for loans can be written as

$$L_i = \frac{r_L - r + \kappa L^T}{c_{Li} + \kappa} \tag{10}$$

A bank's loan supply increases along with the spread between the retail lending rate and the interbank lending rate. Furthermore, a bank will increase its supply for loans if the PBoC raises the target level of loans.

From Eq. (7), the optimal amount of excess reserves is expressed as

$$E_i = \frac{1}{\beta}(r_E - r) + E_i^T \tag{11}$$

From Eq. (8), the deposit demand function is

$$D_i = \frac{1}{c_{Di}}(r - r_D - \alpha(r - r_R)) \tag{12}$$

Banks demand more deposits if the net gain of lending out the deposits in the interbank market, $r - r_D$, increases; they demand fewer deposits when the opportunity cost of the required reserves, $\alpha(r - r_R)$, rises.

Assuming there are N banks in the interbank market, the market clearing condition is

$$\sum_{i=1}^{N} M_i = 0 \tag{13}$$

The supply of central bank bills is exogenous and set through OMOs. r_B or r is determined by the interbank market clearing condition (Eq. 13).

Thus far, we have assumed that banks maximize profits by choosing deposits, loans, excess reserves and central bank bill holdings given interest rates and their cost functions. The net position M_i of each bank can be positive, zero, or negative, while the sum of M_i equals zero, as shown in Eq. (13). Plugging Eqs. (10) through (12) into Eq. (13), we have three unknowns to be determined: the interbank market rate, r; the deposit rate, r_D; and the retail lending rate, r_L. In the next section, we study the model solution and the impact of changes in policy instruments on interbank rate and lending.

The Impact on the Interbank Rate and Bank Loans

We first discuss the solution for the standard case in which the interest rates for lending and deposits are market determined and there is no window guidance.

Case 1: r_L and r_D are market determined, and $\kappa = 0$.

In the standard case, the retail lending rate, r_L, and deposit rate, r_D, are endogenously determined. To capture the demand side of the loan market, we simply assume that the aggregate loan demand is negatively related to the lending rate and positively related to the real GDP and the price level:

$$L^d = L^d\left(\overset{-}{r_L}, \overset{+}{Y}, \overset{+}{P}\right) \tag{14}$$

Loan supply is the sum of the loan supply of the individual bank:

$$L^s = \sum_{i=1}^{N} \frac{r_L - r}{c_{Li}} \tag{15}$$

so that the equilibrium lending rate, r_L^*, is implicitly determined by

$$L^d\left(\overset{-}{r_L}, \overset{+}{Y}, \overset{+}{P}\right) = \sum_{i=1}^{N} \frac{r_L - r}{c_{Li}} \tag{16}$$

Thus, we can solve for r_L^*:

$$r_L^* = h\left(\overset{+}{r}, \overset{+}{Y}, \overset{+}{P}\right) \tag{17}$$

where h is assumed to be continuously differentiable. Thus, r_L^* is positively related to the interbank rate, r; the real GDP, Y; the price level, P; and the loan management costs, as captured by c_{Li}. Furthermore, we assume that the supply of deposits is a function of the deposit rate, the real GDP, and the price level:

$$D^s = D^s\left(\overset{+}{r_D}, \overset{+}{Y}, \overset{-}{P}\right) \tag{18}$$

In equilibrium, we have

$$D^s\left(\overset{+}{r_D}, \overset{+}{Y}, \overset{-}{P}\right) = D^d = \sum_{i=1}^{N} D_i = \sum_{i=1}^{N} \frac{1}{c_{Di}}(r - r_D - \alpha(r - r_R)) \tag{19}$$

By solving Eq. (19), the equilibrium deposit rate, r_D^*, is obtained:

$$r_D^* = f\left(\overset{+}{r}, \overset{-}{Y}, \overset{+}{P}, \overset{+}{r_R}, \overset{\pm}{\alpha}\right) \tag{20}$$

where f is assumed to be continuously differentiable. Thus, r_D^* is positively related to the interbank rate, r, and negatively related to the price level, P, and the real GDP, Y. Additionally, r_D^* is positively related to the remuneration rate on required reserves, r_R, if the opportunity cost of required reserves, $r - r_R$, is non-zero. Furthermore, if $r - r_R > 0$, r_D^* falls with the required reserve ratio, α, then the opposite is true when $r - r_R < 0$. If $r - r_R = 0$, the equilibrium deposit rate is independent of α.[12] Substituting r_L and r_D in Eqs. (10) and (12) with r_L^* and r_D^*, respectively, and substituting M_i with D_i, L_i, E_i, and B, the sum of the aggregate net position, that is, Eq. (13), can be expressed as

$$F(\cdot) = \sum_{i=1}^{N} M_i = \sum_{i=1}^{N} [(1-\alpha)D_i - L_i - E_i] - B$$

$$= (1-\alpha)D^* - L^* - \sum_{i=1}^{N} E_i - B \tag{21}$$

where

$$D^* = D^s\left(\overset{+}{f}\left(\overset{+}{r}, \overset{-}{Y}, \overset{+}{P}, \overset{+}{r_R}, \overset{\pm}{\alpha}\right), \overset{+}{Y}, \overset{-}{P}\right) = \sum_{i=1}^{N} \frac{1}{c_{Di}}\left(r - f\left(\overset{+}{r}, \overset{-}{Y}, \overset{+}{P}, \overset{+}{r_R}, \overset{\pm}{\alpha}\right) - \alpha(r - r_R)\right) \tag{22}$$

and

$$L^* = L^d\left(\overset{-}{h\left(\overset{+}{r}, \overset{+}{Y}, \overset{+}{P}\right)}, \overset{+}{Y}, \overset{+}{P}\right) = \sum_{i=1}^{N} \frac{h\left(\overset{+}{r}, \overset{+}{Y}, \overset{+}{P}\right) - r}{c_{Li}} \tag{23}$$

The aggregate net position $F(\cdot)$ depends on four factors: the fraction of aggregate deposits that is not held as required reserves, $(1-\alpha)D^*$; aggregate loans, L^*; aggregate excess reserves, $\sum_{i=1}^{N} E_i$; and the aggregate amount of central bank bills, B, which is determined by the central bank's open-market operations and is exogenous. The equilibrium interbank rate, r^*, clears the interbank market and is given by

$$r^* = g(\alpha, r_R, r_E, B, Y, P) \tag{24}$$

The partial effect of adjusting the monetary policy instruments on the equilibrium loan level is given by Proposition 1.

Proposition 1. When the deposit rate, r_D, and lending rate, r_L, are market determined, and there is no window guidance policy, the impact of increasing the rate of remuneration on excess reserves and sales of central bank bills on interbank rates, that is, $\partial r/\partial r_E$ and $\partial r/\partial B$, is positive, and their impact on loans, that is, $\partial L/\partial r_E$ and $\partial L/\partial B$, is negative. The same impact of increasing RRR, $\partial r/\partial \alpha$ and $\partial L/\partial \alpha$, depends on $r - r_R$.

The proof of Proposition 1 is in the appendix. The intuition is as follows: increasing the remuneration on excess reserves leads banks to hold more excess reserves, which results in a negative aggregate position in the interbank market, $F(\cdot)<0$, at the original equilibrium interbank rate. Hence, the equilibrium interbank rate must increase to clear the interbank market, which results in a higher lending rate and a lower loan level.

Sales of bills by the central bank have the same effect on the interbank rate and loans as increasing the remuneration on excess reserve does by making the aggregate net position negative. The impact of a change in RRR depends on two factors. First, higher RRR reduces the funds available in the interbank market. Moreover, a higher RRR also raises the demand for deposits if there is a net interest gain on required reserves, that is, if $r_R - r$ is positive. It reduces the deposit demand if there is a net interest loss on required reserves, that is, if $r - r_R > 0$. It has no effect on deposit demand if $r_R - r = 0$. Thus, if $r - r_R \geq 0$, raising RRR reduces the liquidity in the interbank market and hence raises the interbank rate and reduces the lending, while the effect is ambiguous otherwise. These effects on the interbank rate and loans are summarized in Tables 3 and 4, respectively.

Thus far, we have discussed a model in which the interbank rate is determined in a competitive equilibrium under the assumptions that the interest rates on deposits and retail lending are fully liberalized and that the central bank does not have a loan target. This case is relevant for economies where central banks conduct monetary policy through interbank markets and where the interest rate transmission from wholesale to retail market is effective. While this is the case in advanced economies such as the United States and the Euro area, the PBoC continues to rely on direct regulation. We therefore consider how the introduction of regulated lending and deposit interest rates and a loan target change the conclusions from the above analysis.

Case 2: The central bank sets a loan target, a floor of r_L and a ceiling of r_D.

The existence of a loan target and the regulation of interest rates for deposits and lending imply that the central bank can intervene the liquidity at the retail level.

Table 3. Impact of Changes in Policy Instruments on the Interbank Money Market Rate.

Instrument	Case 1	Case 2.1	Case 2.2
	No regulation of retail interest rates and credit growth	$r_L^B < r_L^*$	$r_L^B \geq r_L^*$
		$r_D^B < r_D^*$	$r_D^B < r_D^*$
a	+ *if* $r - r_R \geq 0$ ambiguous otherwise	+	+
B	+	+	+
r_E	+	+	+
r_L^B	/	0	−
r_D^B	/	−	−
L^T	/	+	0

Note: The table shows the effect of raising each policy instrument on the interbank money market rate. "+" represents a positive effect, "−" represents a negative effect, and 0 denotes no effect. "/" denotes that raising the instrument in the corresponding row is not an option for the central bank in the case of the corresponding column. α is the required reserve ratio; **B** is the issuance of central bank bills through OMO; r_E is the remuneration on excess reserves; r_L^B is the regulated lending rate; r_D^B is the regulated deposit rate; L^T is the target level of loan growth set by the central bank.

Table 4. Impact of Changes in Policy Instruments on the Loans.

Instrument	Case 1	Case 2.1	Case 2.2
	No regulation of retail interest rates and credit growth	$r_L^B < r_L^*$	$r_L^B \geq r_L^*$
		$r_D^B < r_D^*$	$r_D^B < r_D^*$
a	$-$ *if* $r - r_R \geq 0$ ambiguous otherwise	$-$	0
B	$-$	$-$	0
r_E	$-$	$-$	0
$\mathbf{r}_L^B$	/	0	$-$
r_D^B	/	+	0
L^T	/	$\pm$	0

Note: The table shows the effect of raising each policy instrument on the interbank money market rate. "+" represents a positive effect, "−" represents a negative effect, and 0 denotes no effect. "/" denotes that raising the instrument in the corresponding row is not an option for the central bank in the case of the corresponding column. α is the required reserve ratio; B is the issuance of central bank bills through OMO; r_E is the remuneration on excess reserves; r_L^B is the regulated lending rate, r_D^B is the regulated deposit rate; L^T is the target level of loan growth set by the central bank.

First, with the introduction of a loan target, the individual bank's loan supply function is augmented, as in Eq. (10), and the resulting equilibrium retail lending rate is also negatively related to the loan target, that is,

$$r_L^* = h\left(\overset{+}{r}, \overset{+}{Y}, \overset{+}{P}, \overset{-}{L^T}\right) \tag{25}$$

Therefore, the equilibrium loan supply is

$$L^* = \sum_{i=1}^{N} \frac{h\left(\overset{+}{r^*}, \overset{+}{Y}, \overset{+}{P}, \overset{-}{L^T}\right) - r^* + \kappa L^T}{c_{Li} + \kappa} = L^d\left(\overset{-}{h\left(\overset{+}{r^*}, \overset{+}{Y}, \overset{+}{P}, \overset{-}{L^T}\right)}, \overset{+}{Y}, \overset{+}{P}\right) \tag{26}$$

Proposition 2. Raising the target loan level will result in a credit expansion if the perceived penalty of not obeying the loan target is large enough. The proof is available in the appendix.

Raising the target level for loans shifts the loan supply curve to the right, resulting in a lower lending rate and greater lending, given the interbank rate, r. On the other hand, a higher demand for liquidity by banks pushes up the interbank rate, which, in turn, tends to reduce the loan supply of banks. However, in deciding whether to increase lending, banks must consider the perceived penalty for deviating from the target loan level. If the perceived penalty is high enough, banks will choose to increase their loan supply.

The restrictions on deposit and retail lending rates complicate the analysis in case 1 above. The main issue is whether the restrictions are binding or not, which is unclear.

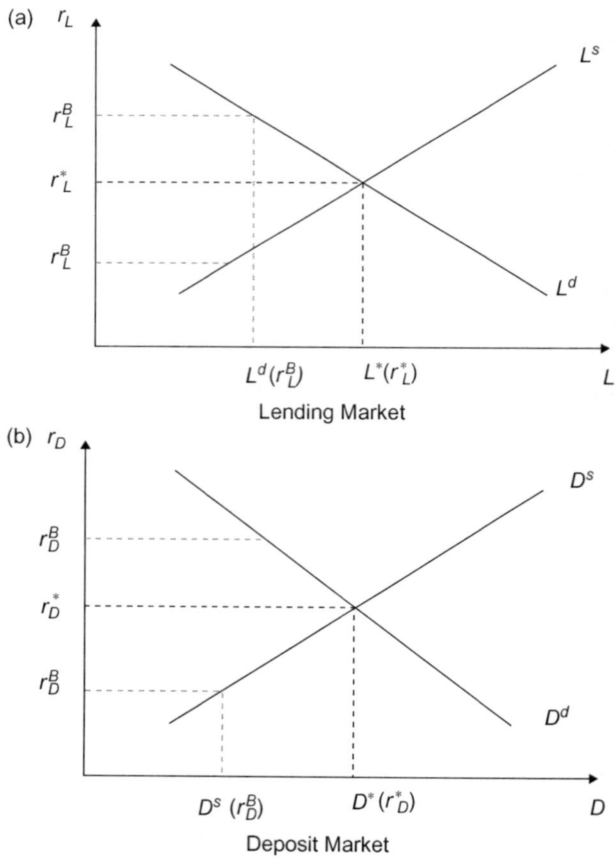

Fig. 6. Interest Rates in Lending and Deposit Markets.

Beginning in October 2004 to the present, the PBoC only imposes a floor on the retail lending rate and a ceiling on the deposit rate. Fig. 6 illustrates the equilibrium loan and deposit rates within this framework. The equilibrium levels of loans and lending rates are the same as those without restriction when the floor of the lending rate is not binding. However, when it is binding, the actual loan level is determined by loan demand, which is exogenous to banks. Similarly, if the ceiling for the deposit rate is below the equilibrium level without regulation, the actual level of deposit is determined by deposit supply. Consequently, whether the ceiling or floor for interest rates is binding or not is crucial because that determines whether the quantity of deposits and loans will rise, fall, or remain the same following a change in benchmark interest rates. As discussed in the second section, the ceiling for deposit rates in China is believed to be binding (i.e., the regulated deposit rate is below equilibrium), while it is unclear whether the floor for lending rates is binding. As the equilibrium deposit and lending rates without restrictions are unobservable, it is difficult for policy makers to know them, which leads to the risk that the consequences of a change in policy rates might be inconsistent with the policy intentions. In the following analysis, we focus on two sub-cases.

Case 2.1: The ceiling for the deposit rate is binding, and the floor for the lending rate is not binding ($r_L^B < r_L^*$ *and* $r_D^B < r_D^*$*).*

In this case, both the benchmark lending and deposit rates are below their equilibrium levels, which implies that the lending market equilibrium is unregulated, and deposits are supply determined. We can solve for r_L^* using Eq. (25), and the loan level is then given by Eq. (26). The aggregate net position in the interbank market is therefore given by

$$F(\cdot) = (1-\alpha)D^s\left(r_D^B\right) - L\left(h\left(\overset{+}{r}, \overset{+}{Y}, \overset{+}{P}, \overset{-}{L^T}\right), \overset{+}{Y}, \overset{+}{P}\right)^{-} - \sum_{i=1}^{N}\left(\frac{1}{\beta}(r_E - r) + E_i^T\right) - B \tag{27}$$

The effect of changes in policy instruments is presented in Proposition 3.

Proposition 3. When r_L^B provides a floor for the retail lending rate and r_D^B provides a ceiling for the deposit rate and these two rates are both below their equilibrium levels in the absence of regulation, increasing RRR or the remuneration rate on excess reserves or sales of central bank bills to the banking system raises the interbank rate and is contractionary.

Increasing the benchmark deposit rate lowers the interbank rate and expands bank credit, providing it remains below the equilibrium level. Changes in the regulated lending rate do not have any effect on the interbank rate and the level of loans if the lending rate remains below the equilibrium level. Raising the target level of loans can have an expansionary effect if the perceived penalty of defying the target level is high enough.

The proof of Proposition 3 is in the appendix. In this case, a higher RRR, a higher remuneration on excess reserves or sales of central bank bills reduces liquidity in the interbank market, which, in turn, pushes up the interbank rate and lowers lending. Therefore, these policies are all contractionary. Increasing the benchmark deposit rate attracts more deposits, assuming the elasticity of the deposit supply is positive. This will increase the liquidity of the interbank market, which will result in a lower interbank rate and higher lending. These policies are therefore expansionary. Raising the regulated lending rate does not change the level of loans and actual lending rate, as long as the increased level of lending rate remains below the equilibrium rate. Raising the target level of loans will have the same effect as in the case without the regulation of interest rates.

Case 2.2: Both the ceiling for the deposit rate and the floor for the lending rate are binding ($r_L^B \geq r_L^*$ and $r_D^B < r_D^*$). When the floor for the lending rate exceeds the equilibrium level in the absence of regulation, it is binding, and the level of loans is demand determined. As in Case 2.1, the deposit level is supply driven. Therefore, the aggregate net position in the interbank market is given by

$$F(\cdot) = (1-\alpha)D^s\left(r_D^B\right) - L^d\left(r_L^B\right) - \sum_{i=1}^{N}\left(\frac{1}{\beta}(r_E - r) + E_i^T\right) - B \quad (28)$$

In this case, only the change in the benchmark lending rate will affect the total amount of loans. As the loan level is solely determined by the aggregate loan demand, other monetary policy instruments have no effect on the loan level. An increase in the benchmark lending rate will reduce the total loan level. Moreover, raising the benchmark lending rate lowers the interbank rate, as banks will have less need to borrow from the interbank market, given that the total loan demand is reduced.

This partial effect of raising the benchmark lending rate on loans is given by

$$\frac{\partial L}{\partial r_L^B} = \frac{\partial}{\partial r_L^B} L^D\left(\overset{-}{r_L^B}, \overset{+}{Y}, \overset{+}{P}\right) < 0 \tag{29}$$

The effect on the interbank rate is

$$\frac{\partial r}{\partial r_L^B} = -\frac{\partial F / \partial r_L^B}{\partial F / \partial r} = -\frac{-\partial L^d\left(r_L^B\right) / \partial r_L^B}{\partial F / \partial r} < 0 \tag{30}$$

However, other monetary policy instruments also influence the interbank rate, as in Case 2.1. Thus, a rise in the benchmark deposit rate lowers the interbank rate, providing it remains below the equilibrium, while raising RRR or increasing remuneration on excess reserves or sales of central bank bills raises the interbank rate.

In this case, the central bank can directly influence the loan level by changing the benchmark lending rate. The interbank market plays no role in the transmission of monetary policy action. This means that the change in the interbank rate does not transmit to the retail lending rate and total level of lending. Therefore, all other policy instruments, such as a change in RRR or in the remuneration on excess reserves, and sales of central bank bills that only affect the interbank rate will have no effect on the total lending. In this sense, there is a disconnect between policy intention and total lending.

A summary of the individual effects of each policy tool for these two cases is presented in Tables 3 and 4. The implication for Chinese monetary policy transmission can be summarized as follows.

First, raising the deposit rate ceiling distorts the contractionary effects of raising RRR and contractionary OMOs when the deposit rate ceiling is binding. The distortion can reduce, offset, or dominate the effects, depending on the amount of liquidity it attracts to the banking system. Therefore, the interbank rate and bank lending resulting from a combination of these three actions may go in an unexpected direction. This explains the uncertainties in the 2006 episode presented in Table 2.

Second, the transmission of liquidity conditions from the interbank market to the retail lending market is blocked when both the ceiling for the deposit rate and the floor for the lending rate are binding. The only instrument that influences the bank lending is the floor for the lending rate.

Hence, the presence of interest rate regulation and the intervention on the interest rate at the retail level make it difficult for the interbank rate to signal monetary policy and transmit its effect further to the real economy.

One should bear in mind that our analysis is essentially a comparative static analysis. We also did not model the demand side of loans or the supply side of deposits. Our model is a one-period general equilibrium model that does not consider the intertemporal dynamics. In practice, monetary policy tightening or loosening usually occurs over several periods. It is carried out alternatively in a cyclical way. In this case, the monetary policy stance is usually not difficult to identify. With continuous tightening or loosening, the monetary policy can be effective in slowing down total commercial lending. However, given that there are other channels for firms to raise funds, such as bond or equity markets, the effectiveness of the monetary policy instruments, which only target the liquidity condition in the banking system, is more or less diluted.

CONCLUSION

In this chapter, we analyze the effects of changes in the monetary policy instruments in China. While central banks in advanced countries, at least before the financial crisis, implemented monetary policy by focusing solely on short-term interest rates in the interbank market, the PBoC's use of regulatory controls and moral suasion makes this an interesting question.

This chapter uses an extended version of the model developed by Porter and Xu (2009a) to show the effects of different monetary policy instruments in China. We find that the transmission of the effect of monetary policy instruments through bank lending channels depends on whether the floor on the lending rate and/or the ceiling on the deposit rate are binding. Our analysis leads to the following implications.

First, the interbank money market rates, such as SHIBOR and the interbank repo rates, are incomplete and potentially misleading indicators of the PBoC's policy intention, although they are determined by policy instruments. The reason is that, among the instruments, the regulation on deposit and lending rates impairs the transmission of the effect of other instruments, such as OMOs and changes in RRR. To properly characterize the central bank's policy intention requires information from all policy instruments. To develop the interbank rate as a benchmark interest rate and as a signal of the monetary policy stance, it would be necessary to liberalize the retail lending and deposit rates. Most recently, steps have been taken to speed up the interest rate liberalization. Effective 20 July 2013, the PBoC removed the floors of the benchmark lending rates.

Second, lack of information on the equilibrium retail interest rates in the absence of regulation leads to risks of policy errors. The combination of the effects of different policy instruments might not be consistent with the policy intention, which makes window guidance and other administrative measures necessary as policy tools.

Third, the monetary policy actions of PBoC since the global financial crisis have been effective. They showed that using several policy instruments simultaneously within a short period of time enabled them to achieve the desired outcome in terms of credit and money growth, which helped controlling the inflation.

NOTES

1. He and Pauwels (2008) and Shu and Ng (2010) construct indicators of the stance of monetary policy using PBoC statements or data on the policy instruments instead.
2. For more details, please see Porter and Xu (2009).
3. Exceptions are rural credit cooperatives, for which the ceiling for lending rates remains.
4. The interbank market is a misnomer. In China, it is not just a market between banks. Its participants include banks, large corporates, fund management companies, and securities companies.
5. Data source: China Financial Market Development Report 2012, People's Bank of China, and authors' calculation.
6. The defined tightening periods are consistent with the findings in Shu and Ng (2010).
7. We do not explicitly model other standing facilities such as central bank lending through the discount window, as they are fine tuning measures intended to maintain the interbank rate at the target level, and their effect on interbank rates is similar to that of open market operations.
8. We deviate from Porter and Xu (2009a), in that we distinguish between required and excess reserves, as the PBoC sets different interest rates for these two types of reserves, and we also consider window guidance.
9. Costs include implicit source costs to attract depositors, i.e., labor, physical capital, and material costs to produce services to depositors (Sealey & Lindley, 1977, p. 1254); costs to attract lenders; and costs to manage bond investment portfolios.
10. Reserves play the role of liquidity. Banks typically set a target level of reserves to finance unexpected inflow or outflow from banks' reserve accounts (Campbell, 1987, p. 61).
11. The penalty for deviating from the target loan level is difficult to measure, as it is usually implicit. However, PBoC, from time to time, sells a certain amount of central bank bills to banks whose loan levels are higher than the policy target level

(PBoC Monetary Policy Annual Report 2009). In this case, κ can be represented by $r_L - r_B$.

12. The U.S. Federal Reserve and the ECB typically set interest rates for required reserves to be close to the interbank rates in general. However, the sign of $r_R - r$ changed over time in China.

ACKNOWLEDGMENTS

This paper was written while Stefan Gerlach was Professor of Economics at the University of Frankfurt and when Qianying Chen was an economist at the Hong Kong Institute for Monetary Research. The views expressed in it are those of the authors, and do not necessarily reflect the institutions they are affiliated with. We thank Kenneth Chow and Amy Miao for excellent research assistance. All errors belong to the authors.

REFERENCES

Bartolini, L., Bertola, G., & Prati, A. (1999). Banks' reserves management, transaction costs, and the timing of the federal intervention. *Journal of Banking and Finance*, *25*, 1281–1317.

Campbell, J. Y. (1987). Money announcements, the demand for bank reserves, and the behavior of the federal funds rate within the statement week. *Journal of Money, Credit, and Banking*, *19*, 56–67.

Freixas, X., & Rochet, J.-C. (2008). *Microeconomics of banking*. Cambridge, MA: MIT Press.

Geiger, M. (2006). *Monetary policy in China (1994-2004): Targets, instruments and their effectiveness*. Wurzburg Economic Papers, No. 68.

Green, S., & Chang, J. (2006). The PBoC's big money problem, on the ground, Asia. *Standard Chartered*, June.

He, D., & Pauwels, L. L. (2008). *What prompts the people's bank of china to change its monetary policy stance?* Evidence from a Discrete Choice Model. HKMA Working Paper No. 06/2008. Hong Kong Monetary Authority, Hong Kong.

Laurens, B. J., & Maino, R. (2007). *China: Strengthening monetary policy implementation*. IMF Working Paper No. 07/14. International Monetary Fund, Washington, DC.

Liu, L.-G., & Zhang, W. (2007). *A new Keynesian model for analysing monetary policy in mainland China*. HKMA Working Paper No. 18/2007. Hong Kong Monetary Authority, Hong Kong.

Podpiera, R. (2006). *Progress in China's banking sector reform: Has bank behavior changed?* IMF Working Paper No. 06/71. International Monetary Fund, Washington, DC.

Porter, N., & Xu, T. T. (2009). *What drives China's interbank market?* IMF Working Paper No. 09/189. International Monetary Fund, Washington DC.

Sealey, C. W., & Lindley, J. T. (1977). Inputs, outputs, and theory of production cost at depository financial institutions. *Journal of Finance*, *32*, 1251–1266.

Shu, C., & Ng, B. (2010). Monetary stance and policy objectives in China: A narrative approach. *HKMA China Economic Issues*, *1*(10), Hong Kong Monetary Authority.

Zhou, X. (2005). *Q&A between Zhou and the journalists*. Retrieved from www.XINHUANET.com

Zhou, X. (2010). *A speech at first Caixin summit*. November 5, 2010.

Zhou, X. (2012). *Main characteristics of China's monetary policy in the new century: A speech at 2012 Caixin summit*. November 17, 2012.

APPENDIX

Proof of Proposition 1

The aggregate net position is given by

$$F(\cdot) = (1-\alpha)D^s - L^D - \sum_{i=1}^{N} E_i - B \tag{A.1}$$

$$= (1-\alpha)D^s\left(f\left(\overset{+}{r}, \overset{-}{Y}, \overset{\overset{+}{+}}{P}, \overset{+}{r_R}, \overset{\pm}{\alpha}\right), \overset{+}{Y}, \overset{-}{P}\right).$$

$$- L^D\left(h\left(\overset{+}{r}, \overset{+}{Y}, \overset{\overset{-}{+}}{P}\right), \overset{+}{Y}, \overset{+}{P}\right)$$

$$- \sum_{i=1}^{N}\left(\frac{1}{\beta}(r_E - r) + E_i^T\right) - B$$

The partial effect of a change in interbank market rate on the aggregate net position is

$$\partial F(\cdot)/\partial r = (1-\alpha)\frac{\partial}{\partial r}D^s - \frac{\partial L^D}{\partial r} - \frac{\partial}{\partial r}\sum_{i=1}^{N} E_i - \frac{\partial B}{\partial r} \tag{A.2}$$

$$\begin{aligned} &= \underbrace{(1-\alpha)\frac{\partial}{\partial r}D^s\left(f\left(\overset{+}{r}, \overset{-}{Y}, \overset{\overset{+}{+}}{P}, \overset{+}{r_R}, \overset{\pm}{\alpha}\right), \overset{+}{Y}, \overset{-}{P}\right)}_{>0} \\ &\quad \underbrace{-\frac{\partial}{\partial r}L^D\left(h\left(\overset{+}{r}, \overset{+}{Y}, \overset{\overset{-}{+}}{P}\right), \overset{+}{Y}, \overset{+}{P}\right)}_{<0} + \underbrace{\frac{N}{\beta}}_{>0} \end{aligned} \tag{A.3}$$

which implies

$$\frac{\partial F(\cdot)}{\partial r > 0} \tag{A.4}$$

The partial effects of raising remuneration on excess reserves on aggregate position is given by

$$\frac{\partial F(\cdot)}{\partial r_E} = -\frac{\partial}{\partial r_E}\sum_{i=1}^{N} E_i = -\frac{N}{\beta} < 0 \tag{A.5}$$

Assuming that h and f are continuously differentiable functions and a point satisfying $F(\cdot) = 0$ and $\partial F(\cdot)/\partial r$ is non-zero, using the implicit function theorem, we obtain the partial effect of remuneration on excess reserves on interbank rate as follows:

$$\frac{\partial r}{\partial r_E} = -\frac{\partial F(\cdot)/\partial r_E}{\partial F(\cdot)/\partial r} > 0 \tag{A.6}$$

In turn, the impact on loans is

$$\frac{\partial L}{\partial r_E} = \frac{\partial L^D}{\partial h}\frac{\partial h}{\partial r}\frac{\partial r}{\partial r_E} = -\frac{\partial L^D}{\partial h}\frac{\partial h}{\partial r}\frac{\partial F(\cdot)/\partial r_E}{\partial F(\cdot)/\partial r} < 0 \tag{A.7}$$

Similarly, the partial effect of changes in remuneration on required reserves on the interbank rate and loans is

$$\frac{\partial F(\cdot)}{\partial r_R} = (1-\alpha)\frac{\partial}{\partial r_R}D^s > 0 \tag{A.8}$$

$$\frac{\partial r}{\partial r_R} = -\frac{\partial F(\cdot)/\partial r_R}{\partial F(\cdot)/\partial r} < 0 \tag{A.9}$$

$$\frac{\partial L}{\partial r_R} = \frac{\partial L^D}{\partial h}\frac{\partial h}{\partial r}\frac{\partial r}{\partial r_R} = -\frac{\partial L^D}{\partial h}\frac{\partial h}{\partial r}\frac{\partial F(\cdot)/\partial r_R}{\partial F(\cdot)/\partial r} > 0 \tag{A.10}$$

The impact of RRR is given by

$$\frac{\partial F(\cdot)}{\partial \alpha} = \underbrace{-D^s}_{<0} + \underbrace{(1-\alpha)\frac{\partial}{\partial \alpha}D^s}_{>0} >/<0 \tag{A.11}$$

$$\frac{\partial r}{\partial \alpha} = -\frac{\partial F(\cdot)/\partial \alpha}{\partial F(\cdot)/\partial r} </>0 \tag{A.12}$$

$$\frac{\partial L}{\partial \alpha} = \frac{\partial L^D}{\partial h}\frac{\partial h}{\partial r}\frac{\partial r}{\partial \alpha} = -\frac{\partial L^D}{\partial h}\frac{\partial h}{\partial r}\frac{\partial F(\cdot)/\partial \alpha}{\partial F(\cdot)/\partial r} >/<0 \tag{A.13}$$

The impact of sales of central bank bills is thus:

$$\frac{\partial F(\cdot)}{\partial B} = -1 \tag{A.14}$$

$$\frac{\partial r}{\partial B} = -\frac{\partial F(\cdot)/\partial B}{\partial F(\cdot)/\partial r} >0$$

$$\frac{\partial L}{\partial B} = \frac{\partial L^D}{\partial h}\frac{\partial h}{\partial r}\frac{\partial r}{\partial B} = -\frac{\partial L^D}{\partial h}\frac{\partial h}{\partial r}\frac{\partial F(\cdot)/\partial B}{\partial F(\cdot)/\partial r} <0 \tag{A.15}$$

Q.E.D

Proof of Proposition 2

The equilibrium levels of deposit and loan are given by

$$D^* = D^s\left(f\left(\overset{+}{r}, \overset{-}{Y}, \overset{+}{\overset{+}{P}}, \overset{+}{r_R}, \overset{\pm}{\alpha}\right), \overset{+}{Y}, \overset{+}{P}\right) = \sum_{i=1}^{N}\frac{1}{c_{Di}}\left(r - f\left(\overset{+}{r}, \overset{-}{Y}, \overset{+}{P}, \overset{+}{r_R}, \overset{\pm}{\alpha}\right) - \alpha(r - r_R)\right) \tag{A.16}$$

$$L^* = {}_{i=1}^{N}\frac{h\left(\overset{+}{r}, \overset{+}{Y}, \overset{+}{P}, \overset{-}{L^T}\right) - r + \kappa L^T}{c_{Li} + \kappa}$$

and the aggregate net position is given by

$$F(\cdot) = (1-\alpha)D^s - L^D - \sum\nolimits_{i=1}^{N} E_i - B \tag{A.17}$$

$$= (1-\alpha)D^s\left(\overset{+}{f}\left(\overset{+}{r}, \overset{-}{Y}, \overset{+}{P}, \overset{+}{r_R}, \overset{\pm}{\alpha}\right), \overset{+}{Y}, \overset{+}{P}\right).$$

$$- L^D\left(\overset{-}{h}\left(\overset{+}{r}, \overset{+}{Y}, \overset{+}{P}, \overset{-}{L^T}\right), \overset{+}{Y}, \overset{+}{P}\right)$$

$$- \sum\nolimits_{i=1}^{N}\left(\frac{1}{\beta}(r_E - r) + E_i^T\right) - B$$

The partial effect of a change in the interbank market rate on the aggregate net position is

$$\frac{\partial F(\cdot)}{\partial r} = (1-\alpha)\frac{\partial}{\partial r}D^s - \frac{\partial L^D}{\partial r} - \frac{\partial}{\partial r}\sum\nolimits_{i=1}^{N} E_i - \frac{\partial B}{\partial r} \tag{A.18}$$

$$= \underbrace{(1-\alpha)\frac{\partial}{\partial r}D^s\left(\overset{+}{f}\left(\overset{+}{r}, \overset{-}{Y}, \overset{+}{P}, \overset{+}{r_R}, \overset{\pm}{\alpha}\right), \overset{+}{Y}, \overset{+}{P}\right)}_{>0} \underbrace{-\frac{\partial}{\partial r}L^D\left(\overset{-}{h}\left(\overset{+}{r}, \overset{+}{Y}, \overset{+}{P}, \overset{-}{L^T}\right), \overset{+}{Y}, \overset{+}{P}\right)}_{<0} + \underbrace{\frac{N}{\beta}}_{>0} > 0 \tag{A.19}$$

which implies

$$\frac{\partial F(\cdot)}{\partial r} > 0 \tag{A.20}$$

$$\frac{\partial F(\cdot)}{\partial L^T} = -\left(\frac{\partial L^D\left(\overset{-}{h}\left(\overset{+}{r}, \overset{+}{Y}, \overset{+}{P}, \overset{-}{L^T}\right), \overset{+}{Y}, \overset{+}{P}\right)}{\partial h}\frac{\partial h}{\partial L^T}\right) < 0 \tag{A.21}$$

$$\frac{\partial r}{\partial L^T} = -\frac{\partial F(\cdot)/\partial L^T}{\partial F(\cdot)/\partial r} > 0 \tag{A.22}$$

$$\frac{\partial L}{\partial L^T} = \underbrace{\frac{\partial L^D\left(\overset{-}{h(\cdot)}, \overset{+}{Y}, \overset{+}{P}\right)}{\partial h}\frac{\partial h}{\partial r}\frac{\partial r}{\partial L^T}}_{<0} + \underbrace{\frac{\partial L^D\left(\overset{-}{h(\cdot)}, \overset{+}{Y}, \overset{+}{P}\right)}{\partial h}\frac{\partial h}{\partial L^T}}_{>0} </> 0 \tag{A.23}$$

If the perceived penalty of defying the loan target κ is high enough, then

$$\left|\frac{\partial h}{\partial L^T}\right| > \left|\frac{\partial h}{\partial r}\frac{\partial r}{\partial L^T}\right| \tag{A.24}$$

$$\frac{\partial L}{\partial L^T} > 0 \tag{A.25}$$

Q.E.D.

Proof of Proposition 3

In this case,

$$\frac{\partial F(\cdot)}{\partial r} = \frac{\partial}{\partial r}(1-\alpha)D^s\left(r_D^B\right) - \frac{\partial}{\partial r}L^D\left(\overset{-}{h\left(\overset{+}{r}, \overset{+}{Y}, \overset{+}{P}, \overset{-}{L^T}\right)}, \overset{+}{Y}, \overset{+}{P}\right) \tag{A.26}$$

$$-\frac{\partial}{\partial r}\sum_{i=1}^{N} E_i - \frac{\partial}{\partial r}B$$

$$= \underbrace{-\frac{\partial L^D}{\partial h}\frac{\partial h}{\partial r}}_{>0} + \frac{N}{\beta} > 0 \tag{A.27}$$

The impact of a change in regulated lending rates on aggregate net position is given by

$$\frac{\partial F(\cdot)}{\partial r_L^B} = 0 \tag{A.28}$$

Assuming that h is a continuously differentiable function and a point satisfying $F(\cdot) = 0$ and $\partial F(\cdot)/\partial r$ is non-zero, and by applying the implicit function theorem, this impact on interbank rate becomes

$$\frac{\partial r}{\partial r_L^B} = -\frac{\partial F(\cdot)/\partial r_L^B}{\partial F(\cdot)/\partial r} = 0 \tag{A.29}$$

and the impact on loans is therefore:

$$\frac{\partial L}{\partial r_L^B} = \frac{\partial L^D}{\partial h}\frac{\partial h}{\partial r}\frac{\partial r}{\partial r_L^B} = -\frac{\partial L^D}{\partial h}\frac{\partial h}{\partial r}\frac{\partial F(\cdot)/\partial r_L^B}{\partial F(\cdot)/\partial r} = 0 \tag{A.30}$$

Similarly, the impact of a change in the regulated deposit rate on net aggregate position, interbank rate, and loans is given by

$$\frac{\partial F(\cdot)}{\partial r_D^B} = (1-\alpha)\frac{\partial}{\partial r_D^B} D^s\left(r_D^B\right) > 0 \tag{A.31}$$

$$\frac{\partial r}{\partial r_D^B} = -\frac{\partial F(\cdot)/\partial r_D^B}{\partial F(\cdot)/\partial r} < 0 \tag{A.32}$$

$$\frac{\partial L}{\partial r_D^B} = \frac{\partial L^D}{\partial h}\frac{\partial h}{\partial r}\frac{\partial r}{\partial r_D^B} = -\frac{\partial L^D}{\partial h}\frac{\partial h}{\partial r}\frac{\partial F(\cdot)/\partial r_D^B}{\partial F(\cdot)/\partial r} > 0 \tag{A.33}$$

The effect of raising remuneration on excess reserves is

$$\frac{\partial F(\cdot)}{\partial r_E} = -\frac{\partial}{\partial r_E}\sum_{i=1}^{N} E_i = -\frac{N}{\beta} < 0 \tag{A.34}$$

$$\frac{\partial r}{\partial r_E} = -\frac{\partial F(\cdot)/\partial r_E}{\partial F(\cdot)/\partial r} > 0 \tag{A.35}$$

$$\frac{\partial L}{\partial r_E} = \frac{\partial L^D}{\partial h}\frac{\partial h}{\partial r}\frac{\partial r}{\partial r_E} = -\frac{\partial L^D}{\partial h}\frac{\partial h}{\partial r}\frac{\partial F(\cdot)/\partial r_E}{\partial F(\cdot)/\partial r} < 0 \tag{A.36}$$

and the effect of raising remuneration on required reserves is

$$\frac{\partial F(\cdot)}{\partial r_R} = 0 \tag{A.37}$$

$$\frac{\partial r}{\partial r_R} = -\frac{\partial F(\cdot)/\partial r_R}{\partial F(\cdot)/\partial r} = 0 \tag{A.38}$$

$$\frac{\partial L}{\partial r_R} = -\frac{\partial L^D}{\partial h}\frac{\partial h}{\partial r}\frac{\partial F(\cdot)/\partial r_R}{\partial F(\cdot)/\partial r} = 0 \tag{A.39}$$

and the impact of a higher RRR is given by

$$\frac{\partial F(\cdot)}{\partial \alpha} = -D^s\left(r_D^B\right) < 0 \tag{A.40}$$

$$\frac{\partial r}{\partial \alpha} = -\frac{\partial F(\cdot)/\partial \alpha}{\partial F(\cdot)/\partial r} > 0$$

$$\frac{\partial L}{\partial \alpha} = -\frac{\partial L^D}{\partial h}\frac{\partial h}{\partial r}\frac{\partial F(\cdot)/\partial \alpha}{\partial F(\cdot)/\partial r} < 0 \tag{A.41}$$

The impact of sales of central bank bills is

$$\frac{\partial F(\cdot)}{\partial B} = -1 < 0 \tag{A.42}$$

$$\frac{\partial r}{\partial B} = -\frac{\partial F(\cdot)/\partial B}{\partial F(\cdot)/\partial r} > 0$$

$$\frac{\partial L}{\partial B} = \frac{\partial L^D}{\partial h}\frac{\partial h}{\partial r}\frac{\partial r}{\partial B} = -\frac{\partial L^D}{\partial h}\frac{\partial h}{\partial r}\frac{\partial F(\cdot)/\partial B}{\partial F(\cdot)/\partial r} < 0$$

The impact of raising the loan target level is

$$\frac{\partial F(\cdot)}{\partial L^T} = -\left(\frac{\partial L^D\left(\overset{-}{h}\left(\overset{+}{r}, \overset{+}{Y}, \overset{+}{P}, \overset{-}{L^T} \right), \overset{+}{Y}, \overset{+}{P} \right)}{\partial h} \frac{\partial h}{\partial L^T} \right) < 0 \tag{A.43}$$

$$\frac{\partial r}{\partial L^T} = -\frac{\partial F(\cdot)/\partial L^T}{\partial F(\cdot)/\partial r} > 0 \tag{A.44}$$

$$\frac{\partial L}{\partial L^T} = \underbrace{\frac{\partial L^D\left(\overset{-}{h}(\cdot), \overset{+}{Y}, \overset{+}{P} \right)}{\partial h} \frac{\partial h}{\partial r} \frac{\partial r}{\partial L^T}}_{<0} + \underbrace{\frac{\partial L^D\left(\overset{-}{h}(\cdot), \overset{+}{Y}, \overset{+}{P} \right)}{\partial h} \frac{\partial h}{\partial L^T}}_{>0} < / > 0 \tag{A.45}$$

Q.E.D.

NON-CORE BANK LIABILITIES AND CREDIT GROWTH: EVIDENCE FROM AN EMERGING ECONOMY☆

Zubeyir Kilinc, Hatice Gokce Karasoy and Eray Yucel

ABSTRACT

The composition of bank liabilities has captured a lot of attention especially after the global financial crisis of 2008–2009. It is argued that a compositional change in non-core liabilities reflects the different stages of financial cycle. Banks usually fund their credits with core liabilities, which grow with households' wealth, but when there is a faster growth in credits compared to deposits, the banks often resort to non-core liabilities to meet the excess demand for loans. This chapter analyses the relationship between non-core liabilities and credits in a small open economy, namely Turkey. It investigates the relationship under alternative settings and presents consistent evidence on a robust relationship between credits and non-core liabilities under all frameworks. The study also verifies

☆The views expressed here are those of the authors and do not reflect the views of the Central Bank of the Republic of Turkey.

Global Banking, Financial Markets and Crises
International Finance Review, Volume 14, 71–90

ISSN: 1569-3767/doi:10.1108/S1569-3767(2013)0000014006

that elevated demand for credit may induce some increase in non-core liabilities. Finally, the relationship between non-core liabilities and credit growth is also affirmed in the long run.

Keywords: Core liabilities; non-core liabilities; credits; small open economy; VAR; VECM

JEL classifications: E44 – Financial markets and the macroeconomy; E51 – money supply; credit; money multipliers

INTRODUCTION

The composition of bank liabilities has captured a lot of attention especially after the 2008–2009 global financial crisis. The literature identifies two types of bank liabilities: core liabilities and non-core liabilities. Core liabilities are defined as banks' liabilities to the claimholders other than financial intermediaries, in other words, deposits. Non-core liabilities include those held by other financial intermediaries and foreign creditors. Shin and Shin (2011) along with others claim that the relative size of non-core liabilities can increase banks' exposures to the risks and therefore can be used as an indicator of the stage of financial cycle and the degree of vulnerability of financial institutions.

Hahm, Shin, and Shin (2012) point out that the core liabilities, which are the main source of funding available to the bank, grow with the size of the economy and wealth of the households. However, when credits grow faster than the core liabilities, the deposits are likely to be insufficient and banks turn to non-core liabilities to finance this excessive credit growth. Thus, it suggests a close association between non-core liabilities and credit growth. Based on this finding along with the others, non-core liabilities have become a target for macro-prudential policies. Therefore, more work is required regarding the dynamics of non-core liabilities as well as the relationship between non-core liabilities and credit growth.

There is a growing literature that investigates the abovementioned subject. Shin and Shin (2011), for instance, examine the dynamics of non-core liabilities in the Korean banking sector and find that they are closely related to the risk-taking behaviours of the banking sector. Hahm et al. (2012), with a very extensive list of countries, show that alternative measures for non-core liabilities have a significant predictive power on explaining currency and credit crises. Alichi, Ryoo, and Hong (2012) document that over the last decade, bank credits have moved beyond the cycle; but they also show that non-core liabilities are the main vehicle for the expansion of bank credits.

Despite these studies, the literature still lacks of country-specific analyses. This study aims at contributing to this strand of research. In particular, it intends to enlarge the avenue of research by presenting evidence from a small open economy and shedding light on the relationship between non-core liabilities and credit growth in Turkey. Ozen, Sahin, and Unalmis (2013) investigates the behaviour of non-core liabilities for Turkish economy during a financial stress abroad. It focuses on the turbulent times since during those times external financing sources is a crucial factor to maintain domestic financial stability. This study, however, tests the statement in the literature and sheds light on the particular relationship between non-core liabilities and credit growth for the Turkish economy.

Financial integration of the Turkish economy to global markets and deepening of the credit markets have gained speed after 2000s. Accordingly, our analysis starts from 2001.[1] It initially documents the basic features of non-core liabilities of Turkey and tests the basic hypothesis presented by the recent literature whether credit growth is indeed accompanied by non-core liabilities. Although recent literature makes it clear that the increased demand for credit may force banks to pull non-core liabilities, our analysis starts without any prior assumption. Next, it examines the relationship within a closed and a small open economy framework. Finally, it investigates the long-run relationship through a Vector Error Correction Model (VECM) analysis.

While constructing the data set, the literature is followed and two measures for non-core liabilities and one measure for core liabilities are built. In a closed economy set-up the basic variables are augmented with interest rate and real GDP. In an open economy framework, exchange rates and VIX are included. The details of the variables are discussed in the next section. The results are as follows. There is a robust relationship between the two variables – non-core banking liabilities and credit growth – under all frameworks. As is the case in the previous studies, non-core liabilities respond to the credit growth. In other words, the credit growth in the Turkish economy pulls non-core liabilities. This relation remains valid in the long run.

The second section introduces the data used in the analysis. The third section elaborates on empirical strategy and presents the results. The fourth section concludes the chapter.

VARIABLES AND DATA

The conceptual distinction between the core and non-core liabilities can be made according to whether the liability is to an ultimate domestic creditor, as discussed by Shin and Shin (2011). They provide the classification, as shown in Table 1, and argue that the claims held by domestic non-financial firms are not straightforward. Therefore, the researchers use alternative measures for non-core liabilities. Following mainly Hahm et al. (2012), we construct two measures. The first measure is the sum of total liabilities to non-residents and the difference between M3 and M2 aggregates of money. The second measure, on the other hand, includes only the total liabilities to non-residents.[2] For the core liabilities, there are alternative measures such as the sum of demand, time, savings and foreign currency deposits and restricted deposits, or monetary aggregates like M1 and M2. Following the literature, in this study we only consider M1 for the core liabilities. The last critical variable of this study, which is credits, is defined as the sum of the claims to the private sector and claims to the public non-financial sector.

Our data set covers the period of 2001Q4–2012Q1. The key variables of interest in this study, core liabilities, non-core liabilities and credits, are collected from the International Financial Statistics (IFS) of the International Monetary Fund (IMF). We provide the summary statistics for these variables in Table 2. The other variables are collected from IFS and the Electronic Data Dissemination System of the Central Bank of the Republic of Turkey except the interest rate Organization for Economic Co-operation and Development (OECD) Turkey overnight money rate and VIX, which

Table 1. Classification of Core and Non-Core Liabilities.

	Core Liability	Intermediate	Non-Core Liability
Highly liquid	Cash Demand deposits (households)	Demand deposits (non-financial corporate)	Repos Call loans Short-term FX bank debt
Intermediate	Time deposit & CDs (households)	Time deposit & CDs (non-financial corporate)	Time deposit & CDs (banks & securities firms)
Illiquid	Trust accounts (households) Covered bonds (households)	Trust accounts (non-financial corporate)	Long-term debt securities (bank & Securities firms) ABS & MBS

Source: Shin and Shin (2011).

Table 2. Summary Statistics for Key Variables.

	CORE1	CRED1	NCL1	NCL2
Mean (Turkish lira)	56.20	243.00	87.60	69.10
Median	36.50	202.00	87.20	65.30
Range	2.89–161.00	33.50–670.00	18.80–226.00	15.60–188.00
Standard deviation	48.10	185.00	58.70	49.10
Skewness	0.63	0.81	0.80	1.03
Kurtosis	2.21	2.70	3.00	3.38
Jarque-Bera	4.93	4.78	4.49	7.63
p-value	0.09	0.09	0.11	0.02
Sample size	53	42	42	42

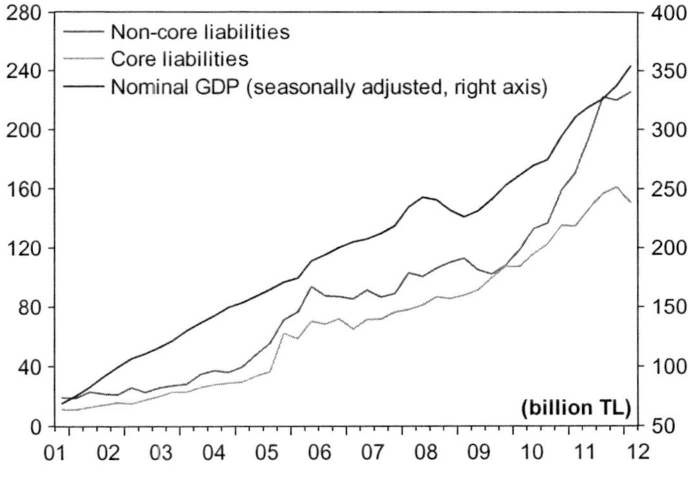

Fig. 1. Core and Non-core Liabilities.

are taken from Bloomberg. We use OECD Turkey overnight money rate for the interest rate. We also use the Chicago Board Options Exchange Market Volatility Index (VIX) as the measure of the market's stock market volatility. See the Appendix for details.

Fig. 1 presents the core and non-core liabilities across time along with the nominal GDP in Turkey during the period 2001–2012, and Fig. 2 lays out the evolution of the liabilities and credits as a ratio to GDP over time. The figures suggest that, especially after the 2008–2009 global financial

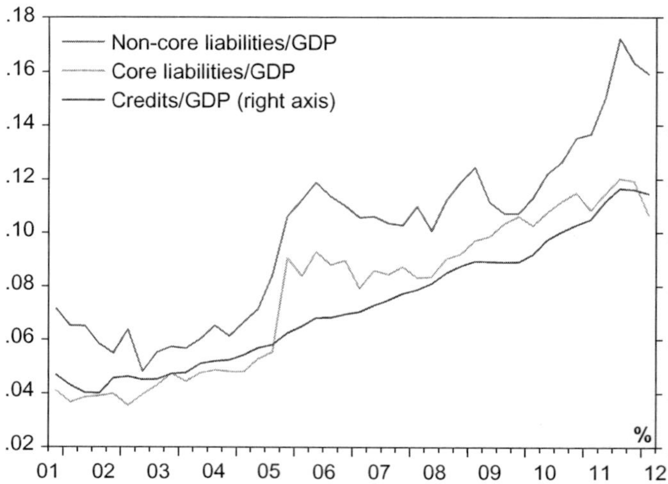

Fig. 2. The Ratio of Credits and Liabilities to GDP.

crisis, non-core liabilities in the Turkish economy has significantly increased. The figures roughly suggest that non-core liabilities are more fluctuating and cyclical than the core liabilities whereas the cyclicality in credits is very low.[3]

MODEL ESTIMATES AND IMPLICATIONS

For our analysis, we use the growth rates of variables as well as the changes in their ratios to GDP. As the main findings stay intact for both we report only the results from using the ratio definition and do not report for the growth rates to save space.[4] Before investigating the relationship between non-core liabilities and credits, we have applied standard unit root tests to our variables (not reported). Wherever applicable the series have been seasonally adjusted. Since our sample period includes the 2008–2009 crisis, we include three dummy variables. The first dummy variable captures all rehabilitating period after 2008, and the other two dummy variables capture the first and second quantitative easing (QE) decisions of the Federal Reserve Bank of the United States.[5]

We start the analysis using a two-by-two Vector Autoregression (VAR) model to set the ground. For the lag length, we choose one lag after checking for alternative information criteria.[6] Although the literature suggests that credits are more exogenous than non-core liabilities, we check for alternative orderings as well. In both orderings the relationship between non-core liabilities and credits is well-established. The literature suggests that the financial sector will rely more on non-core liabilities in the case that core liabilities are not sufficient to fund the demand for credit. However, since 2010, there has been a surge of capital flows from advanced economies to the emerging market economies. Meanwhile, some of the countries, such as Turkey, have dealt with excessive growth in credits. Therefore, the reverse ordering may also provide a plausible story.[7] Despite this rationale, we follow the literature and report the results for only the ordering of credits and non-core liabilities. Fig. 3 shows the impulse responses of the two variables of non-core liabilities and credit growth to each other for 90 and 95 percent confidence intervals. The impulse response functions reveal that when there is an increase in the demand for credit, financial institutions increase non-core liabilities up to four- to five-quarters since the credit shock arrives. Moreover, the dummy variables that we have created to capture the 2008–2009 crisis do not alter the main results. The strong responses of non-core liabilities to credits are found to remain the same when non-core liabilities to non-residents only are used in the analysis.

The Closed Economy Set-Up

After establishing a significant relationship between non-core liabilities and credits in the simplest framework, we embed these in a closed economy framework. We include the first difference of the interest rate and real GDP growth rate and maintained the ordering of [*interest rate, GDP, credits, non-core liabilities*]. The impulse response functions show that the growth in credits pulls non-core liabilities (Fig. 4). Quite interestingly, non-core liabilities seem to be unresponsive to the rest of the variables other than credits. The impact of non-core liability shock to credits is also shown to last up to three-quarter period. Other findings are as follows: the interest rates respond to credits positively. Although it is insignificant, the interest rate respond to GDP positively, which is appropriate for an inflation-targeting economy. GDP responds to the interest rate and non-core liabilities negatively.

When alternative Cholesky orderings are used, the results are shown to be affected, but not in a very significant way. If, for instance, non-core

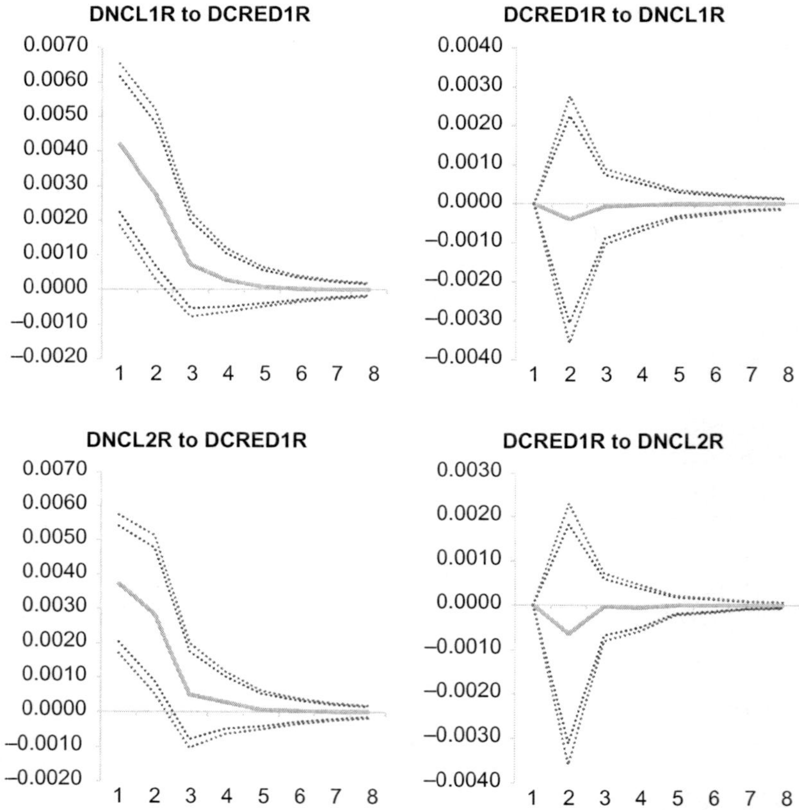

Fig. 3. Impulse Response Functions (ORDERING: DCRED1R, DNCL1R). *Note*: The inner and outer envelopes are the 90 and 95 percent confidence intervals, respectively.

liabilities are more exogenous than credits, the responses of both variables to each other become positive and statistically significant.[8]

The Open Economy Set-Up

Next we test whether the relationship between credits and non-core liabilities is still valid or not within a small open economy framework. To do

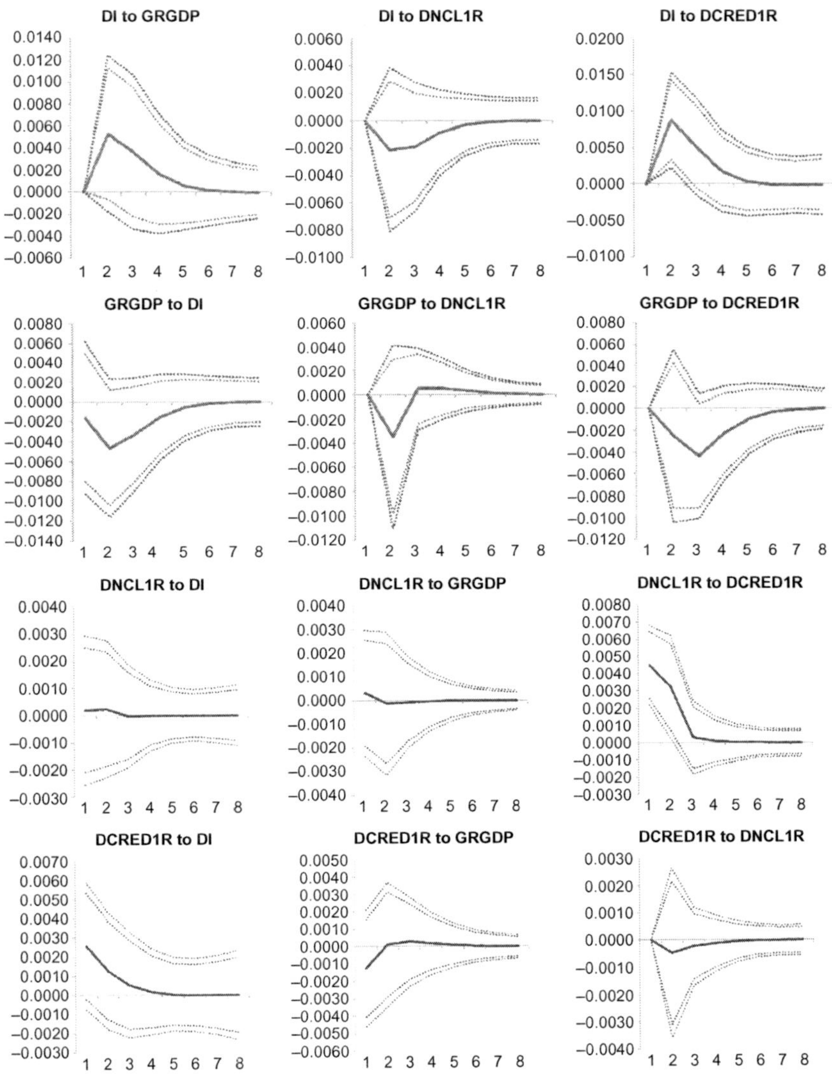

Fig. 4. Impulse Response Functions (ORDERING: DI, GRGDP, DCRED1R, DNCL1R). *Note*: The inner and outer envelopes are the 90 and 95 percent confidence intervals, respectively.

that, we add real exchange rate and VIX to the closed economy framework. We also adopt the Chicago Board Options Exchange Market VIX as the measure of market volatility in the global financial markets, and introduce to the open-economy model as an exogenous variable to the system. For the initial ordering without VIX, we assume that [*interest rates, exchange rate, GDP, credits, non-core liabilities*].

The impulse responses presented in Fig. 5 justify our storyline. The response of non-core liabilities to credits is significantly positive. Another finding under this specification is the significantly positive response of the interest rate to credits, and last up to three-quarter period. Finally, and

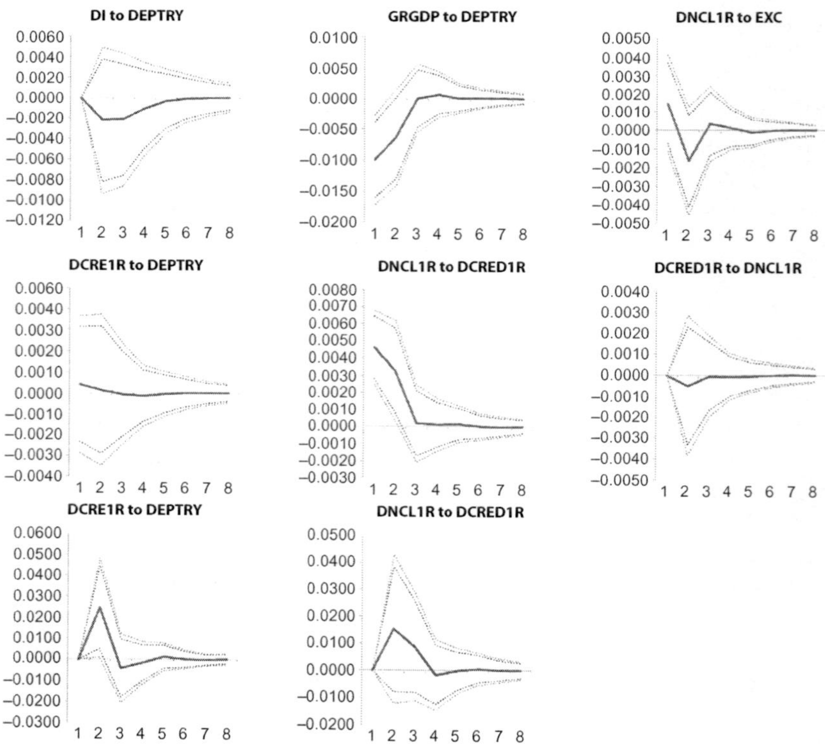

Fig. 5. Impulse Response Functions (ORDERING: DI, DEPTRY, GRGDP, DCRED1R, DNCL1R). *Note*: The inner and outer envelopes are the 90 and 95 percent confidence intervals, respectively.

interestingly, an increase in non-core liabilities causes depreciation in the exchange rate. This can be interpreted by the change in the risk perceptions in international financial markets. If there is an increase in the foreign liabilities of the economy, repayment concerns arise causing the Turkish lira to depreciate. If we alternate non-core liabilities and credits, both of the variables respond to each other statistically significantly as is the case under the previous specifications.[9,10]

The Relation between Credits, Non-Core Liabilities and Core Liabilities

Up to this point, we mainly focused on the argument that credit pulls non-core liabilities. However, it might be an interesting exercise to detect the dynamics of credits, core liabilities and non-core liabilities. To do that, we initially assume that credits are the most exogenous variable and the credit growth is initially financed by core liabilities. We use core 1 measure as the proxy for the core liabilities. Fig. 6 shows the impulse responses for the ordering of [*dcred1r, dncl1r, dcore1r*]. The response of non-core liabilities to the credit growth is significantly positive verifying the results found above. Meanwhile, the core liabilities respond to both credits and non-core liabilities positively. These findings may indicate an intuitive diversification story such that the core liabilities may alter the flow of non-core liabilities, which may strengthen the response of non-core liabilities to credits.

As an alternative ordering we use [*dcred1r, dcore1r, dncl1r*]. Under this specification, as shown in Fig. 7, non-core liabilities respond positively to both core liabilities and credits and core liabilities respond positively to credits. A positive response of core to non-core liabilities can be observed at the 90 percent confidence level.

The final ordering we consider is [*dcore1r, dcred1r, dncl1r*]; the impulse response functions for these are presented in Fig. 8. Under this ordering, credits respond to core liabilities positively. Non-core liabilities positively respond to the core liabilities and credits.

To sum up, the above analysis delivers the following results. Under all specifications, credits respond to non-core liabilities, whereas non-core liabilities respond to credits and core liabilities positively and statistically significantly. This can be interpreted as evidence that non-core liabilities responds to the credit growth, more than core liabilities, in the Turkish economy.

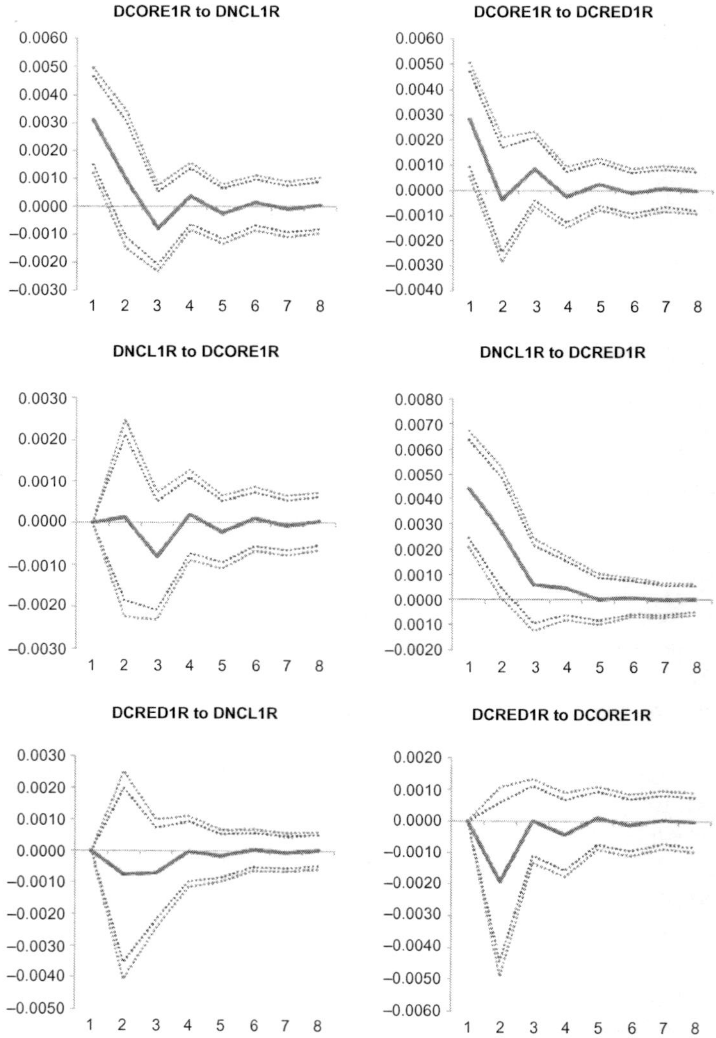

Fig. 6. Impulse Response Functions (ORDERING: DCRED1R, DNCL1R, DCORE1R). *Note*: The inner and outer envelopes are the 90 and 95 percent confidence intervals, respectively.

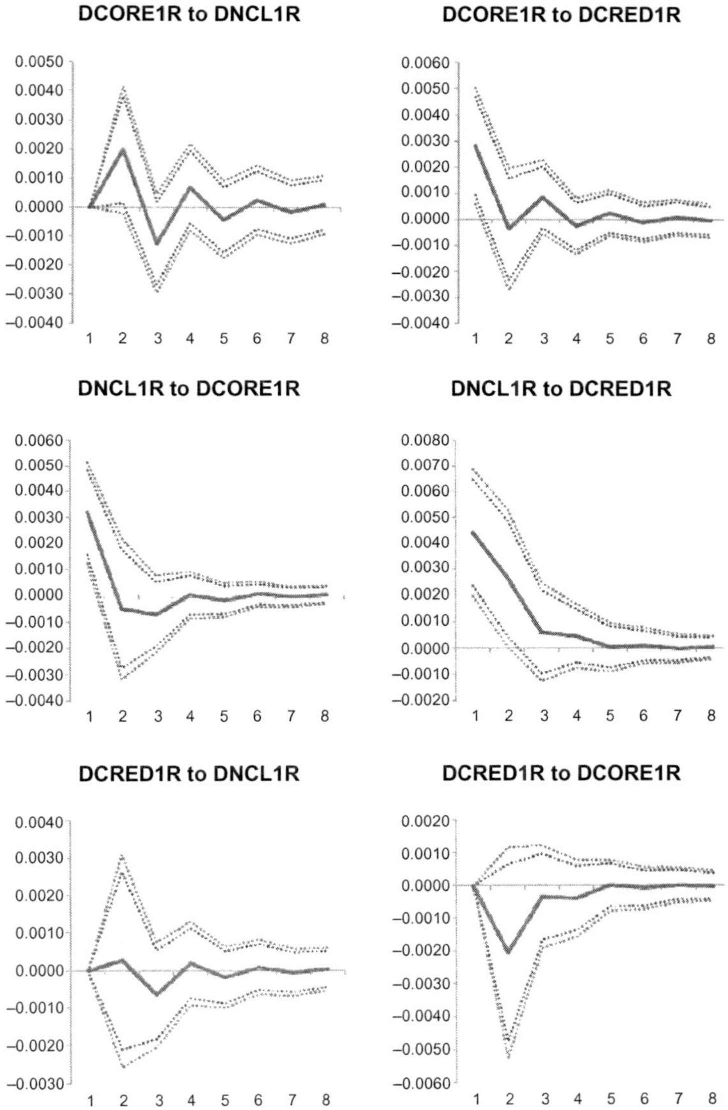

Fig. 7. Impulse Response Functions (ORDERING: DCRED1R, DCORE1R, DNCL1R). *Note*: The inner and outer envelopes are the 90 and 95 percent confidence intervals, respectively.

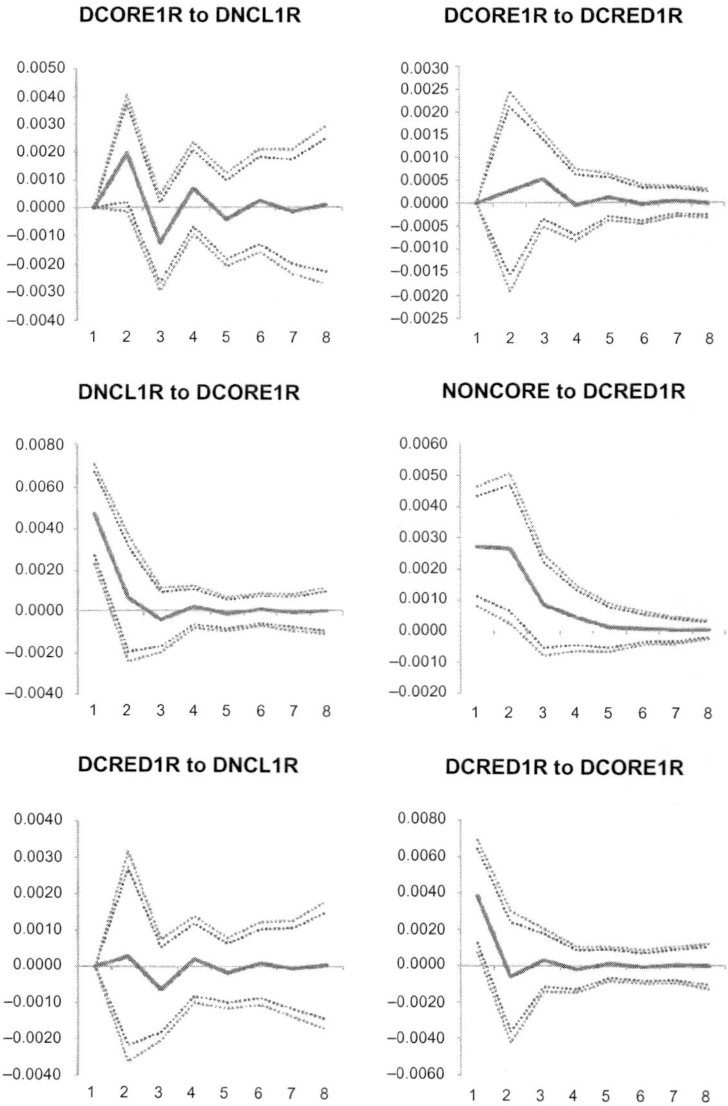

Fig. 8. Impulse Response Functions (ORDERING: DCORER, DCREDR, DNCL1R). *Note*: The inner and outer envelopes are the 90 and 95 percent confidence intervals, respectively.

Long-Run Relationship Investigation

As a final exercise we search for a long-run relationship between core liabilities, non-core liabilities, credits and GDP.[11] All variables are deflated using the GDP deflator and seasonally adjusted whenever applicable.

We order the variables as follows: credits, core liabilities, non-core liabilities and GDP. We have chosen this ordering since as the literature claims, following an increase in credits (mostly arising from demand side) banks will first try to finance this increased credit demand using core liabilities first. If they are not enough, banks will increase their financing for credit supply using non-core liabilities. As these interactions are involved in the bank financing mechanism, aggregate demand will affect total real GDP. The estimates are as below where boldfaced figures are significant at the 10 percent level.[12]

$$\begin{bmatrix} \Delta\ln cred_t \\ \Delta\ln core_t \\ \Delta\ln ncore_t \\ \Delta\ln gdp_t \end{bmatrix} = \begin{bmatrix} \mathbf{-0.063} \\ \mathbf{-0.071} \\ \mathbf{0.091} \\ \mathbf{-0.001} \end{bmatrix} \left[\begin{bmatrix} 1.000 \\ -0.478 \\ \mathbf{-1.190} \\ \mathbf{79.004} \\ \mathbf{-237.569} \end{bmatrix}^T \begin{bmatrix} \ln cred_{t-1} \\ \ln core_{t-1} \\ \ln ncore_{t-1} \\ \ln gdp_{t-1} \\ 1 \end{bmatrix} \right]$$
$$+ \begin{bmatrix} 0.225 & -0.089 & -0.117 & \mathbf{15.593} \\ -0.424 & -0.158 & 0.181 & 11.527 \\ \mathbf{0.693} & 0.169 & \mathbf{-0.260} & -2.845 \\ -0.001 & 0.001 & -0.002 & \mathbf{0.382} \end{bmatrix} \begin{bmatrix} \Delta\ln cred_{t-1} \\ \Delta\ln core_{t-1} \\ \Delta\ln ncore_{t-1} \\ \Delta\ln gdp_{t-1} \end{bmatrix}$$
$$+ \begin{bmatrix} \mathbf{-0.260} & 0.128 & \mathbf{0.185} & 9.469 \\ 0.257 & 0.068 & 0.093 & 11.527 \\ 0.693 & \mathbf{0.169} & -0.260 & \mathbf{-2.845} \\ -0.001 & 0.001 & -0.002 & 0.382 \end{bmatrix} \begin{bmatrix} \Delta\ln cred_{t-2} \\ \Delta\ln core_{t-2} \\ \Delta\ln ncore_{t-2} \\ \Delta\ln gdp_{t-2} \end{bmatrix}$$

The cointegrating vector states that the hypothesis is valid in the long run. Credits move in the same direction as both core and noncore liabilities. However, it moves in the opposite direction to GDP. This result can be interpreted that the long run estimates are consistent with the financial crisis literature which emphasises the property of credit growth as a leading indicator of downturns mainly caused from developments in financial markets. Importantly, non-core liabilities move in the opposite direction of the core liabilities, supporting the changes in the bank behaviour of financing credit supply using core liabilities and non-core liabilities, as discussed earlier.

The impulse responses are provided in Fig. 9. Though some of the responses seem not to be stabilizing over eight quarters, they do for longer horizons. The responses of core liabilities, non-core liabilities and GDP to credits are statistically significant. The responses of non-core liabilities to the core liabilities and GDP to core liabilities are marginally statistically significant. The most important finding is that the response of non-core liabilities to credits is positive and statistically significant, whereas the response of credits to non-core liabilities is positive but statistically insignificant. Therefore, we can conclude that the relationship between credits and non-core liabilities is also sustained in the long run.

CONCLUDING REMARKS

There are two types of bank liabilities; core and non-core. The recent global financial crisis has attracted a lot of attention on especially the non-core type of liabilities since the relative size of these liabilities can increase banks' exposures to risks and therefore be used as an indicator of the stage of the financial cycle of the economy. The main findings in the literature suggest that the core liabilities grow with the economy and credits grow fast, the banks turn to non-core liabilities to finance the credit demand. However, it is claimed that there is a close relationship between credits and non-core liabilities; the literature still lacks country-specific analyses investigating this relationship. This study aims at providing evidence from a small open economy, namely Turkey, and enlarging the avenue of research on this issue.

The financial integration of the Turkish economy to the global markets has picked up after 2000s. Accordingly, our analysis covers the period from 2001 to 2012. This chapter basically tests the hypothesis that the growth of credits is accompanied by an increase in non-core liabilities under alternative frameworks, and presents consistent evidence supporting the hypothesis.

We start with a two-by-two VAR model and then examine the relationship between credit growth and non-core bank liabilities in a closed and a small open economy framework. The most important finding of this exercise is that the relationship stays intact under all specifications. Next, we include both the core and non-core liabilities in the same framework. Even

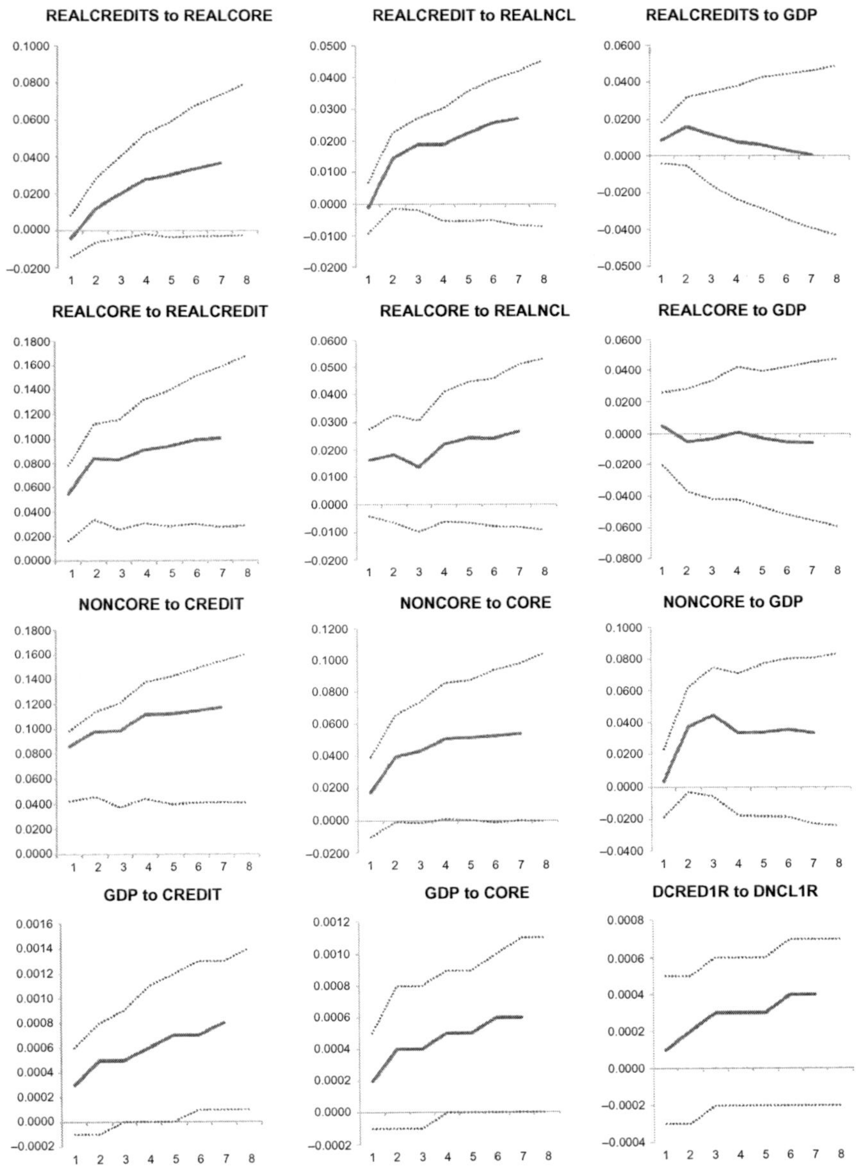

Fig. 9. Impulse Response Functions. Vector Error Correction Model. *Note*: The envelopes show the 90 percent confidence intervals.

though the impulse responses differ when the different orderings of the variables are adopted in the VAR analysis, one pattern stays robust for all specifications: non-core liabilities respond significantly and positively to both credits and core liabilities. Finally, we verify the relationship to hold in the long run within a VECM framework. To sum up, we interpret all these results as a verification of the strong association between credits to non-core liabilities.

This study can be extended towards a few directions. One direction might be a search for an asymmetric relation between non-core liabilities and credits during expansionary and contractionary fiscal and monetary policy periods. Our analysis can also be extended by taking into account the role of macro-prudential policies that are designed to be countercyclical. Better understanding of the dynamic relationship between core liabilities, non-core liabilities and credit growth can be done by setting up a structural model and identifying the specific role of non-core liabilities in the financial stability and crisis build-up in a small open economy.

NOTES

1. Although studies for the United States and Korea show that the peaks in non-core liabilities coincide with the crisis years and this finding is worth to test for the Turkish economy, late financial integration of the Turkish economy to the global markets and the nature of the 2008–2009 global crisis make us leave that research focusing on crisis years to future studies.

2. Although it is an important point to consider the funds that the commercial banks generate from repo transactions from the Central Bank, for the sake of consistency and comparability with the related literature, we solely use the IMF data and ignore the repo transactions.

3. As suggested by the referee, excess volatility of non-core liabilities is an interesting point; however, it is beyond the scope of this study and is left to future research.

4. Another reason behind this choice is the recent emphasis of the Central Bank of the Republic of Turkey (CBRT) on the growth rate of the credit-to-GDP ratio.

5. For the first [second] QE, the dummy variable is 1 for the period of 2008Q3–2010Q1 [2010Q3–2011Q2] and 0 for the rest of the sample.

6. Throughout the chapter we use this lag specification controlling the optimality at each time.

7. We also look at the generalized responses and detect a bi-directional response.

8. We consider orderings that seem to be suitable for a closed economy set-up and check for the results where credits and non-core liabilities alternate. The interpretation remains the same. Some of orderings that we consider are (1) grgdp,

dcred1r, di, dncl1r, (2) grgdp, di, dncl1r, dcred1r, (3) dncl1r, di, grgdp, dcred1r, (4) dcred1r, dncl1r, di, grgdp. For generalized responses, both of the variables respond to each other, which are significant at the 95 percent confidence interval.

9. Estimating the VAR model, with different orderings, does not result in a significant difference. Particularly, we take into account the following orderings and for each we also alternate non-core liabilities and credits: (1) di, deptry, grgdp, dcred1, dncl1r, (2) grgdp, deptry, dcred1, di, dncl1r, (3) deptry, grgdp, di, dncl1r, dcred1r, (4) dncl1, deptry, di, grgdp, dcred1r and (5) di, dcred1r, deptry, dncl1r, grgdp.

10. Note that, we did not include control variables, like current account balance, fiscal stance or overall debt of the economy, which might also impact the ability of the banking sector to attract more non-core liabilities. However, this exercise is left to a further research.

11. The VECM for these four variables embeds the VECM which is constructed with three variables – noncore liabilities, credits and GDP.

12. The lag order of 2 is based on economic intuition.

REFERENCES

Alichi, A., Ryoo, S. C., & Hong, C. (2012). *Managing noncore liabilities and leverage of banking system: A building block for macroprudential policy making in Korea*. Working Paper No. 27. International Monetary Fund, Washington, DC.

Hahm, J., Shin, H. S., & Shin, K. (2012). *Non-core bank liabilities and financial vulnerability*. Working Paper Series No. 18428. National Bureau of Economic Research, Cambridge, MA.

Ozen, E., Sahin, C., & Unalmis, I. (2013). External financial stress and external financing vulnerability in Turkey: Some policy implications for financial stability. *Central Bank Review*, *13*(Special Issue), 63–72.

Shin, H. S., & Shin, K. (2011). *Procylicality and monetary aggregates*. Working Paper Series No. 16836. National Bureau of Economic Research, Cambridge, MA.

APPENDIX

Table A1. Variable Definitions and Data Sources.

Variable	Symbol	Source
Non-core liabilities: Total liabilities to non-residents + M3 − M2	NCL1	IFS
Non-core liabilities as a ratio to seasonally adjusted GDP	NCL1R	
First difference of NCL1R	DNCL1R	
Non-core liabilities: Total liabilities to non-residents	NCL2	IFS
Non-core liabilities as a ratio to seasonally adjusted GDP	NCL2R	
First difference of NCL2R	DNCL2R	
Measure of credits: Sum of claims to the private sector and claims to the public non-financial sector	CRED1	IFS
Credits as a ratio to seasonally adjusted GDP	CRED1R	
First difference of CRED1R	DCRED1R	
Core liabilities: M1	CORE1	IFS
Core liabilities as a ratio to seasonally adjusted GDP	CORE1R	
First difference of CORE1R	DCORE1R	
First difference of interest rates	DI	CBRT
Growth rate of GDP: Growth of (seasonally adjusted) real GDP of Turkey	GRGDP	CBRT
Depreciation of exchange rate: The depreciation rate of TL across USD	DEPTRY	CBRT
Chicago board options exchange market VIX	VIX	Bloomberg

FOREIGN BANKS, MONETARY POLICY, AND CRISES: EVIDENCE FROM BANK-LEVEL PANEL DATA IN ASIA

Bang Nam Jeon and Ji Wu

ABSTRACT

This chapter examines how foreign banks respond to domestic monetary policy in host countries during crisis periods, in particular, the response shown toward the Asian financial crisis of 1997–1999 and the global financial crisis of 2008–2009. By observing 283 domestic and foreign banks in seven emerging Asian economies, we find that foreign banks are slower than domestic banks in adjusting the growth of their loans to changes in host monetary policy. This inertia by foreign banks is found to be more pronounced in the recent 2008–2009 global crisis than in the 1997–1999 Asian regional crisis, suggesting that the buffering/hampering effects of foreign banks on the effectiveness of the domestic monetary policy transmission mechanism become stronger in a recent global crisis originating from outside Asia than a regional crisis imploded within Asia a decade earlier. We also find that foreign banks' lower sensitivity than domestic banks to host monetary policy during the crisis periods is

Global Banking, Financial Markets and Crises
International Finance Review, Volume 14, 91–113

ISSN: 1569-3767/doi:10.1108/S1569-3767(2013)0000014007

heterogeneous, depending on factors such as the extent of the adverse impact of crises on parent banks, the scope of business operation by parent banks, and foreign banks' mode of entry into host banking markets.

Keywords: Foreign banks; monetary policy transmission; global financial crisis

JEL classifications: E44; F43; G21

INTRODUCTION

This chapter addresses the impact of foreign bank penetration on the effectiveness of domestic monetary policy, in particular, during the 1997–1999 Asian financial crisis and the recent 2008–2009 global financial crisis for emerging Asian economies. Since the mid-1990s, multinational banks have expanded their business and established local presence steadily in developing and emerging markets (see Appendix A for selected Asian host economies), which brings about concerns and questions regarding its implication on efficiency, competition, and stability in host financial markets (see, e.g., Claessens & van Horen (2012); Claessens, Demirguc–Kunc, & Huizinga (2001); Cull & Martinez Peria (2010); Jeon, Olivero, & Wu (2011)). As many studies find that foreign banks can be a stabilizing force in *local* crises that hit host markets (Crystal, Dages, & Goldberg (2001); Cull & Martinez Peria (2007); Goldberg (2001), etc.), the financial crisis started in 2008 raises the question how foreign banks perform in a *global* crises that originated outside host economies.

Our chapter is closely related to the literature of the "bank lending channel," which studies how the effects of monetary policy would be transmitted via banks' credit to real economy heterogeneously, depending on characteristics of individual banks such as liquidity, solvency, and size (see, e.g., Bernanke & Blinder (1988, 1992); Kashyap & Stein (2000); Kishan & Opiela (2000)). However, foreign/domestic ownership is another factor that may contribute to the heterogeneity of the efficiency of the monetary policy transmission mechanism (Arena, Reinhart, & Vázquez (2006); Wu, Luca, & Jeon (2011)). As affiliates of global financial conglomerates, foreign banks differ from their domestic peers in their access to internal funds that can be moved globally across headquarters and to its subsidiaries abroad. Parent banks can allocate their assets on a global base, causing their foreign subsidiaries' loans to be less affected by the economic conditions in host markets. During the recent financial crisis, financial resources could be shifted from a specific subsidiary to more secure markets or the headquarters that urgently need capital or liquidity to fix their balance sheet. Global banks' management of capital and liquidity on the global basis may counteract the effectiveness of economic policies in host economies (see Cetorelli & Goldberg (2010, 2012)).

As an extension of some earlier research supporting foreign banks' lower sensitivity to host monetary policy, Wu et al. (2011) provide evidence that foreign banks' insensitivity is more pronounced during crisis periods than in tranquil periods. In this chapter, we examine how foreign banks affected the efficiency of Asian central banks' monetary policies differently during two separate crises, namely, the 1997–1999 Asian crisis and the 2008–2009 global crisis. The results can shed some insight on how likely Asian economies are prone to be affected by the contagion of global financial crisis via foreign banks' lending behavior.[1]

We find that the strength of domestic monetary policy on affecting banks' credit is significantly dampened in the periods of crisis by increasing presence of foreign banks in the region, and the cushioning effect was found more pronounced in the recent global crisis than the earlier regional crisis. However, foreign banks' inertia in adjusting loans to changes in host monetary policy is heterogeneous, depending on factors such as how severely their parent banks are impacted in crisis periods, the business scope of parent banks, and the entry mode into the host banking markets.

There are some important policy implications based on our findings. First, although foreign banks bring about a healthy force to increase the competition in host financial markets and maintain credit in the face of local economic difficulties, they may also be a channel to transmit adverse shocks from the outside and to destabilize domestic economies. They may also dampen the effectiveness of local monetary policy. This monetary policy ineffectiveness due to the increasing presence of foreign banks should be taken into account by host monetary authorities when designing appropriate policies. Second, the finding that foreign banks play a buffering role on host monetary policy differently, depending on factors such as the parent banks' operation scope and the entry mode, suggests that a gradual internationalization of banking sector with a diversity of foreign bank origins may be a better strategy for emerging economies' financial market liberalization.

The remaining part of the chapter is constructed as below. The second section introduces our econometric model and the third section describes the data. The fourth section first reports the baseline empirical results, then various tests on if and how our results may change depending on the severity of the impact of global crisis on subsidiaries' parent banks, on the regional/global operation scope, and the entry mode of foreign banks in host economies. The fifth section concludes the chapter.

MODEL

The model can be described as the following:

$$\begin{aligned}Y_{i,j,t} = {} & c + \alpha \cdot Y_{i,j,t-1} + \beta \cdot mp_{j,t} + \chi \cdot crises + \delta \cdot foreign_{i,j,t} + \phi \cdot mp_{j,t} \times crises \\ & + \varphi \cdot foreign_{i,j,t} \times crises + \gamma \cdot foreign_{i,j,t} \times mp_{j,t} + \eta \cdot foreign_{i,j,t} \times mp_{j,t} \times crises \\ & + \lambda \cdot characteristics_{i,j,t} + \mu \cdot characteristics_{i,j,t} \times mp_{j,t} \\ & + \theta \cdot characteristics_{i,j,t} \times mp_{j,t} \times crises + \rho \cdot hostmacro_{j,t} + f_{i,j} + \varepsilon_{i,j,t}\end{aligned}$$

where $Y_{i,j,t}$ represents the growth rate of loans (in real terms) of bank i in country j in year t, and $Y_{i,j,t-1}$ is its one-year lag. We use $mp_{j,t}$ to denote the monetary policy shock in country j in year t, measured by the first-order difference of average monthly money market rate.[2] *crises* is a set of two crisis dummies, respectively for the Asian financial crisis of 1997–1999 and the recent global crisis of 2008–2009.[3] $foreign_{i,j,t}$ represents an ownership dummy, which is equal to 1 if bank i in country j is foreign-owned in year t, and 0 otherwise. $characteristics_{i,j,t}$ is a vector of individual bank characteristics, including *liquidity*, *capitalization*, *size*, and *riskiness*. To mitigate the concern on potential endogeneity between the dependent variable and bank characteristics, we use one-year lag values of the bank characteristics variables. $hostmacro_{j,t}$ includes a set of variables measuring the macroeconomic condition in the host Asian countries in our sample. $f_{i,j}$ is the time-invariant bank-specific effect, and $\varepsilon_{i,j,t}$ is the idiosyncratic error.

Following the literature of the bank lending channel, which suggests that banks play a nonneutral role in transmitting monetary policy shocks, we expect the sign of the coefficient on $mp_{j,t}$ to be negative in our estimation, implying that banks would reduce (increase) their lending in response to a tightened (relaxed) monetary policy due to their limited capacity to compensate for the reduced resources for lending after a contractionary monetary policy.

We introduce the following interaction terms to the estimation equation to detect the marginal effects of monetary policy conditional on the economic stress and bank ownership. We expect that $mp_{j,t} \times crises$ will reflect the differences in the effectiveness of monetary policy during the 1997–1999 and 2008–2009 crisis periods relative to noncrisis, tranquil periods. The coefficient on $foreign_{i,j,t} \times mp_{j,t}$ will indicate if foreign banks show different responses to changes in monetary policy from domestic banks during noncrisis periods. In order to examine foreign banks' distinctive behavior in adjusting loan granting during crisis periods from domestic banks, independent of host countries' monetary policy, we add the interaction terms, $foreign_{i,j,t} \times crises$.

We also include two three-way interaction terms, $foreign_{i,j,t} \times mp_{j,t} \times crisis$ 1997–1999 and $foreign_{i,j,t} \times mp_{j,t} \times crisis$ 2008–2009, to examine if foreign banks respond differently from domestic banks to changes in monetary policy during the 1997–1999 and 2008–2009 crisis periods. If global banks use internal capital markets to manage their assets and liquidity on a global scope and to reallocate assets toward headquarters during the crisis periods, we expect the sign of the coefficient on $foreign_{i,j,t} \times mp_{j,t} \times crises$ to be positive in the estimation. We interpret this as the evidence that foreign banks only adjust their lending at a lower magnitude in crisis periods than during tranquil periods, thus cushioning the effectiveness of host monetary policy.

Since foreign banks may behave differently from domestic banks simply because of their different bank characteristics, say, *liquidity, capitalization, size* and *riskiness*, we include in our model the variables of bank-specific characteristics. As the literature of the bank lending channel suggests, banks that are more liquid, more capitalized, and larger in size would be less responsive to monetary policy shock due to their increased capacity of access to alternative options for financing loans. To isolate the effect of monetary policy on foreign-owned banks during the global crisis period, independent of their different bank characteristics, we interact the bank characteristics variables with $mp_{j,t}$ and *crises*.

In order to control for the demand-side effects on bank credit, we use a vector of host country macroeconomic variables, $hostmacro_{j,t}$, which includes the real GDP growth rate, inflation rate, and unemployment rate.

DATA

We construct an unbalanced panel dataset using both bank-level data and macroeconomic data. We collect the bank-level data from Bureau van

Dijk's *BankScope* database, which contains financial information (balance sheet data, income, and expenses, ratios, and other annual financial data) on over 28,000 banks worldwide and covers, on an average, more than 90 percent of banking sector assets worldwide.[4] We include only commercial banks in Asia in the dataset to reduce the possible bias due to the different nature and business scope among banks that have different objectives and conduct businesses in different specializations. The selected economies from Asia include: Hong Kong SAR, Indonesia, Korea, Malaysia, the Philippines, Singapore, and Thailand, all of which have witnessed a high or an increasingly higher degree of foreign bank penetration among Asian countries. We use annual data for the period 1997–2009.

We define a bank as a foreign bank if more than 50 percent of its capital is owned by foreign banks, firms, or individuals.[5] To identify foreign-owned banks, we resort to various sources in addition to *BankScope*, taking the following steps. First, we check the brief overview of each bank recorded in *BankScope*, which identifies ownership for only some banks for limited years. Second, we review each bank's history from its own website. Third, we obtain banks' mergers and acquisitions (M&A) information using the *SDC Platinum* database. Finally, if ownership has not yet been identified after following these three steps, we resort to various other available sources, such as banks' annual reports, central banks' publications, and news reports from the Internet.

The constructions of other variables are quite standard by following the literature. The volume of loan is adjusted by using consumer price index (CPI) to get its real value, and its growth rate is approximated by the first-order difference of its natural logarithms. Liquidity is calculated as the ratio of liquid assets to total assets, and capitalization is measured by the ratio of equity to total assets. The size in our model captures the relative dominance (share) of banks in banking markets, calculated as the ratio of a bank's assets to the entire banking sector assets in a host economy. Alternatively, we replaced this relative measure of size by an absolute measure, the natural log of bank assets (converted to constant US dollars), but our main results do not change. Riskiness is measured by using the ratio of loan loss provision to total loans.

In order to mitigate the effects of abnormally extreme and irregular values on the estimates, we drop the highest and lowest first percentile of growth rates of total assets, growth rates of loans, liquidity, capitalization, riskiness, and profitability. Additionally, we also remove the banks when at least three consecutive yearly observations are not available for consistency. Consequently, we end up with 2313 observations for 283 banks.

Before we proceed to estimate the econometric model, it is worthwhile to conduct a simple analysis on the difference between foreign and domestic banks in Asian economies (Appendix B). Domestic banks are observed to provide loans at a higher growth rate than foreign banks in terms of both mean and median. However, foreign banks, although smaller in their market size, have higher liquidity and capitalization ratios than their domestic counterparts. The identified distinction between foreign banks and domestic banks in their bank characteristics confirms the necessity to control for these factors in order to isolate foreign banks' different behavior from domestic banks' caused by their foreign ownership. Since some of the bank characteristics variables may be correlated with each other, they may generate the problem of multicollinearity if included in the model simultaneously. Accordingly, we examine the pair-wise correlation between the bank characteristics variables, and do not observe substantially high correlation coefficients between these variables. This result indicates little evidence on multicollinearity.

EMPIRICAL RESULTS

Econometric Methodology

We estimate our empirical model using three alternative econometric methodologies, namely, pooled ordinary least squares (OLS), the fixed effects estimator, and the system generalized method of moments (GMM) estimator. In all estimations, we control for a full set of year-specific effects, and in pooled OLS and the system GMM estimation we also control for the host country-specific effects. We use robust standard error, adjusted for heteroskedasticity and within-panel serial correlation, in all three estimators.

The choice of fixed effects estimators is based on the Hausman test, which justifies that fixed effects are preferred over random effects because the regressors are shown to be correlated with the bank-specific variables. However, including the lagged dependent variable in the fixed effects estimation may cause inconsistent estimators when the time dimension is limited (Nickell, 1981). Accordingly, we drop the first-year lag of dependent variable in the fixed effects estimation.

To obtain unbiased, consistent, and asymptotically efficient coefficients of the dynamic specification model which has a lagged dependent variable among the regressors, as in our cases of the loan growth estimation, we need to correct the possible endogeneity issue. To this end, we adopt the system GMM estimator, following the methodology developed by Arellano and Bover (1995) and Blundell and Bond (1998), and use both level and differenced equations for estimation. It also instruments the lagged dependent variable by using lagged differences for the level equation and lagged levels for the differenced equation.

Because the system GMM estimator requires no autocorrelation in the idiosyncratic errors, we test the first- and second-order autocorrelation in the first-differenced errors. We find that they are first-order, serially correlated but not second-order, serially correlated in all tests. This supports the moment conditions used by the system GMM estimator as valid. To test whether the instruments are exogenous by group, we perform Hansen's J–test for overidentifying restrictions, and find that in all tests the null of the valid model cannot be rejected.

The Baseline Estimation

We first estimate how individual banks adjust their credit provision with monetary policy shocks in host markets. The results are reported in Table 1. In all estimations, it is found that the monetary policy indicator (*mp*) shows a negative sign and is highly statistically significant, suggesting a tightened (eased) money supply leads banks to reduce (increase) their lending. Quantitatively, an increase of one percentage point in the money market interest rate would cause a decrease in banks' growth rate by 0.88–1.59 percent.

Foreign bank subsidiaries may help domestic monetary policy work by responding more greatly to the adjustment of monetary indicator, during the noncrisis periods, as the two-way interaction term between foreign bank dummy and the monetary policy indicator, $foreign \times mp$, is found consistently negative but statistically significant in only half of all estimations. The two crisis dummy variables, crisis 97–99 and crisis 08–09, are negative, as expected, and statistically significant in pooled OLS and GMM system estimations, indicating both crises caused considerable decrease in all banks' lending.

As our most interested variables, the three-way interaction terms between foreign dummy, monetary policy and crises are found to be positive in almost all regressions. This finding suggests evidence of the inertia of foreign bank subsidiaries in adjusting their loans to changes in host monetary policy in both the regional crisis of 1997–1999 and the global

Table 1. The Effect of Changes in Monetary Policy on Loan Growth of Domestic and Foreign Banks in Asia, 1997 – 2009.

Dependent Variable:	Pooled OLS		GMM System		Fixed Effects	
$\Delta ln(loans)_{i,j,t}$	(1)	(2)	(3)	(4)	(5)	(6)
Δln(loans)$_{i,\ j,\ t-1}$	.161***	.170***	.120***	.132***		
	(.000)	(.000)	(.004)	(.003)		
foreign	−3.069**	−3.073**	−3.858**	−3.831**	−1.421	−1.371
	(.046)	(.047)	(.026)	(.024)	(.730)	(.740)
crisis 1997 – 1999	−9.621***	−8.479***	−6.426*	−3.349	−1.046	−1.996
	(.000)	(.002)	(.063)	(.262)	(.727)	(.515)
crisis 2008 – 2009	−9.768***	−11.115***	−6.799**	−6.902***	−1.637	−2.264
	(.001)	(.000)	(.014)	(.003)	(.541)	(.405)
mp	−1.512***	−1.585***	−1.340***	−1.024*	−.879***	−1.296**
	(.000)	(.001)	(.000)	(.091)	(.004)	(.014)
foreign × crisis 1997 – 1999	1.601	1.149	3.112	2.081	3.543	3.295
	(.050)	(.628)	(.218)	(.415)	(.207)	(.238)
foreign × crisis 2008 – 2009	.563	1.505	−.777	.463	−2.583	−2.147
	(.840)	(.558)	(.800)	(.867)	(.419)	(.479)
mp × crisis 1997 – 1999	1.492***	2.232***	1.637***	1.892**	1.093***	2.203***
	(.000)	(.000)	(.000)	(.011)	(.000)	(.000)
mp × crisis 2008 – 2009	−.058	−3.920*	.907	−5.156**	.443	−1.390
	(.948)	(.098)	(.338)	(.032)	(.635)	(.563)
foreign × *mp*	−.642	−.963*	−.793	−1.250**	−.570	−1.015**
	(.244)	(.078)	(.155)	(.014)	(.294)	(.041)
foreign × *mp* × crisis 1997 – 1999	1.363**	1.796***	1.337**	1.867***	1.157**	1.724***
	(.022)	(.002)	(.025)	(.001)	(.042)	(.000)
foreign × *mp* × crisis 2008 – 2009	3.347**	3.406**	3.576**	3.629**	2.379	2.141
	(.033)	(.032)	(.025)	(.021)	(.117)	(.176)

Table 1. *(Continued)*

Dependent Variable:	Pooled OLS		GMM System		Fixed Effects	
$\Delta ln(loans)_{i,j,t}$	(1)	(2)	(3)	(4)	(5)	(6)
Bank characteristics						
liquidity	.096	.074	.300***	.262***	.384***	.345***
	(.127)	(.227)	(.000)	(.000)	(.000)	(.000)
liquidity × *mp*		−.018***		−.030***		−.015**
		(.004)		(.007)		(.014)
liquidity × *mp* × crisis 1997 – 1999		.010		.017		−.003
		(.288)		(.159)		(.715)
liquidity × *mp* × crisis 2008 – 2009		.127**		.169***		.081
		(.033)		(.006)		(.201)
capitalization	.031	.050	.171	.209*	.469***	.543***
	(.718)	(.569)	(.101)	(.059)	(.003)	(.002)
capitalization × *mp*		.043*		.042**		.063***
		(.060)		(.030)		(.010)
capitalization × *mp* × crisis 1997 – 1999		−.059**		−.055***		−.069***
		(.012)		(.004)		(.003)
capitalization × *mp* × crisis 2008 – 2009		.013		.110		.010
		(.937)		(.478)		(.941)
size	.029	.050	−.026	.003	−1.069**	−1.115**
	(.567)	(.319)	(.704)	(.957)	(.023)	(.016)
size × *mp*		.058***		.047**		.059**
		(.007)		(.016)		(.017)
size × *mp* × crisis 1997 – 1999		−.016		−.010		−.054
		(.628)		(.759)		(.111)
size × *mp* × crisis 2008 – 2009		−.032		.030		−.161*
		(.670)		(.611)		(.064)

riskiness	−.128	−.071	.163	.328	−.225	−.141
	(.591)	(.772)	(.550)	(.241)	(.424)	(.646)
riskiness × *mp*		.019		.051		.050
		(.653)		(.237)		(.345)
riskiness × *mp* × crisis 1997 – 1999		−.023		−.054		−.065
		(.605)		(.245)		(.221)
riskiness × *mp* × crisis 2008 – 2009		.511		.086		.300
		(.548)		(.914)		(.680)
Macroeconomic variables						
Real GDP growth rate	1.155***	1.296***	1.139***	1.169***	1.141***	1.235***
	(.000)	(.000)	(.000)	(.000)	(.000)	(.000)
Inflation	−.914***	−1.058***	−1.092***	−1.165***	−.969***	−1.065***
	(.000)	(.000)	(.000)	(.000)	(.000)	(.000)
Unemployment	−.982*	−.487	−.752	−.564	−1.703***	−1.516**
	(.065)	(.489)	(.218)	(.379)	(.003)	(.018)
Year dummy	Yes	Yes	Yes	Yes	Yes	Yes
Country dummy	Yes	Yes	Yes	Yes	No	No
Observations (banks)	1932	1932	1932	1932	1932	1932
	(269)	(269)	(269)	(269)	(269)	(269)
R^2	.268	.282			.281	.297
$AR(1)/AR(2)$			.000/.181	.000/.324		
Hansen *J*-test			.467	.271		

Notes: *p*-value in parenthesis. ***: 1 percent significance level; **: 5 percent significance level; *: 10 percent significance level.

crisis of 2008–2009, cushioning the effects of host monetary policy in affecting domestic credit.[6] Meanwhile, we find the magnitude of the positive coefficient on $foreign \times mp \times crisis$ 2008–2009 is consistently and notably higher than that on $foreign \times mp \times crisis$ 1997–1999, implying a more pronounced counteracting behavior by foreign banks in response to changes in host monetary policy during the recent global financial crisis.

Foreign banks' lower responses to host monetary policy than domestic banks', in both crises, may be attributed to the movement of capital and liquidity across headquarters and subsidiaries on a global base using the global banks' established internal capital markets. As the Asian financial crisis imploded, central banks raised interest rates to deter the outflow of foreign capital and stabilize exchange rates.[7] The tightened monetary condition caused drastic credit crunch among operating banks, however, foreign banks could receive emergency credit lines and other forms of support from parent banks, which were not severely affected by the crisis, and thus avoid a large scale-down of their loans.[8] By contrast, the 2008–2009 global turmoil differs from the 1997–1999 Asian crisis in the origin of crisis. Parent global banks, which incurred a substantial amount of asset loss on their own balance sheet, conducted redistribution of their resources to strengthen the financial status of the headquarter, causing an upstream capital flow out of subsidiaries and lower credit growth in host markets, although host central banks generally conducted expansionary monetary policy in attempt to ease firms' access to bank loans.[9]

Our results shed some light on how host Asian emerging economies are prone to contagious shocks in their banking sector, in particular what role foreign banks play in crises. When shocks are from internal sources, such as the crisis in 1997–1999, foreign banks can stabilize firms' access to credit by shipping funds from headquarter (or other affiliates) to subsidiaries in need. The ineffectiveness of monetary policy (on foreign banks' lending) may be welcome by central bankers, since they can adjust interest rates to stabilize foreign exchange market without causing a sudden crunch in banking market. However, when shocks are introduced due to the distress in parent banks, like the global financial crisis in 2008–2009, subsidiaries' funds could be siphoned upstream to headquarter. Although host central banks can respond to the economic woes by using expansionary monetary policy, its intended impact on domestic credit would likely be buffered or even reversed in foreign banks. Consistent with some others (see, e.g., De Haas and van Lelyveld (forthcoming)), our result suggests a "double-edged sword" role played by foreign banks. The finding that foreign banks' insensitivity to host monetary policy is more pronounced in the recent global financial crisis than in the local crisis in 1997–1999 suggests that the commitment of foreign banks to host markets is conditional on the financial status of their parent banks.

In order to further study how and under what conditions foreign banks affected the monetary policy transmission mechanism differently from domestic banks in the 2008–2009 global crisis, in comparison to the 1997–1999 Asian crisis, we conducted the following additional tests using subsample estimation.

Subsample Estimation 1: The Extent of Suffering from Crises by Parent Banks

We first divide our foreign bank samples into two subgroups using the criterion if their parent banks are more severely impaired in the global financial crisis or less. We defined more severely impaired banks as the banks whose decrease in its conglomerate assets lies within the lowest 10 percentile of the distribution of the growth of total assets. In this estimation, we replace the previous dummy variable, *foreign*, by two new dummy variables, *foreign (parent more affected)* and *foreign (parent less affected)*, and add their interactions with *mp* and *crises*.

The results, reported in Table 2, show that foreign banks' lower sensitivity to host monetary policy during the global crisis of 2008–2009 is mainly driven by the subsidiaries whose parent banks are more adversely impacted during the crisis. In contrast, the same subsidiaries are not found to be less sensitive in the 1997–1999 Asian crisis. Our finding is consistent with that of Cetorelli and Goldberg (2010, 2012), which show that a lower responsiveness of foreign subsidiaries to changes in host country monetary policies during the 2008–2009 global financial crisis may be caused by the reduced support from their parent banks in home countries. This finding supports the proposition that foreign banks' lower credit growth in the 2008–2009 global crisis is more related to parent banks' loss and the subsequent global-wide asset reallocation than in the 1997–1999 Asian crisis.[10]

Subsample Estimation 2: Where do Foreign Banks Come from?

In this section, we examine if the buffering effects of host monetary policy are different between foreign banks whose headquarters are located in Asia and foreign banks whose headquarters are located outside Asia. Stated

Table 2. The Effect of Changes in Monetary Policy on Loan Growth of Domestic and Foreign Banks in Asia, 1997 – 2009: Foreign Bank Subsidiaries whose Parent Banks were More Adversely Affected Versus. Subsidiaries whose Parent Banks were Less Adversely Affected in the 2008 – 2009 Crisis.

Dependent Variable:	Pooled OLS		GMM System		Fixed Effects	
$\Delta ln(loans)_{i,j,t}$	(1)	(2)	(3)	(4)	(5)	(6)
mp	−1.526***	−1.653***	−1.440***	−.802	−.894***	−1.562***
	(.000)	(.000)	(.000)	(.203)	(.004)	(.004)
foreign (parent more adversely affected) × *mp*	.475	.143	.800	.450	.518	.008
	(.467)	(.829)	(.278)	(.484)	(.469)	(.990)
foreign (parent less adversely affected) × *mp*	−.987	−1.153*	−1.434**	−1.848***	−1.007	−1.275**
	(.110)	(.051)	(.023)	(.000)	(.122)	(.021)
foreign (parent more adversely affected) × *mp* × crisis	−.060	.456	−.447	.050	−.259	.494
1997 – 1999	(.937)	(.538)	(.569)	(.939)	(.728)	(.493)
foreign (parent less adversely affected) × *mp* × crisis	1.903***	2.055***	2.181***	2.663***	1.839***	2.172***
1997 – 1999	(.004)	(.001)	(.001)	(.000)	(.006)	(.000)
foreign (parent more adversely affected) × *mp* × crisis	10.124***	9.443***	8.886***	7.825***	9.331***	8.801***
2008 – 2009	(.000)	(.000)	(.000)	(.003)	(.000)	(.000)
foreign (parent less adversely affected) × *mp* × crisis	1.522	1.680	2.695	2.804	1.217	.805
2008 – 2009	(.434)	(.347)	(.172)	(.115)	(.497)	(.649)
Year dummy	Yes	Yes	Yes	Yes	Yes	Yes
Country dummy	Yes	Yes	Yes	Yes	No	No
Observations (banks)	1932	1932	1932	1932	1932	1932
	(269)	(269)	(269)	(269)	(269)	(269)
R^2	.287	.296			.299	.309
$AR(1)/AR(2)$			.000/.137	.000/.194		
Hansen *J*-test			.330	.275		

Notes: *p*-value in parenthesis. ***: 1 percent significance level; **: 5 percent significance level; *: 10 percent significance level.

differently, we test whether the lower monetary policy effectiveness would differ, depending on the regional versus global orientation of foreign banks.[11] It is expected that global foreign banks would show lower reaction to host monetary policy in the 2008–2009 crisis than in the 1997–1999 crisis, if their parent banks are more adversely affected in the global financial crisis.

We divide foreign banks into two groups according to the geographical range of the presence of their parents and affiliates. We define a foreign bank as a "regional" bank if its headquarters is located in one of the Asian economies and its subsidiaries abroad are concentrated mainly in Asia. We define a foreign bank as "global" if its headquarters is registered outside the Asian countries and most of their foreign subsidiaries operate in continents other than Asia. In order to test the possible heterogeneity of the impact of monetary policy on "regional" and "global" foreign banks, we replace the original dummy, *foreign*, by using two dummies, *foreign(regional)* and *foreign(global)*, and interact them with *mp* and *crises*, respectively and jointly. The estimation results are reported in Table 3.

We find consistent evidence that host monetary policy loses its strength mainly in global foreign banks in both crises, and the policy ineffectiveness is more pronounced in the 2008–2009 global crisis than the 1997–1999 Asian crisis. This finding provides evidence consistent with the hypothesis that the more severe hit on global banking conglomerates causes a larger scale of capital shift across headquarters and subsidiaries in the recent global crisis, thus dampens the strength of host monetary policy more greatly, than in the earlier Asian regional crisis. For regional foreign banks' subsidiaries, we also find they may also tend to be more policy–insensitive during the recent global crisis than in the earlier 1997–1999 crisis, but not statistically significant. Our result also suggests a lower integration of global banks with host banking markets in Asia than regional banks.

Subsample Estimation 3: What are Foreign Banks' Modes of Entry to Host Markets?

We next test if foreign bank subsidiaries' responsiveness to monetary policy in crises is associated with their heterogeneous entry modes. Multinational banks may establish their affiliates abroad from scratch or by merging/acquiring a local bank. It is widely expected that de novo subsidiaries are more closely connected with their headquarters at home than their peers established via M&A, thus more likely affected by the capital movement

Table 3. The Effect of Changes in Monetary Policy on Loan Growth of Domestic and Foreign Banks in Asia, 1997 – 2009: Regional Versus Global Foreign Bank Subsidiaries.

Dependent Variable:	Pooled OLS		GMM System		Fixed Effects	
$\Delta ln(loans)_{i,j,t}$	(1)	(2)	(3)	(4)	(5)	(6)
mp	−1.496***	−1.552***	−1.344***	−.968	−.864***	−1.221**
	(.000)	(.001)	(.000)	(.125)	(.005)	(.021)
foreign (regional) × *mp*	.013	−.375	−.149	−.643	.012	−.554
	(.981)	(.536)	(.790)	(.227)	(.983)	(.335)
foreign (global) × *mp*	−1.416*	−1.550**	−1.648*	−1.868**	−1.286	−1.472**
	(.074)	(.030)	(.058)	(.012)	(.101)	(.025)
foreign (regional) × *mp* × crisis 1997–1999	.269	.962	.388	1.134*	.301	1.170*
	(.689)	(.134)	(.572)	(.064)	(.635)	(.063)
foreign (global) × *mp* × crisis 1997–1999	2.388***	2.484***	2.373***	2.529***	2.071**	2.234***
	(.004)	(.001)	(.009)	(.001)	(.012)	(.002)
foreign (regional) × *mp* × crisis 2008–2009	1.658	1.771	2.141	2.082	.830	.452
	(.247)	(.372)	(.229)	(.320)	(.619)	(.816)
foreign (global) × mp × crisis 2008 –2009	5.207**	4.696*	5.400**	5.136**	4.321**	3.698*
	(.041)	(.058)	(.026)	(.033)	(.048)	(.097)
Year dummy	Yes	Yes	Yes	Yes	Yes	Yes
Country dummy	Yes	Yes	Yes	Yes	No	No
Observations (banks)	1932	1932	1932	1932	1932	1932
	(269)	(269)	(269)	(269)	(269)	(269)
R^2	.283	.293			.293	.306
AR(1)/*AR*(2)			.000/.268	.000/.376		
Hansen *J*-test			.544	.306		

Notes: *p*-value in parenthesis. ***: 1 percent significance level; **: 5 percent significance level; *: 10 percent significance level.

within their conglomerates than the latter (De Haas & Lelyveld, 2006, 2010).

We replace the dummy, *foreign*, by two dummies representing the different entry modes of foreign banks, *foreign(de novo)* and *foreign(M&A)*. We report the empirical results in Table 4. Consistent with our expectation, de novo foreign subsidiaries are more insulated from the domestic monetary policy in both 1997–1999 and 2008–2009 crises. In particular, the dampening effect on monetary policy is found stronger in the latter, implying a more substantial scale and scope of fund shift between headquarters and subsidiaries in the 2008–2009 crisis than in 1997–1999. The subsidiaries established by M&A are not found significant different from domestic banks in their response to host monetary policy in both crises, seemingly suggesting a looser link between parent banks and M&A subsidiaries.[12]

CONCLUSION

Our chapter presents consistent evidence that domestic monetary policy may lose its force in economies in the presence of higher foreign banks. We also find that the policy ineffectiveness is even more pronounced in the global crisis of 2008–2009, a crisis originated and centered outside Asia, than in the Asian regional crisis of 1997–1999. Foreign banks' insensitivity to host country monetary policy during the global financial crisis of 2008–2009 is driven by factors such as parent banks' divergent exposure to the crisis, operational scope, and entry modes into the host markets.

There are some important policy implications of our finding. First, central bankers need to take into account the buffering/hampering effects of foreign banks on the monetary policy transmission mechanism when they design appropriate monetary policy to bail out their economies during financial turmoil, otherwise the effectiveness of monetary policy may be lower than expected. Second, a gradual financial market opening to multinational banks seems a better strategy to avoid a swift and large-scale transmission of crisis from the country of origin to host economies via foreign banks.

Finally, as the impact of foreign banks on the monetary policy transmission mechanism in host economies depends on various different factors as identified in the chapter, financial regulators should welcome and encourage a higher diversity of the foreign entrants with favorable conditions, including divergent home country origins and entry modes.

Table 4. The Effect of Changes In Monetary Policy on Loan Growth of Domestic and Foreign Banks in Asia, 1997 – 2009: De Novo Versus M&A Foreign Bank Subsidiaries.

Dependent Variable:	Pooled OLS		GMM System		Fixed Effects	
$\Delta ln(loans)_{i,j,t}$	(1)	(2)	(3)	(4)	(5)	(6)
mp	−1.506***	−1.774***	−1.378***	−1.381**	−.869***	−1.448***
	(.000)	(.000)	(.000)	(.020)	(.005)	(.006)
foreign (de novo) × *mp*	−1.195*	−1.624***	−1.389**	−1.931***	−1.090*	−1.673***
	(.054)	(.006)	(.025)	(.000)	(.082)	(.001)
foreign (merger) × *mp*	.564	.337	.549	.146	.472	.194
	(.434)	(.615)	(.445)	(.826)	(.485)	(.762)
foreign (de novo) × *mp* × crisis 1997–1999	2.036***	2.536***	2.056***	2.637***	1.775***	2.425***
	(.002)	(.000)	(.001)	(.000)	(.005)	(.000)
foreign (merger) × *mp* × crisis 1997–1999	−.564	−.078	−.601	−.000	−.543	.037
	(.502)	(.908)	(.380)	(.999)	(.391)	(.949)
foreign (de novo) × mp × crisis 2008–2009	4.651	4.926*	6.025**	5.541**	5.047**	5.163**
	(.121)	(.067)	(.024)	(.031)	(.039)	(.038)
foreign (merger) × mp × crisis 2008–2009	1.753	1.761	1.198	1.646	.133	−.198
	(.192)	(.244)	(.433)	(.323)	(.930)	(.907)
Year dummy	Yes	Yes	Yes	Yes	Yes	Yes
Country dummy	Yes	Yes	Yes	Yes	No	No
Observations (banks)	1932	1932	1932	1932	1932	1932
	(269)	(269)	(269)	(269)	(269)	(269)
R^2	.275	.289			.288	.303
$AR(1)/AR(2)$			.000/.138	.000/.283		
Hansen *J*-test			.394	.204		

Notes: *p*-value in parenthesis. ***: 1 percent significance level; **: 5 percent significance level; *: 10 percent significance level.

NOTES

1. Seven Asian economies, namely, Hong Kong SAR, Indonesia, Korea, Malaysia, Philippines, Singapore, and Thailand, are selected in our sample.

2. We follow existent literature by using the change in money market rate to proxy the adjustment of central banks' monetary policy. Money market rate is selected because it is universally available for all of our selected Asian economies, thus making the changes in host monetary policy across countries comparable.

3. Different from many others, we extend the duration of Asian financial crisis from 1997 to 1999 because many Asian countries in our sample experienced industry-wide distress in banking markets even after 1998 (see Caprio & Klingebiel (2003); Laeven & Valencia (2008)).

4. In the literature, the quality of *BankScope* data has been assessed as good overall. For example, using 1999 as a reference year, Cunningham (2001) observes that in 15 of 19 emerging market economies, *BankScope* data covers more than 90 percent of the total banking sector assets. The countries considered for the assessment are Argentina, Brazil, Chile, Colombia, Venezuela, Mexico, China, India, Indonesia, Korea, Malaysia, the Philippines, Taiwan, Thailand, the Czech Republic, Hungary, Poland, Russia, and Turkey, many of which overlap with our country data set of Asia.

5. Most of the foreign banks in our dataset are foreign-owned subsidiaries.

6. Our result is in line with some earlier works that also found foreign banks played a stabilizing role in host crises before 2008. Dages, Goldberg, and Kinney (2000) found that foreign banks had higher growth rate and lower volatility of loans during crisis periods in Mexico and Argentina. Detragiache and Gupta (2006) found some evidence, although only weak, that non-Asia-oriented foreign banks provided loans at a higher rate than domestic banks.

7. During the financial crisis in 1997–1999, Asian central banks lowered interest rates only when peace returned to foreign exchange markets and economies started to recover. In our sample, there are in total 12 country-year observations of tightened monetary policy, and 9 observations of eased monetary policy. By contrast, expansionary monetary policy was adopted almost unanimously in the entire duration of 2008–2009 global financial crisis.

8. Foreign banks might view the crises in host countries as an opportunity to expand their market share, hence increased their lending when domestic credit was shrinking (see Cull and Martinez Peria (2007)).

9. We also test our results by excluding the observations that host central banks conducted expansionary monetary policy, or put differently, we focus on the comparison between the scenario when central banks conducted contractionary monetary policy in the Asian crisis and the scenario when expansionary monetary policy was carried out in the global crisis. Our finding is qualitatively consistent and still statistically significant. Tightened (eased) monetary policy is dampened by foreign banks in the regional (global) financial crisis. Analogously, we then exclude the observations that central banks conducted contractionary monetary policy in the 1997–1999 Asian financial crisis, and test our results again. The results are still qualitatively consistent although not significant in all regressions. Foreign banks were less responsive to eased monetary condition in the late period of 1997–1999 Asian

crisis probably because parent banks discontinued their support to subsidiaries when it was not emergently needed any more.

10. Alternatively, we divide our sample according to parent banks' dependence on wholesale funding markets. Parent banks that are more dependent on wholesale bond and money markets as the main funding sources of lending are expected to suffer from credit crunch more seriously than others in the recent global crisis. These parent banks may withdraw funds more aggressively from their subsidiaries abroad, thus resulting in a lower response to host monetary policy. However, the same subsidiaries are not expected to show a similar lukewarm response to host monetary policy in the earlier Asian crisis since the global wholesale funding markets were not as dysfunctional in the 1997–1999 Asian crisis as was so in the 2008–2009 global crisis. We find that, during the 2008–2009 global crisis the subsidiaries of the global banks with higher dependence on wholesale funding are more sluggish to adjust their loans to changes in host monetary policy than other foreign banks in the global financial crisis. The estimation is statistically significant in half of our tests and only marginally not in the others. This phenomenon is not found during the earlier Asian financial crisis of 1997–1999. For the subsidiaries whose parent banks have lower reliance on nondeposit sources for funding, they show more similar insensitivity in both crises. This finding as well implies that foreign banks' lower sensitivity to host monetary policy during the 2008–2009 global crisis than in the 1997–1999 Asian crisis is attributed to external factors rather than internal ones. The results are available upon request.

11. Detragiache and Gupta (2006) find significant behavioral difference between non-Asia-oriented foreign banks and Asia-oriented foreign banks in the Asian financial crisis, similarly defined as the global and regional foreign banks in this chapter. The finding that non-Asian-oriented foreign banks fared better in the crisis is explained, albeit partially, by the financial assistance received from their parent banks which were not affected in the Asian regional crisis.

12. For a more detailed discussion how entry mode may affect subsidiaries' access to internal capital markets, see Jeon, Olivero, and Wu (2013).

REFERENCES

Arellano, M., & Bover, O. (1995). Another look at the instrumental variable estimation of error-component models. *Journal of Econometrics*, *58*, 5–28.

Arena, M., Reinhart, C., & Vázquez, F. (2006). *The lending channel in emerging economies: Are foreign banks different?* NBER Working Paper No. 12340. National Bureau of Economic Research, Cambridge, MA.

Bernanke, B., & Blinder, A. (1988). Is it money or credit, or both or neither? Credit, money and aggregate demand. *American Economic Review*, *78*, 435–439.

Bernanke, B., & Blinder, A. (1992). The federal fund rate and the channels of monetary transmission. *American Economic Review*, *82*, 901–921.

Blundell, R., & Bond, S. (1998). Initial conditions and moment restrictions in dynamic panel data models. *Journal of Econometrics*, *87*, 115–143.

Caprio, G., & Klingebiel, D. (2003). *Episodes of systemic and borderline financial crises*. World Bank Working Paper. The World Bank, Washington, DC.

Cetorelli, N., & Goldberg, L. S. (2010). *Global banks and international shock transmission: evidence from the crisis*. NBER Working paper No. 15974. National Bureau of Economic Research, Cambridge, MA.

Cetorelli, N., & Goldberg, L. S. (2012). Banking globalization and monetary transmission. *Journal of Finance*, *67*, 1811–1843.

Claessens, S., Demirguc-Kune, A., & Huizinga, H. (2001). How does foreign entry affect domestic banking markets? *Journal of Banking and Finance*, *25*, 891–911.

Claessens, S., & van Horen, N. (2012). *Foreign banks: Trends, impacts and financial stability*. IMF Working Paper WP/12/10. International Monetary Fund, Washington, DC.

Crystal, J. S., Dages, B. G., & Goldberg, L. S. (2001). *Does foreign ownership contributes to sounder banks in emerging markets? The Latin American experience*. Staff Reports 137. Federal Reserve Bank of New York, NY.

Cull, R., & Martinez Peria, M. S. (2007). *Foreign bank participation and crises in developing countries*. World Bank Policy Research Working Paper 4128. The World Bank, Washington, DC.

Cull, R., & Martinez Peria, M. S. (2010). *Foreign bank participation in developing countries: What do we know about the drivers and consequences of this phenomenon?* World Bank Policy Research Working Paper 5398. The World Bank, Washington, DC.

Cunningham, A. (2001). Assessing the stability of emerging market economies' banking systems. *Financial Stability Review*, *11*(December), 187–192.

Dages, B. G., Goldberg, L. S., & Kinney, D. (2000). Foreign and domestic bank participation in emerging markets: Lessons from Mexico and Argentina. *Economic Policy Review*, *6*, 17–36.

De Haas, R., & van Lelyveld, I. (2006). Foreign banks and credit stability in Central and Eastern Europe: A panel data analysis. *Journal of Banking and Finance*, *30*, 1927–1952.

De Haas, R., & van Lelyveld, I. (2010). Internal capital market and lending by multinational bank subsidiaries. *Journal of Financial Intermediation*, *19*, 1–25.

De Haas, R., & van Lelyveld, I. (forthcoming). Multinational banks and global financial crisis: Weathering the perfect storm? *Journal of Money, Credit and Banking*.

Detragiache, E., & Gupta, P. (2006). Foreign banks in emerging market crises: Evidence from Malaysia. *Journal of Financial Stability*, *2*, 217–242.

Goldberg, L. (2001). *When is U.S. bank lending to emerging markets volatile?* NBER Working Paper No. 8209. National Bureau of Economic Research, Cambridge, MA.

Jeon, B. N., Olivero, M. P., & Wu, J. (2011). Do foreign banks increase competition? Evidence from emerging Asian and Latin American banking markets. *Journal of Banking and Finance*, *35*, 856–875.

Jeon, B. N., Olivero, M. P., & Wu, J. (2013). Multinational banking and the international transmission of financial shocks: Evidence from foreign subsidiaries. *Journal of Banking and Finance*, *37*, 952–972.

Kashyap, A., & Stein, J. (2000). What do a million observations on banks say about the transmission of monetary policy? *American Economic Review*, *90*, 407–428.

Kishan, R., & Opiela, T. (2000). Bank size, bank capital and bank lending channel. *Journal of Money, Credit and Banking*, *32*, 121–141.

Laeven, L., & Valencia, F. (2008). *Systemic banking crises: A new database*. IMF Working Paper WP/08/224. International Monetary Fund, Washington, DC.

Nickell, S. (1981). Biases in dynamic models with fixed effects. *Econometrica*, *49*, 1417–1426.

Wu, J., Luca, A. C., & Jeon, B. N. (2011). Foreign bank penetration and the lending channel in emerging economies: Evidence from bank-level panel data. *Journal of International Money and Finance*, *30*, 1128–1156.

APPENDIX A: FOREIGN BANK PENETRATION LEVELS IN ASIA (1997–2009)

	1997	1998	1999	2000	2001	2002	2003	2004	2005	2006	2007	2008	2009
Hong Kong	87.522	88.514	88.511	88.608	91.168	91.874	92.082	92.282	91.802	91.803	91.655	93.058	93.181
Indonesia	5.378	9.923	4.739	5.025	4.325	6.426	15.435	22.109	26.380	25.499	27.994	28.289	27.869
Korea	.828	.629	5.692	4.499	4.412	4.560	13.050	16.454	16.445	17.395	16.197	17.879	16.570
Malaysia	24.086	24.970	22.768	26.240	23.507	22.474	24.092	24.265	22.243	22.386	23.577	23.459	22.327
Philippines	1.946	3.584	4.525	2.595	1.338	2.565	2.486	1.486	1.619	1.716	1.171	1.058	.972
Singapore	3.776	3.722	3.891	4.754	6.305	6.881	5.767	4.016	5.059	4.818	5.918	5.658	5.133
Thailand	.804	6.227	7.312	6.197	6.257	6.025	5.856	3.961	4.836	4.712	5.315	5.504	6.626

Note: Foreign bank penetration level is measured by the share of foreign banks' assets in banking sector total assets.

APPENDIX B: THE SUMMARY DESCRIPTIVE STATISTICS: DOMESTIC VERSUS FOREIGN BANKS IN ASIA, 1997–2009

	Panel A: Mean, Standard Deviation and Median			Panel B: Correlation Coefficient				
	Mean	Std. dev	Median	Δln(loans)	Liquidity	Capitalization	Size	Riskiness
Domestic banks								
Δln(loans)	9.197	22.059	8.403	1				
liquidity	21.989	15.044	18.417	.153***	1			
capitalization	10.228	6.297	9.245	−.063**	.050*	1		
size	5.094	6.697	2.065	−.032	−.104***	−.186***	1	
riskiness	1.545	2.688	.934	−.091***	−.039	−.039	.027	1
Foreign banks								
Δln(loans)	5.393	28.539	4.584	1				
liquidity	27.517	17.226	24.246	.011	1			
capitalization	15.011	10.275	12.138	.037	.106***	1		
size	2.213	6.227	.601	.012	−.038	−.236***	1	
riskiness	1.619	4.192	.621	−.128***	−.070**	−.032	−.068*	1

Note: ***: 1 percent significance level; **: 5 percent significance level; *: 10 percent significance level.

SUPER-SIZE BANKS: IS RISK-TAKING REWARDING?

Jinyong Kim and Yong-Cheol Kim

ABSTRACT

U.S. bank holding companies (BHCs) have experienced dynamic changes over a period of 2000–2010. We find that the size distribution of sample banks becomes highly positively skewed with a small number of big banks becoming super-sized, and these big banks tend to take extra risk by holding derivative positions for trading purposes. The ten largest risk-taking banks hold about 70% of total assets of all the sample banks in 2010. We investigate whether the risk-taking activities of the BHCs translate into higher risk-adjusted return performance. In extensive panel regression analyses, we find that the risk-taking strategies of large banks by holding derivative positions for trading purpose do not show the clear evidence of enhancing risk-adjusted performance. We find that negative impacts of extra risk-taking on the risk-adjusted performance become bigger with the size of banks.

Keywords: Bank holding companies; risk-taking; derivatives; efficiency

JEL classifications: G21; G24

Global Banking, Financial Markets and Crises
International Finance Review, Volume 14, 115–140

ISSN: 1569-3767/doi:10.1108/S1569-3767(2013)0000014008

INTRODUCTION

Banking industry and financial intermediation in the United States have experienced slow and steady changes into the direction of deregulation during the past several decades, and at the same time, created several crises such as the savings and loan crisis in 1980s, the Long-Term Capital Management debacle in 1998, and the global financial crisis in 2007/2008. The main role of traditional banking is "capital intermediation" in which banks take deposits and provide loan capital to households and firms. However, U.S. banks have expanded into nontraditional banking businesses, and the repeal of the Glass–Steagall (G–S) Act eliminated the firewall between commercial and investment banking activities by one institution, allowing banks to conduct "broad banking"[1] and to expand into other financial services. At the same time, nonbank financial service firms could also expand into traditional banking businesses. The expanded opportunities for U.S. bank holding companies (BHCs) allow banks to engage in "risk intermediation" through securitization and the enhancement of credit risk of loan portfolios, in addition to capital intermediation. The double role of capital and risk intermediation poses an interesting question of whether newly created BHCs are able to achieve efficiency gains via the channels of both scale and scope economies.

Do large banks improve efficiency? Banks can benefit from scale economy by extending traditional banking activities of taking deposit and making loans, and from scope economy by expanding into other related financial services. The deregulation on interstate bank branching allows large national banks to benefit from cost-savings and scale economy. Beck, Levine, and Levkov (2010) find that removal of restrictions on interstate branching improves income inequality as small firms that rely on bank lending can hire more workers, which in turn help relative wage rates, and working hours of unskilled workers increased.

Empirical evidence on scope economies of banks is mixed. On the negative side, most empirical analysis on banking firms is consistent with the results of industrial firms, showing the dark side of diversification. The literature on bank diversification documents some benefits of revenue diversification but with more volatile noninterest activities, resulting in no improvement in risk-adjusted performance (Stiroh & Rumble, 2006; Laeven & Levine, 2007). The positive side of diversification benefit is stated in the studies on the effects of the repeal of the G–S Act, which prohibited commercial banks from entering into activities what typical investment banks do, such as underwriting or dealing with corporate securities. It was enacted after the Great Depression with a belief that universal banking would be detrimental to the stability of financial system, but repealed in 1999 by the Gramm–Leach–Bliley (GLB) Act of 1999, also known as the Financial Services Modernization Act, in response to most researches that raised issues of the unnecessary burdens and restrictions on banking activities.[2] While the empirical evidence has been inconclusive with some research in support of and others against the G–S Act, one main argument for the proponents was that the combination of commercial and investment banks would create conflicts of interest since commercial banks, not only as lenders to certain corporations but also as stockholders of the same corporations, are likely to prop up weak and failing firms. Kroszner and Rajan (1994, 1997), in their study of universal banking during 1921–1929, showed that commercial banks underwrite only high quality securities as the investors incorporate potential conflicts of interest in the pricing of securities. On the other hand, the argument to repute the alleged ill-effects of universal banking emphasizes the risk-taking patterns of universal banks. White (1986) finds that banks show no significant differences in earning volatilities no matter whether the banks engage in securities business or not.

As banks grow in size by both extending its scale and by expanding the scope of financial services, larger banks enter into risk management and risk-taking activities. The research question is whether increased risk-taking by large banks enhances bank performance. In this chapter, we focus on a specific dimension of risk-taking activities based on derivative positions held by the U.S. BHCs. In other words, we classify a bank possessing positive notional amount of derivative securities especially for trading purposes as a type of bank that takes extra risk. While derivative positions held by hedging purposes can be regarded as an effective tool for risk management, derivatives held for trading can be considered as evidence that the banks are actively taking additional risk and targeting for extra profit. Accordingly, we call the banks to hold derivatives for trading purposes as "risk-taker." If we look at these risk-taking banks from the perspective of size distribution, a small number of big banks become super-sized, which makes the size distribution of sample banks become highly positively skewed over time, and these big banks tend to be the ones who take extra risk by holding derivative positions for trading purposes. It is observed that the size of the risk-taking banks are more than 80% of the total size of the sample banks, and especially the ten largest risk-taking banks hold about 70% of total assets of all the banks in 2010.

Considering the importance of super-size risk-taking banks in the banking industry, we investigate whether the active risk-taking activities, as well as their increased size and diversified business structure, turn out to generate any efficiency gain and to translate into higher risk-adjusted return. We apply the panel regression approach with the two types of performance measures: return on asset (ROA) and return on equity (ROE). We use risk-adjusted returns as the main dependent variables in order to evaluate the contribution of risk-taking in addition to the size and diversification structure of the sample banks. The results show that, during the full sample period, the extra risk-taking by holding derivatives with trading purpose is not shown to significantly enhance the risk-adjusted return performance. Subsequent subsample analysis shows that while the banks seem to get some positive benefits by taking advantage of more risky instruments for extra revenue generation during the normal times before the crisis, the benefits are wiped out during the crisis period.

This chapter is organized as follows. The second section describes data and variables. The third section presents various descriptive statistics to show historical changes of banks. The results of the regression analyses are reported in the fourth section. In addition to the full sample, we also consider the two subsamples, before and after the financial crisis, in order to highlight the difference in the pattern of contribution of the risk-taking to the performance between two different time periods. The fifth section concludes.

DATA AND VARIABLE DEFINITION

Data and Performance Measures

The quarterly Federal Reserve (FR) Y-9C form reports notional amounts of four types of derivative contracts such as interest rate, foreign exchange, equity, and commodity and others, in addition to the basic financial information (balance sheets and income statements) of the U.S. BHCs. More specifically, the form reports the total gross notional amount of each derivative contract held for trading purpose and for purposes other than trading separately. Accordingly, from the FR Y-9C form, we classify the reported banks into two criteria, risk-taker and non-risk-taker, based on information about their derivative positions. We call a bank as a risk-taker if the bank reports positive notional amount for at least one type of derivative contracts for trading purpose, since it is likely that the derivatives are utilized to actively seek for speculative gains by taking riskier positions. The remaining banks in the sample are considered to be non-risk-taker. A bank that reports a derivative position for purposes other than trading is included in the non-risk-taker group, since the derivatives are likely to help hedge existing risky assets or liabilities and reduce variability of the bank portfolio.

With this classification, we choose the sample BHCs from the FR Y-9C form with (i) total assets of 500 million dollars or more, (ii) the interest income share, the ratio of interest income to total income, between zero and one, and (iii) positive sum of net income and book equity, for the sample years of 2000–2010.[3] Then, in order to construct the risk measures in the time-varying short-window manner, we impose further sample selection criteria such that a bank should have previous consecutive eight quarters' report records to be included in the sample.[4] Our selection criteria provide a total of 26,852 sample quarter-banks.

As the main performance variables, we consider two types of risk-adjusted measures for each ROA and ROE by considering volatility and bank beta as the adjustment factors for bank risk. ROA is constructed as the ratio of net income attributable to a BHC to the total assets, while ROE is as the ratio of net income to total book equity of the bank, in place of the total assets. Detailed procedure to derive the risk-adjusted performance measures by incorporating bank volatility and beta risk components are described in detail in the later sections. Naturally, in order to explicitly consider the risk-taking measure in our regression analyses, we use the dummy variable for the risk-taking bank, that is, for the bank that reports positive notional amount of derivative for trading purpose.

Size and Diversification Measures

As a size measure, we use the relative size that is defined as the total asset of an individual bank relative to the cross-sectional average of the total assets of the sample banks, for each sample year. The relative size is employed to emphasize the effect of a bank size in terms of distribution, that is, whether the bank's relative size in comparison with the cross-sectional average of distribution has an effect on its performance.

For business scope and diversification of banks, we use three measures. Laeven and Levine (2007) suggest two diversification measures based on assets and income-generating activities of banks. The asset-based measure is calculated by the share of total loans out of total assets, and the income-based measure is calculated by the share of net interest income out of net operating income. Detailed derivations of these measures are derived as follows. First, the income diversification measure DIV_{Income} is such that

$$\begin{aligned} SH_{interest} &= \frac{\text{Net interest income}}{\text{Net interest income} + \text{Non-interest income}}, \\ SH_{nonint} &= 1 - SH_{interest}, \\ DIV_{Income} &= 1 - (SH^2_{interest} + SH^2_{nonint}) \end{aligned} \tag{1}$$

This variable is effectively used as a diversification measures since the value is maximized as one half when a bank holds the interest income and noninterest income as exactly half and half out of total income, while the value is minimized at zero when the bank purely depends on either interest or noninterest income so that one share value takes one and the other share value takes zero.

Second, the asset diversification measure DIV_{Asset} is calculated as

$$\begin{aligned} SH_{loan} &= \frac{\text{Total loan}}{\text{Total asset}}, \quad SH_{nonloan} = 1 - SH_{loan}, \\ DIV_{Asset} &= 1 - (SH^2_{loan} + SH^2_{nonloan}) \end{aligned} \tag{2}$$

In addition, we develop the third diversification measure based on the liability components of bank balance sheets. The liability diversification measure $DIV_{Liability}$, is calculated by the share of total deposit out of total liability and derived as

$$\begin{aligned} SH_{deposit} &= \frac{\text{Total deposit}}{\text{Total liability}}, \quad SH_{nondeposit} = 1 - SH_{deposit}, \\ DIV_{Liability} &= 1 - (SH^2_{deposit} + SH^2_{nondeposit}) \end{aligned} \tag{3}$$

By including the three diversification measures, we try to capture the diversifying effects in all the three aspects of the balance sheets, asset and liability, as well as the income statement structures.

In addition to size, diversification and risk-taking measures, we use the total liability to total asset ratio as another control variable to consider the effect of leverage on the bank return performance. We also include the year dummy variables with 2000 as the base year, and control for the bank fixed effects so that the regression can further consider unobserved individual bank characteristics.

DESCRIPTIVE ANALYSIS OF RISK-TAKER VERSUS NON-RISK-TAKER

Table 1 reports the average and median values of total assets, as well as the numbers, of risk-taker and non-risk-taker banks across the sample years, based on the report of the last quarter for each year. The total assets are presented in real terms deflated by the personal consumption expenditures price index, with the 2005 as the base year. First, it is noted that the average size of risk-taking banks is much bigger than that of the non-risk-taking banks, by more than thirty times. And the average total assets of the banks in the whole sample tended to increase up to the mid-2000s and

Table 1. Numbers and Total Assets of Risk-Taking and Non-Risk-Taking Banks.

	Total			Non-Risk-Taker			Risk-Taker		
Year	Num	Mean	Med	Num	Mean	Med	Num	Mean	Med
2000	452	19.381	1.968	384	4.101	1.595	68	105.673	39.311
2001	497	20.551	1.625	422	3.844	1.333	75	114.558	34.302
2002	544	20.172	1.536	459	3.074	1.242	85	112.500	35.507
2003	590	21.015	1.479	500	3.719	1.203	90	117.105	34.608
2004	611	22.395	1.356	526	3.673	1.167	85	138.254	35.026
2005	652	20.505	1.351	556	3.654	1.164	96	118.096	23.680
2006	675	17.537	1.237	589	2.968	1.101	86	117.324	17.343
2007	709	16.305	1.154	615	2.948	1.037	94	103.700	8.558
2008	701	14.338	1.097	603	2.712	0.979	98	85.875	8.386
2009	686	14.956	1.053	589	2.848	0.976	97	88.475	8.643
2010	679	17.288	1.021	577	3.102	0.948	102	97.537	6.975

This table reports the number of sample banks and the average and the median values of total assets of the banks in total as well as in risk-taker and non-risk-taker group over the years of 2000–2010. If BHCs are reported to have a positive notional amount for at least one type of derivative contracts for trading purpose, then the BHC is classified as a risk-taker. The remaining BHCs in the sample are classified as a non-risk-taker. "Num" column reports the number of banks included in the sample, and "Mean" and "Med" columns report the sample mean and median of total assets, respectively. Total assets are presented in real terms with 2005 as the base year. Units are in billion USD.

decreased afterwards, while the median asset size steadily decreased over the years. On the other hand, the number of especially smaller-sized non-risk-taking banks, accordingly the total number of sample banks, continued to increase up to 2007. For the risk-taking banks, with the relatively stable numbers over time, the gap between the mean and median asset size is extremely wide and becomes even wider up to 2006. From the viewpoint of the cross-sectional size distribution, the results in Table 1 indicate that the size distribution of the sample banks is transformed into more right skewed one with smaller number of banks with much bigger size (e.g., by merger and acquisition) and larger number of banks with smaller size.

These patterns of the size distribution can be more clearly presented in Table 2, which indicates the high and increasing degrees of concentration of total assets in the sample. It is shown that the ratio of total assets of risk-taking banks to total assets of all the sample banks are relatively stable at 82–85% and the share of total number of the risk-takers are also stable around 12–15%. However, the ratio of asset size of the ten largest risk-taking banks to total assets of all banks shows that the small number

Table 2. Size Distribution of Sample Banks.

Year	Number of Risk-Takers/ Number of Total Banks	Size of Risk-Takers/ Size of Total Banks	Size of 10 Biggest Risk-Takers/Size of Total Banks
2000	15.04	82.03	57.54
2001	15.09	84.12	57.74
2002	15.63	87.14	56.67
2003	15.25	85.00	55.35
2004	13.91	85.88	61.03
2005	14.72	84.80	57.02
2006	12.74	85.23	61.17
2007	13.26	84.32	66.70
2008	13.98	83.73	65.30
2009	14.14	83.65	65.20
2010	15.02	84.75	69.31

This table presents the summary statistics for the relative size and number distribution of the sample banks for the years of 2000–2010. The second column presents the ratio of the number of risk-takers to the number of all sample banks, the third column presents the ratio of total size of the risk-taking banks to the size of all sample banks, and the fourth column presents the ratio of total assets of the ten biggest risk-takers out of total size of sample banks. If a BHC is reported to have a positive notional amount for at least one type of derivative contracts for trading purpose, then the BHC is classified as a risk-taker. The remaining BHCs in the sample are classified as a non-risk-taker. Size is measured in the real values of total assets. Units are in percentage.

of largest banks becomes even larger in total assets and concentration in size becomes stronger. These results support the argument that the cross-sectional size distribution becomes more highly skewed to the right over time.

Table 3 summarizes the time-series patterns of compositions of total assets, total liabilities, and total loans for the risk-taking and non-risk-taking banks. The compositions of the non-risk-taking banks are listed on the top panel, while those of the risk-taking banks are listed on the bottom panel. For the total assets, the compositions are relatively stable. The non-risk-takers show higher and slightly increasing dependence on loan, with relatively higher percentage to security, while the risk-takers show higher percentage of cash, trading assets, and fed fund sold and reverse repo. For the total liabilities, the non-risk-takers show overall high and increasing dependence on deposit especially since 2000. However, the risk-takers show much smaller dependence on deposit, no higher than 70% during 2000–2006. Fed fund purchased and repo, and other borrowed money compositions are higher for the risk-takers. If we look at the compositions of total loans more in detail, both the non-risk-takers and the risk-takers show decreasing dependence on commercial and industrial (C&I) loan and consumer loan, and increasing dependence on real estate loans. The ratios of C&I loans to total loans are higher for the risk-takers, while the real estate to total loan ratios are higher for the non-risk-takers. While not presented in the table, the loans secured by residential properties out of real estate loans show less weights over time, and the loans secured by nonfarm and nonresidential, or commercial, properties gain more weights, and these patterns are more clearly shown for the non-risk-taking banks.

Table 4 presents the results that the bank ROA and ROE performance turned to negative, especially for the risk-taking banks, during 2008–2009 because of the net loss of the BHCs as a result of the financial crisis. While the statistical significance is not strong, by simply comparing the values it seems that the return performance of the risk-taking banks was better in the earlier 2000s but tended to be worse during the periods of 2005–2008, in comparison with the non-risk-taking banks.

We also take a more detailed look at one of the main performance measures, ROA, in terms of the income statement compositions over the sample years. Table 4 also reports the average ROA interest, measured by the net interest income to total asset ratio, in the top panel, which shows stable but slightly decreasing pattern. ROA interest of non-risk-taking banks becomes significantly higher than that of risk-taking banks over the all sample years, indicating higher dependence on the revenue generated by

Table 3. Compositions of Total Asset, Total Liability, and Total Loan.

	Total Asset						Total Liability					Total loan			
	Cash	Security	Trading	Loan	Fed repo	Other	Deposit	Trading	Fed repo	Borrow	Other	C&I	Consumer	Real est	Other
							Non-risk-taker								
2000	0.040	0.246	0.001	0.649	NA	0.064	0.826	0.000	NA	NA	0.174	0.181	0.120	0.642	0.057
2001	0.039	0.238	0.001	0.651	NA	0.070	0.837	0.000	NA	0.092	0.070	0.171	0.109	0.667	0.053
2002	0.041	0.246	0.000	0.643	0.020	0.049	0.844	0.000	0.045	0.091	0.019	0.167	0.096	0.688	0.049
2003	0.037	0.254	0.001	0.641	0.014	0.053	0.840	0.000	0.048	0.091	0.021	0.161	0.083	0.709	0.048
2004	0.031	0.235	0.000	0.662	0.016	0.055	0.834	0.000	0.044	0.088	0.034	0.155	0.077	0.722	0.047
2005	0.034	0.214	0.000	0.680	0.014	0.057	0.839	0.000	0.041	0.087	0.033	0.146	0.069	0.741	0.044
2006	0.032	0.194	0.000	0.698	0.017	0.058	0.852	0.000	0.039	0.075	0.034	0.146	0.058	0.755	0.042
2007	0.029	0.180	0.002	0.717	0.013	0.059	0.836	0.000	0.042	0.089	0.033	0.147	0.054	0.759	0.041
2008	0.034	0.178	0.001	0.718	0.010	0.060	0.834	0.000	0.039	0.097	0.031	0.147	0.049	0.761	0.042
2009	0.058	0.191	0.001	0.680	0.008	0.063	0.866	0.000	0.032	0.072	0.029	0.139	0.051	0.766	0.045
2010	0.064	0.213	0.001	0.651	0.007	0.065	0.887	0.000	0.028	0.056	0.028	0.138	0.050	0.764	0.049
							Risk-taker								
2000	0.056	0.186	0.027	0.628	NA	0.102	0.631	0.014	NA	NA	0.355	0.298	0.119	0.465	0.118
2001	0.058	0.208	0.032	0.583	NA	0.119	0.625	0.014	NA	0.114	0.248	0.274	0.112	0.494	0.120
2002	0.062	0.219	0.030	0.569	0.045	0.074	0.599	0.016	0.111	0.130	0.144	0.251	0.126	0.497	0.125
2003	0.049	0.227	0.030	0.567	0.042	0.085	0.590	0.016	0.115	0.137	0.142	0.221	0.136	0.512	0.131
2004	0.047	0.223	0.027	0.587	0.036	0.080	0.605	0.015	0.115	0.132	0.133	0.224	0.121	0.539	0.115
2005	0.048	0.212	0.023	0.602	0.032	0.084	0.676	0.010	0.100	0.111	0.103	0.218	0.112	0.569	0.100
2006	0.045	0.196	0.024	0.610	0.041	0.084	0.663	0.010	0.100	0.118	0.109	0.213	0.088	0.596	0.103
2007	0.039	0.180	0.017	0.657	0.029	0.078	0.718	0.008	0.086	0.104	0.083	0.205	0.079	0.642	0.074
2008	0.058	0.169	0.014	0.669	0.015	0.076	0.736	0.007	0.062	0.119	0.075	0.200	0.090	0.645	0.064
2009	0.063	0.191	0.012	0.638	0.015	0.081	0.779	0.006	0.056	0.084	0.074	0.198	0.081	0.648	0.073
2010	0.067	0.202	0.013	0.624	0.011	0.083	0.797	0.007	0.047	0.077	0.072	0.192	0.073	0.658	0.078

This table presents the composition of total assets, total liability, and total loans for the non-risk-taker (above panel) and the risk-taker banks (below panel) during the sample years from 2000 to 2010. Each column corresponds to the share of the component, titled in the second row, out of the total asset, total liability, or total loan, as indicated in the first row. The results are from the December reports of the FR Y-9C form of sample banks for each year.

Table 4. Comparison of Average Performance.

	Non-Risk-Taker	Risk-Taker	Difference (*t*-value)	Non-Risk-Taker	Risk-Taker	Difference (*t*-value)
		ROA			ROE	
2000	0.011	0.012	−0.000 (−0.53)	0.129	0.140	−0.011 (−1.56)
2001	0.011	0.011	−0.000 (−0.06)	0.111	0.110	0.001 (0.10)
2002	0.012	0.012	−0.000 (−0.10)	0.112	0.118	−0.006 (−0.66)
2003	0.011	0.013	−0.002 (−1.86)	0.111	0.128	−0.017 (−2.68)
2004	0.011	0.012	−0.001 (−0.88)	0.123	0.133	−0.010 (−1.58)
2005	0.012	0.011	0.001 (1.06)	0.129	0.122	0.008 (1.22)
2006	0.011	0.011	0.000 (0.10)	0.123	0.121	0.001 (0.21)
2007	0.009	0.007	0.002 (1.84)	0.099	0.075	0.024 (2.01)
2008	0.003	−0.001	0.004 (2.41)	0.018	−0.018	0.036 (1.79)
2009	0.000	−0.002	0.002 (1.45)	−0.025	−0.016	−0.010 (−0.61)
2010	0.004	0.004	0.000 (0.17)	0.025	0.036	−0.012 (−0.94)
		ROA interest			ROA noninterest	
2000	0.036	0.032	0.004 (3.70)	−0.017	−0.010	−0.007 (−6.02)
2001	0.036	0.031	0.005 (3.70)	−0.018	−0.011	−0.007 (−5.79)
2002	0.037	0.033	0.004 (2.37)	−0.016	−0.010	−0.006 (−3.90)
2003	0.035	0.031	0.003 (2.38)	−0.016	−0.008	−0.008 (−4.71)
2004	0.034	0.030	0.004 (3.63)	−0.017	−0.010	−0.007 (−5.84)
2005	0.035	0.028	0.006 (6.12)	−0.017	−0.011	−0.006 (−6.33)
2006	0.035	0.028	0.007 (6.20)	−0.017	−0.010	−0.007 (−6.66)
2007	0.034	0.029	0.004 (4.54)	−0.018	−0.015	−0.003 (−3.47)
2008	0.032	0.029	0.003 (4.18)	−0.019	−0.018	−0.002 (−1.29)
2009	0.032	0.029	0.003 (3.90)	−0.020	−0.017	−0.003 (−2.57)
2010	0.034	0.031	0.003 (3.47)	−0.020	−0.017	−0.003 (−3.12)

This table reports the average values of ROA, ROE, ROA interest (net interest income to total asset ratio), and ROA noninterest (net noninterest income to total asset ratio) for the non-risk-taker and the risk-taker banks, for the sample years from 2000 to 2010. The results are from the December reports of FR Y-9C form of sample banks for each year. The last "Difference" column presents the difference in values between the non-risk-taker and the risk-taker banks and *t*-value in parenthesis under the null hypothesis that the mean values between the two groups are the same.

the interest income components. The ROA noninterest, which is the ratio of net noninterest income to total asset, is also reported in the bottom panel of Table 4. While the net noninterest income is shown to have negative contribution to the overall return, that of the risk-taking banks is less negative on average, probably because noninterest income includes service charges or trading revenues.

REGRESSION RESULTS

Preliminary Regressions

We apply the panel regression approach to analyze the impacts of size, scope and risk-taking strategies of the sample banks on their return performance. Accordingly, the regression equation is such that

$$y_{it} = x_{it}\beta + z_i\alpha + d_t\gamma + \varepsilon_{it}, \tag{4}$$

where y_{it} in our analyses are bank ROA and ROE return measures, x_{it} includes the size, diversification and leverage variables of the individual banks over time, z_i include the risk-taking (i.e., holding derivatives for trading purpose) bank dummy and the bank fixed effects, as well as the constant, and d_t corresponds to the year dummy variables. For each performance measure, we report the results of two regressions: Regression 1 and Regression 2. Regression 1 includes the leverage, relative size, three diversification measures and their related share variables, and the risk-taker dummy variables as well as the year dummy variables and the bank fixed effects as the explanatory variables. Regression 2 adds the interaction terms of the size with diversification and risk-taking measures, in order to investigate whether the scope and risk-taking activities are shown to have an extra impact on the bank returns when they are interacted with the bank size.

Table 5 presents the results of Regression 1 and Regression 2 with ROA and ROE variables before adjustment of risk, as a preliminary stage. It is shown that the risk-taking activities ("Risk" dummy) does not have a significant impact on both the ROA and ROE performance, and there is no significant evidence of scale economies or diseconomies by looking at the coefficients on the relative size at the preliminary regression stage. However, we can observe more distinguished diversification effects in these regressions. For the ROA, the overall effect of diversification seems to be negative, while there is a positive interaction effect of size and income diversification, in the sense that the diversified income structure tends to help enhancing ROA when it is implemented in relatively big banks. On the other hand, the income and liability diversification strategies are positively effective for bank performance when ROE is considered as the bank return measures, even if the diversified asset structure shows significantly negative coefficients. The leverage, or the total liability to total asset ratio, are also presented to have negative significant effects on the ROA and ROE performance.

Table 5. ROA and ROE Regressions.

	ROA				ROE			
	Regression 1		Regression 2		Regression 1		Regression 2	
	Coefficient	*t*-value	Coefficient	*t*-value	Coefficient	*t*-value	Coefficient	*t*-value
Leverage	−0.133**	−49.51	−0.133**	−49.49	−0.747**	−24.28	−0.748**	−24.31
Size	0.000	0.49	−0.000	−0.67	0.000	1.02	0.001	0.26
Income div.	−0.003*	−2.27	−0.004**	−2.79	0.155**	10.16	0.153**	9.82
Asset div.	−0.015**	−9.02	−0.015**	−8.81	−0.192**	−10.10	−0.190**	−9.97
Liability div.	−0.007**	−5.90	−0.007**	−5.84	0.044**	3.19	0.046**	3.30
Interest	−0.015**	−12.99	−0.015**	−13.26	0.004	0.30	0.003	0.20
Loan	−0.002	−1.72	−0.002	−1.70	−0.032*	−2.37	−0.032*	−2.31
Deposit	−0.024**	−17.63	−0.024**	−17.55	−0.084**	−5.41	−0.083**	−5.34
Risk	−0.000	−1.23	−0.000	−1.10	0.002	0.68	0.002	0.58
Size*Income			0.001**	2.62			0.002	0.55
Size*Asset			−0.001	−1.52			−0.001	−0.39
Size*Liability			0.000	0.36			−0.002	−1.04
Size*Risk			−0.000	−0.28			0.000	0.20
2001	−0.002**	−9.26	−0.002**	−9.24	−0.025**	−9.73	−0.025**	−9.73
2002	−0.002**	−8.18	−0.002**	−8.18	−0.028**	−10.70	−0.028**	−10.70
2003	−0.003**	−12.33	−0.003**	−12.29	−0.033**	−12.52	−0.033**	−12.51
2004	−0.002**	−9.86	−0.002**	−9.80	−0.024**	−9.24	−0.024**	−9.23
2005	−0.002**	−9.44	−0.002**	−9.38	−0.024**	−9.32	−0.024**	−9.31
2006	−0.002**	−10.06	−0.002**	−9.97	−0.025**	−9.84	−0.025**	−9.84
2007	−0.004**	−16.08	−0.004**	−15.95	−0.042**	−16.26	−0.042**	−16.25
2008	−0.007**	−31.65	−0.007**	−31.48	−0.088**	−33.28	−0.088**	−33.21
2009	−0.010**	−43.57	−0.010**	−43.43	−0.124**	−47.27	−0.124**	−47.20
2010	−0.007**	−32.06	−0.007**	−31.99	−0.094**	−35.38	−0.094**	−35.35
Adj. R^2	0.539		0.539		0.355		0.355	

This table presents the results of regressions of ROA in the left panel and ROE in the right panel on the two different groups of explanatory variables, classified as Regression 1 and Regression 2. Leverage is total liability to total asset ratio, Size is the relative size, div. denotes the diversification measures, Interest, Loan, and Deposit are the three share variables used to derive the income, asset, and liability diversification measures, Risk is the dummy variable for the risk-taking banks, and Size* indicates the interaction term with size, respectively. All the regressions include year dummies from 2001 to 2010, the bank fixed effects, and the constant. Adj. R^2 means the adjusted R^2 value. ** indicates significance at 1% level and * indicates significance at 5% level.

In addition, all of the year dummy variables from 2001 to 2010 turn out to be negative and statistically significant. The years before the financial crisis in 2007 are characterized by low market interest, and big banks became even bigger with some banks being super-sized during these periods, as shown in Table 2. The deterioration of ROA over time shows that the overall efficiency loss for bank performance turned out to dominant when the market interest was low and as the size distribution of banks became highly skewed over time.

However, the effects of the above stated bank strategies would be more clearly understood when they are evaluated with respect to the risk-adjusted performance, since a strategy is likely to be accompanied by its risk and return tradeoff. That is, it is possible that a bank activity from larger scale and broader scope would enhance its return performance, but this better performance can be more than offset by the increased risk resulting in negative net effect, or vice versa. Accordingly, in the next section we consider the risk-adjusted ROA and ROE measures as the main performance variables and investigate the net effects of the above listed explanatory variables.

Risk-Adjusted Performance

In the previous section, simple ROA and ROE are used as main performance measures to analyze the unconditional effects of the main business activities, including the derivative holdings for trading purpose, on the bank return. This section provides further analyses of the effects of the bank activities on the risk-adjusted performance measures, to evaluate whether their size, diversification and risk-taking strategies are proven to contribute to efficiency gain in performance-enhancing or risk-reducing perspectives.

Risk Measures

There is no consensus about appropriate risk measure for banking firms, and different risk measures are used in different contexts. For example, the literature on systemic risk investigates both institution level and financial industry level components of risk. Acharya and Viswanathan (2011) consider an institution-risk component, that is, the expected loss on its guaranteed liabilities, and a systemic-risk component, that is, the expected systemic costs that is the institution's percentage contribution to the undercapitalization of the overall financial sector, in a crisis period. Hovakimian, Kane, and Laeven (2012) compare the stand-alone risk and the systemic risk, and suggest the value of banking-sector loss from systemic default as a measure of systemic risk in the U.S. banks.

We use two risk measures at an institution level, total volatility and bank beta calculated from ROA and ROE. First, Stiroh and Rumble (2006) show that volatile activities that generate noninterest income of big banks more than offset diversification benefits with a net effect of lower risk-adjusted profits, where their risk adjustment is based on volatility risk of banks. Similar to Stiroh and Rumble (2006), we develop a volatility-adjusted ROA and ROE (VROA and VROE). For the VROA and VROE, their volatilities are calculated as the standard deviations for the current and past eight quarters' window periods, for each quarter. Then the original ROA and ROA are divided by the corresponding nine quarters' volatilities.

Second, bank beta is used as a measure of systematic risk to derive beta-adjusted abnormal ROA and ROE (BROA and BROE). We consider a bank beta measure as the one to capture "market risk" of the bank. The standard CAPM intends to capture market risk by estimating market beta of individual stocks. We try to capture dynamic changes in return performance of an individual bank relative to the overall changes in the banking sector by bank beta, which is also considered to measure contribution of the particular bank to the riskiness of portfolio of banks.[5] Bank beta is defined as a sensitivity of ROA and ROE of each bank to the change in the average performance of overall banks in the sample, and measured as a coefficient from the regression of individual returns on the cross-sectional averages for the nine quarters that are the same window periods used to calculate the volatilities. Then beta-adjusted measures are calculated by subtracting the fitted values, which are betas multiplied by the sample averages, from the raw ROA and ROE, to derive an abnormal returns on individual banks over the normal performance based on market risk of the bank.

Regressions with Risk-Adjusted Performance

Table 6 shows the results of regressions with the volatility- and beta-adjusted ROA and ROE. Again, this table presents the two regressions, Regression 1 and Regression 2, by varying the set of explanatory variables with and without the interaction terms, for each dependent variable. First, for the results of VROA and VROE, there seems to be some degree of, even if not strong, the benefit of relative size. In Regression 1, the

Table 6. Regressions with Risk-Adjusted Measures.

$N = 26,852$	Regression 1		Regression 2		Regression 1		Regression 2	
	Coefficient	*t*-value	Coefficient	*t*-value	Coefficient	*t*-value	Coefficient	*t*-value
	VROA				BROA			
Leverage	−7.505**	−16.72	−7.515**	−16.74	−0.127**	−46.95	−0.126**	−46.92
Size	0.004	1.36	−0.001	−0.05	−0.000	−0.44	−0.001**	−3.13
Income div.	1.938**	8.70	1.922**	8.45	−0.012**	−8.68	−0.013**	−9.30
Asset div.	−1.626**	−5.87	−1.595**	−5.73	−0.010**	−6.15	−0.010**	−6.03
Liability div.	0.555**	2.75	0.553**	2.72	−0.010**	−8.35	−0.010**	−8.29
Interest	−0.656**	−3.48	−0.667**	−3.51	−0.020**	−17.95	−0.021**	−18.30
Loan	0.391	1.96	0.388	1.95	−0.003*	−2.26	−0.003*	−2.33
Deposit	−1.098**	−4.87	−1.095**	−4.85	−0.027**	−19.82	−0.027**	−19.73
Risk	0.009	0.23	−0.005	−0.13	−0.001*	−2.22	−0.001*	−2.38
Size*Income			0.012	0.25			0.001**	4.07
Size*Asset			−0.071	−1.30			−0.000	−0.96
Size*Liability			0.014	0.48			0.000	0.39
Size*Risk			0.026	1.27			0.000	0.98
Adj. R^2	0.323		0.323		0.274		0.274	
	VROE				BROE			
Leverage	−3.972**	−8.82	−3.993**	−8.86	−0.809**	−28.77	−0.808**	−28.73
Size	0.005*	2.03	0.006	0.20	0.000	0.55	−0.007**	−3.34
Income div.	1.684**	7.53	1.668**	7.31	0.055**	3.94	0.044**	3.11
Asset div.	−1.661**	−5.98	−1.619**	−5.80	−0.127**	−7.31	−0.127**	−7.29
Liability div.	0.493*	2.43	0.504*	2.47	0.018	1.45	0.019	1.51
Interest	−0.855**	−4.52	−0.868**	−4.55	−0.081**	−6.87	−0.087**	−7.28
Loan	0.233	1.16	0.235	1.17	−0.047**	−3.74	−0.047**	−3.80
Deposit	−1.325**	−5.85	−1.317**	−5.81	−0.083**	−5.88	−0.082**	−5.79

Risk	0.015	0.37	−0.004	−0.09	−0.002	−0.62	−0.002	−0.69
Size*Income			0.010	0.20			0.012**	4.03
Size*Asset			−0.083	−1.50			0.001	0.28
Size*Liability			−0.001	−0.03			−0.001	−0.39
Size*Risk			0.033	1.60			0.001	0.42
Adj. R^2	0.325		0.325		0.254		0.254	

This table presents the results of regressions of two risk-adjusted ROA measures, VROA and BROA, and two risk-adjusted ROE measures, VROE and BROE, on the two different groups of explanatory variables (Regression 1 and Regression 2), over the periods of 2000–2010. Leverage is total liability to total asset ratio, Size is the relative size, div. denotes the diversification measures, Interest, Loan, and Deposit are the three share variables used to derive the income, asset, and liability diversification measures, Risk is the dummy variable for the risk-taking banks, and Size* indicates the interaction term with size, respectively. All three regressions include the year dummie variables from 2001 to 2010, the bank fixed effects, and the constant. Adj. R^2 means the adjusted R^2 value. ** indicates significance at 1% level and * indicates significance at 5% level.

coefficients on the size are all positive with that in the VROE regression being significant evaluated at the 95% confidence interval. For the BROA and BROE regressions, the coefficients on the size are insignificant in Regression 1 or negatively significant in Regression 2. However, the coefficients on the interaction between size and income diversification become strongly positively significant both in BROA and BROE regressions, indicating that the increased relative size are likely to create certain efficiency gain when it is combined with diversified income structure, that is, by utilizing the income sources other than the interest income components.

In terms of the diversification benefits more in detail, the volatility-adjusted performance regressions show positive and significant benefits by income and liability diversifications, while the diversified asset structure leads to significantly negative impacts on all the risk-adjusted performance. Considering that our performance measures are closely related to the ratio of net income to total assets, while the diversified income from noninterest components are somewhat helpful in enhancing return performance, the effect is not strong enough to dominate the effect of increased asset size. Accordingly, even if the significant and positive sign of the income-based diversification measure seems to indicate that there are benefits from economies of scope in the income statement composition at the first sight, contrasting the positive income-based diversification and negative asset-based diversification also indicate that diversified assets did not necessarily contribute to the higher return.

Third, by focusing on the coefficients on the risk dummy variable, overall the extra risk-taking behavior does not provide a significant impact in enhancing the bank performance, with the significantly negative signs in case of the BROA regressions. Based on these results, it could be concluded that the extra risk-taking by holding the derivative positions for trading purpose has not been fruitful in generating enough extra revenue. However, one thing we need to further investigate is that, as our sample periods include the low-interest boom markets in the earlier years and the financial crisis in the later years, it is possible that the contribution of risk-taking to the generation of extra revenue may look quite different across the earlier and later periods, in that a discounted value of derivative instruments might adversely affect bank revenue during the crisis. Corresponding to this issue, we apply the same regression analyses with the risk-adjusted performance to two subsamples in the next section, where the first subsample consists of the periods of 2000–2006 before the financial crisis, and the second subsample is for 2007–2010 including the crisis periods.

Subsample Analysis: Before versus after the Financial Crisis

Tables 7 and 8 present the results of risk-adjusted performance regressions in two subsamples before and after the year of 2007, leading to the sample size of 15,641 and 11,211 quarter-banks, respectively. First, for the risk-taking activities, it turns out that, in Table 7, the signs of coefficients on the risk-taking dummy variable are significantly positive in the VROA and VROE regressions before the crisis periods, even if the contribution of the risk-taking activity becomes insignificant for the beta-adjusted performance measures. These results are clearly distinguished from those of the full sample analysis, and indicate that there were at least some dimensions of efficiency gain by holding the derivatives for trading purpose and taking extra risk. However, the observed benefits of extra risk-taking are swept away during the crisis periods, as all variables capturing the contribution of risk-taking lose statistical significance. Furthermore, when we look at the sign of interaction terms between size and risk-taking, the signs are all negative, even if they are not statistically significant, somehow indicating that the negative impacts of extra risk-taking on the risk-adjusted performance become bigger with the size of banks.

For the leverage effects, while taking higher leverage was shown to enhance the risk-adjusted ROE performance before the crisis, during the crisis periods the increased liability to asset ratio generated highly strong negative impacts on all measures of risk-adjusted performance. Highlighting for the volatility-adjusted measures, the income diversification brings strong positive impacts on the bank performance, possibly by increasing revenues from noninterest income sources. The result is in contrast to the findings of insignificant role of liability diversification in earlier sample periods reported in Table 7. However, if we look at the results of Table 8 during the crisis periods, the contribution of the income diversification becomes insignificant, and instead the diversified liability structure shows strong positive impacts on the VROA and VROE. This result may indicate that, at least during the crisis periods, benefits from diversification mainly came from funding diversification, when we consider the fact that deposits are main source of bank financing.

Regarding the effects of relative size, Table 7 shows that the bigger relative size has significant and positive contribution to VROA and VROE indicating that there observed some economies of scale effects when the performance are adjusted for the volatility risk factor before the crisis periods. While the coefficients on the size are overall negative and significant especially in Regression 2 for BROA and BROE, it is also noted that the interactions between the size and income diversification measure provide

Table 7. Regressions with Risk-Adjusted Measures: Before the Financial Crisis.

$N = 15{,}641$	Regression 1		Regression 2		Regression 1		Regression 2	
	Coefficient	*t*-value	Coefficient	*t*-value	Coefficient	*t*-value	Coefficient	*t*-value
	VROA				BROA			
Leverage	−3.758**	−6.42	−3.843**	−6.55	−0.121**	−37.02	−0.121**	−36.89
Size	0.019**	3.00	0.104	1.89	0.000	−1.92	−0.001**	−4.64
Income div.	1.927**	6.88	2.026**	6.97	−0.024**	−15.15	−0.026**	−15.94
Asset div.	−2.609**	−7.11	−2.531**	−6.79	−0.008**	−3.80	−0.007**	−3.60
Liability div.	−0.062	−0.24	−0.021	−0.08	−0.023**	−15.97	−0.022**	−15.58
Interest	−0.628**	−2.66	−0.579*	−2.42	−0.027**	−20.77	−0.029**	−21.31
Loan	0.075	0.29	0.105	0.41	−0.003	−1.84	−0.003	−1.91
Deposit	−1.115**	−4.13	−1.101**	−4.06	−0.037**	−24.38	−0.036**	−23.95
Risk	0.183**	3.21	0.158*	2.57	0.000	0.43	0.000	0.05
Size*Income			−0.139	−1.43			0.003**	5.15
Size*Asset			−0.067	−0.77			−0.001	−1.17
Size*Liability			−0.045	−0.93			0.000	1.05
Size*Risk			0.033	1.04			0.000	0.92
Adj. R^2	0.111		0.111		0.227		0.228	
	VROE				BROE			
Leverage	1.973**	3.38	1.870**	3.20	0.027	1.32	0.028	1.38
Size	0.019**	2.94	0.114*	2.09	−0.000	−0.85	−0.009**	−4.96
Income div.	1.135**	4.06	1.243**	4.29	−0.100**	−10.36	−0.118**	−11.72
Asset div.	−2.559**	−6.99	−2.480**	−6.67	−0.056**	−4.38	−0.053**	−4.12
Liability div.	−0.062	−0.25	−0.002	−0.01	−0.052**	−5.90	−0.048**	−5.43
Interest	−1.058**	−4.49	−1.005**	−4.20	−0.181**	−22.19	−0.190**	−22.97
Loan	−0.024	−0.09	0.012	0.05	−0.039**	−4.37	−0.039**	−4.41
Deposit	−1.483**	−5.51	−1.461**	−5.40	−0.068**	−7.34	−0.064**	−6.83

Risk	0.162**	2.84	0.135*	2.21	−0.001	−0.48	−0.001	−0.55
Size*Income			−0.154	−1.59			0.022**	6.50
Size*Asset			−0.052	−0.60			−0.004	−1.20
Size*Liability			−0.073	−1.51			0.000	0.27
Size*Risk			0.034	1.09			0.000	0.23
Adj. R^2	0.122		0.123		0.332		0.333	

This table presents the results of regressions of two risk-adjusted ROA measures, VROA and BROA, and two risk-adjusted ROE measures, VROE and BROE, on the two different groups of explanatory variables (Regression 1 and Regression 2), over the periods of 2000–2006. Leverage is total liability to total asset ratio, Size is the relative size, div. denotes the diversification measures, Interest, Loan, and Deposit are the three share variables used to derive the income, asset, and liability diversification measures, Risk is the dummy variable for the risk-taking banks, and Size* indicates the interaction term with size, respectively. All three regressions include the year dummie variables from 2001 – 2006, the bank fixed effects, and the constant. Adj. R^2 means the adjusted R^2 value. ** indicates significance at 1% level and * indicates significance at 5% level.

Table 8. Regressions with Risk-Adjusted Measures: During the Financial Crisis.

$N = 11{,}211$	Regression 1		Regression 2		Regression 1		Regression 2	
	Coefficient	t-value	Coefficient	t-value	Coefficient	t-value	Coefficient	t-value
	VROA				BROA			
Leverage	−18.671**	−20.34	−18.755**	−20.40	−0.156**	−27.53	−0.156**	−27.56
Size	0.006	0.83	0.143	1.95	0.000	1.12	0.001	1.49
Income div.	0.213	0.50	0.255	0.59	0.003	1.13	0.003	1.24
Asset div.	−2.514**	−4.21	−2.470**	−4.10	−0.016**	−4.27	−0.016**	−4.21
Liability div.	1.989**	4.37	2.022**	4.40	0.014**	4.82	0.013**	4.74
Interest	−1.873**	−5.00	−1.871**	−4.99	−0.007**	−3.03	−0.007**	−2.98
Loan	0.310	0.61	0.349	0.68	−0.000	−0.03	0.000	0.01
Deposit	−1.037	−1.91	−1.028	−1.89	−0.001	−0.29	−0.001	−0.32
Risk	0.079	1.13	0.101	1.40	0.000	0.09	0.000	0.43
Size*Income			−0.104	−1.26			−0.001	−1.07
Size*Asset			−0.016	−0.18			0.000	0.23
Size*Liability			−0.039	−0.77			0.000	0.06
Size*Risk			−0.062	−1.16			−0.000	−1.26
Adj. R^2	0.482		0.526		0.504		0.504	
	VROE				BROE			
Leverage	−16.377**	−17.77	−16.442**	−17.82	−2.768**	−37.45	−2.776**	−37.52
Size	0.004	0.63	0.113	1.54	0.001	1.01	0.014*	2.44
Income div.	0.353	0.83	0.401	0.93	0.151**	4.41	0.161**	4.65
Asset div.	−2.693**	−4.49	−2.664**	−4.41	−0.302**	−6.29	−0.303**	−6.26
Liability div.	1.722**	3.77	1.767**	3.83	0.019	0.53	0.022	0.59
Interest	−1.888**	−5.03	−1.893**	−5.03	−0.006	−0.20	−0.003	−0.12
Loan	−0.069	−0.14	−0.048	−0.09	−0.092*	−2.25	−0.091*	−2.22
Deposit	−1.484**	−2.73	−1.473**	−2.70	−0.181**	−4.16	−0.182**	−4.15

Risk	0.067	0.96	0.068	0.93	0.004	0.75	0.006	1.08
Size*Income			−0.125	−1.52			−0.016*	−2.45
Size*Asset			−0.043	−0.49			0.004	0.53
Size*Liability			−0.052	−1.03			−0.003	−0.85
Size*Risk			−0.005	−0.09			−0.006	−1.39
Adj. R^2	0.479		0.479		0.435		0.436	

This table presents the results of regressions of two risk-adjusted ROA measures, VROA and BROA, and two risk-adjusted ROE measures, VROE and BROE, on the two different groups of explanatory variables (Regression 1 and Regression 2), over the periods of 2007–2010. Leverage is total liability to total asset ratio, Size is the relative size, div. denotes the diversification measures, Interest, Loan, and Deposit are the three share variables used to derive the income, asset, and liability diversification measures, Risk is the dummy variable for the risk-taking banks, and Size* indicates the interaction term with size, respectively. All three regressions include the year dummie variables from 2001–2006, the bank fixed effects, and the constant. Adj. R^2 means the adjusted R^2 value. ** indicates significance at 1% level and * indicates significance at 5% level.

significantly positive contribution to the beta-adjusted performance, indicating that there was an efficiency gain by the diversified income structure, toward noninterest income components, for the bigger-sized banks. However, the economies of scale seem to disappear and the coefficients on the size become insignificant during the crisis periods, as shown in Table 8. Even if there is one case of positive significance in Regression 2 with BROE, in this case the interaction term between the size and income diversification turns to be negatively significant, offsetting the potential effect of scale economy.

CONCLUDING REMARKS

The chapter documents dynamic changes in U.S. BHCs over the periods of 2000–2010. We find that size distribution of the sample banks has become highly positively skewed, with a small number of big banks becoming super-sized, and these big banks tend to take extra risk by holding derivative positions for trading purposes. The ten biggest risk-taking banks hold about 70% of total assets of all the sample banks in 2010. The bigger size of risk-taking banks does not translate into higher profitability. Non-risk-taking banks earn higher positive interest income, and the risk-takers earn lower average returns since mid-2000s. In extensive regression analysis, while we find that big banks become bigger and super-sized by expanding both scale and scope, the increased size and scale of banks do not necessarily contribute to higher risk-adjusted performance that is measured by total volatility-adjusted return and bank beta-adjusted abnormal return.

We investigate efficiency gain from scale and scope economies of U.S. banks as the largest banks become more concentrated and tend to take more risks by holding derivatives for trading purpose. For the whole sample period, we find banks benefit from income and liability diversification. However, these positive effects are wiped out by asset diversification, resulting in net negative effects from all three measures of diversification. Furthermore, majority of the largest banks are also risk-takers and the risk-taking marginally contributes to better risk-adjusted performance for the whole sample period. However, the negative impacts of extra risk-taking on the risk-adjusted performance become bigger with the size of banks during the crisis period. The results that banks expand their size and take riskier asset positions including derivative instruments with no visible efficiency gain in the form of enhanced return or reduced risk pose further interesting research question: do banks manage assets and liabilities and take positions on derivatives with implicit expectations of government bailout especially during financially distressed periods?

This chapter contributes to current literature of the financial crisis in 2007–2008 and dynamic changes in the banking and financial industry. First, we show that super-size banks exhibit diversification discount, and poor performance of big and super-size banks occurs as a result of taking excessive risky operations and naked positions on derivatives. Second, dynamic changes of U.S. BHCs pose heated debate on the merits of big and super-size banks and financial holding companies among academics, policy makers, regulators or banking industry practitioners. We find that, while a group of super-size banks expand their scale and scope into related financial service sectors and take risky position on derivatives, we do not find efficiency gains such as improved return or reduced risk during the sample periods.

NOTES

1. Barth, Dan Brumbaugh, and Wilcox (2000) characterize the financial holding companies as broad banking, different from universal banking.
2. The GLB Act of 1999 is an act of the 106th United States Congress (1999–2001). It was signed into law by President Bill Clinton and it repealed part of the G–S Act of 1933, opening up the market among banking, security and insurance companies. The G–S Act prohibited any one institution from consolidating an investment bank, a commercial bank, and an insurance company, and the GLB Act allowed the consolidation. For example, the Citicorp (a commercial bank) were merged with the Travelers Group (an insurance company) in 1998 to form the conglomerate Citigroup, a corporation combining banking, security and insurance services under a house of brands that included Citibank, Smith Barney, Primerica, and Travelers. This combination, announced in 1998, would have violated the G–S Act and the Bank Holding Company Act of 1956, even if not for a temporary waiver process. The law was passed to legalize these mergers on a permanent basis. The GLB Act also repealed the conflict of interest prohibitions "against simultaneous service by any officer, director, or employee of a securities firm as an officer, director, or employee of any member bank" of the G–S Act.
3. Effective March 31, 2006, the FR Y-9C filing threshold was increased from $150 million to $500 million or more and the reporting exception that required each lower-tier bank holding company with total consolidated assets of $1 billion or more to file the FR Y-9C was eliminated.
4. It means that the data for 1998–1999 are used as the sample for the initial window periods.
5. In this sense, bank beta is related to systemic risk, which measures the risk of a crisis in the financial sector and a spillover to the economy at large.

REFERENCES

Acharya, V. V., & Viswanathan, S. (2011). Leverage, moral hazard, and liquidity. *Journal of Finance*, *66*(1), 99–138.

Barth, J., Dan Brumbaugh, R. Jr., & Wilcox, J. (2000). The repeal of Glass-Steagall and the advent of broad banking. *Journal of Economic Perspectives*, *14*(2), 191–204.

Beck, T., Levine, R., & Levkov, A. (2010). Big bad banks: The winner and losers from bank deregulation in the United States. *Journal of Finance*, *65*(5), 1637–1667.

Hovakimian, A., Kane, E. J., & Laeven, L. (2012). Variation in systemic risk at us banks during 1974–2010. NBER Working Paper No. 18043. National Bureau of Economic Research, Cambridge, MA.

Kroszner, R. S., & Rajan, R. G. (1994). Is the Glass-Steagall Act justified? A study of the U.S. experience with universal banking before 1933. *American Economic Review*, *84*(4), 810–832.

Kroszner, R. S., & Rajan, R. G. (1997). Organization structure and credibility: Evidence from commercial bank securities activities before the Glass–Steagall act. *Journal of Monetary Economics*, *39*(3), 475–516.

Laeven, L., & Levine, R. (2007). Is there a diversification discount in financial conglomerates? *Journal of Financial Economics*, *85*(2), 331–367.

Stiroh, K., & Rumble, A. (2006). The dark side of diversification: The case of US financial holding companies. *Journal of Banking and Finance*, *30*, 2131–2161.

White, E. (1986). Before the Glass–Stegall act: An analysis of the investment banking activities of national banks. *Explorations in Economic History*, *23*, 33–55.

WHAT DETERMINES BANK PRODUCTIVITY? INTERNATIONAL EVIDENCE ON THE IMPACT OF BANKING COMPETITION, BANK REGULATION, AND THE GLOBAL FINANCIAL CRISIS

Sheng-Hung Chen

ABSTRACT

This chapter examines the impact of banking competition, bank regulation, and the global financial crisis (GFC) of 2008–2009 on banks' productivity changes. For the empirical analysis, I apply a semi-parametric two-step approach of Malmquist index estimates and bootstrap regression to a cross-country panel data of 8,451 commercial banks from 82 countries over the period 2004–2012. Empirical results show that (1) banking competition and capital regulation significantly enhance bank productivity, (2) a tighter bank supervision have a positive impact on bank productivity, and (3) bank productivity decreases during the GFC, but starts to increase as the GFC recovers. I also present

Global Banking, Financial Markets and Crises
International Finance Review, Volume 14, 141–171

ISSN: 1569-3767/doi:10.1108/S1569-3767(2013)0000014009

consistent evidence that commercial banks in countries with better national governance have higher productivity growth before, during and after the GFC.

Keywords: Bank productivity; banking competition; bank regulation and supervision; global financial crisis

JEL classifications: D24; G21; G28

INTRODUCTION

The recent global financial crisis (GFC) of 2008–2009 and European Sovereign Debt Crisis (ESDC) of 2010–2012 have been observed to inflict some harmful impacts on global syndicated lending (de Haas & van Horen, 2012, 2013; Giannetti & Laeven, 2012), bank performance (Beltratti & Stulz, 2012; Fahlenbrach, Prilmeier, & Stulz, 2012), and competition (Sun, 2011) in global banking. This observation invoked a strong interest to academic researchers and policy makers in examining whether changes in banking competition and bank regulations enhance bank productivity, performance, and stability or not (Barth, Lin, Ma, Seade, & Song, 2013). There has been little consensus as to what consists of good regulation and supervision, or how specific regulations influence the performance and stability in the banking industry (see Barth, Caprio, & Levine, 2004; Barth et al., 2013; Beck, Demirgüç-Kunt, & Levine, 2006; Delis, Molyneux, & Pasoiras, 2011; Demirgüç-Kunt, Detragiache, & Tressel, 2008). Furthermore, there are very few research which show the substantial influences of bank competition, regulation and supervision on bank performance, particularly in the context of GFC. To do this end, this chapter aims to contribute to the literature by investigating the differential impacts of banking competition, national governance, bank regulations and supervision on banks' total factor productivity (TFP) growth in the global banking sector.

More specifically, we focus on examining the impacts of (1) regulatory and supervisory policies related to the three pillars of Basel II and (2) restrictions on bank activities, on TFP growth of commercial banks in global banking. The existing banking literature, such as Tirtiroglu, Daniels, and Tirtigoglu (2005), provides some findings that banking deregulation may help explain bank productivity growth, although other single-country studies find no such relationship (Grifell-Tatje & Lovell, 1996). There is also a lack of cross-country evidence in previous studies. This chapter, therefore, attempts to not only link bank productivity to a number of both internal and external determinants, but also aim to shed some light on the effects of GFC on global banks' productivity (Casu, Girardone, & Molyneux, 2004).

Therefore, based on the study of Delis et al. (2011), we first apply the Malmquist index methodology to calculate the growth rate of TFP of 4,518 commercial banks operating in 82 countries from 2004 to 2012. We thus use a robust bootstrap procedure combining the approach presented in Simar and Wilson (2007) as well as Khan and Lewbel (2007) to regress the TFP growth on measures characterizing the banking regulatory conditions across countries. The bank regulatory conditions are associated closely with the Basel II framework of capital requirements (CAP) (Pillar 1), supervision by the authorities (Pillar 2), and market discipline (Pillar 3). Besides, we also examine the impact of restrictions to bank activities as a potential factor influencing banks' TFP changes.

Empirical results indicate that bank regulations enhancing private monitoring (PMON) have a positive impact on productivity growth of banks. Furthermore, restrictions on bank activities relating to securities, insurance, real estate, and ownership of nonfinancial firms, promote bank productivity as well. In contrast, CAP and official supervisory power (SPR) have a statistically significant effect on TFP growth over the whole sample period of 2004–2012. Especially their influences persist during and after GFC. It confirms that tougher standards of capital requirements and SPR matter in terms of influencing bank productivity during and after GFC. Empirical findings also suggest that regulations and their enforcement are contributed to shaping bank performance (Barth, Caprio, & Levine, 2007; Delis & Staikouras, 2011).

The remainder of the chapter is organized as follows. The second section presents a review of the related literature on bank performance in global banking. The third section provides the methodology for estimation and regression equation specification. The fourth section presents variables and data sources. The fifth section discusses some empirical results, and finally, the sixth section concludes.

RELATED LITERATURE

Exploring the association between bank's TFP growth and the regulatory environment broadly relates to twofold strands of the empirical banking literature. The first encompasses studies that examine the relationship between regulatory reforms and productivity growth. The second includes studies that examine the impact of regulations on various aspects of bank performance in a cross-country setting. The following sections discuss these strands of the literature.

Determinants of Bank Productivity

The first strand of literature focuses on the impact of regulatory reform on productivity growth. Tirtiroglu et al. (2005) explore the impact of U.S. intrastate and interstate deregulations on bank TFP growth and find that intrastate branching liberalization has a positive long-run impact on productivity growth of banks. Isik (2007) empirically investigates financial reform programs that took place in Turkey during the 1980s and finds that the productivity of banks improved significantly as the reform process accelerated. Similar results are obtained by Aysan and Ceyhan (2008) who test Turkish banking-sector reforms (BSRs) post-2001. Additionally, Gilbert and Wilson (1998) indicate that Korean banks responded to privatization and deregulation during the 1980s and early 1990s by altering their mix of inputs and outputs, generating large changes in productivity.

In comparison to the above findings, Tırtıroglu, Daniels, and Tirtiroglu (1998) find a negative association between regulatory initiatives and TFP growth in U.S. commercial banking over the period 1946–1995. Regulatory changes in banking include the Federal Deposit Insurance Act of 1950, the Competitive Equality Banking Act of 1987, the Depository Institutions Act of 1982, and the Depository Institutions Deregulation and Monetary Control Act of 1980, as the most influential regulatory initiatives. Furthermore, Grifell-Tatje and Lovell (1996) remark that the relaxation and removal of regulatory constraints in the Spanish savings bank sector cause an increase in branching and merger activity, though this case could not explain the magnitude or nature of productivity decreasing, which was found over the study period.

Typically, the literature that focuses on regulations and productivity tends to (1) examine individual countries, (2) evaluate overall regulatory reforms (usually captured by dummy variables) and productivity change over deregulation periods, and (3) generally yield conflicting findings. Regarding some studies on bank performance in transition countries, these studies, many of which focus on the new EU member states, explore various issues including the impact of ownership and privatization on bank efficiency (Bonin, Hasan, & Wachtel, 2005) and profitability (Naaborg &

Lensink, 2008), efficiency convergence (Mamatzakis, Staikouras, & Koutsomanoli-Filippaki, 2008), whether technical progress reduces bank costs (Kasman & Kirbas-Kasman, 2006), how competition impacts bank efficiency and TFP growth (Brissimis, Delis, & Papanikolaou, 2008), and whether BSRs influence efficiency (Fries, Neven, Seabright, & Taci, 2006; Koutsomanoli-Filippaki, Mamatzakis, & Staikouras, 2009) or TFP growth (Brissimis et al., 2008).

In general, the findings of the aforementioned literature are rather mixed. Only Brissimis et al. (2008) consider the impact of regulations on Banks' TFP growth. Using time dummies and the European Bank for Reconstruction and Development (EBRD) BSR index, they find that in the newly acceded 10 EU economies productivity is only positively affected in the latter stages of regulatory reform.

Cross-Country Impacts of Banking Regulations on Bank Performance

There is a relatively new literature examining the impact of supervision and regulatory policies on bank performance using cross-country data. Barth, Dopico, Nolle, and Wilcox (2002) focus on how regulatory features impact on various components of the CAMELS model – a bank-rating systems where supervisory authorities rate institutions according to six factors: capital adequacy, asset quality, management quality, earnings, liquidity, and sensitivity to market risks (Barth, Caprio, & Levine, 2003), or net interest margins and overhead costs (Demirgüç-Kunt, Laeven, & Levine, 2004). Moreover, Barth et al. (2004) show complete theoretical and empirical findings and focus on how the regulatory environment influences both banking industry development, the incidence of crises, via using a variety of conventional measures on bank performance.

More recent studies apply some frontier techniques to investigate the impacts of banking regulations and supervision on bank efficiency (Barth et al., 2013; Gaganis & Pasiouras, 2013; Pasiouras, 2008; Pasiouras, Tanna, & Zopounidis, 2009). However, others consider more general indicators such as bank credit ratings (Demirgüç-Kunt et al., 2008; Pasiouras, Gaganis, & Zopounidis, 2006). Generally, these studies suggest that banking regulations, empowering private sector monitoring, pose a positive impact on performance. Some empirical evidence regarding the impact of other key regulations, however, appears mixed in previous related studies. For example, Barth et al. (2004) indicate that there is no strong association between banking-sector development, performance, and official SPR. Other studies show that the presence of more powerful government supervisors is linked to higher levels of nonperforming loans (NPLs) (Barth et al., 2002) and the former could be harmful to the banking-sector development in countries with closed political systems (Barth et al., 2003). In contrast, Pasiouras (2008) presents a positive and statistically significant impact of SPR on bank technical efficiency, and Pasiouras et al. (2009) confirm this finding as cost and profit efficiency. These results suggest that tougher supervisory regimes result in more efficient banking systems.

Regarding the effects of activity restrictions (ACTR), Barth et al. (2004, 2006) find that ACTR negatively impact banking-sector development and stability. The impact of ACTR on bank-level indicators of performance, however, seems inconclusive. For instance, Demirgüç-Kunt et al. (2004) indicate that ACTR boost net interest margins while Barth, Caprio, and Levine (2001) present mixed results on their impact on margins and overheads. Besiades, Pasiouras et al. (2009) argue that ACTR on banks appear to reduce cost but improve profit efficiency, although Pasiouras (2008) show no significant relation with technical efficiency.

Furthermore, Barth et al. (2004) suggest that CAP do not appear to have a robust impact on banking-sector development, the incidence of banking crises, margins, or bank overhead costs. Yet, more stringent capital regulations are associated with lower levels of NPLs. Evidence from the bank efficiency literature also provides conflicting results, indicating that stricter CAP improve bank cost and technical efficiency, although they tend to reduce profit efficiency (Barth et al., 2013; Gaganis & Pasiouras, 2013; Pasiouras, 2008; Pasiouras et al., 2009).

Finally, Delis et al. (2011) recently indicate that various aspects of regulation and supervision can be important determinants of bank performance. However, a certain deal of ambiguity still remains given the different banking systems and time periods examined, as well as the variation in performance measures employed.

METHODOLOGY

Stage 1: Estimation of Bank's Total Factor Productivity

To investigate the impact of regulations on bank productivity growth, we use a two-stage approach. In the first stage, we derive output-oriented Malmquist indices to measure bank TFP growth. As a sensitivity analysis, we also use input-oriented scores. Productivity scores are estimated using separate frontiers for each country (productivity growth is relative to each country's own frontier), so as to avoid incorporating the effects of different countries economic environments in the estimated measures. As a robustness check, we also estimate TFP growth for the pooled cross-country sample. In the second stage, the productivity growth measures are regressed against a variety of regulatory and other control variables.

In order to apply TFP growth measures in the first stage, we adopte the output-oriented Malmquist method, which was introduced by Caves, Christensen, and Diewert (1982) and estimated using data envelopment analysis (DEA) methodology by Färe, Grosskopf, and Weber (2004). This approach is the most popular nonparametric method used to obtain TFP growth estimates. Based on Delis et al. (2011), we also use the output-oriented method for the estimation for two reasons. First, regulators are more concerned about bank outputs (risk-related asset-based variables) rather than inputs. Also some of our inputs (in particular those relating to physical capital) are sticky downward in the short run, while banks are more likely to expand outputs than reduce inputs in order to increase productivity.

Consistent with Färe, Grosskopf, Norris, and Zhang (1994), a mixture of constant and variable returns to scale (CRS and VRS, respectively) are used. To introduce some notation, we assume that for N observations there exist P inputs producing Q outputs. Hence, each observation n uses a nonnegative vector of inputs denoted $\boldsymbol{x}^n = (x_1^n, x_2^n, \ldots, x_k^n) \in R_+^P$ to produce a nonnegative vector of outputs, denoted $\boldsymbol{y}^n = (y_1^n, y_2^n, \ldots, y_l^n) \in R_+^Q$. Production technology $F = \{(y,\ x)\!: x \text{ can produce } y\}$ defines the set of feasible input–output vectors, and the input sets of production technology $PT(y) = \{x\!: (y,\ x) \in F\}$ defines the sets of input vectors that are feasible for each output vector. TFP change is then estimated in the spirit of Färe et al. (1994) defining the Malmquist index as:

$$\Phi_0(y_T, x_T, y_t, x_t) = \left[\frac{d_0^T(y_t, x_t)}{d_0^T(y_T, x_T)} \times \frac{d_0^t(y_t, x_t)}{d_0^t(y_T, x_T)}\right]^{1/2} \tag{1}$$

where Φ_0 measures the productivity change between periods T (base period) and t, and $d_0^T(y_t, x_t)$ represents the distance from the period t observation to the period T technology. $\Phi_0 > 1$ indicates positive TFP growth from period s to period t, $\Phi_0 < 1$ indicates a decline, and $\Phi_0 = 1$ indicates constant TFP growth.

Stage 2: Determinants of Bank Productivity Change

In the second stage, we use the TFP growth scores as the dependent variable in the estimation of the following equation:

$$\Phi_{i,j,t} = \alpha_0 + \sum_{j=1}^{k} \alpha_j \times Z_{k,j,t} + \sum_{l=1}^{m} \alpha_l \times M_{l,j,t} + \sum_{s=1}^{q} \alpha_s \times B_{i,j,t} + \varepsilon_{i,j,t} \quad (2)$$

where the TFP change, $\Phi_{i,j,t}$, of bank i operating in country j at year t is specified as a function of time-dependent banking sector in terms of regulation variables, Z; some variables that capture the macroeconomic conditions common to all banks, M; a vector of bank level variables, B; and the error term, ε.

Next, we investigate interactive impacts of banking competition, national governance, and regulatory variable before, during, and after GFC, namely, on bank productivity changes, using the following specification.

$$\Phi_{i,j,t} = \beta_0 + \sum_{T=1}^{3}\sum_{k=1}^{4} \beta_{T,j} \times GFC_{T,t} \times W_{k,j,t} + \sum_{l=1}^{4} \beta_l \times M_{l,j,t} + \sum_{s=1}^{q} \beta_s \times B_{i,j,t} + \varepsilon_{i,j,t} \quad (3)$$

where GFC is the dummy variable with T periods, defining before GFC ($T=1$), during GFC ($T=2$), and after GFC ($T=3$). W is a number of variables of interest with banking competition, country governance, and regulatory indicator (CAP, SPR, PMON, and ACTR).

For estimating Eqs. (2) and (3), we pool the data across banks, countries, and years and then regress the TFP growth measures on range of variables, including banking competition, governance, and the regulatory indicators that are of central interest in this chapter. The panel regression with fixed effects is used for estimation and conducted in terms of a bootstrapping procedure (Simar & Wilson, 2007).

VARIABLES AND DATA

Variables of Bank's Inputs and Outputs

We select inputs and outputs for the estimation applying Malmquist index on the basis of the intermediation approach, which assumes that banks collect funds, using labor and physical capital, to transform them into loans and other earning assets (OEA). Accounting for the increasing involvement of banks in fee-generating services, we also include noninterest income (NII) as an additional output. Thus, we assume that banks have three outputs, respectively: (1) net loans (NL) (gross loans net of reserves for impaired loans/NPLs), (2) OEA, and (iii) NII. The three inputs used to generate the above outputs are (1) fixed assets (FA), (2) customer deposits and short-term funding (DEP), and (3) overhead expenses (OH).

Key Measures on Banking Regulation and Supervision

For the construction of the CAP, power of supervisory agencies (SPR), market discipline and PMON, and ACTR indices, we use the information from the database provided by World Bank, compiled and updated by Barth, Caprio, and Levine (2013), which provides regulator responses to a series number of questions by central bankers. We discuss briefly these indices below and provide detail information shown in the appendix.

CAP is an index of capital requirements accounting for both initial and overall capital stringency. This index is measured by considering the sources of funds used as capital and taking into account various issues that emerge during the calculation of the capital-to-assets ratio. The index can take values between 0 and 8, with higher values indicating greater capital stringency. SPR is a measure of the power of SPR indicating the extent to that these authorities can take specific actions against bank management and directors, shareholders, and bank auditors. This index shows values between 0 and 14 with higher values, indicating more SPR. PMON is an indicator of market discipline and means the degree to which those banks are enforced to disclose accurate information to the public and whether there are incentives to increase market discipline. This index ranges from 0 and 8 with higher values showing greater PMON. Finally, ACTR is a proxy for the level of restrictions on banks' activities in each country. It is determined by considering whether participation in securities, insurance, real estate activities, and ownership of nonfinancial firms are unrestricted, permitted, restricted, or prohibited. ACTR shows values between 1 and 4 with higher values indicating higher restrictions.

We include average values for these variables for all 82 countries included in panel data. These values indicate that Denmark, Dominican Republic, Japan, Swaziland, and Turkey have the strictest CAP while Netherlands is the least. Official SPR appears to be greater in Indonesia, Hungary, Malta,

United States, Panama, and Slovenia, although Swaziland and Sweden record the lowest indicators. DeYoung, Hughes, and Moon (2001) find a similar trade-off across the United States, suggesting that supervisors allow banks with high productive efficiency more flexibility in their investment strategies and risk-taking activities. Moreover, PMON appears to be higher in Indonesia, Japan, Paraguay, Peru, and Ukraine, but lowest in Belgium, Qatar, Sweden, United Kingdom, and Uruguay. Finally, restrictions on bank activities (ACTR) are the most onerous in Bangladesh, Nigeri, and Lithuania, but the most liberal in United Kingdom and Nicaragua.

Control Variables

To control for other potential determinants of bank productivity, we use a number of bank- and country-specific variables. Country averages for these variables indicate that global banking systems are relatively highly capitalized (average ratio of equity to total assets up to 14%) and less competitive (Boone Index averaging −0.003), have lower levels of foreign ownership (11.38% of banking-sector assets across the sample), and nearly all experienced relatively high levels of inflation (INF) (averaging 7.02%) and real GDP growth (GDPG) (2.20%) over 2004–2012. In particular, we employ the ratio of equity to total assets as a proxy for bank capitalization. Capitalization is expected to be positively related to productivity growth to the extent that capital is used for productive purposes.

Note, however, that in 82 countries banks have inherited high capitalization levels; this can harm future productivity because accumulated capital is an expensive source of financing. To capture potential nonlinearity, we additionally use the squared term of ratio of equity to total assets in our empirical specification. Next, we control for bank size by using the natural logarithm of real total assets and again we also consider a nonlinear relationship between size and productivity by introducing the squared term of the bank size variable among all regressors. Generally, the effect of bank size on bank performance has been proved to be positive up to a certain extent although for banks that become extremely large, productivity growth could be negative due to bureaucratic and other reasons.

Following previous studies that focus on bank performance (Barth et al., 2004; Demirgüç-Kunt et al., 2004; Fries & Taci, 2002; Pasiouras, 2008; Pasiouras et al., 2006), We additionally control for cross-country differences in structural and macroeconomic conditions. First, we control for the national governance using the composite indicator from "World Governance Indicators." We use this variable because in the countries considered, many general policies aiming at increased ECFR may have affected country productivity, including banking. Thus, we want to prevent our indices of bank regulation capturing the effects of these general economic reforms. Besides, we use (1) Boone index for the degree of banking competition, and (2) the percentage of assets held by foreign (FOR) banks. In the banking literature, the expected effect of banking competition on bank performance is ambiguous, while it is generally expected that higher foreign and less government ownership are associated with higher bank productivity growth. In the countries considered, foreign ownership increased substantially during the sample period, so we anticipate the impact of FOR on TFP growth to be highly significant.

Additionally, we control for the impact of macroeconomic and monetary conditions using real GDPG and the INF rate, respectively (Barth et al., 2003; Pasiouras, 2008). In economies with favorable macroeconomic and stable monetary conditions, productivity growth of banks would be higher. Finally, to cope with the impact of the financial crisis from 2007 to 2009, we include an indicator of credit risk, the country-level ratio of NPLs to total loans in all regressions.

Data

The panel data in this chapter is unbalanced and consists of a maximum of 21,420 observations from 4,518 commercial banks operating in 82 countries over the period 2004–2012. Following the suggestion by Delis et al. (2011), we focus on commercial banks for two main reasons. First, this provides a more homogenous sample in terms of services and consequently inputs and outputs, which in turn enhances the comparability of banking markets. Second, as mentioned in Demirgüç-Kunt et al. (2004), because regulatory data of the World Bank database are for commercial banks, it is more appropriate to use bank-level data only for these types of banks.

We collect related information from various sources. All bank-level data are obtained from the *BankScope* database of Bureau van Dijk and converted to U.S. dollars and reported in real 2000 terms using country-specific GDP deflators. Information on bank regulations and supervision are obtained from the World Bank database on "Bank Regulation and Supervision" developed and updated by Barth et al. (2013). Data for proxies for the financial crisis are collected from the 2012 version of the

World Bank database on "Financial Development and Structure," which was initially constructed by Beck, Demirgüç-Kunt, and Levine (2000). Information on macroeconomic conditions is collected from the World Bank database. Data for composite index of national governance are collected from the World Bank's "Worldwide Governance Indicators" database (Kaufmann, Kraay, & Mastruzzi, 2010), including six indicators of "voice and accountability," "government effectiveness," "rule of law," "political stability," "quality of regulation," and "control of corruption," respectively.

EMPIRICAL RESULTS

Bank Productivity Changes Before, During, and After GFC

We obtain TFP change estimates by country before, during, and after GFC. Table 1 shows the mean values of the estimates of TFP changes. As already mentioned, an index greater than one indicates a positive TFP growth while a value less than one suggests a decline. The results indicate that over the sample period most countries experienced significant TFP growth, representative of banking systems experiencing major bank regulation. In particular, average TFP growth has been substantial in Ireland, Australia, Belgium, Spain, Netherlands, and Luxembourg, while it has been declining in Ecuador, Ghana, Lesotho, Dominican Republic, and Paraguay.

Sharply declining in TFP growth before and after GFC are observed in Thailand, Russian Federation, Indonesia, Lesotho, and Paraguay; while a noticeable upward trend is observed for Vietnam, Czech Republic, India, United Arab Emirate, Lebanon, and Norway. Overall, transition banking systems appear to exhibit relatively high TFP growth (Casu et al., 2004).

Differences in Key Variables Before, During, and After GFC

We further test whether key variables are statistically significantly different before, during, and after GFC using analysis of variance (ANOVA). Table 1 reports the statistically significant difference in bank's TFP change, financial characteristics, banking market structure, regulation, and macroeconomic conditions before, during, and after GFC. Fig. 1 shows that

Table 1. Mean Valus and Test of Key Variables Before, During, and After GFC on Bank Productivity Change.

Variables	All Period (2004–2012)	Global Financial Crisis (GFC) Prior (2004–2006)	During (2007–2009)	Post (2010–2012)	Mean Difference F-statistics	(p-Value)
Bank's total factor productivity (TFP) change	1.525	1.681	1.283	1.513	5***	(0.008)
Bank financial characteristics						
Logarithm of total assets	18.145	12.120	20.497	20.786	13,573***	(0.000)
Ratio of equity to total assets	0.140	0.137	0.131	0.153	4**	(0.028)
Banking market structure						
Bank competition (Boone Index)	−0.030	−0.022	−0.022	−0.042	14***	(0.000)
Foreign ownership (%)	11.382	10.978	11.034	11.915	53***	(0.000)
National governance	0.976	0.843	0.996	1.016	247***	(0.000)
Proxies for the financial crisis						
Ratio of nonperforming loans (NPLs) to total loans	84.078	119.820	79.969	72.505	13,716***	(0.000)
Banking-sector Z-score (Z)	19.545	19.061	18.671	20.641	703***	(0.000)
Macroeconomic conditions						
GDP Growth (%)	2.204	4.272	0.613	2.852	11,009***	(0.000)
Inflation (%)	7.018	5.175	11.453	3.415	11***	(0.000)
Bank regulation						
Capital requirements (CAP)	7.145	6.106	6.893	7.461	5,431***	(0.000)
Supervisory power (SPR)	0.899	0.777	0.923	0.931	2,061***	(0.000)
Market discipline and private monitoring (PMON)	4.290	3.188	4.153	4.940	6,046***	(0.000)
Activity restrictions (ACTR)	7.522	7.208	6.912	8.282	10,004***	(0.000)

Note: ** and *** denote statistical significance at the 5% and 1% levels, respectively.

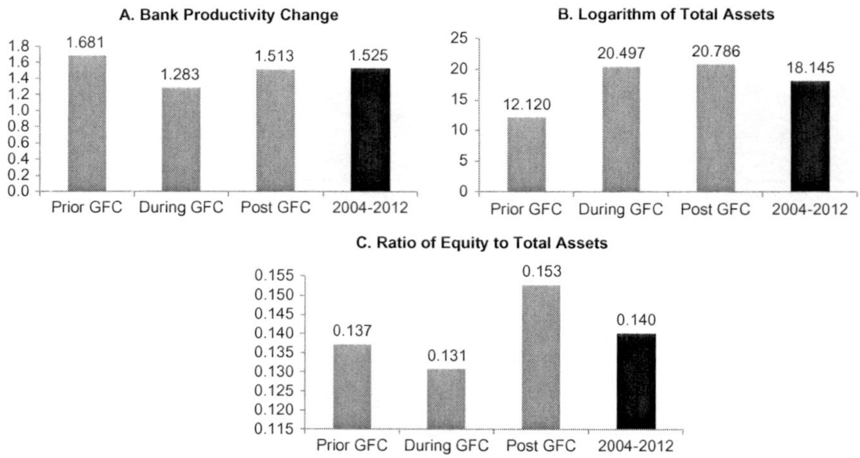

Fig. 1. Bank Productivity Change and Financial Characteristics Prior, During, and Post GFC.

increasing trend in bank size before, during and after GFC while bank's capital ratio slightly decreased during GFC but jumped after GFC. Regarding the change in banking competition, Fig. 2 demonstrates the increasing competition in global banking industry while the foreign bank shares remarkably increase after GFC.

In addition, national governance shows steady trend over the period 2004–2012 while banking stability deteriorated during GFC but NPL ratio decreased sharply. It is noted that GDP fell significantly during GFC but recovers after GFC. The inflation rate also experienced a higher level during GFC but immediately decreased after GFC. Finally, as shown in Fig. 3, besides ACTR, the trend in major regulatory variables present the upward over the period 2004–2012. This implies that the global banking industry have undergone a higher standard of banking regulation as result from Basel II. Interestingly, ACTR fell during GFC but sharply increased after GFC.

Determinants of Banks' Productivity Changes

For the estimation of the second empirical specification, we use the bootstrap procedure described in Brissimis et al. (2008). The bootstrap

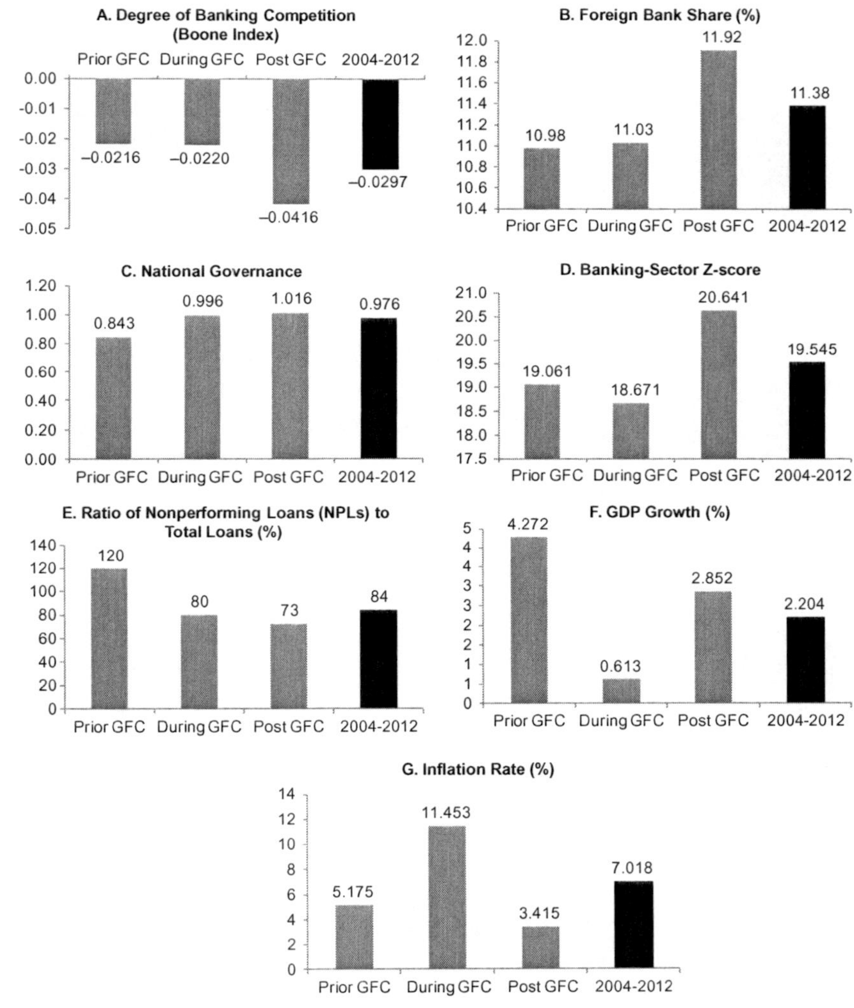

Fig. 2. Banking Market Structure, Goveranance Macroeconomic, and National Conditions Prior, During, and Post GFC.

procedure accounts for potential endogeneity of some of right-hand-side variables, which are in our case the capital ratio and the squared term of capital ratio. The main results of the second-stage analysis are reported in Table 2. We estimate various models, where we control for alternative

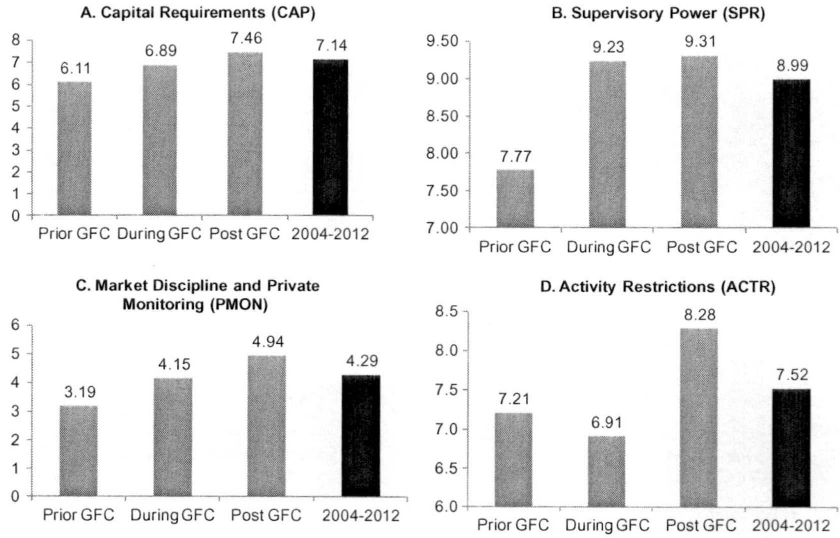

Fig. 3. Bank Regulation Prior, During, and Post GFC.

bank regulatory-specific factors. In all cases, we control for bank-specific characteristics and country effects using dummy variables. Model 1 is the base model where we examine the impact of banking market structure on bank productivity change, while controlling for bank-specific characteristics, macroeconomic conditions and the NPLs to total loans ratio. The coefficients on foreign ownership (FOR) and banking competition (Boone index) are positive, statistically significant, and holds across all specifications (Models 1–7). These results indicate that increasing foreign bank ownership in domestic banking industry and higher banking competition would enhance bank productivity.

In Model 2, we include additional variables in the regression equation, which represent various aspects of national governance. The coefficient on national governance shows a positive sign and statistically significance and this finding holds across all specifications (Models 2–7). This empirical evidence is consistent to the findings of Barth et al. (2013) and also confirms that banks in better national governance demonstrate better productivity growth. In Models 3–6, we individually control for bank regulation measures of CAP, SPR, PMON, and ACTR. In Model 3, CAP has a positive and statistically significant coefficient, suggesting higher bank capital

Table 2. Determinant of Bank Productivity Change: The Impacts of Banking Competition, National Governance, and Bank Regulation.

Independent Variables	Dependent Variable: Bank Total Factor Productivity (TFP) Change						
	Model (1)	Model (2)	Model (3)	Model (4)	Model (5)	Model (6)	Model (7)
Banking market structure							
Foreign ownership (FOR)	1.911***	1.522***	1.539***	1.563***	1.372***	1.555***	1.460***
	(10.799)	(8.510)	(9.022)	(8.788)	(7.833)	(8.718)	(8.641)
Bank competition (Boone Index)	0.889**	1.474***	1.403***	1.236***	0.858**	1.211***	0.900***
	(2.436)	(4.024)	(4.017)	(3.392)	(2.389)	(3.308)	(2.592)
National governance		1.583***	1.464***	1.458***	1.730***	1.487***	1.517***
		(12.479)	(12.099)	(11.538)	(13.918)	(11.722)	(12.578)
Bank regulation							
Capital requirements (CAP)			0.164***				0.141***
			(41.124)				(33.932)
Supervisory power (SPR)				0.625***			0.192***
				(14.212)			(4.439)
Market discipline and private monitoring (PMON)					0.181***		0.115***
					(27.078)		(16.857)
Activity restrictions (ACTR)						0.065***	0.013**
						(9.924)	(1.970)
Bank financial characteristics							
Logarithm of total assets	−5.227***	−5.324***	−4.386***	−5.166***	−4.947***	−5.250***	−4.215***
	(−33.627)	(−34.362)	(−29.343)	(−33.457)	(−32.474)	(−33.941)	(−28.427)
(Logarithm of total assets)^2	0.169***	0.170***	0.142***	0.165***	0.159***	0.168***	0.137***
	(42.347)	(42.666)	(36.797)	(41.523)	(40.494)	(42.234)	(35.747)
Ratio of equity to total assets	1.525***	1.385***	1.291***	1.376***	1.341***	1.361***	1.269***
	(13.848)	(12.570)	(12.285)	(12.556)	(12.426)	(12.382)	(12.189)

Table 2. *(Continued)*

Independent Variables	Dependent Variable: Bank Total Factor Productivity (TFP) Change						
	Model (1)	Model (2)	Model (3)	Model (4)	Model (5)	Model (6)	Model (7)
(Ratio of equity to total assets)^2	0.024***	0.022***	0.020***	0.022***	0.021***	0.022***	0.020***
	(12.790)	(11.700)	(11.487)	(11.688)	(11.588)	(11.750)	(11.454)
Proxies for the financial crisis							
Ratio of nonperforming loans (NPLs)	−0.011***	−0.010***	−0.008***	−0.010***	−0.009***	−0.010***	−0.007***
to total loans	(−30.026)	(−27.506)	(−21.509)	(−27.379)	(−24.284)	(−26.685)	(−20.011)
Banking-sector Z-score (Z)	0.016***	0.015***	0.019***	0.012***	0.018***	0.013***	0.019***
	(3.602)	(3.521)	(4.565)	(2.751)	(4.267)	(3.034)	(4.559)
Macroeconomic conditions							
GDP growth (GDPG)	0.009***	0.013***	0.005**	0.014***	0.011***	0.011***	0.005**
	(3.579)	(5.244)	(2.242)	(5.612)	(4.767)	(4.494)	(2.284)
Inflation (INF)	−0.051***	−0.046***	−0.050***	−0.047***	−0.043***	−0.045***	−0.048***
	(−15.806)	(−14.299)	(−16.231)	(−14.724)	(−13.708)	(−14.174)	(−15.695)
Constant	1.985***	1.999***	1.920***	1.985***	1.964***	1.990***	1.903***
	(129.908)	(131.067)	(130.919)	(130.644)	(131.022)	(130.583)	(130.715)
Observations	21420	21420	21420	21420	21420	21420	21420
Number of bank	4518	4518	4518	4518	4518	4518	4518
Adjusted R^2	0.196	0.203	0.276	0.213	0.236	0.208	0.290
Sigma	1.137	1.132	1.079	1.125	1.108	1.128	1.068

Note: *, **, and *** denote statistical significance at the 10%, 5%, and 1% levels, respectively.

requirement standard do influence bank productivity. In Model 4, SPR shows a positive and statistically significant coefficient, indicating more powerful supervisors do influence bank productivity as well. This is, however, inconsistent to the result of Delis et al. (2011).

Moreover, PMON has a positive and statistically significant coefficient. This result strongly supports the view that empowering PMON, through disclosure requirements that allow private agents to overcome information and transaction costs (Hay & Shleifer, 1998) as well as other incentives such as the use of subordinated debt and the absence of deposit insurance, increases bank's productivity.

In Model 6, empirical results also confirm that ACTR has a positive and significant impact on bank's productivity growth. Barth et al. (2003) argued that fewer restrictions could provide greater profit opportunities, but banks may systematically fail to manage a diverse set of financial activities beyond traditional banking, and hence experience lower profitability. Finally, in Model 7, we include all bank regulatory measures in the regression and find that all coefficients of those measures are positive and statistically significant, the same results as in individually specified regressions. It is interesting that SPR has relatively higher influence on banks' productivity changes.

The effect of the control variables is shown to be as expected. Bank size is positively and significantly related to TFP growth, which is intuitive since large banks, especially in global banking industry, are likely to benefit from economies of scale. The same holds for bank capitalization, indicating that those banks with a sound capital position are able to pursue business opportunities more effectively, thus achieving higher productivity growth. Similar to the findings on bank size, the impact of capital ratio on TFP growth is also positive and statistically significant at the 1% level, indicating that high levels of capital tend to enhance TFP growth.

Turning to the country-specific control variables, we find that, as expected, FOR has a positive sign which supported by the literature that suggests a number of benefits from foreign bank entry in the international banking industry. For example, Levine (1996) mentions three major benefits from the presence of foreign banks: (1) improvements in the quality and availability of financial services in the domestic market as result from increased bank competition, the adoption of modern banking skills, and better technology, (2) development in the domestic bank supervisory and legal framework, and (3) enhancement of the country's access to international financial markets.

Furthermore, the presence of foreign banks may encourage nonfinancial foreign firms to invest in the host country since in many cases foreign banks follow their customer's abroad (Brealey & Kaplanis, 1996). Lensink and Hermes (2004) confirmed that foreign banks may also enhance the quality of human capital in the banking system, not only by importing high skilled bank managers to work in their branches, but also by training local employees. The effects of GDPG on TFP growth are also positive and show that favorable macroeconomic conditions benefit substantially banks' TFP growth. In addition, Banking-sector *Z*-score also carries a positive sign, indicating that higher financial stability in the banking industry significantly increases the productivity of banks, which is consistent with findings in the efficiency literature of Pasiouras (2008). Finally, as expected, INF and the NPLs ratio, are all negatively correlated with TFP growth.

Impacts of Banking Competition, Governance, and Regulation Before, During, and After GFC

Table 3 reports the results from impacts of banking competition, national governance, and bank regulation before, during and after GFC on bank productivity changes. Regarding the effect of banking competition on bank productivity, higher banking competition before and during GFC significantly enhances bank productivity, while this effect becomes negative, indicating decreased productivity of bank. Moreover, banks in better country governance present higher productivity regardless before, during and after GFC. This implies that national governance have beneficial impacts on increasing bank productivity. However, banks which have the stringent standard of bank capital requirements substantially increase bank's productivity during and after GFC, while banks in a country with more stringent CAP would decline the productivity of bank.

Finally, we find the similar results from SPR, PMON, and ACTR, indicating that stringent bank regulation is beneficial to bank's productivity growth, especially when banks are hit by financial crises. One of the most important policy implications of these findings is that bank regulations play the crucial role in enhancing banks' productivity during the GFC of 2008–2009.

Table 3. The Impacts of Banking Competition, National Governance, and Bank Regulation Before, During, and After GFC on Bank Productivity Change.

Independent Variables	Dependent Variable: Bank Total Factor Productivity (TFP) Change					
	Interactions of Key Variables (W) with Global Financial Crisis (GFC)					
	Banking competition	National governance	Capital requirements (CAP)	Supervisory power (SPR)	Market discipline and private monitoring (PMON)	Activity restrictions (ACTR)
Global financial crisis (GFC)						
Prior GFC*W	49.841***	2.436***	−0.223***	−1.291***	−0.216***	−0.177***
	(54.530)	(20.580)	(−26.841)	(−27.639)	(−23.036)	(−23.085)
During GFC*W	9.369***	2.848***	0.044***	0.129***	0.052***	0.030***
	(20.823)	(23.929)	(8.847)	(3.306)	(6.852)	(4.022)
Post GFC*W	−5.880***	3.599***	0.231***	1.642***	0.274***	0.191***
	(−15.492)	(29.334)	(61.468)	(42.730)	(43.503)	(26.529)
Bank financial characteristics						
Logarithm of total assets	4.342***	3.888***	3.484***	2.513***	3.095***	2.051***
	(30.941)	(26.613)	(25.720)	(19.011)	(21.830)	(16.223)
(Logarithm of total assets)^2	−0.132***	−0.134***	−0.115***	−0.088***	−0.105***	−0.071***
	(−36.127)	(−35.877)	(−32.678)	(−25.552)	(−28.571)	(−21.637)
Ratio of equity to total assets	0.848***	1.532***	1.163***	1.164***	1.364***	1.098***
	(8.535)	(15.043)	(12.299)	(12.789)	(13.934)	(12.679)
(Ratio of equity to total assets)^2	−0.012***	−0.025***	−0.018***	−0.018***	−0.020***	−0.017***
	(−7.300)	(−14.376)	(−11.544)	(−12.038)	(−12.218)	(−11.354)
Proxies for the financial crisis						
Ratio of nonperforming loans (NPLs) to total loans	−0.005***	−0.005***	−0.007***	−0.002***	−0.006***	−0.003***
	(−15.067)	(−15.586)	(−22.109)	(−8.036)	(−17.233)	(−9.246)

Table 3. *(Continued)*

Independent Variables	Dependent Variable: Bank Total Factor Productivity (TFP) Change					
	Interactions of Key Variables (W) with Global Financial Crisis (GFC)					
	Banking competition	National governance	Capital requirements (CAP)	Supervisory power (SPR)	Market discipline and private monitoring (PMON)	Activity restrictions (ACTR)
Banking-sector *Z*-score (*Z*)	0.008**	−0.014***	−0.015***	−0.009**	0.002	−0.024***
	(2.001)	(−3.421)	(−3.868)	(−2.411)	(0.573)	(−6.554)
Macroeconomic conditions						
GDP growth (GDPG)	0.008***	0.001	−0.007***	−0.019***	−0.010***	−0.010***
	(3.479)	(0.460)	(−3.303)	(−8.808)	(−4.338)	(−4.179)
Inflation (INF)	−0.053***	−0.068***	−0.065***	−0.064***	−0.050***	−0.037***
	(−17.971)	(−22.496)	(−23.911)	(−24.309)	(−17.799)	(−12.412)
Banking market structure						
Foreign ownership (FOR)	1.423***	1.372***	1.603***	1.976***	1.393***	1.833***
	(8.967)	(8.228)	(10.568)	(13.478)	(8.822)	(13.139)
Constant	1.965***	1.854***	1.861***	1.771***	1.818***	1.748***
	(143.094)	(128.737)	(140.574)	(137.623)	(131.565)	(142.427)
Observations	21,420	21,420	21,420	21,420	21,420	21,420
Number of bank	4,518	4,518	4,518	4,518	4,518	4,518
Adjusted R^2	0.354	0.319	0.409	0.452	0.365	0.504
Sigma	1.019	1.046	0.975	0.938	1.010	0.893

Note: *, **, and *** denote statistical significance at the 10%, 5%, and 1% levels, respectively.

CONCLUDING REMARKS

This chapter empirically investigates how banks' productivity are affected by country-level bank regulations of CAP, official SPR, market discipline, and restrictions on bank activities at various different stages of financial crises. For the empirical analysis, we first use the Malmquist index to estimate the TFP growth of 582 banks operating in 82 countries during the period 2004–2012. Then, we apply a robust bootstrap procedure to utilize the estimated TFP growth scores from the first stage which are regressed on a number of key variables including regulatory, governance, and banking market structure, while controlling for country- and bank-specific characteristics.

Empirical results suggest that commercial banks in countries with better national governance have higher productivity growth before, during and after the GFC. Furthermore, all three pillars of Basel II are shown to have a positive and significant impact on productivity growth during GFC. These findings suggest that policy makers should direct their efforts toward ensuring adequate and timely disclosure of information and promote a framework of adequate bank surveillance which incorporates an incentive system of market discipline and PMON in the banking sector during financial crises, in particular.

ACKNOWLEDGMENTS

I gratefully acknowledge the financial support from National Science Council (NSC) of Taiwan (NSC-101-2410-H-343-005). I also thank for very helpful comments from Sergio Masciantonio, Dorota Skala, Malgorzata Pawlowska, and participants at the 2013 INFINITI Conference on International Finance (Aix-en-Provence, France) and the 2013 Taiwan Productivity and Efficiency Conference (Taipei).

REFERENCES

Aysan, A. F., & Ceyhan, S. P. (2008) What determines the banking sector performance in globalized financial markets? *The case of Turkey*. *Physica A*, *387*, 1593–1602.

Barth, J. R., Caprio, G. Jr., & Levine, R. (2001). Banking systems around the globe: Do regulations and ownership affect performance and stability? In F. S. Mishkin, (Ed.), *Prudential supervision: What works and what doesn't* (pp. 31–88). Chicago, IL: University of Chicago Press.

Barth, J. R., Caprio, G. Jr., & Levine, R. (2003). Bank regulation and supervision: Lessons from a new database. In J. A. M. Garza (Ed.), *Macroeconomic stability, financial markets, and economic development*. Mexico: Banco de Mexico.

Barth, J. R., Caprio, G. Jr., & Levine, R. (2004). Bank regulation and supervision: What works best? *Journal of Financial Intermediation, 13*, 205–248.

Barth, J. R., Caprio, G. Jr., & Levine, R. (2007). *Bank regulations are changing: But for better or worse?* World Bank Working Paper No. 4646. Washington, DC: World Bank.

Barth, J. R., Caprio, G. Jr., & Levine, R. (2013). *Bank regulation and supervision in 180 countries from 1999 to 2011*. National Bureau of Economic Research Working Paper No. 18733. Cambridge, MA: NBER.

Barth, J. R., Dopico, L. G., Nolle, D. E., & Wilcox, J. A. (2002). Bank safety and soundness and the structure of bank supervision: A cross-country analysis. *International Review of Finance, 3*, 163–188.

Barth, J. R., Lin, C., Ma, Y., Seade, J., & Song, F. M. (2013). Do bank regulation, supervision and monitoring enhance or impede bank efficiency? *Journal of Banking and Finance, 37*, 2879–2892.

Beck, T., Demirgüç-Kunt, A., & Levine, R. (2000). A new database on financial development and structure. *World Bank Economic Review, 14*, 597–605.

Beck, T., Demirgüç-Kunt, A., & Levine, R. (2006). Bank concentration, competition, and crises: First results. *Journal of Banking and Finance, 30*, 1581–1603.

Beltratti, A., & Stulz, R. M. (2012). The credit crisis around the globe: Why did some banks perform better? *Journal of Financial Economics, 105*(1), 1–17.

Bonin, J. P., Hasan, I., & Wachtel, P. (2005). Bank performance, efficiency and ownership in transition countries. *Journal of Banking and Finance, 29*, 31–53.

Brealey, R. A., & Kaplanis, E. C. (1996). The determination of foreign banking location. *Journal of International Money and Finance, 15*, 577–597.

Brissimis, S. N., Delis, M. D., & Papanikolaou, N. I. (2008). Exploring the nexus between banking sector reform and performance: Evidence from newly acceded EU countries. *Journal of Banking and Finance, 32*, 2674–2683.

Casu, B., Girardone, C., & Molyneux, P. (2004). Productivity change in European banking: A comparison of parametric and non-parametric approaches. *Journal of Banking and Finance, 28*, 2521–2540.

Caves, D. W., Christensen, L. R., & Diewert, W. E. (1982). The economic theory of index numbers and the measurement of input, output, and productivity. *Econometrica, 50*, 1393–1414.

de Haas, R., & van Horen, N. (2012). International shock transmission after the Lehman Brothers collapse: Evidence from syndicated lending. *American Economic Review, Papers & Proceedings, 102*(3), 231–237.

de Haas, R., & van Horen, N. (2013). Running for the exit? International bank lending during a financial crisis. *Review of Financial Studies, 26*(1), 244–285.

Delis, M. D., Molyneux, P., & Pasoiras, F. (2011). Regulations and productivity growth in banking: Evidence from transition economies. *Journal of Money, Credit and Banking, 43*, 735–764.

Delis, M. D., & Staikouras, P. K. (2011). Supervisory effectiveness and bank risk. *Review of Finance. Review of Finance, 15*(3), 511–543.

Demirgüç-Kunt, A., Detragiache, E., & Tressel, T. (2008). Banking on the principles: Compliance with basel core principles and bank soundness. *Journal of Financial Intermediation, 17*, 511–542.

Demirgüç-Kunt, A., Laeven, L., & Levine, R. (2004). Regulations, market structure, institutions, and the cost of financial intermediation. *Journal of Money, Credit and Banking, 36*, 593–622.

DeYoung, R. E., Hughes, J. P., & Moon, C. (2001). Efficient risk-taking and regulatory covenant enforcement in a deregulated banking industry. *Journal of Economics and Business, 53*, 255–282.

Fahlenbrach, R., Prilmeier, R., & Stulz, R. M. (2012). This time is the same: Using bank performance in 1998 to explain bank performance during the recent financial crisis. *Journal of Finance, 67*(6), 2139–2185.

Färe, R., Grosskopf, S., Norris, M., & Zhang, Z. (1994). Productivity growth, technical progress, and efficiency change in industrialized countries. *American Economic Review, 84*, 66–83.

Färe, R., Grosskopf, S., & Weber, W. L. (2004). The effect of risk-based capital requirements on profit efficiency in banking. *Applied Economics, 36*, 1731–1743.

Fries, S., Neven, D. J., Seabright, P., & Taci, A. (2006). Market entry, privatization and bank performance in transition. *Economics of Transition, 14*, 579–610.

Fries, S., & Taci, A. (2002). *Banking reform and development in transition countries*. European Bank for Reconstruction and Development Working Paper No. 71. Retrieved from http://www.ebrd.com/downloads/research/economics/workingpapers/wp0071.pdf

Gaganis, C., & Pasiouras, F. (2013). Financial supervision regimes and bank efficiency: International evidence. *Journal of Banking and Finance*. Forthcoming.

Giannetti, M., & Laeven, L. (2012). The flight home effect: Evidence from the syndicated loan market during financial crises. *Journal of Financial Economics, 104*(1), 23–43.

Gilbert, R. A., & Wilson, P. W. (1998). Effects of deregulation on the productivity of Korean banks. *Journal of Economics and Business, 50*, 133–155.

Grifell-Tatje, E., & Lovell, C. A. K. (1996). Deregulation and productivity decline: The case of Spanish savings banks. *European Economic Review, 40*, 1281–1303.

Hay, J. R., & Shleifer, A. (1998). Private enforcement of public laws: A theory of legal reform. *American Economic Review Papers and Proceedings, 88*, 398–403.

Isik, I. (2007). Bank ownership and productivity developments: Evidence from Turkey. *Studies in Economics and Finance, 24*, 115–139.

Kasman, A., & Kirbas-Kasman, S. (2006). Technical change in banking: Evidence from transition countries. *International Journal of the Economics of Business, 13*, 129–144.

Kaufmann, D., Kraay, A., & Mastruzzi, M. (2006). Governance Matters V: Worldwide governance indicators, 1996–2005. World Bank Policy Research Working Paper No. 4012. Washington, DC: World Bank.

Kaufmann, D., Kraay, A., & Mastruzzi, M. (2010). *The worldwide governance indicators: Methodology and analytical issues*. World Bank Policy Research Working Paper No. 5430. Washington, DC: World Bank.

Khan, S., & Lewbel, A. (2007). Weighted and two-stage least squares estimation of semiparametric truncated regression models. *Econometric Theory, 23*, 309–347.

Koutsomanoli-Filippaki, A., Mamatzakis, E., & Staikouras, C. (2009). Structural reforms and banking efficiency in the new EU states. *Journal of Policy Modeling, 31*, 17–21.

Lensink, R., & Hermes, N. (2004). The short-term effects of foreign bank entry on domestic bank behaviour: Does economic development matter? *Journal of Banking and Finance, 28*, 553–568.

Levine, R. (1996). *Financial development and economic growth: Views and agenda*. World Bank Policy Research Working Paper Series 1678.

Mamatzakis, E., Staikouras, C., & Koutsomanoli-Filippaki, A. (2008). Bank efficiency in the new European Union member states: Is there convergence? *International Review of Financial Analysis*, *17*, 1156–1172.

Naaborg, I., & Lensink, R. (2008). Banking in transition economies: Does foreign ownership enhance profitability? *European Journal of Finance*, *14*, 545–562.

Pasiouras, F. (2008). International evidence on the impact of regulations and supervision on banks' technical efficiency: An application of two-stage data envelopment analysis. *Review of Quantitative Finance and Accounting*, *30*, 187–223.

Pasiouras, F., Gaganis, C., & Zopounidis, C. (2006). The impact of bank regulations, supervision, market structure, and bank characteristics on individual bank ratings: A cross-country analysis. *Review of Quantitative Finance and Accounting*, *27*, 403–438.

Pasiouras, F., Tanna, S., & Zopounidis, C. (2009). The impact of banking regulations on banks' cost and profit efficiency: Cross-country evidence. *International Review of Financial Analysis*, *18*, 294–302.

Simar, L., & Wilson, P. W. (2007). Estimation and inference in two-stage, semi-parametric models of production processes. *Journal of Econometrics*, *136*, 31–64.

Sun, Y. (2011). *Recent developments in European bank competition*. IMF Working Paper, No. 11/146. Washington, DC: International Monetary Fund.

Tirtiroglu, D., Daniels, K. N., & Tirtigoglu, E. (2005). Deregulation, intensity of competition, industry evolution, and the productivity growth of U.S. commercial banks. *Journal of Money, Credit and Banking*, *37*(2), 339–360.

Tirtiroglu, D., Daniels, K. N., & Tirtiroglu, E. (1998). Total factor productivity growth and regulation in U.S. commercial banking during 1946–1995: An empirical investigation. *Journal of Economics and Business*, *50*, 171–189.

APPENDIX: VARIABLE DESCRIPTION AND DATA SOURCES

Variable	Description	Data Sources
Stage 1: Estimation of total factor productivity		
Bank inputs		
Fixed assets (FA)	Assets related to physical capital	Bankscope
Deposits and short-term funding (DEP)	Incoming funds used to generate bank outputs	Bankscope
Overheads (over)	Operating expenses used in the production process of bank outputs	Bankscope
Bank outputs		
Net loans (NL)	Bank gross loans net of reserves for impaired loans/NPLs	Bankscope
Other earning assets (OEA)		Bankscope
Noninterest income (NII)		Bankscope
Stage 2: Determinants of total factor productivity change		
Internal determinants		
Logarithm of total assets (LNTA)	Proxy for bank size	Bankscope
Ratio of equity to total assets (EQTA)	Proxy for bank capitalization	Bankscope
External determinants		
Regulatory conditions		
Capital requirements (CAP)	This variable is determined by adding 1 if the answer is yes to questions 1–6 and 0 otherwise, and the opposite occurs for questions 7 and 8 (i.e., yes = 0, no = 1). The questions are: (1) Is the minimum required capital asset ratio (risk weighted) in line with Basel guidelines? (2) Does the ratio vary with market risk? (3–5) Before determining minimum capital adequacy, are any of the following are deducted from the book value of capital? (a) Market value of loan losses not realized on the financial	Bank Regulation and Supervision Database, World Bank, Barth et al. (2013)

Appendix. *(Continued)*

Variable	Description	Data Sources
	statements, (b) unrealized losses on securities portfolios, and (c) unrealized foreign exchange losses. (6) Have regulatory/supervisory authorities verified the sources of funds to be used as capital? (7) Can assets other than cash or government securities provide the initial or subsequent injections of capital? (8) Can borrowed funds provide the initial disbursement of capital?	
Supervisory power (SPR)	This variable is determined by adding 1 if the answer is yes and 0 otherwise, for each of the following 14 questions: (1) Does the supervisory agency have the right to meet with external auditors to discuss their report without the approval of the bank? (2) Are auditors legally required to communicate directly to the supervisory agency any presumed involvement of bank directors or senior managers in illicit activities, fraud, or insider abuse? (3) Can supervisors take legal action against external auditors for negligence? (4) Can the supervisory authorities force a bank to change its internal organizational structure? (5) Does the institution disclose off-balance-sheet items to supervisors? (6) Can the supervisory agency order the bank's directors or management to constitute provisions to cover actual or potential losses? (7) Can the supervisory agency suspend directors' decisions to distribute dividends? (8) Can the supervisory agency suspend directors' decisions to distribute bonuses? (9) Can the supervisory agency suspend directors' decisions to distribute management fees? (10) Can the supervisory agency supersede bank shareholder rights and declare the bank insolvent? (11) Does banking law allow a supervisory agency or any other government agency (other than a court) to suspend some or all ownership rights at a problem bank? (12) Regarding bank restructuring and reorganization,	Bank Regulation and Supervision Database, World Bank, Barth et al. (2013)

	can the supervisory agency or any other government agency (other than a court) supersede shareholder rights? (13) Regarding bank restructuring and reorganization, can the supervisory agency or any other government agency (other than a court) remove and replace management? (14) Regarding bank restructuring and reorganization, can the supervisory agency or any other government agency (other than a court) remove and replace directors?	
Market discipline and private monitoring (PMON)	This variable is determined by adding 1 if the answer is yes to questions 1–7 and 0 otherwise, and the opposite occurs for questions 8 and 9 (i.e., yes = 0, no = 1). (1) Is subordinated debt allowed (or required) capital? (2) Are financial institutions required to produce consolidated accounts covering all bank and any nonbank financial subsidiaries? (3) Are off-balance-sheet items disclosed to the public? (4) Must banks disclose their risk-management procedures? (5) Are directors legally liable for erroneous/misleading information? (6) Do regulations require credit ratings for commercial banks? (7) Is an external audit by certified/licensed auditor mandatory for banks? (8) Does accrued, unpaid interest/principal on nonperforming loans appear on the income statement? (9) Is there an explicit deposit-insurance protection system?	Bank Regulation and Supervision Database, World Bank, Barth et al. (2013)
Activity restrictions (ACTR)	The score for this variable is determined on the basis of the level of regulatory restrictiveness for bank participation in: (1) securities activities, (2) insurance activities, (3) real estate activities, and (4) bank ownership of nonfinancial firms. These activities can be unrestricted, permitted, restricted, or prohibited and receive values of 1, 2, 3, or 4, respectively. We create an overall index by calculating the average value of the four categories.	Bank Regulation and Supervision Database, World Bank, Barth et al. (2013)

Appendix. *(Continued)*

Variable	Description	Data Sources
Banking market structure		
Banking competition	I use Boone index as the proxy of degree of banking competition	Author's estimation
Foreign ownership (FOR)	Asset share of foreign-owned banks in percent	Author's estimation
Macroeconomic conditions		
GDP growth (GDPG)	Real GDP growth	World Bank
Inflation (INF)	CPI inflation	World Bank
Proxies for the financial crisis		
Ratio of nonperforming loans (NPLs) to total loans	Proxy for credit risk	Financial Development and structure database, World Bank
Banking-sector *Z*-score (*Z*)	Indicator of the overall soundness of the banking sector. It is calculated as (ROA + (equity/assets))/sd(ROA), with the standard deviation of ROA, sd(ROA), being estimated over a five-year moving window	Financial Development and structure database, World Bank
National goveranance measures		
Voice and accountability	The indicator measures the extent to which a country's citizens are able to participate in selecting their government, as well as freedom of expression, freedom of association, and free media.	Kaufmann, Kraay, and Mastruzzi (2006)
Government effectiveness	The indicator measures the quality of public services, the quality of the civil service and the degree of its independence from political pressures, the quality of policy formulation and implementation, and the credibility of the government's commitment to such policies.	Kaufmann et al. (2006)

Rule of law	The indicator measures the extent to which agents have confidence in and abide by the rules of society, and in particular the quality of contract enforcement, the police, and the courts, as well as the likelihood of crime and violence.	Kaufmann et al. (2006)
Political stability	The indicator measures the perceptions of the likelihood that the government will be destabilized or overthrown by unconstitutional or violent means, including political violence and terrorism.	Kaufmann et al. (2006)
Quality of regulation	The indicator measures the ability of the government to formulate and implement sound policies and regulations that permit and promote market competition and private-sector development.	Kaufmann et al. (2006)
Control of corruption	The indicator measures the extent to which public power is exercised for private gain, including both petty and grand forms of corruption, as well as "capture" of the state by elites and private interests.	

Note: All information is mainly adopted from Delis et al. (2011).

PART III
FINANCIAL MARKETS AND CRISES

THE IMPACT OF DOMESTIC AND INTERNATIONAL MONETARY POLICY NEWS ON U.S. AND GERMAN BANK STOCKS

Suk-Joong Kim, Linda Lee and Eliza Wu

ABSTRACT

This chapter investigates the impact of policy interest rate news from the U.S. Federal Reserve (Fed) and the European Central Bank (ECB) on stock returns and volatilities of U.S. NYSE and German DAX listed commercial banks. We find that Fed news has the most influence on both U.S. and German listed bank stocks and an unexpected policy rate increase (decrease) lowers (raises) returns and raises volatility in the majority of cases. On the other hand, ECB news generally increases bank stock volatility in the United States but has little impact within its own domestic banking industry. While our results for the U.S. listed banks confirm that their stock prices are more responsive in bad economic times and also during periods of monetary tightening, we find disparities for German banks suggesting that U.S. and European banking industries respond heterogeneously to monetary policy news but the

Global Banking, Financial Markets and Crises
International Finance Review, Volume 14, 175–210

ISSN: 1569-3767/doi:10.1108/S1569-3767(2013)0000014010

Global Financial Crisis increased the sensitivity of all banks to monetary policy news.

Keywords: Federal Reserve; European Central Bank; banking; spillovers; volatility

JEL classifications: E43; E44; G21

INTRODUCTION

Since the mid-1980s central banks in many advanced economies have moved to targeting official interest rates and the procedures for announcing the targets have well been established from the early 1990s. Considering the important role that official interest rates play in the banking sector, financial markets and the broader economy, it comes as no surprise that official interest rate announcements are keenly watched for any deviations from expectations. In the days approaching a scheduled target rate announcement, market participants aim to forecast the direction and magnitude of future target rate changes so that they can protect themselves from potential interest rate risk. Market participants need to accurately anticipate future monetary policy actions of not only their own domestic central bank, but also the policy actions imposed by the U.S. Federal Reserve (Fed) as it is highly influential on the world economy (Bernanke & Kuttner, 2005). These anticipated changes should already be factored into market prices observed immediately prior to the announcement of policy interest rate changes. If the announced interest rate differs from what is expected, then the market will significantly react to this news. Therefore, central banks influence financial markets through their control of the target interest rate, by how well they communicate the impending changes of the target interest rate to market participants, and by their policy credibility.

The segment of the economy that is most directly impacted by changes in the target rate is the commercial banking sector due to the nature of their business model which results in a mismatch of maturities in their holdings of assets and liabilities and the cyclicality of the banking industry. As shown by Fuertes, Heffernan, and Kalotychou (2010) using a sample of UK banks, changes in central bank rates affect a large range of financial products offered. Hence, changes in target interest rates are likely to flow through to influence banks' stock prices. In this chapter we investigate the policy interest rate news effects of the U.S. Fed and the European Central

Bank (ECB) on the commercial banks listed in the United States (U.S. banks, Canadian and Latin American banks, and European banks) and in Germany (German banks) over the different phases of business and monetary policy cycles. To our best knowledge, this is the first firm-level banking study to examine in detail, the international spillover effects of monetary policy news in the global financial system.

There is an extensive literature on the impact of the U.S. Fed's monetary policy surprises on various segments of the U.S. financial markets dating back to the early 1980s. During the modern era of inflation and interest rate targeting, market participants have concentrated on the news contents of the Fed's regular target interest rate announcements. In particular, the news impacts on stock markets are generally found to be negative in sign, that is unexpected rate increase lowers stock returns (inter alia Bernanke & Kuttner, 2005; Ehrmann & Fratzscher, 2004; Jensen, Mercer, & Johnson, 1996; Rigobon & Sack, 2004; Thorbecke, 1997). Furthermore, Bernanke and Blinder (1992) and Kashyap, Stein, and Wilcox (1993) report stronger reactions of unexpected monetary tightening on firms that are highly dependent on bank-sourced funds. The central message from this literature is that only the unexpected target rate change has an impact with an unexpected hike (cut) decreasing (increasing) the stock market returns on the days of announcement. The usual negative association is also reported for the ECB's target interest rate news by Bohl, Siklos, and Sondermann (2008) where stock market indexes from the four largest markets in Europe (Germany, France, Italy, and Spain) are significantly lower (higher) following unexpected rate increases (cuts).

Considering the significant information leadership of the U.S. stock market, it comes as no surprise that what drives the U.S. stock market would have both direct and indirect effects (via stock market spillovers) on non-U.S. stock markets. In particular, Bernanke and Kuttner (2005) find that an unanticipated 25-basis point cut in the Fed funds target rate would lead to a 1% point increase in foreign stock markets in their samples. In addition, Wongswan (2009) reports foreign stock market reactions ranging from 0.5% to 2.5% for the stock markets in Asia, Europe and Latin America. Using intraday data, Ammer, Vega, and Wongswan (2010) show that foreign firms in cyclical industries[1] exhibit even stronger responses to the Fed's interest rate surprises. In contrast, the interest rate news from the ECB does not seem to have a significant impact on the U.S. market. For example, Funke and Matsuda (2002) find that unexpected changes in the German interest rate do not have a significant impact on U.S. stock prices. Similarly, Ehrmann, Fratzscher, and Rigobon (2010) find that Euro area markets account for only 8% of U.S. asset price changes, compared to the

25% of Euro area financial market movements that are explained by U.S. financial market developments.

It has been documented that interest rate news effects are dependent on economic conditions and monetary policy direction. There is evidence of heightened stock market sensitivity to interest rate news during recessions (Basistha & Kurov, 2008; Chen, 2007). In addition, there is much evidence of asymmetric interest rate news effects on stock markets (inter alia Conover, Jensen & Johnson, 1999; Jensen & Johnson, 1995; Jensen et al., 1996). In general, stock markets show higher sensitivity for unexpected interest rate increases than decreases.

The segment of a stock market that is likely to be most sensitive to interest rate news would be the financial sector in general and the commercial banking sector in particular due to the need to manage balance sheet mismatches of interest rate sensitive assets and liabilities. It has been amply documented in the literature that the effect of interest rate changes on financial institutions' stock prices are related to the maturity composition of a firm's net nominal asset holdings (Akella & Greenbaum, 1992; Flannery & James, 1984; Madura & Zarruk, 1995). The literature also documents how various bank characteristics also influence bank stock reactions to monetary policy news (Elyasiani & Mansur, 1998; Fraser, Madura & Weigand, 2002; Madura & Schnusenberg, 2000). However, there is little evidence outside of the United States. The recent literature reports that U.S. banks with large size, low capital ratio, higher degree of business diversification or greater international exposure are more sensitive to unexpected changes in the Fed funds target rate. Furthermore, banks that rely more heavily on nonbanking revenue or nondeposit funding are more sensitive to interest rate changes, and sounder banks are less sensitive to unexpected Fed funds target rate movements (Yang & Yin, 2009; Yin, Yang, & Handorf, 2010). This suggests that the trend of commercial banks tapping into capital markets for both asset and liability operations has potentially increased their exposure to interest rate risk, making them more sensitive to interest rate news in recent years.

This chapter explores the following research questions on three levels. First, we explore the own market and international spillover interest rate news effects of the U.S. Fed and the ECB on the U.S. and German market listed banks, as these two countries operate under the two largest and most influential central banks and have the largest banking sectors in the world economy.[2] Second, we ask if the impacts of monetary policy surprises on bank stocks are state-dependent (on the business cycle, Global Financial Crisis (GFC) period or monetary policy regime)? We employ a sample of

14 banks incorporated and operating in the U.S. (U.S. listed banks) for the period January 1 1995 to June 30 2009 and 5 German listed German banks for the period February 18, 1999 to June 30, 2009 to investigate the above research questions. While there is some understanding on the own market impacts of monetary policy news, little is known at the bank firm level about the international spillover effects of central bank interest rate decisions in the global economy and is warranted in light of the current environment of international banking sector turmoil.

The major results of our investigations are summarized as follows. First, we find that Fed news has both own market and international spillover effects on bank stock returns and volatilities, whereas ECB news has less price or volatility impact on its' own domestic market but there are significant volatility spillover effects to U.S. listed bank stocks. Second, we report that the U.S. listed banks are more sensitive to news in bad economic times, while the German listed banks are more sensitive to both ECB and Fed news in *good* economic times. In addition, we find that the U.S. listed and German listed banks are more responsive to own market interest rate news during a tightening monetary policy phase (but spillover effects are more severe in an expansionary phase). Consistent with this, volatility responses to all interest rate shocks were heightened during the onset of the GFC.

The implications of our study are of interest to policy makers, bank managers and investors alike. In particular, greater transparency and timely communications from the central banks would reduce the likelihood of disruptions in financial markets when unexpected interest rate decisions are communicated. In addition, there is an important impaction for academic researchers in relation to the modelling of international transmission mechanisms of business cycles and monetary policy shocks.

DATA DESCRIPTIONS

Target Interest Rate Announcement Data

The U.S. Federal Open Market Committee (FOMC) began announcing changes in its policy stance in 1994, and it began to explicitly state its target level for the Fed funds rate from 1995. The FOMC holds 8 scheduled meetings a year, with additional ad hoc meetings as needed, and the interest rate decisions are announced at 2:15 pm Eastern Standard Time (EST). Our sample of U.S. Fed interest rate news is thus from January 1995.

The Governing Council of the ECB is responsible for setting the key interest rates for the entire Euro area. The interest rate on the main refinancing operations is perceived to be the policy interest rate as it provides the bulk of liquidity to the banking system, and it plays a pivotal role in the ECB's open market operations. The Eurosystem may execute its tenders in the form of fixed rate or variable rate tenders. The Governing Council meet on the first Thursday of each month.[3] At this meeting they assess the economic situation in the Euro area and make their monetary policy decisions, after which a press release announcing their decision on the key ECB interest rate is issued at 1:45 pm Central European Time (CET). The ECB's first announcement of their target for the refinancing rate was on February 18, 1999. Hence, this is the starting point of our sample for the ECB interest rate announcements.

The target interest rate data for the FED and ECB are obtained from their respective web sites.[4] Table 1 reports the breakdown of target rate announcements into rate rises, rate cuts and unchanged decisions for the full sample period available for the Fed and the ECB, respectively.[5] Of these, the Fed made 54 announcements where there was a change (25 rate rises and 29 cuts), and 81 no change announcements. The ECB made 31 announcements of interest rate change (16 rate rises and 15 cuts), and 129 no change announcements. Most of the scheduled interest rate announcements have been unchanged decisions; 60% for the Fed, 81% for the ECB. For each of the central bank target rate announcements, we disaggregate the announcements into the expected and the unexpected components and concentrate on the latter for our analyses as the literature reports significant market responses only for the surprise component.

In order to isolate the unexpected component in the target interest rate announcements, researchers have made use of both market-based surveys of rate expectations (Reinhart & Simin, 1997) or Fed funds futures rate (Kuttner, 2001) as predictors of the Fed funds target rate. The early literature on the ECB interest rate news used price based proxies (Gaspar, Perez-Quiros, & Sicilia, 2001) to account for the market's expectations of the official interest rate changes. Alternatively, Ehrmann and Fratzscher (2004) use survey data as a proxy for the market expectations. However, following Bernoth and Von Hagen's (2004) finding that the three-month EURIBOR futures rate is an unbiased predictor of ECB target rate announcements, the literature suggests that a market-based approach using futures rates is the most appropriate measure for generating expectations data.

In this chapter, we employ Kuttner's (2001) methodology to extract the unexpected components of the Fed's and ECB's target interest rate announcements using relevant interest rate futures. The news component is

Table 1. Target Interest Rate Announcements and Interest Rate News from the Fed and the ECB.

Panel A: Target Interest Rate Announcements

	Fed funds target rate Announcements				ECB target rate announcements			
	Total	Rate rise	Rate cut	No change	Total	Rate rise	Rate cut	No Change
No. of announcements	135	25	29	81	160	16	15	129
Proportions	100%	19%	21%	60%	100%	10%	9%	81%

Panel B: Target Interest Rates News

	Fed target rate News				ECB target rate News			
	Total	Unexpected rise	Unexpected fall	No news	Total	Unexpected rise	Unexpected fall	No news
No. of announcements	135	45	57	33	160	78	66	16
Proportions	100%	33%	42%	24%	100%	49%	41%	10%
Summary statistics								
Mean	−0.0024	0.0812	−0.2583		0.0001	0.0407	−0.0427	
Variance	0.0026	0.0068	0.1284		0.0002	0.0023	0.0024	
Skewness	−23.6086	1.5182	−2.4841		0.9528	3.0748	−2.5075	
Excess Kurtosis	741.22	1.9050	7.7501		161.57	11.7793	7.5334	
Min	−1.9140	0.0055	−1.9140		−0.2700	0.0050	−0.2700	
Max	0.2400	0.2400	−0.0050		0.2950	0.2950	−0.0050	

This table shows the distribution of target interest rate announcements and news events, defined as a deviation of actual from expected rates for both the U.S. Federal Reserve (Fed) Bank and the European Central Bank (ECB) over the time period from January 2, 1995 for the United States and February 18, 1999 for the ECB to June 30, 2009.

formally defined as the difference between the actual target interest rate change and the expected change. In order to extrapolate the Fed's unexpected component, we look at the current-month Fed funds futures contracts traded on the Chicago Board of Trade (CBOT). For ECB news, we use three-month EURIBOR futures contracts traded on the European Exchange (EUREX). We obtained these futures data from Datastream.

Kuttner's (2001) methodology proceeds as follows. The news component of the Fed's target interest rate announcement on day d of month m can be derived from the implied change in the price of the Fed funds futures. Given that the Fed funds futures settlement price is based on the monthly average of the spot Fed funds rate, we must account for this by scaling equation (1) for the number of days affected by the announcement in that particular month. However, since the 3-month EURIBOR futures settlement price is based on the reference interest rate (EURIBOR) for the three-month Euro term deposits on the last trading day, it is not necessary to scale Eq. (1) for the ECB announcements.

$$\Delta i^{u} = \frac{D}{D-d}(f^{0}_{m,d} - f^{0}_{m.d-1}) \tag{1}$$

where

- Δi^{u}: the unexpected change in the target rate announcement
- D: the number of days in the month
- $D-d$: the number of days in the month affected by the announcement
- $f^{0}_{m,d}$: the current month (superscript 0) Fed funds futures rate on the day of the announcement, d.
- $f^{0}_{m,d-1}$: the current month (superscript 0) Fed funds futures rate on the day prior to the announcement, $d-1$.

An exception to the above calculation is when the target rate announcement is made within the last three days of the month, or the first day of the month.[6] In these cases, the surprise component is instead calculated as

$$\Delta i^{u} = y_{m,D} - y_{m-1,d} \tag{2}$$

where

- $y_{m,D}$: is the yield (100 minus the futures price) for the current month Fed funds futures corresponding to the date of the target rate announcement
- $y_{m-1,d}$: is the yield corresponding to the last day of the previous month.

Panel B of Table 1 reports the summary statistics for the expected and unexpected components of the target rate decisions for the two central banks. For the Fed, 102 of the target rate announcements contained news (45 unexpected rises and 57 unexpected falls), and 33 announcements contained no news. For the ECB, 144 of the announcements contained news (78 unexpected rise and 66 unexpected falls), and 16 contained no news.[7] There were more negative surprises than positive surprises for the Fed, whereas more positive surprises than negative surprises were made by the ECB. The Fed had a greater proportion of announcements that were correctly anticipated by market commentators (42%) than the ECB's announcements (10%).

Bank Stock Data

Our sample includes stock price data for 14 U.S. (NYSE) listed commercial banks for the period January 2, 1995 to June 30, 2009.[8] We only include commercial banks whose main business line is intermediation of loanable funds. In this sample there are 5 U.S. banks, 4 non-U.S. American banks (1 Canadian and 3 Latin American banks), and 5 European banks. In addition, we use 5 large German banks listed in the German stock market (DAX) for the period February 18, 1999 to June 30, 2009.[9] Appendix A lists the details of the banks in our sample.[10]

The open and close stock prices for these 19 banks were collected from the Thomson Reuters Datascope Tick History (RDTH) database and Thomson's Datastream. The banks we examine are among the larger commercial banks in each country. From opening and closing stock prices we generate intraday (open to close at day t) and overnight (close at day $t-1$ to open at day t) return horizons. The intraday and overnight return characteristics of the bank stocks show typical non-normal patterns, significant skewness and kurtosis. In the majority of cases, the return series show evidence of significant serial correlation in the first and second moments, with the exception of some U.S. listed bank returns. These diagnostics suggest that a GARCH type model is suitable for modelling our bank stock return data. We do not report the details of these summary statistics to save space. However, detailed statistics are available upon request.

EMPIRICAL MODELLING ISSUES

The GARCH family of models are known to be appropriate in modelling the stylized characteristics of daily and intraday financial return series. In particular, Exponential GARCH (EGARCH) models have been applied in the literature to capture the potential negative influence of regressors in the conditional variance equations. In this chapter, we model both intraday and overnight returns of bank stocks with domestic and foreign interest rate news as regressors for the first two moments of the return distributions.[11]

We adopt a parsimonious AR(1)-EGARCH (1,1)-in-Mean model and its baseline specification is shown in equation (1a) and (1b) below

$$\begin{aligned} y_t^{HP} = {} & \alpha_c + \alpha_{Lag} y_{t-1}^{HP} + \alpha_{Mon} Mon_t + \alpha_{Hol} Hol_t + \alpha_{ErCh} ErCh_t \\ & + \alpha_{SD_{Index}} SD_{Index_t} + \alpha_h \sqrt{h_t} + \varepsilon_t \end{aligned} \tag{1a}$$

$$ln\, h_t^{HP} = \beta_c + \beta_h\, ln\, h_{t-1}^{HP} + \beta_{\varepsilon 1} \frac{|\varepsilon_{t-1}|}{\sqrt{h_{t-1}}} + \beta_{Mon} Mon_t + \beta_{Hol} Hol_t + \beta_{ErSq} ErSq_t \tag{1b}$$

We estimate our bank stock returns over two holdings periods (HP); the intraday holding period (ID: from Open to Close at day t) which will capture own market news effects (Fed news effects on the U.S. listed bank stocks, and ECB news effects on German listed German bank stocks), and the overnight holding period (ON: from Close at day $t-1$ to Open at day t) which will capture the spillover news effects of the interest rate news that arrived overnight from the other market (ECB news for U.S. listed banks and Fed news for German listed German banks).[12] The advantage of disaggregating the typical close-to-close trading day into intraday and overnight holding periods is that it smooths out the relatively noisier results that are found when estimating returns over a standard daily horizon.

The conditional mean equation for the returns (y_t) is expressed as a function of the previous holding period return, a Monday dummy (*Mon*), a holiday dummy (*Hol*), exchange rate changes (*ErCh*), standard deviation of the country's aggregate stock market index (SD_{Index}) and the EGARCH-in-Mean term ($\sqrt{h_t}$).[13] The *Mon* dummy takes the value of one for Mondays and zero otherwise, and the *Hol* dummy takes on a value determined by the number of days of market closure due to holidays between two consecutive market prices. These two indicator variables are used to capture any unusual trading due to the start of the week and holiday effects, respectively. The change in the USD/EUR exchange rate is used for each country.[14] This is used to capture the degree of internationalization of each bank under consideration, and the impact a change in the exchange rate may have on the bank stock returns (foreign exchange exposure).[15]

We also control for the volatility of the aggregate stock market index and the conditional volatility of the stock itself. The market indexes for the United States and Germany are the S&P500 and the DAX, respectively.[16] This allows us to investigate the impact of market volatility and the stocks' own volatility on the stock returns. Elyasiani and Mansur (1998) employ a similar methodology and they find a significant volatility effect of a trade-off between expected returns and risk. Their results show a negative coefficient for volatility in the mean equation, and this negative relationship holds across different bank portfolios. The conditional variance equation (h_t) is expressed as a function of the previous holding period variance and the absolute value of the residuals, the Monday dummy (*Mon*), the holiday dummy (*Hol*), and the change in the exchange rate squared (*ErSq*).

The interest rate news effect is then investigated separately by including domestic news over the intraday (ID) holding period and foreign interest rate news over the overnight period (ON) as regressors in the conditional mean and variance equations. The baseline model shown in equations (1a) and (1b) is augmented with a news term to form Eqs. (2a) and (2b) to capture the overall target rate news effect on bank stock returns.

$$y_t^{HP} = [RHS\ of\ 1a] + \alpha_{News} News_t \tag{2a}$$

$$lnh_t^{HP} = [RHS\ of\ 1b] + \beta_{News} |News_t| \tag{2b}$$

The contemporaneous domestic news to be included in Eqs. (2a) and (2b) above are Fed news for the U.S. and ECB news for Germany and the relevant holding period (HP) is intraday (ID). In addition, to capture the effects of overnight foreign news, we use lagged foreign news terms that occur before the domestic market opens. For the United States we use ECB news and for Germany we use Fed news with a one day lag and the relevant holding period is overnight (ON). Furthermore, a dummy for macroeconomic announcements other than target rate changes that are made on the same day as a monetary policy announcement is also included in the variance equation for Germany[17] (Fig. 1).

In general, we expect the own market news coefficient for stock market indices to be negative in sign. An inverse relationship between surprise changes in the target interest rate and equity returns has been well documented in the literature (Bernanke & Kuttner, 2005; Ehrmann & Fratzscher, 2004; Wongswan, 2009). For our individual banking stocks, depending on their balance sheet exposure to interest rate risk, we may observe positive or negative coefficients on the news term.

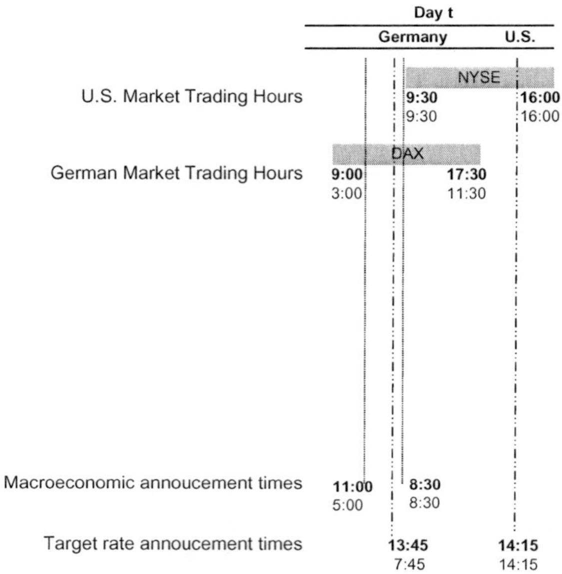

Fig. 1. Timeline of Stock Exchange Opening Hours, Central Bank Target Interest Rate Announcements, and Macroeconomic Announcements. *Notes*: This figure shows trading hours of the DAX and NYSE, the times of the target interest rate announcements made by the ECB and the Fed, and the times of the macroeconomic announcements made in Germany and the United States. Local times are in bold and non-bolded times are in Eastern Daylight Savings; and daylight savings for Germany. Times are shown for the opening and closing of each stock market. The longer, thick dashed lines show the times of each regions target interest rate announcements. For the U.S. it is made at 2:15 pm local time (14:15 EDST), and for Germany is it made at 1:45 pm local time (3:00 EDST). The shorter, finely dashed lines show the times of the macroeconomic announcements made in each region. For the U.S. they are made at 8:30 am local time (8:30 EDST), before the NYSE opens for trading, and for Germany they are made at 11:00 am local time (5:00 EDST).

The sign of the news term in the volatility equation depends on whether the news adds to or resolves the level of information heterogeneity in the market. If the news stimulates information heterogeneity regarding the future direction of the target interest rate, then this would lead to an increase in volatility that is (a positive coefficient). Alternatively, if the arrival of news resolves the level of uncertainty in the market, then a market calming effect would be found, which would be shown as a negative coefficient.

EMPIRICAL RESULTS: AGGREGATE NEWS EFFECTS

Baseline EGARCH(1,1) Estimations

We do not report the full estimation results of the baseline EGARCH(1,1) models for the intraday and overnight horizon bank stock returns. Instead, we provide summaries of the estimation results which show typical patterns of financial return series.[18]

The coefficient of the first lag in the mean equation is generally significant, although we observe both positive and negative signs. For the *Mon* and *Hol* dummy we find that intraday estimations for both the U.S. and German bank returns generally have insignificant Monday and Holiday effects while the Holiday effects tend to be widely significant for the overnight return horizon in German bank returns. The coefficient on the change in the exchange rate (*ErCh*) is mostly positive for Germany and mixed for the U.S. market for both intraday and overnight return horizons suggesting that German banks are more likely to benefit from currency movements. The volatility of the stock market index (SD_{Index}) for each country is found to be significant and positive in the majority of cases, suggesting that an increase in the volatility of the representative stock market index results in an increase in the mean stock price consistent with a risk-return trade off. Moreover, the EGARCH-M term, $\sqrt{h_t}$, is generally significant.

In the variance specification, the coefficient on β_h is consistently significant and close to one in all cases, suggesting volatility persistence as commonly identified for financial returns. We find that the coefficient on $\beta_{\varepsilon 1}$ is consistently significant and positive in all cases suggesting the presence of volume effects in the innovations, where unexpected changes in the mean, of any direction, has a significant impact on raising the conditional volatility. The *Mon* and *Hol* dummy variables generally have a positive coefficient suggesting a generally higher volatility on the days following holidays and weekends.

Overall Contemporaneous Own Market News Effects

Panel A1 of Table 2 reports the impact of Fed news on individual U.S. listed bank stock returns as well as on the aggregate S&P 500 market index returns. A majority (11 out of 14 banks) shows a significant drop in their stock prices following an unexpected increase in the policy rate, but only

Table 2. Fed and ECB Interest Rate News on U.S. Listed and German Listed Bank Stocks.

This table presents the estimated interest rate effects from the following EGARCH-M model for our sample of U.S. and German listed banks (individual and portfolio) as well as for the S&P 500 index and the DAX. Panel A contains domestic interest rate news effects while Panel B reports the international spillover effects. ***, **, * denotes statistical significance at the 1, 5 and 10% levels respectively.

$$y_t^{ID} = \alpha_c + \alpha_{Lag} y_{t-1} + \alpha_{Mon} Mon_t + \alpha_{Hol} Hol_t + \alpha_{ErCh} ErCh_t + \alpha_{SD_{Index}} SD_{Index_t} + \alpha_h \sqrt{h_t} + \alpha_{News} DomesticNews_t + \varepsilon_t \quad (2a)$$

$$\ln h_t^{ID} = \beta_c + \beta_h \ln h_{t-1}^{ID} + \beta_{\varepsilon 1} \frac{|\varepsilon_{t-1}|}{\sqrt{h_{t-1}}} + \beta_{Mon} Mon_t + \beta_{Hol} Hol_t + \beta_{ErSq} ErSq_t + \beta_{News} |DomesticNews_t| \quad (2b)$$

where y_t^{ID} and $\ln h_t^{ID}$ are intraday returns and return volatilities, *DomesticNews* is Fed news for the U.S. and ECB news for the German stock markets, respectively.

Panel A: Contemporaneous Own Market News Effects

A1. Fed news effects on U.S. listed Banks

U.S. Banks	**BAC**	**CIT**	**JPM**	**USB**	**WFC**	**SP500**
αNews	−2.292***	−2.138***	−2.955***	−0.597	−1.280***	−1.265***
	{0.000}	{0.000}	{0.000}	{0.256}	{0.008}	{0.000}
βNews	0.088	0.171	0.264**	0.091	0.094	−0.023
	{0.564}	{0.254}	{0.021}	{0.602}	{0.537}	{0.857}
Non-U.S. American Banks	**BBV**	**RBC**	**BST**	**TRD**		
αNews	−1.692***	−1.980***	−1.514***	−1.720***		
	{0.001}	{0.000}	{0.006}	{0.000}		
βNews	0.263**	0.399**	0.111	0.089		
	{0.037}	{0.016}	{0.347}	{0.626}		
European banks	**BCS**	**CRS**	**DTB**	**HBC**	**UBS**	
αNews	−1.181***	−0.701	−0.735	−1.630***	−1.083***	
	{0.001}	{0.248}	{0.300}	{0.000}	{0.002}	
βNews	0.172	0.355*	0.211	0.081	−0.162	
	{0.142}	{0.067}	{0.305}	{0.421}	{0.401}	

A2. ECB news effects on Germany listed banks

German banks	BEB	DBK	CBK	CRI	IKB	DAX
αNews	2.929**	1.291	−2.354	−0.907	3.149***	0.873
	{0.048}	{0.455}	{0.259}	{0.672}	{0.000}	{0.522}
βNews	−3.542***	−0.052	−1.336*	−0.071	−0.354	0.185
	{0.000}	{0.945}	{0.067}	{0.864}	{0.538}	{0.766}

$$y_t^{ON} = \alpha_c + \alpha_{Lag} y_{t-1} + \alpha_{Mon} Mon_t + \alpha_{Hol} Hol_t + \alpha_{ErCh} ErCh_t + \alpha_{SD_{Index}} SD_{Index_t} + \alpha_h \sqrt{h_t} + \alpha_{News} ForeignNews_{t-1} + \varepsilon_t$$

$$\ln h_t^{ON} = \beta_c + \beta_h \ln h_{t-1}^{ON} + \beta_{\varepsilon 1} \frac{|\varepsilon_{t-1}|}{\sqrt{h_{t-1}}} + \beta_{Mon} Mon_t + \beta_{Hol} Hol_t + \beta_{ErSq} ErSq_t + \beta_{News} |ForeignNews_{t-1}|$$

where y_t^{ON} and $\ln h_t^{ON}$ are overnight returns and return volatilities, *ForeignNews* is Fed news for the German stock market and ECB news for the U.S. stock market.

Panel B: International Spillover News Effects

BI. ECB news effects on U.S. listed banks

U.S. Banks	BAC	CIT	JPM	USB	WFC	SP500
αNews	3265***	−1.629*	−0.855	−0.501	−0.126	0.403***
	{0.000}	{0.076}	{0.655}	{0.904}	{0.883}	{0.000}
βNews	15.215***	0.668***	8.367***	37.278***	1.928***	1.005
	{0.000}	{0.000}	{0.000}	{0.000}	{0.000}	{0.198}
Non-U.S. American Banks	**BBV**	**RBC**	**BST**	**TRD**		
αNews	−2.171	0.334	0.437	−0.907		
	{0.132}	{0.924}	{0.751}	{0.119}		
βNews	1.442***	71.358***	0.759	−0.233		
	{0.001}	{0.000}	{0.567}	{0.667}		

Table 2. (*Continued*)

Panel B: International Spillover News Effects						
BI. ECB news effects on U.S. listed banks						
European banks	**BCS**	**CRS**	**DTB**	**HBC**	**UBS**	
αNews	−58.393***	0.270	−1.202	−2.822	0.989***	
	{0.000}	{0.937}	{0.670}	{0.128}	{0.000}	
βNews	8.635***	2.301***	2.265***	−0.091***	2.690***	
	{0.000}	{0.014}	{0.001}	{0.835}	{0.000}	
B2. Fed news on Germany listed banks						
German banks	**BEB**	**DBK**	**CBK**	**CRI**	**IKB**	**DAX**
αNews	−1.843***	−0.632**	−0.571**	−0.396*	0.018	−0.010
	{0.000}	{0.024}	{0.010}	{0.076}	{0.939}	{0.325}
βNews	1.112	0.459***	−0.371***	−0.318***	0.375***	−0.639***
	{0.000}	{0.001}	{0.005}	{0.010}	{0.000}	{0.000}

4 banks show a significantly higher conditional return variance. Whereas eight out of nine North American based banks show a significant negative response, the responses by the U.S. listed European banks are generally weaker – three out of five banks show a significant response but with smaller magnitudes. In general, the impact of Fed news on U.S. listed bank stocks is well understood by U.S. market participants as reflected in immediate price changes without significant impact on volatility in most cases. The relationship between an unexpected target rate change by the Fed and U.S. listed bank stock returns is consistently negative, which is in line with the existing literature. The volatility responses are generally weak. Only 4 out of 14 U.S. listed banks show significant volatility responses. In these cases, higher volatilities are observed on the announcement days suggesting a mild increase in the level of market uncertainly.

Panel A2 of Table 2 shows ECB news effects on German listed German bank stock returns. Only 2 out of 5 bank stocks show significant mean or variance responses. In those two cases, the stock returns increased (decreased) and the volatilities fell in response to an unexpected interest rate hike (cut). The responses, in general, are opposite to the U.S. listed banks' response to Fed news. We speculate that there is little diversity of opinion amongst German market participants regarding the impact of an ECB target rate change on the bank stocks in their own country. This is likely to arise from a more efficient and transparent monetary policy, and indeed, past studies have found that the ECB is efficient at communicating its policy decisions to market participants (see Bohl et al., 2008). Furthermore, the insignificant responses in the back stock returns might stem from the culture of the conservative way of business that is common in German financial institutions.

International Spillover Effects of Interest Rate News

The news spillover effects are investigated in the overnight holding period which contains the respective foreign news releases from the previous day (see Fig. 1). The results of our estimations are reported in Panel B of Table 2.

We find that an unexpected increase in the Fed funds target rate has a consistently significant and negative impact on the German bank stock returns (Panel B2). Although the literature reports an inverse relationship between unexpected Fed funds changes and the broad German equity market (Bohl et al., 2008), our study confirms that these results are even stronger when examining the impact on the banking sector alone.

In terms of the spillover impact of Fed news on the volatility of the German banks, we find somewhat mixed results. A volatility reduction is noticeable in two cases and the opposite is observed in the other three cases. In general, the German stock market as a whole (DAX) show a volatility reduction in relation to Fed news. We conjecture that the mixed results may arise because of the long period spanning the announcement of Fed news and the opening of the German stock market. As can be seen from Fig. 1, there is a time span of 13 hours between the release of Fed news and the opening of the German stock market. During this period, market participants in Germany would have more time to develop opinions on the impact of Fed news on German bank stocks, and by the time the stock market opens, the diversity of opinions would be vast, hence our results show evidence of both market calming and volatility increasing effects following the arrival of Fed news.

As for ECB news' spillover impact on U.S. Banks (reported in Panel B1), we find that the price impact of ECB news is weak and inconsistent across the three groups of banks. Only two out of 5 U.S. banks show a significant response. Moreover the two banks that responded to ECB news show opposite responses (unexpected ECB rate hike increased Bank of America and lowered Citigroup). There is no visible response from the non-U.S. American banks and this might be due to their limited exposure to Eurozone markets. In addition, the European banks also show lacklustre responses – only Barclays and USB showing significant (and opposite) responses. The general indifference to ECB news is not unusual as the literature also finds inconclusive results for the impact of ECB news on aggregate U.S. stock index returns. Funke and Matsuda (2002) find that German interest rates do not impact significantly on the U.S. stock market, while Ehrmann et al. (2010) find an inverse relationship between the short term interest rate in the Euro area and aggregate U.S. equity prices. For our sample period, we find a positive and significant effect of ECB news on the S&P 500 index returns. We conjecture that these mixed results might arise because market participants in the U.S. have different opinions on how changes in the ECB's main refinancing rate impact on U.S. stock market performance depending on the industry concerned.

On the other hand we find that in 11 out of 14 cases, the volatility impact is positive and significant. This further implies that U.S. market participants are less clear about the potential impact of ECB news and this is translated in higher U.S. bank stock volatilities.

In sum, we observe that the U.S. listed banks responded in a uniform fashion to Fed news whereby an unexpected rate hike (cut) led to a significant price drop and volatility increase. On the other had their responses to the overnight ECB news were bank specific in terms of price response. The responses may be dependent on the extent to which their cross border activities include the Eurozone. For instance, the non-U.S. American banks do not respond to ECB news, whereas the U.S. and European multinational banks show mixed responses. The latter would have more exposure to Eurozone markets. However, we report a consistent volatility response to ECB news in all cases.

The German listed banks show consistently negative mean responses to Fed news as per the U.S. listed banks, however, the volatility responses are a mixture of both positive and negative responses suggesting that bank specific characteristics tend to be more important in determining volatility responses. The mean responses to ECB news are generally positive for the banks that show significant responses (BEB and IKB) and the volatility responses are negative for the ones that are significant. This is opposite to what we observed for their responses to Fed news. That is, the participants in the German stock market viewed the Fed and ECB news conveying different messages to the German market.

EMPIRICAL RESULTS: SUBSAMPLE ANALYSES

There is much evidence that stock markets react differently to macroeconomic news under different economic climates. An unexpected rise in economic activities might be considered good news during recessions but might be regarded as potentially inflationary during boom periods. Similarly, an unexpected policy interest rate change may have different market implications during various business conditions. Furthermore, the literature finds that stock returns are generally more sensitive to monetary policy news in times of recession (Basistha & Kurov, 2008), and when an expansionary monetary policy regime is in place (Conover et al., 1999). As such, we model the potential for differential market responses to policy interest rate news on commercial bank stock returns and volatilities conditioned on the states of the economy.

Business Cycle Estimations

We use the business cycle classification of the National Bureau for Economic Research (NBER) to investigate the differential impact of domestic and international monetary policy news on bank stocks in good versus bad economic times.[19,20]

Contemporaneous Own Market News over the Business Cycle
The business cycle estimations for Fed news on U.S. listed banks are presented in Panel A1 of Table 3. We find that U.S. listed bank stock returns have a consistently negative response to own market interest rate news in both good and bad times. However, the magnitude of the response is greater, in general, in bad economic times. This is consistent with Basistha and Kurov (2008) and Chen (2007) who also find that U.S. bank returns are generally more sensitive to interest rate news in bad times, and this supports the credit channel of monetary policy transmission. An alternative explanation is that banks may be less capable of capitalising on growth opportunities in bad times (Fraser et al., 2002). From the volatility equation, we observe that Fed news causes U.S. bank stocks to become more volatile in bad times, whereas there is less profound impact on volatility in good times. We conjecture that this is because in bad times, market participants are wary of the arrival of any news for trading guidance, whether good or bad due to uncertain and volatile market conditions.

The German bank stocks responses to ECB news are summarized in Panel A2 of Table 3. We find that for the banks that show significant responses in Table 2 (whole sample) their responses were entirely coming from the boom period. This may result from the Euro area having a different economic cycle to the US and world economy at large.

International News Spillover Effects over the Business Cycle
The international spillover effects under both recession and boom periods are reported in Panel B of Table 3. We find that German bank stocks are more responsive (shown in Panel B2) to Fed news only in good economic times (4 out of 5 banks show significant and negative mean responses) and this helps to understand the reason why Germany was less affected by the subprime crisis than the United States. Although Germany was severely affected by the subprime crisis, the extent to which German banks needed explicit assistance from the government was minimal compared to the U.S. – only €130 million (USD$200 million) was injected into the German banking system, compared with the USD$700 million that was injected into the U.S. banking system.[21]

Similarly, in response to ECB news, the U.S. banks are more responsive under good economic conditions (Panel B1). Hence, we find that the transmission of international monetary policy news is most prominent in good

Table 3. Target Interest Rate News during Recession and Booms in the Business Cycle.

Panel A: Contemporaneous Own Market News Effects

A1. Fednews effects on U.S. listed Banks

U.S. Banks	**BAC**	**CIT**	**JPM**	**USB**	**WFC**	**SP500**
αNews: Boom	−1.943***	−2.047***	−3.207***	−1.512***	−1.039**	−1.623***
αNews: Recession	−3.467***	−3.227*	−2.292***	0.937	−2.206*	0.206
Test of equality	2.214	0.449	0.868	3.988**	0.759	4.080
βNews: Boom	−0.229	−0.022	0.256*	−0.334	0.015	−0.266
βNews: Recesssion	0.458**	0.469*	0.260	0.467***	0.182	0.314
Test of equality	5.748**	2.553	0.000	7.490***	0.332	0.339

Non-U.S. American Banks	**BBV**	**RBC**	**BST**	**TRD**
αNews: Boom	−1.680***	−1.795***	−1.768***	−1.925***
αNews: Recesssion	−1.989*	−2.275***	−0.709	−1.636**
Test of equality	0.061	0.236	0.750	0.099
βNews: Boom	0.134	0.176	−0.259**	−0.149
βNews: Recesssion	0.452**	0.677**	0.481**	0.391
Test of equality	1.534	2.239	8.907***	2.389

European banks	**BCS**	**CRS**	**DTB**	**HBC**	**UBS**
αNews: Boom	−0.840**	−0.110	−1.098	−1.432***	−0.988**
αNews: Recesssion	−2.488**	−1.557*	−0.272	−2.672***	−2.910***
Test of equality	2.519	1.673	0.304	2.714*	3.176*
βNews: Boom	−0.104	−0.897**	−0.172	−0.249	−0.599***
βNews: Recesssion	0.481**	0.583***	0.310	0.371**	0.288
Test of equality	5.114**	10.765***	1.086	7.164***	10.287***

A2. ECB news Effects on Germany listed banks

German banks	**BEB**	**DBK**	**CBK**	**CRI**	**IKB**	**DAX**
αNews: Boom	3.235***	3.064	−3.763	0.224	5.700***	0.821
αNews: Recesssion	0.387	-0.991	−1.725	−2.301	1.594	0.649
Test of equality	0.476	0.699	0.172	0.373	0.767	0.003
βNews: Boom	−8.696***	−2.347*	−4.166***	−0.977	−0.830	−1.330
βNews: Recesssion	−0.139	1.142	0.236	0.519	0.345	1.037
Test of equality	28.036***	3.326*	9.049***	1.674	0.885	3.254*

Panel B: International Spillover News Effects

B1. ECB news effects on U.S. listed banks

U.S. Banks	**BAC**	**CIT**	**JPM**	**USB**	**WFC**	**SP500**
αNews: Boom	1.731***	−1.903	−0.175	14.991***	0.773	−0.045
αNews: Recesssion	3.431	−2.310	1.167	1.603**	−3.208	−0.787***

Table 3. *(Continued)*

Panel B: International Spillover News Effects

B1. ECB news effects on U.S. listed banks

U.S. Banks	**BAC**	**CIT**	**JPM**	**USB**	**WFC**	**SP500**
Test of equality	0.519	0.015	0.130	272.186***	3.280*	2.814*
βNews: Boom	−7.402***	7.392***	10.220***	−11.447***	−10.828***	5.320***
βNews: Recession	0.771***	−0.488**	1.453***	4.872***	6.979***	3.112***
Test of equality	20980.9***	1124.16***	545.958***	126.015***	569.540***	21.890***

Non-U.S. American Banks	**BBV**	**RBC**	**BST**	**TRD**
αNews: Boom	−2.781*	1.276	0.314	−0.820
αNews: Recesssion	−2.054	−0.373	1.689	−0.167
Test of equality	0.044	0.115	0.200	0.149
βNews: Boom	−0.292	79.893***	−1.263	1.338
βNews: Recesssion	2.362***	11.391***	2.919	0.129
Test of Equality	8.660***	946.684***	2.536	0.136

European Banks	**BCS**	**CRS**	**DTB**	**HBC**	**UBS**
αNews: Boom	−72.806***	2.057	0.083	−2.830	0.239
αNews: Recesssion	5.320	−6.100	−7.724	−2.666***	5.073
Test of Equality	170.494***	0.526	0.489	0.006	0.084
βNews: Boom	9.235***	−2.967*	−2.273	−1.002	2.304***
βNews: Recesssion	4.713**	4.727***	3.971***	0.361	7.918***
Test of equality	5.593**	14.477***	14.506***	1.968	2079***

B2. Fed news on Germany listed banks

German banks	**BEB**	**DBK**	**CBK**	**CRI**	**IKB**	**DAX**
αNews: Boom	−2.948***	−0.707**	−0.733***	−0.657	−0.199***	−0.030
αNews: Recesssion	0.038	−0.201	−0.101	0.224	0.230	0.259
Test of Equality	25.038***	0.278	0.596	0.517	0.244	0.724
βNews: Boom	1.832***	0.431**	−0.582***	0.080	−0.541***	−1.658***
βNews: Recesssion	−0.397	0.527	−0.067	−1.146***	0.804***	0.531**
Test of Equality	41.239***	0.060	4.083**	16.366***	70.238***	16.432***

This table presents the estimated interest rate news effects on bank returns and volatilities over recession and boom periods in the business cycle. Panel A contains domestic interest rate news effects while Panel B reports the international spillover effects. ***, **, * denotes statistical significance at the 1%, 5%, and 10% levels respectively.

economic times for the global economy, whereas in bad economic times, the actions of the two main central banks in the global financial system have little impact on the stock return of foreign banks. This relates to the asymmetric news impact of monetary policy decisions as it is consistent with interest rate hikes (used to curb inflation) being more significant than cuts on banks' funding costs in international financial markets.

In regards to the volatility responses, we find that the volatility impact of Fed news on German markets is less clear with a mixture of both volatility raising and reducing influences being found (Panel B2). We interpret this to mean that there are heterogeneous interpretations of Fed news impacts on German bank stocks. ECB news imparts the same informational spillover effects on U.S. bank stock return volatility, which is a mixed impact in good times but a significant volatility increasing effect in bad times. We conjecture that these responses arise because U.S. market participants are unsure of what a change in the ECB target rate would imply for their domestic banks, hence the arrival of news causes an increase in the level of market heterogeneity in volatile (bad) times, and a mixed effect in stable times. The differential volatility impact between good and bad times is statistically significant in most cases.

Subprime Analysis

In light of the dramatic economic and financial market impacts of the GFC on the world economy, we explore whether monetary policy actions and their impact on commercial banks is statistically different for the period prior to and during the subprime crisis. We conservatively take June 30, 2007 as the date to separate our sample into the pre-subprime and subprime period. The pre-subprime period is dominated by mostly stable market condition, while the subprime period corresponds closely with the most recent recession period as defined by the NBER. Hence, we expect our subprime crisis results to be largely in line with our business cycle results, in which we find a statistically different impact of monetary policy news on bank stocks in good and bad times.

Contemporaneous Own Market News Effects during the Subprime Crisis

The impacts of own market monetary policy news on commercial bank stock returns and volatilities are summarized in Panel A of Table 4. The results of the subprime analysis are largely similar to the business cycle results as we find that all three groups of the U.S. listed banks are more

Table 4. Fed and ECB Interest Rate News Effects Pre-and during the Subprime Crisis.

Panel A: Contemporaneous Own Market News Effects

A1. Fed news effects on U.S. listed Banks

U.S. Banks	**BAC**	**CIT**	**JPM**	**USB**	**WFC**	**SP500**
αNews: Pre-subprime	−1.967***	−2.153***	−2.943***	−0.732	−1.064**	−1.652***
αNews: Post-subprime	−4.102***	−3.613**	−4.250**	−0.220	−2.948*	0.432
Test of equality	4.262**	0.659	0.921	0.212	1.785	4.952**
βNews: Pre-subprime	−0.206	−0.119	0.110	0.028	−0.055	0.362***
βNews: Post-subprime	0.548**	0.747***	0.695***	0.184	0.357	0.529***
Test of equality	6.463**	7.842***	5.852**	0.235	1.862	13.387***

Non-U.S. American Banks	**BBV**	**RBC**	**BST**	**TRD**
αNews: Pre-subprime	−1.771***	−1.212***	−1.491**	−1.930***
αNews: Post-subprime	−1.588	−7.545***	−2.070**	−2.063**
Test of equality	0.023	17.732***	0.246	0.016
βNews: Pre-subprime	0.103	−0.051	−0.177	−0.220
βNews: Post-subprime	0.542***	1.232***	0.518***	0.646***
Test of equality	2.829	13.486***	7.999***	6.164**

European banks	**BCS**	**CRS**	**DTB**	**HBC**	**UBS**
αNews: Pre-subprime	−1.026***	0.126	−0.121	−1.708***	−1.097***
αNews: Post-subprime	−2.377*	−2.330**	−1.698	−1.416*	−2.602**
Test of equality	1.070	4.503**	1.141	0.124	1.650
βNews: Pre-subprime	0.037	−0.868***	−0.713*	−0.147	−0.745***
βNews: Post-subprime	0.420*	0.708**	0.401*	0.388**	0.804***
Test of equality	2.072	15.207***	4.697**	6.564**	34.564***

A2. ECB news effects on Germany listed banks

German banks	**BEB**	**DBK**	**CBK**	**CRI**	**IKB**	**DAX**
αNews: Pre-subprime	3.024	0.904	−2.349	−0.710	2.809***	0.704
αNews: Post-subprime	4.537*	2.178	0.526	−0.927	2.358	0.576
Test of equality	0.246	0.013	0.060	0.000	0.001	0.001
βNews: Pre-subprime	−2.316***	−1.006	−3.177***	−0.562	−3.540***	−0.723
βNews: Post-subprime	−7.457***	2.611	3.963**	1.688	8.956***	2.209**
Test of equality	6.410**	2.941*	16.421***	2.461	73.212***	5.024**

Panel B: International Spillover News Effects

B1. ECB news effects on U.S. listed banks

U.S. Banks	**BAC**	**CIT**	**JPM**	**USB**	**WFC**	**SP500**
αNews: Pre-subprime	1.059*	−1.261	−1.207	−0.060***	−2.034***	−0.102***
αNews: Post-subprime	−3.565	8.742	3.454	−0.414	8.278	−0.957

Table 4. (*Continued*)

Panel B: International Spillover News Effects

B1. ECB news effects on U.S. listed banks

U.S. Banks	**BAC**	**CIT**	**JPM**	**USB**	**WFC**	**SP500**
Test of equality	0.482	1.652	0.446	0.002	4.093**	0.949
βNews: Pre-subprime	0.209	−0.633***	8.700***	4.303***	−3.216***	2.757***
βNews: Post-subprime	7.289***	3.705***	5.519***	0.021	9.378***	−1.672***
Test of equality	34.4***	147.6697***	16.525***	31.750***	238.934***	2269.666***
Non-U.S. American banks	**BBV**	**RBC**	**BST**	**TRD**		
αNews: Pre-subprime	−2.030	1.642	0.820	−0.372		
αNews: Post-subprime	−4.146	1.268	−0.246	−9.894***		
Test of equality	0.076	0.007	0.045	16.109***		
βNews: Pre-subprime	0.450	74.291***	−2.979**	0.350		
βNews: Post-subprime	3.924***	25.443***	9.981***	3.711		
Test of equality	11.404***	264.160***	17.262***	0.338		
European banks	**BCS**	**CRS**	**DTB**	**HBC**	**UBS**	
αNews: Pre-subprime	−69.557***	1.606	−0.307	−3.159	15.800***	
αNews: Post-subprime	2.375	−3.622	−3.076	−1.211***	1.750**	
Test of equality	58.071***	0.257	0.056	1.001	285.297***	
βNews: Pre-subprime	11.083***	−2.765*	−2.503*	−0.579	−12.087***	
βNews: Post-subprime	7.149***	4.522***	4.100***	1.933**	4.733	
Test of equality	2.491	13.086***	15.903***	5.405**	26***	

A2. Fed News On Germany listed banks

German banks	**BEB**	**DBK**	**CBK**	**CRI**	**IKB**	**DAX**
αNews: Pre-subprime	−2.799***	−0.557**	−0.564***	−0.435	−0.100	−0.033***
αNews: Post-subprime	−0.012	−2.459***	−3.410***	0.149	3.492	0.239
Test of equality	20.626***	5.374**	15.952***	0.612	1.678	0.373
βNews: Pre-subprime	1.691***	0.183	−0.754***	−0.233	−0.490**	−2.063***
βNews: Post-subprime	−0.389	1.390***	0.652***	−0.562***	1.624	1.358***
Test of equality	32.357***	13.975***	29.893***	1.609	3.645*	36.499***

This table presents the estimated interest rate news effects on bank returns and volatilities over subsample periods before and during the Subprime crisis. Panel A contains domestic interest rate news effects while Panel B reports the international spillover effects. ***, **, * denotes statistical significance at the 1%, 5%, and 10% levels respectively.

sensitive to Fed news in the period after the breakout of the subprime crisis (bad economic times) than in the period prior to the subprime crisis (good economic times). However, there are no significant differences in the response of German listed bank stock returns to ECB news before and during the subprime crisis (Panel A2).

The volatility impact of Fed news on U.S. bank stocks show that Fed news has a greater impact on stock return volatilities in bad times than in good times, and this impact is exhibited as a market calming effect in good times, and a volatility increasing effect in bad times (Panel A1). We conjecture that the generally insignificant impact of news on the return volatilities in good times is because market participants understand the impact of Fed news on bank stock prices and this is reflected immediately as a change in the stock prices. However, in bad times when markets are more volatile, market participants are more wary of the implications of interest rate changes, and hence Fed news leads to a significant increase in market volatility in the subprime crisis period.

German banks have a similar response to domestic news from the ECB, that is, there is a market calming effect for the period prior to the subprime crisis, and a heightened volatility increasing effect for the period after the subprime crisis (Panel A2). This unambiguous result suggests that in the subprime crisis period, international monetary policy makers need to factor in increased market sensitivity when using domestic monetary policy as a recovery tool in order to avoid unintended destabilizing effects (however, short term).

International Spillover News Effects during the Subprime Crisis
International spillover effects before and during the subprime crisis are presented in Panel B of Table 4. The international news spillover results are similar to the business cycle estimations in which we find that German bank stocks react more to Fed news in the period prior to the subprime, that is, in *good* economic times, and that U.S. listed bank stocks generally do not respond to ECB news. Hence, our subprime results further support the findings from the business cycle analyses that monetary policy impact is felt by foreign banks mostly during good global economic conditions when the concern is more on unexpected interest rate hikes. This suggests that banks' funding costs are a key monetary transmission channel internationally. Moreover, despite shared downturns during the GFC, European and American banking industries have actually become more segmented in their pricing of monetary policy news in the post-GFC era. The respective

markets have become more sensitive to local instead of common global monetary influences.

The impact of foreign monetary policy news on the return volatilities of banks also largely concurs with the impacts found in the business cycle analyses. For both U.S. listed and German banks we find that foreign monetary policy news exerts a mixed influence on volatility in the pre-subprime period (good times), but then reverts to a volatility increasing effect for the subprime crisis period (bad times). Hence, monetary policy spillover effects have induced greater uncertainty into bank operations in both economies echoing heightened market sensitivity to monetary policy news worldwide.

Monetary Regime Estimation Results

We also test whether news effects depend on monetary policy regimes at the time, defined as loose (interest rate cutting) or tight (interest rate hiking) policy stance. The literature reports that stock prices in the United States are generally higher under a loose monetary stance and hence, in line with the existing literature, we would expect to find our commercial banks to exhibit asymmetric responses to different monetary policy stances. We summarize our results on this briefly.

The impact of domestic monetary policy news during both tight and loose policy periods is first explored and displayed in Panel A of Table 5. The most striking finding is that U.S. listed bank stocks display significant asymmetries over the monetary policy cycle. (Panel A1). Specifically, we reveal that U.S. listed bank stock returns fall to a greater extent during monetary tightening than loosening phases and this difference is statistically significant. This result quadrates with the established inverse relationship between interest rate surprises and bank stock returns. Furthermore, we find that volatility is higher during tightening phases but lower during loosening phases in response to Fed news. Our results for the responses of German banks to domestic ECB interest rate news (Panel A2) reveal less asymmetry than for the U.S. listed stocks.

The international effects of monetary policy news can be seen in Panel B of Table 5. We show that there are opposing spillover effects from the FED and ECB. In most instances, Fed news has a market calming effect for German banks under a tightening phase while a volatility increasing effect is displayed under a loose monetary environment (Panel B2). In contrast, ECB news has the opposite effect on the U.S. listed bank stock volatilities under different monetary policy stances (Panel B1). This difference in

Table 5. Fed and ECB Interest Rate News over Monetary Policy Regimes.

Panel A: Contemporaneous Own Market News Effects

A1. Fed news effects on U.S. listed Banks

U.S. Banks	**BAC**	**CIT**	**JPM**	**USB**	**WFC**	**SP500**
αNews: Loose	−1.199*	−0.165	0.937	0.311	−0.400	1.112
αNews: Tight	−2.679***	−2.907***	−4.302***	−0.929	−1.485***	−1.603***
Test of equality	3.346*	8.889***	21.776***	0.771	0.718	8.518***
βNews: Loose	−0.409	−0.964	−0.671	−0.262	−0.046	−0.745
βNews: Tight	0.127	0.090	−0.017	0.012	0.099	0.061
Test of equality	0.617	2.179	2.066	0.288	0.073	2.045

Non-U.S. American Banks	**BBV**	**RBC**	**BST**	**TRD**
αNews: Loose	0.106	−0.939	1.011	−0.933
αNews: Tight	−2.072***	−2.242***	−2.064***	−1.901***
Test of equality	1.838	1.200	5.492**	0.815
βNews: Loose	−0.011	−0.415	−0.523	−1.264*
βNews: Tight	0.377***	0.461***	0.179	0.069
Test of equality	0.406	1.813	2.360	2.991*

European banks	**BCS**	**CRS**	**DTB**	**HBC**	**UBS**
αNews: Loose	−0.008	−0.537	1.452	−0.824	0.535
αNews: Tight	−1.428***	−1.046	−1.956*	−1.918***	−1.188***
Test of equality	1.499	0.195	4.338**	2.773*	2.508
βNews: Loose	0.103	−0.317	−0.339	−0.438	−0.554
βNews: Tight	0.160	1.551***	0.144	−0.021	−0.064
Test of equality	0.017	4.649**	0.209	0.568	0.228

A2. ECB news effects on German listed banks

German banks	**BEB**	**DBK**	**CBK**	**CRI**	**IKB**	**DAX**
αNews: Loose	1.269	1.734	−1.900	−0.951	1.756	0.424
αNews: Tight	8.622**	0.256	−4.004	−0.598	6.906***	1.665
Test of equality	3.638*	0.106	0.139	0.006	5.901**	0.152
βNews: Loose	−4.479***	−0.216	−1.347	−0.509	−0.466	0.474
βNews: Tight	−0.048	0.140	−1.398	0.802	−0.309	−0.425
Test of equality	11.144***	0.036	0.001	1.172	0.014	0.468

Panel B: International Spillover News Effects

B1. ECB news Effects on U.S. Listed Banks

U.S. Banks	**BAC**	**CTT**	**JPM**	**USB**	**WFC**	**SP500**
αNews: Loose	−1.401	−2.676	−2.061	−1.823	−4.253**	0.081
αNews: Tight	4.436***	1.767	1.814	6.051	0.644	−0.178

Table 5. *(Continued)*

Panel B: International Spillover News Effects

B1. ECB news Effects on U.S. Listed Banks

U.S. Banks	**BAC**	**CTT**	**JPM**	**USB**	**WFC**	**SP500**
Test of equality	4.511**	3.991**	0.578	1.067	5.617**	3.876**
βNews: Loose	0.040	1.998***	10.119***	3.149**	6.496***	−5.020***
βNews: Tight	0.756***	0.549***	2.196***	39.678***	1.219***	1.325***
Test of equality	86.6***	566.46***	522.382***	614.438***	91.278***	2152.033***
Non-U.S. American banks	**BBV**	**RBC**	**BST**	**TRD**		
αNews: Loose	−5.460***	3.476	−2.332***	0.544		
αNews: Tight	0.587	-0.666	3.827	1.074		
Test of equality	4.860**	0.196	6.118**	0.130		
βNews: Loose	−0.861	90.766***	−14.499***	1.432		
βNews: Tight	1.930***	8.244***	5.179***	−2.044**		
Test of equality	8.877**	121.645***	75.524**	1.228		
European banks	**BCS**	**CRS**	**DTB**	**HBC**	**UBS**	
αNews: Loose	−0.098	−0.440	−1.932	−3.392***	−4.803***	
αNews: Tight	−155.322***	2.446	2.151	−1.962	8.116***	
Test of equality	694.420***	0.192	0.453	0.296	18.009***	
βNews: Loose	−8.696***	−7.484***	−3.083	−1.682	4.321***	
βNews: Tight	21.875***	5.119***	3.625***	0.466	6.390***	
Test of equality	203.701***	29.013***	9.711***	3.724*	245***	

B2. Fed news on Germany listed banks

German banks	**BEB**	**DBK**	**CBK**	**CRI**	**IKB**	**DAX**
αNews: Loose	0.097	−0.705	−0.555	−0.371	0.009	−0.006***
αNews: Tight	9.816***	−0.255	−0.552	0.740	−0.871***	0.015
Test of equality	523.905***	0.475	8.810	2.288	4.813	0.041
βNews: Loose	0.635***	0.705***	−0.164	−0.243*	0.694***	−0.183
βNews: Tight	4.717***	−1.274***	−1.431***	−0.697***	−1.018***	−1.939***
Test of equality	351.662***	16.908***	19.726***	2.914*	114.292***	9.664***

This table presents the estimated interest rate news effects on bank returns and volatilities over subsample periods of monetary policy tightening and easing. Panel A contains domestic interest rate news effects while Panel B reports the international spillover effects. ***, **, * denotes statistical significance at the 1%, 5%, and 10% levels respectively.

volatility is statistically significant in nearly all cases. This suggests that inflationary concerns in the U.S. are of a major concern for trading in German bank stocks whereas the U.S. listed bank stocks are affected more by weakening economic conditions in Europe.

CONCLUSION

This chapter provides new evidence on the domestic and international transmission of monetary policy news on U.S. listed and German listed bank stock prices and their volatilities. First, we find that in general, U.S. Fed interest rate news has the greater impact in both countries. A negative relationship between target rate news and stock price movements is revealed in all cases. On the other hand, ECB news generally increases bank stock volatility in the U.S. but has little impact within its own domestic banking industry.

Second, we find that over the global business cycle, U.S. listed bank stocks are more sensitive to news in bad economic times, whereas the German banks respond more in *good* economic times.

Third, we find evidence of a significant asymmetric effect in our monetary regime estimations. The results for the U.S. are consistent with the literature, in which we find that stocks are more responsive to a domestic tightening monetary policy stance but ECB monetary policy shocks have much less asymmetric effects on German bank stocks.

Fourth, the results of our detailed analyses over both intraday and overnight horizons help to explain how German banks have managed to remain relatively less affected by the GFC than the U.S. economy. This comes from our findings that German bank returns are more responsive to U.S. monetary policy in good economic times and in general, have opposing asymmetric reactions to monetary policy. Put together, we reveal that German and U.S. banking industries largely decoupled from each other via the international monetary policy transmission channel during the GFC.

There are important implications of our findings for policy makers, bank managers and investors alike. With a deeper understanding of the impact of their monetary policy decisions on banks at home and abroad policy makers will be able to tailor their monetary policy decisions to impact the financial system in the direction and magnitude they desire. More importantly, if policy makers are able to improve the transparency of their monetary policy decisions so that target rate announcements do not surprise market participants unnecessarily then potential financial instabilities can be minimised. Given the highly interest rate sensitive nature of banks in the international financial system, a greater understanding of the impacts of domestic and international monetary policy news on bank stock prices will aid bank managers in developing more effective hedging strategies to minimise the adverse impacts of monetary policy shocks on their balance sheets, or even benefit from surprise monetary movements. On the other hand, investors, with a better understanding of bank stock price reactions to domestic and foreign monetary policy news, may be able to improve their trading strategies, risk management practices and also portfolio composition. In addition, we contribute to the academic research community in terms of providing empirical evidence of international transmission mechanisms of business cycles and monetary policy shocks.

NOTES

1. Cyclical industries are those that are more sensitive to general business conditions such producers of nondurable consumption goods.

2. However, by 2012 Asia Pacific banks (mostly Chinese banks) have replaced the North American banks as the second most important group in terms of global share of assets with their global asset share of 33.5% compared to 45% of the Western European banks (The Banker, 2012).

3. Prior to 2002, the Governing Council met twice a month.

4. These data are available at http://federalreserve.gov/monetarypolicy/fomccalendars.htm for the Fed and http://www.ecb.int/stats/monetary/rates/html/index.en.html for the ECB.

5. The full sample period for each country begins at different dates (January 1, 1995 for the US and February 18, 1999 for Germany), and they both end at June 30, 2009.

6. There is one further exception that applies for the date of 15 October, 1998. Typically, the Fed makes their target rate announcements at 2:15 pm EST and trading in Fed funds futures contracts ends at 3:00 pm EST. Therefore, the closing futures price on the day of the announcement used in equation (1) would have incorporated the news of the Fed's decision. However, on 15 October, 1998, the Fed surprised the markets by announcing an interest rate change at 3:15 pm EST, after the futures market had closed. Therefore, in this case, a better measure of the unexpected change in interest rates involves taking the difference between the closing futures rate on 16 October, 1998 less the closing futures rate on October 15, 1998.

7. Although there are only 54 and 31 announcements of target rate changes for the Fed and the ECB, respectively, the number of unexpected rate changes are much larger. This is because the latter includes those no change announcements when a change was expected by financial market participants.

8. The sample period captures the period of aggressive post GFC monetary easing by the two central banks which includes many newsworthy announcements such as bigger than expected rate cuts from the Fed (75 basis point cuts on January 22, March 18, and December 16, 2008). The last in the series of large (50 basis points+) cuts from the Fed was on 16 Dec 2008 and the ECB's last rate cut was of 25 basis points on 5 May 2009. Since then the Fed has only one rate change (25 basis point increase on 19 Feb 2010) and the ECB had five but the rate has stayed around 1% range with mostly predictable changes announced. Extending the sample to include these additional announcements, therefore, would not yield much different results to the analyses we present in the current paper due to the small number of announcements involved (1 in the case of Fed).

9. Despite the U.S. and German bank stock sample periods being different, we do not expect there being a qualitative difference in the results if the U.S. sample is shortened to coincide with that of the German bank stock sample period. This is because the sensitivity of the U.S. and German banks' stock returns to the U.S. monetary policy news over the nonoverlapping years of 1995–1998 is unlikely to be substantially different given that most of the hard work in terms of developing credibility in anchoring (low) inflation was already achieved by the mid 1990s post the Gulf-War related recession.

10. We limited the choice of bank stocks in each country to the ones that are large commercial banks with intradaily price data being available.

11. In our study we look at analysing whether monetary policy announcements have a positive or negative effect on volatility, that is, whether unexpected interest rate decisions increase volatility in markets, or have a volatility calming effect. In the case of an increase in volatility, this would exhibit itself as a positive coefficient on the news term, and there would not be a problem in employing a GARCH model. However, in the case of a volatility calming effect, this would exhibit itself as a negative coefficient on the news term which the EGARCH model is able to capture since the dependent variable is in log form. The dependent variables in the mean equation is also in log forms – $\ln(Y_t/Y_{t-1})$ over various holding periods.

12. The Fed news is release while the German stock market is closed so the Fed news effect can be investigated when the German market is open at day $t+1$. Similarly, the ECB news is released when the U.S. stock market is closed. Therefore, the relevant horizon for investigating international spillover effects are the overnight horizon at day t (close at day $t-1$ to open at day t) for the U.S. market for the investigation of the ECB news, and the overnight horizon at day t for the German market for the investigation of the Fed news.

13. We find that one lag of the dependant variable addresses the residual serial correlation found in our return series in most cases. For the sake of consistency, we employ the use of one lag for all of our models.

14. The exchange rate data are obtained from Datastream.

15. Choi et al. (1992) are the first to examine the joint interaction of interest rates and exchange rates on bank stock returns and found that exchanges rates are significant in explaining bank stock returns, although the significance and sign for the exchange rate may differ depending on the time period estimated, the nature of the bank under consideration, and whether risk factors are measured in aggregate or decomposed into the expected and unexpected components.

16. We also tried collecting data for the financial indexes and banking indexes in each region, but this was not possible due to data availability. Hence, we compensate for this by forming our own portfolio (*PORT*), which is a market capitalisation weighted average of the returns of each of our stocks, calculated separately for each region and holding period.

17. For German bank estimations, we include a U.S. and Euro area macroeconomic announcement dummy in the variance equation as a contemporaneous term since these announcements are made during the trading hours of the DAX, as can be seen in Fig. 1. For the U.S. bank estimations, we do not include a dummy for U.S. macroeconomic announcements because the U.S. releases most of their macroeconomic announcements at 8:30 am EST, before the NYSE opens for trading at 9:30 am EST as can be seen in Fig. 1. The U.S. macroeconomic announcements we include for the United States are GDP, CPI, unemployment, trade deficit, and retail trade. The macroeconomic announcements we include for the euro area are GDP, CPI, employment, unemployment, external trade, current account and retail trade.

18. Interested readers may obtain full estimation results of the baseline model and full model specifications with various news terms upon request from the corresponding author.

19. The boom periods in our sample include the periods January 1, 1995 to Feburary 28, 2001 and November 1, 2001 to November 31, 2001. The recessions are for the periods March 1, 2001 to October 31, 2001 and December 1, 2007 to June 30, 2009 (end of our sample period).

20. There are potential shortfalls in using the NBER classifications. First, the variability of the business cycles may be small and that may have an impact on the investigation results. Second, the pre- and post-GFC subsample results that are similar to those of the NBER business cycle estimations might be attributable to the NBER classifications closely matching the crisis/noncrisis breakdowns. We are grateful for an anonymous referee for pointing these issues out.

21. *Source*: Bank of England, Financial Stability Report 24, October 27, 2008.

ACKNOWLEDGMENT

We greatly appreciate the insightful comments and suggestions from an anonymous referee and helpful suggestions made by the editors.

REFERENCES

Akella, S. R., & Greenbaum, S. R. (1992). Innovations in interest rates, duration transformation, and bank stock returns. *Journal of Money, Credit, and Banking*, *24*, 27–42.

Ammer, J., Vega, C., & Wongswan, J. (2010). International transmission of U.S. monetary policy shocks: Evidence from stock prices. *Journal of Money, Credit and Banking*, *42*, 179–198.

Basistha, A., & Kurov, A. (2008). Macroeconomic cycles and the stock market's reaction to monetary policy. *Journal of Banking and Finance*, *32*, 2606–2616.

Bernanke, B. S., & Blinder, A. S. (1992). The federal funds rate and the channels of monetary transmission. *American Economic Review*, *82*, 901–921.

Bernanke, B. S., & Kuttner, K. N. (2005). What explains the stock market's reaction to federal reserve policy? *Journal of Finance*, *60*, 1221–1257.

Bernoth, K., & Von Hagen, J. (2004). Euribor futures market: Efficiency and the impact of ECB policy announcements. *International Finance*, *7*, 1–24.

Bohl, M. T., Siklos, P. L., & Sondermann, D. (2008). European stock markets and the ECB's monetary policy surprises. *International Finance*, *11*, 117–130.

Chen, S. (2007). Does monetary policy have asymmetric effects on stock returns? *Journal of Money, Credit and Banking*, *39*, 667–688.

Conover, C. M., Jensen, R. G., & Johnson, R. (1999). Monetary environments and international stock returns. *Journal of Banking and Finance*, *23*, 1357–1381.

Ehrmann, M., & Fratzscher, M. (2004). Taking stock: Monetary policy transmission to equity markets. *Journal of Money, Credit, and Banking*, *36*, 719–737.

Ehrmann, M., Fratzscher, M., & Rigobon, R. (2010). Stocks, bonds, money markets and exchange rates: Measuring international financial transmission. *Journal of Applied Econometrics*, *26*(6), 948–974.

Elyasiani, E., & Mansur, I. (1998). Sensitivity of the bank stock returns distribution to changes in the level and volatility of interest rate: A GARCH-M model. *Journal of Banking and Finance*, *22*, 535–563.

Flannery, M. J., & James, C. M. (1984). The effect of interest rate changes on the common stock returns of financial institutions. *The Journal of Finance*, *39*(4), 1141–1153.

Fraser, D. R., Madura, J., & Weigand, R. A. (2002). Sources of bank interest rate risk. *The Financial Review*, *37*, 351–368.

Fuertes, A.-M., Heffernan, S., & Kalotychou, E. (2010). How do UK banks react to changing central bank rates? *Journal of Financial Services Research*, *37*(2), 99–130.

Funke, N., & Matsuda, A. (2002). *Macroeconomic news and stock returns in the United States and Germany*. International Monetary Fund Working Paper Series No. 239. Retrieved from http://www.imf.org/external/pubs/ft/wp/2002/wp02239.pdf

Gaspar, V., Perez-Quiros, G., & Sicilia, J. (2001). The ECB monetary policy strategy and the money market. *International Journal of Finance & Economics*, *6*, 325–342.

Jensen, G. R., & Johnson, R. R. (1995). Discount rate changes and security returns in the U.S., 1962–1991. *Journal of Banking and Finance*, *19*, 79–95.

Jensen, G. R., Mercer, J. M., & Johnson, R. R. (1996). Business conditions, monetary policy, and expected security returns. *Journal of Financial Economics*, *40*, 213–237.

Kashyap, A. K., Stein, J. C., & Wilcox, D. W. (1993). Monetary policy and credit conditions: Evidence from the composition of external finance. *American Economic Review*, *83*, 78–98.

Kuttner, K. N. (2001). Monetary policy surprises and interest rates: Evidence from Fed funds futures market. *Journal of Monetary Economics*, *47*, 523–544.

Madura, J., & Schnusenberg, O. (2000). Effect of federal reserve policies on bank equity returns. *The Journal of Financial Research*, *23*(4), 421–447.

Madura, J., & Zarruk, E. R. (1995). Bank exposure to interest rate risk: A global perspective. *The Journal of Financial Research*, *18*(1), 1–13.

Reinhart, V. R., & Simin, T. (1997). The market reaction to federal reserve policy action from 1989-1992. *Journal of Economics and Business*, *49*, 149–169.

Rigobon, R., & Sack, B. P. (2004). The impact of monetary policy on asset prices. *Journal of Monetary Economics*, *51*, 1553–1575.

The Banker. (2012). Top 1000 world banks 2012 – Cover story. *The Banker*, July, pp. 114–130. Retrieved from http://www.thebankerdatabase.com/files/pdf_downloads/Top1000WorldBanksIntroduction.pdf

Thorbecke, W. (1997). On stock market returns and monetary policy. *Journal of Finance*, *52*(2), 635–654.

Wongswan, J. (2009). The response of global equity indices to US monetary policy announcements. *Journal of International Money and Finance*, *28*, 344–365.

Yang, J., & Yin, H. (2009). Bank characteristics and stock reaction to federal funds rate target changes. *FMA Program*, *24*(October).

Yin, H., Yang, J., & Handorf, W. (2010). State dependency of bank stock reaction to federal funds rate target changes. *Journal of Financial Research*, *33*, 289–315.

APPENDIX A: U.S. AND GERMAN BANKING STOCK CODES USED

U.S. Listed Banks		Germany Listed Banks	
U.S. Banks			
BAC	Bank of America	BEB	LB Berlin Holding
CIT	Citigroup Inc.	DBK	Deutsche Bank
USB	U.S. Bankcorp	CRI	Unicredit S.P.A.
WFC	Well Fargo and Co.	IKB	IKB Deutsche Induestrie bank AG
Non-U.S. American Banks			
BBV	Banco Bilao Vizcaya Argentina		
RBC	Royal Bank of Canada		
STD	Banco Santander		
TRD	Toronto Dominion		
European Banks			
BCS	Barclays PLC		
CRS	Credit Suisse		
DTB	Deutsche Bank		
HBC	HSBC Holdings PLC		
UBS	UBS AG		

WHAT ARE THE CHALLENGES AND PROBLEMS FACING CHINA'S OUTWARD PORTFOLIO INVESTMENT? EVIDENCE FROM THE QUALIFIED DOMESTIC INSTITUTIONAL INVESTOR SCHEME

Aidan Yao and Honglin Wang

ABSTRACT

Since their inception in late 2007, the Qualified Domestic Institutional Investor (QDII) funds, which help Chinese investors to invest in foreign capital markets, have experienced significant portfolio losses and persistent fund outflows. While these losses are large in absolute terms, QDII funds, on average, performed better than Chinese A-share funds, but slightly worse than a group of foreign mutual funds. Our study focuses on the QDII industry, and asks three interrelated questions: (1) why have there been large fund outflows from the industry? (2) what explains

Global Banking, Financial Markets and Crises
International Finance Review, Volume 14, 211–242

ISSN: 1569-3767/doi:10.1108/S1569-3767(2013)0000014011

QDII funds' poor performance? and (3) why have QDII funds been so heavily exposed to the Hong Kong market? Our empirical analysis shows that the persistent capital outflows were primarily a result of disappointing fund performance. This poor performance can, in turn, be explained by the deficiency of knowledge required of QDII fund managers to successfully invest in foreign capital markets and manage global portfolios. Finally, our study goes some way to explain the phenomenon of QDII funds' large asset allocation in the Hong Kong market. This 'Hong Kong bias' is shown to be consistent with the well-documented 'home bias' behaviour in cross-border portfolio investment, but is greatly exacerbated by the lack of global investing experience of QDII managers.

Keywords: China economy; capital account liberalisation; outward portfolio investment; QDII

JEL classifications: F21; F34; O53

INTRODUCTION

China has entered an important stage of its structural economic transformation and capital market reform. In recent years, substantial policy progress has been made on improving the flexibility of the exchange rate, aligning the interest rate setting mechanism with market forces, and reducing regulatory controls on the capital account (PBC, 2012). In this study, we look at one of the key developments relating to the liberalisation of China's capital account: the establishment of the Qualified Domestic Institutional Investor (QDII) programme, which helps Chinese capital to be invested in foreign financial markets. In particular, we focus our study on a number of pressing issues currently facing the QDII industry, and ask three important and interrelated questions: (1) why have there been massive capital outflows from the industry? (2) what explains QDII funds' poor performance? and (3) why have QDII funds been so heavily exposed to the Hong Kong market?

Our empirical results show that the large investor withdrawals were primarily driven by the poor performance of QDII funds. While this result seems obvious and is widely discussed in the existing literature, our study is the first to provide empirical support to the relationship. In addition, we find that the magnitude of investors' withdrawals tends to be more sensitive to the absolute return of funds, rather than the relative return over benchmark or risk-adjusted return. This could be consistent with the general perception that Chinese investors tend to focus more on 'return maximisation' for portfolio investment, with insufficient consideration given to benchmark performance and portfolio risk (Shenzhen Stock Exchange, 2012).

Turning to the issue of fund performance, we show that the lack of global investing experience of fund managers and limited research capacity of QDII funds are significant in explaining poor returns. Interestingly, these factors are also important in explaining why most QDII funds have significant exposure to the Hong Kong market. It appears that the deficiency of knowledge about offshore markets has constrained fund managers in pursuing a more globally diversified portfolio, and exacerbated the 'home bias' behaviour in their asset allocation. Furthermore, QDII funds, on average, show a tendency to repatriate funds back to Hong Kong following significant portfolio losses. This is also consistent with the 'home bias' behaviour relating to capital repatriation during times of rising risk aversion. Our analysis however cannot rule out of the possibility that this 'Hong Kong bias' is also influenced by fund managers attempting to add value to the portfolio, using their previous local-market (i.e. A-share market) investing experience.

Finally, we discuss the importance of the QDII industry in a broader context of China's financial market reforms, and the role it can play in enhancing the portfolio performance of Chinese investors. We show that A-share investors could have benefited significantly by allocating part of their risky portfolio in QDII funds in the last few years, achieving both higher returns and lower portfolio volatility. Looking ahead, as restrictions on capital controls are gradually lifted, and investor awareness of global diversification improves, demand for offshore investment should increase substantially, creating a favourable backdrop for the future development of the QDII industry.

Notwithstanding the bright future, the industry is currently facing a number of hurdles both internally (e.g. lack of capable managers, small fund size, and limited resources to support research) and externally (e.g. reduced investor interest, poor market performance, and elevated uncertainty). In this regard, we believe that there are a number of things the authorities can help.

On the demand side, the authorities can help to expand the size of the QDII market by encouraging large state-owned institutions, such as pension funds and sovereign wealth funds, to invest in QDII funds for greater portfolio diversification. In addition, the authorities should continue to improve the financial literacy of the general public, particularly raising investors' awareness of risk management and the importance of international portfolio diversification. This should raise retail-investors' demand for QDII funds. On the supply side, regulators could set higher eligibility standards for QDII managers, in order to improve the overall professional quality of the industry. This improvement should lead to better fund performance and capital inflows into the industry, according to our study. Furthermore, tax incentives could be offered to stimulate the demand for and supply of QDII funds, such as lowering dividend/capital gain taxes for investors, reducing stamp duties for transactions, and cutting levies imposed on fund companies. Finally, the government should continue to push for the exchange rate reform, reducing the negative impact of persistent currency appreciation on QDII performance, and thereby increasing its investment appeal to Chinese investors.

Overall, we think that given the clear policy direction towards greater openness of capital markets, outward portfolio investment from China will likely rise substantially in the coming years (He, Cheung, Zhang, & Wu, 2012). This will create a favourable regulatory backdrop for the QDII industry. But in order to capitalise on this growth, the industry needs to first address its existing problems, and make efforts to regain investor trust. Only when the proper infrastructure is put in place (quality managers, capable research teams, right institutional/regulatory frameworks etc.), can the industry truly excel and fulfil its role in China's financial market liberalisation and economic transformation.

The rest of the chapter is structured as follows. In the second section, we provide a brief background discussion on the evolution of China's capital account liberalisation, and how the QDII scheme fits into this broad context. We present our three key research questions in the third section and discuss the results from our empirical analysis. Finally, we conclude and discuss policy implications in the fourth section.

INSTITUTIONAL BACKGROUND AND CURRENT SITUATION

China has made significant progress in opening up its financial markets over the past two decades. Of the three key components of financial market reforms, progress on exchange rate liberalisation has been most noticeable, with major policy initiatives including: (1) a gradual appreciation of the

RMB, (2) the creation of offshore currency centres, (3) the push to make the RMB a trade settlement currency and (4) the establishment of currency swap facilities with other central banks. On the interest rate market reform, while the People's Bank of China (PBC) remains in control over the setting of short-term lending and deposit rates and the amount of credit banks are allowed to disburse, policy supports have been given to the development of inter-bank funding markets that have increasingly exerted influence on interest rate formation in the economy (He & Wang, 2012).

Regarding capital account liberalisation, China has taken a cautious and gradualist approach, although significant progress has been made over time (Shu, Su, Chang, & Miao, 2008). Within the capital account, a selective opening for direct investment has been underway since the early 1990s, under strict regulatory screening and approval. The extent of control has been gradually lifted over the years, allowing inward foreign direct investment (FDI) to increase substantially over the past two decades. Relative to inbound investment (whose stock exceeded USD$1,400 billion in 2010), the growth for outward FDI (or ODI) has been relatively slow. Recognising the unbalanced nature of the development, Chinese authorities have, in recent years, increased policy support to companies seeking global investment opportunities, and as a result, the stock of ODI has grown rapidly and reached USD$400 billion at the end of 2011 (MoC, 2011).

Relative to direct investment, the pace of liberalisation in the other component of the capital account, the financial account, has lagged behind. Part of this reflects policy makers' concerns about speculative portfolio flows, which can be volatile and difficult to manage (Cheung, Chow, Chang, & Li, 2006). These concerns were reinforced by events, such as the Asian Financial Crisis, where massive capital outflows from a number of South-East Asian countries had exacerbated the effect of the crisis on the financial systems and economies around the region.

Notwithstanding the caution, important steps have been taken to allow for a selective and managed opening of the financial account in recent years. The main policy initiative was the launch of two pilot schemes: Qualified Foreign Institutional Investor (QFII) in 2002 and QDII in 2006. The QFII programme allows licensed foreign investors to buy and sell yuan-denominated financial assets in China. While the industry grew rapidly in the early years, the Global Financial Crisis (GFC) and disappointing A-share market performance in recent years has taken its toll on foreign investor interest in QFII products. In 2011, there were around 100 licensed QFII investors in China, with a combined quota of USD$21.6 billion (SAFE, 2012).

Forming a mirror image with QFII, the QDII programme allows licensed domestic institutions to raise capital from Chinese investors to invest in foreign capital markets. The QDII scheme can trace its origin back to the middle of the last decade, starting with Chinese insurance companies seeking offshore investments for their foreign currency premiums. In 2006, the authorities formerly launched the QDII programme, expanding the investor base to include banks and mutual funds, and broadening the investment scope to include a wider range of fixed income products. However, the industry did not really take off until late 2007, when restrictions were lifted to allow (1) QDII funds to invest in foreign stock markets, and (2) retail investors to participate in the QDII scheme.

Chinese investors embraced QDII with enthusiasm, and financial institutions – banks, insurance companies and mutual funds – moved quickly to tap into new-found investor demand. According to data compiled by WIND, the first four QDII funds established in the second half of 2007 raised a total of RMB119.4 billion, with significant over-subscription.[1] However, this explosive growth fails to repeat itself in subsequent years, as the QDII funds suffered significant losses during the GFC and investor demand for offshore investment plummeted. Although new funds have continued to emerge after the subprime crisis in 2008, the average fund size has dropped substantially and remains low (Fig. 1).

Indeed, some QDII funds that started prior to the GFC did not survive the subsequent losses. According to WIND, funds that were established before 2009 account for less than 1/5 of the QDII industry today (Fig. 2).

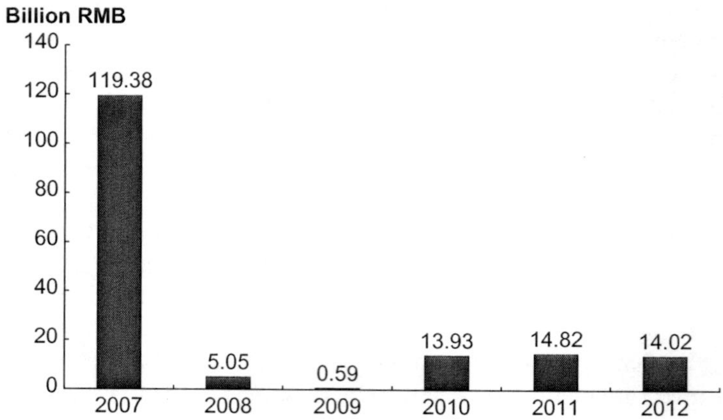

Fig. 1. Total Issuing Units of QDII Funds.

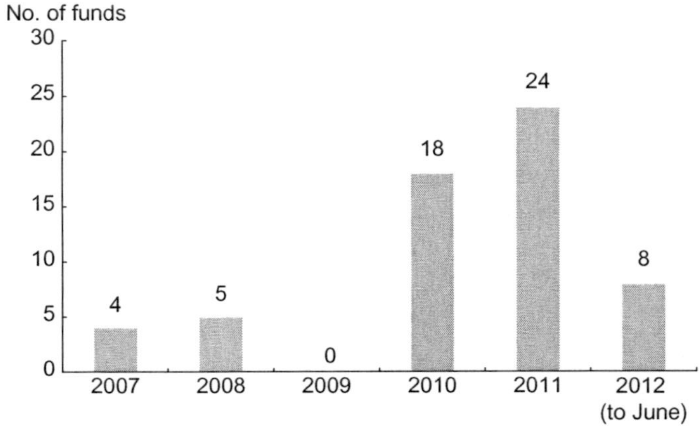

Fig. 2. Year of Inception of Existing QDII Funds.

But in terms of assets-under-management, the older funds remain much larger than those launched post-GFC.

In terms of asset allocation, today's QDII funds invest in diverse locations and asset classes. Over 50% of the industry is made up of equity funds, investing primarily in publicly listed companies across the globe. About one quarter of the funds focus on commodity investment, with the rest specialising in other investments, such as real estate and fixed income products (Fig. 3). There are a number of fund of funds, which focus their investment on foreign mutual funds and ETFs, although much of their investment eventually ends up in equity markets. Geographically, around two thirds of the industry has a global mandate, while a majority of the remaining funds invest in emerging markets, such as BRIC countries and the Asia Pacific region (Fig. 4).

EMPIRICAL ANALYSIS

What Explains The Massive Outflows From QDII Funds?

Since the industry started to open up to retail investors in 2007, there have been significant and persistent outflows of funds from the QDII industry. In fact, of the 50 funds we track in our sample, only three experienced net

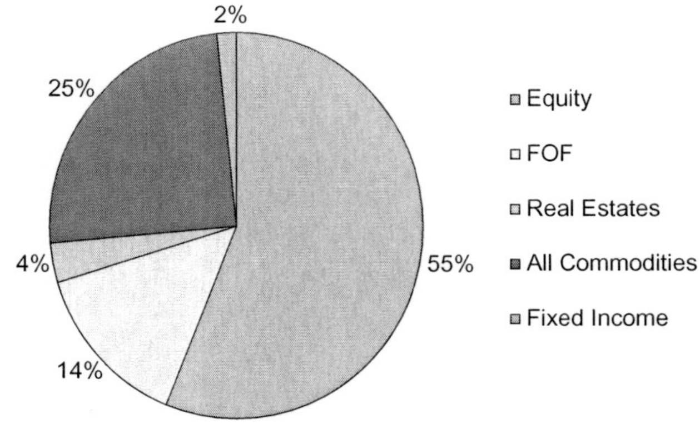

Fig. 3. Investment Category.

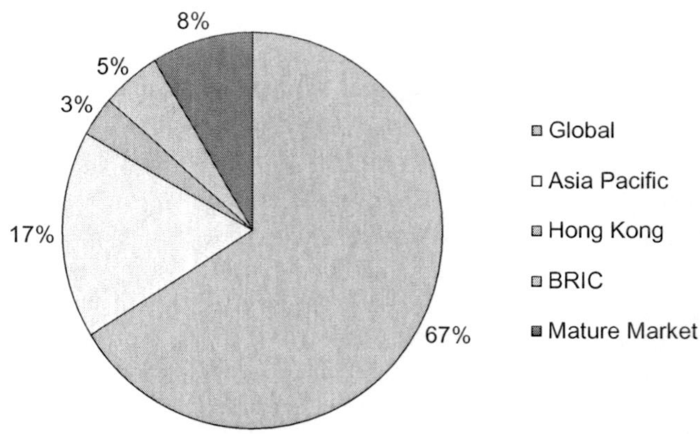

Fig. 4. Stated Investment Region.

inflows over the investment period, while the remainder experienced outflows of between 3% and 48% of their initial size. Fig. 5 shows the change in size of the nine oldest QDII funds since their inception.[2] As shown, more than 1/3 of the funds have been withdrawn in the past four years, with outflows occurring in a persistent and sometimes aggressive manner.

What caused investors to withdraw their investment so aggressively? Disappointing fund performance appears to be an obvious answer (Ba, 2007; Cao, 2010). Indeed, the return generated by QDII funds has

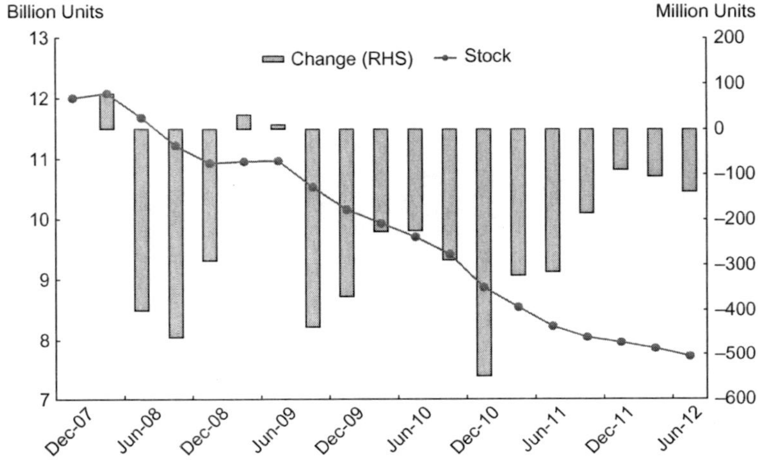

Fig. 5. Assest under Management of Nine Oldest QDII Funds.

been abysmal in recent years, with only 6 out of the 50 funds in our sample reporting positive holding period returns. Obviously, a large part of this poor performance was due to the bleak global environment, as the starting time of the industry coincided with the peak of global equity markets. Shortly after the first batch of QDII funds was launched, global markets collapsed in light of the US subprime crisis, which later degenerated into a full-blown financial crisis of global proportions. On average, QDII funds that started in late 2007 lost over 50% of their value during 2008, and despite the subsequent market recovery, remain about 26% under water as at the end of Q2 this year (Fig. 6).

Indeed, the terrible market backdrop means that QDII funds were not alone in suffering massive portfolio losses and large capital outflows. Table 1 compares QDII funds' performance and net flows against those of A-share funds in China and large foreign mutual funds. All three groups of funds experienced substantial negative returns between Q4 2007 and Q2 2012, with QDII funds ranking ahead of A-share funds, but trailing behind offshore funds. Similarly, all three groups of funds have experienced significant capital outflows of around 30% over the holding period. These simple comparisons suggest that the sharp losses of QDII funds are not unique, and their experiences were similar to those of their local and overseas counterparts'.[3]

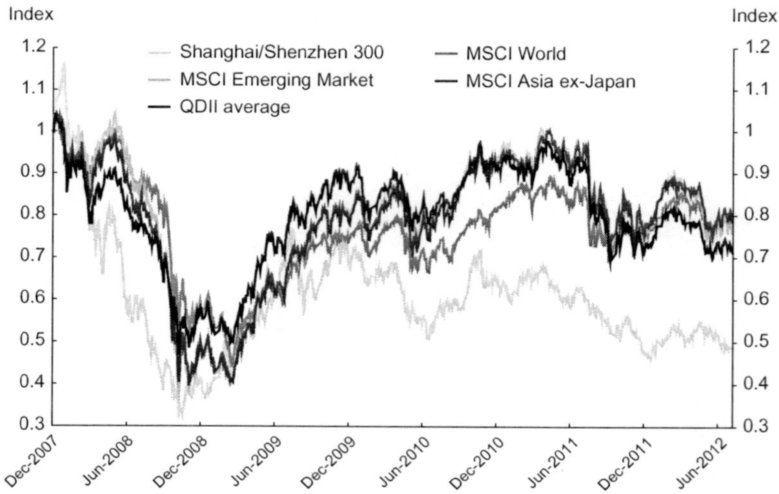

Fig. 6. QDII Performance and Global Equity Index.

Table 1. Performance and Net Flows of QDII, A-share and Offshore Funds.

	Q4 2007 ~ Q2 2012	
Funds	Performance[a]	Net Capital Flows
QDII funds	*−29%*	*−26.3%*
A-share funds	−35%	−27.8%
Offshore funds[b]	−20%	−33.0%

[a]Average holding period return, unweighted.
[b]Offshore funds include global equity funds from Allianz, AXA, Fidelity and Vanguard.

Besides the declining equity markets, QDII performance was also negatively affected by the persistent appreciation of the RMB. Since QDII funds raise yuan-denominated capital for foreign investment, and are required to convert their portfolio back to the RMB for reporting and redemption, the gradual appreciation in the CNY/USD (and CNY/HKD) exchange rate has reduced QDII's foreign investment returns. In developed markets, this currency risk can be completely or partially hedged, depending on the degree of discretion of fund managers. However in China, the relatively underdeveloped currency market and strict capital controls mean that QDII managers have limited scope to hedge this risk. Even if they could hedge (using currency forwards in recent time, for example), the relatively high costs of such transactions would also subtract from funds' total returns.

Unfortunately, we do not have information about whether and how much each QDII fund hedges against currency risk, and therefore, we calculate fund performance before and after exchange rate adjustment. Upon examining the data, there is little difference between the two measures, as the impact of currency appreciation on total returns is small relative to investment-driven returns. Therefore, in the regression analysis below, we use mainly the unadjusted return (as it gives a clearer measure of performance), and use the currency-adjusted return where appropriate for robust checks.

To see whether there is a relationship between fund performance and the size of capital outflows, Fig. 7 plots two variables for the 50 QDII funds in our sample. As expected, there is indeed a positive relationship between the two, suggesting that better performing funds have tended to see *lower outflows (or inflows)* than those that have performed poorly. We will test this relationship more formally below.

Besides the simple holding period (or absolute) return used in Fig. 7, we calculate three other performance measures: excess return over QDII fund benchmark, risk-adjusted return, and excess return over the Shanghai/Shenzhen 300 index (CSI 300). These measures can be seen as measuring

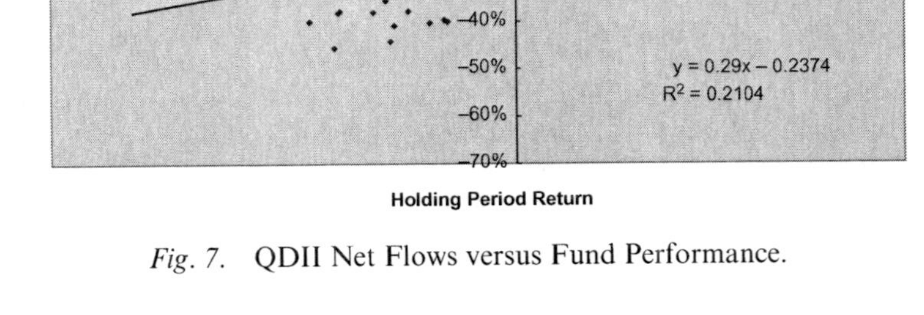

Fig. 7. QDII Net Flows versus Fund Performance.

QDII fund performance against various control groups. The excess return against benchmark is a standard performance measure in the fund management industry, aimed at separating managers' performance from that of the broad market. The risk-adjusted return goes a step further, taking into account the degree of risk that fund managers take in order to generate the excess return. Finally, we measure QDII fund performance relative to the CSI 300 index, which is a standard performance benchmark for Chinese A-share funds. The rationale for creating such a measure is to reflect the choice facing an average Chinese investor between investing in the local market and in the foreign market. If the A-share market performs better than offshore markets, investors will have an incentive to shift money away from QDII funds to the local market, and vice versa. We think this is an important measure to consider, as most Chinese investors view QDII funds as a simple alternative to A-share equity funds (Gu, 2008).[4]

To properly test the empirical relationship, we run a number of bivariate regressions of QDII fund net capital flows on various measures of performance.[5,6] The results are shown in models (1)–(4) in Table 2. As expected, all four measures of fund performance are shown to have a positive and significant relationship with net flows. Of the four measures, the simple holding period return has the largest and most significant correlation with net flows, as reflected in the size and the statistical significance of its coefficient. This is consistent with the general perception of Chinese investors that they tend to evaluate the success of their investment based on absolute returns (i.e. whether they have made money), without giving adequate consideration to benchmark performance or portfolio risk (Shenzhen Stock Exchange, 2012).[7]

In models (5) and (6), we expand our regressions by introducing a number of control variables. The full equation can be written as the following:

$$\text{Net flow}_i = \beta_0 + \beta_1\,\text{performance}_i + \beta_2\,\text{equity\_}d_i + \beta_3\,\text{size}_i + \beta_4\,\text{ownership}_i + u_i \tag{1}$$

where

Net flow_i is the percentage net flow of funds.
performance_i is the holding period return.[8]
$\text{equity\_}d_i$ is a dummy variable for equity-oriented QDII funds.
size_i denotes the size of the fund.
ownership_i is the percentage ownership of a fund by retail investors.
u_i is the idiosyncratic term.

Table 2. Cross Section Regression Results (Dependent: Percentage Net Flow).

	Absolute (1)	Benchmark (2)	Risk Adjusted (3)	CSI 300 (4)	Absolute (5)	Absolute (6)
Constant	−0.24***	−0.26***	−0.26***	−0.28***	−0.26***	−0.27**
	(−13.18)	(−16.9)	(−15.7)	(−17.3)	(−9.9)	(−2.08)
Return (abs)	**0.29*** **				**0.35*** **	**0.32*** **
	(3.36)				**(3.7)**	**(3.34)**
Return (bench)		**0.24*** **				
		(2.4)				
Return (IR)			**0.03* **			
			(1.77)			
Return (SZ300)				**0.29** **		
				(2.33)		
Equity dummy					0.025	0.02
					(0.86)	(0.59)
Size					0.001	**0.001* **
					(1.47)	**(1.66)**
Retail ownership						**−0.001* **
						(−1.67)
R^2	0.2	0.12	0.07	0.11	0.26	0.31
Observations	50	50	50	50	50	50

*statistical significance at a 10% level.
**statistical significance at a 5% level.
***statistical significance at a 1% level.
Numbers in the parentheses are T-statistics.
The numbers appearing in parentheses in the column heads indicate equation numbers mentioned in the text.

These control variables are designed to capture the influence on net flows from sources other than fund performance. The 'equity dummy' assesses whether net flows vary across funds that invest in different sectors. Its coefficient, as shown in Eqs. (5) and (6), takes on a positive value, suggesting that equity funds on average see less outflows than other funds, although the coefficient is not statistically significant.

The 'size' of the fund is used as a proxy for the reputation of the fund management company. We expect it to be positively correlated with net flows, as larger and more reputable funds ought to see fewer outflows than smaller and less well-known funds, holding performance constant. Indeed, the results are consistent with our prior, and the coefficient is statistically significant in Eq. (6).

The last control variable is 'ownership', which measures the percentage of the fund owned by retail investors. Retail investor ownership of QDII funds is very high, averaging around 85% for the whole industry (the remaining 15% is held by institutional investors and fund managers themselves). The rationale for including this variable is to capture the more speculative nature of Chinese retail investors, who tend to have a shorter investment horizon, and are less tolerant of large market downturns than institutional investors (Shenzhen Stock Exchange, 2012). Thus, we expect the 'ownership' variable to have a negative sign, indicating that funds with a large retail-investor base should experience greater outflows owing to the market turbulence of recent years. The negative coefficient in Equation 6 is consistent with this hypothesis. Overall, our results from Eqs. (5) and (6) suggest that even after controlling for fund specific characteristics, the influence of performance on net flows remains positive and significant.

It is worth noting that while the above cross-sectional analysis allows us to assess the sign of the relationship between net flows and performance, it does not necessarily reveal causality. In other words, we do not know whether the poor performance of funds causes capital outflows, or the outflows themselves lead to worse performance. Although this question cannot be fully addressed by the regressions, we think some economic reasoning can help to shed light on the issue. It seems reasonable to expect a causal relationship to run from performance to fund flows (i.e. better performing funds attract capital inflows, and vice versa), as this is consistent with the rational behaviour of investors. However, explaining the reverse causality – from net flows to performance – is much less straightforward. It is true that funds that experience larger investor withdrawals would need to hold a higher amount of cash to meet redemptions. This might lead to underperformance of the funds in a persistent bull market, because their portfolio is not as fully invested. The reverse will also be true that, in a persistent bear market, larger cash holdings could reduce the extent of losses from the risky portfolio, allowing the funds to outperform their peers. However, this cash holding-induced under/out performance is likely to be fairly small, provided the variation in net flows across funds is not large. Perhaps more importantly, the investment environment over our sample period *as a whole* was neither a persistent bull market, nor a bear market (e.g. there were bull and bear phases over time), suggesting some ambiguity as to whether holding more cash would lead to superior or inferior performance. Because of these, we think the negative relationship found between performance and net flows is more likely driven by the former leading the latter.

What Explains Funds' Performance?

Since fund performance plays an important role in determining the extent of capital outflows, the next question to ask is what explains performance? To examine this question, we run a series of regressions to see what characteristics of QDII funds are correlated with their returns.

For the explanatory variables, we first construct a 'manager quality index', which consists of three components: (1) the number of managers in a fund, (2) whether the managers have foreign financial market working experience and (3) whether the managers have tertiary (or above) education in foreign universities. The first component should have an obvious and positive relationship with returns, as funds with a large investment team are more likely to outperform those with fewer managers, all else equal.[9] The second and the third components are designed to capture the relevance of managers' past work/study experience in investing foreign capital markets. Our expectation is that, since QDII funds are mandated to invest overseas, the funds with managers who have foreign experience should outperform those who do not.[10,11] We construct two dummy variables based on the managerial information provided by WIND, taking a value of 1 for managers with foreign experience and 0 otherwise. The overall 'manager quality' index is the sum of the 3 components.

The second explanatory variable is the percentage of manager ownership in a fund. We expect this variable to be positively correlated with returns, as greater manager ownership reduces the principal-agency problem by better aligning the interest between investors (i.e. principal) and managers (i.e. agent) (Evans, 2008; Eichberger, 1999).

The third variable is fund size, but the sign of it is ambiguous. On the one hand, large funds should have more resources to support better research, and can hire more capable managers. They should also be more cost effective, as fixed trading/operation costs can be spread over a large number of fund units (Indro, 1999). On the other hand, large funds tend to be more difficult to manoeuvre, when it comes to altering portfolio allocations in a fast changing market. Indeed, the difficulty to sell illiquid securities during periods of market turmoil could significantly undermine a fund's performance. By contrast, smaller funds may be able to reposition their portfolios more easily in a turbulent market and hence improve their performance (Chen, Hong, Huang, & Kubik, 2004). Finally, we include two dummy variables to account for the differences in geographical and investment sector allocations.[12] The empirical models can be written as follows:

$$\begin{aligned} \text{performance}_i = \alpha_0 + \alpha_1\,\text{quality}_i + \alpha_2\,\text{ownership}_i + \alpha_3\,\text{size}_i + \alpha_4\,\text{global}_i \\ + \alpha_5\,\text{equity\_}d_i + \varepsilon_i \end{aligned} \tag{2}$$

where

performance_i is measured as absolute returns, excess returns relative to benchmark and risk adjusted returns.
quality_i is the manager quality index.
ownership_i is the percentage of manager ownership of a fund.
size_i is the size of a fund.
$\text{equity\_}d_i$ is a dummy variable for equity funds.
global_i is a dummy variable for funds that have a global investment focus.
ε_i is the idiosyncratic term.

The results, shown in Table 3, generally conform to our expectations.[13] The manager quality index is significantly positive across all three measures of performance.[14] The coefficient in Eq. (1) suggests that for every one unit increase in the index, the performance improves by 9% over the holding period. The manager ownership is also correctly signed, although the coefficient is not statistically significant in the first three equations. Interestingly, the size variable is negatively correlated with returns, suggesting that smaller funds, that can more readily change their asset allocation, tend to outperform larger funds over the sample period. However, this variable is insignificant for excess and risk-adjusted returns, perhaps reflecting the ambiguity discussed above.

Table 3. Cross-Section Regression Results (Dependent: Return).

	Absolute	Benchmark	IR	*With HK*
Constant	**−0.23*** **	**−0.13*** **	**−0.71*** **	**−0.26*** **
	(−4.24)	**(−2.4)**	**(−2.53)**	**(−4.45)**
Manager quality	**0.09***	**0.09****	**0.51****	**0.09***
	(1.91)	**(2.04)**	**(2.08)**	**(1.98)**
Manager ownership	0.001	0.001	0.1	**0.003***
	(1.3)	(1.19)	(0.99)	**(1.84)**
Size	**−0.002*** **	0.0002	−0.001	**−0.002*** **
	(−3.63)	(0.25)	(−0.03)	**(−3.39)**
Global dummy	**0.07***	−0.05	−0.32	**0.14*** **
	(1.65)	(−1.26)	(−1.29)	**(3.14)**
Equity dummy	0.03	0.05	0.19	0.04
	(0.62)	(1.36)	(0.71)	(0.76)
HK average				**−0.11***
				(−1.67)
R^2	0.37	0.19	0.18	0.58
Observations	50	50	50	50

*statistical significance at a 10% level.
**statistical significance at a 5% level.
***statistical significance at a 1% level.
Numbers in the parentheses are T-statistics.

The global dummy is positively correlated with the absolute return, but the sign turns negative (albeit insignificant) for the excess return. This could be due to the fact that globally-diversified funds tend to have a larger exposure to mature markets (e.g. United States, United Kingdom, Australia etc.), which performed strongly following the subprime crisis in 2008. In contrast, many EM equity markets performed poorly in 2010 and 2011 (recall that China's A share market was the second worst performing market in 2011 after Greece, and continued to trail other markets in 2012. This would have affected stocks of Chinese companies listed overseas, which are the preferred investment for many regional-focused QDII funds). The better performing mature markets would have helped the global-focused funds to outperform regional funds in terms of absolute returns. However, it is much more difficult for QDII funds to beat their global benchmark, as they are up against fund managers all over the world that track the same indices, such as the MSCI World Index. Managing a global fund requires extensive knowledge about foreign markets, and skills to trade a wide range of securities. This puts Chinese funds in a disadvantageous position relative to their western counterparts (Ba, 2010). Finally, the equity dummies are positive in all three equations, although the coefficients are insignificant.[15]

Finally, in our investigation of the determinants of performance, we include a variable representing QDII funds' average asset allocation in the Hong Kong market. The motivation is that QDII funds, especially those specialising in equity investment, tend to significantly overweight the Hong Kong market in their portfolio. As shown in Fig. 8,[16] the industry's average allocation to Hong Kong is around 50%, with some equity funds almost exclusively investing in this market. Given such a high concentration, we are interested to see whether this 'Hong Kong bias' has any systematic impact on fund performance, and if so, in what direction.

Fig. 9 shows a simple plot of fund performance and the proportion of the fund invested in the Hong Kong market.[17] A casual observation suggests that there is a negative relationship between the two.[18] We put this relationship to a more rigorous test by adding a variable representing the Hong Kong allocation to the performance equation. The result, shown in the final column of Table 3, confirms that the Hong Kong exposure is indeed negatively correlated with returns, suggesting that funds with a larger exposure to Hong Kong tend to underperform those with a smaller position. We will discuss this issue further in the following section.

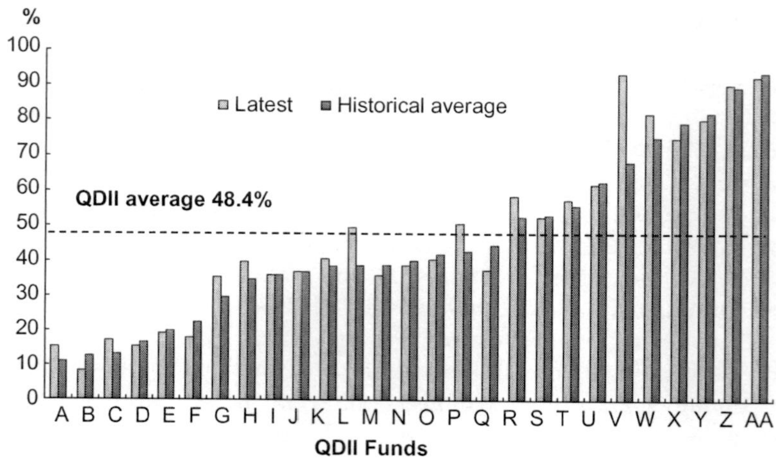

Fig. 8. Equity-Oriented QDII Funds' Allocation HK.

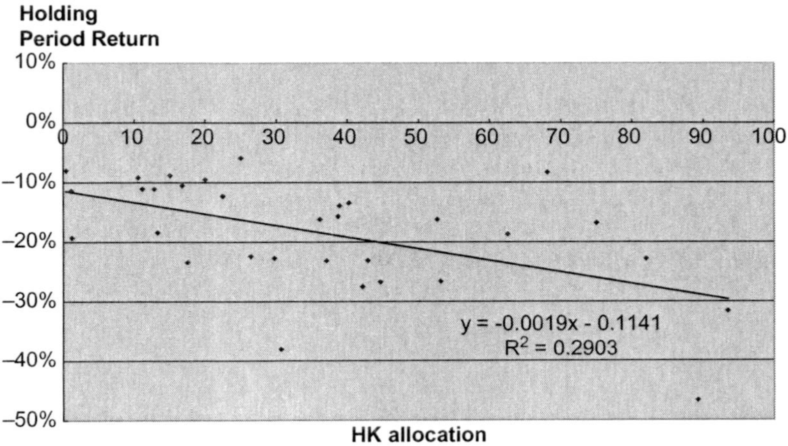

Fig. 9. HK Allocation versus QDII Performance.

What Explains QDII Funds' Allocation to Hong Kong?

The extraordinarily high concentration of QDII funds in the Hong Kong market is an interesting and puzzling phenomenon, particularly given the negative relationship between fund performance and the proportion of the asset invested in this market.[19] Furthermore, since many QDII funds measure their performance against a global or regional benchmark, of which the Hong Kong market generally accounts for a very small weight, the large exposure to Hong Kong therefore represents a significant departure from the benchmark composition. In this section, we aim to explore what factors have contributed to this 'Hong Kong bias'? (Fig. 10).

One explanation for this 'Hong Kong bias' relates to the deficiency of the knowledge required of QDII fund managers to successfully invest in foreign capital markets and manage global portfolios. Industry contacts suggest that it is difficult for QDII funds to attract experienced and qualified fund managers from overseas, because a lack of resources constrains compensation.[20] This has forced many funds to employ local-trained managers (i.e. those who have previously worked in A-share funds) to specialise investment in Hong Kong listed Mainland companies (Liang, 2004).

Theoretically, the phenomenon of investors favouring their home markets for portfolio investment is well documented by the 'home bias' theory (Chan, Covrig, & Ng, 2005; Lütje, 2007; Tesar, 1995). Empirical studies

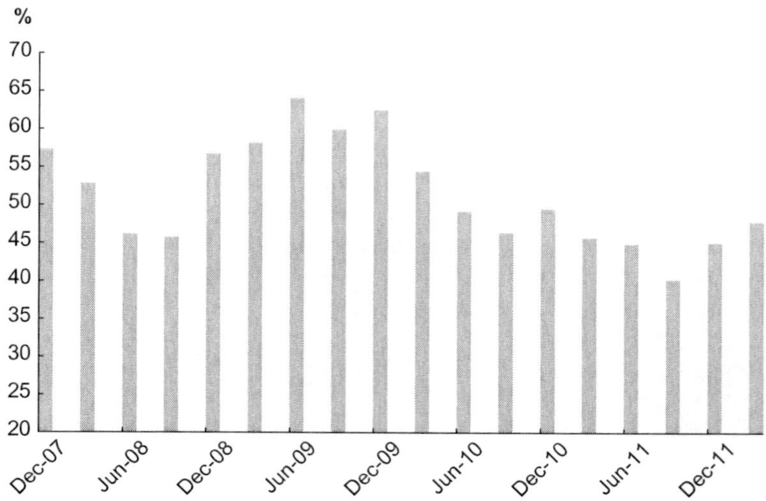

Fig. 10. Average Asset Allocation to Hong Kong for Equity-Oriented QDII Funds.

have shown that this 'home bias' can be driven by a number of behavioural traits, such as investors' perceived information advantage about the home market and a better understanding of the local rule of law leading to overconfidence and a reluctance to diversify. Since QDII funds are prohibited from investing in A-shares, the Hong Kong market is naturally seen by many managers as the closest proxy for their 'home market'.[21]

To properly test if managers' lack of foreign investing experience has any impact on their decision to overweight Hong Kong, we use one of the components from our 'manager quality index', which directly measures a manager's previous work experience, in the regressions.[22] We expect it to be negatively correlated with Hong Kong allocation, as foreign-trained managers would not face the same knowledge constraint about global markets as those with only local experience.

As for the control variables, we use the fund 'size' to account for the level of resources possessed by QDII funds. Not only is a large fund more capable of hiring more experienced managers, it also has more resources to build a good research team to support foreign investment. On the flipside, if a fund is small, with limited research capacity to cover wider markets, the manager is more likely to invest in his more familiar 'home' market

(Gong, 2009). As a result, we expect a negative relationship between fund size and the Hong Kong allocation.

We also include fund performance in the equation for completeness, as we already know it is negatively correlated with the Hong Kong allocation from previous results. But as with cross-section regressions, we do not know about the nature of the causal relationship, that is, does more allocation in Hong Kong cause poorer fund performance, or do poor returns lead the funds to be in favour of the Hong Kong market. We will address this question by running a set of Granger causality tests between performance and the Hong Kong allocation. Finally, we include an equity dummy to separate equity oriented funds from others. The above discussion can be written into an equation below:

$$HK\_\text{average}_i = \gamma_0 + \gamma_1 \text{Experience}_i + \gamma_2 \text{size}_i + \gamma_3 \text{performance}_i + \gamma_4 \text{equity}\_d_i + \upsilon_i \tag{3}$$

where

Experience is a dummy variable that represents whether fund managers have overseas investment experience.

HK_average_i, size_i, performance_i and equity_d_i are defined in the same as Eq. (2).

υ_i is the idiosyncratic term.

The results are presented in Table 4. The manager experience dummy – the variable in which we are interested the most – is significantly negative across all equation specifications. The coefficient in Eq. (1) suggests that funds, managed by foreign-trained managers, have on average 22.4% less weight on Hong Kong than those managed by local managers. In addition, fund 'size' and 'performance' are also negatively correlated with the Hong Kong allocation, consistent with our expectations.

To address the causal relationship between performance and asset allocation, we put together a small sample QDII funds, with large exposure to the Hong Kong market and a long data record. We run two Granger causality tests: one is constructed as return leading allocation (Eq. (4)), and the other as allocation leading return (Eq. (5)).

$$HK\_\text{average}_t = \delta_0 + \delta_1 \text{Performance}_{t-1} + \upsilon_t \tag{4}$$

$$\text{Performance}_t = \kappa_0 + \kappa_1 HK\_\text{average}_{t-1} + \upsilon_t \tag{5}$$

Table 4. Cross-Section Regression Results (Dependent: Percentage HK Allocation).

	(1)	(2)	(3)	(4)
Constant	**35.4*** **	**45.7*** **	**33.64*** **	10.2
	(6.26)	**(7.61)**	**(3.88)**	(0.91)
Manager experience	**−22.4*** **	**−24.5*** **	**−20.6*** **	**−12.7***
	(3.0)	**(3.65)**	**(−3.01)**	**(−1.89)**
Size		**−4.01*** **	**−3.16*** **	−1.07
		(−3.21)	**(2.45)**	(−0.78)
Return			**−63.6***	**−74.3*** **
			(−1.87)	**(−2.4)**
Equity dummy				**21.5*** **
				(2.96)
R^2	0.19	0.37	0.42	0.54
Observations	50	50	50	50

*statistical significance at a 10% level.
**statistical significance at a 5% level.
***statistical significance at a 1% level.
Numbers in the parentheses are T-statistics.

where

Performance is the average quarterly return of the funds
HK_average is the average quarterly allocation to the Hong Kong market
υ_t is the idiosyncratic term.

As shown in Table 5, the lagged return carries a significantly negative sign for the Hong Kong allocation, while the reverse relationship is wrongly signed and insignificant. These results suggest that it is fund performance that drives the investment in the Hong Kong market. While this finding may not seem intuitive at a first glance, we think it is again consistent with the 'home bias' behaviour in cross-border portfolio investment. Studies in the literature have shown that not only do investors tend to overweight their 'home' market, they also have the tendency to repatriate funds back to the local market amid rising risk aversion (Chan et al., 2005; Lütje, 2007). Indeed, the negative sign on the lagged return for 'HK allocation' suggests that QDII funds do indeed raise their local (i.e. Hong Kong) market allocation when they experience losses in the previous quarter. This increase was found to be particularly acute following sharp global market sell-offs during the peak of the financial crisis.

Table 5. Granger Causality Test.

Dependent Variable: HK Allocation		Dependent Variable: Return	
Constant	1.15	Constant	0.008
	(0.84)		(0.22)
Return (−1)	**−16.54***	HK allocation (−1)	0.003
	(−1.67)		(0.45)
R-square	0.17	R-square	0.014
Observations	16	Observations	16

*statistical significance at a 10 % level.
**statistical significance at a 5% level.
***statistical significance at a 1% level.
Numbers in the parentheses are T-statistics.

Overall, our results suggest that the choice to overweight Hong Kong is related to a lack of human expertise about foreign investment exacerbating the 'home bias' behaviour of QDII fund managers. And poorly performing funds have tended to revert back to the 'home market' after experiencing large portfolio losses.

The above results and discussions give the perception that QDII funds have been *forced* to invest in Hong Kong by constraints on human resources and disappointing performance. There is, however, another possible explanation, and that is, the managers have willingly and intentionally chosen Hong Kong because: (1) they might have expected Hong Kong to outperform other markets, so the overweight was simply a tactical choice to enhance return; (2) managers with previous A-share investing experience can easily switch their expertise to investing in Hong Kong-listed Mainland companies and (3) some large QDII fund management companies have presence in Hong Kong with research capacity, so funds with large Hong Kong investment can readily tap into these existing resources. Unfortunately, we cannot measure fund managers' ex-ante market expectations, and it is also difficult to know to what extent a manager's asset allocation decision was influenced by the Hong Kong market presence of his parent company. Having said that, one thing we do observe from the data is that QDII funds often increase their Hong Kong weight in times of *underperformance* of the Hang Seng and China H-share indexes relative to other regional and global benchmarks (the most obvious episode is between Q2-2011 and Q2-2012, see Fig. 11). If overweighting Hong Kong was truly a tactical choice to enhance return, one would expect such

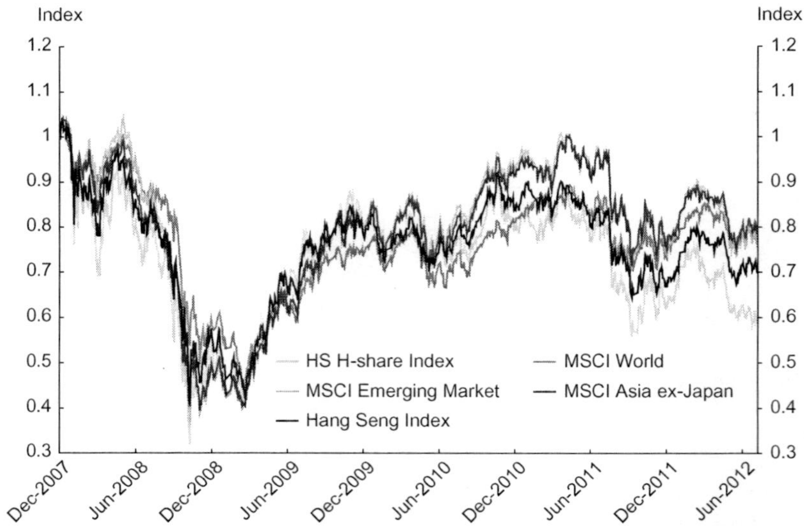

Fig. 11. Global Equity Market Index.

persistent underperformance to lead to a reduction in the Hong Kong weight, rather than an increase.

The finding that QDII managers with only local market investing experience tend to overweight Hong Kong does not eradicate the possibility that fund managers' are attempting to add value by investing in markets that they are most familiar with. Some QDII funds, in fact, explicitly state that their investment strategy is to explore undervalued Chinese stocks listed overseas. And because the Hong Kong market houses a majority of foreign-listed Mainland companies, overweighting the market can be justified by their investment mandate.

As sensible as that seems at a micro level, such a high concentration in the Hong Kong market undermines the key policy objective of the QDII scheme in helping Chinese investors to diversify their portfolio risk and reduce investment bias towards the home market. Given the high correlation between the Hong Kong and Mainland stock markets, the 'Hong Kong bias' tends to reduce the diversification benefit of QDII funds, even though the choice may be entirely justifiable given the current skill set of QDII fund managers.

CONCLUDING REMARKS AND POLICY-RELATED DISCUSSIONS

The QDII fund industry has suffered significant losses since its inception in late 2007. This poor performance has, in turn, led to substantial outflows of funds from the industry and markedly reduced investor interest. Our research adds to the existing QDII literature by providing empirical evidence for the negative relationship between fund performance and the size of capital outflows. In addition, we find that the performance of QDII funds is strongly correlated with an index of manager quality, which measures the level of human resources and the relevance of managers' past work/study experience in investing foreign capital markets. We find two other factors also influence returns: (1) the size of fund, which we think is correlated with a fund's research and analytical capacity, and (2) the level of managerial ownership in the fund, which can influence the degree of principal-agency problems.

Our research also provides an explanation for the significant exposure of QDII funds to the Hong Kong market. We argue that QDII funds, on average, are forced to stay in Hong Kong, because the lack of foreign market experience of fund managers exacerbates the 'home bias' tendency in their portfolio allocation. While this 'Hong Kong bias' could also be a strategy to enhance return, we find some contradicting evidence to the argument, as exposures to Hong Kong tend to increase during periods of local market underperformance.

Overall, our study uncovers some important issues facing the QDII industry today, and provides empirical evidence on the root causes of these issues. As mentioned earlier, the establishment of the QDII scheme is an integral part of China's financial market reform and economic restructuring. As China becomes more integrated into the world economy, the QDII industry should play an important role in this transition by channelling Chinese capital to global financial markets. However, the current problems in the QDII industry are restraining its growth and limiting its diversification benefits for Chinese investors. Below, we describe these benefits in detail, and discuss how the Chinese authorities can help the industry to overcome the existing challenges:

(1) Despite the fact that QDII funds, on average, are 30% below their initial value, they easily beat the average performance of A-share funds since late 2007 (Table 1). In addition, QDII returns were less volatile

than those of A-share funds, with the correlation of returns also quite low. These suggest that a typical Chinese investor could gain significantly by allocating part of his/her equity portfolio to a QDII fund, achieving both enhanced return and reduced risk.[23]

(2) More specifically, the QDII industry can play an important role in helping Chinese investors to diversify portfolio risk and reduce the extent of 'home bias' in their investment (Gong, 2009). This is indeed one of the key motivations for establishing the QDII scheme in the first place. At the moment though, Chinese investors tend to focus more on maximising returns for their investment, with insufficient consideration given to diversification and risk management. [24] However, as household wealth rises and investors' financial literacy improves, managing portfolio risk will likely become a more important consideration. This should increase investors' demand for QDII funds.

(3) The QDII industry is currently facing a vicious cycle of poor performance leading to capital outflows, which reduce funds' ability to hire good managers and further undermines performance. Our results suggest that this cycle has led to a high concentration of funds in the Hong Kong market, which reduces QDII funds' diversification benefit for Chinese investors.

(4) To break this vicious cycle, we believe there are a number of implications for the policy design of regulatory authorities in China. Firstly, tax incentives could be provided to investors to stimulate demand for QDII funds, while levies charged on QDII fund companies could be lowered. Secondly, the government can encourage state-owned institutions, such as pension funds, local governments, state-owned insurance companies and banks, to invest in QDII funds to gain international exposure and to diversify risk. This would increase the size of the QDII industry, thereby giving it the resources to attract more qualified managers from overseas. Thirdly, the authorities should continue to improve the financial literacy of the public, particularly raising investors' awareness of risk management and the importance of global portfolio diversification. This will go some way to accentuate the core benefits of QDII funds in helping investors to build a more complete and balanced portfolio. Fourthly, given the importance of global experience of fund managers in determining performance, regulators may set higher eligibility standards for managers of QDII funds. By raising the overall professional quality of the industry, this could improve fund performance and investors' interest. In addition, the

government could help to attract qualified fund managers from overseas through policy incentives, or encourage local fund companies to train their own managers. Fifthly, regulators could lift the restrictions on QDII funds' investment operation, expanding their investment scope and instruments. Some industry contacts suggest that if QDII funds are allowed to operate like feeder funds, coming under the operation of large and reputable global fund companies, Chinese investors would have fewer concerns about manager quality, and can enjoy greater economies of scale. Finally, industry contacts indicate that a large portion of fees charged by QDII funds (particularly front/back loads) are paid to commercial banks for using them as issuing platforms. If there are policies that enable QDII funds to retain more of these fees for internal use (i.e. to attract better managers and improve investment research), fund performance could be improved.

(5) Turning to China's macroeconomic policies, measures that allow for more Chinese capital to be invested abroad are an important part of capital account liberalisation. The QDII industry can play a significant role in this process (Hu, 2005). In addition, the outflows of the RMB could serve as a counter-balance to the QFII-related capital inflows, improving the two-way liquidity in the RMB currency market (Ba, 2010). In the past few years, a gradual but persistent appreciation of the RMB has affected the foreign investment performance of QDII funds (Yang, 2012; You, 2007). Going forward, as the currency moves towards its equilibrium value, the negative impact from a one-sided appreciation should diminish, increasing QDII's appeal to local investors.

(6) Finally, Chinese policy makers have shown a strong commitment to financial market reform, setting up explicit goals and implementation steps in the 12th Five-Year Plan. Regarding cross-border capital investment, the authorities are likely to continue to reply on the QDII and QFII schemes to push for further convertibility and liberalisation of the capital account. Given this, we are likely to see substantial growth in portfolio-related flows into and out of China in future years. He et al. (2012) predicts that outward portfolio investment from China will grow from USD 257 billion (or 4% of GDP) in 2010 to about USD 5,500 billion (or 29% of GDP) in 2020, assuming the capital account is fully liberalised – a timeline that is consistent with the recent proposals by the PBC. These underlying structural changes should provide strong growth impetus for the QDII industry.

NOTES

1. In China, QDII licensed institutions can be broken down into three main categories: fund management companies, banks and insurance companies. The insurance companies tend to use their QDII quotas (obtained from the SAFE) for their own investment of insurance premiums, and do not open to other investors. Banks mainly use the quotas to support their wealth management products, and tend to focus on fixed income investment. Our study focuses on QDII mutual funds, which are the most diverse and least restrictive (in terms of asset selection) of the three groups. The QDII fund industry is also the largest of the three, commanding a combined quota of RMB 440 billion as of Q3 2012, more than those of banks and insurance companies put together (RMB 330 billion).

2. We measure net flows using units of funds, rather than nominal yuan, as this captures the 'real' change in the fund size that is not influenced by performance.

3. The numbers in Table 1 are designed to put QDII fund performance in a broad context. The underlying message is that the GFC has affected all mutual funds that invest in risk-sensitive asset classes (such as equity) given the synchronized decline in global markets. However, directly comparing QDII fund performance with that of A-share funds is not strictly appropriate, as these two funds belong to different asset classes, according to modern financial theories, such as the Capital Asset Pricing Model (CAPM).

4. As a cross check, we substitute the CSI 300 index with the performance index of A-share equity mutual funds. The empirical results, not shown in the chapter, remain the same.

5. The QDII fund data used in this study are taken from WIND, while benchmark and market-related data are from Bloomberg. Apart from daily net value of funds, QDII data are in quarterly frequency, extracted from their quarterly reports by WIND. There are in total 59 QDII funds in China as of September 2012, nine of which are new funds that have no records of fund flow information, we therefore exclude them from our sample.

6. While the relatively small size of the sample may not give us very precise estimates of the coefficients, it, in fact, raises the hurdle for rejecting the null hypothesis of the statistical t-tests. In other words, the statistical significance of the coefficients will likely improve as the sample size gets larger, all else equal.

7. This is particularly true for less financially-literal retail investors, who dominate the QDII industry (see below for details). It is also worth noting that the interpretation of investors' tendency to focus on returns, and not paying as much attention to risk, is solely based on the results derived in Table 2. A more proper examination of how investors evaluate QDII fund performance in their portfolio requires an explicit modelling of variance-co-variance matrix between QDII and other assets in their portfolio. This is not the focus of our study, and thus, beyond the scope of our analysis.

8. We use the absolute return in the full model to reflect the results from the bilateral regressions. As a robust check, we replace the absolute return with other performance measures, and the coefficients remain statistically significant.

9. Because many QDII funds in our sample have experienced turnover of managers, we account for the time overlap by using fractional numbers. For example if

a fund has two managers for half of the investment period, and one manager for the other half, we assign a score of 1.5 for the fund.

10. The issue of limited foreign investing experience of QDII fund managers leading to poor performance is well recognized and documented in the existing literature (see Gong, 2009; Gu, 2008; Yang, 2012). However, none of the existing research has provided empirical evidence of the relationship.

11. Gu (2008) highlighted a number of deficiencies of local-trained fund managers in managing global portfolios. These include (1) insufficient risk management skills, particularly around the time of the GFC, (2) a lack of knowledge in using derivative products to manage risk and enhance returns, (3) a 'typical' style of trading on 'inside' information in the A-share market is not useful in mature markets and (4) excessive speculation, such as betting on high P/E conceptual stocks and corporate restructuring, which is highly profitable in A-share markets, is less effective in developed markets, where the focus tends to be on long-term value investing.

12. A globally focused fund will take a value of 1 in the global dummy, and 0 if it is a regional-focus fund, which include emerging market funds and BRIC funds.

13. As mentioned before, the small sample size could have reduced the statistical significance of the coefficients, although the signs of the coefficients are less affected. We therefore focus on the signs, and see if they are consistent with our hypothesis.

14. The results generally stay the same, if we replace the performance variable with currency-adjusted returns.

15. We also tried a dummy variable to capture whether a QDII fund has an overseas investment consultant. However, the variable is insignificant and has a negative sign, contrary to our expectation. Ba (2010) and Ye (2011) discuss this issue and document the disappointing performance of funds with foreign consultants. Ye (2011) notes that some QDII funds actually saw their performance improved after they separated from their partners.

16. See the appendix for the names of the funds represented by the alphabetical letters.

17. We use the absolute return here, since it is found to be the most significant performance measure on which investors' withdrawal/injection decisions are based. If the excess return relative to the benchmark is used instead, one needs to adjust for the funds' over/under exposure to Hong Kong relative to the benchmark weights.

18. QDII funds that do not invest in the Hong Kong market are excluded from the plot. Most of the omitted funds are non-equity funds.

19. For example, Cheung et al. (2006) predicts that Hong Kong will capture around 10% of outward portfolio investment from China. In fact, even under their most optimistic scenario, Hong Kong would only capture around 20% of the total investment, which is much lower than the proportion of QDII funds invested in Hong Kong currently.

20. We have talked to some QDII fund managers and informed market participants, who follow the industry closely.

21. A number of QDII funds employ Hong Kong based fund managers, in which case the Hong Kong market is their 'home market'.

22. Note that a manager's working experience in Hong Kong and Taiwan is not qualified as overseas experience in our construction. Also, we do our best, based on the available information, to distinguish those that truly worked overseas from those that worked for a foreign institution in China.

23. We constructed a hypothetical two-asset optimal equity portfolio for a Chinese investor, consisting of domestic equity (CSI 300 Index) and foreign equity (MSCI Developed World Index), based on historical data going back to 1991. Using the 10-year Chinese government bond yield as the rate-free rate, the portfolio assigns 43% weight to domestic equity and 57% to foreign equity respectively. In reality, one would expect the domestic market weight to be much higher, given investors' home-bias tendency and market frictions (such as capital controls) that limit foreign investment.

24. Our results from Table 2 showing that QDII investors tend to base their withdrawal/injection decisions on absolute returns, as opposed to risk-adjusted returns, are consistent with this observation.

ACKNOWLEDGMENTS

The authors thank Dong He and an anonymous referee for their constructive comments on the chapter, and Jonathan Kam and Michael Dai for research assistance.

The views expressed in this chapter are those of the authors, and do not necessarily reflect those of the Hong Kong Monetary Authority, Hong Kong Institute for Monetary Research, its Council of Advisers or the Board of Directors.

REFERENCES

Ba, S. S. (2007). Why QD II encounters 'cold'. *Xi'an Finance*, *3*, 12–15.

Ba, S. S. (2010). The future of QDII and QFII in China. *China Logistic Journal, Opinion*, *9*.

Cao, G. S. (2010). Review of commercial bank QDII products and a discussion of its future. *Modern Finance*, *011*, 11–12.

Chan, K., Covrig, V., & Ng, L. (2005). What determines the domestic bias and foreign bias? Evidence from mutual fund equity allocations worldwide. *The Journal of Finance*, *60*(3), 1495.

Chen, J., Hong, H., Huang, M., & Kubik, J. D. (2004). Does fund size erode mutual fund performance? the role of liquidity and organization. *The American Economic Review*, *94*(5), 1276–1302.

Cheung, L., Chow, K., Chang, J., & Li, U. (2006, September). *Outward portfolio investment from mainland China: How much do we expect and how large a share can Hong Kong expect to capture?* HKMA Working Papers, No. 0613, Hong Kong Monetary Authority.

Retrieved from http://www.hkma.gov.hk/media/eng/publication-and-research/research/working-papers/pre2007/RM13-2006.pdf

Eichberger, J. (1999). On relative performance contracts and fund manager's incentives, *European Economic Review*, *43*(1), 135.

Evans, A. L. (2008). Portfolio manager ownership and mutual fund performance. *Financial Management Tampa*, *37*(3), 513.

Gong J. G. (2009). *Current situation of QDII and an analysis of its future development.* Productivity Research, No. 23.

Gu, L. M. (2008). QDII: A poor start waiting for a turnaround. *China Securities Journal*, *4*, 47–49.

He, D., Cheung, L., Zhang, W. L. & Wu, T., (2012). *How would capital account liberalization affect China's capital flows and the renminbi real exchange rate?* HKIMR Working Paper No. 09/2012, Hong Kong Institute for Monetary Research. Retrieved from http://www.hkimr.org/uploads/publication/17/ub_full_0_2_316_wp-no-09_2012-final-.pdf

He, D., & Wang, H. L. (2012). Dual-track interest rates and the conduct of monetary policy in China. *China Economic Review*, *23*(4), 928–947.

Hu, F. (2005). Capital flows, overheating, and the nominal exchange rate regime in china. *Cato Journal*, *25*(2), 357.

Indro, D. C. (1999). Mutual fund performance: Does fund size matter? *Financial Analysts Journal*, *55*(3), 74.

Liang, Y. (2004). Hong Kong stock market is the biggest beneficiary of the QDII scheme. Shanghai Securities News.

Lütje, T. (2007). What drives home bias? evidence from fund managers' views. *International Journal of Finance Economics*, *12*(1), 21.

Ministry of Commerce (MoC) of People's Republic of China. (2011). *2011 statistical bulletin of China's outward foreign direct investment.*

PBC. (2012). Improving the exchange rate reforms and the liberalisation of the capital accounts. *China Securities Journal.*

Shenzhen Stock Exchange. (2012). Investor structure of the Shenzhen stock market. Investor education column, Risk education. Retrieved from http://www.szse.cn/main/investor/fxjy/tzfx/39747560.shtml

Shu, C., Su, X. J., Chang, J., & Miao, H. (2008). China's monetary regime in dealing with large BoP surpluses: framework, effectiveness and costs. *China Economic Issues, Hong Kong Monetary Authority*, (03/2008).

State Administration of Foreign Exchange (SAFE). (2012), *Annual report: Monitoring China inward/outward capital flows* (2011).

Tesar, L. L. (1995). Home bias and high turnover. *Journal of International Money and Finance*, *14*(4), 467.

Yang, J. Y. (2012). The implementation of the QDII scheme in China, problems and solutions. *Chinese Market*, *9*, 70–71.

Ye G. (2011), Analysis: China QDII fund 'relying on its own FT «Ignites Asia».

You, Y. X. (2007). The problems and solutions in the sales of QDII products. *Science and Technology Journal*, *29*.

APPENDIX

Fund	English Name	Chinese Name
A	ICBC Credit Suisse Global Selected Stock Fund	工銀瑞信全球精選
B	CHINA MERCHANTS MERCHANTS GLOBAL RESOURCES EQUITY FUND	招商全球資源
C	China International Emerging Markets Stock Fund	上投摩根新兴市场
D	CCB Principal Emerging Markets Selected Stock Fund	建信新興市場
E	UBS SDIC Emerging Markets Stock Fund	國投瑞銀新興市場
F	Changsheng Global Prosperity Industrial Large-cap Selected Stock Fund	長盛環球景氣行業
G	Huatai-PineBridge Asia Leading Enterprise Stock Fund	華泰柏瑞亞洲
H	China International Asia-Pacific Advantage Stock Fund	上投摩根亞太優勢
I	CCB Principal Global Opportunity Stock Fund	建信全球機遇
J	China Southtern BRICs Index Fund	南方金磚
K	ICBC Credit Suisse China Opportunity Global Balanced Stock Fund	工銀端信全球配置
L	GF Asia-Pacific (ex Japan) Selection Stock Fund	廣發亞太
M	Bank of Communictions Schroder Global Selected Value Fund	交銀環球精選
N	China Unversal Asia Australia Mature Market (expect Japan) Advanced Selected Stock Fund	汇添富亞澳
O	China Merchants S and P BRICs Index Fund (LOF)	招商標普金磚
P	E Fund Asia Selected Stock Fund	易方达亚洲
Q	China Global Selected Stock Fund	華夏全球精選
R	Bosera Greater China Asia-Pacific Selected Stock Fund	博時大中華亞太
S	Fortis Haitong Greater China Selected Stock Fund	海富通大中華
T	Invesco Great Wall Greater China Stock Fund	景順長城大中華
U	Hua An Greater China Upgrade Stock Fund	華安大中華升級
V	China Southern China Mid and Small Cap Index Fund	南方中小盘
W	Fortune SGAM Overseas China Growth Stock Fund	華寶興業中國成長
X	Fortis Haitong China Overseas Selected Stock Fund	海富通海外精選
Y	Hua An Hong Kong Selection Stock Fund	華安香港
Z	Harvest Overseas China Stock Fund	嘉實海外中國股票
AA	Harvest Hang Seng China Enterprises Index Fund (QDII-LOF)	嘉實恒生中國

ARE THERE RETURN AND VOLATILITY SPILLOVERS FROM MAJOR BANK STOCKS TO THE NATIONAL STOCK MARKET IN THE UK?

Panagiotis Dontis-Charitos, Orla Gough, K. Ben Nowman and Sheeja Sivaprasad

ABSTRACT

We investigate the return and volatility spillovers from major UK banks to Financial Times Stock Exchange 100 (FTSE 100) index using Gaussian estimation and continuous time models as well as discrete time multivariate GARCH (MGARCH) modelling approaches. Using daily, weekly and monthly data over the period December 1999–December 2010, which includes the recent 2007–2009 global financial crisis, empirical estimates of uni- and/or bi-directional return and volatility spillovers are provided. The bivariate MGARCH results reveal strong return spillovers from the FTSE to the banks, and no return spillover from the latter to the FTSE. Nevertheless, strong bi-directional volatility

Global Banking, Financial Markets and Crises
International Finance Review, Volume 14, 243–268

ISSN: 1569-3767/doi:10.1108/S1569-3767(2013)0000014012

transmission is verified. The continuous time analysis provides mixed evidence of feedback effects over the different models.

Keywords: Return; volatility; spillovers; bank stocks; stock market

JEL classifications: E44; G01; C32

INTRODUCTION

The current global economic system is characterized by strong interdependencies, both within and between economies/sectors. With spillover effects being the norm rather than the exception, if an economy experiences a major shock it is very difficult to contain the damage from spreading. The recent banking crisis caused the S&P500 index to shed more than 45% of its value between June 2007 and November 2008, while the effects rapidly spilled over to the rest of the world and developed into a global economic shock, resulting in plummeting stock markets and widespread bank failures. As such, it is not a coincidence that the unprecedented trend towards convergence[1] in the financial services industry – as witnessed in mega-mergers and the creation of financial conglomerates – raises considerable concerns regarding the effects on the stability of the financial system (Herring & Santomero, 1990). These concerns mainly stem from a wider appreciation of the role of financial conglomerates in propagating shocks and the inherent difficulties in regulating those complex institutions (Herring & Carmassi, 2009; Wagner, 2008).

As a matter of fact, the concerns regarding convergence are based on the notion that risk may spill over more easily across financial institutions (FIs) if the latter are highly interconnected (Carey & Stulz, 2005), something that may lead to system-wide problems such as those experienced during the financial crisis. The latter serve to remind all stakeholders of the inherent flaws within the current financial regulatory system, and trigger the debate on the future form of the regulatory and supervisory arena (Harrington, 2009; Moshirian, 2011a, 2011b). A white paper released in June 2009 by the U.S. Department of the Treasury (2009) outlines proposals for financial regulatory reform. The white paper attributes much of the blame for the financial crisis on the failure of large and interconnected FIs.

There is no question that the various causes of the financial crisis will be probed and debated for the decades to come. Yet, one of the most important issues attracting recent scrutiny from both academics and regulators alike is the effect of convergence in the financial sector and the interconnectedness of large FIs on systemic risk. However, despite the growing attention on this matter, the question still remains on convergence. Nonetheless, the conclusions to this debate are of extreme importance to all stakeholders, as they will determine the future architecture, regulation and supervision of the financial system and FIs.

The majority of past contributions are limited to the modelling of risk–return spillovers across FIs, within and/or across national boundaries. Nonetheless, the nature of systemic risk is such that the latter transcends sectoral boundaries and can cause extreme turbulence to the global economy. In effect, although the existing contributions do indeed shed light on the interconnectedness of these institutions – through the ever growing linkages among the first and/or second moments of their returns – they do not provide evidence on whether shocks from these institutions are transmitted to the economy. Given the fact that systemic risk is nowadays of utmost importance for regulators and policymakers alike, it is necessary to also look into whether the stock market as a whole is prone to return and volatility spillovers from these institutions.

The aim of the chapter is to fill this gap by testing for the presence of return and volatility spillovers from three major UK banks to the Financial Times Stock Exchange 100 (FTSE 100) index, which includes the 100 largest companies by market value on the London Stock Exchange.[2] The UK market offers an ideal landscape for the purposes of this study. Specifically, three out of the five largest banks in the world are based in the UK.[3] Given that the prior literature has established that spillover effects are stronger with size, if any effects do exist in our context, these should be observable in the UK market.

On the methodological side, we add to the debate on modelling in discrete as well as continuous time, which has long been a choice in empirical econometric modelling. The problem with the estimation of continuous time models is that we only have discrete data typically at daily, monthly and quarterly intervals, so a considerable amount of research has concentrated on developing estimation methods to use this available discrete time data (see Bergstrom, 1976, 1984, 1990, 1996; Bergstrom & Nowman, 2007; Phillips & Yu, 2009). General Gaussian estimation methods have been developed by Bergstrom (1990) for the estimation of general continuous time dynamic models with discrete time series data and have been applied in different areas (see Bergstrom and Nowman (2007) for a major application to a UK macroeconomic model and for other applications). Nowman (1997) first applied Gaussian estimation methods in finance to interest rate modelling and these methods are used in this chapter (see also Nowman, 2001, 2002, 2003, 2006).

There are a number of benefits of modelling in continuous time. For example, since the economy and financial markets are continuously operating and the underlying decision processes we are trying to model involve millions of decisions by economic agents within the recorded data observation interval, realistic models will depend on the continuous passage of time and should therefore be formulated in differential equation form. Another advantage is that continuous time formulations allow for a more precise description of the partial adjustment mechanisms to the equilibrium level to be modelled. There are a number of other advantages of continuous time modelling (see Bergstrom, 1990, Chapter 1, 1996; Bergstrom & Nowman, 2007, Chapter 1).

The main contribution of the chapter is twofold. First, we extend previous spillover work to model return and volatility transmissions from large UK banks to the FTSE and vice versa. Second, the application of a continuous time approach in this context and the comparison with discrete time results allow us to gauge the sensitivity of the latter to a change of modelling approach. By way of preview, the discrete time analysis does not reveal any return-related spillovers from any of the banks to the index, but does provide some evidence of uni-directional return spillovers across bank pairs. On the contrary, we find strong volatility spillovers across the majority of bank pairs and/or bank-index pairs. The continuous time analysis provides mixed evidence of feedback effects over the different models. These results help inform the debate on the structure, regulation and supervision of systemically important FIs. In particular, they highlight the need for measures to minimize the probability of failures of such institutions and/or shield the financial system from the aftershocks such failures could create.

The rest of the chapter is organized as follows: the second section provides related literature and the third section outlines the continuous time models and discrete time models used. The fourth section presents the data. Empirical results are given in the fifth section and some conclusions in the sixth section.

RELATED LITERATURE

Several studies on the equity returns of FIs reveal strong linkages caused by information flows across these (Flannery, 1998). By way of preview, they verify the existence of wealth spillover effects across FIs (Elyasiani, Mansur, & Pagano, 2007) and, in particular, those caused by banking/insurance failures or distress announcements (Aharony & Swary, 1983, 1996; Brewer & Jackson, 2002; Kaufman, 1994). The risk-spillover effects, however, have received attention only recently, with Elyasiani, Mansur, and Pagano (2007) reporting strong volatility spillover effects across FIs and Elyasiani and Mansur (2003) pointing to strong interest-rate and idiosyncratic volatility spillover effects in the equity prices of banks across the United States, Japan and Germany. Unlike the findings above, Carson, Elyasiani, and Mansur (2008) report weak evidence on volatility spillovers across insurance companies.

More specifically, Elyasiani, Mansur, and Pagano (2007) examine the risk-return linkages across all U.S. commercial banks, securities firms and life insurance companies traded on the NYSE, AMEX and Nasdaq between 1991 and 2001. They investigate the transmission of changes in the level and volatility of stock returns across these firms using a multivariate GARCH (MGARCH) model. Their results verify the presence of wealth spillover effects across smaller FIs and the presence of strong volatility spillover effects across large institutions. The latter finding provides additional support to concerns discussed above; in particular, those related to the interconnectedness of large FIs and their role in the diffusion of the financial crisis across sectors and borders. In a similar vein, Elyasiani and Mansur (2003) use a sample of 47, 85 and 7 large banking institutions for the United States, Japan and Germany, respectively. Their results suggest strong interest-rate and idiosyncratic volatility spillover effects in the equity prices of banks across these countries. The return and volatility spillover effects across sectors of the U.S. insurance industry, from 1991 to 2001, are examined in Carson, Elyasiani, and Mansur (2008). They report strong return spillovers but fail to establish the presence of volatility spillovers across insurance sectors, with the exception of a uni-directional volatility transmission from the accident and health sector to the life segment.

Another issue of particular interest that has been examined in the academic literature is that of spillover effects caused by banking/insurance failures or distress announcements. For example Aharony and Swary (1983) look into the three largest bank failures in the 1970s to examine the presence of contagion effects.[4] They fail to find any contagion effects for the two cases where the failure was caused by firm specific factors, but report strong contagion effects for one of the cases examined, where the failure was induced by external factors. In a similar fashion, Brewer and Jackson (2002) look into the inter-industry spillover effects of three distress-related announcements across 134 banks and 61 life insurance companies. Although they find evidence of strong inter-industry contagion, the results suggest that the effects are not purely contagious in nature but directly linked to factors such as geographic proximity, asset portfolio composition, liability portfolio composition and regulatory expectations. These results give rise to the issue of the so-called 'pure panic' versus 'information based' contagion discussed in Aharony and Swary (1996).

CONTINUOUS AND DISCRETE TIME MODELLING OF SPILLOVERS

In what follows, the continuous and discrete time approaches are introduced.

Continuous Time Model

Continuous time modelling has been extensively applied in the economic and financial modelling of variables. Bergstrom (1990, 1996) and Bergstrom and Nowman (2007) provide extensive advantages of modelling in continuous time and the development of Gaussian estimation methods and applications. In modelling interest-rate behaviour a general continuous time interest rate model was developed by Chan, Karolyi, Longstaff, and Sanders (1992) and included the special cases of Cox, Ingersoll, and Ross (1985, CIRSR) and Brennan and Schwartz (1980, BRSC). One approach in the literature to estimating these models by Nowman (1997) uses an approximate discrete model and the general Gaussian estimation methods of Bergstrom (1990) (see also Bergstrom & Nowman, 2007). Applications of this methodology include Episcopos (2000), Nowman (2002, 2006) and Nowman and Yahia (2008). Gaussian estimation of multi-factor versions of the CKLS model with feedback effects in the mean and volatility correlation was considered in Nowman (2001, 2003) for the CKLS and CIRSR models. We apply the model specifications in Nowman (2003) in the analysis of the feedbacks in this chapter.

The CKLS continuous time model is specified as follows:

$$dr(t) = \{\alpha + \beta r(t)\}dt + \sigma r^{\gamma}(t)\zeta(dt) \quad (t \geq 0) \tag{1}$$

where $\{r(t), t>0\}$ is the dependent variable which in this application is defined as the logarithm of the variable, α and β are the unknown drift and mean reversion parameters; σ is the volatility and γ is the elasticity of the relationship between the level of the variable to the volatility. This is called the '*Level-Effect*'. The error term $\zeta(dt)$ is defined as white noise as in Nowman (1997).

The CKLS and CIRSR models with $\gamma=0.5$ with conditional mean feedback effects were considered in Nowman (2003) which we also now include in the BRSC model assumption with $\gamma=1.0$.

$$dr_1(t)=\{\alpha_1+\beta_1 r_1(t)+\beta_2 r_2(t)\}dt+\zeta_1(dt) \quad (t\geq 0) \tag{2}$$

$$dr_2(t)=\{\alpha_2+\beta_3 r_2(t)+\beta_4 r_1(t)\}dt+\zeta_2(dt) \quad (t\geq 0) \tag{3}$$

The $r_1(t)$ and $r_2(t)$ present the log of the stock market and bank variables and α_1, α_2, β_1, β_2, β_3 and β_4 are the unknown parameters. The error term is assumed in Nowman (2003) to satisfy Assumption 1:

Assumption 1. ζ_1 and ζ_2 are random measures defined on all subsets of the half line $0 < t < \infty$ with finite Lebesgue measure, such that: $E[\zeta_1(dt)]=0, E[\zeta_2(dt)]=0$ and $E[\zeta_1(dt)\zeta_2(dt)]=(dt)\sum(r,t)$ where $\sum(r,t)$ was a positive definite matrix assumed in Nowman (2003) to be given below which allows for correlation between them.

$$\sum(r,t)=\begin{bmatrix}\sigma_1^2 r_1^{2\gamma_1}(t) & \rho_{12}\sigma_1\sigma_2 r_1^{\gamma_1}(t)r_2^{\gamma_2}(t)\\ \rho_{21}\sigma_2\sigma_1 r_2^{\gamma_2}(t)r_1^{\gamma_1}(t) & \sigma_2^2 r_2^{2\gamma_2}(t)\end{bmatrix}$$

The discrete model used in Nowman (2003) to obtain the estimates of the continuous time models parameters is given below:

$$r_t=e^{\beta}r_{t-1}+\left(e^{\beta}-I\right)\beta^{-1}\alpha+\varepsilon_t \quad (t=1,\ldots,T) \tag{4}$$

where

$$E\left(\varepsilon_t\varepsilon_t'\right)=\int_0^1 e^{r\beta}\sum^{*}(r,t)e^{r\beta'}dr=\Omega(r,t)$$

$$\alpha=\begin{bmatrix}\alpha_1\\ \alpha_2\end{bmatrix},\quad \beta=\begin{bmatrix}\beta_1 & \beta_2\\ \beta_4 & \beta_3\end{bmatrix},\quad e^{\beta}=I+\sum_{i=1}^{\infty}\frac{1}{i!}\beta^i$$

and $\sum^*$ is defined in Nowman (2003) which has the same structure as $\sum$. The Gaussian estimates are obtained from the Gaussian likelihood function (see Nowman, 2003) below:

$$L(\theta) = \sum_{t=1}^{T} \log(|\Omega(r,t)|) + \sum_{t=1}^{T} \varepsilon_t' \Omega^{-1}(r,t)\varepsilon_t \tag{5}$$

Discrete Time Model

MGARCH models are now widely used in the academic literature due to their applicability on modelling the relations between the mean and volatility of various asset classes. The most popular approaches are the VECH model proposed by Bollerslev, Engle, and Wooldridge (1988), the CCC model (Bollerslev, 1990), the factor ARCH model (Engle, Ng, & Rothschild, 1990) and the BEKK model (Engle & Kroner, 1995).[5]

The discrete time analysis of the return and risk spillover effects across three major UK banking firms and the FTSE is based on the MGARCH methodology. The MGARCH approach used here facilitates the modelling of the relationship between the returns, volatilities (conditional variances) and cross-volatilities (conditional co-variances) of the above series. Specifically, the modelling of the return transmission is achieved by inflating the mean equations with cross-return terms ($R_{j,t-1}$ and R_{k-1}, where $j \neq k \neq i$). In turn, we also extend the traditional GARCH specification for the volatility with cross-volatility terms ($h_{jj,t-1}$ and $h_{kk,t-1}$, where $j \neq k \neq i$). The econometric analysis is carried out as a two-stage process. In the first stage, we employ a bivariate specification. In this case, the risk–return spillover effects from each of the three banks to the FTSE and vice versa are modelled using the following specifications:

$$R_{1,t} = \alpha_1 + \beta_2 R_{1,t-1} + \beta_{21} R_{2,t-1} + \varepsilon_{1,t} \tag{6}$$

$$h_{11,t} = \omega_1 + \lambda_{11}^2 \varepsilon_{1,t-1}^2 + \gamma_{11}^2 h_{11,t-1} + \vartheta_{21} h_{22,t-1} \tag{7}$$

$$R_{2,t} = \alpha_2 + \beta_3 R_{2,t-1} + \beta_{12} R_{1,t-1} + \varepsilon_{2,t} \tag{8}$$

$$h_{22,t} = \omega_2 + \lambda_{22}^2 \varepsilon_{2,t-1}^2 + \gamma_{22}^2 h_{22,t-1} + \vartheta_{12} h_{11,t-1} \tag{9}$$

In the second stage, we extend the specification to a trivariate case. Here, we model the risk–return spillover effects across groups comprising two banks and the FTSE. Both the bivariate and trivariate models require the respective equations to be estimated three times to account for all possible combinations. The detailed specification of the trivariate model is provided below:

$$R_{1,t} = \alpha_1 + \beta_2 R_{1,t-1} + \beta_{21} R_{2,t-1} + \beta_{31} R_{3,t-1} + \varepsilon_{1,t} \tag{10}$$

$$h_{11,t} = \omega_1 + \lambda_{11}^2 \varepsilon_{1,t-1}^2 + \gamma_{11}^2 h_{11,t-1} + \vartheta_{21} h_{22,t-1} + \vartheta_{31} h_{33,t-1} \tag{11}$$

$$R_{2,t} = \alpha_2 + \beta_3 R_{2,t-1} + \beta_{12} R_{1,t-1} + \beta_{32} R_{3,t-1} + \varepsilon_{2,t} \tag{12}$$

$$h_{22,t} = \omega_2 + \lambda_{22}^2 \varepsilon_{2,t-1}^2 + \gamma_{22}^2 h_{22,t-1} + \vartheta_{12} h_{11,t-1} + \vartheta_{32} h_{33,t-1} \tag{13}$$

$$R_{3,t} = \alpha_3 + \beta_4 R_{3,t-1} + \beta_{13} R_{1,t-1} + \beta_{23} R_{2,t-1} + \varepsilon_{3,t} \tag{14}$$

$$h_{33,t} = \omega_3 + \lambda_{33}^2 \varepsilon_{3,t-1}^2 + \gamma_{33}^2 h_{33,t-1} + \vartheta_{13} h_{11,t-1} + \vartheta_{23} h_{22,t-1} \tag{15}$$

The properties of the error term from both the bivariate and the trivariate specifications are represented in Eq. (16), while the specification of the conditional covariances is represented in Eq. (17).

$$\varepsilon_{i,t} \sim N(0, h_{ii,t}) \tag{16}$$

$$h_{ij,t} = h_{ji,t} = \omega_{ij} + \lambda_{ii}\, \varepsilon_{i,t-1}\, \varepsilon_{j,t-1}\, \lambda_{jj} + \gamma_{ii} h_{ij,t-1} \gamma_{jj}, \quad i \neq j \tag{17}$$

In all the above specifications, indexes i and j are integers taking the values of 1 and 2 (bivariate) and 1, 2 and 3 (trivariate) to represent the returns and conditional variances of a combination of either one banking firm and the FTSE (bivariate), or groups of two banking firms and the FTSE (trivariate), respectively; $R_{i,t}$ is the return of bank/index i at time t; $\varepsilon_{i,t}$ is the error term with properties described in Eq. (16), whereas $\alpha, \beta, \omega, \lambda$ and ϑ are the parameters to be estimated, with the latter (ϑ_{ji}) capturing the volatility transmission from bank/index j to bank/index i. Furthermore, $h_{ii,t}$ and $h_{ij,t}$ are the conditional variances and conditional covariances, respectively. These are derived from H_t, a conditional variance–covariance matrix parameterized using the diagonal BEKK approach, where H_t is modelled as follows:

$$H_t = C'C + A'\varepsilon_{t-1}\varepsilon_{t-1}'A + B'H_{t-1}B \tag{18}$$

where C is an upper triangular matrix, while A and B are diagonal matrices.

DATA

The data used in this study are daily, weekly and monthly prices for Royal Bank of Scotland (RBS), HSBC, Barclays Bank (BARC) and the FTSE level over the period December 1999–December 2010 giving a total of 2,782 daily observations, 574 weekly observations and 132 monthly observations. Table 1 shows the basic summary statistics for the log level and returns. The first six auto-correlations of the levels decay slowly and the first differences are small. The ADF statistics do not reject the null hypothesis of a unit root at the 5% level. Figs. 1–3 display the levels and the returns. As can be seen the impact of the recent financial crisis increased volatility in the market dramatically.

EMPIRICAL EVIDENCE[6]

Continuous Time Model

The Gaussian estimates (standard errors in brackets) of the different continuous time models are presented in Table 2. Following Nowman (1997, 2006) the explanatory power of each model is compared to the unrestricted model using the maximized Gaussian log likelihood function value.

For the daily data for the two-factor CKLS model for RBS-FTSE volatility level effects are $\gamma_1 = -2.5727; \gamma_2 = -1.7375$; and significant. There is weak evidence of feedback effects in the mean return from the FTSE in the CKLS model and evidence of feedback in the BRSC model. Based on the log-likelihood values the CIRSR and then the BRSC model perform

Table 1. Summary Statistics: 1999–2010.

Variable	Mean	S.D.	ρ_1	ρ_2	ρ_3	ρ_4	ρ_5	ρ_6	ADF
Daily RBS									
$r(t)$	5.5701	0.9747	0.99	0.99	0.99	0.99	0.99	0.99	−1.5000
$\Delta r(t)$	−0.0007	0.0390	0.11	−0.05	0.06	0.04	−0.06	−0.08	−22.811
HSBC									
$r(t)$	6.5633	0.1457	0.99	0.98	0.98	0.97	0.96	0.96	−3.4516
$\Delta r(t)$	−0.0001	0.0188	−0.02	−0.06	−0.03	0.02	−0.03	−0.07	−40.003
BARC									
$r(t)$	6.0789	0.3756	0.99	0.99	0.98	0.98	0.97	0.97	−2.4304
$\Delta r(t)$	−0.0002	0.0322	0.04	0.03	−0.02	0.02	−0.06	−0.07	−50.455
FTSE									
$r(t)$	8.5568	0.1633	0.99	0.99	0.98	0.98	0.98	0.98	−1.9769
$\Delta r(t)$	−0.0001	0.0132	−0.07	−0.05	−0.08	0.09	−0.05	−0.05	−25.385
Weekly RBS									
$r(t)$	5.5768	0.9696	0.99	0.98	0.97	0.97	0.96	0.96	−1.5624
$\Delta r(t)$	−0.0034	0.0878	−0.00	−0.13	−0.06	0.09	0.15	0.02	−19.293
HSBC									
$r(t)$	6.5630	0.1453	0.96	0.93	0.90	0.87	0.85	0.82	−2.9775
$\Delta r(t)$	−0.0002	0.0397	−0.12	0.05	−0.08	0.07	−0.03	−0.03	−26.915
BARC									
$r(t)$	6.0797	0.3785	0.97	0.95	0.94	0.92	0.91	0.89	−2.7733
$\Delta r(t)$	−0.0008	0.0815	−0.07	−0.13	0.04	−0.03	−0.01	0.13	−20.077
FTSE									
$r(t)$	8.5575	0.1639	0.98	0.97	0.95	0.94	0.93	0.92	−2.2379
$\Delta r(t)$	−0.0002	0.0269	−0.08	0.06	−0.14	−0.04	0.07	0.06	−25.941
Monthly RBS									
$r(t)$	5.5811	0.9642	0.97	0.94	0.91	0.87	0.84	0.80	−1.2981
$\Delta r(t)$	−0.0154	0.1532	0.19	0.04	0.08	0.08	−0.02	−0.17	−9.5013
HSBC									
$r(t)$	6.5629	0.1419	0.88	0.76	0.66	0.53	0.42	0.30	−2.8286
$\Delta r(t)$	−0.0011	0.0682	0.02	−0.06	0.09	−0.02	−0.04	−0.16	−11.370
BARC									
$r(t)$	6.0824	0.3630	0.93	0.84	0.77	0.72	0.64	0.56	−2.2185
$\Delta r(t)$	−0.0040	0.1226	0.24	−0.17	−0.09	0.16	−0.01	−0.23	−8.8548
FTSE									
$r(t)$	8.5570	0.1644	0.95	0.91	0.87	0.82	0.76	0.70	−2.0114
$\Delta r(t)$	−0.0017	0.0442	0.07	−0.07	0.04	0.19	0.02	0.02	−10.782

Note: The variable $r(t)$ is the log level and $\Delta r(t)$ is the change, and ρ_j is the autocorrelation coefficient of order$j$.

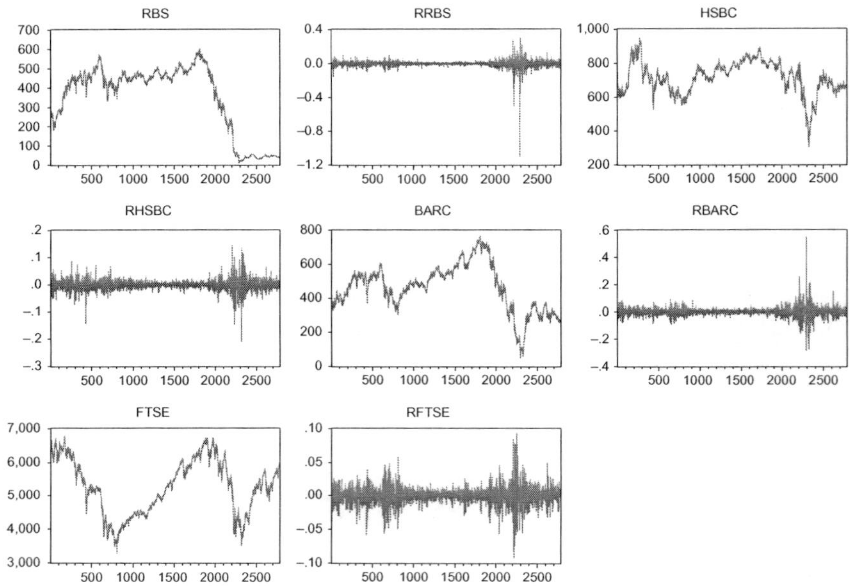

Fig. 1. Daily Level and Returns.

the best. The correlation evidence varies from 47% to 61% over the different models. For the CKLS model for HSBC–FTSE the volatility level effects are $\gamma_1 = -2.5689; \gamma_2 = -2.3995$; and significant. There is evidence of feedback effects in the mean returns from HSBC to the FTSE in the CIRSR and BRSC models. Based on the log-likelihood values the CIRSR model and then the BRSC model perform the best. The correlation varies from 47% to 72% over the different models. Lastly for the CKLS model for BARC–FTSE the volatility level effects are $\gamma_1 = -3.9720$; $\gamma_2 = -3.0000$; and significant. There is weak evidence of feedback effects in the mean returns from the FTSE to BARC in the CKLS model and feedback from BARC in the BRSC model. Based on the log-likelihood values the CIRSR model and then the BRSC model perform the best. The correlation varies from 47% to 69% over the different models.

For the monthly data for the two-factor CKLS model for RBS-FTSE volatility level effects are $\gamma_1 = -2.3378; \gamma_2 = -0.6741$; and significant for RBS. There is no evidence of feedback effects in the mean returns for the different models. For the two-factor CKLS model for HSBC–FTSE the

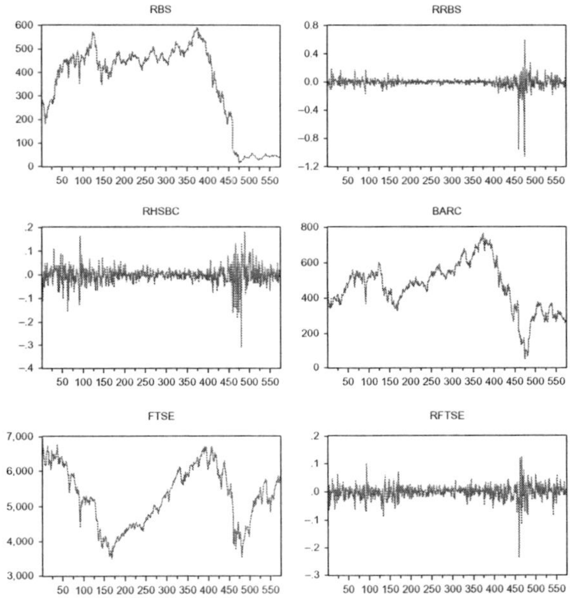

Fig. 2. Weekly Level and Returns.

volatility level effects are $\gamma_1 = -1.8550; \gamma_2 = -0.9200$; and significant for HSBC. There is no evidence of feedback effects in the mean returns for the different models. Lastly for the CKLS model for BARC–FTSE the volatility level effects are $\gamma_1 = -1.9074; \gamma_2 = 0.0653$; and significant. There is evidence of feedback effects in the mean returns from the FTSE to BARC in the CKLS model. For the weekly data for the two-factor CKLS model for RBS-FTSE volatility level effects are $\gamma_1 = -2.2637; \gamma_2 = -2.2037$; and significant. There is no evidence of feedback effects in the mean returns for the different models. For the two-factor CKLS model for HSBC–FTSE the volatility level effects are $\gamma_1 = -2.1620; \gamma_2 = -1.6372$; and significant. There is no evidence of feedback effects in the mean returns for the different models apart from weak evidence from HSBC to the FTSE in the BRSC model. Lastly for the CKLS model for BARC–FTSE the volatility level effects are $\gamma_1 = -3.1633; \gamma_2 = -2.8724$; and significant. There is weak evidence of feedback effects in the mean returns from the FTSE to BARC in the CKLS model.

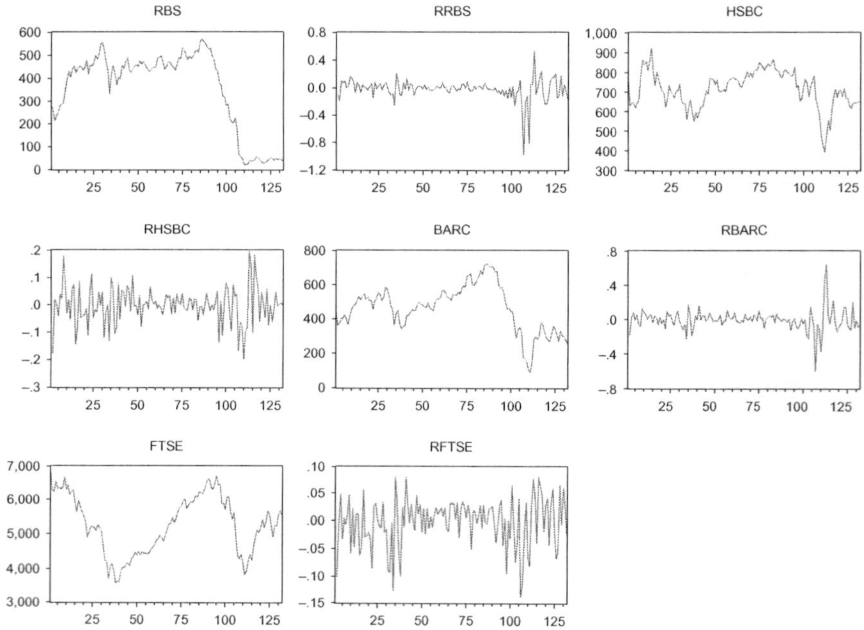

Fig. 3. Monthly Level and Returns.

Discrete Time Model

Two-Factor Models

Table 3 presents the results from the estimation of the system represented by Eqs. (6)–(9). The first two columns of the table describe the coefficients while the respective coefficient estimates are presented under the subsequent columns. Specifically, the bivariate analysis performed here involves the estimation of three sets of models, each one capturing the risk–return spillover effects between a UK bank and the FTSE. The results for these three models are presented under each of the respective headings (Models 1–3).

Looking at the coefficients designed to capture return spillovers, the results reveal the existence of negative return spillovers from the FTSE to both RBS (Model 1) and HSBC (Model 3), that are significant at the 5% and 1% levels, respectively. On the contrary, the returns of BARC

Table 2. Daily Gaussian Estimates of Two-Factor Models.

Parameters	CKLS	CIRSR	BRSC
RBS–FTSE			
α_1	0.0223	0.0274	0.0004
	(0.0201)	(0.0743)	(0.0001)
α_2	0.0338	0.0318	0.0012
	(0.0126)	(0.0174)	(0.0252)
β_1	0.0011	−0.0007	−0.0045
	(0.0011)	(0.0007)	(0.0011)
β_2	−0.0034	−0.0028	0.0012
	(0.0022)	(0.0088)	(0.0001)
β_3	−0.0038	−0.0036	−0.0018
	(0.0015)	(0.0020)	(0.0029)
β_4	−0.0002	−0.0003	0.0039
	(0.0002)	(0.0002)	(0.0005)
γ_1	−2.5727	0.5	1.0
	(0.0078)		
γ_2	−1.7375	0.5	1.0
	(0.0795)		
σ_1^2	5.0067	0.0004	0.0001
	(1.0023)	(0.0001)	(0.0001)
σ_2^2	0.2943	0.0001	0.0001
	(0.0997)	(0.0001)	(0.0001)
ρ_{12}	0.6138	0.4605	0.4707
	(0.0117)	(0.0147)	(0.0455)
Log LF	9,927	9,076	8,141
HSBC–FTSE			
α_1	0.0454	0.0485	0.0006
	(0.0263)	(0.0205)	(0.0129)
α_2	0.0355	0.0377	0.0012
	(0.0191)	(0.0150)	(0.0185)
β_1	−0.0084	-0.0097	−0.0034
	(0.0039)	(0.0025)	(0.0001)
β_2	0.0011	0.0017	0.0026
	(0.0036)	(0.0022)	(0.0027)
β_3	−0.0021	−0.0020	−0.0025
	(0.0024)	(0.0018)	(0.0015)
β_4	−0.0027	−0.0032	0.0043
	(0.0025)	(0.0021)	(0.0013)
γ_1	−2.5689	0.5	1.0
	(0.0071)		
γ_2	−2.3995	0.5	1.0
	(0.0062)		
σ_1^2	5.0023	0.0001	0.0001
	(1.0020)	(0.0001)	(0.0001)

Table 2. *(Continued)*

Parameters	CKLS	CIRSR	BRSC
σ_2^2	5.0012	0.0001	0.0001
	(1.0004)	(0.0001)	(0.0001)
ρ_{12}	0.7243	0.7160	0.4707
	(0.0089)	(0.0092)	(0.0432)
Log LF	10772	10629	9805
BARC–FTSE			
α_1	0.0422	0.0533	0.0005
	(0.0226)	(0.0277)	(0.0158)
α_2	0.0294	0.0313	0.0012
	(0.0122)	(0.0113)	(0.0193)
β_1	−0.0007	−0.0034	−0.0040
	(0.0018)	(0.0018)	(0.0018)
β_2	−0.0045	−0.0038	0.0018
	(0.0030)	(0.0037)	(0.0023)
β_3	−0.0035	−0.0035	−0.0024
	(0.0015)	(0.0015)	(0.0024)
β_4	0.0001	−0.0002	0.0041
	(0.0007)	(0.0007)	(0.0014)
γ_1	−3.9720	0.5	1.0
	(0.0074)		
γ_2	−3.0023	0.5	1.0
	(1.0002)		
σ_1^2	1.0034	0.0002	0.0001
	(1.0200)	(0.0001)	(0.0001)
σ_2^2	6.3923	0.0001	0.0001
	(1.7468)	(0.0001)	(0.0001)
ρ_{12}	0.6881	0.6047	0.4707
	(0.0099)	(0.0120)	(0.0627)
Log LF	10,254	9,610	8,659

(Model 2) do not exhibit any sensitivity to lagged FTSE returns, and thus, no return spillovers prevail in this case. Similar conclusions can be drawn from the cross-return term which is attached to the FTSE (Columns 6–8). All the respective coefficients are insignificant, suggesting no return-related spillovers from any of the banks to the index. However, the results from the volatility equations reveal significant volatility spillovers across the majority of models. Specifically, with the exception of the HSBC–FTSE pair – where only uni-directional volatility transmission is present (from the FTSE to HSBC) – bi-directional volatility spillovers are prevalent for

Table 3. Daily MGARCH Estimates of Two-Factor Models.

Parameters		Model 1		Model 2		Model 3	
		RBS ($i=1, j=2$)	FTSE ($j=2, i=1$)	BARC ($i=1, j=2$)	FTSE ($j=2, i=1$)	HSBC ($i=1, j=2$)	FTSE ($j=2, i=1$)
				Frequency: daily (N = 2,780)			
α_i	Intercept	0.000	0.000	0.001	0.000	0.000	0.000
		(0.928)	(2.677)***	(1.592)	(2.645)***	(1.477)	(2.341)**
β_i	AR (1)	0.049	−0.086	0.020	−0.067	0.019	−0.094
		(1.527)	−(3.670)***	(0.753)	−(2.665)***	(0.590)	−(3.592)***
β_{ji}	Return spillover	−0.122	0.004	−0.042	0.004	−0.115	0.026
		−(2.543)**	(0.429)	−(0.814)	(0.336)	−(3.119)***	(1.399)
ω_i	Intercept	0.000	0.000	0.000	0.000	0.000	0.000
		(3.365)***	(5.452)***	(3.375)***	(4.177)***	(3.125)***	(4.494)***
λ_{ii}^2	$ARCH^2$	0.227	0.081	0.099	0.076	0.062	0.084
		(6.640)***	(14.382)***	(14.064)***	(17.066)***	(14.762)***	(18.562)***
γ_{ii}^2	$GARCH^2$	0.781	0.910	0.899	0.917	0.936	0.907
		(31.890)***	(203.055)***	(140.901)***	(228.030)***	(296.068)***	(205.276)***
ϑ_{ji}	Volatility spillover	0.098	0.001	0.202	0.001	0.013	0.004
		(2.021)**	(1.983)**	(2.902)***	(1.994)**	(1.240)	(1.750)*
$\lambda_{ii}^2 + \gamma_{ii}^2$	Persistence	1.008	0.991	0.998	0.994	0.998	0.991
Log LF		16,068.27		16,257.38		17,602.85	

Note: The numbers in brackets are z-statistics. In addition, ***, ** and * represent statistical significance at the 1%, 5% and 10% levels, respectively.

all other bank-index combinations. The fact that volatility is transmitted from these banks to the FTSE indicates how large/important these institutions are and how, otherwise pure, idiosyncratic shocks can manifest into system-wide shocks.

Results for the weekly and monthly frequencies are now briefly discussed. These results reveal a different pattern. For the weekly data, the coefficients attached on the cross-return terms are insignificant across all models. When the volatility is considered, the results are diametrically different from those reported in Table 3 and point to insignificant volatility spillovers. The only case where volatility spillovers are present is the HSBC–FTSE pair, where there is weak statistical evidence (10% significance) of volatility transmission from the FTSE to HSBC. The monthly data estimates, on the other hand, point to a negative and significant return spillover from the FTSE to HSBC, something consistent with daily estimates. Interestingly, the monthly results also provide weak evidence of a return spillover from BARC to FTSE; the coefficient on the cross-return is positive and significant at the 10% level. Shifting our attention to the volatility, the monthly results are comparable to the weekly ones.

Three-Factor Models

This section extends the previous one by employing three-factor models. Table 4 presents the results from the estimation of the system in Eqs. (10)–(15) and follows the same structure as Table 3.

Looking at the coefficients designed to capture return spillovers, the results from the second cross-return term point to the existence of negative and significant return spillovers from the FTSE to both RBS and BARC (Model 1), RBS and HSBC (Model 2) and, finally, from the FTSE to HSBC (Model 3). Moreover, the results from the first cross-return term only reveal a uni-directional feedback effect from RBS to BARC that is positive and significant at the 1% level. Interestingly, the cross-return terms attached to the FTSE across all models fail to capture a significant return spillover from any of the three banks to the index, something consistent with the results from the bivariate models.

In line with the results from the bivariate models, the volatility equations reveal some interesting results. Looking at the cross-volatility terms, the coefficients show strong bi-directional volatility transmissions across the RBS–BARC (Model 1) and RBS–HSBC (Model 2) pairs. On the contrary, when the BARC–HSBC pair is considered (Model 3) the results only point to uni-directional volatility feedback, that is from HSBC to

Table 4. Daily MGARCH Estimates of Three-Factor Models.

Parameters		Model 1			Model 2			Model 3		
		RBS ($i=1$)	BARC ($i=1$)	FTSE ($i=1$)	RBS ($i=1$)	HSBC ($i=1$)	FTSE ($i=1$)	BARC ($i=1$)	HSBC ($i=1$)	FTSE ($i=1$)
					Frequency: daily ($N=2780$)					
α_i	Intercept	0.000	0.001	0.000	0.000	0.000	0.000	0.001	0.000	0.000
		(1.366)	(1.617)	(2.792)***	(0.697)	(1.643)	(2.508)**	(1.660)*	(1.771)*	(2.586)***
β_i	AR (1)	−0.008	−0.023	−0.088	0.050	−0.005	−0.112	0.018	0.000	−0.078
		−(0.204)	−(0.672)	−(2.466)**	(1.651)*	−(0.158)	−(3.883)***	(0.656)	−(0.012)	−(2.637)***
β_{ji}	Return spillover	0.070	0.090	0.010	0.027	0.013	−0.006	0.028	−0.002	−0.001
		(1.365)	(3.105)***	(0.685)	(0.636)	(0.836)	−(0.596)	(0.703)	−(0.095)	−(0.095)
β_{ki}	Return spillover	−0.146	−0.145	−0.009	−0.140	−0.125	0.026	−0.069	−0.095	0.013
		−(1.664)*	−(1.802)*	−(0.705)	−(2.255)**	−(3.061)***	(1.286)	−(1.144)	−(2.238)**	(0.691)
ω_i	Intercept	0.000	0.000	0.000	0.000	0.000	0.000	0.000	0.000	0.000
		(2.415)**	(2.379)**	(3.672)***	(3.779)***	(3.497)***	(6.437)***	(3.913)***	(3.256)***	(5.068)***
λ_{ii}^2	ARCH^2	0.140	0.048	0.048	0.198	0.047	0.064	0.080	0.043	0.062
		(8.124)***	(8.195)***	(10.076)***	(6.664)***	(17.098)***	(15.409)***	(16.505)***	(18.148)***	(20.285)***
γ_{ii}^2	GARCH^2	0.869	0.948	0.945	0.807	0.951	0.926	0.916	0.955	0.929
		(81.849)***	(153.371)***	(195.188)***	(39.362)***	(451.366)***	(263.663)***	(209.194)***	(526.106)***	(318.034)***
ϑ_{ji}	Volatility spillover	0.120	0.313	0.000	0.105	0.005	0.000	0.064	0.005	0.001
		(3.343)***	(3.174)***	(0.326)	(3.017)***	(2.108)**	(1.255)	(2.267)**	(1.194)	(1.264)
ϑ_{ki}	Volatility spillover	−0.069	1.008	0.002	0.040	0.007	0.004	0.205	0.004	0.003
		−(0.871)	(3.206)***	(1.412)	(0.674)	(0.621)	(1.540)	(2.465)**	(0.290)	(1.124)
$\lambda_{ii}^2+\gamma_{ii}^2$	Persistence	1.009	0.997	0.993	1.004	0.998	0.989	0.996	0.998	0.991
Log LF		23741.99			24927.66			25158.33		

Note: The numbers in brackets are z-statistics. In addition, ***,** and * represent statistical significance at the 1%, 5% and 10% levels, respectively.

BARC. As for volatility spillovers from the FTSE to the banks, the results only indicate positive and significant feedback effects from the FTSE to BARC, the coefficients on the other two banks being insignificant. Finally, the trivariate models fail to corroborate the results from the bivariate case where the FTSE was found to be prone to past volatility shocks coming from UK banks. In this case, the respective cross-volatility coefficients are insignificant across all models.

We now briefly discuss the results for the weekly and monthly frequencies. Similar to the respective results from the bivariate case, the weekly and monthly results for the trivariate model reveal a different pattern. For the estimates using weekly data, the coefficients attached on the cross-return terms are insignificant across all models with the exceptions of a negative return spillover from HSBC to RBS and a positive spillover from the FTSE to RBS. When the volatility is considered, the results point to bi-directional volatility spillovers between RBS and BARC. We also find uni-directional spillovers from the FTSE to the above banks and from the FTSE to HSBC.

The monthly data estimates, on the other hand, point to a positive and significant uni-directional return spillover from BARC to RBS and a negative and significant return spillover from the FTSE to RBS. Interestingly, the results here also provide evidence of a return spillover from BARC to FTSE. The results also reveal positive return spillovers from both RBS and BARC to HSBC. Shifting our attention to the volatility, the results reveal a volatility spillover from RBS to FTSE and HSBC to BARC, the coefficients being negative and significant at the 1% and 5% levels, respectively. Finally, the results point to a uni-directional volatility feedback effect from the FTSE to BARC and HSBC.

Figs. 4–6 contain plots of the time-varying (daily) variances, covariances and correlations of our sample of banks and the FTSE. Looking at the conditional variances of our series (Fig. 4), there is an interesting pattern emerging across banks and the index. Starting in 2000, the conditional variances remain at relatively low levels, and then shoot up during the 2007–2009 financial crisis. This is expected as the degree of investor uncertainty during the crisis manifested into extreme volatility in the markets. Consistent with recent work on systemic risk (Wagner, 2010), Figs. 5 and 6 reveal that the conditional covariances and correlations of our sample of banks and the FTSE also increase during the crisis. This gives further support to the argument that diversification at FIs and the creation of financial conglomerates (such as RBS, BARC and HSBC) increase the probability of systemic crises.

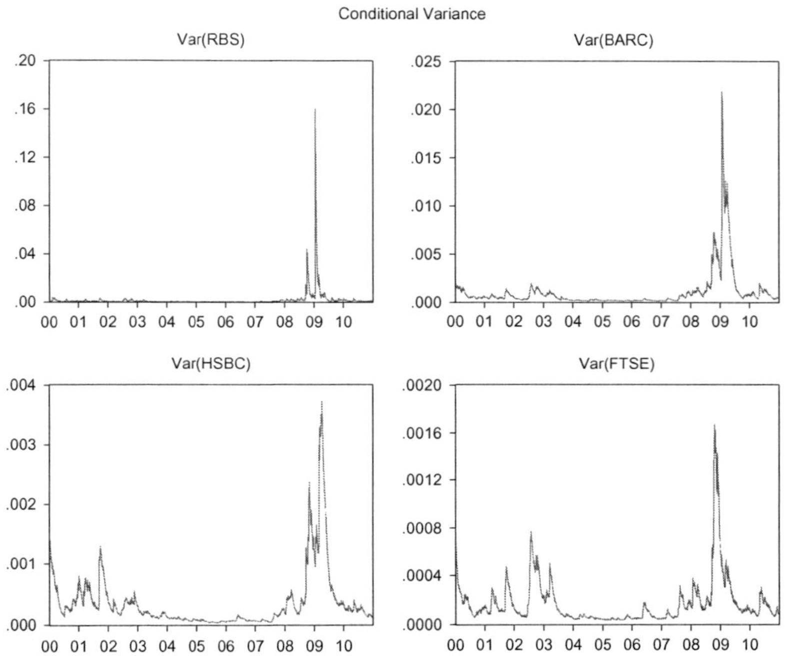

Fig. 4. Daily Plots of the Conditional Variance.

CONCLUSIONS

The recent financial crisis has caused renewed attention on the scale and interconnectedness of large FIs. The main concern among regulators and policymakers is that shocks from these institutions can no longer be contained with the effects transcending the financial sector and impacting upon the economy. Despite the emergence of a growing body of academic research investigating the extent to which returns and risk can spillover across these, there is lack of empirical evidence on whether shocks from large FIs can spill over to their peers and the market, posing a significant threat to the economy as a whole.

The aim of this chapter was to formally test the hypothesis that shocks from large FIs are transmitted across these and to the economy. As such, we investigate the return and volatility spillovers from major UK banks to FTSE and vice versa, using both continuous and discrete time methods.

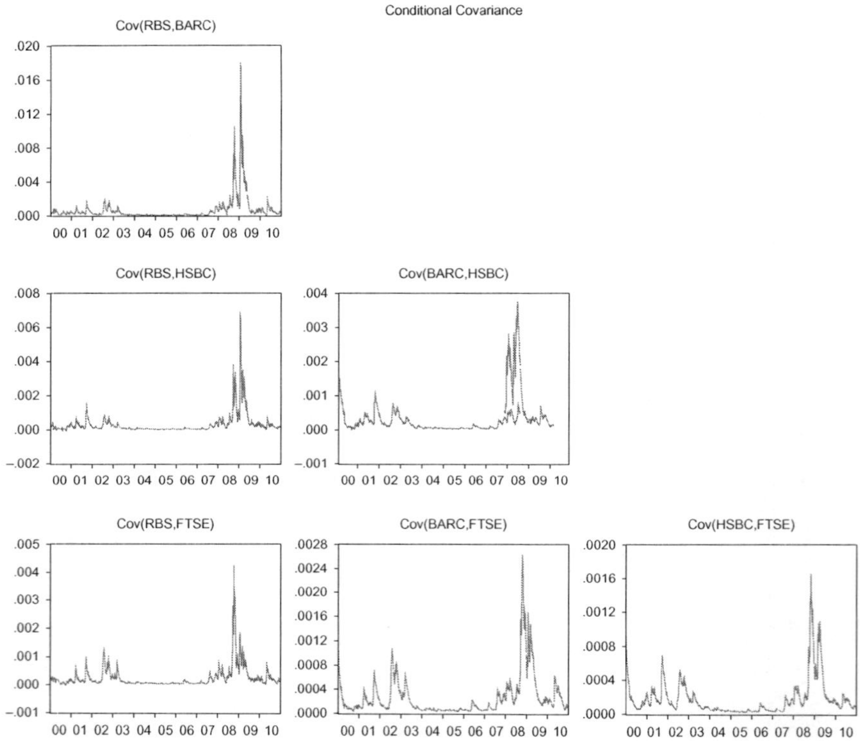

Fig. 5. Daily Plots of the Time-Varying Covariance.

Using daily, weekly and monthly data empirical estimates of uni- and/or bi-directional return and volatility spillovers are provided. The bivariate MGARCH results reveal strong return spillovers from the FTSE to the banks, and no return spillover from the latter to the FTSE. Nevertheless, strong bi-directional volatility transmission is verified.

The continuous time analysis finds mixed evidence of feedback effects in some cases. Overall, we provide evidence that the results are sensitive to the choice of modelling approach. The discrete time results show that volatility is indeed transmitted from large banks to the FTSE and highlight how large/important these institutions are and how easily idiosyncratic shocks can manifest into system-wide problems. The implication of the

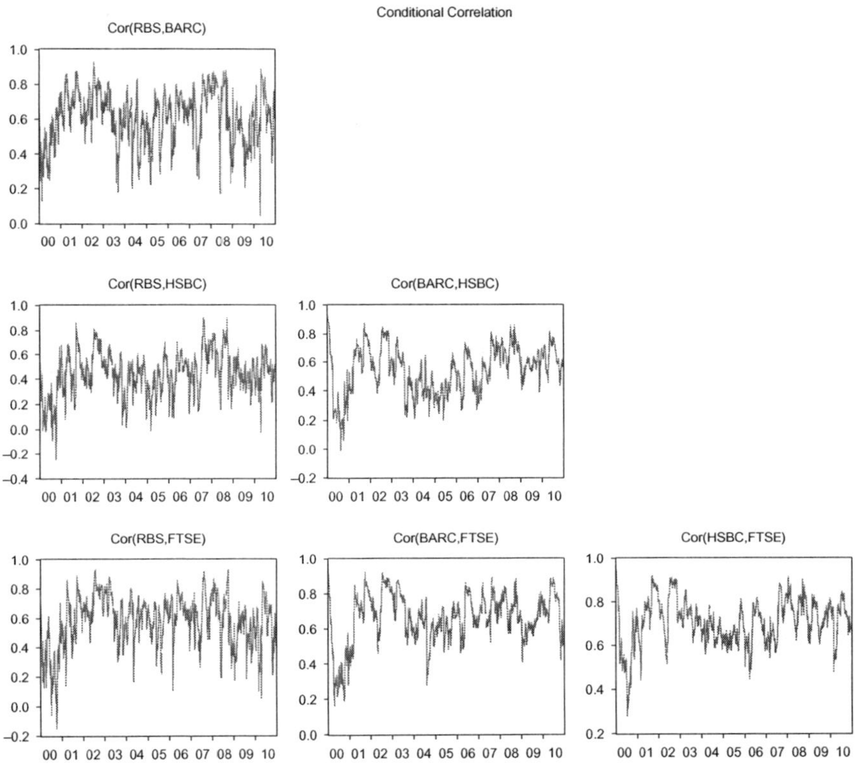

Fig. 6. Daily Plots of the Time-Varying Correlation.

above result is that large FIs should narrow the scale and/or scope of their operations and/or be closely monitored and regulated to avoid financial crises such as the recent one.

NOTES

1. Elyasiani, Mansur, and Pagano (2007) define convergence as the increased similarity of products across different financial institutions, and the resulting blurring of their differences.
2. For ease of exposition, we shall be using the term FTSE when referring to the FTSE 100 index.

3. The three banks are HSBC, Barclays and Royal Bank of Scotland (RBS, hereafter), and also represent the banks in our sample. Ranking is based on total assets (2010 figures).

4. Aharony and Swary (1983) define contagion in the context of bank failures as the case in which a negative shock to the stock of the failing institution is also transmitted to other institutions in the industry. They measure contagion by examining the relationship between abnormal returns of failing banks and those of the banking industry.

5. A detailed analysis of the above models as well as their benefits and shortcomings falls beyond the scope of this study. The interested reader is referred to Bauwens, Laurent and Rombouts (2006) and Kroner and Ng (1998).

6. We report daily results in full with tables and figures. To conserve space, we describe very briefly the results using weekly and monthly data, while detailed tables and figures are available upon request from the authors.

REFERENCES

Aharony, J., & Swary, I. (1983). Contagion effects of bank failures: Evidence from capital markets. *The Journal of Business*, *56*, 305–322.

Aharony, J., & Swary, I. (1996). Additional evidence on the information-based contagion effects of bank failures. *Journal of Banking and Finance*, *20*, 57–69.

Bauwens, L., Laurent, S., & Rombouts, J. V. K. (2006). Multivariate garch models: A survey. *Journal of Applied Econometrics*, *21*, 79–109.

Bergstrom, A. R. (Ed.) (1976). *Statistical inference in continuous time economic models*. Amsterdam: North-Holland.

Bergstrom, A. R. (1984). Continuous time stochastic models and issues of aggregation over time. In Z. Griliches & M. D. Intriligator (Eds.), *Handbook of econometrics* (*Vol. 2*, pp. 1145–1212). Amsterdam: Elsevier Science.

Bergstrom, A. R. (1990). *Continuous time econometric modelling*. Oxford: Oxford University Press.

Bergstrom, A. R. (1996). Survey of continuous time econometrics. In W. A. Barnett, G. Gandolfo, & C. Hillinger (Eds.), *Dynamic disequilibrium modelling* (pp. 3–25). Cambridge: Cambridge University Press.

Bergstrom, A. R., & Nowman, K. B. (2007). *A continuous time econometric model of the united kingdom with stochastic trends*. Cambridge: Cambridge University Press.

Bollerslev, T. (1990). Modelling the coherence in short-run nominal exchange rates: A multivariate generalized ARCH model. *The Review of Economics and Statistics*, *72*, 498–505.

Bollerslev, T., Engle, R. F., & Wooldridge, J. M. (1988). A capital asset pricing model with time-varying covariances. *The Journal of Political Economy*, *96*, 116–131.

Brennan, M. J., & Schwartz, E. S. (1980). Analyzing convertible bonds. *Journal of Financial and Quantitative Analysis*, *15*, 907–929.

Brewer, E., & Jackson, W. E. (2002). *Inter-industry contagion and the competitive effects of financial distress announcements: Evidence from commercial banks and life insurance companies*. Working Paper No. WP-02-23. Federal Reserve Bank of Chicago, Chicago, IL. Retrieved from http://econpapers.repec.org/paper/fipfedhwp/wp-02-23.htm

Carey, M., & Stulz, R. M. (2005). *The risks of financial institutions*. Dice Center Working Paper No 2005-13, Department of Finance, Ohio State University, Columbus, OH. SSRN eLibrary.

Carson, J. M., Elyasiani, E., & Mansur, I. (2008). Market risk, interest rate risk, and interdependencies in insurer stock returns: A system-garch model. *Journal of Risk and Insurance*, *75*, 873–891.

Chan, K. C., Karolyi, G. A., Longstaff, F. A., & Sanders, A. B. (1992). An empirical comparison of alternative models of the short-term interest rate. *Journal of Finance*, *47*, 1209–1227.

Cox, J. C., Ingersoll, J. E., & Ross, S. A. (1985). A theory of the term structure of interest rates. *Econometrica*, *53*, 385–407.

Elyasiani, E., & Mansur, I. (2003). International spillover of risk and return among major banking institutions: A bivariate garch model. *Journal of Accounting, Auditing and Finance*, *18*, 303–330.

Elyasiani, E., Mansur, I., & Pagano, M. S. (2007). Convergence and risk-return linkages across financial service firms. *Journal of Banking and Finance*, *31*, 1167–1190.

Engle, R. F., & Kroner, K. F. (1995). Multivariate simultaneous generalized arch. *Econometric Theory*, *11*, 122–150.

Engle, R. F., Ng, V. K., & Rothschild, M. (1990). Asset pricing with a factor-arch covariance structure: Empirical estimates for treasury bills. *Journal of Econometrics*, *45*, 213–237.

Episcopos, A. (2000). Further evidence on alternative continuous time models of the short-term interest rate. *Journal of International Financial Markets, Institutions and Money*, *10*, 199–212.

Flannery, M. J. (1998). Using market information in prudential bank supervision: A review of the U.S. empirical evidence. *Journal of Money, Credit and Banking*, *30*, 273–305.

Harrington, S. E. (2009). The financial crisis, systemic risk, and the future of insurance regulation. *Journal of Risk and Insurance*, *76*, 785–819.

Herring, R. J., & Carmassi, J. (2009). The corporate structure of international financial conglomerates: Complexity and its implications for safety and soundness. In A. N. Berger, P. Molyneux, & J. O. S. Wilson (Eds.), *The Oxford handbook of banking* (pp. 195–229). Oxford: Oxford University press.

Herring, R. J., & Santomero, A. M. (1990). The corporate structure of financial conglomerates. *Journal of Financial Services Research*, *4*, 471–497.

Kaufman, G. G. (1994). Bank contagion: A review of the theory and evidence. *Journal of Financial Services Research*, *8*, 123–150.

Kroner, K. F., & Ng, V. K. (1998). Modeling asymmetric comovements of asset returns. *The Review of Financial Studies*, *11*, 817–844.

Moshirian, F. (2011a). The global financial crisis and the evolution of markets, institutions and regulation. *Journal of Banking and Finance*, *35*, 502–511.

Moshirian, F. (2011b). Global financial crisis, international financial architecture and regulation. *Journal of Banking and Finance*, *35*, 499–501.

Nowman, K. B. (1997). Gaussian estimation of single-factor continuous time models of the term structure of interest rates. *Journal of Finance*, *52*, 1695–1706.

Nowman, K. B. (2001). Gaussian estimation and forecasting of multi-factor term structure models with an application to Japan and the United Kingdom. *Asia Pacific Financial Markets*, *8*, 23–34.

Nowman, K. B. (2002). The volatility of Japanese interest rates: Evidence for certificate of deposit and gensaki rates. *International Review of Financial Analysis*, *11*, 29–38.

Nowman, K. B. (2003). A note on gaussian estimation of the CKLS and CIR models with feedback effects for Japan. *Asia Pacific Financial Markets*, *10*, 275–279.

Nowman, K. B. (2006). Continuous time interest rate models in Japanese fixed income markets. In J. A. Batten, T. A. Fetherston, & P. G. Szilagyi (Eds.), *Japanese fixed income markets* (pp. 321–346): Amsterdam: Elsevier.

Nowman, K. B., & Yahia, B. H. H. (2008). Euro and fibor interest rates: A continuous time modelling analysis. *International Review of Financial Analysis*, *17*, 1029–1035.

Phillips, P. C. B., & Yu, J. (2009). Maximum likelihood and Gaussian estimation of continuous time models in finance. In T. G. Andersen, R. A. Davis, J.-P. Kreiß, & Th. Mikosch (Eds.), *Handbook of financial time series*. Heidelberg: Springer-Verlag.

U.S. Department of the Treasury. (2009). *Financial regulatory reform – A new foundation: Rebuilding financial supervision and regulation*. Washington, DC: U.S. Department of the Treasury.

Wagner, W. (2008). The homogenization of the financial system and financial crises. *Journal of Financial Intermediation*, *17*, 330–356.

Wagner, W. (2010). Diversification at financial institutions and systemic crises. *Journal of Financial Intermediation*, *19*, 373–386.

PART IV
CRISIS SPILLOVERS TO EMERGING ECONOMIES

ECONOMIC IMPACT OF EUROZONE SOVEREIGN DEBT CRISIS ON DEVELOPING ASIA

Minsoo Lee, Donghyun Park, Arnelyn Abdon and Gemma Estrada

ABSTRACT

This chapter investigates the impact of the euro crisis on Asia's short-term economic outlook. This chapter tries to answer this question by examining both the trade and financial channels of crisis transmission. More specifically, it looks at the effect of euro crisis on Asian exports and growth, contagion from EU financial markets to Asian financial markets, and influence of EU bank lending on credit growth in Asia. The chapter also touches upon Asia's policy space to assess how well the region is positioned to weather another major external shock. This chapter finds that the impact of euro crisis on developing Asia points to a sizable but manageable short-term impact. Furthermore, our analysis points to a significant effect on the region's financial systems, especially its banking sector. This chapter informs policymakers of the impact of the

Global Banking, Financial Markets and Crises
International Finance Review, Volume 14, 271–304

ISSN: 1569-3767/doi:10.1108/S1569-3767(2013)0000014013

euro crisis and advice to continue to keep a close eye on eurozone developments and their ramifications for their economies.

Keywords: Euro crisis; developing Asia; financial channel; international trade; equity and bonds market

JEL classifications: G01; F32; F36

INTRODUCTION

Notwithstanding developing Asia's (henceforth Asia) growing weight and stature in the world economy, it is premature to talk of the region's decoupling from the advanced economies. The 2008–2009 global financial and economic crisis gave a vivid reminder of Asia's continued vulnerability to the G3 – the United States (US), the European Union (EU), and Japan – business cycle. Despite the negligible exposure of the region's banking system to subprime assets, the crisis hit the region hard through the trade channel. The adverse impact of the crisis on the region peaked during fourth quarter of 2008 and first quarter of 2009, when a collapse of exports triggered widespread fears about a deep and protracted recession. Bold and decisive countercyclical macroeconomic policy, in particular big fiscal stimulus packages which were quickly implemented, staved off recession and laid the foundation for a robust V-shaped recovery. The budding recovery gained full momentum when world economy and trade stabilized and normalized.

Just a few years after the global crisis, Asia now faces another major threat to its growth from the G3, this time from Europe. More specifically, the sovereign debt crisis afflicting Greece and other eurozone economies (henceforth euro crisis) is the single biggest downside risk to the current global outlook. From Asia's viewpoint, both the 2008 and 2009 global crisis and the ongoing euro crisis represent external shocks originating from large economies outside the region. On the other hand, there are some key differences between the two crises. The euro crisis is essentially a fiscal crisis associated with governments borrowing too much and taking on unsustainable levels of debt. In contrast, the global crisis was a banking crisis resulting from banks lending too much money to borrowers with poor credit histories. The euro crisis is a public sector crisis whereas the global crisis was a private sector crisis. In terms of impact on Asia, the single most significant difference between the two is that the euro crisis is, so far, limited to the eurozone whereas the global crisis was a synchronized G3 crisis that spread from its US epicenter to the EU and Japan. The simultaneous recession in the G3 had a predictably marked adverse impact on the global outlook.

The impact of the euro crisis on Asia will depend heavily on how the crisis plays out. There remains a great deal of uncertainty about the future evolution of the crisis, notwithstanding the massive injection of liquidity by the European Central Bank (ECB) in late 2011 and early 2012. While the tail risk of the euro crisis morphing into a second global crisis still cannot be ruled out, market consensus seems to be gravitating toward some type of resolution in the near future. That is, the probability of a full-blown contagion infecting US and Japan, and resulting in another synchronized G3 recession, remains relatively small. Therefore, the analysis here will center on a baseline scenario of the euro crisis being largely confined to the eurozone and largely to a recession in the real economy rather than a full-blown financial crisis. The limited exposure of US banks to eurozone periphery government bonds strengthens the case for this baseline scenario. In striking contrast, due to the heavy exposure of EU banks to subprime assets, the US subprime crisis spread like a wildfire across the Atlantic and brought the global financial system, trade, and economy to its heels.

The EU has traditionally been an important economic partner for Asia. In particular, during the region's pursuit of export-oriented industrialization, the high-income economies of Western Europe, along with the US, served as the main markets for the region's exports. Initially, low income levels and purchasing power of Asia and other parts of the developing world limited the scope for exports to markets outside the two regions. Even today, the EU and US play outsize roles as importers of final goods due to their high consumption levels. In addition to absorbing a significant share of the region's exports, the EU has been a major source of FDI and other capital flows into the region. More recently, mirroring Asia's emergence as a third hub of the world economy as a result of its rapid growth, the region is now an increasingly significant import market and source of investment for the EU.

In light of such close trade and, to a lesser extent, financial linkages between the EU and Asia, the euro crisis will undoubtedly influence Asia's short-term macroeconomic outlook. However, the key question is not whether the euro crisis will have an impact on Asia but how big the impact will be. This chapter tries to answer this question by examining both the trade and financial channels of crisis transmission. More specifically, it looks at the effect of euro crisis on Asian exports and growth, contagion from EU financial markets to Asian financial markets, and influence of EU bank lending on credit growth in Asia. The chapter will also touch upon Asia's policy space to assess how well the region is positioned to weather another major external shock. The chapter concludes with an overall assessment of how Asia's short-term economic outlook is affected by the euro crisis.

TRADE CHANNEL: IMPACT OF EURO CRISIS ON ASIAN EXPORTS AND GROWTH

Trade is the primary channel through which the euro crisis will be transmitted from the EU to Asia. While there are significant and growing financial linkages between EU and Asia, they pale in comparison to their extensive, well-established trade linkages. The EU has long been a major market for Asian exports. The main impact of the 2008–2009 global crisis fell on Asian exports and growth (Figs. 1 and 2), and this will be the case for the euro crisis. While Asia's relative lack of financial integration with the US minimized trans-Pacific financial contagion, the synchronized recession of the advanced economies had a predictably pronounced effect on Asian exports and growth. Similarly, the adverse impact of the euro crisis on the EU's real economy will crimp its appetite for imports from Asia. The EU is now widely expected to contract this year, and this will harm Asian exports and growth. What matters for Asia is the magnitude of the impact. In this context, a key factor is the relative importance of EU market for Asian exporters.

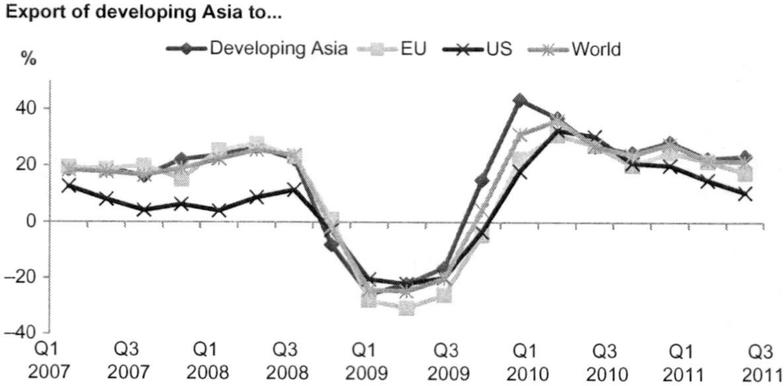

Fig. 1. Developing Asia's Exports, Q1 2007–Q3 2011. *Source*: Authors' calculations based on Direction of Trade Statistics (accessed on January 27, 2012).

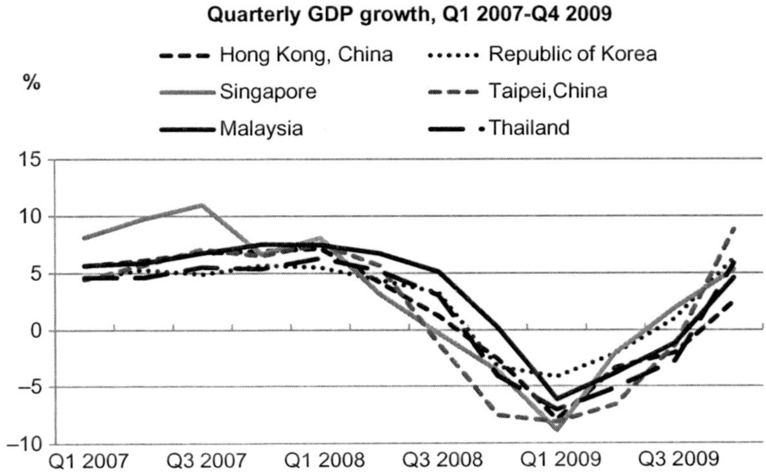

Fig. 2. Quarterly GDP Growth, Selected Developing Asian Countries. *Source*: CEIC Data Company (accessed on March 5, 2012).

There has been a visible shift in Asia's export markets from the Group of 3 (G3) – US, EU, and Japan – to developing countries since 1995. The share of the G3 in Asia's exports fell from about one-half in 1995 to a little more than one-third in 2011. During the same period, there has been a corresponding increase in the share of developing countries. The shift parallels the sustained shift in the center of gravity of the world economy from advanced economies to developing countries, and has gained further momentum since the global crisis. That crisis originated in the advanced economies, which were consequently hit harder and are recovering more slowly than developing countries. Between 2007 and 2011, the share of the G3 in Asia's exports fell further, with the decline most pronounced for the US, while the shares of Africa and Latin America rose (Table 1). Furthermore, the share of intra-Asian trade rose from 39.9% in 2007 to 42.1% in 2011. Asia's export dependence on EU is much less than Africa and more or less the same as Latin America. Interestingly, the EU has now become a larger export market for Asia than the US. However, the more fundamental trend is that both are declining in relative significance. In and of itself, this suggests that a recession in the US will have a smaller impact on Asian exports and growth than it did in the past.

Table 1. Export Share by Region, 2007 and 2011, % of Total Exports.

Destination	Exporting Region					
	Africa		Developing Asia		Latin America	
	2007	2011	2007	2011	2007	2011
Africa	8.5	9.5	2.3	2.7	1.6	1.4
Developing Asia	15.1	23.3	39.9	42.1	9.0	15.5
EU 27	37.8	31.2	15.6	14.0	13.4	13.0
Other Europe	3.6	3.2	5.0	4.8	2.5	2.6
Japan	2.7	2.7	7.8	7.3	2.4	2.6
Latin America	3.6	3.9	3.2	4.4	17.3	16.8
US	21.6	17.7	15.2	12.4	44.8	36.8
Other	7.1	8.6	11.1	12.3	9.0	11.3

Note: Data up to September 2011.
Source: Authors' calculations based on Direction of Trade (accessed on January 23, 2012).

Besides the relative importance of exports to EU in Asia's total exports, another key indicator in assessing the trade impact of the euro crisis on Asia is the relative importance of the growth of exports to EU in growth of Asia's total exports. A higher contribution of EU to Asia's export growth portends a bigger effect of an EU recession on the region's export and growth momentum. After bottoming out in the fourth quarter of 2008 and first quarter of 2009, Asia's exports grew at a robust pace between late 2009 and early 2010 when global trade normalized. However, since then the region's export growth has slowed down noticeably, reflecting external uncertainties intensified by the euro crisis. Predictably, in light of the post-crisis weakening of its growth, the EU's relative contribution to Asia's export growth has shrunk since the global crisis (Fig. 3). Prior to the crisis, the EU accounted for 16.5% of the region's export growth but after the crisis this Fig. dropped by 4 percentage points to 12.4%. Therefore, not only is the EU declining in importance as an export market for Asia, but also as a source for Asia's export growth. Both are consistent with the relative decline of the EU in the world economy in recent years, especially since the global crisis.

The level of trade exposure to Europe varies widely across Asia's subregions and countries. As noted earlier, Asia as a whole is much less exposed to Europe than Africa and has a similar exposure to Latin America. However, this region-wide exposure level contains a great deal of diversity. Therefore, some subregions and countries are more vulnerable to a European downturn than others. In particular, the share of exports to

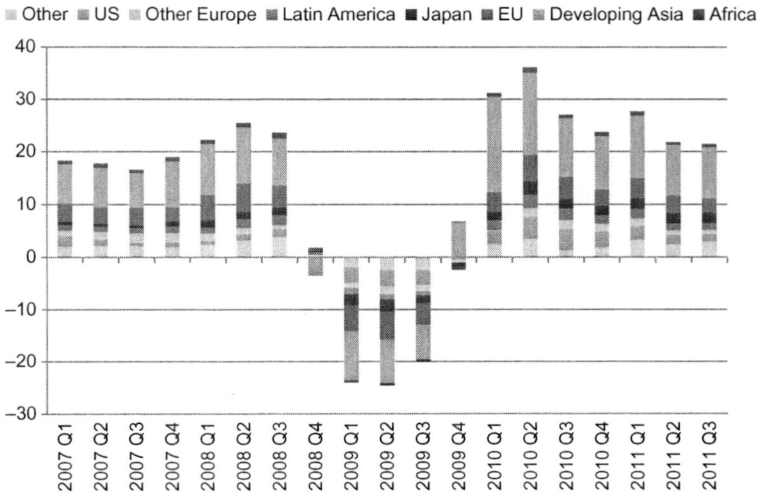

Fig. 3. Contributions to Developing Asia's Export Growth. EU = European Union, US = United States. *Note*: Data up to September 2011. *Source*: Authors' calculations based on Direction of Trade Statistics (accessed on January 23, 2012).

Europe is highest for Central Asia than it is for other subregions (Fig. 4). In 2011, Europe took in 56% of Central Asia's exports with the EU absorbing 37% and other European countries absorbing the rest. Between 1995 and 2011, there has been a visible reorientation of Central Asia's exports from the Russian Federation and Eastern Europe to the EU. While the geographic distribution of Central Europe's exports implies that it is the most vulnerable to a euro crisis, the product composition of its exports implies otherwise. This is because the subregion's exports to the EU are primarily commodities, which are less sensitive to the business cycle than manufactured goods. On the other hand, the exports of East and Southeast Asia, Asia's traditional manufacturing hubs, are heavily skewed toward manufactured goods and hence more vulnerable to an EU recession (Fig. 5). During the global crisis, highly open exporters of manufactured goods such as the newly industrialized economies, Malaysia, and Thailand were hit harder than other groups of countries.

Another indicator of the relative importance of exports to EU in economic performance is the ratio of exports to EU to gross domestic product (GDP). The higher this ratio, the greater the importance of exports to EU in a country's economic performance. Table 2 confirms that the ratio varies

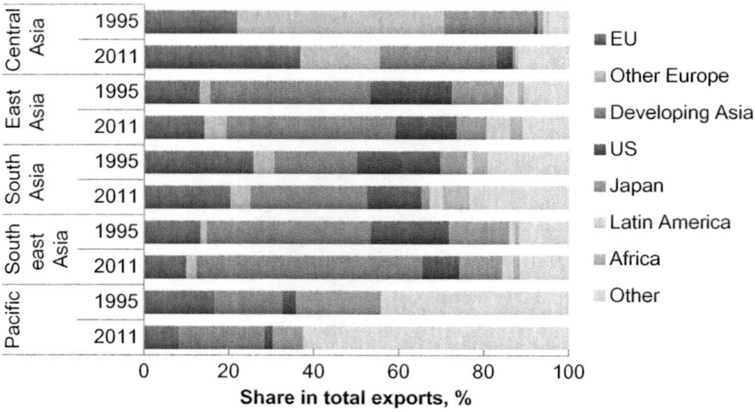

Fig. 4. Export Share by Subregion, % of Total Exports (1995 and 2011). EU = European Union, US = United States. *Source*: Authors' calculations based on Direction of Trade Statistics (accessed on January 23, 2011).

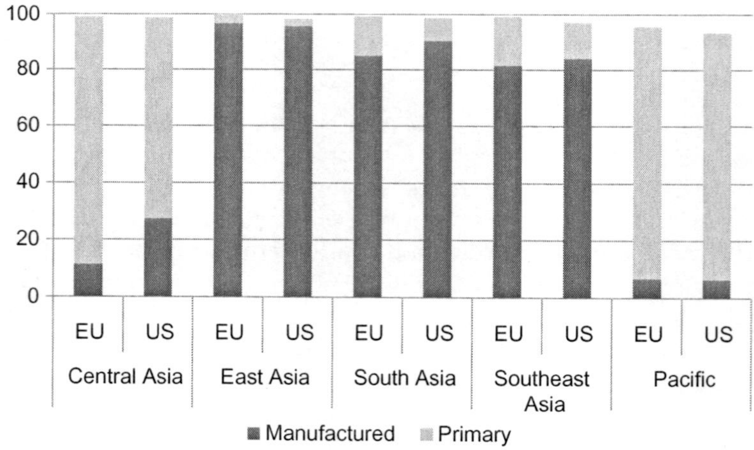

Fig. 5. Share of Primary and Manufactured Exports to the US and EU, 2005–2010 Average (%). EU = European Union, US = United States. *Source*: Authors' calculations based on UN Comtrade database (accessed on January 27, 2012).

greatly across subregions and countries, as it does for geographic distribution and product composition of exports. Table 2 shows exposure to the US for the sake of comparison and includes both direct and total export exposure. Total exposure includes potential reexports – for example,

Table 2. Export Exposure to US and EU, % of GDP.

	Exposure to the US						Exposure to EU					
	Direct			Total			Direct			Total		
	2006	2008	2010	2006	2008	2010	2006	2008	2010	2006	2008	2010
Central Asia	*0.6*	*2.1*	*0.9*	*1.2*	*2.9*	*1.4*	*8.5*	*11.9*	*4.6*	*13.0*	*16.5*	*6.4*
Armenia	1.0	0.5	0.9	1.6	0.7	1.1	7.2	4.3	3.6	10.8	6.3	5.6
Azerbaijan	0.5	13.0	3.1	1.3	15.5	4.1	16.8	57.0	18.1	20.1	67.4	21.5
Georgia	0.8	0.8	1.5	1.1	1.4	1.9	2.2	1.5	1.4	3.6	3.2	2.8
Kazakhstan	1.1	1.1	1.2	1.9	1.9	2.0	16.0	14.2	10.3	20.5	19.0	13.4
Kyrgyz Republic	0.3	0.1	0.1	0.9	0.7	0.3	0.9	2.8	0.3	4.9	7.0	1.8
Tajikistan	0.0	0.0	0.0	1.0	0.5	0.5	21.2	10.6	0.4	34.0	17.6	1.7
Turkmenistan	0.3	0.6	0.2	0.6	1.1	0.6	1.9	2.9	2.0	4.2	7.9	3.0
Uzbekistan	0.8	0.9	0.2	1.4	1.3	0.4	2.0	1.6	0.6	5.9	3.8	1.6
East Asia	*10.2*	*8.5*	*7.3*	*14.6*	*12.1*	*10.5*	*9.0*	*9.9*	*7.1*	*14.8*	*16.0*	*11.9*
China, People's Rep. of	7.5	5.6	4.8	10.1	7.4	6.2	6.3	5.8	4.7	10.3	9.4	7.4
Hong Kong, China	25.2	21.5	19.1	34.5	29.0	25.9	22.0	21.4	17.9	35.0	34.3	29.0
Korea, Rep. of	4.6	5.0	4.9	6.8	7.4	7.1	4.5	5.0	3.9	7.9	9.1	7.5
Mongolia	3.5	2.0	0.2	7.2	4.6	2.7	3.1	7.5	1.7	6.0	11.2	4.0
South Asia	*2.6*	*1.9*	*1.5*	*3.1*	*2.3*	*1.8*	*3.8*	*3.7*	*2.9*	*4.9*	*4.9*	*3.7*
Afghanistan	0.6	0.8	0.5	0.7	0.8	0.6	0.7	0.6	0.4	0.9	1.0	0.5
Bangladesh	4.4	3.3	3.1	4.9	3.8	3.4	8.2	7.6	7.0	10.3	9.6	8.7
India	2.0	1.7	1.4	2.7	2.3	2.0	2.8	2.9	2.4	4.1	4.4	3.6
Maldives	0.2	0.2	0.1	0.9	0.6	0.3	3.9	4.4	2.0	5.1	5.4	2.5
Nepal	1.1	0.5	0.4	1.3	0.7	0.5	1.1	0.8	0.6	1.5	1.1	0.9
Pakistan	2.8	2.1	1.9	3.3	2.5	2.2	2.9	2.8	2.4	4.0	3.9	3.3
Sri Lanka	7.1	4.6	3.4	7.7	5.1	3.7	6.8	6.9	5.1	8.5	9.1	6.7

Table 2. *(Continued)*

	Exposure to the US						Exposure to EU					
	Direct			Total			Direct			Total		
	2006	2008	2010	2006	2008	2010	2006	2008	2010	2006	2008	2010
Southeast Asia	*10.2*	*7.1*	*6.2*	*14.6*	*10.4*	*9.0*	*7.8*	*6.4*	*5.7*	*13.7*	*11.7*	*10.1*
Brunei Darussalam	4.6	0.7	0.1	6.9	3.0	2.0	1.1	0.1	0.1	3.4	2.4	1.8
Cambodia	26.1	17.5	16.4	29.3	20.3	20.0	8.9	6.7	7.9	13.3	10.9	13.3
Indonesia	3.1	2.6	2.0	4.8	3.8	2.9	3.2	2.9	2.3	5.6	5.2	3.9
Lao PDR	0.2	0.8	0.9	2.6	2.5	2.6	3.1	3.2	3.1	5.9	5.5	5.2
Malaysia	19.2	11.2	8.0	26.4	16.1	12.1	12.4	9.5	8.5	23.0	18.1	15.4
Myanmar	0.0	0.0	0.0	2.2	1.2	0.6	2.2	0.8	0.4	4.5	2.2	1.2
Philippines	7.0	4.7	3.8	9.8	6.4	5.2	7.0	4.8	3.5	12.1	8.2	6.1
Singapore	19.0	12.8	10.3	34.3	24.3	19.3	20.4	17.6	14.9	38.7	33.7	27.7
Thailand	9.5	7.2	6.3	13.8	10.8	9.3	8.2	7.5	6.0	14.3	13.4	11.0
Viet Nam	12.9	13.2	13.7	16.2	16.0	16.2	11.1	11.2	10.3	16.6	17.0	15.6
Pacific	*1.9*	*1.5*	*1.5*	*3.5*	*3.4*	*2.4*	*2.9*	*3.9*	*2.5*	*4.9*	*6.6*	*4.0*
Fiji	5.1	5.0	6.1	5.5	5.4	6.5	4.3	4.2	1.6	5.1	5.1	2.3
Papua New Guinea	1.4	1.3	1.0	3.6	3.1	2.3	8.3	10.3	7.6	12.0	14.7	10.8
Samoa	1.0	0.9	0.7	1.2	1.1	0.8	0.2	0.1	0.3	0.5	0.5	0.5
Solomon Islands	0.6	0.2	0.2	3.6	3.0	2.5	2.9	6.0	4.3	6.0	9.7	7.2
Tonga	2.9	1.5	0.6	3.1	1.7	0.9	0.1	0.3	0.2	0.3	0.5	0.4
Vanuatu	0.5	0.2	0.2	4.2	5.8	1.7	1.6	2.3	1.0	5.6	9.2	2.6
Developing Asia	*5.1*	*4.1*	*3.4*	*7.4*	*6.0*	*4.9*	*6.4*	*7.1*	*4.5*	*10.4*	*11.1*	*7.2*

EU = European Union, US = United States.
Source: Authors' calculations based on Direction of Trade Statistics (accessed on January 23, 2012).

Malaysia exports to the People's Republic of China (PRC), which reexports to the EU. Overall, exposure to EU is higher for East and Southeast Asia than it is for the other subregions. This is plausible since those two subregions export a lot of manufactured goods, much of it to the EU. For developing Asia as a whole, in contrast to the earlier period of 1994–2006 (IMF, 2008), export exposure to EU has declined in 2006–2010, lending further support to Asia's declining vulnerability to an EU slowdown.

The impact of the euro crisis on Asia's GDP growth will differ from country to country but the overall impact is likely to be significant but manageable. This is consistent with the overall picture of a declining role of EU in Asia's exports and export growth. In our baseline scenario of a recession which is largely confined to the eurozone, Oxford Economic Forecasting model simulations indicate that 2012 GDP growth for Emerging Asia[1] will drop by a little more than 1%. For individual countries, the impact varies from 0.4% to 2% (Fig. 6). Predictably, the negative impact on the region is bigger for two worse case scenarios – a eurozone recession combined with a US recession and a second global crisis. Since Emerging Asia includes the most open Asian countries with the highest degree of exposure to the EU, the impact on the GDP growth of the rest of developing Asia to be smaller. At a broader level, the simulation results point to a moderation rather than derailment of Asia's growth momentum.

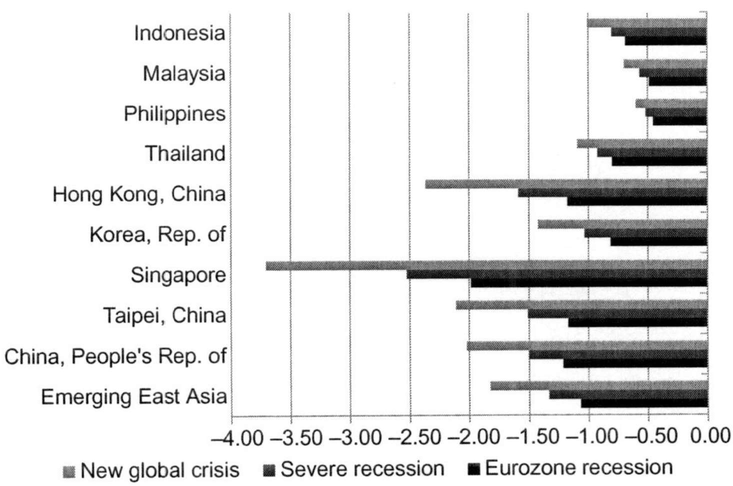

Fig. 6. Impact of Eurozone Crisis on Selected Asian Countries. (Deviation from the Baseline Forecast, Percentage Points.) *Source*: Asian Development Bank (2011).

Finally, the vector autoregression (VAR) model is another empirical avenue for analyzing the potential impact of an EU recession on developing Asia's GDP growth.

The VAR model allows to assess the relative contribution of EU's imports, US's imports, and PRC's imports to the GDP of nine countries between Q1 2000 and Q4 2011. Following Park and Shin (2009) we include the PRC in light of its growing importance as an export market for Asian countries although its relative role differs a lot across countries (Fig. 7). The nine countries in the sample are Hong Kong, China; India; Indonesia; the Republic of Korea; Malaysia; the Philippines; Singapore; Thailand; and Viet Nam. So, for example, we can use the VAR model to estimate the relative role of EU's imports from Malaysia – that is, Malaysia's exports to EU – in Malaysia's GDP. The VAR model includes the following four variables: Malaysia's real GDP, EU's real imports from Malaysia, US's real imports from Malaysia, and the PRC's real imports from Malaysia.

The first step toward measuring the effect of EU's imports from Malaysia is to compute the dynamic responses of Malaysia's GDP to

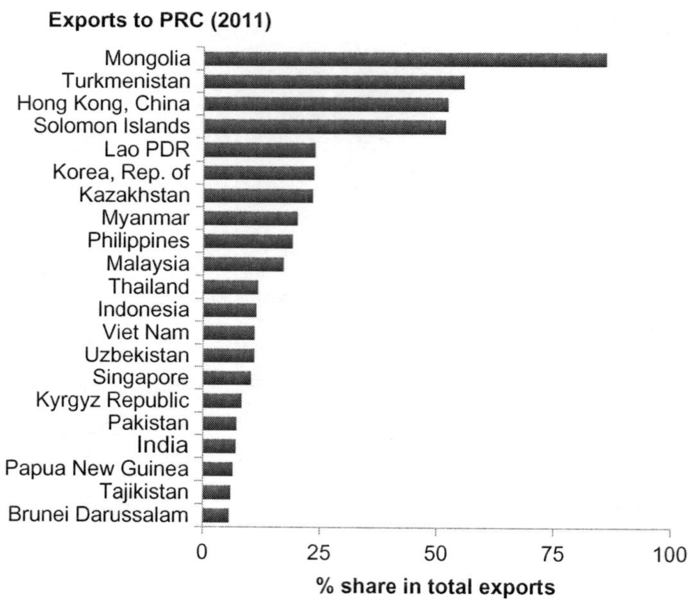

Fig. 7. Share of Exports to PRC, 2011. *Note*: Economies whose export to PRC is less than 5% are not shown. Data up to September 2011. *Source*: Authors' calculations based on Direction of Trade Statistics (accessed on January 23, 2012).

positive shocks to EU's imports. More precisely, we compute impulse responses, which refer to the responses of the level of domestic output to a one standard deviation shock to the EU's imports. Summing up the impulse responses gives us the cumulative effect of the positive EU import shocks on Malaysia's GDP over time. Likewise, we can sum up impulses to compute the cumulative effect of positive shocks to the US's and the PRC's imports on Malaysia's GDP over time. The impulse response functions indicate a substantial response of the GDP of three Asian countries – namely Hong Kong, China; India; and the Republic of Korea – to positive EU import demand shocks.

A more fundamental issue than impulse responses is the relative importance of the import demand shocks of PRC, EU, and the US in the domestic GDP fluctuations in the nine sample countries. This depends not only on the size of the impulse responses in the face of a given size shock but also the frequency and average size of shocks hitting the economy. More specifically, variance decompositions, which measure the percentage of the forecast error variance of domestic output at various forecast horizons that is attributable to each shock, indicate the relative importance of demand shocks of the PRC, the EU, and the US.

Table 3 shows an example of variance decomposition (VD) results, for Indonesia. Model 1 in Table 3 reports the results of the VD for the estimated four-variable VAR model. After 10 quarters, for example, exports to the EU account for about 25% of Indonesia's output fluctuations. Besides Indonesia, VD results indicate that the EU's imports also played a significant role in the GDP fluctuations of Hong Kong, China; the Republic of Korea; and the Philippines. The six-variable Model 2 adds the PRC's exports to the EU and the US to take into account the fact that the PRC imports a lot of parts and components from other Asian countries, and assembles them for export to the EU and the US. That is, to some extent, the PRC's import demand is not an independent demand but derived demand based on final demand from the EU and the US. Model 2 VD results indicate that the EU's import demand is no longer a significant source of Indonesia's GDP fluctuations once we take into account the PRC's derived import demand. However, Model 2 results for other countries indicate that exports to the EU remain an important source of fluctuations for Hong Kong, China; India; Malaysia; the Philippines; and Viet Nam.

The overall pattern from the VD analysis is that import demand from both the EU and the US are significant sources of GDP fluctuations in our nine sample countries. The VD results confirm that under our baseline

Table 3. Variance Decomposition Results for Indonesia, %.

Period	(1)				(2)					
	Exports to US	Exports to EU	Exports to PRC	Other shocks	Exports to US	Exports to EU	PRC's export to US	PRC's export to EU	Exports to PRC	Other shocks
1	0.6	15.2	3.5	80.7	0.9	12.6	10.1	4.1	1.1	71.1
	(3.5)	(9.2)	(6.1)	(11.5)	(3.8)	(9.4)	(7.8)	(5.3)	(3.0)	(12.1)
2	4.0	29.0	8.7	58.3	2.9	18.6	8.9	4.0	5.0	60.5
	(8.4)	(12.8)	(9.6)	(12.8)	(7.5)	(11.5)	(9.8)	(5.6)	(5.9)	(10.8)
3	18.8	23.0	8.3	49.9	18.4	13.7	9.4	4.1	4.2	50.1
	(14.4)	(12.5)	(9.8)	(12.6)	(14.0)	(9.0)	(12.3)	(4.7)	(6.5)	(11.0)
10	42.2	25.4	9.5	22.9	23.5	5.4	20.9	22.0	10.7	17.4
	(17.3)	(14.4)	(8.4)	(10.8)	(13.4)	(10.0)	(16.1)	(11.7)	(11.1)	(11.1)

EU = European Union, PRC = People's Republic of China, US = United States.
Source: Authors' calculations. Numbers inside the parenthesis are standard errors.

scenario of a recession which is confined to the EU, the impact on Asia's exports and hence growth will be tangible but manageable. Once we incorporate the PRC's derived import demand, the PRC's exports to the EU and the US emerge as a new significant source of GDP fluctuations in many Asian countries. This points to the importance of derived demand in the PRC's demand for Asian exports. In addition, for many Asian countries, exports to the PRC lose much of their significance.

Overall, our analysis indicates that the impact of the euro crisis on Asia via the trade channel will be tangible but not pronounced. Asia's exports and growth will definitely feel the effect of a euro recession but the impact is likely to be noticeably smaller than the pronounced effect observed during the global crisis. Some subregions and countries will be hit harder than others but the impact will be manageable even in the hardest hit subregions and countries. The EU remains an important export market for Asia but its relative importance has been declining, a decline which has accelerated since the global crisis. Furthermore, the evidence points to a visible but not pronounced effect of an EU recession on Asian countries' growth. The one big difference between the global crisis and the euro crisis is that the former was a synchronized G3 recession which led to a collapse of global trade, whereas the latter is a recession which is limited to the EU and hence a reduction of demand from only the EU. While we should be careful not to downplay the role of the EU, especially since it continues to play a disproportionate role as a consumer of final goods from Asia, the overall picture is such that a euro crisis will dent but not arrest the momentum of growth.

FINANCIAL CHANNEL: IMPACT OF EURO CRISIS ON ASIA'S FINANCIAL SYSTEM

The dominant channel of transmission of the euro crisis to Asia will be the trade channel but there will be effects on Asia's financial sector as well. During the global crisis of 2008–2009, Asia's financial systems were largely immune from the credit crunch which engulfed the EU and the US except for sporadic bouts of turbulence in a few countries such as Indonesia and the Republic of Korea. But by and large, credit continued to flow uninterrupted from the financial system to the real economy and Asia was largely spared the financial paralysis which almost brought financial intermediation to a standstill in the West. On the other hand, the onslaught of recession in the G3's real economies and consequent collapse of their import demand had a pronounced impact on Asia's export and growth. This asymmetry between the transmission of the crisis to the real and financial sectors reflects the fact that Asia's trade integration with the West is at a much more advanced state than its financial integration.

For this fundamental reason behind the asymmetrical effect of the global crisis on Asia during the global crisis, we can expect the euro crisis to leave a bigger and deeper mark on Asia's exports and growth than on Asia's financial stability. Just as relatively low level of financial integration with the US protected Asian financial systems from the global crisis, we can expect relative lack of financial linkages with the EU to shelter them this time around. Asian banks and financial institutions had minimal exposure to US subprime assets during the global crisis, and they have minimal exposure to eurozone government bonds this time around. Furthermore, the massive injection of liquidity by the ECB has bolstered the contingent balance sheets of eurozone banks and financial institutions, and thus significantly reduced the risk of a full-blown financial crisis in the eurozone, at least in the short term. The abatement of the risk of a euro financial meltdown due to decisive ECB action further reinforces the likelihood that the primary transmission channel will be the trade channel via a eurozone recession, and the financial channel will play at most a secondary role.

Impact of Euro Crisis on Asia's Equity and Bond Markets

Nevertheless, while the financial channel will play a visibly smaller role than the trade channel, the sizable and growing financial linkages – albeit overshadowed by trade linkages – between Asia and the EU imply that the euro crisis will have at least some potential negative spillovers on Asian financial systems. One possible route for financial contagion is via capital markets – that is, equity and bond markets – but the balance of evidence indicates only a limited scope for this type of financial contagion. The collapse of capital markets, especially the equity markets, along with freefalling exchange rates, was perhaps the most dramatic symptoms of crisis during the Asian financial crisis of 1997–1998. One way to get some idea of the risk of financial contagion from the eurozone to Asian equity and bond markets is to look at the movement of eurozone financial indicators and Asian financial markets. Table 4 indicates there is no systematic positive correlation between eurozone financial indicators and Asian financial markets. A more rigorous, in-depth analysis of financial contagion to Asian equity and bond markets via the event study methodology also yields

Table 4. Correlation between Eurozone Financial Indicators and Emerging Market Stock and Bond Market Indices.

Whole Sample: January 1, 2003–December 12, 2011		Euro Financial Indicators			Equity MSCI Indices ($)				Bond EMBI Indices ($)			
		EONIA	iTraxx	Pr (Default)	Global EM	ASIA	EEMA	LATM	Global EM	ASIA	EEMA	LATM
Euro Financial Indicators	EONIA											
	iTraxx	−0.5255*										
	Pr(Default)	−0.3076*	0.6529*									
Equity MSCI Indices (US$)	Global EM	0.1038*	−0.0193	−0.4809*								
	ASIA	0.0644*	−0.0097	−0.4868*	0.9954*							
	EEMA	0.6581*	−0.4620*	−0.6060*	0.8934*	0.8714*						
	LATM	−0.0887*	0.2022*	−0.3616*	0.9789*	0.9679*	0.8159*					
Bond EMBI Indices (US$)	Global EM	−0.5628*	0.5902*	−0.1573*	0.8472*	0.8439*	0.5524*	0.9104*				
	ASIA	−0.4873*	0.3627*	−0.2520*	0.8314*	0.8241*	0.6112*	0.8507*	0.9221*			
	EEMA	−0.3894*	0.5240*	−0.1857*	0.8865*	0.8739*	0.6419*	0.9472*	0.9751*	0.8763*		
	LATM	−0.5551*	0.5720*	−0.1713*	0.8471*	0.8440*	0.5553*	0.9095*	0.9969*	0.9230*	0.9644*	

Pre-Euro-Crisis: January 1, 2003–October 7, 2009		Euro Financial Indicators			Equity MSCI Indices ($)				Bond EMBI Indices ($)			
		EONIA	iTraxx	Pr (Default)	Global EM	ASIA	EEMA	LATM	Global EM	ASIA	EEMA	LATM
Euro Financial Indicators	EONIA											
	iTraxx	−0.4268*										
	Pr(Default)	−0.6360*	0.8595*									
Equity MSCI Indices ($)	Global EM	0.6786*	−0.2538*	−0.4443*								
	ASIA	0.6344*	−0.2579*	−0.4532*	0.9938*							
	EEMA	0.8358*	−0.4882*	−0.5872*	0.9593*	0.9406*						
	LATM	0.5781*	−0.002	−0.3003*	0.9768*	0.9590*	0.9074*					

Table 4. *(Continued)*

Pre-Euro-Crisis: January 1, 2003–October 7, 2009		Euro Financial Indicators			Equity MSCI Indices (S)				Bond EMBI Indices (S)			
		EONIA	iTraxx	Pr (Default)	Global EM	ASIA	EEMA	LATM	Global EM	ASIA	EEMA	LATM
Bond EMBI Indices (S)	Global EM	0.0603*	0.5108*	0.0093	0.8402*	0.8169*	0.7013*	0.9138*				
	ASIA	0.1685*	−0.1213*	−0.1654*	0.7855*	0.7596*	0.7296*	0.7848*	0.8251*			
	EEMA	0.2442*	0.4336*	−0.0551*	0.8517*	0.8227*	0.7331*	0.9263*	0.9826*	0.7724*		
	LATM	0.0996*	0.4391*	−0.0171	0.8559*	0.8319*	0.7250*	0.9289*	0.9928*	0.8256*	0.9700*	

Euro-Crisis: October 8, 2009–December 12, 2011		Euro Financial Indicators			Equity MSCI Indices (S)				Bond EMBI Indices (S)			
		EONIA	iTraxx	Pr (Default)	Global EM	ASIA	EEMA	LATM	Global EM	ASIA	EEMA	LATM
Euro Financial Indicators	EONIA											
	iTraxx	0.1789*										
	Pr(Default)	−0.5368*	0.5737*									
Equity MSCI Indices (S)	Global EM	0.7006*	−0.3353*	−0.8570*								
	ASIA	0.7359*	−0.2840*	−0.8400*	0.9951*							
	EEMA	0.6878*	−0.4391*	−0.8496*	0.9534*	0.9357*						
	LATM	0.4881*	−0.5227*	−0.8677*	0.9475*	0.9177*	0.9057*					
Bond EMBI Indices (S)	Global EM	0.8830*	0.4044*	−0.4147*	0.6661*	0.7045*	0.5713*	0.4505*				
	ASIA	0.7913*	0.5890*	−0.2215*	0.5119*	0.5588*	0.3965*	0.2764*	0.9662*			
	EEMA	0.8253*	−0.1751*	−0.7483*	0.8370*	0.8396*	0.8461*	0.7313*	0.7728*	0.5960*		
	LATM	0.8543*	0.5223*	−0.2886*	0.5580*	0.6037*	0.4536*	0.3269*	0.9860*	0.9788*	0.6800*	

Note: * denotes statistical significance at 10% level.

EEMA = Eastern Europe, Middle East, and Africa, EONIA = Euro Overnight Index Average Swap Index 3-Month, EMBI = JP Morgan Emerging Markets Bond Index, Global EM = Global emerging markets, iTraxx = iTraxx Europe 5-Year Credit Default Swap Index, LATM = Latin America, MSCI = Morgan Stanley Capital International, Pr(Default) = Fitch's Probability of Eurozone Default. *Source*: Table 5, Aizenman, et al. (2012).

the same conclusion – that is, little evidence of financial contagion (Aizenman, Jinjarak, Lee, & Park, 2012).

Aizenman et al. (2012) assessed the likelihood of financial contagion from the eurozone to Asian financial markets using event study. More specifically, the event study methodology was used to measure the responses of equity and bond markets in developing countries to bad news from the eurozone – for example, sudden spike in the risk of sovereign default by a eurozone periphery country. The authors assume that financial markets' expectations about the future effects of distinct news are recorded by the observed reaction of asset prices in the days following the news. That is, asset prices capture and incorporate the effect of relevant shocks and developments. The event study methodology allowed the authors to trace the impact of distinct eurozone news on the dynamics of equity and bond prices in developing countries.

Thin and underdeveloped financial markets are often subject to wild gyrations in asset prices which are detached from fundamentals. For example, sales or purchases by a single large market player can exert disproportionate influence on asset prices. Therefore, we limit our analysis to a subset of developing countries with relatively deep and well-developed financial markets where asset prices are more responsive to news.

The 20 countries covered are Brazil, Chile, the PRC, Colombia, Czech Republic, Egypt, Hungary, India, Indonesia, the Republic of Korea, Malaysia, Mexico, Peru, the Philippines, Poland, the Russian Federation, South Africa, Taipei-China, Thailand, and Turkey. Since eurozone news may have different effects for different regions, we analyze three different regions – developing Asia (eight countries), Latin America (five countries) and Eastern Europe, Africa, and Middle East (seven countries) – in addition to the whole sample.

Table 5 reports the baseline regression results for the sample of 20 developing countries. The first two columns use cumulative normal return of equity and bond market as the dependent variable, while the third and fourth columns use cumulative abnormal returns. Our key variable of interest, in terms of assessing the risk of financial contagion from the eurzone to developing countries is bad news from the eurozone. The results provide some evidence of contagion – negative eurozone news has a significant negative effect on normal returns in the equity markets. Table 6 reports the regression results for the subsample of eight developing Asian countries. Negative eurozone news does have a significant effect on either normal or abnormal returns in both the equity or bond markets. This suggests that the risk of a financial contagion from the eurozone to Asia via financial

Table 5. Impact of Eurozone Bad News on Returns in Developing Countries' Equity and Bond Markets.

Variable\Return	Normal Return						Abnormal Return					
	Equity			Bond			Equity			Bond		
	Coeff.	(S.E.)		Coeff.	(S.E.)		Coeff.	(S.E.)		Coeff.	(S.E.)	
Global crisis period	−0.690	(0.29)	**	−0.336	(0.08)	***	−0.038	(0.44)		−0.683	(0.10)	***
Euro Crisis: bad news	−1.122	(0.54)	**	0.165	(0.14)		0.990	(0.82)		0.207	(0.19)	
Euro Crisis: good news	−0.432	(0.39)		0.012	(0.10)		1.429	(0.59)	**	−0.110	(0.14)	
(bad news)x(exposure)	−0.051	(0.04)		−0.004	(0.01)		−0.038	(0.06)		−0.022	(0.01)	*
constant	−1.178	(0.22)	***	0.075	(0.06)		−3.605	(0.33)	***	0.056	(0.08)	
country-events	1900			1900			1900			1900		
R^2	0.016			0.011			0.004			0.030		

Standard errors are in parentheses. ***, **, * denote statistical significance at 1%, 5%, 10%, respectively.

Table 6. Impact of Eurozone Bad News on Returns in Developing Asian Countries' Equity and Bond Markets.

Variable\Return	Normal Return						Abnormal Return					
	Equity			Bond			Equity			Bond		
	Coeff.	(S.E.)		Coeff.	(S.E.)		Coeff.	(S.E.)		Coeff.	(S.E.)	
Global crisis period	0.198	(0.42)		−0.194	(0.11)	*	1.293	(0.68)	*	−0.642	(0.16)	***
Euro Crisis: bad news	−2.273	(1.53)		0.082	(0.41)		1.528	(2.47)		0.039	(0.58)	
Euro Crisis: good news	−0.807	(0.56)		0.061	(0.15)		1.077	(0.91)		0.189	(0.21)	
(bad news)x(exposure)	0.185	(0.28)		0.016	(0.08)		0.025	(0.46)		0.057	(0.11)	
constant	−1.914	(0.32)	***	−0.065	(0.09)		−4.783	(0.51)	***	−0.174	(0.12)	
country-events	760			760			760			760		
R^2	0.008			0.004			0.015			0.022		

Standard errors are in parentheses. ***, * denote statistical significance at 1%, 10%, respectively.
Source: Table 2, Aizenman et al. (2012).

markets is limited. This is plausible in light of limited financial integration between the two regions.

Impact of Euro Crisis on Asia's Banking Sector

While one channel of financial contagion from the eurozone to Asia is via the equity and bond markets, another channel is through the banking sector. Within the banking channel, there are two possibilities. First, Asia's banks and financial institutions may have exposure to the government bonds of eurozone periphery countries at the heart of the euro crisis. However, anecdotal evidence suggests that this exposure is minimal. Second, eurozone banks may sharply cut back their lending to Asia to repair balance sheets damaged by the euro crisis – for example, losses incurred on holdings of eurozone periphery government bonds. Unlike the first channel, the second channel is relevant in light of the large amounts of eurozone bank lending to Asia. From Asia's viewpoint, a cutback in eurozone bank lending could seriously tighten external financing conditions, especially for countries which depend heavily on foreign bank loans.

Developing Asia's Exposure to Eurozone Lending

Overall, eurozone has been an important source of foreign bank loans for developing Asia. According to data from the Bank for International Settlements, in September 2011 Asia's borrowings from eurozone banks amounted to around $440 billion, equivalent to 14% of the region's total foreign bank financing.[2] The exact impact of eurozone bank loans in an Asian economy will depend on the extent to which that economy relies on eurozone banks as source of external financing. In East Asia, South Asia, and Southeast Asia, eurozone banks provide about 12–17% of their total foreign bank borrowings. In Central Asia and the Pacific, the shares are even higher at nearly 50% (Table 7). This suggests that the two subregions are most at risk of disruptions to their credit flows should eurozone cross-border lending be sharply reduced. Even for developing Asia as a whole, there is a fairly high dependence on eurozone banks in the context of borrowing from foreign banks.

However, just a few economies account for the lion's share of the region's exposure to eurozone bank financing. Only five economies – the PRC; Hong Kong, China; the Republic of Korea; India; and Singapore – jointly took in about three-fourths of Asia's total borrowing from eurozone banks. In terms of the sheer size of funding, these economies might seem

Table 7. Asia's Borrowings from Eurozone Banks, September 2011.

Region/Economy	Amount ($ Billion)	Share by Each Region/ Economy (%)	Share of Borrowings from Eurozone in Total Foreign Bank Borrowings	Borrowings from Eurozone Banks as Share of Domestic Credit
Central Asia	13.3	3.0	49.2	–
East Asia	228.9	51.9	12.4	–
People's Rep. of China	96.4	21.9	14.1	0.9
Hong Kong, China	63.8	14.5	9.8	12.4
Rep. of Korea	44.0	10.0	13.0	4.1
Taipei,China	24.7	5.6	14.2	4.1
South Asia	60.4	13.7	17.2	–
India	57.5	13.0	17.9	4.4
Southeast Asia	114.8	26.0	14.3	–
Indonesia	18.8	4.3	16.2	6.6
Malaysia	10.2	2.3	7.0	3.0
Philippines	8.2	1.9	20.7	7.7
Singapore	63.6	14.4	16.9	27.4
Thailand	7.1	1.6	7.5	1.5
Viet Nam	6.4	1.5	26.2	4.6
Pacific	23.5	5.3	49.8	–
Developing Asia	440.9	100.0	14.3	2.9

– = means data not available.
Note: Data for developing Asia are based on the 11 economies with data.
Source: Authors' calculations based on Table 9b (Consolidated foreign claims, immediate borrower basis), Bank for International Settlements.

most vulnerable to large cutbacks in borrowings from eurozone banks. However, a much more accurate indicator of vulnerability to credit tightening by eurozone banks is the share of eurozone bank borrowing as a share of domestic credit. This share indicates the relative role of eurozone bank borrowing in domestic financial intermediation. Borrowings from eurozone banks are equivalent to 4–8% of domestic credit in India, Indonesia, the Republic of Korea, Malaysia, the Philippines, and Viet Nam. As expected, the shares in Asia's two major financial centers – Hong Kong, China and Singapore – are higher. However, those very high shares probably reflect their role as financial centers rather than a disproportionate dependence in financial intermediation. While there are differences across countries, developing Asia as a whole does not seem at high risk of a credit crunch from a pullback of eurozone bank lending.

Lending further support to such a benign projection is the healthy state of the region's banking sector. The good health of developing Asia's banks will help cushion adverse fallout from a eurozone banking crisis. So far private credit continues to expand at a healthy pace, which indicates that the effects of the euro crisis on the region's banking sector are quite limited (Fig. 8). Furthermore, key indicators of financial soundness such as risk-weighted capital adequacy ratio and ratio of nonperforming loans point to a robust and resilient banking sector capable of absorbing external shocks

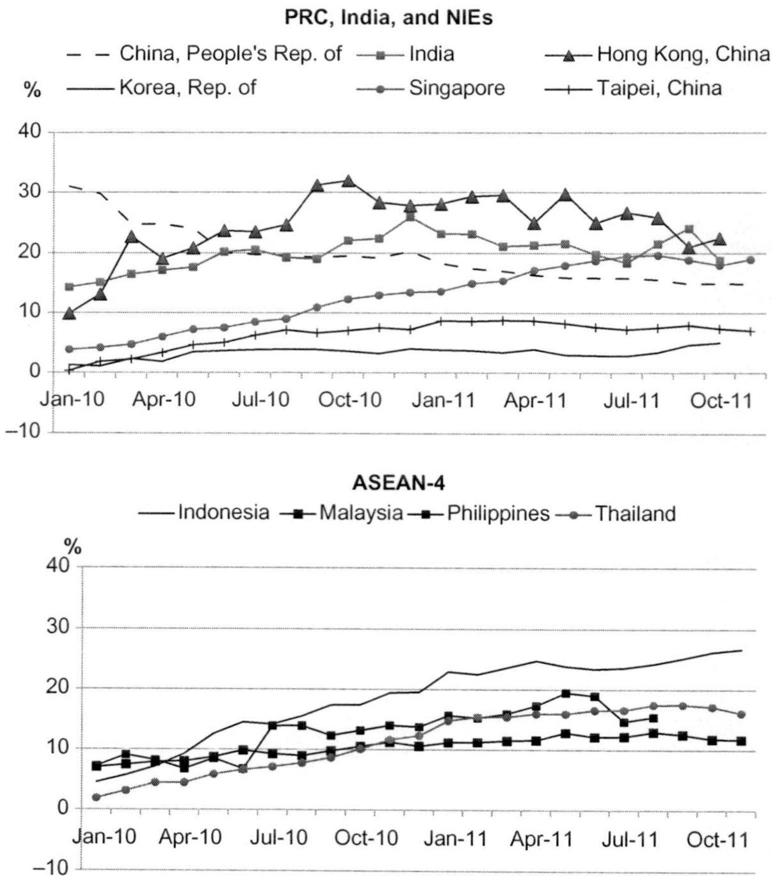

Fig. 8. Growth in Private Credit. NIE = Newly industrialized economies. *Source*: CEIC Data Company; International Monetary Fund, *International Financial Statistics* online database (both accessed on February 7, 2012).

Table 8. External and Financial Vulnerabilities (%).

Economy	External Debt/GDP (2011)	Foreign Exchange Reserves, Months of Imports (2011)[a]	Short-Term External Debt/ Reserves (2011)[b]	Risk-Weighted Capital Adequacy Ratio (March 2011)[c]	Bank Nonperforming Loans to Total Loans (2010/2011)[d]
China, People's Rep. of	9.5	20.1	15.8	11.8	1.1
Hong Kong, China	376.7	6.2	250.0	16	0.7
India	17.4	7.3	25.9	13.6	2.4
Indonesia	28.6	6.3	35.3	17.6	2.9
Korea, Rep. of	34.9	5.8	45.6	14.3	1.9
Malaysia	29.1	7.5	24.1	16.4	2.9
Philippines	27.5	10.6	10.7	16.7	3.8
Singapore	246.9	6.0	199.6	17.8	1.8
Taipei, China	27.1	14.4	27.9	–	0.4
Thailand	33.5	7.9	23.2	15.5	3.5

"–" means data not available.
[a]Data for India refer to 2010.
[b]Data are as of September 2011 for India, Singapore, and Taipei, China; 2010 for Thailand.
[c]Data are as of June 2011 for Malaysia.
[d]Data are as of March 2011 for the People's Rep. of China; Hong Kong, China; and Thailand; March 2010 for India; May 2011 for Indonesia; June 2011 for Malaysia; Dec. 2010 for the Rep. of Korea and the Philippines; Sep. 2010 for Singapore; Dec. 2011 for Taipei, China.
Sources: Authors' calculations using data from CEIC Data Company and International Monetary Fund, International Financial Statistics; *Asian Development Outlook* data base; International Monetary Fund, *Financial Soundness Indicators*, September 2011.

(Table 8). External debt indicators in Asia are also favorable; other than Hong Kong, China and Singapore – the two financial centers, external debt is low as a share of GDP. Although the overall picture of the impact on Asia's banking sector remains benign, there is no room for complacency among policymakers. In this connection, our formal empirical analysis below reveals that borrowing from eurozone banks has had a significant positive effect on private credit growth for a group of 11 major Asian economies.

Impact of Bank Borrowings from Eurozone on Asia's Private Credit Growth – An Econometric Analysis

We performed panel data regression analysis to examine the relationship between Asia's private credit and borrowings from eurozone banks. This exercise uses data from the first quarter of 2000 to the third quarter of 2011 and covers 11 Asian economies (the PRC; Hong Kong, China; India; Indonesia; the Republic of Korea; Malaysia; the Philippines; Singapore; Taipei,China; Thailand; and Viet Nam). The basic specification of the model is:

$$\mathrm{PCgr}_{i,t} = \beta_0 + \beta_1 \mathrm{EBgr}_{i,t-1} + \beta_2 \mathrm{GDPgr}_{i,t-1} + \beta_3 i_{i,t-1} + \beta_4 \mathrm{Dgr}_{i,t} + \beta_5 \mathrm{FFRch}_{i,t}$$

The dependent variable is growth in private credit ($\mathrm{PCgr}_{i,t}$), while the key independent variable is lagged growth in eurozone borrowings ($\mathrm{EBgr}_{i,t-1}$). The model controls for lagged GDP growth ($\mathrm{GDPgr}_{i,t-1}$), lagged interest rate ($i_{i,t-1}$), growth in deposits ($\mathrm{Dgr}_{i,t}$), and change in US federal funds rate ($\mathrm{FFRch}_{i,t}$). GDP growth is an indicator of the demand for credit; a more vibrant economy is expected to lead to higher growth in domestic credit. Interest rate is used as proxy for overall monetary stance, since a restrictive monetary policy can lead to slower credit growth. Growth of deposits is used to account for the importance of domestic deposits as source of loanable funds. Change in US federal fund rates is included as a measure of global liquidity conditions. Country fixed effects are controlled in the regressions. The empirical model is largely based on Guo and Stepanyan (2011), who analyzed the determinants of bank credit based on a sample of over 80 emerging market economies.

The regression results reported in Table 9 indicate that lagged growth in eurozone borrowings has a positive and significant impact on private credit growth; however, its magnitude is negligible. This implies that a sharp cutback or reversal of eurozone bank loans from Asia may disrupt domestic financial intermediation in the region but its impact would be minimal.

DEVELOPING ASIA'S POLICY SPACE TO COPE WITH THE EURO CRISIS

Any meaningful discussion of the potential effect of the euro crisis on Asia must include a discussion of policy space available to the region's policymakers. To the extent that the policymakers have ample policy space, they will be able to use policy tools to mitigate the adverse impact of the euro crisis. On the other hand, lack of policy space will amplify the adverse effects of the euro crisis on the region. The region's experiences during the global crisis served as a vivid reminder of the importance of policy space in

Table 9. Regression Results: Dependent Variable–Growth in Private Credit.

	A	B	C
Lagged growth in borrowings from eurozone banks	0.044***	0.042***	0.041***
	(0.013)	(0.012)	(0.012)
Lagged GDP growth	0.362***	0.349***	0.460***
	(0.102)	(0.097)	(0.104)
Lagged interest rate	−0.974***	−1.103***	−1.166***
	(0.235)	(0.224)	(0.223)
Growth in deposits		0.413***	0.422***
		(0.059)	(0.059)
Change in federal funds rate			−0.540***
			(0.190)
Constant	6.426***	24.832***	23.950***
	(1.177)	(2.693)	(2.689)
Observations	440	440	440
Adjusted R^2	0.627	0.664	0.670

Standard errors in parentheses; *** $p < 0.01$.
Note: The estimation controls for country fixed effects. Standard errors are in parentheses.
Source: Authors' calculations.

determining the impact of a large external shock. It is widely agreed that the region's ample policy space enabled the region's policymakers to aggressively pursue countercyclical macroeconomic policy which helped stave off a deep and protracted recession. In particular, fiscal space allowed the region's governments to quickly unleash large fiscal stimulus programs which supported aggregate demand and growth in the face of collapsing exports and feeble private domestic demand.

More specifically, policy space refers to the scope for using fiscal, monetary, and financial policy to counter the effects of an external shock. For example, relatively low public debt to GDP ratios allows governments to raise spending and cut taxes without triggering adverse reactions from financial markets about fiscal sustainability. Likewise, a history of anti-inflationary credibility expands the scope for interest rate cuts and a clearly defined lender of last resort function strengthens the effectiveness of financial policy during a crisis. While the region's stimulus during the global crisis used up some of its policy space, nevertheless Asian economies still appear to have ample room to respond through monetary, fiscal, or financial policy. Strong macroeconomic fundamentals can once again cushion the region from a large external shock.

Above all, Asian countries still have the luxury of fiscal space which would enable them to unleash a forceful fiscal stimulus in the event of a major slowdown. Fiscal balances of many Asian countries in the region remain at healthy levels. In the PRC, India, the Republic of Korea, the Philippines, and Thailand, fiscal position has improved in 2011 relative to the 3 previous years as a result of the unwinding of the stimulus implemented during the global crisis (Fig. 9). Furthermore, Asian countries' public debt to GDP ratios are well below those of the advanced economies and generally quite close to their desirable medium-term levels. Furthermore, financial markets' concerns about the fiscal sustainability of the region's countries have abated since escalating in October 2011 despite lingering uncertainty about the euro crisis, as evident in the decline of sovereign spreads (Fig. 10).

Developing Asia's economies also have some scope to ease monetary policy. To stem rising inflation and to unwind the monetary stimulus response to the global crisis, several economies have gradually tightened monetary policy over the last 2 years or so. Since nominal benchmark rates

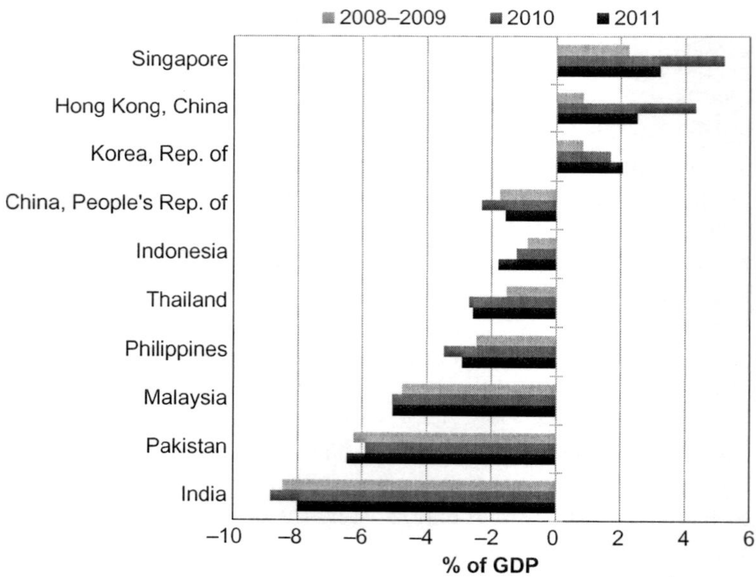

Fig. 9. Fiscal Balances, Selected Developing Asian Countries. *Source*: International Monetary Fund, September 2011 Fiscal Monitor "Addressing Fiscal Challenges to Reduce Economic Risks."

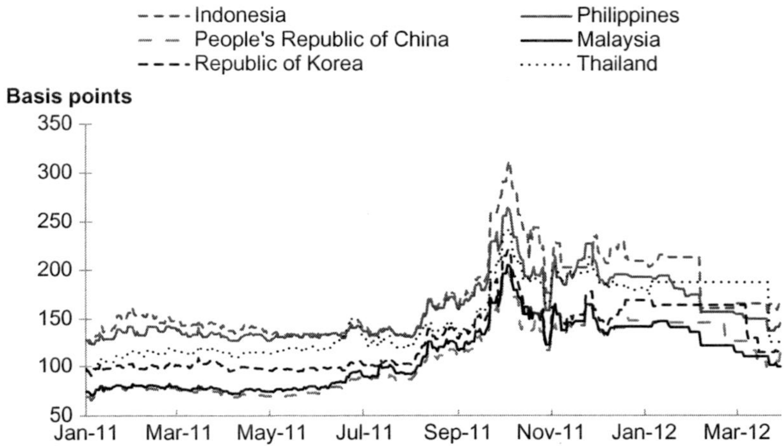

Fig. 10. Credit Default Swap Spreads, 5 Year, Selected Developing Asian Countries. *Source*: Bloomberg (accessed on March 9, 2012).

are above the zero floor, monetary authorities have sufficient room to lower the rates should there be a need for monetary easing to prop up their financial systems and economies (Fig. 11). Inflation rates have also been declining, stemming concerns that inflationary pressures may limit the scope for monetary policy. In the PRC, Indonesia, Republic of Korea, and the Philippines, inflation rates are moving closer to targets set by monetary authorities. Turning to financial policy, the region's central banks have ample foreign exchange reserves to help them cope with any unexpected shortage of foreign currency liquidity. Furthermore, they have clearly specified lender of last resort facilities and flexible collateral arrangements. Sound financial supervision and regulation has resulted in healthy financial systems. For example, a large share of bank loans is financed through deposits rather than wholesale funding (Table 10).

Notwithstanding the region's ample policy space, the region should closely monitor the euro area as there is still a great deal of uncertainty on how the euro crisis will unfold. Economies should be ready to adjust fiscal, monetary, and financial policy in response to new major developments in the eurozone, especially a sudden and sharp deterioration. How the region fares in the event of another major external shock will ultimately depend on how effectively it manages its policy space. In addition, the region should be careful to preserve its tradition of fiscal prudence and macroeconomic stability, which is what gave it its highly valuable

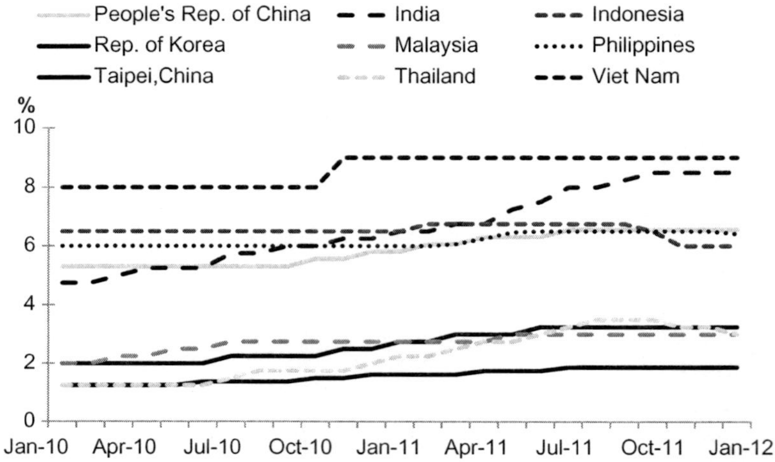

Fig. 11. Benchmark Interest Rates, Selected Developing Asian Economies. *Source*: CEIC Data Company (accessed on March 9, 2012).

Table 10. Banks' Loan to Deposit Ratio (%), Selected Developing Asian Countries.

Economy	2007	2008	2009	2010	2011
Brunei Darussalam	74.1	70.0	61.7	58.4	51.7
Cambodia	68.8	103.1	81.0	79.1	83.4
China, People's Rep. of	74.1	69.6	72.6	73.1	73.4
Hong Kong, China	45.8	47.3	49.1	58.3	63.3
India	74.5	75.3	71.4	76.3	75.1
Indonesia	70.0	80.1	76.3	81.2	90.1
Japan	76.3	73.9	69.2	66.1	64.2
Korea, Republic of	135.6	134.1	126.3	118.3	118.5
Lao PDR	33.4	48.8	70.8	71.1	–
Malaysia	90.9	92.7	91.7	93.4	92.6
Myanmar	47.0	43.4	39.2	37.2	39.7
Philippines	59.2	59.6	58.6	59.3	64.5
Singapore	82.9	85.3	77.9	81.5	86.7
Taipei, China	68.4	64.3	60.6	61.7	63.2
Thailand	99.1	97.7	95.2	96.6	97.1
Viet Nam	96.4	98.0	105.9	102.2	107.3

Source: Authors' calculations using data from International Financial Statistics, International Monetary Fund and national sources.

policy space in the first place. That is, policy space should be used primarily in response to a clear and present danger, such as another global crisis, rather than during every episode of uncertainty and instability. In addition, the region's ample fiscal space may be more apparent than real once we take into account the wide range of medium-term fiscal demands looming on the region's horizon. These include rising pension and health care costs associated with the region's rapid demographic transition as well as social protection expenditures required for a more inclusive growth.

CONCLUDING OBSERVATIONS AND POLICY IMPLICATIONS

Our analysis of the impact of euro crisis on developing Asia points to a sizable but manageable short-term impact. Put differently, the euro crisis will slow down but not derail the robust momentum of the region's recovery since the global crisis of 2008–2009. The EU will remain an important economic partner for the region in the foreseeable future. Above all, the EU is a key export market for a region which still depends heavily on exports for growth. Furthermore, our analysis points to a significant effect on the region's financial systems, especially its banking sector. However, overall, the magnitude of the shock from the euro crisis will be significantly smaller than the shock from the global crisis. A critical but often overlooked structural difference between the two crises is that the global crisis was a synchronized crisis which simultaneously affected the EU, Japan, and the US, but the euro crisis is largely confined to Europe. Within developing Asia, some subregions and countries, especially the most open economies which export manufactured goods to EU, will be hit harder than others but even those economies should be able to cope.

A further cause for guarded optimism is that developing Asia still has relatively ample policy space to cushion a major external shock. Therefore, not only is the magnitude of the shock smaller relative to the global crisis, but the region has monetary, fiscal, and financial policy tools to mitigate the impact of another external shock. During the global crisis, countercyclical macroeconomic policy, in particular large fiscal stimulus programs, laid the foundation for a V-shaped recovery. Likewise, developing Asia's policymakers remain relatively well equipped in the tail-risk event that the euro crisis morphs into another global crisis. However, the broader policy lesson from Asia's global crisis experience is that the region's tradition of fiscal prudence can yield huge benefits in times of severe crisis. Furthermore, the region faces a number of medium-term fiscal demands, for example, those associated with an aging population and fostering inclusive growth, which further strengthen the case for fiscal responsibility.

Going forward, the impact on developing Asia will fall primarily on trade but the region should be able to weather a euro slowdown. The euro crisis is still far from fundamentally resolved and its evolution will clearly impinge heavily on its future impact. The most practical and immediate implication for policymakers is that they should continue to keep a close eye on eurozone developments and their ramifications for their economies. Of particular concern to the region is the tail risk of a sharp, abrupt deterioration of the euro crisis and its transformation into another global financial crisis. However, for the moment, the risk of this worst-case scenario of a full-fledged financial crisis appears to be receding due to large liquidity injections by the ECB. The much more likely scenario is that of medium term weakening of the growth momentum in Europe due to governments consolidating their finances and banks repairing their balance sheets. The consequent weakening of Asia's exports to Europe will have a visible but not pronounced effect on Asia's growth. Furthermore, in line with its weakening since the global crisis, the EU's share of Asia's exports has already been falling for some time.

Beyond the very short term, the euro crisis further strengthens the case for developing Asia's rebalancing toward domestic sources of growth. In a fundamental sense, the euro crisis is simply part and parcel of the broader, long-term shift of global economic power from the North to the South. Europe had already been weakened by the global crisis and the euro crisis merely reflects an intensification of the medium-term structural problems which stand in the way of a firmer recovery in the advanced economies. The euro crisis did not precipitate Europe's slow growth but it has complicated its efforts to mount a firm and durable postglobal crisis recovery. From Asia's viewpoint, this reinforces a two-speed world economy which combines robust, sustained growth in the South with feeble, sputtering recovery in the North. Therefore, Asia should continue and reinforce its efforts to stimulate domestic demand, along with South–South trade, to compensate for lacklustre demand from its traditional G3 markets.

Slow Down

Developing Asia can and should make bigger contributions toward fostering global financial stability. Global financial turmoil is a global public bad and, by the same token, global financial stability is a global public good. The postglobal crisis world is likely to be characterized by moderation due to slower growth in the advanced economies. Another defining characteristic of the postcrisis world is greater global instability since the advanced countries, which used to be bedrocks of stability, have now themselves become the sources of stability. While Asia can protect itself from heightened global volatility by structural measures such as rebalancing and financial sector development, the region has now grown large enough to make significant contributions of its own to global financial stability. Regardless of the pros and cons of recent calls for Asia to contribute financial resources toward resolving the euro crisis, such calls bring up a bigger point. In particular, the region should not only contribute more resources but also actively take part in global discussions on strengthening the global financial architecture. One specific avenue is through the International Monetary Fund where an expanded Asian role would go hand in hand with increased Asian contributions.

NOTES

1. Emerging Asia includes the PRC; Hong Kong, China; Indonesia; the Republic of Korea; Malaysia; the Philippines; Singapore; Taipei, China; Thailand; and Viet Nam.
2. Data are based on 30 economies that provide consolidated worldwide banking data to the Bank for International Settlements. The economies are Australia; Austria; Belgium; Brazil; Canada; Chile; Denmark; Finland; France; Germany; Greece; Hong Kong, China; India; Ireland; Italy; Japan; Luxembourg; Mexico; The Netherlands; Norway; Panama; Portugal; Singapore; Spain; Sweden; Switzerland; Taipei-China; Turkey; the United Kingdom; and the United States. For eurozone, nine countries (Austria, Belgium, France, Germany, Greece, Italy, the Netherlands, Portugal, and Spain) with individual country data on developing Asia are included.

REFERENCES

Aizenman, J., Jinjarak, Y., Lee, M., & Park, D. (2012). *Developing countries' financial vulnerability to the Euro crisis: An event study of equity and bond markets*. NBER Working Paper Series No. 18028. National Bureau of Economic Research, Cambridge, MA.

Asian Development Bank. (2011). *Asian economic monitor*. Manila: Asian Development Bank.
Guo, K., & Stepanyan, V. (2011). *Determinants of ban credit in emerging market economies*. IMF Working Paper WP/11/51, International Monetary Fund, Washington, DC.
IMF. (2008). *World economic and financial surveys, Regional economic outlook: Asia and Pacific*. April. International Monetary Fund, Washington DC.
Park, D., & Shin, K. (2009). *The people's republic of China as an engine of growth for developing Asia? Evidence from vector autoregression models*. ADB Economics Working Paper Series No.175. Asian Development Bank, Manila.

FINANCIAL INTEGRATION AND FOREIGN BANKS IN LATIN AMERICA: HOW DO THEY IMPACT THE TRANSMISSION OF EXTERNAL FINANCIAL SHOCKS?

Arturo J. Galindo, Alejandro Izquierdo and Liliana Rojas-Suarez

ABSTRACT

This chapter explores the impact of international financial integration on credit markets in Latin America, using a cross-country dataset covering 17 countries between 1996 and 2008. It is found that financial integration amplifies the impact of international financial shocks on aggregate credit and interest rate fluctuations. Nonetheless, the net impact of integration on deepening credit markets dominates for the large majority of states of nature. The chapter also uses a detailed bank-level dataset that covers more than 500 banks for a similar time period to explore the role of financial integration – captured through the participation of foreign banks – in propagating external shocks. It is found that interest rates charged and loans supplied by foreign-owned banks respond more to

Global Banking, Financial Markets and Crises
International Finance Review, Volume 14, 305–339

ISSN: 1569-3767/doi:10.1108/S1569-3767(2013)0000014014

external financial shocks than those supplied by domestically owned banks. This does not hold for all foreign banks. Spanish banks in the sample behave more like domestic banks and do not amplify the impact of foreign shocks on credit and interest rates.

Keywords: Foreign Banks; credit; interest rates; financial shocks

JEL classifications: F36; G0; G21

INTRODUCTION

Since the 1990s, most countries in Latin America have embarked on a process of financial integration characterized by a reduction of impediments to cross-border financial transactions and increased participation of foreign banks in the local banking systems.[1] By 2007, Latin America as a whole was the most financially open region in the developing world (see the third section). Accompanying these developments, a growing amount of literature on this topic has emerged. However, no consensus has been reached regarding the relative benefits and perils of both increased financial integration and greater participation of foreign banks.

This debate was further exacerbated by the global financial crisis that started in 2007 in major industrialized countries. In the view of some analysts, the propagation of the crisis from developed countries to emerging market economies in general – and Latin America in particular – through financial channels is proof of the need to impose limits on financial integration. The sharp reduction in access to international capital markets experienced by Latin American countries in the latter part of 2008 and the beginning of 2009, and the resulting adverse effects on growth and economic stability, is cited as evidence of the dangers of liberalized capital accounts (see, e.g., Stiglitz, 2009).

Others, however, focus on the rapid growth experienced by the region in the five years that preceded the crisis and argue that greater financial integration and active participation of foreign banks played an important role in that outcome. While acknowledging the adverse effects of contagion during the crisis, this group of experts argues that the low savings rates prevalent in most countries in the region impose a greater constraint on long-term growth than the short-term negative impact of the international crisis.

The importance of financial integration and foreign banks in Latin America, however, goes beyond its effect on economic growth. These two factors also play a crucial role in the behavior of real credit growth and real interest rates. Interestingly enough, when analyzing these issues, most of the analytical literature deals with the response of local financial variables to *real shocks*, such as a reduction in economic activity either in the local economy or in the home country of foreign banks (see the literature discussion in the second section). In contrast, analyses of the role of financial integration and foreign banks in the transmission of *external financial shocks* (such as a sharp increase in the U.S. high-yield spread) to domestic credit and interest rates in Latin America are extremely limited.

This chapter aims to help fill that vacuum and complement existing literature by conducting an empirical investigation of the relationship between domestic financial variables (real credit growth and real interest rates) and external financial shocks that lead to changes in investors' perception of risk. We measure these as a drastic increase in the VIX index, the EMBI spread or the spread of U.S. high-yield bonds. The novelty of the analysis lies in determining the role of both financial integration and foreign banks in this interrelationship. Thus, the key questions answered in this chapter for Latin America are:

(a) Does financial integration exacerbate the adverse effect of a foreign shock on domestic credit growth and its cost?
(b) Does the behavior of foreign banks differ from that of domestic banks in terms of the response of credit to an adverse external financial shock?
(c) Do foreign banks increase interest rates more than domestic banks when a negative external financial shock hits the local financial system?

The empirical investigation provides a positive answer to these questions. However, despite this pernicious effect, the research also concludes that the net impact of financial integration supports real credit growth and lower real interest rates. Thus, while financial integration is a channel through which adverse financial shocks lead to credit contractions and increases in interest rates, it also helps credit markets to deepen and the cost of finance to decline in the absence of adverse external financial shocks. Moreover, this latter effect dominates the former.

The rest of this chapter is organized as follows. The second section presents a brief review of the literature on the benefits and risks of financial integration and foreign banks in emerging markets. The third section discusses the extent of financial integration in Latin America using both de jure and de facto measurements. This section also shows some changes in the characteristics of international loans to the region that accompanied the process of financial integration. The fourth section conducts an empirical analysis to determine the role of financial integration in the relationship between external financial shocks and domestic real credit growth and real interest rates. The section also explores whether, in the presence of an external financial shock, the behavior of domestic banks differs from that of foreign banks. The fifth section provides our conclusions.

FINANCIAL INTEGRATION AND FOREIGN BANKS IN EMERGING MARKETS: A BRIEF LITERATURE REVIEW

Financial integration has been the subject of much debate, particularly following the crises in emerging markets in the late 1990s. Much of the debate has focused on identifying the pros and cons of capital account liberalization policies. Despite the large provision of funding supporting growth processes in emerging markets, stark financial crises stemming from supply shocks to the provision of international credit and their associated output meltdowns (as shown, e.g., by Calvo, Izquierdo, & Talvi, 2006) led to a rethinking of financial integration strategies. The current global financial crisis poses similar questions about desired integration levels in a context of repeated international financial volatility. Although capital account liberalization seems to have brought several benefits to those who engaged in these policies – as evidenced by large expansionary cycles during the mid-2000s – it has not been without costs. However, recent work by Rancière, Tornell, and Westermann (2008) suggests that the benefits seem to outweigh the costs considering countries that have experienced occasional financial crises have, on average, grown faster than countries with stable financial conditions, suggesting a positive effect of integration with systemic risk on growth.[2] Thus, situations of greater incidence of crisis are compatible with higher mean growth. As a matter of fact, Rancière, Tornell, and Westermann (2006) provide an empirical decomposition of the effects of financial liberalization on growth and on the incidence of crises, and show that the direct effect of financial liberalization on growth outweighs by far the negative indirect effect of a higher propensity to crisis.[3] Recent work by Calvo and Loo-Kung (2009) also suggests that, in terms of consumption welfare, periods of financial liberalization coming hand in hand with high growth do not need to be very long to beat the alternative of lower growth, closed capital account processes.[4]

In many cases, larger participation by foreign banks has accompanied financial integration. Thus, it is relevant to understand how foreign banks contribute to or detract from credit volatility. Foreign banks may play a stabilizing role in that they can better diversify risk, and they can rely on liquidity from the parent company and capital back up in the event of host-country shocks. For example, Goldberg (2002) shows that the international activities of foreign banks headquartered in the United States are not influenced by host-country economic conditions. Moreover, Goldberg (2005) finds that local and cross-border claims on Latin American customers of U.S. banks are not robustly related to country-specific business cycle variables. Galindo, Micco, and Powell (2003) provide additional support for these findings by establishing that foreign banks can stabilize credit during domestic deposit crunches.

In a similar vein, Martínez Peria, Powell, and Vladkova-Hollar (2005) present evidence that the sensitivity of foreign bank claims to host-country factors diminishes as banks' aggregate exposure rises. They also infer that foreign bank claims react more to positive than to negative host shocks and that they are not significantly curtailed during crises. De Haas and Lelyveld (2006) find additional evidence from Central and Eastern Europe that during crisis periods domestic banks contract their credit and deposit bases, whereas foreign banks do not. More recently, Cull and Martínez Peria (2007) report that, although countries that experienced a banking crisis tended to have higher levels of foreign bank participation than those that did not, foreign participation increased as a result of crises rather than prior to them.

However, research also indicates that foreign banks can amplify credit cycles driven by changes in business opportunities in the domestic economy. For example, although Morgan and Strahan (2003) show that foreign banks may dampen the effect of a general bank capital shock on firm investment in the host country – in line with the literature mentioned above – they also find that foreign banks can amplify firm collateral shocks in the host country by reallocating their portfolio when changes in expected risk/return take place. In this way foreign banks exploit alternative investment opportunities abroad, an option that may not be available to domestic banks. Similarly, Galindo, Micco, and Powell (2003) determine that when foreign banks suffer a shock to expected returns in the host country, they may cut back on local operations at a faster pace than less diversified domestic banks. These findings point to the fact that under particular conditions there may be a positive association between a host country's business cycle and foreign bank credit supply.

Apart from the above-mentioned reaction to host-country shocks, also known as "pull" factors, several studies have focused on "push" factors linked to the impact of source-country shocks on host-country lending by foreign banks. Goldberg (2005) finds that the claims of U.S. banks on European markets have been generally positively correlated with U.S. GDP growth, implying that net claims abroad increase when the U.S. economy is expanding. Peek and Rosengren (2000) present similar evidence on pro-cyclical flows when studying U.S. exposure to the Japanese cycle. They find that exposure to the Japanese real estate bubble of the early 1990s led to a contraction of credit from Japanese banks to U.S. customers. Kamil and Rai (2009) show that liquidity constraints in U.S. money markets reduce cross-border lending and foreign bank subsidiary lending to Latin American countries.

However, Goldberg (2005) finds that cross-border claims on Latin American markets are not robustly related to the U.S. business cycle, and thus U.S. banks do not appear to be strong conduits for transmitting U.S. cycles to smaller markets. Despite this finding on "push" factors indicating that apparently foreign banks do not seem to import source-country shocks into Latin America, little has been explored in terms of the relevance of external shocks related to changes in risk aversion – such as sharp changes in U.S. high-yield spreads, global EMBI spreads or the VIX index – on foreign bank lending behavior compared with that of domestic banks. Similarly, although much has been written about financial integration and banking crises, there is a need to explore whether larger financial integration significantly affects domestic credit fluctuations and real interest rates when systemic risk aversion rises. This issue will be tackled empirically in the fourth section.

LATIN AMERICA'S FINANCIAL INTEGRATION

Two alternative measures of international financial integration are de jure and de facto. The former assesses the regulatory restrictions (or lack of) on cross-border financial transactions of financial institutions. The latter measures the extent to which cross-border holdings of financial assets and liabilities have *actually taken place*. While in general one could expect that, in an increasingly globalized world, both measures would be highly correlated, it is also quite possible to envision situations in which such correlation does not materialize. For example, a country with a fully liberalized capital account might encounter very little interest from foreign investors in the country's assets and financial instruments due to its high economic and/or political instability. Likewise, it is possible that a large accumulation of foreign assets and liabilities occurs in spite of existing capital account controls if those controls prove to be ineffective (see, e.g., Edwards, 1999). A review of the literature shows that examples of both cases abound in the recent history of Latin America.[5]

Regardless of the desirability and effectiveness of capital controls – a topic not addressed in this chapter – it is relevant to understand the degree and evolution of financial integration in Latin America, both de jure and de facto. This section explores those matters. At the outset, however, it is important to clarify that the measures discussed here are approximations and that it is extremely difficult to fully distinguish between these two kinds of measurements. As explained above, unstable macro policies can de facto be an impediment to financial integration, even in the absence of de jure capital controls.

De Jure Financial Integration

There are a number of alternative measures of capital account liberalization (or, conversely, capital controls). For the purpose of allowing country comparisons, all these measures are based on information provided by the IMF's *Annual Report on Exchange Arrangements and Exchange Restrictions* (AREAER), which reports the extent of rules and regulations affecting cross-border financial transactions (see, e.g., Glick & Hutchison, 2001; Quinn, 2003). In this chapter we use the index of financial openness developed by Chinn and Ito (2008), which attempts to capture the extent and intensity of restrictions on capital mobility. To achieve its purpose, the Chinn and Ito index, which is also based on information from AREAER, uses a principal components methodology. The higher the value of the index, the more open the capital account.[6]

Fig. 1 presents the evolution of the financial openness index by regions.[7] As the chart clearly shows, the Latin American index of capital account liberalization has been increasing since the 1990s. By 2006, Latin America was the most financially open region in the world, second only to developed countries. Indeed, by 2006, Latin America's index of financial openness was triple that of Eastern Europe and Central Asia.

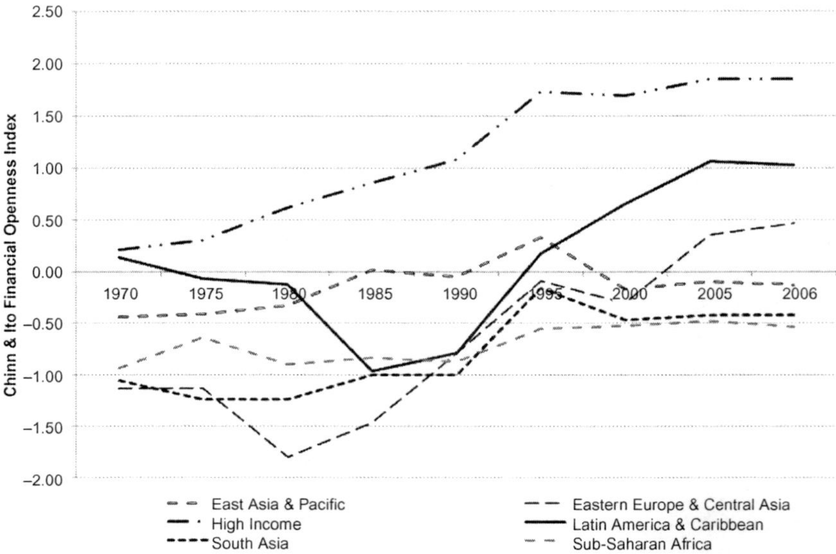

Fig. 1. Financial Openness. *Source*: Chinn and Ito (2008).

Moreover, as Table 1 shows, the majority of Latin American countries display a very high degree of financial openness and an increasing trend. By 2006, only four countries presented limited openness – Argentina, Colombia, Honduras, and Venezuela – with the indicator significantly deteriorating in the cases of Argentina and Venezuela. Although the index is not estimated after 2006, recent policy decisions in Ecuador imply that this country has joined Argentina and Venezuela in the imposition of restrictions on the capital account. By contrast, Colombia has recently lifted a number of capital controls.

A discussion of the factors behind the high level of financial openness in Latin America can be found elsewhere. For the purpose of this chapter, it is sufficient to recall that the impetus toward capital account liberalization started in the 1990s with the implementation of the Brady Plan. This plan allowed for the *securitization* of governments' external liabilities as a way to resolve the debt crisis of the 1980s that had *paralyzed* the region for a decade. Since then, a highly liquid market for international bonds and other securities issued by Latin American countries has developed. This, together with extremely low national savings rates, implies that most

Table 1. Financial Openness Index in Latin America, 1970–2006.

Country	1970	1980	1990	2000	2006
Argentina	0.72	–0.09	–1.13	1.73	–0.76
Bolivia	1.27	1.27	0.60	1.50	1.50
Brazil	–1.80	–1.80	–1.80	–1.13	–1.27
Chile	–1.80	–0.09	–1.80	–1.13	2.54
Colombia	–1.80	–1.80	–1.13	–1.13	–0.09
Costa Rica	1.27	–0.49	–1.80	1.27	1.27
Dominic an Republic	–1.13	–1.80	–1.80	–0.44	2.54
Ecuador	0.99	0.60	–0.98	–0.09	2.27
El Salvador	–1.13	–1.13	–1.80	2.54	2.54
Guatemala	–1.13	–0.05	–0.22	1.27	2.54
Honduras	2.54	0.99	–1.80	–0.09	–0.09
Mexico	2.54	2.54	–0.76	1.19	1.19
Nicaragua	2.54	–1.26	–1.13	2.54	2.54
Panama	2.54	2.54	2.54	2.54	2.54
Paraguay	–1.13	–0.76	–1.13	1.50	1.50
Peru	–0.71	0.06	–1.80	2.54	2.54
Uruguay	–0.59	0.72	1.27	2.54	2.54
Venezuela	0.60	1.87	–0.09	2.54	–0.71

Source: Chinn and Ito (2008).

countries in the region depend on foreign capital to meet their financing needs and are subject to the volatility of capital flows.

While increased access to international capital markets has certainly supported growth prospects in the region, it has also brought about important risks, especially as demonstrated by the current international financial crisis. However, in spite of the current uncertainties in international capital markets, there are no indications that Latin America as a whole will cease to be the most financially open developing region in the foreseeable future. Instead, most countries have placed the achievement (or maintenance) of investment grade among their top priorities and, to this end, have made significant progress in avoiding deviations from macroeconomic stability.[8]

De Facto Financial Integration

A well-known measure of *actual* financial integration is that developed by Lane and Milesi-Ferretti, hereafter LM-F (2007), who assembled a dataset on foreign assets and liabilities of 145 countries over the period 1970–2004 and also produced an updated and extended version using the same methodology covering the period 1970–2007. Since this measure of financial integration cannot fully capture the participation of foreign financial institutions (beyond foreign direct investment and other forms of external financing), a separate subsection presents data on the participation of foreign banks in the region.

The Value of Cross-Border Holdings in Latin America

Following LM-F, a measurement of de facto financial integration is defined as the sum of the stocks of (the absolute value of) external assets plus external liabilities as a percentage of GDP. Data for the period 1970–2007 are directly taken from LM-F (2007 and updates). Fig. 2 shows the evolution of this indicator for Latin America.[9]

Consistent with global developments, the trend in accumulation of international assets and liabilities has been significantly positive in Latin America throughout the time period under analysis – except for the decline in the latter part of the 1980s, mainly as a consequence of the debt crisis that stormed the region at that time. LM-F data also show that, although

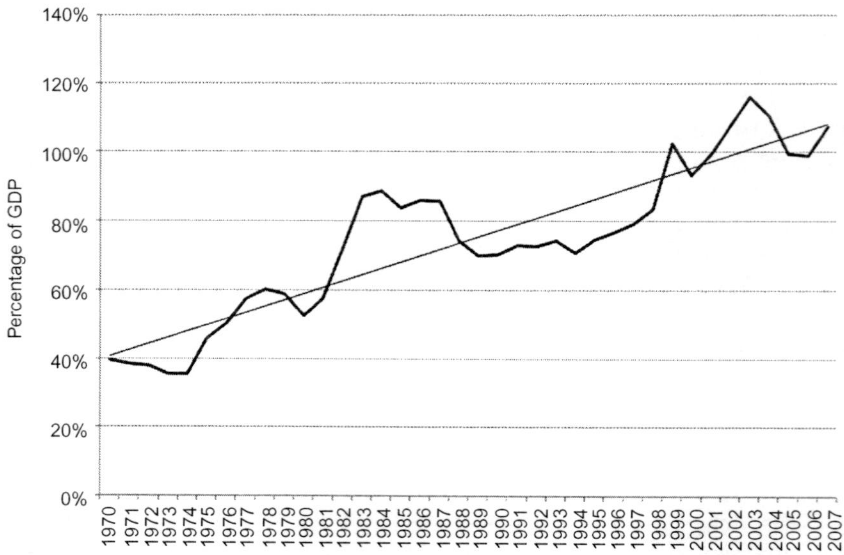

Fig. 2. Sum of Latin American External Assets and Liabilities 1970–2007. (as a Percentage of Regional GDP) *Source*: Lane and Milesi Ferretti (2009).

lagging significantly behind industrial countries in terms of financial integration, Latin America is de facto one of the most financially integrated regions in the developing world.

But increased financial integration has not only meant increased values of cross-border financial assets and liabilities. It has also implied important changes in some of the characteristics of these stocks. For example, information from the Bank for International Settlements (BIS) allows us to illustrate two features of international bank lending to Latin America that have been changing dramatically since the 1990s. The first deals with the composition of international bank claims between the public and private sectors. As shown in Fig. 3, in the early 1990s, when the process of financial integration was at its early stage, a large proportion (about 50%) of lending from BIS reporting banks to the region was directed to the public sector. In sharp contrast, by 2007, more than 90% of international bank lending was directed to the private sector. This development is consistent with the market-led growth model adopted by most countries in the region in the past decade.

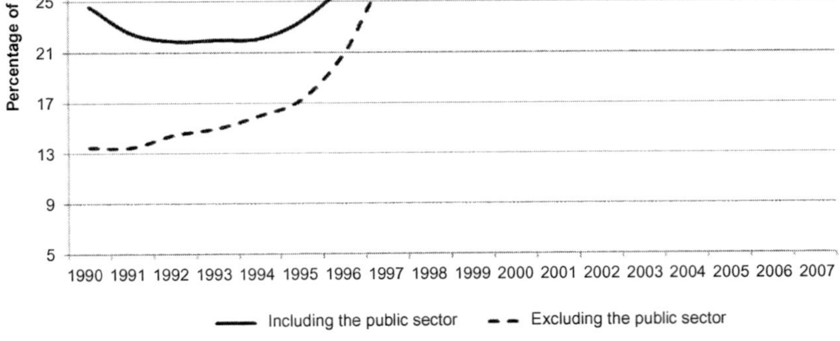

Fig. 3. Loans from International Banks to latin America 1990–2007. *Source*: BIS (Reporting bank claims vis a vis banks, non banks, the public sector, and local currency) and Lane and Milesi Ferretti.

The second feature is the maturity of international loans to the region. In the mid-1990s, more than 50% of international claims to Latin America had a maturity of one year or less. In some countries, such as El Salvador and Guatemala, this value reached over 80%. Since then, the average maturity of these loans has increased consistently and, by 2008, short-term international bank claims as a percentage of total international bank claims had declined to 40% (see Fig. 4).

In the context of a favorable external environment in the 2003–2007 period, increased financial integration of Latin America and improved regulatory and supervisory domestic frameworks improved the availability of financing on better terms and conditions than in the previous two decades.

The Participation of Foreign Banks in Local Financial Systems

An important component of the process of financial integration in Latin America that is not captured by data on cross-border transactions is the participation of foreign banks in local financial systems. Two major factors, depending on the country, increased participation of foreign banks beginning in the mid-1990s. First, consistent with capital account liberalizations,

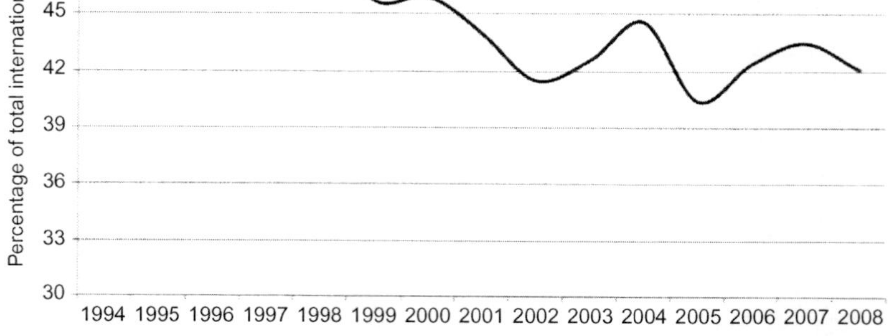

Fig. 4. International Bank Claims up to and including One Year to Latin American Countries 1983–2008. *Source*: BIS.

many countries in the region liberalized their domestic financial systems, which significantly reduced government interference in commercial banking. Together with privatization of public banks, this liberalization created incentives for foreign investment in local banking systems. Second, the need to recapitalize banks in the context of the severe banking crises experienced by the region in the 1990s required efforts to attract foreign capital into local banking systems. Mexico is an example of this development.

Measured by the percentage of total assets in the local banking system, the participation of foreign banks varied widely across Latin American countries by 2007. As shown in Table 2, El Salvador and Mexico stand out (by a large margin) as the countries with the highest participation of foreign banks in the region (with over 85% of total assets of the banking system). In contrast, foreign bank participation is very low in Ecuador and Venezuela. Moreover, while in most countries foreign bank participation has increased or remained stable, in some cases, the participation of foreign banks has significantly declined. Argentina is a clear example. As a result of the inadequacies in the resolution of the banking crisis in 2001, parent companies of several international banks reduced their presence in that country.

Table 2. Participation of Foreign Banks (as a Percentage of Total Assets).

Country	2000	2007
Argentina	37.4%	19.2%
Bolivia	55.1%	37.7%
Brazil	19.5%	16.8%
Chile	43.6%	40.3%
Colombia	28.5%	21.8%
Costa Rica	18.0%	20.5%
Dominican Republic	13.3%	9.9%
Ecuador	6.8%	4.5%
El Salvador	56.8%	93.1%
Guatemala	8.1%	9.9%
Honduras	36.6%	36.1%
Mexico	59.3%	85.4%
Nicaragua	16.1%	20.5%
Paraguay	77.1%	58.9%
Peru	55.1%	50.6%
Uruguay	30.4%	43.7%
Venezuela	4.3%	1.8%

Source: Bankscope.

PROPAGATION OF INTERNATIONAL FINANCIAL SHOCKS AND FOREIGN BANKS: AN EMPIRICAL INVESTIGATION

The literature review presented in the second section discussed the response of foreign bank operations in Latin America to shocks generated in local economies and to changes in economic activity in the home country of foreign banks. Here, we empirically assess the response of foreign banks to external financial shocks, reflecting a change in risk aversion – a key issue in the context of the current international financial crisis.

We explore the effect of external financial shocks on domestic financial variables from two complementary angles. First, we use cross-country data for a set of Latin American countries to assess the impact of changes in external financial conditions reflecting investors' perceptions of risk on the real growth rate of credit and on real interest rates. As part of this investigation, we explore the role played by financial integration in propagating external financial fluctuations to domestic variables. Second, we use a database of detailed bank-level balance sheets to analyze the response of real credit growth and real interest rates of specific banks to external financial fluctuations. We then explore whether the response varies according to the ownership structure of the bank; namely whether the bank is domestic or foreign owned.

Cross-Country Methodology and Results

We use a quarterly dataset for 18 Latin American and Caribbean[10] countries spanning the period 1996–2008, including data from the IMF's International Financial Statistics (IFS), Bloomberg and data collected from country-specific statistical agencies to estimate the impact of changes in international financial conditions on the real growth rate of credit and real interest rates in Latin American countries.

We measure international financial conditions using two indicators of investors' perceptions of risk: the spread of high-yield bonds and the VIX index (both in logs).[11] Our main objectives are to assess the correlation between the *riskiness* of international financial conditions and domestic financial variables and to analyze whether this relationship depends on the degree of integration with international financial markets.

We estimate the following regression:

$$X_{it} = \alpha_1 \Delta\log(IP_{it-1}) + \alpha_2 \Delta\log(IP_{it-1}) \times \mathrm{Int}_{it-1} + \beta_1 Y_t + \beta_2 Y_t \times \mathrm{Int}_{it-1} + \gamma \mathrm{Int}_{it-1} + \mu_i + d + \varepsilon_{it} \tag{1}$$

where i denotes a country and t a time period, and X is either the real growth rate of credit or the real interest rate. Real credit growth is calculated as the difference in the logarithm of real credit, which is nominal credit supplied by the domestic banking system to the private sector deflated by the Consumer Price Index (CPI). The real interest rate is calculated using the one-period ahead observed inflation rate as a measure of inflation expectations.[12] *IP* is the country's industrial production. *Int* is a measure of financial integration, which corresponds to the de facto measure of financial integration discussed in the third section, namely the measure developed by LM-F (2007). Y is a variable measuring international financial conditions (in some specifications we use the log of the high-yield spread, in others the log of the VIX index), μ_i are country fixed effects, d are seasonal dummies and ε is a residual.[13]

In Eq. (1) we allow the dependent variable of interest to relate to changes in the lagged level of economic activity measured by the industrial production index, to international financial conditions (U.S. high-yield spread or VIX), to lagged financial integration and to relevant interactions.

We are aware that endogeneity is a relevant issue in this regression in several dimensions. Specifically, we acknowledge that both industrial production and financial integration can be endogenous to developments in credit markets, and that is the reason for using lags of industrial production and financial integration as independent variables to estimate OLS regressions.[14] We also deal with the endogeneity problem by carrying out IV estimations using Chinn and Ito's de jure integration measure as an instrument for the de facto integration proxy.

Table 3 reports the results of estimating Eq. (1) for both dependent variables using the two alternative measures of international financial market volatility and alternative estimation techniques (OLS and IV). Columns 1 and 3 report OLS results when the real growth rate of credit is used as the dependent variable, and columns 5 and 7 report the results when using the real interest rate. Columns 2, 4, 6, and 8 report similar results using panel IV methods. In all specifications we allow for the relationship between external and domestic variables to depend on the degree of financial integration.

Table 3. Cross-Country Results.

Dependent Variable	1	2	3	4	5	6	7	8
	Δlog (Real Credit)$_{it}$				Real Interest Rate$_{it}$			
Δlog (IP$_{it-1}$)	0.0567***	0.0364*	0.0611***	0.0319	−0.0365	−0.0332	−0.0462*	−0.0417
	[0.017]	[0.020]	[0.017]	[0.019]	[0.028]	[0.030]	[0.025]	[0.028]
Δlog (IP$_{it-1}$) × Integration$_{it-1}$	0.0157	−0.0307	0.0245*	−0.0291	−0.0230	−0.00515	−0.0302*	−0.0227
	[0.012]	[0.020]	[0.012]	[0.020]	[0.018]	[0.028]	[0.017]	[0.026]
log (High Yield Spread$_t$)	−0.00131	0.0114			−0.0252**	−0.0265*		
	[0.007]	[0.009]			[0.012]	[0.014]		
log (High Yield Spread$_t$) × Integration$_{it-1}$	−0.0203***	−0.0314***			0.0411****	0.0431***		
	[0.005]	[0.006]			[0.008]	[0.010]		
log(VIX$_t$)			0.00215	0.0118			−0.00918	−0.0489***
			[0.008]	[0.010]			[0.011]	[0.015]
log(VIX$_t$) × Integration$_{it-1}$			−0.0218***	−0.0314***			0.0424***	0.0781***
			[0.005]	[0.008]			[0.008]	[0.012]
Integration$_{it-1}$	0.147***	0.217***	0.0831***	0.108***	−0.255**	−0.258**	−0.133***	−0.235***
	[0.034]	[0.042]	[0.018]	[0.026]	[0.055]	[0.068]	[0.026]	[0.038]
Observations	724	711	812	799	809	793	893	880
Over all R^2	0.129	0.126	0.110	0.103	0.0553	0.0711	0.0562	0.0598
Between R^2	0.0116	0.00449	0.00820	0.00243	0.0254	0.124	0.0457	0.00138
Within R^2	0.166	0.149	0.136	0.112	0.0697	0.0705	0.0849	0.0635
Number of countries	18	18	18	18	18	18	18	18
Country fixed effects	Yes	Yes	Yes	Yes	Yes	Yes	Yes	Yes
Seasonal dummies	Yes	Yes	Yes	Yes	Yes	Yes	Yes	Yes
Estimation method	OLS	IV	OLS	IV	OLS	IV	OLS	IV
Sample	1997.I–2008.IV		1996.I–2008.IV		1997.I–2008.IV		1996.I–2008.IV	

*** $p<0.01$, ** $p<0.05$, * $p<0.1$; Standard errors in brackets. IV regressions use lags of a measure of de jure integration (China and Ito) and of the de facto integration measure (Lane and Milesi Ferretti) as instruments.

The results reported in columns 1–4 suggest that there is a strong correlation between real credit growth and the variables measuring international financial conditions, and that the correlation is stronger the higher the degree of financial integration. In all regressions, the coefficients of the log of the high-yield spread and the log of the VIX index interacted with the financial integration proxy have a negative sign and are statistically significant. This evidence suggests that financial integration amplifies the impact of changes in external financial risk on domestic financial markets.

A noteworthy economic implication can be derived from the estimated coefficients. A one standard deviation increase in the log of the high-yield spread (0.41) in our sample is associated with a 1.0% decline in real credit for a country with average financial integration.[15] This is a sizeable value given that the average real growth rate of credit in the sample is close to 1%. Similarly a one standard deviation increase in the log of the VIX index (0.33) is associated with a 0.8% decline in real credit.[16]

Panels (a) and (b) of Fig. 5 plot the marginal impact of increasing the high-yield spread and the VIX index, respectively, on the real growth rate of credit. Note that, according to the regressions, this impact depends on the level of integration. Specifically, the marginal impact of an increase in these measures is given by:

$$\frac{\partial X_{it}}{\partial Y_t} = \beta_1 + \beta_2 \mathrm{Int}_{it-1} \tag{2}$$

where, as above, X represents either real credit growth or the real interest rate, and Y is either the log of the high-yield spread or the log of the value of the VIX index. Panels (a) and (b) of Fig. 5 depict Eq. (2) for the range that the integration measure takes in our sample, with appropriate confidence intervals.[17] The figure clearly shows that there is a range where financial integration is so low that real credit growth is not affected by external financial shocks. As financial integration rises, the impact of external shocks becomes negative and highly significant.[18]

Turning to the behavior of the real interest rate, columns 5–8 of Table 3 show that the coefficients of the interactions between the high-yield spread and the VIX index with the integration measure are positive and significant, indicating that the correlation between external and domestic financial variables increases with the degree of integration.

Once again, the estimated coefficients can be used to derive additional important implications. A one standard deviation increase in the log of the high-yield spread or in the log of the VIX index is associated with

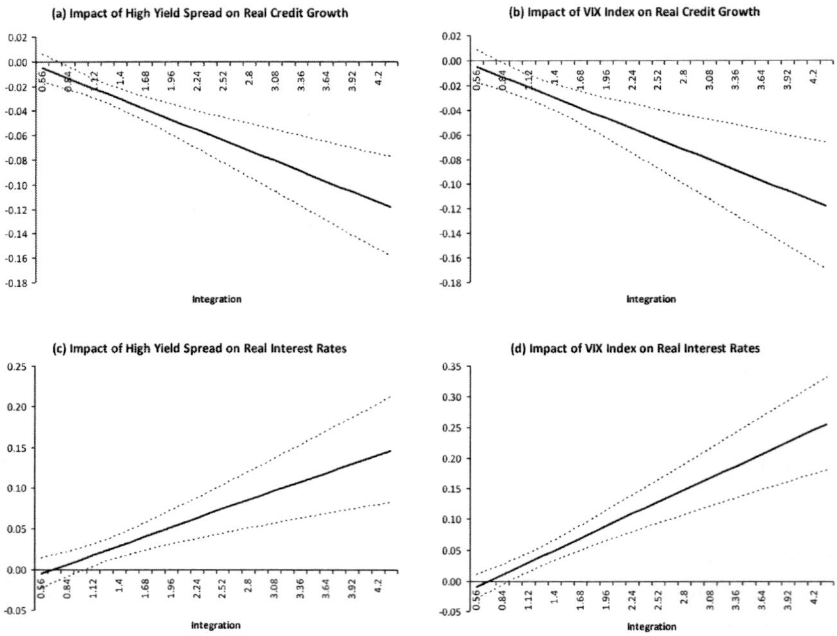

Fig. 5. Marginal Effects of Foreign Financial Shocks on Real Credit Growth and Real Interest Rates.

1.0 and 1.2 percentage point increases in the real interest rate, respectively, for a country with average financial integration.[19] These are also meaningful figures considering the average real interest rate for the sample period was 1.8%.

Panels (c) and (d) in Fig. 5 depict the estimated marginal impact of an increase in the high-yield spread and the VIX index, respectively, on the real interest rate. We find a positive and significant impact at most levels of integration, and as with credit, we also find that at very low levels of integration the impact is not statistically significant.

A central conclusion that is worth noting from Table 3 is that for a wide range of international financial shocks there is a positive association between financial integration and real credit growth *even when factoring in the negative effect on credit growth brought about by foreign financial shocks.* In other words, the sum of the coefficient estimated for integration and the coefficient estimated for the interaction between the foreign shock and integration is positive for most levels of the foreign shock. Fig. 6 depicts

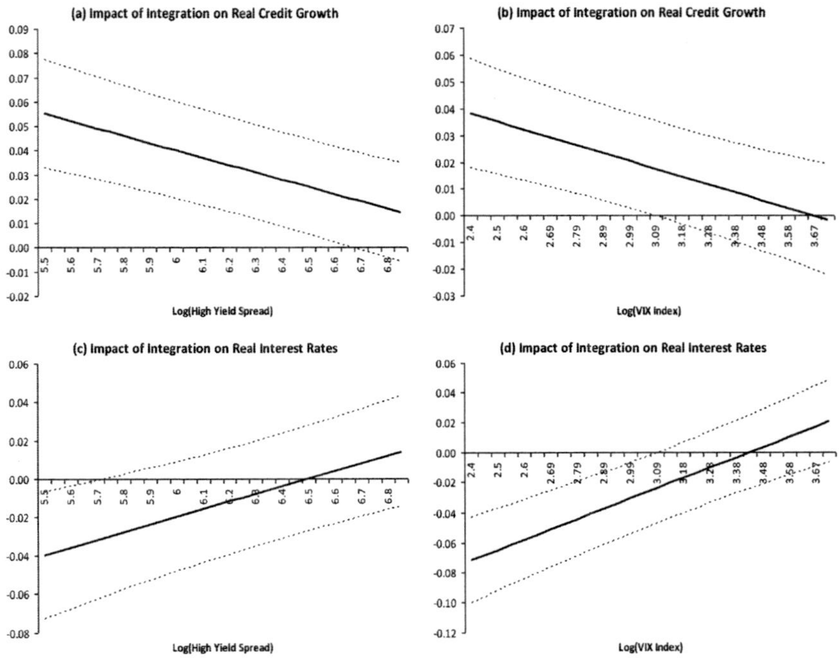

Fig. 6. Marginal Effects of Financial Integrationon Real Credit Growth and Real Interest Rates.

estimates similar to those in Fig. 5 but focuses on the marginal impact of financial integration on real credit growth and the real interest rate. Namely it plots:

$$\frac{\partial X_{it}}{\partial \mathrm{Int}_{i,t-1}} = \gamma + \beta_2 Y_t + \alpha_2 \Delta \log(IP_{it-1}) \tag{3}$$

Panels (a) and (b) in Fig. 6 report results for real credit growth and (c) and (d) for the real interest rate.[20] The panels show that for most levels of the high-yield spread and of the VIX index, integration has a positive and significant effect on real credit growth. The effect diminishes as external risks increase and becomes nonsignificant for high levels of risk. In other words, in tranquil times, the positive effects of financial integration dominate, while in times of crisis the negative effects of financial integration net out the benefits. It is worthwhile noting that in times of crisis the overall impact of financial integration is not statistically significant. When measuring risk with the high-yield spread, the positive and significant impact of financial integration on credit growth prevails, except for a few tail observations. When measuring it with the VIX index, the positive and significant effect prevails up to a value of 3.09 of the log of the VIX index that in our sample corresponds to approximately the 65th percentile.

Similarly, columns 5–8 of Table 3 suggest that greater integration with international financial markets is associated with, on average, lower interest rates for most levels of financial risk. Panels (c) and (d) of Fig. 6 support these findings; however, the results are not as clear cut as with the evidence on credit growth. When risk is measured using the high-yield spread, we find that, through most of the range, the impact of financial integration is not statistically significant. When measuring risk with the VIX index, we find that for most of the distribution, and up to the 65th percentile of the distribution within our sample, the impact of integration on interest rates is negative and significant.

Thus, while it is true that deeper financial integration may be a channel through which negative external financial shocks amplify domestic credit contractions and increases in interest rates, it is also true that financial integration may deepen credit markets and reduce the cost of financing. Moreover, Fig. 6 demonstrates that, under the vast majority of states of nature, financial integration has a positive effect on deepening credit markets. It is only in cases of very high financial risk that greater financial integration can be related to a decline in real credit growth.

Bank-Level Methodology and Results

This subsection complements the results above by using bank-level data to explore additional conduits through which financial integration may help to propagate international financial shocks in Latin American and Caribbean economies. As noted above, an important mechanism of increased financial integration in Latin America has been through the presence of foreign banks.

To assess whether foreign banks have played a role in exacerbating international financial market fluctuations, we use a yearly bank-level dataset that covers 476 banks in 17 Latin American and Caribbean countries between 1996 and 2007.[21] For that purpose, we estimate regressions of the following type:

$$X_{bit} = \alpha X_{bit-1} + \gamma C_{bit-1} + \delta_1 \Delta\log(IP_{it-1}) + \delta_2 \Delta\log(IP_{it-1}) \times \text{Foreign}_{bi} + \beta_1 Y_t + \beta_2 Y_t \times \text{Foreign}_{bi} + \mu_b + \varepsilon_{bit} \quad (4)$$

where b denotes a specific bank, i denotes a country and t a time period. X is either the real growth rate of credit supplied by bank b in country i at time t (we measure the change in the logarithm of the stock of real credit of each bank, computed as the bank's nominal credit stock divided by the country's CPI) or the real interest rate (which is obtained by subtracting the observed inflation rate in period $t+1$ from an implicit interest rate – estimated from individual banks' income statements and balance sheets). C is a set of bank-specific controls that include measures of liquidity and capitalization.[22] *IP* is the country's industrial production, Foreign is a dummy indicating if the bank is foreign owned, μ_b are bank fixed effects, ε is a residual and Y is the variable measuring international financial conditions. As above, we measure international financial conditions using the logs of the high-yield spread and the VIX index. In addition, we use the log of the global EMBI spread.[23] We did not use the global EMBI spread in the cross-country regressions because it was likely to be an endogenous variable given the inclusion of large emerging market countries in the sample. Since we are now using bank-level data, endogeneity of the global EMBI spread is not a relevant issue.

Given that real credit growth and real interest rates are highly persistent at the bank level,[24] we allow for a lagged dependent variable in our specification. The inclusion of a lagged dependent variable in the context of a panel with fixed effects is well known to generate biased and inconsistent estimates. This is the case because, by construction, the lagged dependent variable will be correlated with the error term. To deal with these issues, and following Arellano and Bover (1995) and Blundell and Bond (1998), we use the system GMM estimator.[25]

Table 4 reports results of the bank-level regressions using the real growth rate of credit as the dependent variable.[26] Columns 1, 3, and 5 report regression results without allowing for differential effects from foreign banks. These results suggest that there is a significant negative association between external financial variables and real credit growth. These relationships are important and sizable from an economic perspective. A one standard deviation increase in the logs of the high-yield spread, the

Table 4. Bank-Level Results: Real Credit Growth.

Dependent Variable: Δlog (Real Credit)	1	2	3	4	5	6
Δlog (Real Credit) [*t*−1]	0.175***	0.168***	0.163***	0.156***	0.166***	0.159***
	[0.039]	[0.040]	[0.039]	[0.039]	[0.040]	[0.040]
Log(Liquid Assests/Total Assets) [*t*−1]	0.0730***	0.0734***	0.0618***	0.0623***	0.0739***	0.0754***
	[0.019]	[0.020]	[0.019]	[0.019]	[0.019]	[0.019]
Log(Capital/Assets) [*t*−1]	0.0405	0.0447	0.013	0.0145	0.0.346	0.0355
	[0.028]	[0.028]	[0.032]	[0.033]	[0.035]	[0.035]
Δlog(*IP*) [*t*−1]	0.255***	0.252***	0.246***	0.245***	0.250***	0.250***
	[0.037]	[0.033]	[0.036]	[0.032]	[0.037]	[0.032]
Δlog(*IP*) [*t*−1] × Foreign		0.0143		−0.000611		0.00259
		[0.106]		[0.107]		[0.105]
Log(High Yield Spreads)	−0.0406***	−0.0393***				
	[0.009]	[0.009]				
Log(High Yield Spreads) × Foreign		−0.00759**				
		[0.003]				
Log(VIX)			−0.0512***	−0.0472***		
			[0.015]	[0.015]		
Log(VIX) × Foreign				−0.0143**		
				[0.006]		
Log(EMBI)					−0.0389***	−0.0371***
					[0.010]	[0.010]
log(EMBI) × Foreign						−0.00702**
						[0.003]

Observations	2773	2773	2773	2773	2773	2773
Number of banks	520	520	520	520	520	520
Number of countries	17	17	17	17	17	17
Bank fixed effects	Yes	Yes	Yes	Yes	Yes	Yes
p-Value AR1	0.000	0.000	0.000	0.000	0.000	0.000
p-Value AR2	0.740	0.712	0.988	0.987	0.840	0.866
p-Value Hansen Stat	0.404	0.417	0.388	0.405	0.336	0.327
p-Value *F*-test 1		0.008		0.016		0.012
p-Value *F*-test 2		0.000		0.000		0.000
Sample			Yearly: 1996–2008			

*** $p<0.01$, ** $p<0.05$, Clustered standard errors in brackets. *F*-test 1 is a test under the null hypothesis that the sum of the coefficient of *IP* growth and the coefficient of *IP* growth interacted with the foreign bank dummy is zero. *F*-test 2 is a test under the null hypothesis that the sum of the coefficient of the external variable (high yield spread, VIX, or EMBI) and the coefficient of it interacted with the foreign bank dummy is zero. Regressions are estimated using the bank's relative size in each country and time period as a weight.

VIX index and the EMBI spread leads to contractions of 2.0%, 1.9%, and 2.1% in real credit, respectively.[27] These numbers are considerable compared to the real growth rate of credit during the sample period, which was 9.3%.

When we allow for a differential effect of foreign banks in columns 2, 4, and 6, we find that domestic banks play a role in propagating the impact of the external financial shock, but that the impact of the shock is amplified by foreign banks. In all three regressions, the coefficient of the external financial variable is negative and significant, which should be interpreted as evidence that real credit growth by domestic banks adjusts to foreign financial shocks. Moreover, the coefficient of the interaction between each of the external financial variables and the foreign bank dummy is also significant and negative. These results provide statistical evidence that the adjustment made by foreign banks to their real credit flow is stronger than that of domestic banks. The additional adjustment of foreign banks, according to our estimates, is economically important. Depending on the specification considered, we find that foreign banks adjust their real credit growth between 20% and 30% more than the adjustment made by domestic banks.

It is worth noting that the estimated effects are symmetrical, meaning when the global economy goes through favorable financial conditions (high-yield spreads, the VIX index and the EMBI spread are low), the expansion of real credit by foreign banks is larger than that of domestic banks. When negative financial shocks hit the global economy, the contraction shown by foreign banks is stronger.

As for the rest of the controls, we find that real credit growth is persistent and that lending activity is positively and significantly linked to bank liquidity. We find a positive association between real credit growth and capitalization, but this relationship is not estimated precisely. We also find that real credit growth at the bank level is highly pro-cyclical with respect to industrial production. The coefficient associated with growth in industrial production is consistently significant across alternative specifications. However, we do not find evidence of differential behavior between foreign banks and domestic banks regarding pro-cyclicality.

In Table 5 we report similar results using an implicit real interest rate on deposits as the dependent variable. The implicit interest rate is computed as the ratio of interest payments during a given year with respect to the stock of deposits at the beginning of the year. As explained above, the real rate of interest is obtained by subtracting the observed rate of inflation in the following year from the nominal interest rate. Results are similar to and consistent with those reported in Table 4. An increase in any of the

Table 5. Bank-Level Results: Real Interest Rate.

Dependent Variable: Real Interest Rate	1	2	3	4	5	6
Real interest rate [$t-1$]	0.431***	0.429***	0.434***	0.432***	0.435***	0.433***
	[0.054]	[0.056]	[0.050]	[0.052]	[0.051]	[0.052]
Log(Liquid Assests/Total Assets) [$t-1$]	−0.33	−0.56	−2.814***	−2.948***	−2.928***	−3.073***
	[0.604]	[0.623]	[0.946]	[0.971]	[0.844]	[0.870]
Log(Capital/Assets) [$t-1$]	1.579	1.471	0.424	0.594	0.645	0.77
	[2.042]	[1.940]	[1.431]	[1.425]	[1.920]	[1.911]
$\Delta\log(IP)$ [$t-1$]	−5.083**	−0.956	−4.263*	0.0407	−4.754*	−0.389
	[2.220]	[1.314]	[2.410]	[1.337]	[2.436]	[1.372]
$\Delta\log(IP)$ [$t-1$] × Foreign		−16.02		−16.40*		−16.65*
		[9.728]		[9.674]		[9.894]
Log(High Yield Spreads)	2.873***	2.649***				
	[0.564]	[0.570]				
Log(High Yield Spreads) × Foreign		0.280***				
		[0.134]				
Log(VIX)			2.969***	2.747***		
			[0.655]	[0.624]		
Log(VIX) × Foreign				0.631**		
				[0.296]		
Log(EMBI)					1.383***	1.308***
					[0.470]	[0.451]
Log(EMBI) × Foreign						0.281*
						[0.147]
Observations	2026	2026	2026	2026	2026	2026
Number of banks	439	439	439	439	439	439
Number of countries	17	17	17	17	17	17
Bank fixed effects	Yes	Yes	Yes	Yes	Yes	Yes

Table 5. (*Continued*)

Dependent Variable: Real Interest Rate	1	2	3	4	5	6
p-Value AR1	0.005	0.005	0.002	0.002	0.002	0.002
p-Value AR2	0.522	0.454	0.959	0.905	0.934	0.989
p-Value Hansen Stat	0.519	0.471	0.685	0.686	0.652	0.633
p-Value *F*-test 1		0.077		0.091		0.084
p-Value *F*-test 2		0.000		0.000		0.001
Sample				Yearly: 1996–2008		

*** $p<0.01$, ** $p<0.05$, * $p<0.1$. Clustered standard errors in brackets. *F*-test 1 is a test under the null hypothesis that the sum of the coefficient of *IP* growth and the coefficient of *IP* growth interacted with the foreign bank dummy is zero. *F*-test 2 is a test under the null hypothesis that the sum of the coefficient of the external variable (high yield spread, VIX, or EMBI) and the coefficient of it interacted with the foreign bank dummy is zero. Regressions are estimated using the bank's relative size in each country and time period as a weight.

three measures of international financial conditions is accompanied by an increase in domestic real interest rates. Also, increases in the interest rates of foreign banks are larger than those of domestic banks.

For the average bank (without distinguishing between domestic and foreign banks), a one standard deviation increase in the log of the high-yield spread is accompanied by an increase of 122 basis points in the real interest rate. The corresponding increases in the real interest rate when the log of the VIX index or the log of the EMBI spread rises by one standard deviation are 99 and 77 basis points, respectively.

Results reported in columns 2, 4, and 6 indicate that foreign banks react more than domestic ones to external financial shocks. In the case of the high-yield and EMBI spreads, the estimated coefficients reveal that the increase in real interest rates by foreign banks is between 10% and 20% larger than that of domestic banks. Independent of the magnitude, the qualitative importance of these results ought to be highlighted: foreign banks tend to amplify external financial shocks.

Regarding the rest of the controls, the results of the regressions show that, similar to the behavior of real credit growth, real interest rates are highly persistent. With respect to changes in growth in industrial production, the results indicate an inverse relationship with real interest rates and there is evidence of differential behavior between domestic and foreign banks. In particular, we find that foreign banks reduce real interest rates more than domestic banks in good times and increase real interest rates more in bad times. With respect to bank-specific controls, while it is notable that the coefficients are estimated imprecisely, we find some evidence indicating a negative correlation between interest rates and liquidity.

An important question that comes out of the analysis above is whether all foreign banks behave equally. There is ample discussion on how different types of foreign banks follow different models when locating abroad. In particular in Latin America, there is a wide perception that the model followed by Spanish banks is different, and that their home office has given them guidelines to behave as a domestic bank. To test whether there are differences in the way foreign banks from different origins behave, we reestimate Eq. (4) separating foreign banks into three categories: banks of U.S. origin, banks of Spanish origin and other foreign banks. The last category includes mostly European banks from countries other than Spain, some Canadian banks, and some additional banks from Australia, Israel, Japan, Korea, and Taiwan. Table 6 reports results of these estimations, once again

Table 6. Bank-Level Results: By Bank Origin.

Dependent Variable	1	2	3	4	5	6
	Δlog (Real Credit)			Real interest rate		
Δlog (Real Credit)	0.173***	0.164***	0.166***			
	[0.034]	[0.033]	[0.033]			
Real interest rate [$t-1$]				0.432***	0.434***	0.435***
				[0.055]	[0.052]	[0.052]
Log(Liquid Assets/Total Assets) [$t-1$]	0.0707***	0.0566***	0.0713***	−1.034*	−3.168***	−3.378***
	[0.017]	[0.016]	[0.016]	[0.609]	[0.980]	[0.878]
Log(Capital/Assets) [$t-1$]	0.0482*	0.0311	0.0539*	0.63	0.467	0.506
	[0.025]	[0.027]	[0.029]	[1.769]	[1.335]	[1.797]
Δlog(*IP*) [$t-1$]	0.262***	0.255***	0.262***	−1.486	−0.367	−0.802
	[0.032]	[0.032]	[0.032]	[1.445]	[1.423]	[1.462]
Δlog(*IP*) [$t-1$] × Foreign USA	−0.0212	−0.0545	−0.0627	−2.46	−2.813	−3.088
	[0.231]	[0.224]	[0.230]	[7.194]	[6.947]	[6.985]
Δlog(*IP*) [$t-1$] × Foreign Spain	0.00274	−0.00257	−0.0108	−9.818	−9.158	−9.095
	[0.132]	[0.136]	[0.135]	[10.004]	[9.566]	[9.758]
Δlog(*IP*) [$t-1$] × Foreign Other	0.131	0.139	0.149	−43.63**	−43.35**	−45.42**
	[0.116]	[0.109]	[0.108]	[19.631]	[19.047]	[18.979]
Log(High Yield Spreads)	−0.0391***			2.332***		
	[0.008]			[0.540]		
Log(High Yield Spreads) × Foreign USA	−0.0152***			0.103		
	[0.005]			[0.166]		
Log(High Yield Spreads) × Foreign Spain	0.000271			0.202		
	[0.004]			[0.177]		
Log(High Yield Spreads) × Foreign Other	−0.00832***			0.487***		
	[0.003]			[0.155]		

Log(VIX)		−0.0539***			3.102***	
		[0.013]			[0.668]	
Log(VIX) × Foreign USA		−0.0275***			0.352	
		[0.009]			[0.405]	
Log(VIX) × Foreign Spain		0.000924			0.218	
		[0.008]			[0.392]	
Log(VIX) * Foreign Other		−0.0168***			1.181***	
		[0.006]			[0.347]	
Log(EMBI)			−0.0419***			1.565***
			[0.009]			[0.443]
Log(EMBI) × Foreign USA			−0.0142***			0.186
			[0.005]			[0.185]
Log(EMBI) × Foreign Spain			0.00135			0.0555
			[0.004]			[0.203]
Log(EMBI) × Foreign Other			−0.00824***			0.569***
			[0.003]			[0.166]
Observations	2773	2773	2773	2018	2018	2018
Number of banks	521	521	521	439	439	439
Number of countries	17	17	17	17	17	17
p-Value AR1	0.000	0.000	0.000	0.003	0.002	0.001
p-Value AR2	0.613	0.924	0.925	0.956	0.594	0.513
p-Value Hansen Stat	0.470	0.415	0.392	0.453	0.643	0.636
Sample	Yearly: 1996–2008					

$^{***}p < 0.01$, $^{**}p < 0.05$, $^{*}p < 0.1$. Clustered standard errors in brackets. Regressions are estimated using the bank's relative size in each country and time period as a weight.

using the real growth rate of credit (columns 1–3) and the real interest rate (columns 4–6) as dependent variables.

The estimated coefficients for the relevant interactions reveal that foreign banks from different origins follow different behaviors. Most notably, we find no significant differences between the behavior of Spanish banks and domestic banks regarding the behavior of either real credit or real interest rates.[28] Our results suggest U.S. banks strongly amplify the effects of external shocks on real credit growth, but we do not find differences in the way they adjust interest rates. Foreign banks of other origins also amplify external financial shocks by contracting credit more than domestic banks, but they also increase real interest rates more than domestic banks. Thus, other foreign banks largely account for the result (reported in Table 5) that foreign banks increase interest rates more than domestic banks in the presence of an adverse financial shock. Note that these results are consistent across alternative measures of external financial conditions used throughout the analysis.

CONCLUDING REMARKS

Financial integration in Latin America and the Caribbean, as measured by alternative methodologies, is high. Both from a de jure and a de facto point of view, the region appears to be notoriously more integrated with international financial markets than other regions of the developing world. The propagation of the recent crisis from developed economies to emerging economies, including Latin America, through financial channels has raised concerns about the appropriateness of maintaining a highly open capital account. This chapter contributes to the literature by providing evidence that, in most states of nature, financial integration has a positive effect by deepening local financial markets. It is only in cases of very high international financial risk that greater financial integration can be related to a decline in real credit growth. Indeed, the empirical analysis demonstrates that while financial integration amplifies the impact of international financial shocks on aggregate real credit and real interest rate fluctuations, the net impact of integration on deepening credit markets prevails in most occasions. Evidence that financial integration reduces interest rates in most states of nature is not as conclusive.

One crucial dimension of financial integration that has been developing rapidly in Latin America in the past decade is greater participation of foreign-owned banks. The impact of foreign bank penetration in developing countries has been studied widely, and in general points to favorable conclusions, such as improvements in technology, improved methods for financial and risk management, and greater competition. In this chapter we explored the role of foreign banks in propagating foreign financial shocks to the local financial systems of Latin America. Our main finding is that, in general, foreign banks tend to amplify the impact of foreign financial fluctuations on domestic financial variables. However, the results also show that origin matters, and that Spanish banks tend to react less than other foreign banks to changes in risk conditions in the international capital markets.

From a policy perspective, these findings need to be interpreted with caution. They do not call for banning or reducing foreign bank participation in Latin America, but rather for strategies that avoid excessive transmission of foreign financial shocks into domestic economies while preserving the gains of greater financial depth obtained through financial integration. Policies such as ring-fencing, or the incorporation of agreements with foreign supervisors, ought to be considered to prevent financial weakness in Latin American financial systems when international capital markets are in turmoil.

NOTES

1. Exceptions to this trend include Venezuela and, more recently, Argentina and Ecuador.
2. On similar lines, Galindo, Micco and Ordoñez (2002) show that financial liberalization exerts a positive impact on the growth rate of economic sectors that rely more on external finance.
3. Other work showing positive effects of financial liberalization on growth includes Galindo, Schiantarelli and Weiss (2007), who show that the allocation of investment is more efficient where financial liberalization is greater.
4. This does not mean that processes of high growth accompanied by crises are desirable. Indeed, emerging markets are continuously struggling to integrate financially in ways that do not pose significant danger leading to financial crises.
5. The literature on the desirability and effectiveness of capital controls is quite extensive, especially for Latin America. For a review, see Magud and Reinhart (2007). This chapter does not deal with this issue.
6. In this index, by construction, the value of the series has a mean of zero.
7. Each regional value for every year is simply the average of the value of the index for all countries within the region.
8. Not surprisingly, the countries with weaker macroeconomic indicators – Argentina, Ecuador, and Venezuela – are also the countries with more controls on

cross-border transactions. Also, Argentina and Ecuador defaulted on their external debt obligations in the early 2000s.

9. The sum of (the absolute value of) external assets and liabilities for all Latin American countries is expressed as a share of regional GDP in US dollars.

10. The countries included in the dataset are determined by data availability. The countries in the sample are: Argentina, Bolivia, Brazil, Chile, Colombia, Costa Rica, Ecuador, Guatemala, Honduras, Haiti, Mexico, Nicaragua, Peru, Paraguay, El Salvador, Trinidad and Tobago, Uruguay, and Venezuela. Data was also available for Panama, but this country was not included in the analysis because it is a financial center and our data sources do not allow for a distinction between domestic and international banking activities.

11. The high-yield spread is the difference between the return of U.S. high-yield bonds (noninvestment grade, speculative-grade or junk bonds) and the return of U.S. Treasuries. A higher spread indicates higher risk. The VIX is the ticker symbol for the Chicago Board Options Exchange Volatility Index. This is a commonly used measure of the implied volatility of S&P 500 index options. A high value corresponds to a more volatile market.

12. For simplicity, the real interest rate (r) is computed as $(1+i)/(1+\pi^e)-1$ where i is the nominal interest rate and π^e is the one-period-ahead observed CPI inflation rate (i.e., assuming perfect foresight).

13. Data on credit to the private sector, interest rates and CPI were taken from IFS; high-yield spreads and the VIX index were taken from Bloomberg; and industrial production was taken from domestic sources.

14. An alternative measurement of de facto financial integration is BIS data that includes external claims of international banks on Latin America as well as local claims of foreign banks on the region. This variable, however, suffers from more serious endogeneity problems than the LM-F measure. The reason is that local claims of foreign banks are, to a large extent, a component of total domestic credit.

15. Average financial integration refers to the mean of the measure of financial integration for countries in the sample throughout the sample period.

16. To provide additional context for these estimations, for a country with average financial integration, the rise in the high-yield spreads and in the VIX index observed during the recent financial crisis would predict 2.3% and 1.8% declines in real credit, respectively. This rise in our sample corresponds to the change in the high-yield spreads and the VIX index between the second and fourth quarters of 2008. Such rises account for approximately 1,000 basis points (bps) in the high-yield spread and for 16 points in the VIX index.

17. Note that the relevant standard error for the estimated marginal impact is given by: $\sigma = \sqrt{\text{var}(\beta_1) + \text{var}(\beta_2)^*\text{int}^2_{i,t-1} + 2\text{cov}(\beta_1\beta_2\text{int}_{i,t-1})}$

18. Graphs in this figure are constructed using IV estimates.

19. As above, the fluctuations in the high-yield spreads and the VIX index observed during the recent financial crisis (between the second and fourth quarters of 2008 in our sample) suggest that real interest rates should increase by 200 and 190 basis points, respectively.

20. In order to plot Eq. (3) in the two dimensional graph, we evaluate it in the median value of $\Delta\log(IP)$, that in our sample is equal to zero.

21. The source of bank-level data is BankScope. We use all information available for privately owned banks in Argentina, Bolivia, Brazil, Chile, Colombia, Costa Rica, Ecuador, El Salvador, Guatemala, Honduras, Mexico, Nicaragua, Peru, Paraguay, Trinidad and Tobago, Uruguay, and Venezuela.

22. Our specification and selection of bank-specific controls follows closely that in Arena, Reinhart, and Vázquez (2006). Liquidity is computed as the share of liquid assets in total assets. Liquid assets include cash and reserves, government bonds and other marketable securities. Capitalization is defined as the ratio of equity capital to total assets.

23. We use the log of most variables to reduce their high variance and ease the interpretation of results so that changes can be interpreted as proxies of growth rates.

24. Real credit growth is particularly persistent since real credit usually has a trend.

25. This method relies on differencing the equation to address the problem of possible omitted-variable bias induced by the presence of the bank fixed effects. In addition, and to address the problem of joint endogeneity, lagged values of both the independent and dependent variables are used as instruments for contemporaneous values of the independent variables. The results that we report use the system estimator that improves on the standard first differenced GMM estimator by exploiting instruments available for the equations in levels. This improves the precision and reduces the finite sample bias when these additional moment conditions are valid.

26. We restrict the instrument matrix to avoid biases resulting from over-fitting and weak instruments. We allow up to four lags on the relevant variables as instruments.

27. To provide further context for these estimates, we also simulate the impact of the recent international financial crisis on real credit growth. During the last year of our sample (2008), the high-yield spread increased 1,220 bps, the VIX index increased 17.5 points and the EMBI spread increased 475 bps. According to our estimates, these increases should lead to a contraction in real credit of 4.5%, 3.1%, and 4.1%, respectively.

28. Because (in contrast with other foreign banks) Spanish banks fund themselves mostly through domestic deposits, this result using bank-level data may be similar to that of Kamil and Rai (2009) who, using BIS aggregate data, find that total foreign bank lending is less sensitive to changes in TED spreads and expected default probabilities when banks fund themselves through domestic deposits.

ACKNOWLEDGMENT

The chapter represents the views of the authors and do not necessarily reflect the views of any institution including the IDB, its Executive Directors or the countries they represent. We thank Eduardo Cavallo, Gian Maria Milesi-Ferretti and seminar participants at the Center for

Global Development for their valuable comments, as well as Verónica Gonzales and Cesar Tamayo for superb research assistance. We also thank Gian Maria Milesi-Ferretti for providing us with an update of the financial integration data.

REFERENCES

Arellano, M., & Bover, O. (1995). Another look at the instrumental variable estimation of error-components models. *Journal of Econometrics*, *68*(1), 29–51.

Arena, M., Reinhart, C., & Vázquez, F. (2006). *The lending channel in emerging economies: Are foreign banks different?* NBER Working Papers 12340. Cambridge, MA: National Bureau of Economic Research.

Blundell, R., & Bond, S. (1998). Initial conditions and moment restrictions in dynamic panel data models. *Journal of Econometrics*, *87*, 115–143.

Calvo, G., Izquierdo, A., & Talvi, E. (2006). *Phoenix miracles in emerging markets: Recovering without credit from systemic financial crises*. NBER Working Paper 12101. National Bureau of Economic Research, Cambridge, MA.

Calvo, G., & Loo-Kung, R. (2009). *Should We Rush to Further Regulate Financial Institutions?* New York, NY: Mimeographed document.

Chinn, M., & Ito, H. (2008). A new measure of financial openness. *Journal of Comparative Policy Analysis*, *10*(3), 307–320.

Cull, R., & Martínez Peria, M. S. (2007) *Foreign bank participation and crises in developing countries*. World Bank Policy Research Working Paper 4128. World Bank, Washington, DC.

De Haas, R., & Lelyveld, I. V. (2006). Foreign banks and credit stability in central and eastern europe: A panel data analysis. *Journal of Banking and Finance*, *30*, 1927–1952.

Edwards, S. (1999). How effective are capital controls? *Journal of Economic Perspectives*, *13*, 65–84.

Galindo, A., Micco, A., & Ordoñez, G. (2002). Financial liberalization: Does it pay to join the party? *Economia*, *3*(1), 231–261.

Galindo, A., Micco, A., & Powell, A. (2003). *Loyal lenders or fickle financiers: Foreign banks in latin America*. Research Department Working Paper 529. Inter-American Development Bank, Washington, DC.

Galindo, A., Schiantarelli, F., & Weiss, A. (2007). Does financial reform improve the allocation of investment? micro evidence from developing countries. *Journal of Development Economics*, *83*, 562–587.

Glick, R., & Hutchison, M. (2001). Banking and currency crises: How common are twins? In R. Reuven et al. (Eds.), *Financial Crisis in Emerging Markets*. New York, NY: Cambridge University Press.

Goldberg, L. (2005). *The international exposure of U.S. banks*. NBER Working Paper 11365. National Bureau of Economic Research, Cambridge, MA.

Goldberg, L. (2002). When is foreign bank lending to emerging markets volatile? In S. Edwards & J. Frankel (Eds.), *Preventing currency crises in emerging markets*. Chicago, IL: University of Chicago Press.

Kamil, H., & Rai, K. (2009). *On the eve of retrenchment? the effect of the global credit crunch on foreign banks' lending in emerging markets*. Washington, DC: International Monetary Fund.

Lane, P. R., & Milesi-Ferretti, G. M. (2007). The external wealth of nations mark II: Revised and extended estimates of foreign assets and liabilities, 1970–2004. *Journal of International Economics*, *73*(2), 223–250.

Magud, N., & Reinhart, C. (2007). *Capital controls: An evaluation*. NBER Working Paper 11973. National Bureau of Economic Research, Cambridge, MA.

Martínez Peria, M. S., Powell, A., & Vladkova-Hollar, I. (2005). *Banking on foreigners: The behavior of international bank claims on latin America, 1985–2000*. Staff Paper 52. International Monetary Fund, Washington, DC, MA.

Morgan, D., & Strahan, P. (2003). *Foreign bank entry and business volatility: evidence from U.S. states and other countries*. NBER Working Paper 9710. National Bureau of Economic Research, Cambridge, MA.

Peek, J., & Rosengren, E. (2000). Collateral damage: Effects of the japanese bank crisis on real activity in the united states. *American Economic Review*, *90*(1), 30–45.

Quinn, D. (2003). Capital account liberalization and financial globalization, 1890–1999: A synoptic view. *International Journal of Finance and Economics*, *8*(3), 189–204.

Rancière, R., Tornell, A., & Westermann, F. (2006). Decomposing the effects of financial liberalization: Crises vs. growth. *Journal of Banking & Finance*, *30*, 3331–3348.

Rancière, R., Tornell, A., & Westermann, F. (2008). Systemic crises and growth. *Quarterly Journal of Economics*, *123*(1), 359–406.

Stiglitz, J. (2009). *The UN takes charge*. Retrieved from http://www.project-syndicate.org/commentary/stiglitz114

EUROZONE DEBT CRISIS: IMPLICATIONS FOR THE INDIAN BANKING SECTOR

Vighneswara Swamy

ABSTRACT

The Eurozone debt crisis has indeed jeopardized the recovery plans put in place post global crisis by regulators, policymakers, and the sovereigns. Though the crisis is epicentered in the Eurozone, the knock-on effects of the crisis are felt all across the globe. The emerging and developing economies (EDEs) are also expected to post lower growth on account of worsening external environment and a weakening internal demand. This chapter analyzes the causes for sovereign debt crisis, presents the implications of sovereign debt crises, and draws lessons for banking sectors more particularly in the context of emerging markets like that of India.

Keywords: Sovereign debt crisis; credit risk; endogenous default; banking crisis

JEL classifications: E05; E32; E42; F33; F36; G01

Global Banking, Financial Markets and Crises
International Finance Review, Volume 14, 341–362

ISSN: 1569-3767/doi:10.1108/S1569-3767(2013)0000014015

INTRODUCTION

The Eurozone debt crisis has led to a crisis of confidence in the global financial markets amid growing market turmoil and the risk of contagion. The Eurozone economies are struggling with a combination of high levels of indebtedness, budget deficits, and frail or deficient growth. In addition, concern about the mounting government deficits and alarming debt levels across the globe has also added to the fretfulness in the financial markets.

The probability of default on sovereign debt has further compounded in congruence with the macro-economic misalignments. Starting from Greece, Ireland, Portugal, Spain, and more recently Italy, these Eurozone economies have witnessed a severe downgrade in the rating of their sovereign debt, fears of default, and a sudden rise in borrowing costs. These developments apart from threatening other Eurozone economies and even the future of the euro have indeed triggered a global debate on the management of sovereign debts and their implications on other emerging markets.

The objective of this chapter is twofold: first to analyze the nature and causes of sovereign debt crises in the context of the Eurozone debt crisis and second to present the implications of sovereign debt crises and draw lessons for banking sector. Remainder of this chapter is structured as follows: section titled "Nature of Sovereign Debt Crises" illustrates the nature, significance, and indicators of sovereign debt crises. Section titled "Impact of Sovereign Debt Crises" presents the economic impact of sovereign debt crisis from a theoretical perspective. Impacts of Eurozone sovereign debt crisis on the Indian economy in general are analyzed in section titled "Impact of Eurozone Sovereign Debt Crisis on the Indian Economy." Implications for the banking sector are analyzed in section titled "Implications for the Banking Sector" and conclusion is provided in section titled "Conclusion."

NATURE OF SOVEREIGN DEBT CRISES

Sovereign debt differs from corporate debt in that it is not enforceable by the courts, as a sovereign cannot credibly commit to hand over assets in the event of default. Sovereign debt storm erupts when nations and companies act as delinquent individuals and those responsible for monitoring them are slumbering on the job (e.g., of debt crises; Russia, Argentina, Turkey). Defining a debt crisis as a period of debt-service default for a specific country would lead to detecting only a few crises, with the extreme ones corresponding to official defaults (Argentina, 2001; Russia, 1998).

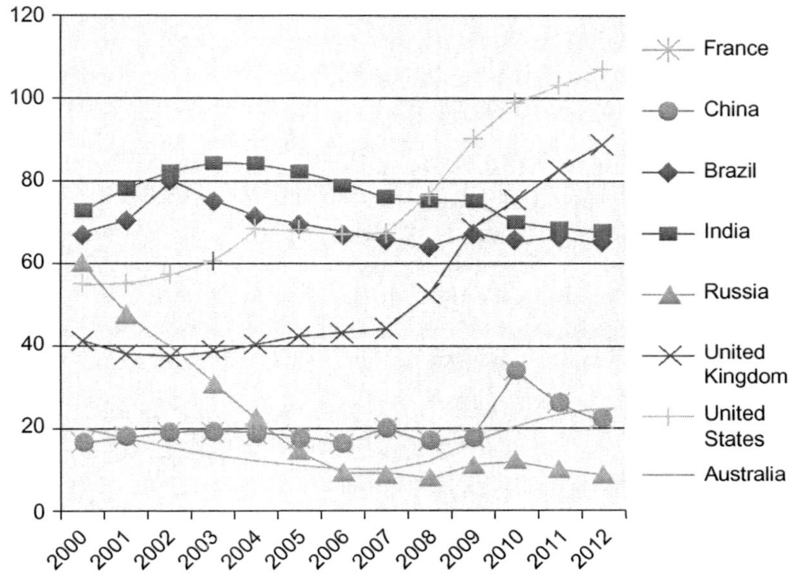

Fig. 1. Government Debt (percent of GDP) – Developed economies and BRIC Countries. *Source*: Compiled by author based on S&P publications. Source data are from GFSR data of IMF.

In practice, countries rarely officially announce that they are defaulting, since the consequences for their credibility would be terrible. For more detailed fiscal positions of the Eurozone economies, see the appendix.

We present the trend of government debt to GDP of select developed economies and BRIC countries, as shown in Fig. 1. It is shown that the increasing government debt in European countries is associated with Eurozone sovereign debt crisis since 2007. Among the BRICs countries, government debt ratio to GDP is higher in India and Brazil, but lower in China and Russia.

IMPACT OF SOVEREIGN DEBT CRISES

Banking Crises

The Eurozone debt crisis has brought to light that international financial integration will not automatically lead to an efficient allocation of capital, and has raised doubts about the ability of free markets to efficiently allocate capital (Volz, 2012). Though there have been notable sovereign debt crises, to mention, like the ones faced by Russia and Latin American countries during the 1990s, the current Eurozone sovereign debt crisis is significant in terms of the transition that is taking place globally in the geopolitical context.

The seminal model of Flood and Garber (1984) provides a theoretical explanation for the occurrence of a currency crisis stemming from incoherent macroeconomic policies, and in particular, an uncontrolled monetary expansion, which can be easily extended for monetized excessive public deficits (Corsetti & Mackowiak, 2006). On the contrary, only few papers have scrutinized the potential mutation of banking crises into sovereign debt ones. However, Reinhart and Rogoff (2011) in their detailed study on the topic argue that (1) external debt surges are an antecedent to banking crises and (2) banking crises are often preceded or accompanied by debt crises. In addition, they also observe that public borrowing surges ahead of external sovereign default, as governments have "hidden domestic debts" that exceed the better documented levels of external debt. Sovereign debt crises impact the cross-border capital flows and corporate market access (Reinhart, Kenneth, & Savastano, 2003).

The most prominent channel linking sovereign and private sector balance sheets is the insolvency of banks. The largest ticking bomb for public balance sheets is the debt of the banking sector. Banking crises often develop into sovereign debt crises, or vice versa. Since the crisis started in 2008, we have witnessed unprecedented write-down by financial institutions and large-scale government bailouts. The collateral damage from banking crises spills over to public balance sheets in the form of increasingly unsustainable debts. Given that the sovereign debt of the affected countries is present in the balance sheets of banks and insurance companies across the world, contagion effects and financial instability could spread through the global financial system. The financial crisis has demonstrated that the globalized banking system can play a crucial role in transmitting the crisis from the advanced economies to various parts of the world, particularly emerging markets. The Eurozone debt crisis also bears lessons for making a choice on the manner in which foreign banks operating in emerging economies should be allowed by the regulators to expand, that is, through the route of subsidiaries or through branches.

The extent of the impact on banks has been broadly in line with the perceived deterioration in the credit worthiness of the home sovereign suggesting that investors focus on the banks' jurisdictions as well as their creditworthiness. According to the BIS (2011), there are, broadly, four channels through which sovereign risk affects banks' funding costs, given the pervasive role of government debt in the financial system: First, losses associated with government debt weaken balance sheets of banks making funding more costly and difficult to obtain. Second, higher sovereign risks reduce the value of the collateral that banks can use to raise wholesale funding and central bank liquidity. Third, sovereign rating downgrades generally flow through to lower ratings for domestic banks, as banks are more likely than other sectors to be affected by sovereign distress. As the banks' credit ratings decline, their wholesale funding costs rise. Fourth, a weakening of the sovereign reduces the funding benefits that banks could derive from implicit and explicit government guarantees.

Debt Crises and Procyclicality

Financial markets are prone to overshooting, which in turn adds to the pro-cyclicality inherent in asset valuations. Typically, during "good times," (when risk appetite is zealous and economic conditions are favorable) asset prices tend to be high and risk spreads tend to be low. On the other hand during "bad times" (when the degree of risk aversion heightens and GDP growth shrinks), asset prices tend to decline and risk spreads rise. Further, during bad times, the procyclicality gets amplified by market overshooting/overreaction, as investors tend to overprice certain types of risk and thus underpricing the respective financial assets.

Pro-cyclicality of this type with multiplier effects has hit the sovereign bond market during the debt crisis. Besides, it has exerted severe adverse effects on other segments of financial markets, such as the funding markets for banks and financial institutions. Accordingly, the funding costs of those Indian banks who were expecting to raise funds from global markets would escalate severely though not the liquidity.

IMPACT OF EUROZONE SOVEREIGN DEBT CRISIS ON THE INDIAN ECONOMY

With the Eurozone seeming to head for a recession and the global growth decelerating again after a dumpy recovery, growth in India too has toned-down more than that was expected earlier. Upsurge in global uncertainty, feeble industrial growth, slowdown in investment activity, and deceleration in the resource flow to commercial sector led to dip in output growth. Inflation risks emanating from suppressed domestic energy prices, incomplete pass-through of rupee depreciation, and slippage in fiscal deficit, further fuelled by food and commodity inflation, have led to monetary policy tightening.

Europe being one of the largest trading blocs for India, the austerity measures by the European countries and falling consumer expenditures have negatively affected exports, more so services exports from India. According to RBI (*RBI Monthly Bulletin*, June 2012), share of India's exports to the Eurozone countries to total exports has come down from 20.1% in 2009–2010 to 18.6% in 2010–11 and 17.5% in 2011–12. In view of the weak position of the European banks, capital has flown back, leading to a sharp depreciation of the Indian rupee (INR), which is already weak (Fig. 2 presents the impact of the crisis on GDP growth and Indian currency).

Impact on Capital Flows

Investments into Indian economy have also slowed down significantly due to protracted Eurozone sovereign debt crisis. Foreign direct investment (FDI) to India (excluding disinvestments/repatriation) during April–December 2012 at US$ 21.1 billion stood lower as compared to the level attained during the corresponding period of previous year (US$ 28.7 billion). The moderation in FDI to India was recorded under both equity and debt flows. Net FDI inflows to India (inward FDI minus

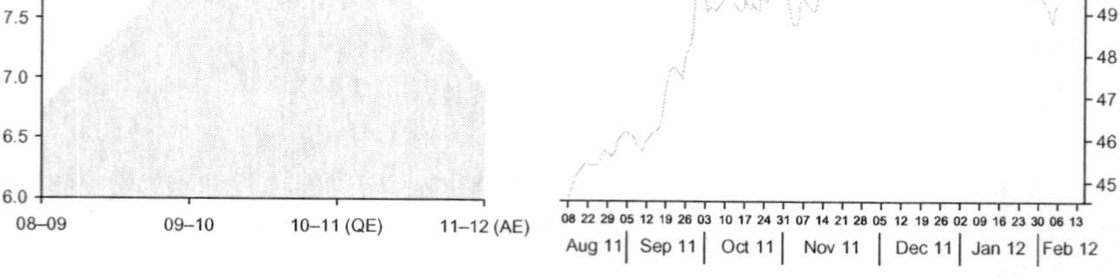

Fig. 2. Impact on GDP Growth and the Indian Rupee. *Source*: RBI (2012).

Table 1. Disaggregated Items of Financial Account.

	October-December 2011	October-December 2012	April-December 2011	April-December 2012
Foreign direct investment (FDI) to India	6.9	4.8	28.7	21.1
FDI into India – financial services	2.4	2.2	–	–
FDI into India – business services	1.3	0.5	–	–
Loans to India	8.1	7.2	15.7	14.4
External commercial borrowings (ECB)	−0.8	3.1	6.9	4.7
Loans by India – ECB	0.5	−0.1	1.2	−0.2
Reserve assets	12.8	−0.8	7.1	−1.1

Note: Figures in US$ billion.
Source: Developments in India's balance of payments during third quarter (October–December) of 2012–2013, *RBI Monthly Bulletin*, June 2013. Available at www.rbi.org.in.

outward FDI), however, declined during April–December 2012 to US$ 2.5 billion from US$ 5.0 billion in April–December 2011. Net inflows under financial account rose to US$ 31.1 billion during April–December 2012 (US$ 20.6 billion during April–December in previous year). This was mainly on account of net portfolio inflows of US$ 8.6 billion during April–December 2012 as compared with an inflow of US$ 1.8 billion during April–December 2011 (Table 1).

Net external loans availed by banks stood at US$ 2.7 billion during April–December 2012 as against outflows of US$ 8.7 billion during April–December 2011 mainly due to drawing down of Nostro balances and higher overseas borrowings by the banks. Sector-wise, the decline in FDI inflows during the period was mainly in case of manufacturing, financial services, business services, and communication services (Table 2).

IMPLICATIONS FOR THE BANKING SECTOR

In the run up to the crisis, the Eurozone experienced strong credit booms as the Eurozone banks could easily borrow from international financial markets in their own currency – euro. Further, lower interest rates and easy credit availability stimulated the consumption and mortgage

Table 2. Sector-wise FDI Inflows.

FDI into India	April-December 2011	April-December 2012
Financial services	2.4	2.2
Business services	1.3	0.5
Communication services	1.5	0.1
Manufacture	8.0	4.8
Electricity and other	1.0	1.0
Computer services	0.5	0.2
Construction	1.7	1.0
Restaurants and hotels	0.7	3.1
Others	2.1	1.0
Total	19.2	13.9

Note: Figures in US$ billion.
Source: Developments in India's balance of payments during third quarter (October–December) of 2012–2013, *RBI Monthly Bulletin*, June 2013. Available at www.rbi.org.in.

borrowing (Fagan & Gaspar, 2007). This led to sharp shooting up of the domestic credit levels in the Eurozone.

Fig. 3 illustrates the growth of domestic credit in select Eurozone countries viz., Portugal, Ireland, Italy, Greece, Spain, and Sweden. One of the key predictors of a banking crisis is the scale of the domestic credit preceding the boom (Gourinchas & Obstfeld, 2012). There was a sudden upshot in the dispersion of domestic credit and heating up of current account deficits during 2003–2007 though not during the onset of euro in 1999 (Lane & McQuade, 2012; Lane & Pels, 2012).

The crisis has posed serious challenges for the banking sector. Deficient policy actions and not enough reforms of the banking sector have left segments of the global banking system vulnerable to further shocks. Many institutions – particularly weaker European banks – are caught in a maelstrom of interlinked pressures that are intensifying risks for the system as a whole (Fig. 4).

In order to address the challenges posed by the debt crises the affected countries could consider some of the solutions like: (i) restructuring the portfolios of the banks to strengthen the tail, (ii) providing policy clarity on the private sector bail-ins to address the investor concerns, (iii) reducing the reliance on short-term wholesale funding to relieve the funding pressures, (iv) introducing rigorous stress tests and transparency in governance mechanisms to address to the asset-quality concerns, (v) tightening fiscal consolidation and being prudent in macro-economic management than

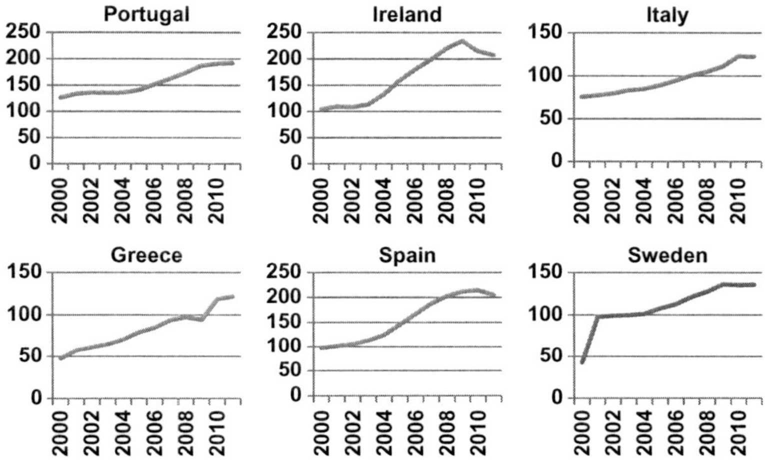

Fig. 3. Growth of Domestic Credit in the Eurozone Countries. *Note*: The figure captures domestic credit to private sector (percent of GDP) select Eurozone countries. *Source*: The figure is developed based on the data sourced from World Development Indicators of Data Bank of the World Bank.

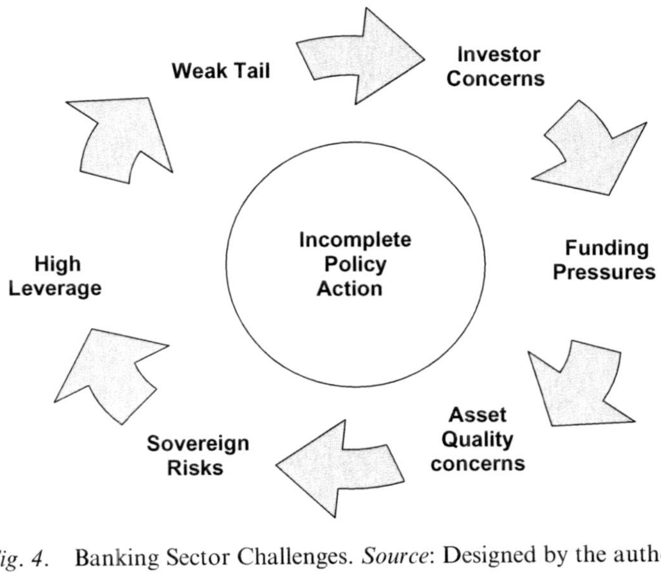

Fig. 4. Banking Sector Challenges. *Source*: Designed by the author.

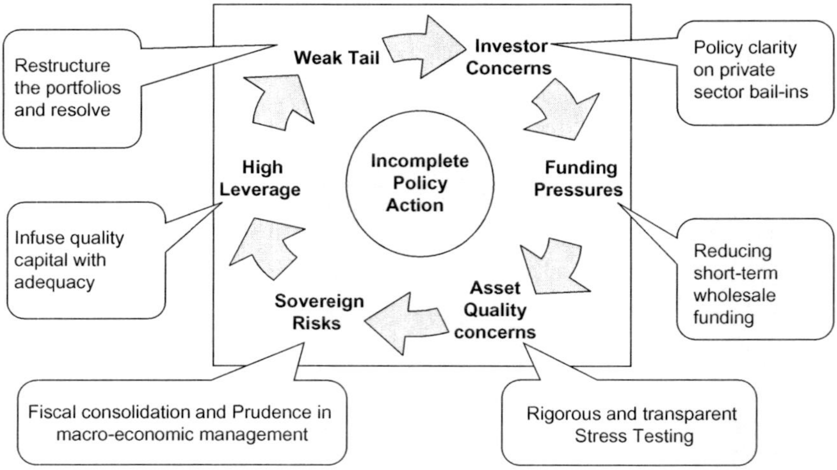

Fig. 5. Banking Sector Challenges – Suggested Measures. *Source*: Designed by the author.

populist to address the sovereign risks, and (v) infusing the enough quality capital to address leverage concerns (Fig. 5).

The worries about Europe's banks have been teeming in the background for some time as inadequately capitalized banks are holding up poorly financed governments, which in turn are expected to support those banks. After a brief lull reflecting the hefty liquidity injection by the European Central Bank (ECB), concerns have again arisen about a sustainable solution to the sovereign debt crisis and the escalating vulnerability of the banking sector. Heightened risk aversion and the ensuing decline in capital flows will have an adverse impact on emerging economies including India.

For the emerging markets like China and India, Europe and the Eurozone account for a significant market. Therefore, stagnation or a downturn in the Eurozone will undoubtedly dent their export growth. While for the Chinese – who are looking for opportunities to make bargains during the fire sales of assets, the Eurozone debt crisis poses both the threats and opportunities, however, for India – for whom EU is a major trading partner accounting for almost 20% of India's exports and 13% of imports, is a serious threat. This apart FDI from EU during 2010 amounted to €3.0 billion while India invested about €0.6 billion in the EU. Per se, a slowdown in the Eurozone and the EU is likely to have a major

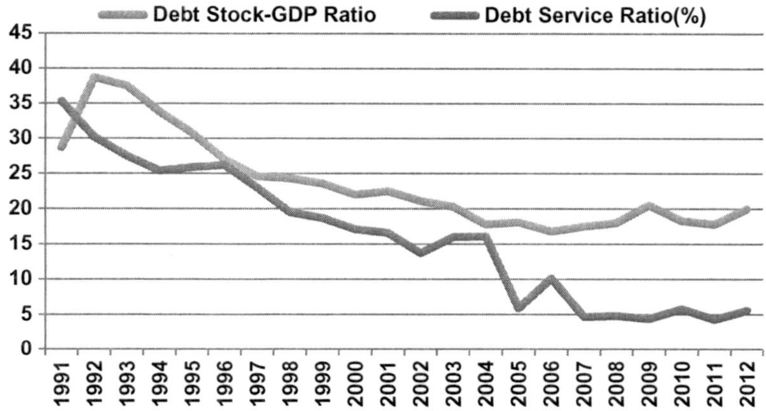

Fig. 6. India's External Debt, 1991–2012. *Source*: Data sourced from RBI database.

adverse impact on India's exports. Fig. 6 presents the India's external debt position and its debt–service ratio.

Implications for the Indian Banking Sector

Though trade is the dominant channel of transmission of the Eurozone crisis contagion to India, there are negative spillovers on India's financial sector as well. Aizenman, Jinjarak, Lee, and Park (2012) assessing the likelihood of financial contagion from the Eurozone to Asian financial markets using event study have traced the impact of distinct Eurozone news on the dynamics of equity and bond prices in developing countries.

In general, the Eurozone economy has been a vital source of foreign bank loans for developing Asia. The conflux of funding strains and sovereign risks led to fears of a precipitous deleveraging process that could hurt financial markets and the wider economy via asset sales and contractions in credit. Many European banks have announced medium-term business plans for reducing assets. The impact is likely to differ significantly across regions, with larger effects expected in emerging Europe than in Asia or Latin America.

In the Indian context, the claims of European banks, amounting to US$ 146 billion, formed 53% of total consolidated foreign claims. Of this, 56% pertained to claims of banks in United Kingdom. According to data from the Bank for International Settlements, in September 2011 India's borrowings from Eurozone banks amounted to around $57 billion. While share of borrowings from the Eurozone in total foreign bank borrowings was to the extent of 17.9%, borrowings from Eurozone banks as share of domestic credit was at 4.4%.

Indian banking system has not been notably impacted by the Eurozone debt crisis as neither does it have any significant presence in countries impacted by the current crisis nor Indian banks have any significant exposures to bonds issued by them. Though there is no first-order impact of the sovereign debt crisis, there could, however, be second-order impact through various channels including trade. There could be funding constraints for Indian bank branches operating overseas if European banks deleverage. The cost of borrowing for banks and corporates, as a result, may go up leading to concerns over refinancing foreign currency liabilities. Due to the slump in the overseas demand and the associated downturn in investment activity, there has already been some sluggishness in the credit as well as asset growth of Indian banking sector during 2011–2012.

The direct impact of the Eurozone crisis on Indian banks is expected to be limited as the Indian banking sector is largely dominated by domestic banks with foreign banks accounting for only 8% of total banking sector assets and 5% of banking sector credit. However, there could be indirect impact on Indian banks due to their exposures to other countries, especially in the Eurozone. Further, though the direct impact of deleveraging is not expected to be significant on domestic credit availability, there definitely would be an impact on specialized types of financing like structured long-term finance, project finance, and trade finance.

According to RBI data, at the end-September 2011, there are only 37 branches and 3 subsidiaries of Indian banks in the EU, and none of them is in Portugal, Italy, Greece, and Spain. Out of the 37 branches, 30 branches are in the UK, 3 branches in Belgium, and 2 each in Germany and France. All of the three subsidiaries are in the UK. Their combined share in the aggregate banking sector assets stood at 3% as at end-September 2011. Moreover, none of the Indian banks have any exposure to bonds issued by Portugal, Greece and Spain while exposures to Italian bonds are insignificant.

One significant lesson from the Eurozone debt crises for the Indian financial system comes from the fact that the Indian financial system is relatively more open than that of Chinese. For example, wholesale debt funding has been the undoing for banks in the Eurozone economies. Though it is hard to argue that banks should only raise debt resources through retail deposits, at the same time, the current episode shows that large-scale reliance on wholesale debt, specifically, from across borders can tilt the financial stability. Of course, though the Indian banking system has conventionally relied on retail deposits, which despite higher cost serve as a stable source of funding, any substantial shift toward wholesale debt funding may not be desired.

The second important inference we can draw from the Eurozone debt crisis is that India's continuance of making the banks hold the public debt (due to its high fiscal deficit) hitherto as a vestige of the era of financial repression may not hold prudent all the time as the Eurozone debt crisis raises the question of whether sovereign debt of a country can be held largely outside a country in portfolios that keep getting churned and subject to day-to-day re-pricing. Fig. 7 presents the amount of investments in T-Bills of the Government of India by the Indian banks.

Sovereign debt crises have far-reaching consequences and usually go hand in hand with (or can be traced to) banking and – in many cases – currency crises. Hence, managing and resolving sovereign debt crises pose unexpected challenges to policymakers. Crucial actions and reforms have been taken over the past two years to tackle the current European debt crisis. However, given their numerous transmission channels, these measures have been the subject of intense debate among decision-makers, experts,

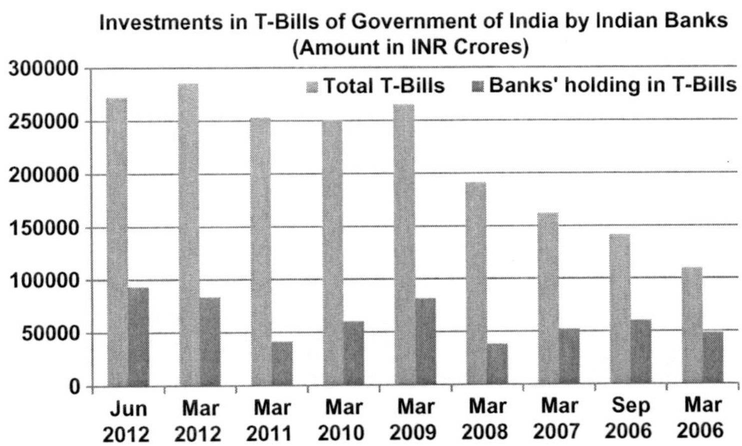

Fig. 7. Indian Banks' Investments in T-Bills of India. *Source*: Data sourced from RBI database.

the media, and the general public. Though the Eurozone sovereign debt crisis can impact Indian economy through five broad channels such as banking sector, commodity markets, currency markets, investments, and trade, this chapter has focused exclusively on the implications for the banking sector, as its all pervasive nature interacts with all the other channels too.

The global financial crisis and the current Eurozone crisis have severely impacted the banking sectors in the advanced economies and the spillover is ricocheting on banks in emerging economies including India. The Indian banking sector has not been impacted by Eurozone debt crisis, as it does not have any substantial presence in Eurozone countries nor the Indian banking sector has any significant exposures to bonds issued by them. Though there is no first-order impact of the Eurozone debt crisis, there could, however, be second-order impact through various channels including trade. There could be funding constraints for Indian bank branches operating overseas if European banks deleverage. The cost of borrowing for Indian banks and corporates has shoot up leading to concerns over refinancing foreign currency liabilities. Owing to the drop in the overseas demand and the associated downturn in investment activity, there has already been some sluggishness in the credit as well as asset growth of Indian banking sector.

Consequent to the European banks suffering huge losses and liquidity constraints, the supply of foreign credit to emerging markets has dried up. This has added to the pressure on investing in emerging markets that are already struggling to cope with rising capital costs due to tight monetary policies. India is experiencing similar situation and the Indian banks are forced to look inward and explore domestic sources of capital though relatively costlier to compensate for the shrinking global market. As European banks suffered due to the sovereign debt crisis, capital has flown back, leading to a sharp depreciation of the rupee, which was already weak. A falling rupee has hurt the industries and their profit margins both within and outside the country. This has negatively affected the profitability and credit deployment activity of the banking sector.

Impact of Foreign Claims on the Indian Banks

In view of the prolonged Eurozone debt crisis, net external loans availed by banks stood at US$ 2.7 billion in third quarter (Q3) of 2012–2013 as against outflows of US$ 8.7 billion in Q3 of 2011–2012. Similarly, the consolidated claims of foreign banks on India have experienced a gradual decline due to the impact of the crisis (Table 3). Particularly on the Indian

Table 3. Consolidated Claims of Reporting Banks – Immediate Borrower Basis on India by Maturity and Sector.

	Total Foreign Claims on a Contractual Basis	Consolidated Cross-Border Claims in all Currencies and Local Claims in Nonlocal Currencies					
		Total International Claims	Maturities			Sectors	
			Up to and Including One Year	Over One Year and up to Two Years	Over Two Years	Banks	Public Sector
		(A)	(B)	(C)	(D)	(E)	(F)
End-September 2011	320,914	224,460	139,213	12,311	51,892	83,553	10,632
End-September 2012	331,902	234,763	139,515	11,598	57,739	81,731	10,530
Percentage change	3.4	4.5	0.2	−5.79	11.26	−2.22	−0.96

Note: Amounts outstanding figures in millions of US dollars.
Source: *BIS Quarterly Review*, March 2012, and *BIS Quarterly Review*, March 2013.

banks, the outstanding consolidated claims of the foreign banks have experienced a negative change of 2.22%, that is, from US$ 83,553 million in end-September 2011 to US$ 81,731 million in end-September 2012. Further, the external positions of foreign banks on India (according to BIS statistics) have nosedived from US$ 36,987 million in December 2010 to US$ 32,194 million in December 2011, US$ 30,092 million in June 2012, and US$ 29,515 million in September 2012.

On a comparison of the consolidated foreign claims and other exposures of foreign banks on ultimate risk basis in India by sector type, we find that, consolidated cross-border claims on the Indian banks experienced downward trend with a negative growth of 3.15% with the outstanding level of US$ 75,413 million in end-September 2011 to US$ 73,039 million in end-September 2012 (Table 4). Similarly, the exposures under derivative contracts have nosedived to negative growth of 30.98%. Guarantees extended have experienced a fall of 19.45% and the credit commitments have declined by 24.60%.

Our observation that the Eurozone sovereign debt crisis has impacted on the Indian banking sector further stands supported by the fact that there has been a significant fall in the claims of the Eurozone banks on India. Table 5 depicts the consolidated foreign claims on India of the foreign banks based on their country of origin. Claims of European banks on India came down from US$ 13,354 million in end-September 2011 to US$ 12,362 million in end-September 2012, thus experiencing a downfall of 7.54%. Most of the foreign claims from countries like Italy, Ireland, Denmark, France, Luxemburg, Cyprus, Norway, and Netherlands have drastically come down during the crisis period.

Impact on the Indian Syndicated Credit Facilities

We also analyze the trend of the international syndicated credit facilities by India for the period from 2010 to 2012 in order to discern the impact of the Eurozone sovereign debt crisis. We observe that international syndicated credit facilities for India have slipped down from US$ 33.6 billion in 2010 to US$ 32.9 billion in 2011 and US$ 25.0 billion in 2012 (see Fig. 8).

This reduced activity under syndicated credit facilities has dampened the fund-raising scenario for the Indian banks, financial institutions, and institutional investors.

Table 4. Consolidated Foreign Claims and Other Exposures of Reporting Banks – The Ultimate Risk Basis on India by Sector and Type.

	Consolidated Cross-Border and Local Claims in All Currencies					Other Exposures (Not Included in Foreign Claims)		
	Total Foreign Claims of 24 Countries	Of Which on			Of Which Cross-Border Claims	Derivative Contracts	Guarantees Extended	Credit Commitments
		Banks	public Sector	Nonbank Private Sector				
End-September 2011	283,645	75,413	32,033	176,039	174,439	17,594	42,465	54,576
End-September 2012	287,707	73,039	37,614	176,838	174,124	12,143	34,202	41,153
Percentage change	1.43	−3.15	17.42	0.45	−0.18	−30.98	−19.45	−24.60

Note: Amounts outstanding figures in millions of US dollars.
Source: *BIS Quarterly Review*, March 2012, and *BIS Quarterly Review*, March 2013.

Table 5. Consolidated Foreign Claims of Reporting Banks by Country: The Ultimate Risk Basis on India.

	End-September 2011	End-September 2012	Percentage change
All countries	44,581	46,198	3.62
Developed countries	27108	26,122	−3.64
Other developed countries	13,754	13,760	0.04
Developing countries	8,735	9,498	8.73
Offshore centers	7,965	9,500	19.27
Europe	**1,3354**	**1,2362**	**−7.54**
Belgium	969	1,122	15.78
Cyprus	197	183	−7.10
Denmark	99	85	−14.14
Finland	45	41	−8.88
France	964	762	−20.95
Germany	2,461	2,077	−15.60
Ireland	258	71	−72.48
Italy	233	160	−31.33
Luxembourg	161	58	−63.97
Malta	275	1	−99.63
Netherlands	1,468	1,276	−13.07
Norway	101	17	−83.16
Portugal	32	34	6.25
Spain	109	125	14.67
Switzerland	684	714	4.38
United Kingdom	5,172	5,361	8.87

Note: Amounts outstanding figures in millions of US dollars.
Source: *BIS Quarterly Review*, March 2012, and *BIS Quarterly Review*, March 2013.

Impact on Portfolio Investments in India

There has been a steady slide in the portfolio investments in India due to the impact of the Eurozone sovereign debt crisis. We find in our analysis that portfolio investments in India (according to RBI Monthly Bulletin June 2011 and June 2013) came down from US$ 32,376 million in 2009–2010 to US$ 31,471 million in 2010–11 and came further down to US$ 27,264 million in 2012–2013 (see Fig. 9).

Eurozone debt crisis, apart from its negative impact on portfolio investments capital inflows, could also affect the European involvement in the merger and acquisition (M&A) activities in Indian corporate sector. With the Eurozone remaining sluggish, the appetite of European companies for M&A in India has declined.

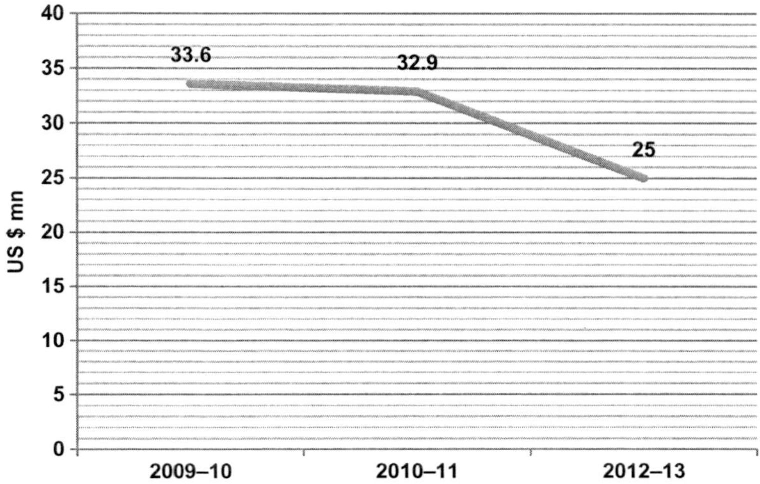

Fig. 8. Portfolio Investments in India. *Source*: Data sourced from *RBI Monthly Bulletin*, June 2011 and June 2013.

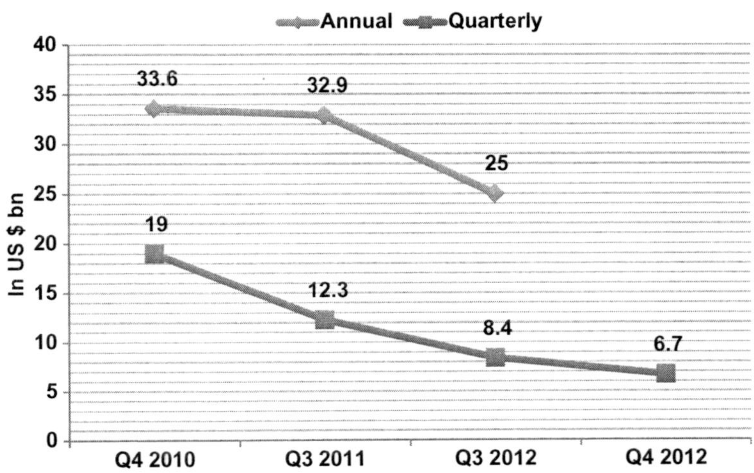

Fig. 9. Signed International Syndicated Credit Facilities by India. *Source*: *BIS Quarterly Review*, March 2012, and *BIS Quarterly Review*, March 2013.

CONCLUSION

When banking markets are closely integrated, each individual country is de facto responsible for preserving the stability of the entire international financial system. As Bolton and Jeanne (2011) rightly observed that by maintaining a sound fiscal position, each country provides a public good to all other countries.

The recent financial crisis has demonstrated that the globalized banking system has played a key role in transmitting the crisis from the advanced economies to other parts of the world, including the emerging economies. The Eurozone debt crisis also holds lessons for making a prudent choice on the manner in which foreign banks should be allowed to expand in emerging economies, that is, whether through the route of subsidiaries or through branches.

This study has analyzed the causes and consequences of the Eurozone debt crisis on the emerging markets' banking sectors in general and the Indian banking sector in particular. I provide an overview and evidence that bank exposures to sovereign debts and the weak economy are perpetuating the financial sector fragility, which in turn is spurring continued deleveraging. It is suggested that the emerging markets need to strengthen their firewalls to protect themselves from the ill effects of spillovers from crises originated from abroad including the Eurozone debt crises.

REFERENCES

Aizenman, J., Jinjarak, Y., Lee, M., & Park, D. (2012). *Developing countries' financial vulnerability to the Euro crisis: An event study of equity and bond markets*. NBER Working Paper Series No. 18028. National Bureau of Economic Research, Cambridge, MA.

Bank for International Settlements (BIS). (2011, July). *The impact of sovereign credit risk on bank funding conditions*. CGFS Papers No. 43. Available at http://www.bis.org/

Bolton, P., & Jeanne, O. (2011). Sovereign default risk and bank fragility in financially integrated economies. *IMF Economic Review*, *59*(2), 162–194.

Corsetti, G., & Mackowiak, B. (2006). Fiscal imbalances and the dynamics of currency Crises. *European Economic Review*, *50*(5), 1317–1338.

Fagan, G., & Gaspar, V. (2007). *Adjusting to the Euro*. ECB Working Paper Series No. 716. Frankfurt am Main: European Central Bank. Retrieved from http://www.ecb.europa.eu/pub/pdf/scpwps/ecbwp716.pdf

Flood, R. P., & Garber, P. M. (1984). Collapsing exchange rate regimes: Some linear examples. *Journal of International Economics*, *17*, 1–13.

Gourinchas, P.-O., & Obstfeld, M. (2012). Stories of the twentieth century for the twenty-first. *American Economic Journal: Macroeconomics*, *4*(1), 226–265.

Lane, P. R., & McQuade, P. (2012). *Domestic credit growth and international capital flows.* Unpublished paper, Trinity College Dublin.

Lane, P., & Pels, B. (2012). *Current account imbalances in Europe*, IIIS Discussion Paper no. 397, Trinity College, Dublin, April.

RBI. (2012, April). Changing contours of global crisis – impact on indian economy. *RBI Monthly Bulletin*, pp. 725–737. Retrieved from http://rbidocs.rbi.org.in/rdocs/Speeches/PDFs/CCGCIEF200312.pdf

Reinhart, C. M., Kenneth, S. R., & Savastano, M. A. (2003). Debt intolerance. *Brookings Papers on Economic Activity*, *34*(1), 1–70.

Reinhart, C. M., & Rogoff, K. S. (2011). From financial crash to debt crisis. *American Economic Review*, *101*(5), 1676–1706.

Volz, U. (2012). *Lessons of the European crisis for regional monetary and financial integration in East Asia.* ADBI Working Paper No. 347. Asian Development Bank Institute, Tokyo. Retrieved from http://www.adbi.org/working-paper/2012/02/21/5007.lessons.european.crisis.east.asia

APPENDIX: FISCAL POSITION OF SELECT ECONOMIES IN THE CONTEXT OF THE EUROZONE DEBT CRISIS

Country	Fiscal and Debt Fundamentals			Financing Needs		External Funding	Banking System Linkages			Sovereign Credit		Sovereign CDS
	Gross General Government Debt 2011	Net General Government Debt 2011	Primary Balance 2011	Gross General Government Debt		General Government Debt Held Abroad	Domestic Depository Institutions' Claims on General Government		BIS Reporting Banks' Consolidated International Claims on Public Sector	Rating/Outlook (Notches Above Speculative Grade/Outlook) (As of 3 October 2011)		Five-Year (basis points) (as of 3 September 2011)
				2011	2012		(Percent of 2010 GDP)	(Percent of 2010 GDP) (Percent of Depository Institutions' Consolidated Assets)				
Australia	24.1	7.8	−2.1	4.5	3.3	43.4	2.2	1.2	3.2	9	Stable	51
Canada	84.2	35.1	−4.1	18.5	16.4	19.6	19.6	10.3	3.6	10	Stable	n.a.
Denmark	45.6	4.4	−3.2	9.3	9.8	41.8	15.5	3.2	6	10	Stable	44
France	87.6	77.9	−3.5	20.6	19.7	64.4	19	4.7	8.8	10	Stable	85
Germany	80.1	54.7	−0.3	11.4	10.5	52.8	25.4	7.6	10.4	10	Stable	48
Greece	152.3	n.a.	−0.9	24	26	61.5	27.4	12.2	23.3	−1	Negative	1,037
Ireland	114.1	95.2	−7.5	19.5	18	59.4	28.2	2.8	8.7	3	Negative	587
Italy	120.3	100.6	0.2	22.8	23.1	47	32.1	13.1	15.2	7	Stable	180
Japan	229.1	127.8	−8.6	55.8	52.5	6.9	76.3	23.7	1.6	7	Negative	77
Korea	28.8	27.5	3.5	8.9	5.8	11.5	6.1	4.4	4.8	5	Stable	98
Netherlands	65.6	30.5	−2.2	19.9	16.6	66.4	13.8	3.6	9.2	10	Stable	47
Portugal	90.6	86.3	−1.6	21.6	21	56.7	15.7	4.8	17.2	5	Negative	498
Spain	63.9	52.6	−4.6	19.3	18.7	49.6	22.3	6.8	7.1	8	Negative	253
Sweden	37.3	−13.8	−0.9	5.4	4.6	45.2	6.5	2.3	5.3	10	Stable	33
UK	83	75.1	−5.5	15.7	13.6	26.8	6.9	1.5	2.9	10	Stable	58
USA	99.5	72.4	−9.0	28.8	25.6	31.9	7.7	5.3	3.7	10	Stable	43

Source: Compiled by the author from World Economic Outlook updates of IMF.

Note: Shaded ones are countries inflicted with Eurozone Sovereign Debt Crisis.

PART V
POLICY IMPLICATIONS AND LESSONS

CORPORATE GOVERNANCE AND INTRA-GROUP TRANSACTIONS IN EUROPEAN BANK HOLDING COMPANIES DURING THE CRISIS

Franklin Allen, Xian Gu, and Oskar Kowalewski

ABSTRACT

In this chapter we study the intra-group transactions between the parent bank and its foreign subsidiaries in European Union (EU) countries during the crisis. We use hand-collected data from annual statements on related party transaction and find that they may create a serious problem for the stability of the foreign banks' subsidiaries. Moreover, as some of those subsidiary banks were large by assets in some of the member states the related party transactions with the parent bank created a serious threat to the host countries' financial system stability. We attribute this transaction to the weak governance in foreign subsidiaries. We suggest

Global Banking, Financial Markets and Crises
International Finance Review, Volume 14, 365–431

ISSN: 1569-3767/doi:10.1108/S1569-3767(2013)0000014016

improvements in governance as well as greater disclosure of related party transactions in bank holding companies in Europe.

Keywords: Multinational banks; corporate governance; internal bank markets; crisis

JEL classifications: G21; G28; G38

INTRODUCTION

The financial crisis of 2008 put most multinational banks under severe funding stress. These banks were not only confronted with mounting losses in their home market but also faced disruption in their numerous foreign subsidiaries at the same time. Hence, as the financial losses increased and the crisis spread across markets cross-border banking activity declined sharply. It was therefore expected that this contraction might result in a considerable tightening of financial conditions in many host countries, which could exacerbate the economic downturn, especially in emerging markets (IMF, 2009). The recent studies, however, about foreign banks transmitting shocks to host countries are not conclusive, since most of the empirical research concentrated so far only on the loan channel (Allen, Hryckiewicz, Kowalewski, & Tumer-Alkan, 2010; De Haas & Van Lelyveld, 2010; Popov & Udell, 2010).

Most of these studies assume that the contraction of credit by foreign banks is the result of lower funds provided by the parent bank. The assumption was based on the findings of De Haas and Van Lelyveld (2010), who documented the existence of internal capital markets (ICMs) in multinational bank holding companies prior to the crisis. Using data for a large number of banks, they showed that foreign subsidiaries with financially strong parent banks were able to expand their lending faster in the host countries. Consequently, it is not surprising that Popov and Udell (2010) found that foreign banks, whose parent banks had low equity ratios or severe losses in financial assets, tightened credit more in host countries during the global crisis.

Although the existence of ICMs in multinational banking has been well-established in literature, little is known about how they function, especially during a financial crisis. Moreover, the existing empirical research used financial data for the parent bank and its subsidiaries without establishing directly the channels of the internal capital flows in multinational bank holding companies. We close the existing gap in the literature by providing an overview of the existing internal bank channels, which have been used to transfer assets and income from the parent bank to its subsidiaries and the other way around during the crisis in the period 2007–2009.

In order to present the different channels we hand-collected financial information from annual statements of multinational banks and their subsidiaries in the European Union (EU). We focus mainly on the EU banking sector as in this region the integration process was especially visible in the recent years as the member states tried to establish a unified internal financial market by encouraging cross-border mergers and acquisitions in the financial industry. The pattern of financial integration in the EU, however, has been unbalanced. Large and concentrated foreign ownership has evolved in the banking sector in the new member states (NMS) of EU.

In these countries foreign ownership constituted between 30% in Slovenia to 99% in the Baltic countries (Allen, Bartilori, & Kowalewski, 2005). The foreign banks were often of small importance from the parent banks' perspective, but systemically important for the host countries. Furthermore, in the Central and Eastern Europe (CEE) member states multinational banks mainly come from Italy, Belgium, or the Netherlands, with the exception of the Baltic States (Estonia, Latvia, and Lithuania) where Swedish banks dominate so far. The concentrated and large exposure of the host countries increases their risk and vulnerability to fluctuations in home countries. The same conversely applies for home countries in the event of excessive concentration of their banks to a few countries as was the case for the Baltic States.

The exposures of the CEE countries to multinational banks and their dominant role in the banking sector make them important for these countries' financial system stability, especially through the risk of intra-group asset transfers. In the past, foreign banks and intra-group transfers were often associated with the stabilization of the financial systems in underdeveloped countries. De Haas and Van Lelyveld (2006) documented that during crisis periods domestic banks contract their credit in CEE countries. In contrast, foreign banks played a stabilizing role by keeping their credit base stable. This study, however, concentrated only on crisis in the host countries and did not take into account potential liquidity problems of the parent banks, which surfaced during the current crisis.

Indeed, we report that during the crisis the intra-group asset transfers may involve substantial risk as they have been used to increase the liquidity of the parent bank and jeopardize the transferor's solvency in the host countries. As the foreign subsidiaries are relatively large those asset transfers may create a serious threat to the countries' banking sector stability. Those transfers were often disadvantageous to the subsidiaries as the parent bank could exercise undue influence over its management. We argue therefore that the governance of foreign subsidiaries should take into account not only the interests of the parent banks, but also the stability of the host countries' financial systems.

In this study we documented intra-group asset transfers of multinational bank holding companies that were conducted during the crisis and created, in our opinion, a risk to the financial systems, often across several countries. Our assumptions are based on the theoretical models of Allen and Gale (2000) that showed that if a bank is hit by a shock, it tries to meet its liquidity need by drawing on its deposits at other banks before liquidating long-term assets. Upper and Worms (2002) expanded this model and presented empirical evidence showing that credit risk associated with interbank lending may lead to domino effects. In their work they documented that a failure of one bank might result in the failure of other banks not directly affected by the initial shock. Employing their findings to our study we argue that the failure of one subsidiary within a multinational bank holding company may have led to the failure of multiple banks across the countries.

Consequently, we advocate for a greater disclosure and monitoring of intra-group transactions between parents and subsidiaries. Today only few banks provide detailed information on third-party transactions in their financial statements. As a result outsiders are often not in the position to assess the risk related to these transactions. At the same time disclosure of information and risk is an important part of market discipline, which helps fulfill supervisory authorities their obligations.

Moreover, the study shows that those transactions often involve banks from different countries. We argue, therefore, that there is also a pressing need to regulate and supervise the multinational banks using transnational financial regulators. Only transnational authorities, with full access to information on third-party transaction within multinational banking holding company across different countries, will be able to monitor and assess the risk of those operations.

The analysis is presented in four parts. The second section presents the development of the EU banking sector with a focus on foreign banks. The third section discusses the problems of the governance of foreign banks. In the fourth section we present the data on intra-group asset transfers, and in the fifth section on intra-group income transfers. Finally, in the sixth section, we discuss the Vienna Initiative that was undertaken by the European

Bank for Reconstruction and Development (EBRD) during the crisis to prevent large scale withdrawal of foreign banks from CEE countries, while the seventh section concludes the chapter.

OVERVIEW OF THE BANKING SECTOR IN THE EU-27

The liberalization of international capital movements within the European internal market has significantly changed the banking systems of the member states. At the same time the integration process, which was encouraged through cross-border mergers, might have caused the banking system to be more vulnerable to financial instability. In this section, we present the development of the European banking sector and its integration process from both the legislative and institutional perspective, and describe the pressing cross-border banking issues.

Development of the Financial System: Legislation and Institutions

The development of the European financial system in the last 30 years was accompanied by an integration process. As a large literature has already pointed out, the European financial system is mainly bank-oriented, due to the dominant role of credit institutions (CIs) in most member states (Allen et al., 2005). Especially, in the CEE countries, domestic credit has undergone decade-long booms since the 1990s, which allowed solid economic growth and financial development. This has also been demonstrated by the narrowing gap of the income and financial deepening level between these countries and western European countries (Cottarelli, Dell's Ariccia, & Hollar, 2003). The problem is that the financial systems of the CEE countries are dominated by banks, most of which are foreign-owned institutions. That is to say, credit provision in these countries depends largely on the behavior of foreign-owned banks.

In this section, we first review the integration process of European banking system in the last 30 years from the legislative perspective and then provide the empirical evidence of the consolidation process and multinational banking development, which had resulted in the steeply increasing foreign banks' market share in CEE countries. We develop the evidence part from two aspects, first, the consolidation process and mergers and acquisitions (M&A) activities, and second, foreign ownership in European banking system. We leave the regulation problems associated with subsidiaries and foreign branches to the last part.

The Integration Process of European Banking: The Legislative Evolution
One reason why cross-border banking is especially widespread in EU countries is due to the legislative efforts that have been made to achieve the long-term goal of creating a single market for financial services in EU. Since the First Banking Directive was published in 1977, which mainly coordinated the laws on CIs and removed obstacles to the establishment of credit institution branches across the borders of EU member states, the integration process of the European banking system has been accelerated. Several major advances followed in the 1980s and 1990s, including the 1985 white paper on *The Completion of the Internal Market* published by the European Commission, the 1986 *Single European Act*, the 1988 Directive on *Liberalization of Capital Flows,* the 1989 Second Banking Directive on single EU banking licenses, the 1992 *Treaty on European Union* (TEU), which opened the way to political integration and started a new stage in European consolidation – the creation of Euro and the launch of Financial Services Action Plan (FSAP) in 1999, which built the legislative framework for the single market in the Euro Area. Then, from 2000 to 2004 there were also several directives on the European banking sector that were published, such as the consolidated banking directive, the directive on e-money, the directive on the reorganization and winding-up of CIs, the financial conglomerates directive, and the new EU takeover directive. Another important event in May 2004 was the entry of 10 NMS, most of which were emerging countries from CEE.[1] Then in December 2005, the European Commission published a white paper on financial service policies for the period from 2005 to 2010, which showed that the Commission would continue to advance the FSAP and eliminate the remaining barriers between the financial sectors of EU member states. Finally, the European Central Bank set up the objective to achieve a single Euro payment area (SEPA) by the end of 2010 and made the first SEPA products available from January 2008. Those products allowed the consumers to benefit from prompt and secure transfers between different bank accounts anywhere in the euro area.

The Consolidation Process and M&A Activities
The level of the consolidation process in European banking has been high in the last 20 years. In the old member states (OMS) the number of CIs fell from 12,256 in 1985 to 7,444 in 2003 (Dermine, 2006). At the end of 2009

the number of CIs had further dropped to 6,360. This means that more than half of the CIs have disappeared in the last 20 years in the EU despite the fact that the internal market has expanded from 15 to 27 countries. Also, the total number of monetary financial institutions (MFI) has also decreased from 9,856 in 1998 to 8,076 in 2009 in the EU.[2] The decrease of the MFI reflects the ongoing consolidation process not only in the banking sector but in the whole financial industry in the EU.

Actually, the downward trend continued until November 2007, and after that the number of CIs grew for a short period until December 2008. Nevertheless, CIs still have a prominent role in the European banking system (see Table 1). In terms of a share to GDP, the total CIs' assets of the EU-27 increased from 275.9% in 2005 to 357.3% in 2009, while they were at 263.5% in 2000 for the EU-15 member states.

Among the EU member countries, changes of CIs' assets in the NMS of EU-12 have a totally different pattern from the OMS of EU-15. The data shows that before the 2007 financial crisis, the total assets of CIs measured relative to GDP in the OMS appeared to decrease, but then increased after the crisis. In the NMS, the ratio rose before the crisis but declined after that. The difference in the ratios before the crisis was mainly due to the foreign banks' entry in the NMS.[3] In the literature some authors have pointed out that since foreign banks are not restrained by the conditions in the domestic market, there is a positive relationship between foreign bank market share and private sector credit growth (Aydin, 2008; Clarke, Cull, Martinez Peria, & Sanchez, 2003; De Haas & Van Lelyveld, 2006).

M&A activities, especially the cross-border M&A deals, appeared to accelerate the consolidation process. Table 2 reveals that after the accession of the NMS in 2004, both the number and value of M&A transactions have increased significantly. Moreover, Fig. 1 shows that even after the outbreak of the financial crisis in the second-half of 2007, the value of M&A transactions was still increasing in the years 2007–2008, in which the EU cross-border and outward transactions played a more and more important role. The year of 2009 saw the value of M&A deals dropping but this was probably only temporary. It is very likely that the cross-border M&A activity will pick up again once economic conditions improve, both within the EU and in particular in the emerging markets (ECB, 2010). With the number dropping and the total assets rising, especially when measured relative to GDP, the M&A activity and international strategy may partially give the reason why the size of CIs are getting larger in EU, which also enhances the bank concentration level in EU.

Table 1. Number and Total Assets of CIs in Euro and as a Share of GDP.

	Number of CIs					Total Assets of CIs (EUR Millions)					CIs Assets as a Share to GDP				
	2000	2005	2007	2008	2009	2000	2005	2007	2008	2009	2000	2005	2007	2008	2009
Austria	848	818	803	803	790	527,933	721,159	890,747	1,067,860	1,036,597	2.5545	2.9606	3.2747	3.7722	3.7788
Belgium	118	100	110	105	104	698,809	1,055,270	1,297,788	1,270,766	1,155,506	2.8201	3.4845	3.8746	3.6868	3.4259
Denmark	210	197	189	171	164	431,756	746,589	1,091,809	1,091,809	1,104,536	2.5163	3.6003	4.8092	4.7055	4.9555
Finland	341	363	360	357	349	127,999	234,519	383,908	383,908	387,630	0.9835	1.4908	2.1364	2.0791	2.2627
France	1099	854	808	728	712	3,502,581	5,073,388	6,682,335	7,225,140	7,155,460	2.4664	2.9393	3.5258	3.7080	3.7519
Germany	2742	2089	2026	1989	1948	6,063,568	6,826,564	7,562,432	7,875,401	7,423,967	2.9870	3.0446	3.1144	3.1555	3.0816
Greece	57	62	63	66	66	191,862	281,067	383,295	461,981	490,134	1.5581	1.4387	1.6927	1.9318	2.0638
Ireland	81	78	81	82	498	355,346	941,908	1,337,356	1,412,198	1,323,584	3.4552	5.8110	7.0480	7.7672	8.0932
Italy	861	792	821	818	801	1,771,126	2,509,436	3,331,829	3,634,559	3,691,965	1.5183	1.7555	2.1549	2.3182	2.4275
Luxemburg	202	155	156	152	147	647,896	792,417	915,446	931,563	797,460	30.4491	26.1679	24.4340	23.6750	21.1837
Netherlands	586	401	341	302	295	1,148,942	1,697,781	2,168,280	2,231,514	2,217,008	2.8560	3.3069	3.8129	3.7449	3.8881
Portugal	218	186	175	175	166	315,312	360,185	439,459	482,126	520,188	2.7288	2.3430	2.6044	2.8044	3.1031
Spain	368	348	357	362	352	1,124,944	2,152,833	3,005,274	3,381,187	3,433,283	1.8450	2.3689	2.8547	3.1063	3.2662
Sweden	211	200	201	182	180	434,669	659,286	854,947	907,536	934,534	1.6724	2.2098	2.5298	2.7153	3.1930
UK	491	394	396	391	389	5,227,636	5,897,712	10,094,508	8,840,240	9,420,998	3.3519	3.2158	4.9173	4.8695	6.0268
OMS total	8433	7037	6887	6683	6961	22,570,379	29,950,114	40,439,413	41,197,788	41,092,850	5.9186	5.5251	5.9806	6.0301	6.2877
Bulgaria	–	34	29	30	30	–	17,447	31,238	36,825	37,950	–	0.7973	1.0809	1.0793	1.1202
Cyprus	–	391	215	163	155	–	62,553	92,897	118,142	139,372	–	4.5796	5.8239	6.8496	8.2245
Czech Republic	–	56	56	54	56	–	100,902	140,168	155,005	160,219	–	1.0071	1.1008	1.0482	1.1674
Estonia	–	11	15	17	18	–	11,876	20,603	22,066	21,340	–	1.0621	1.3184	1.3729	1.5543
Hungary	–	214	206	197	190	–	78,289	108,504	124,672	126,160	–	0.8832	1.0734	1.1813	1.3553
Latvia	–	25	31	34	37	–	15,727	30,816	32,249	29,925	–	1.2087	1.4597	1.3999	1.6142
Lithuania	–	78	80	84	84	–	13,162	23,817	26,542	26,180	–	0.6307	0.8334	0.8242	0.9824
Malta	–	19	22	23	24	–	27,195	37,807	42,283	41,242	–	5.6846	6.9206	7.4468	7.2101
Poland	–	730	718	712	710	–	163,421	233,938	262,591	274,212	–	0.6686	0.7522	0.7246	0.8843
Romania	–	40	42	43	42	–	35,400	72,095	84,541	86,386	–	0.4436	0.5780	0.6049	0.7455
Slovakia	–	23	26	26	26	–	37,834	58,053	65,509	54,473	–	0.9837	1.0575	1.0113	0.8601
Slovenia	–	25	27	24	25	–	30,135	43,493	49,010	53,404	–	1.0479	1.2582	1.3198	1.5305
NMS total	–	1646	1467	1407	1397	–	593,941	893,429	1,019,435	1,050,863	–	1.0901	1.2444	1.2077	1.1085
MU16 total	7521	6704	6391	6175	6458	16,476,318	22,804,244	28,534,207	30,633,483	29,921,272	2.5055	2.7978	3.1666	3.3261	3.3362
EU27 total	8433	8683	8354	8090	8358	22,570,379	30,544,055	41,123,104	42,217,558	42,143,710	2.6345	2.7591	3.3198	3.3745	3.5726

Sources: ECB (2004, 2006, 2010).

Table 2. Share of the Five Largest CIs Assets in Total Assets (%).

	2001	2005	2007	2008	2009
Austria	44.9	45.0	42.8	39.0	37.2
Belgium	78.3	85.3	83.4	80.8	77.1
Denmark	67.6	66.3	64.2	66.0	64.0
Finland	79.5	82.9	82.3	82.8	82.6
France	47.0	51.9	51.8	51.2	47.2
Germany	20.2	21.6	22.0	22.7	25.0
Greece	67.0	65.6	67.7	69.5	69.2
Ireland	42.5	47.8	50.4	55.7	58.8
Italy	29.0	26.8	33.1	33.0	34.0
Luxemburg	28.0	30.7	27.9	27.3	27.8
Netherlands	82.5	84.5	86.3	86.8	85.0
Portugal	59.8	68.8	67.8	69.1	70.1
Spain	43.9	42.0	41.0	42.4	43.3
Sweden	54.6	57.3	61.0	61.9	60.7
United Kingdom	28.6	36.3	40.7	36.5	40.8
OMS average	51.6	54.2	54.8	55.0	54.9
Bulgaria	n.a.	50.8	56.7	57.3	58.3
Cyprus	61.3	59.8	64.9	63.9	65.0
Czech Republic	68.4	65.5	65.7	62.0	62.4
Estonia	98.9	98.1	95.7	94.8	93.4
Hungary	56.4	53.2	54.1	54.5	55.2
Latvia	63.4	67.3	67.2	70.2	69.3
Lithuania	87.6	80.6	80.9	81.2	80.5
Malta	81.1	75.3	70.2	72.8	72.7
Poland	54.7	48.5	46.6	44.2	43.9
Romania	n.a.	59.4	56.3	54.0	52.4
Slovakia	66.1	67.7	68.2	71.5	72.1
Slovenia	67.6	63.0	59.5	59.1	59.7
NMS average	70.6	65.8	65.5	65.5	65.4
MU16 average	51.9	56.7	56.7	57	57
EU27 average	59.1	59.3	59.5	59.6	59.5
MU16 average[a]	39.1	42.8	44.4	44.7	44.6
EU27 average[a]	37.8	42.6	41.5	45.2	44.3

[a]CIs assets weighted averages.
Sources: ECB (2004, 2006, 2010).

Foreign Ownership in European Banking

The market share of foreign banks differs significantly between the OMS and NMS (Figs. 2 and 3). This tendency is consistent with the evidence from other countries, where developed nations tend to have much lower foreign bank ownership shares than developing countries, as the government entry barriers are relatively more implicit and foreign banks always

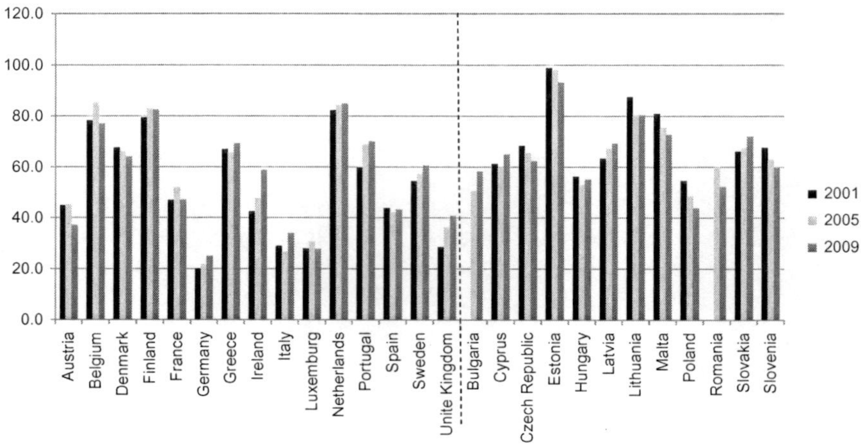

Fig. 1. Share of the Five Largest CIs Assets in Total Assets (%). *Sources*: ECB (2004, 2006, 2010).

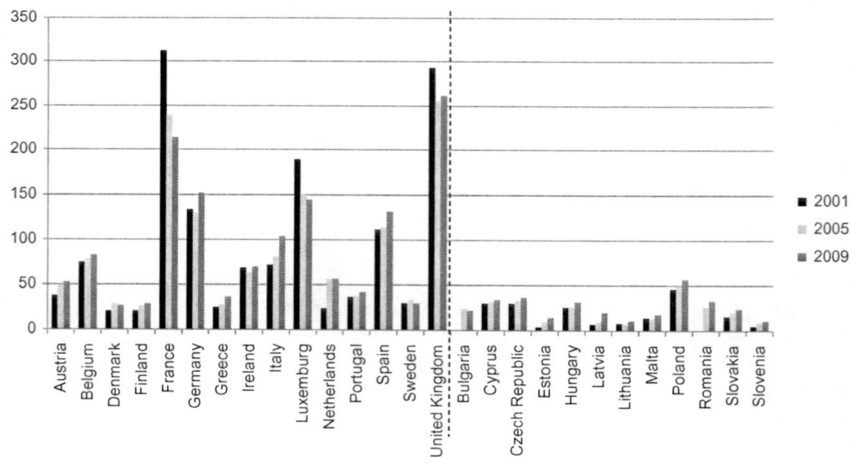

Fig. 2. Number of Foreign-Controlled CIs: Subsidiaries and Branches. *Sources*: ECB (2004, 2006, 2010) and authors' calculations.

have net comparative disadvantages in developed countries, as Berger (2006) has pointed out.

On an average the number of total foreign-controlled CIs in the OMS, including both subsidiaries and branches, was much higher than the

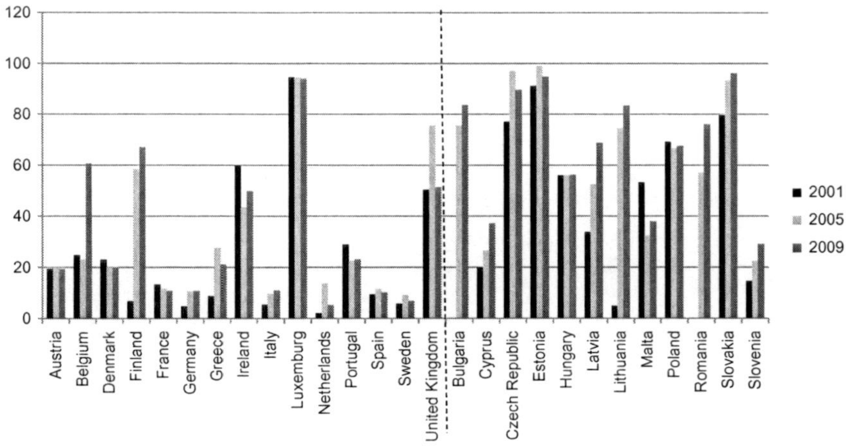

Fig. 3. Share of Foreign-Controlled Assets to Total Assets of CIs (%). *Sources*: ECB (2004, 2006, 2010) and authors' calculations.

number in the NMS. At the same time, the share of foreign-controlled assets to total assets of CIs was higher in most NMS than in the OMS during the past eight years. From 2001 to 2010, the average share of foreign to total banking assets in the NMS was 65.5%, while it was 25.8% in the OMS. During the 2007 financial crisis, the average number of foreign CIs increased in the NMS but dropped in the OMS. This may indicate that multinational banks were looking for opportunities in developing rather than developed countries during the crisis. This is consistent with the findings of Cardenas, Graf, and O'Dogherty (2003), who showed that in emerging markets foreign banks used financial crisis as a reason to enter. In contrast, in mature economies foreign bank entry was more likely related to competitive pressure.

Table 3 shows that among the NMS, the highest percentage of foreign ownership in the banking sector is in Slovakia. In 2009, the foreign-controlled assets accounted for 96.1% of the total assets of CIs, while in 2005 and 2001, the ratio was 93.3% and 79.5%. Estonia and Czech Republic rank second and third respectively, with foreign ownership shares of 94.9% and 89.7% in 2009. At the same time, the CR5 concentration ratio was 72.1% in Slovakia, 93.4% in Estonia, and 62.4% in Czech Republic. Due to the high concentrations in their banking systems, the CEE countries were found to be more prone to financial fragility, whereas

Table 3. Subsidiaries versus Foreign Branches: Number and Its Share in Total Assets.

	Number				CI's Assets to Total Assets in %			
	Branches		Subsidiaries		Branches		Subsidiaries	
	2001	2009	2001	2009	2001	2009	2001	2009
Austria	15	26	23	23	0.78	1.05	18.64	18.35
Belgium	46	50	29	28	5.53	7.59	19.33	53.13
Denmark	11	19	10	10	4.37	3.57	18.81	16.36
Finland	18	20	3	6	6.37	4.36	0.44	62.74
France	83	81	229	159	3.73	2.04	9.49	8.73
Germany	80	89	54	41	2.07	2.45	2.68	8.30
Greece	21	23	4	5	8.80	7.81	0.00	13.29
Ireland	33	32	36	32	13.84	9.46	46.12	40.46
Italy	63	68	9	13	4.28	3.94	1.10	7.04
Luxemburg	63	44	126	107	19.14	14.58	75.42	79.43
Netherlands	5	28	19	28	0.73	2.85	1.33	2.48
Portugal	25	25	12	13	4.96	6.39	24.11	16.72
Spain	56	65	56	49	4.18	6.63	5.19	3.55
Sweden	20	20	10	14	5.41	6.39	0.35	0.47
United Kingdom	200	170	93	86	44.12	38.30	6.35	13.20
OMS total	739	760	713	614	13.64	11.92	8.86	13.32
Bulgaria	–	6	–	18	–	4.40	–	79.31
Cyprus	21	22	9	10	10.52	4.59	9.52	32.66
Czech Republic	10	12	20	21	12.76	11.71	64.24	77.97
Estonia	1	6	3	4	0.02	26.04	91.15	68.83
Hungary	0	3	26	23	0.00	6.19	56.04	50.12
Latvia	1	1	6	9	0.01	12.19	33.84	56.63
Lithuania	4	2	4	5	4.91	17.58	0.05	65.80
Malta	3	2	11	11	19.03	0.00	34.35	38.01
Poland	0	7	46	42	0.00	5.02	69.22	62.59
Romania	–	6	–	20	–	6.61	–	69.44
Slovakia	2	5	14	16	0.00	6.93	79.52	89.20
Slovenia	1	3	4	6	0.01	0.94	14.64	28.19
NMS total	43	75	143	185	4.85	6.87	54.96	59.34

Sources: ECB (2006, 2010) and authors' calculations.

capital regulations spur financial stability across whole Europe (Uhde & Heimeshoff, 2009).

The total number of foreign-controlled assets in the EU was €11.1 trillion in 2009, in which the share of NMS was less than 6.3%, showing that compared to the OMS, the banking sector in NMS is still highly undeveloped and dominated by a small number of foreign institutions. Further, among these subsidiaries or foreign branches, 93.5% are hosted by other EU countries, showing that most cross-border activities in these countries were still within EU area, which is line with the findings of Navaretti, Calzolari, Pozzolo, and Levi (2010).

Among the OMS, France, the United Kingdom, and Luxemburg have the highest number of total foreign-controlled CIs, including both subsidiaries and branches. In contrast, France has a quite a low market share of foreign-controlled assets of CIs, which was 10.8% in 2009. The average market share of foreign-controlled assets to total assets of CIs in the OMS was 25.8% in 2009, while in the NMS it was 65.5%. At the same time the average CR5 bank concentration ratio in the OMS increased from 54.9% to 50.5% in 2000. The M&A activities, especially cross-border deals mentioned above, were enhancing bank concentration in the recent years. Looking further into the foreign ownership in the OMS, the data shows that 69.9% of the foreign CIs were hosted by other EU countries, with the rest from other third countries. Hence, the data indicates that the banking system ownership in the OMS was much more diversified than the NMS. Ekhlom (2010) documented that much of the development in EU cross-border banking was driven by large institutions in a few countries, notably the United States, the United Kingdom, France, Germany, and Netherland.

Subsidiaries Versus Foreign Branches

An important factor affecting regulation of cross-border banks is the choice of the form that foreign banks choose to operate abroad. The banks registered in the EU may use either the form of subsidiary or branch to operate in the other market. The differences between the two forms can be described briefly as follows. Subsidiaries are independent companies governed by host authorities. In contrast, branches follow the single banking license scheme and are therefore regulated by their home countries. This difference provides different incentives for monitoring and supervising banks by the home and host countries' authorities.

Assuming a host country is riskier than the home country; the home country authority would prefer a subsidiary structure to insulate the parent bank from the host country's risk (Kahn & Winton, 2004). In addition when a branch experiences financial difficulties in the host country, it has to rely on a bailout from its home country. The home authority might, however, be reluctant to rescue the branch or its parent bank if it is not systemically important for the home country financial system. At the same time a branch may have a large share in the host country's assets and be systemically important to its financial system, which would then create conflicts of interests. Those problems arising from the dependence on the home country's regulation and bailout action have become evident in European banking system in the aftermath of the financial crisis that started in 2007. In particular, the problems of the Icelandic branches in the United Kingdom have exposed the described conflicts between home and host authorities.[4] Besides these, Navaretti et al. (2010) have also illustrated that different types of foreign bank' entry might give rise to distinct liability structures between the bank's units within the group and hence different functioning of ICMs.

As for the pros and cons of these two types of foreign institutions, subsidiaries could hold more advantages for the parent bank. The most important point is that branches might not address the internal incentive issues within the organization and its units as well as subsidiaries. As Navaretti et al. (2010) reported, subsidiaries can solve the risk-sharing problem and asymmetric information problem better, and hence reassure the shareholder, local management, public, and government. Besides these, Dermine (2006) also pointed out several other factors that influence the decision of multinational banks to choose subsidiaries as their preferred foreign organization form. First, it allows them to keep "business as usual" and does not require them to change the brand after a merger. Second, it provides a more flexible international corporate tax structure. Third, it creates an opportunity to get extra deposit insurance premium contributions made by the host countries. Fourth, it gives the flexibility to sell the business unit at any time. Cerutti, Dell'Ariccia, and Martinez Peria (2007) used the evidence of the world's top 100 banks in Latin America and Eastern Europe to demonstrate that banks were more likely to operate as branches in countries which have higher taxes and lower regulatory restrictions on foreign bank entry. On the other hand, subsidiaries were preferred by banks seeking to establish large retail operations in host countries. Besides these factors, legal differences in parent banks' responsibilities associated with subsidiaries and branches must also be considered.

The data in Table 3 shows that the banking sectors of the member states are experiencing some reversals in the choice of foreign entry modes in recent years, especially between the OMS and NMS, and the periods after and prior to the enlargement of the EU in 2004. In the OMS before the EU accession, foreign banks preferred to enter other European markets using branches, with 739 foreign banks having established branches in host

EU-15 countries and 713 having established subsidiaries. Furthermore, the percentage of banking assets held by foreign branches was 13.6% in 2001, which far outstrips that of subsidiaries, 8.9%. But things seem to have reversed after 2005, with the percentage of banking assets held by foreign branches declining from 14.4% to 11.9% and that of subsidiaries declining from 14.2% to 13.3% in the OMS.

In contrast, our data show that foreign banks preferred to enter other CEE countries using subsidiaries, as subsidiaries far outstripped foreign branches both in total numbers (143 to 43) as well as in percentage of banking assets controlled in each country (55.0% to 4.9%). But after the accession, the number of foreign branches increases dramatically, from 75 in 2005 to 128 in 2009, although the assets held by subsidiaries still dominates the banking sector in emerging countries.

Altman (2006) mentioned the reasons why there exists some dissimilarity between these two regions on the form of foreign bank entry. The study stated that the abundance of branches as compared to subsidiaries can be partially explained as the EU-15 countries have been operating under the Second Banking Co-ordination Directive longer, which permits banks that have a license in any EU country to open branches in another member state without further bureaucratic impediments. Additionally, in the NMS, the relatively small number of branches prior to the EU accession can be attributed to the unfavorable attitudes of host regulators toward branches (Cerutti et al., 2007). Before the accession, regulators in these countries often refused the applications from foreign banks to open branches based on a wider set of criteria than those used for banks seeking to use subsidiaries (Hryckiewicz & Kowalewski, 2010). Another reason explaining the subsidiary structure in the NMS is that many banks entered the CEE market via acquisition of privatized local banks and cross-border banking is thus the result of large scale M&A activity rather than organic growth, which is more the case in the OMS. After the NMS joined the EU in 2004, there were fewer potential targets left to acquire in the region, and thus, entries through branches gained importance, which eventually declined during the global financial crisis.

GOVERNANCE OF FOREIGN-OWNED BANKS

According to the Basel Committee, the commonly used principle to govern and supervise foreign institutions is called "home country control," which means the home country is responsible for the supervision of the consolidated entity, including the worldwide activities in the parent bank, foreign subsidiaries, branches, and other operations, while host country is responsible for ensuring that foreign subsidiaries are well-supervised within its borders (BCBS, 1997). But sometimes national differences in cross-border banking regulation may give rise to divergent incentives and mandates between the home supervisor and the host supervisor, which may cause an inconsistency or mismatch in the regulation of foreign institutions. In this part, we will elaborate the differences in the corporate governance of foreign subsidiaries and branches, in particular the agency problems and weak performance of independent nonexecutive board members in foreign subsidiaries. Today, many regulators attribute the governance of banks as one of the main causes of the global financial crisis (Basel Committee on Banking Supervision, 2010; European Commission, 2010b). As a result the Basel Committee made recommendations on the governance of financial institutions, while the European Commission may propose regulatory measures, in order to remedy any weakness in the corporate governance system in the financial sector. The existing documents, however, show that the problems of governance of subsidiaries have largely been ignored. Basel Committee on Banking Supervision (2010) principle stated that boards of subsidiaries should adhere to the corporate values and governance principles espoused by its parent company. The European Commission (2010a) working documents did not discuss so far the problem of governance in foreign bank subsidiaries. We have presented evidence that foreign banks are often systemically important institutions in the member states' financial systems. Consequently, we advocate that any future recommendations or regulations should also consider foreign subsidiaries separately in more detail, and in particular its relationship to the parent bank.

Foreign Bank Subsidiaries

Under the principle of "home country control," for subsidiaries, the home country is a consolidated supervisor, while the host country supervises the local bank, with a local name, local management, and internal culture (Goldberg, Sweeney, & Wihlborg, 2005). The foreign subsidiaries are separate corporations fully subject to the host country's jurisdiction. Therefore, it may cause significant agency problems between the parent bank and local bank managers. Another important issue in the governance of foreign subsidiaries exists in the independent nonexecutive board members, who have very low incentives to oversee the risk-taking activities by the executive board in the current regulatory system. In this part, we will first discuss the agency problem between home bank and local bank manager, and then show the severe problems with the current system of nonexecutive board members.

Agency Problems

The first important issue for the governance of foreign subsidiaries is the agency problem between parent banks and their subsidiaries. The reason why a principal–agent structure is applied to explain this is that a parent bank and the host country share decision-making authority and responsibility for the foreign subsidiaries, so conflicts of interests may arise among the different parties: bank shareholders, bank managers, depositors, deposit insurers, and borrowers. The asymmetric information between these parties and the monitoring costs make it impossible to draw up a complete contract (Dermine, 2006). Sometimes, different subsidiaries will have different levels of agency problems. Kim, Prescott, and Kim (2005) have pointed out that the extent to which the principal could observe and verify the subsidiaries' activities depends on the strategic roles of the agents, which means various foreign subsidiaries may play different roles due to their strategic objectives and resources thus cast different levels of agency problems to the parent bank. Although we have mentioned that subsidiaries could solve the internal incentive issues better than branches, both of them have supervisory and legitimate worries as well.

First, the information sharing is quite asymmetric between host and home country. Since the home country is responsible for the consolidated supervision, it will have control over most key information about the consolidated bank, while the host supervisor will have greater access to information about the subsidiary operations and local economy. Normally, the host country should keep the home supervisor informed of all the risk-taking activities in the local bank, while the parent bank should disclose relevant information to its subsidiary. Thus, for its own financial stability, the host supervisor always hopes to get more information of the consolidated bank from the home supervisor, such as the overall risk characteristics as well as developments in the home country or other host countries that may affect the consolidated bank or the local subsidiary. On the other hand the home supervisor hopes to obtain more information about the local market since some of this may not be easily available (Krimminger, 2008). Normally the information sharing and disclosure should conform to the Memoranda of Understanding (MOU), but sometimes some special information may not be addressed in a timely and complete manner, especially some risk activities during the crisis. However, Pistor (2010) documented that the home supervisor is unlikely to monitor and respond to risk from activities of subsidiaries in host countries that are subject to their consolidated regulatory supervision. Moreover, she shows that the host regulator may supervise the subsidiary of the parent bank, yet it may rely on the home supervisor to exert regulatory control. As a result the existing framework favors home country regulators and leaves host country regulators without much power to adequately supervise foreign subsidiaries.

Moreover, we argue that in some cases, if the parent bank is large, and the subsidiary is not systemically important to the consolidated bank, it may not have enough incentives to exchange supervisory information with the host country, such as the overall bank's operations or the intended actions by the home country, which leads to a very weak position for the host country. Therefore, communication and coordination is in particular critical for foreign subsidiaries.

Some papers have mentioned that a separate public listing of subsidiaries would solve the asymmetric information problems between uninformed investors, informed investors, and the bank managers (Dermine, 2006). Furthermore, Francis, Hasan, Song, and Yeung (2009) proposed that bank's regulators might rely on the information content in bank stock price to supervise banks and avoid financial volatility in the future. Habib, Johnsen, and Nail (1997) pointed out that the increase in the number of public traded securities could make the pricing system more informative and efficient. However, we are aware that the stock price information content might be biased by the governance problems of the subsidiaries, which we outline in detail later. Hence, in order to increase the information content in stock prices the governance problems in subsidiaries need to be resolved.

Deposit insurance is another issue besides information availability. The deposit insurance rules vary widely among different countries, existing on the types of accounts covered, the maximum limits to coverage, premium assessments, solvency, private or tax-payer involvement, and the government support for coverage (Eisenbeis & Kaufman, 2005). The inconsistent national deposit insurance rules of different countries may create disincentives for effective actions by home or host country and different coverage for depositors in the same country, as Krimminger (2008) has pointed out. For foreign subsidiaries, the EU directives stipulate that foreign subsidiaries in host countries should receive equal treatment with the domestically owned banks, so many of the conditions of prompt reopening are decided by host countries. But as the multinational banks are increasingly managed on a consolidated basis, management and facilities concerning deposit insurance may be held in the parent bank or other foreign subsidiaries, which leaves the host country still in a relatively passive position (Eisenbeis & Kaufman, 2005).

The third existing problem is the asymmetric risk sharing between home and host country. Kahn and Winton (2004) found that the problem of risk-sharing is particularly acute when two entities have different levels of risk. As for foreign subsidiaries, the allocation of the responsibilities of supervision and resolution between parent banks and host-country supervisors is not very clear, which directly leads to a serious risk shifting problem between these two entities. To the parent bank, sometimes losses in one subsidiary may be offset by gains in another one, leaving the subsidiaries to bear the financial fluctuations. The parent bank would have low incentives to give obligations and guarantees to the subsidiaries. Cardenas et al. (2003) pointed out that when the subsidiary has financial difficulties the parent bank's decision about whether to support the subsidiary is totally dependent on the future profits and expenses including their legal and reputation costs. Specifically, if the financial turmoil is overwhelming, a problem parent bank may transfer losses to a host country's subsidiary or remove assets from the host country through intra-group transactions before the foreign subsidiary is approved for bankruptcy protection, which means the bailout or resolution costs will be shifted to the host country.[5] This has already become a huge problem among foreign subsidiaries in European countries during the financial crisis. We will show in the following sections a large quantity of asset transfers from 2007 to 2009, especially in those countries where the foreign bank assets account for a large share in the whole banking system.

Numerous papers discuss the blind spots of the principle of "home country control," especially for CEE countries. Pistor (2010) argues that the home country may not monitor and regulate the risk which is unique to the host country; while the host country has very little regulatory power if the parent bank engages in direct lending practices or channels capital through entities that are not under similar regulations. This point of view is similar to that of Dermine (2006), who argues that the principle of "home country control," which is guiding the European cross-border banking system, is unlikely to be adequate in the future, as some small European countries may not be able to bail out a large international bank if there is any financial difficulty. Our data will also demonstrate this point below.

Independent Nonexecutive Board Members (Supervisory Board Members)

A number of papers have discussed the relationship between bank governance and performance. This literature can be divided into two streams. The first stream studies the relationship between board characteristics and bank performance, while the second discusses bank remuneration policy, which has already attracted considerable attention after 2007 financial crisis. Both streams have led to a range of regulatory proposals in many countries including the EU (European Commission, 2010a).

The impact of board features on bank performance is quite clear according to a number of papers. De Andres and Vallelado (2008) used cross-country evidence and demonstrate that bank performance has an inverted U relationship with board size and more outside directors will improve performance. The latter point has been confirmed by several other papers, like the one written by Pathan (2009), who also argued that more independent directors appear to lead to low risk-taking. Other papers discuss ownership concentration, risk taking, and bank performance. Caprio, Laeven, and Levine (2007) employed cross-country data and found evidence showing that concentrated ownership is consistent with good governance, while strong regulatory power may not improve the governance for a given level of ownership concentration. Also, Lavine and Levine (2008) found that more concentrated ownership will lead to higher risk-taking, which is exactly consistent with the agency theory.

Therefore, the common view among these papers is that nonexecutive independent directors are good for bank governance – they help control risk-taking and improve bank performance. Since the role of nonexecutive board members is in particular important when ownership is highly concentrated as it is in the case of subsidiaries, we inspect the performance and governance of independent directors more deeply, including the expertise and time commitment of those nonexecutive board members, their appointment, the board composition, and the board remuneration policy.

Analyzing the governance structure of listed foreign subsidiaries in the host countries we find that the proportion of independent nonexecutive board members with financial industry expertise was relatively low. Table 4 presents the characteristics of the independent nonexecutive board members in listed companies. We document that most of them have a degree in law or some other discipline and lack any expertise in the financial industry.[6] Moreover, we find that most of the risk or audit committees were dominated by nonexecutive board members, who also hold positions in the parent bank, which could cause severe agency problems.

Table 4. Structure of Supervisory Boards and the Characteristics of Nonexecutive Directors in Listed Foreign Banks Subsidiaries in 2010.

No. of Directors	Of Which Independent Board Members (Nonexecutive Directors)				Other Boards
		Age	Education	Profession	
UniCredit (Poland)					
9	1[a]	63	Ph.D. in engineering	Professor, Warsaw University of Technology	n/a
	2	64	Ph.D. in physics	Founder and President of the Business School WSB–NLU	n/a
	3	59	Ph.D. in economics	Professor, Gdansk University	3
	4	58	High school	CEO, Fiat Auto Poland	n/a
	5	55	M.A. in theater direction	CEO, Allianz Poland	1
Citigroup (Poland)					
12	1[a]	71	Ph.D. in law	Lawyer and Em. Professor, AM University	n/a
	2	63	Ph.D. in economics	Politician	8
	3	44	M.A. in economics and law	Founder and CEO, ICENTIS Corporate Solutions	2
	4	61	M.Sc. in engineering	CEO, ABB Poland	n/a
	5	62	Ph.D. in economics	Professor, Warsaw University	2
	6	61	M.Sc. in engineering	CEO, Can Pack Group	n/a
Commerzbank (Poland)					
10	1[a]	64	M.A. in economics	n/a	n/a
	2	58	M.A. in economics	Founder and CEO, MOKATE	n/a
	3	52	M.Sc. in engineering	Advisor to the Board of CTL Logistics	n/a
	4	59	Ph.D. in economics	President of the Gdańsk Institute for Market Economics	n/a
	5	46	Ph.D. in law	Lawyer and Professor, Warsaw University	5
Erste Bank (Czech Republic)					
9	0			no independent supervisory board members (non executive directors)	
Erste Bank (Slovakia)					
5	0			no independent supervisory board members (non executive directors)	
KBC (Bulgaria)					
3	0			no independent supervisory board members (non executive directors)	

Table 4. *(Continued)*

No. of Directors	Of Which Independent Board Members (Nonexecutive Directors)				Other Boards
		Age	Education	Profession	
KBC (Poland)					
7	1[a]	61	M.A. in law	Lawyer and CEO, PZMot	n/a
	2	66	Ph.D. in economics	Professor, Kozminiski University	n/a
	3	57	M.Sc. in mathematics	Founder and CEO, Capital Strategy	n/a
Société Générale Group (Romania)					
11	1	70	n/a	Independent Financial Advisor	1
	2	46	M.A. in economics	Director, European Bank for Reconstruction and Development	6
	3	57	Ph.D. in economics	Professor, Technical University of Bucharest	n/a
	4	61	n/a	CEO, Romanian Loan Guarantee Fund for Private Entrepreneurs	n/a
Société Générale Group (Czech Republic)					
9	1	67	M.Sc. in engineering	n/a	n/a
	2	61	M.A. in economics	Retired	n/a
ING (Poland)					
8	1[a]	63	M.A. in economics	Professor, Technical University of Lodz	1
	2	59	Ph.D. in law	Lawyer and Professor, University of Silesia	0
	3	49	M.A. in economics	Auditor and CEO, PRO AUDIT	0
Bank Millennium (Poland)					
11	1[a]	70	M.A. in law	Lawyer	1
	2	85	M.Sc. in navigator engineer	n/a	1
	3	54	M.A. in law	Lawyer	1
	4	69	Ph.D. in economics	Rector and Professor, Kozminski University	2
	5	57	Ph.D. in economics	Politicians and Professor, Warsaw School of Economics	4
	6	64	Ph.D. in economics	Politicians and Professor, Warsaw School of Economics	n/a

[a]Chairman (woman) of the Supervisory Board.
Sources: Companies annual statements, ISI Emerging Markets, and Thomson ONE Banker.

For example in the BRE Bank, a listed company on the Warsaw Stock Exchange (WSE), where Commerzbank owns 75% of the equity, the supervisory board consisted of ten members at the end of 2010. Of the ten members five including the Chairman were independent according to the definition of the governance code of the WSE. The function of Chairman was held since 2004 by a former Subsecretary of State at the Ministry of Infrastructure with 22 years of work experience in the central state administration (degree in economics). This person was also the Chairman of the Supervisory Board in the years 1994–2001. The remaining four independent board members in the subsidiary were a CEO and co-owner of a Polish coffer producer (degree in economics), an adviser to the management of a logistics company (degree in engineering), a president of an economic think tank (degree in economics), and a law professor of the University of Warsaw. The remaining five members of the supervisory board were foreigners and senior managers at the parent bank. As a result we may assume that their loyalty to the subsidiary and host country was relatively low.

Moreover, the example shows that even in listed subsidiaries the supervisory boards are dominated by the parent bank board members, who are the only ones with the knowledge and access to information to monitor the bank's risk. In the case of the Commerzbank Polish subsidiary none of the independent board members had any industry experience. Furthermore, two of them did not even have permanent employment. This may make them more likely to follow the directions of the members representing the main shareholder. The performance of the nonexecutive board members, especially their challenges to the aggressive risk-taking activities of the dominant shareholder executed by the management, is extremely important to the subsidiaries. Erkens, Hung, and Matos (2010) found that during the crisis CEOs were more likely to be replaced following large losses if boards had more independent directors and firms were held more by institutional investors, but not when firms were controlled by inside blockholders. Hence, the composition of the board, where a low level of independent directors with financial expertise is present in subsidiaries, may leave the bank under poor supervision and regulation (Nestor Advisors, 2009).

Masulis, Wang, and Xie (2012) found that foreign directors are associated with a significantly poorer performance of the companies. Hence, a large presence of foreigners not only in the supervisory boards but also in the management may result in lower bank performance, especially in nonlisted foreign bank subsidiaries. The size of the management and the

Table 5. Governance Structure of Parent Banks and their Subsidiaries.

	Shares	Listed	Management			Of which foreigners			Board			Of which foreigners			Option plans based on shares	
		Stock exchange	2007	2008	2009	2007	2008	2009	2007	2008	2009	2007	2008	2009	P	S
ING		*Amsterdam, Brussels, New York*	*9*	*7*	*3*				*12*	*11*	*11*				*Yes*	
Poland	75%	Warsaw	7	7	7	3	1	2	8	8	8	4	4	4	Yes	Yes
Unicredit		*Milan, Frankfurt, Warsaw*	*23*	*23*	*23*										*Yes*	
Bulgaria	92%	No	4	5	5	2	2	2	7	7	7	6	6	6	Yes	No
Poland	59%	Warsaw	9	9	7	3	4	3	9	9	9	5	5	5	Yes	Yes
Slovakia	99%	No	4	3	3	1	1	1	9	9	9	5	5	5	Yes	No
Czech Republic	100%	No	4	4	5	2	2	3	9	9	9	6	6	3	Yes	No
Hungary	100%	No	5	5	5	1	1	1	6	9	9	1	6	6	Yes	No
Romania	51%	No		6	5		2	2		9	7		8	5	Yes	No
Commerzbank		*Frankfurt*	*10*	*8*	*9*				*21*	*21*	*21*				*Yes*	
Poland	70%	Warsaw	7	7	7	4	3	4	9	9	10	4	4	5	Yes	Yes
AIB		*Irish, London, NY*	*18*	*21*	*12*										*Yes*	
Poland	71%	Warsaw	10	10	11	2	2	3		8	7	4	4	3	No	Yes
Citigroup		*NY, Tokyo, Mexico*	*15*	*15*	*17*											
Poland	75%	Warsaw	5	5	5	1	1	0	12	12	12	6	6	6	Yes	No
KBC		*Brussels*	*26*	*25*	*22*										*Yes*	

Poland	87%	Warsaw	5	5	5	2	1	1	10	9	10	4	4	5	No	No
Hungary	100%	no	4	3	3											No
Czech Republic	100%	no	5	6	5	2	2	1	9	9	9	5	5	5	No	No
Slovakia	100%	no	6	6		2	2		6	6		3	3		No	No
Deutsche Bank	*Frankfurt, NY*		*4*	*4*	*8*				*20*	*20*	*20*				*Yes*	
Poland	100%	No	3	3	4	0	0	0	6	6	5	5	5	4	No	No
GE	*NY*		*16*	*16*	*16*										*Yes*	
Poland	89%	Warsaw	2	8	8	0	4	4	11	12	13	4	6	4	Yes	No
Czech Republic	100%	No	3	3	4	3	3	4	3	3	3	2	1	1		No
Raiffeisen Bank	*Vienna*	*7*	*6*	*6*				*7*	*6*	*7*					*Yes*	
Czech Republic	51%	No	7	7	7	0	0	0	9	9	8	4	4	4	No	No
Poland	100%	No	5	5	5	0	0	0	5	5	5	4	4	4	No	No
Slovakia	100%	No	6	6	6	1	0	0	6	7	9	3	4	6	No	No

Note: Ownership structure of foreign banks and information on parent (*p*) or subsidiaries (*s*) option plans existing in foreign subsidiaries at the end of 2009. In one-tier board companies the management shows the number of all directors.

Sources: Companies annual statements.

supervisory board in foreign-owned banks is shown the Table 5. We document that in the majority of the subsidiaries the nonexecutive board members are foreigners, who are often senior managers in the parent bank. For example, in Poland in the subsidiaries of Deutsche Bank or Raiffeisen Bank only one member of the supervisory board was Polish out of six and five members, respectively. Furthermore, all the supervisory members including the Polish were senior managers or former employees of the parent bank, who often own the parent bank's shares. Hence, those members will more likely safeguard the interests of the parent bank than the interests of other stakeholders of the subsidiary such as depositors.

For this reason, Cardenas et al. (2003) argued that the governance structures of the subsidiaries should be adequately designed to reflect the interests of both the parent company and the stakeholders of the subsidiary. Such regulations are clearly established in New Zealand and Australia. In those countries the regulation authorities require that banks have constitutions that explicitly prevent directors from damaging the subsidiary and its creditors while pursuing benefits for the holding company. In addition, foreign banks must include independent nonexecutive directors on their boards to make sure that the management is following the regulation and acting in the best interest of the local institution. In 12 of the member countries the law requires employee representation at board level, which may safeguard the interest of the subsidiary. On the other hand their leverage against the other board members and managers is weak.

Moreover, European Commission (2010c) recently reported the large majority of respondents to its public consultation on possible ways forward to improve corporate governance of financial institution were not in favor of creating a specific duty of care to be established for the board of directors to take into account the interests of depositors and other stakeholders during the decision-making procedure. Most of the respondents, where the majority were financial institution and investors from OMS, considered that the primary fiduciary duty of boards are their shareholders.

An existing and important problem of the governance presents also the remuneration policy of executive managers in the foreign bank subsidiaries. The inappropriate pay structures for directors, leading to excessive risk-taking and short-termism, were found to be one of the causes of the financial crisis. Again, however, most of the research and proposed regulations focus only on domestic banks, while ignoring the problem of subsidiaries and their remuneration policy for board members.

Our study shows that the remuneration policy of board member may be biased toward the interest of the parent bank and the expense of the host stakeholders. In Table 4, we list those subsidiaries where the management received, in addition to its salaries, the options for shares in the parent bank. Moreover, we find that managers of subsidiaries that are listed received bonuses in the form of the shares of the parent bank. For example, in 2009 the management of Citibank's subsidiary in Poland, which is also listed on the WSE, received as part of their remuneration Citigroup shares granted in the previous years and options on Citigroup common stock for which exercise rights were granted in 2009. Hence, all the managers of the subsidiary were Citigroup shareholders, while only one held a few shares of the subsidiary itself. In addition, the CEO of the subsidiary was also employed directly by Citigroup and held the position of Citigroup Country Officer as well was member of the Citigroup Management Committee. Consequently, we may assume that the remuneration policy in this foreign subsidiary was rather aimed at protecting the parent bank interest than that of the subsidiaries minority shareholders.

In our opinion the existing governance structure of subsidiaries may explain why the management of the foreign subsidiaries undertook transactions during the crisis, which were often to its disadvantage and moreover as we show later put it at risk.

Foreign Bank Branches

As for foreign branches following the single banking license, it is the responsibility of the home country to regulate the institutions in the host country, as branches are an integral part of the bank and not separately incorporated into the host country's jurisdiction, which is to say, the home country will have principal authority over the branch and all the relevant information. In this case, the host country is in an even weaker position in terms of information availability compared to the form of subsidiaries, so it may not assess the potential risks or externalities its financial system may be exposed to. This information problem is in particular acute in those European countries where foreign banks are significant in the financial system.

Another incentive issue of foreign branches is their resolution by their home countries when there is a financial turmoil. Since the decision of whether and when to bail out is also made by the home supervisor, the host country is totally at the mercy of the home country's willingness to provide the information or take timely actions. Numerous papers have shown that such a mismatch among supervisory control, information access, and legal authority to intervene could cause significant problems during a financial crisis. If the branch is systemically important to the host country, while it only accounts for a small share of business in the consolidated bank, the home country will have low incentives to support the branch if there are financial difficulties (Cardenas et al., 2003; Ekholm, 2010; Goldberg et al., 2005; Krimminger, 2008). In this case, the host regulator is faced with a quite difficult dilemma: it lacks access to the key information about both the local branch and the consolidated bank, the supervisory authority to the institution in its own border, while it still has to bear the insolvency risk of the foreign branch and the potential impact to the whole economy, as shown by Krimminger (2008).

As for the deposit insurance scheme, when the bank is operated as a foreign branch in the host country, it is also the responsibility of the home bank to take on the deposit insurance. In this case, when a large number of foreign branches from different countries coexist in the host country, the different deposit schemes may cause some confusion. Goldberg et al. (2005) has pointed out that normally the home country authorities would have incentives to charge higher deposit insurance premia to be able to cover the potential losses if the branch fails. Even so, when there's an insolvency situation, some countries follow a "separate-entity" doctrine, which means they will put their domestic depositors and creditors before those of other countries, such as Australia and the United States. The other insolvency procedure followed by some countries is called "single-entity" doctrine, which considers the foreign depositors and creditors equal to domestic ones (Cardenas et al., 2003).

ASSET TRANSFERS

In this section we present our findings on the transfer of assets within cross-border banking groups in the EU. While, the intra-group transfer of assets is a common financial transaction between banking group members, we show that it may become sensitive in crisis situations.

During the crisis management, techniques used by multinational banks may take different legal forms such as transfer of capital and collateral, interbank lending, guarantees, and liquidity backup facilities (European Commission, 2008). The aim of using these instruments is to provide financial support from one legal entity to another within the group. There are, however, some limits on how far the support can be granted. According to the European Commission (2008) the transfer of assets is possible as long as all institutions meet the respective prudential requirements. In other words, the asset transfer should not create any risk in the host or home country. On the other hand, there are no explicit regulations showing when the asset transfer may create a risk in the host or home country. Consequently, during the crisis assets were transferred from healthy subsidiaries in host countries to parent banks in financial difficulties. Hence, the results of this study reveal that the intra-group transfer of assets may have created a substantial risk for the host country financial system.

In some member states also particular types of transfers are prohibited or restricted. In Estonia, for example, a general loan restriction is embodied in the commercial code (European Commission, 2008). A subsidiary may grant a loan to its parent provided that this does not harm the financial status of the entity or the interests of the creditor. Also, in other countries, regulations exist or have been introduced that should allow greater control of intra-group asset transfers. In Poland, for example, in 2009 the supervisory authority obligated foreign banks to reports daily on new exposures to foreign entities and warned against any transactions which might have consisted in ungrounded transfers of funds to parent entities.

This step shows that the supervisory authorities are aware of the possible assets transfers form subsidiaries to parent banks using the existing regulatory framework. Our study, however, shows that despite the efforts of the authorities significant transactions between the subsidiaries and their parent banks took place during the crisis, which might have created a risk for financial system stability.

Subsidiaries Conversion to Bank Branches

In the EU the Second Directive allows the conversion of foreign banks' subsidiaries to branches in host countries at any time. The main idea behind this regulation was to allow banks incorporated in one of the member states to conduct further activities using only branches across the unified single market.

The conversion of subsidiaries to branches is implemented in the form of a cross-border merger, and needs to be approved by both the host and home financial regulators. The need for approval by both agencies is related to the transfer of supervision over the bank assets and liabilities from host to home country regulators. Moreover, after the conversion the home country's deposit insurance applies instead of the host country's.

It creates a large regulatory problem, which was described in detail by Dermine (2006).

In the past, foreign banks preferred the structure of subsidiaries to branches in the NMS (Goldberg et al., 2005). According to Kahn and Winton (2004) a parent bank uses the subsidiary structure to protect itself if the host country is considered riskier than the home country. Moreover, Cerutti et al. (2007) found that host countries' economic and political risk matters in the decision to establish a branch or subsidiaries. They found that branches are less common in countries with highly risky macroeconomic environments. Hence, the decision of multinational banks to operate in NMS using subsidiaries was not surprising.

Some multinational banks with banking licenses in one of the OMS also decided to operate branches in riskier NMS. The reason was that those foreign banks' branches were able to provide more loans than subsidiary banks as their loan limits were calculated using the parent banks' capital. Those new branches in the NMS, however, often only supplemented the activities of the subsidiaries. As a result branch operations were quite small in comparison to the subsidiary activities in the NMS.

At the same time multinational banks often owned subsidiaries in the NMS, which then operated in the region using branches. Unicredit, for example, has operated a fully owned subsidiary in Latvia since 2007. It uses branches for its activities in Estonia and Lithuania. This structure allows the parent banks to protect their interest and reduce as well the capital funding needed to provide lending in the region. Similar bank structures for cross-border activity in the CEE countries have been adapted by other multinational banks as SEB, Citigroup, and Société Général.

During the crisis, however, the multinational banks decided to convert subsidiaries to branches in host countries which were economically and politically riskier than the home country. In some of the cases the converted subsidiaries were merged not directly with the parent bank but with other subsidiaries in third countries, which had a more relaxed approach to their supervision. Moreover, this structure created a buffer, which protected the parent bank from any fallout coming from the branches. While, in the past the conversion of the subsidiaries to branches was found to create a risk for the parent bank it may have the opposite effect during a crisis.

As shown in Table 6 the converted subsidiaries were on average more profitable than their parent banks prior to the year of the conversion. Moreover, in most cases the subsidiaries' loan to deposits ratio was significantly lower than one. Hence, we may assume that the conversion improved

Table 6. Conversion from Subsidiaries into Branches in the EU During the Crisis in the Years 2007–2009 (in mln Euro).

	Parent Bank			Subsidiary Converted to Branch						As % of Parent Bank	
	Name	Gross profit	Home country	Host country	Gross profit	Loans	Deposits	Equity	Assets	Equity	Assets
2010	UniCredit Bank AG	1,957	Germany (Italy)	Austria	214	182.6	22,723.5	5,918.1	50,389.8	27.8%	17%
2010	Société Générale	512	Czech Republic (France)	Slovakia	−12.8	180.7	196.8	32	249.3	1.2%	0.9%
2009	AXA	−6.2	Belgium (France)	Hungary	8.4	936.7	1,035.3	32.7	1,090.0	4.0%	4.7%
2009	Citigroup	546.3	Ireland (USA)	Hungary	73.0	672.3	1,409.9	275.0	2,858.8	11.0%	22.2%
2009	Citigroup	546.3	Ireland (USA)	Slovakia	18.4	475.3	1,161.8	114.9	1,404.1	4.6%	10.9%
2009	Citigroup	546.3	Ireland (USA)	Romania	3.4	447.3	689.6	124.1	1,070.5	4.9%	8.3%
2008	Citigroup	374.9	Ireland (USA)	Czech	43.3	1,370.8	3,477.9	320.4	4,906.0	9.1%	71.8%
2008	Danske Bank	2,584.2	Denmark	Estonia	42.1	1,876.5	1,047.5	172.1	2,350.8	1.2%	0.5%

Note: In the first column the year of the conversion is provided, while the financial data for the parent bank and subsidiary is for the year prior to conversion. In the parentheses the home country of the ultimate owner of the parent bank is presented.
Sources: Companies annual statements and Bankscope.

the liquidity position of the parent bank. Therefore, the conversion of subsidiaries to branches may be seen as a substantial asset transfer from host to home country. It is important, as all the parent banks in our sample reported either declining earnings or losses in the year of the conversion. This means that most likely what was happening was that financially distressed parent banks were absorbing healthy subsidiaries.

As a result, the situation of the parent bank may have been improved after the conversion, but it created a risk of financial instability in the host country. The risk may have been substantial because financial intermediaries such as Citigroup requested government help at the same time when they converted their subsidiaries to branches. Moreover, the share of the converted subsidiaries in the host countries was often substantial. The subsidiary of the Danske Bank before conversion represented more than 11% of the total banking assets in Estonia. Citigroup's subsidiaries share in total assets ranged from 1.3% in Romania to 3.5% in the Czech Republic prior to its conversion.

A failure of a converted branch due to the parent bank's losses could have resulted in the instability of the host banking system. Therefore, the conversions of subsidiaries to branches by Nordea and Danske Bank, two pan-Nordic financial groups whose Finnish subsidiaries were among the largest banks in the country, have raised concerns by the authorities (IMF, 2010). As a consequence the conversion of a subsidiary to a branch was put on hold as the host authority argued that it would significantly limit its supervisory effectiveness and power in Finland, including in a crisis situation.

The decision of the Finnish authority may indicate that the conversion of subsidiaries to branches should be limited or forbidden during financial crises or financial system instability. An argument for limiting the conversion of branches is that a healthy subsidiary may be absorbed by a failing bank, which may lead to instability in the host country.

On the other hand, the conversion to branches may also create a risk for home regulators. In the short term a subsidiary conversion may improve parent banks' liquidity. Should the parent bank fail despite the conversion then the cost related to it including the deposit insurance will be covered by the home regulators. Those liquidation costs might be substantial when the multinational bank develops an extensive network of branches across European countries. Consequently, the conversion does not create a risk only to the host country but as well to the home country regulator.

Intra-Group Deposits and Loans

Multinational banks use intra-group transactions to finance their subsidiaries and other operations across various countries. De Haas and Van Lelyveld (2010) have shown that multinational banks employ their internal capital market to allocate scarce capital to their subsidiaries. They found that foreign subsidiaries of stronger parent banks grow faster and that parent banks trade off lending across countries. Hence, the results suggested that the parent bank allocated the capital to subsidiaries in host countries with the greatest growth potential. The results are were in line with an earlier finding that bank lending tends to be influenced by the home country business cycle (Martinez Peria, Powell, & Hollar, 2002; Morgan & Strahan, 2004).

De Haas and Van Lelyveld (2010) found that as a result of parental support subsidiaries do not typically rein in their lending during a financial crisis in the host country, while domestic banks were often forced to do so. Consequently, the results of their study confirmed that multinational banks may dampen host country financial shocks (De Haas & Van Lelyveld, 2006; Peek & Rosengren, 2000b). However, earlier studies also showed that lending by multinational banks tends to transmit home country financial shocks (Peek & Rosengren, 1997, 2000a; Van Rijckeghem & Weder, 2000, 2001). Nevertheless, none of the studies have shown that either host or home country financial shocks may result in financial instability in one of the countries.

A limitation of all these empirical studies is that they were not able to track the actual transactions within ICMs. Hence, they were not able to fully ascertain that the bank-observed patterns are caused by equity flows between parent banks and their subsidiaries. Moreover, most of the studies assumed that those capital flows take either the form of equity, quasi-equity (subordinated loans), or intra-group loans.

We may assume that equity and subordinated loans to subsidiaries cannot be easily withdrawn by the parent bank during a financial crisis. In contrast, intra-group loans to subsidiaries can be significantly reduced or even cancelled during a period of financial distress. Hence, in the literature it is often assumed that any reduction in foreign bank liquidity would be the result of reduced access to loans from the parent bank during the crisis, who suffered themselves from a lack of liquidity in the financial markets.

An explanation for this is that multinational banks have a tendency to centralize the funding of cross-board subsidiaries. Cardens et al. (2003)

showed that multinational banks after acquiring a local bank usually close its foreign funding window to eliminate duplicity of operations. As a result they make the foreign-owned subsidiary dependent on the willingness of its parent bank to provide foreign funding, which might turn out to be crucial during a period of financial distress. Furthermore, according to the authors subsidiaries are competing for funds among themselves as the parent company has the sole power to direct its resources anywhere.

Consequently, the tightness in liquidity and sharp revision of conditions has increased the likelihood of a sudden stop or reversal in foreign-based lending to some emerging markets countries (Maechler & Ong, 2009). In the past, in many emerging markets, the subsidiaries of multinational banks have been one of the major sources of finance for the catching-up process of these economies. Hence, it is not surprising that the bank lending ties have been identified as one of the main channels of transmission of the latest crisis from advanced economies to emerging markets (IMF, 2009). Indeed, recently Popov and Udell (2010) confirmed that the contraction of parent bank's balance sheet caused by losses on financial assets and deterioration of their equity position was transmitted through their subsidiaries to CEE countries. In contrast, Navaretti et al. (2010) reported that multinational banks have a stabilizing role across countries during the period of the recent financial distress.

One of the explanations for the different results is that the multinational banks behaved differently across countries during the crisis. A good example are the Baltic States, where the banking sector relies on Swedish banks. In the Baltic States three Swedish banks were active: SEB, Swedbank, and Nordea. Nordea's operations were mainly done through branches, and its presence was relatively small in the region. In contrast, in 2009 Swedbank accounted for almost 45% of total lending in Estonia, while SEB accounted for 30% of lending in Lithuania. Jointly the Swedbank and SEB market shares represented 67% total lending in Estonia, 40% in Latvia, and 51% in Lithuania (European Commission, 2009). The exposure of Swedish banks in the Baltic countries had significant benefits for them, in particular in terms of new revenue streams due to a credit boom in the region. Nevertheless, when the global crisis emerged, the credit losses started to increase dramatically as the Baltic States entered a serve recession in late 2008.

The uncertainty regarding potential losses of the Baltic subsidiaries and the economic situation in the region resulted in funding problems for the Swedish parent banks. As a consequence, their exposures to the region quickly become an issue for systemic stability in Sweden, where these banks were also dominating the banking sector. This situation prompted the Swedish authorities to introduce measures to support their national banking system and alleviate funding pressures on the effected multinational banks (CGFS, 2010).

Nevertheless, the lending of the Swedish Banks to the subsidiaries in the Baltic States still declined between the years 2008–2009. The lending pattern of Swedbank to its subsidiary in Latvia, which controls the banks in Estonia and Lithuania, is illustrated in Table 6. As can be seen, the lending of the parent bank to its Baltic subsidiary dropped by almost 20% in 2009, while the net exposures of the parent bank to its subsidiaries were down 30%.

While the Swedish exposure to the Baltic region created difficulties for both the home and host countries, it probably prevented greater reductions in the funding channel between the parent banks and their subsidiaries in the region. However, as the Table 1 shows, this was not the case in all the countries of the CEE region. In most of the countries, where the exposure of the multinational banks was relatively small compared to the parent banks' overall assets, the multinational banks dramatically reduced their lending and exposure.

As a result the situation in most of the CEE countries resembled the "nightmare scenario" described by Herring (2007). According to this scenario, multinational banks with a large share of the host market become systemically important, while at the same time, being so small relative to the parent group that it is not regarded as significant to the condition of the parent company. As a consequence, the home country regulator does not see a case for intervention as it is naturally concerned only with the stability of its' own financial system and not in countries were the multinational bank operates a subsidiary. The situation also explains why in most of the countries regulators introduced stability programs as they were forced to substitute for multinational banks.

However, those stability programs did not only stabilize the subsidiaries but also may have provided additional funding for the parent banks. Most of the existing studies on parent bank funding of subsidiaries have assumed the capital flow is either in the form of equity or more likely loans. The crisis, however, has revealed that the intra-group deposits may be an important channel of cross-border asset transfers from foreign subsidiaries to parent bank.

Deposits and loans from the subsidiaries to its parent bank have the same function and provide liquidity, yet how they are regulated can differ substantially. In the EU the Directive relating to the taking up and pursuit of the business of credit institution provides limits on the exposure of the parent bank and/or subsidiaries to each other.[7] According to Article 111 Point 2 a credit institution or/and its subsidiaries may not incur an exposure to the parent undertaking and/or one or more its subsidiaries which exceeds the value of 20% of its capital. The exposure of the credit institution consists of any assets or off-balance sheet item listed in the Directive in Section 3 subsection 1. The subsection lists in Article 79 the exposure classes, which are used to calculate the minimum capital required for credit risk in CIs. However, the Article 113 grants the member states a right to fully or partially exempt from the existing limits exposures incurred by the credit institution to its parent undertaking, to other subsidiaries of that parent undertaking or to its own subsidiaries, in so far as those undertakings are covered by the supervision on a consolidated basis to which the credit institution itself is subject. Moreover, this article also grants the member states a right to fully or partially exempt asset items constituting claims on and other exposures to institutions, with a maturity of one year or less, but not constituting such institutions' own funds.

Most member states implemented those two exceptions into their national banking laws as they assumed that they do not present a serious threat. It was assumed that the supervision on a consolidated basis would prevent any exposure, which would be deemed to be risky. The second exemption affected mainly bank transactions related to the interbank markets. In this case it was assumed that loans granted on the interbank markets would nevertheless fall under further external or internal regulation on credit quality and concentration. On the other hand, bank deposits to institutions were not covered by any other regulations.

We assume that the implementation of these exceptions might have created a loophole in the national banking laws, which allowed parent banks and its subsidiaries to transfer assets without any significant restrictions. A confirmation could be the fact that in 2009 the Polish Financial Supervisory Authority decided to change the law and remove the exception for banks of claims on and other exposures to institutions, with a maturity of one year or less. It did it however gradually and so in 2009 only 50% of claims and other exposure were exempted, while by the end of 2010 no more exemptions in this regard were present anymore.

Nevertheless, we still assume that the risk inside the multinational bank may be substantial, what is the result of existing interconnections between the parent bank and its subsidiaries. An example of existing interconnections in a foreign bank subsidiary is shown in Fig. 4. In this example, we use the subsidiary of UniCredit Bank in Czech Republic, which was one of

UniCredit S.p.A
Italy, *listed*

Assets		Liabilities	
Receivables	221,287	Deposits	144,445
of which CZ	2		
Total	293,526	Total	173,052

Pioneer Asset Management
Czech Republic, Pioneer Global Asset Management SPA (100%)

Assets		Liabilities	
Receivables	na	Deposits	na
of which CZ	13		
Total	na	Total	na

UniCredit Bank Austria AG
Austria, *UniCredit S.p.A. (99.995%)*

Assets		Liabilities	
Receivables	10,664	Deposits	2,937
of which CZ	200	of which CZ	303
Equity	35	Other	
Other		Of which CZ	8
Total	10,872	Total	10,345

UniCredit CAIB AG[a]
Austria, *UniCredit Bank AG (100%)*

Assets		Liabilities	
Receivables	na	Deposits	na
of which CZ	9	of which CZ	286
Total	na	Total	na

UniCredit Bank AG
Germany, *UniCredit S.p.A. (100%)*

Assets		Liabilities	
Receivables	23,378	Deposits	11,587
of which CZ	15	of which CZ	13
Total	26,142	Total	15,142

UniCredit Bank
Czech Republic, *UniCredit Bank Austria AG (100%)*

Assets		Liabilities	
Receivables	809	Deposits	281
Equity	32		
Total	843	Total	281

UniCredit Jezalogbank Zrt[b]
Hungary, *UniCredit Bank Hungary (100%)*

Assets		Liabilities	
Receivables	205	Deposits	251
		of which CZ	24
Total	205	Total	251

UniCredit Bank Serbia Jsc
Serbia, *UniCredit Bank Austria AG (100%)*

Assets		Liabilities	
Receivables	3	Deposits	769
		of which CZ	8
Total	3	Total	771

Fig. 4. Related Parties Transaction of UniCredit Bank Czech Republic as on 31 December 2009 (in mln euro). Receivables or Deposits of UniCredit Czech Republic (CZ) Indicate Transaction with the UniCredit Bank Czech Republic. The Subsidiary Also Conducted Transactions with UniCredit Leasing GmbH and Unicredit Business Partner s.r.o, which are Not Shown Here for Brevity. The Direct Owner of the Subsidiary and His Share in Equity is Presented in Italic. *Note:* [a]In 2010 CAIB AG was merged with UniCredit Bank AG. [b]Data for UniCredit Jezalogbank Zrt (mortgage banks) as on 31 December 2008.

the few banks in our sample that disclosed in its financial statements detailed information who were their counter parts within the multinational banking holding company.

UniCredit Bank in Czech Republic is a subsidiary of UniCredit Bank Austria in Austria, which in turn is the subsidiary of the parent bank UniCredit in Italy. The Italian parent bank owns through UniCredit Bank Austria more than 20 subsidiaries in CEE countries, yet the Czech entity has links only to few banks within the bank holding company. In addition two banks, namely UniCredit Bank Austria and its subsidiary UniCredit CA IB, constitute together over 50% of all the subsidiaries claims. Those claims might signal an incomplete internal bank market structure, whereas Allen and Gale (2000) suggested that those structures are more fragile. Moreover, the subsidiaries significant exposure to only two banks shows that the risk of contagion inside bank holding companies can be much larger than in interbank markets.

Figure 4 shows the Czech subsidiary deposited funds or provided loans to the parent bank and other subsidiaries equal to 809 million euro. The Czech subsidiary as well many other banks in our sample do not report whether its assets are deposits or loans to other entities within the banking group. Therefore, we decided to present only the aggregate amount of claims of the subsidiaries to the parent bank group in Table 7. In this table the first three columns present the loans and advances of the subsidiary to the parent bank group for the years 2007–2009. We excluded here equity investments, which amounted to 32 million euro. Consequently, the reported exposures to the group might be biased downward in Table 7. Nevertheless, we found that the equity investments represented only a small proportion of subsidiaries assets in our sample.

The next three columns in the Table 7 present the amount of deposits and loans, which the subsidiaries received from the parent bank and other subsidiaries in the years 2007–2009. Again we decided to aggregate received deposits and loans as often the financial statements did not provide enough detailed information on the character of the liabilities of the subsidiary to related third-party. In case of the Czech subsidiary such an information was available. Based on it we know that the subsidiary received only deposits, which amounted to 281 million euro at the end of 2009.

Using the subsidiaries assets presented in the first column and liabilities showed in the next columns of the subsidiary we calculated its net position to the group. The difference between subsidiaries assets and liabilities for each year is presented in the following three columns. Table 7 shows

Table 7. Subsidiaries Transactions with the Parent Bank Group (in mln Euro).

	Loans and Advance			Deposits and Loans			Net Position			To Equity		
	2007	2008	2009	2007	2008	2009	2007	2008	2009	2007	2008	2009
Swedbank (Sweden)												
Estonia (Baltic)	371	497	1,314	10,161	10,520	8,541	−9,790	−10,024	−7,227	−5.20	−4.43	−4.04
SEB (Sweden)												
Estonia	330	37	8	2,386	2,028	2,412	−2,055	−1,991	−2,404	−3.98	−3.53	−5.04
Latvia	186	106	308	2,288	2,352	2,223	−2,102	−2,247	−1,915	−5.83	−5.75	−6.17
Lithuania	181	192	884	3,610	4,376	3,865	−3,428	−4,184	−2,980	−5.89	−6.44	−6.75
ING (Netherlands)												
Poland	1,493	2,252	143	126	1,464	831	1,367	788	−689	0.10	0.04	−0.05
Unicredit (Italy)												
Poland	420	311	627	160	1	2	260	310	625	0.01	0.01	0.02
Czech Republic	801	921	809	669	817	285	131	104	524	0.16	0.11	0.53
Bulgaria	433	753	1,005	435	1,469	1,516	−2	−715	−511	0.00	−1.02	−0.61
Citigroup (USA)												
Poland	896	408	285	633	1,001	401	264	−593	−116	0.03	−0.05	−0.01
Ireland	5,819	7,909	6,952	1,958	2,354	310	3,861	5,555	6,642	2.70	2.22	1.88
Deutsche Bank (Germany)												
Poland	1,009	257	158	319	62	28	690	196	130	0.41	0.11	0.13
Erste Bank Group (Austria)												
Slovakia	90	14	961	444	1,815	318	−354	−1,802	643	−0.48	−2.25	0.82
Czech Republic	165	1,068	755	431	409	314	−257	599	441	−0.12	0.24	0.18
Raiffeisen (Austria)												
Czech Republic	76	116	40	230	829	675	−150	−720	−635	−0.54	−1.62	−1.26
Slovakia	61	99	166	9	443	34	52	−343	132	0.09	−0.49	0.16
Hungary		30	213		950	952		−920	−739		−1.48	−1.43
Bulgaria	423	574	294	164	79	25	259	494	269	0.90	1.11	0.57

Table 7. (*Continued*)

	Loans and Advance			Deposits and Loans			Net Position			To Equity		
	2007	2008	2009	2007	2008	2009	2007	2008	2009	2007	2008	2009
GE Capital (USA)												
Czech Republic	42	20	339	207	209	26	−163	−190	314	−0.21	−0.21	0.24
Poland		0	0		2	2		−2	−2		0.00	0.00
Volksbank (Austria)												
Czech Republic	2	11	3	62	47	34	−60	−37	−31	−0.38	−0.18	−0.15
Slovakia	15	15	4	2	44	86	13	−29	−82	0.10	−0.21	−0.64
OPT Hungary												
Slovakia	5	50	62	34	156	0	−29	−106	62	−0.28	−0.92	0.68

Note: When third-party transactions with parent banks were not listed in the annual statements, we used instead the transaction with the parent group.
Sources: Companies annual statements and Bankscope.

that the net position of the Czech subsidiary to the group amounted to 131 million euro in 2007 and then increased to 524 million euro in 2009. It means that during the crisis the Czech subsidiaries net claims to the parent bank group members increased by almost 400 million euro over the period 2007–2009. Finally, we decided to present the net position in relation to subsidiaries equity, what shows the last three columns. In 2007 the Czech subsidiary net position was equal to 17% of its capital and then it increased to 53% of its equity in 2009.

As a result the risk steaming from the exposure to the parent group has increased in the Czech subsidiaries during the risk. Indeed, we assume the risk might be much larger than that shown in Table 7 as the market structure of the claims is incomplete. A good example are lending and borrowing relation between the Czech subsidiary and UniCredit CAIB, which is the investment bank in the UniCredit group. At the end of 2009 the Czech subsidiaries claims to UniCredit CAIB amounted to 55% of its equity, while the deposits of the UniCredit CAIB in the subsidiary were only equal to 2% of its equity. If UniCredit CAIB would fail over one quarter of the Czechs subsidiaries equity would be wiped out assuming a loss rate of 50% of the assets. This example clearly documents the existing risk of contagion inside the multinational bank holding company. We advocate, therefore, for more disclosure of the counterparts as currently little information is provided by the subsidiaries about the actual structure of their bilateral exposure.

The data in Table 7 also provides information on different strategies of the parent groups toward their subsidiaries during the crisis. In Table 7 we documented that the Austrian Erste Bank Group changed its exposure, based on the net position, dramatically toward its subsidiaries in CEE in the period 2007–2009. Prior to the crisis the Erste Bank Group was financing the subsidiaries in our sample. In the year 2009 the situation changed and data shows that the subsidiaries in CEE were financing the parent group. Other banking groups as Swedbank or SEB, for example, reduced significantly their financing in the year 2009. Consequently, the data shows the most of the banking groups limited their financing or even have transferred assets out of CEE in the year 2009.

Most of the subsidiaries in our sample did not disclose whether the asset transfer to the parent group was a deposit or a loan. However, on the few banks that disclosed such information in their financial statements, we were able to establish that most of those transactions were deposits, whereas its terms were not reported.

Using deposits as a way of accessing funding has not been explored in the academic literature as it came to light in the banking industry over the course of the financial crisis. As a result, even new regulations often do not cover deposits. For example, in Ireland a new code that addresses the issues concerning related party lending applies to all loans, quasi-loans, and credit transactions (including guarantees) between the parent bank and subsidiaries. Hence, those transactions need to be disclosed, while the level of disclosure relating to deposits is seriously lacking in certain instances. At the same time the scale and complexity of certain deposit arrangements between banks and their subsidiaries is large and may create a serious problem to the stability of many countries.

On the other hand, countries such as Poland as already mentioned have already introduced new regulations, which gradually remove the exemption provided by the national law and the directive. The data, however, suggest that only a few countries have decided to deal with this problem.

A good example illustrating this problem is the Irish subsidiary of Citibank called Citibank Europe. During the crisis the Irish holding bank converted four subsidiaries to branches in four different CEE countries. All those subsidiaries had high liquidity, which was reflected in a relatively low loan to deposit ratios. Hence, it is also not surprising that this Irish subsidiary used the newly gained funds in order to deposit it in other subsidiaries of the parent banks in other countries. Consequently, the Irish subsidiary currently has a very high exposure to the other operations of Citibank, which equaled on average 200% of equity in the years 2007–2009. The exposure of the Irish subsidiary may be much higher than presented in Table 7, when we take into account that not all the operation can be netted.

If the deposits were allocated to a Citibank operation that failed it would very likely trigger the failure of the Irish operation. The failure of this would mean a default of five banks (branches) in five different EU countries. Hence, the uncontrolled use of deposits to finance parent banks underlying operations creates a serious problem not only to the stability of the host financial system but as well as to the whole EU financial system.

It is also very unlikely that the Irish government would decide to bail out this Citibank operation as it includes mainly deposits and loans of the host countries. As a result it might not create directly a danger to the Irish financial system. Moreover, it might also be difficult to explain to the Irish voters why the government should try to safe deposits of CEE savers, when it cuts its social expenditures at the same time. On the other hand not saving this institution might as well be risky for the Irish financial system as we do not know all the counterparts of the Citigroup operations today. Hence, it may be that through a domino effect the other Irish Citibank subsidiary (with the deposits of the Irish savers) would be affected as well as a consequence of failure of Citibank Europe. Therefore, in our opinion, the regulators should not only monitor and collect information on the third-party transactions in their home country but should also be able to access to information from other host countries were the multinational banks operate.

Off-Balance Sheet Transactions

An area that also lacks sufficient regulation guaranteeing extensive disclosure is derivatives transactions between the parent banks and subsidiaries. The disclosure of those transactions may be important as often they are only partially regulated by the existing law, which also turned out to be a major problem during the recent crisis. Moreover, often the transactions undertaken by the subsidiaries' management do not need the approval of the supervisory board as they are classified as usual business transactions. Hence, parent banks may easily force subsidiaries' management to engage in those types of transaction in order to transfer capital from the host country. Those transfers can take the form of provisions or subsidiaries' losses and are very difficult to trace.

Analyzing the financial statements of the subsidiaries across countries shows a significant increase in the volume of off-balance transactions between the parent bank and its subsidiaries during the crisis, as shown in Table 8. It is necessary, however, to be very careful in the interpretation of the financial data on related party off-balance transactions as most of the banks used different methods to present their exposure, which additionally varied across the time.

Currently, European accounting standards only require entities to determine and report in annual statements their overall off-balance sheet exposure and disclose fair value estimates. At the same time the existing accounting standards do not provide any information on how and to what extent the transactions between the subsidiary and parent bank should be disclosed. As a result the way they are presented varies a great deal and makes their assessment a very difficult task for outsiders. On the other hand given recent experience they may constitute a serious risk to the stability of banks as well as the financial system.

Table 8. Subsidiaries Off-Balance Sheet Transactions with the Parent Bank Group (in mln Euro).

	Contingent Assets and Commitments			Contingent Liabilities and Commitments			Net Position			to Equity		
	2007	2008	2009	2007	2008	2009	2007	2008	2009	2007	2008	2009
SEB (Sweden)												
Estonia	140	42	0	118	0	0	21	42	0	0.02	0.03	0.00
Latvia	0	6	2	0	21	20	0	−15	−18	0.00	−0.04	−0.06
Lithuania	2	2	1	31	18	1	−29	−16	0	−0.05	−0.02	0.00
Unicredit Italiano (Italy)												
Poland	6	1	0	5	0	0	1	1	0	0.00	0.00	0.00
Bulgaria		80	53		0	0		−80	−53		−0.11	−0.06
Commerzbank (Germany)												
Poland	14	165	181	28	159	40	−14	7	141	−0.02	0.01	0.16
AIB (Ireland)												
Poland	132	47	2	132	7	9	0	40	−7	0.00	0.03	−0.01
Millennium (Portugal)												
Poland				124	89	37	−124	−89	−37	−0.23	−0.13	−0.06
Citibank												
Poland		82	52		65	4		17	48	0.00	0.01	0.03
KBC (Belgium)												
Poland	1	14	241	325	452	271	−325	−438	−30	−0.55	−0.60	−0.05
Hungary	58	6	12	57	53	39	−1	47	27	0.00	0.06	0.04
Czech Republic	16	38	29	3	3	2	−13	−35	−27	−1.07	−0.02	−0.01
Deutsche Bank (Germany)												
Poland	35	69	77	24	7	3	11	62	74	0.06	0.36	0.49
Raiffeisen Bank (Austria)												
Slovakia	15	36	20	23	26	36	8	−11	16	0.02	−0.02	0.02
Czech Republic	214	61	25	1	2	28	−213	−59	3	−0.81	−0.13	0.01

Hungary	0	15	36	0	0	0	0	−15	−36	0.00	−0.02	−0.07
Volksbank (Austria)												
Slovakia	13	15	10				13	15	10	−0.12	−0.10	0.01
Czech Republic	291	127	64	1	0	0	−290	−127	−64	−0.22	−0.07	−0.04
Dexia (Belgium)												
Slovakia	45	10	10	0	0	200	−45	−10	190	−0.50	−0.11	1.50
Erste Bank Group (Austria)												
Czech Republic	0	47	0	1	0	0	1	−47	0	0.00	−0.02	0.00
Romania					436	530		436	530		0.27	0.31
Société Générale (France)												
Bulgaria	85	282	48	44	149	133	−41	−133	85	−0.35	−0.94	0.48
Romania	40	49	96	0	0	0	−40	−49	−96	−0.04	−0.04	−0.07
Eurobank EFG Group (Greece)												
Bulgaria		0	1		0	2		0	1		0.00	0.00
Intensa SanPaolo (Italy)												
Hungary	0	0	0	0	0	0	0	0	0	0.00	0.00	0.00
Bayerische Landesbank (Germany)												
Hungary	4	8	8	0	0	0	−4	−8	−8	0.00	−0.01	−0.01
OTP Bank (Hungary)												
Bulgaria	27	27		3	6		−24	−22		−0.05	−0.03	

Sources: Companies annual statements and Bankscope.

One of the propositions to the European Commission was that in the future the loan guarantees of the parent bank to its subsidiaries and vice-versa should also be supervised and disclosed (DBB Law, 2010). Including guarantees in the assessment process is important as they present an obligation. The data in Table 8 shows that during the crisis the guarantees granted to the parent banks has increased significantly. In Poland, for example, the Deutsche Bank subsidiary had contingent assets and liabilities outstanding that increased considerably over the years 2007–2009 and were equal to 50% of equity in 2009. On the other hand, we may assume that most of the contingent assets are covered under the existing banking regulation as they constitute liabilities and are taken into account in the calculation of the capital adequacy of the bank.

Nevertheless, while subsidiaries disclosed to some extent the fair value of their contingent assets and liabilities related to parent bank transactions they seldom reported the valuation of the off-balance derivative instruments. In fact, those instruments seem to have a much higher value than the guarantees issued by the subsidiaries to the parent bank, or vice-versa. The Polish subsidiary of Citibank, for example, reported in 2009 that the balance sheet value in respect of the off-balance sheet derivative instruments amounted to 50.051 billion euro in 2008 and 23.129 billion euro in 2009, or 4.26 and 2.75 times the total asset value of the bank, respectively. Yet, the net balance sheet value of financial derivatives transaction was −2.75 and −1.27 billion euro at the end of the year 2008 and 2009, correspondingly.

According to Citibank's subsidiary's annual report these derivative transactions were opposite to derivatives transactions with the other parent bank entities to close current FX position of the Citigroup and its clients. Again the annual report of the Citibank's subsidiary shows, however, that the FX positions constitute only 10% of the value of all the off-balance sheet liabilities in respect of derivative instruments. The remaining 90% represents mainly interest rate instruments, whereas interest rate swaps make up between 60%–70% of all the derivative instruments in the period 2008–2009. Thus, the large exposure of the subsidiary does not seem to be justified either by the scale of its operation in Poland or by the information provided in the annual statement.

Therefore, in our opinion, due to their large volume the off-balance sheet transactions between the parent bank and its subsidiaries may present a serious threat to the stability of the institution. Consequently, these transactions and instruments need to be disclosed in more detail. More important, however, a unified way of reporting them should be used, that would allow a comparison of the changes in exposure over the time and across institutions.

Other Financial Instruments

Our analysis of the annual reports revealed that the parent banks might also transfer other financial instruments to the subsidiaries and vice-versa. Nevertheless, we found the value of the trading position between parent banks and its subsidiaries to be relatively small in comparison to the intra-group deposits and loans. On the other hand, we encountered problems in identifying the trading positions between the parent banks and subsidiaries as again the disclosure of these transactions in the annual reports was very limited. We advocate, therefore, that also the existing trading positions should be presented in more detail as they might also be used to transfer assets between a bank's entities.

INCOME TRANSFERS

In the previous section we have documented different methods used by parent banks to transfer assets from or to their subsidiaries during a crisis. We have shown that some of these transactions may create a risk for the stability of the financial system as the amount, which is transferred to the parent, can represent a significant proportion of subsidiaries' equity.

In this section we show how asset transfers determine the income and costs of the subsidiaries. Furthermore, we present evidences that those transactions might influence the profitability of the subsidiaries. However, in our opinion, income transfer does not present such a serious threat to the financial stability of the subsidiary as the volume of transactions was relatively small in comparison to asset transfers.

Dividends

Dividend payments are the most important form of income flow from foreign subsidiaries to their parent companies so far. In nonfinancial companies the dividend payments account for approximately 50% of all remittances to US companies (Kim et al., 2005). It is therefore not surprising that dividend payments are often presented as the main way that the subsidiaries can support their parent banks during a crisis. In contrast to the majority of parent banks, the foreign subsidiaries, especially in emerging markets, were still very profitable in the years 2007–2008.

Table 9 shows the net incomes of parent banks and their foreign subsidiaries over the period 2007–2009. As can be seen most of the parent banks reported losses in the year 2008, which resulted in decisions to pay lower dividends in the same year. Moreover, many of the parent banks reported losses on subsidiaries in developed countries in the year 2008. Unicredit, for example, reported losses on its operation in Germany. Those losses have been offset by the profits of its Austrian bank holding company, which includes all the subsidiaries in the CEE countries without Poland. Consequently, overall Unicredit was still profitable in the year 2008. Nevertheless, its profitability declined quite rapidity as the effects of the crisis became felt in the CEE countries too. As a result the net profit fell more than 30% in the year 2008 and more than 50% in the year 2009.

As dividends are the easiest way to transfer capital from abroad but have a direct effect on subsidiaries' own funding level, most countries have some kinds of restrictions regarding the dividend payments of financial institutions. In Portugal, for example, the supervisory authority can introduce an embargo on the distribution of dividends when the bank fails to achieve minimum liquidity or solvency ratios. Similar regulations are also present in many other countries including the United States (Eisenbeis & Kaufman, 2008). Moreover, in some of the countries such as Poland, for example, the supervisory institution advised all the banks not to pay dividends during the crisis. This advice was not legally binding but was followed by most of the banks. As a matter of fact during the crisis subsidiaries delayed or significantly lowered the payments of the regular dividends despite their profitability and presented a reluctance to pay advanced dividends.

Income and Expenses from Related Parties Transactions

Subsidiaries incurred costs and received income on transactions with the parent bank group during the crisis, which were mainly related to the asset transfers within bank holding company' different entities. The amount of income and expenses of the subsidiaries related to the parent bank transactions are shown in Table 10. The first column shows the income of the foreign subsidiaries in the years 2007–2009, where over 90% of it constitutes the interest income from deposits or loans provided to the parent bank

Table 9. Parent Bank's and its Subsidiaries Dividend Payments (in millions of Euro).

	Equity			Net Income			Dividends		
	2007	2008	2009	2007	2008	2009	2007	2008	2009
Citigroup	*77,167*	*103,487*	*107,576*	*2,457*	*−19,892*	*−1,049*	*7,291*	*4,347*	*25*
Belgium	316	269	263	194	−47	−6			
Ireland	1,427	2,507	3,525	328	472	516			
Poland	1,563	1,365	1,510	230	146	123	173	0	120
United Kingdom	2,470	2,876	3,829	252	−94	−644	0	49	
Unicredit	*62,465*	*58,240*	*62,892*	*6,678*	*4,529*	*2,035*	*3,431*	*0*	*550*
Austria	15,334	14,237	14,388	2,364	1,284	1,153	808	808	0
Germany	23,638	23,024	23,998	5,866	−649	884	402	0	1,633
Poland	4,114	3,891	4,474	603	859	603	702	0	185
Erste Bank Group	*11,403*	*11,095*	*14,943*	*1,550*	*1,039*	*977*	*295*	*309*	*347*
Slovakia	733	802	782	138	142	31	53	65	
Czech Republic	2,150	2,428	2,398	465	586	447	171	576	172
Romania	1,346	1,611	1,561	258	516	205	102	94	192
Malta	140	138	134	13	11	7	12	13	7
ING Bank	*27,195*	*24,121*	*31,217*	*3,701*	*703*	*543*	*1,300*	*4,250*	
Belgium	8,776	9,480	10,554	1,161	905	1,241		348	
Poland	1,071	11,014	1,190	178	108	145	42	0	
KBC	*18,487*	*15,376*	*17,177*	*3,403*	*−2,379*	*−2,547*			
Hungary	815	740	777	144	99	37	115	112	27
Ireland	1,000	937	1,031	137	103	92	117		
Bulgaria	101	107	101	30	4	1			
Poland	635	642	630	109	79	8	39	0	0
Raiffeisen Bank	*8,422*	*7,837*	*10,308*	*1,190*	*432*	*571*			
Poland	477	611	686	94	88	36	42	38	47
Bulgaria	287	452	467	61	70	23		70	23

Table 9. *(Continued)*

	Equity			Net Income			Dividends		
	2007	2008	2009	2007	2008	2009	2007	2008	2009
Romania	434	543	518	88	156	69		11	57
Slovenia	59	62	72	8	3	0			
Slovakia	592	663	808	114	131	95	63		
Hungary	599	599	536	110	56	−14	28	37	44
SEB	*8,126*	*7,703*	*9,722*	*1,445*	*926*	*115*	*432*	*410*	*0*
Lithuania	582	658	440	148	76	−412	0	0	0
Estonia	523	572	477	131	50	−88	0	0	0
Latvia	354	399	311	108	43	−183	0	0	0
Denmark	308	315	304	23	34	23			

Sources: Companies annual statements and Bankscope.

Table 10. Subsidiaries Income and Expenses Related to Parent Bank Group Transactions (in mln Euro).

	Income			Expenses			Net Parent Bank			To Profit/Loss Before Taxes		
	2007	2008	2009	2007	2008	2009	2007	2008	2009	2007	2008	2009
Swedbank (Sweden)												
Estonia	48.8	61.7	5.2	402.9	583.2	314.1	354.1	521.5	308.9	0.661	1.234	(0.312)
SEB (Sweden)												
Estonia	7.4	11.3	10.3	96.1	114.3	68.8	88.7	103.1	58.5	0.680	1.898	(0.641)
Latvia	12.4	14.4	6.2	73.0	91.4	56.3	60.6	77.1	50.1	0.473	1.533	0.232
Lithuania	5.7	14.3	4.3	123.2	190.1	147.3	117.6	175.8	143.0	0.709	2.035	(0.288)
ING Bank (Netherlands)												
Poland	55.0	49.7	−2.5	27.3	17.4	15.3	−27.7	−32.3	17.8	(0.133)	(0.217)	0.091
Unicredit (Italy)												
Poland	3.3	7.5	1.1	3.6	5.8	4.5	0.2	−1.6	3.4	0.000	(0.001)	0.004
Slovakia	1.6	1.1	0.1	23.8	33.3	18.9	22.2	32.2	18.8	0.454	0.362	0.211
Czech Republic	24.6	38.5	20.5	25.8	26.0	6.6	1.1	−12.5	−13.9	0.007	(0.054)	(0.109)
Bulgaria	9.5	5.3	3.9	9.8	36.8	30.5	0.3	31.4	26.6	0.002	0.189	0.236
Romania	6.9	23.5	25.8	83.6	553.1	630.9	76.7	529.6	605.1	0.800	4.519	6.663
Commerzbank (Germany)												
Poland	6.8	10.2	3.4	65.0	145.2	123.3	58.2	135.1	119.9	0.231	0.511	2.166
AIB (Ireland)												
Poland	14.4	−82.6	20.1	10.4	26.0	16.6	−4.0	108.6	−3.5	(0.011)	0.339	(0.011)
Millennium (Portugal)												
Poland	0.0	0.9	14.0	1.2	0.2	13.2	1.2	−0.7	−0.7	0.007	(0.005)	(1.828)
Citgroup (USA)												
Poland	26.0	30.0	12.6	18.2	19.2	6.8	−7.8	−10.9	−5.7	(0.028)	(0.054)	(0.033)
Ireland	498.7	430.9	265.7	108.7	160.9	74.2	(390.0)	(270.0)	(191.4)	(1.040)	(0.491)	(0.318)

Table 10. (*Continued*)

	Income			Expenses			Net Parent Bank			To Profit/Loss Before Taxes		
	2007	2008	2009	2007	2008	2009	2007	2008	2009	2007	2008	2009
KBC (Belgium)												
Poland	3.1	2.0	9.5	27.0	46.9	28.7	66.1	94.0	61.5	0.498	0.845	4.987
Hungary	6.4	7.9	1.9	26.7	48.9	45.0	20.3	41.1	43.1	0.102	0.248	0.712
Czech Republic	5.1	23.7	31.0	90.2	69.4	20.2	85.1	45.7	−10.8	0.170	3.051	(0.014)
Deutsche Bank												
Poland	65.6	22.9	8.6	14.8	24.2	0.6	−50.8	50.5	−8.0	(1.532)	2.004	(0.221)
Erste Bank Group (Austria)												
Slovakia	1.2	4.9	14.5	7.7	27.9	5.8	7.1	27.5	−11.7	0.054	0.183	(0.228)
Czech Republic	61.4	−160.7	153.7	13.3	19.7	12.7	−48.2	180.4	−141.0	(0.086)	0.242	(0.246)
Romania	0.6	240.0	770.4	52.5	136.0	532.8	51.9	−104.0	−237.6	0.165	(0.165)	(0.779)
Intensa SanPaolo (Italy)												
Slovakia		6.7	8.1		19.1	20.7		8.8	9.7		1.415	0.060
Hungary				9.9	42.1	35.1	9.9	42.1	35.1	0.060	0.262	1.028
Raiffeisen Bank (Austria)												
Slovakia	2.0	3.5	5.6	1.5	7.7	2.2	1.4	−0.1	−3.4	0.011	(0.000)	(0.028)
Czech Republic	2.8	3.9	1.9	9.3	12.8	23.9	6.4	8.8	22.1	0.159	0.134	0.230
Hungary		8.2	2.2		59.7	31.7		50.9	27.7			
Bulgaria	11.4	17.0	5.8	10.4	12.8	7.9	−1.0	−4.2	2.0	(0.015)	(0.054)	0.080
Dexia (Belgium)												
Slovakia	6.2	4.4	8.3	11.9	17.8	14.8	5.8	13.4	6.6	0.383	(0.152)	(0.412)
OPT (Hungary)												
Slovakia	34.1	195.3	7.2	67.3	78.0	2.6	33.3	−117.3	−4.5	0.117	(0.322)	0.178
Bulgaria	15.1	2.3	3.0	13.2	22.6	8.1	−2.0	20.3	5.0	(0.018)	0.133	0.051

Volksbank (Austria)												
Slovakia	0.3	0.2	0.1	0.6	1.4	0.8	0.4	1.2	0.7	0.033	0.079	(0.096)
Czech Republic	0.4	0.8	0.2	3.3	3.4	1.9	3.0	2.6	1.7	0.179	0.158	0.160
Romania	0.0	0.0	0.0	46.7	117.4	65.0	46.7	117.4	65.0	7.826	2.992	1.271
Société Générale (France)												
Czech Republic	312.4	606.4	565.8	318.5	682.3	516.5	6.2	75.9	−49.4	0.012	0.117	(0.096)
Bulgaria	0.4	1.7	1.5	3.2	14.8	12.7	2.8	13.2	11.2	0.150	0.646	0.997
Romania	4.4	133.0	3.6	47.0	83.7	46.4	42.5	−49.3	42.7	0.117	(0.102)	0.125
GE Capital (USA)												
Czech Republic	10.9	13.0	26.0	24.6	40.5	30.6	13.7	27.5	4.6	0.123	0.198	0.044
Eurobank EFG (Greece)												
Bulgaria							0.8	15.9	1.9	0.014	0.230	0.061
Romania	−21.7	19.8		69.7	113.5		91.4	93.7		2.294	22.404	
Bayerische Landesbank (Germany)												
Hungary	0.6	0.6	2.6	13.7	88.4	8.3	13.1	87.8	5.8	0.157	2.648	0.267
Piraeus (Greece)												
Bulgaria	2.4	4.2		20.2	47.3		17.8	43.1		0.594	1.303	
National Bank of Greece (Greece)												
Bulgaria	0.0	0.0	0.0	6.3	57.7	45.5	6.3	57.7	45.5	0.060	0.513	0.997

Sources: Companies annual statements and Bankscope.

group. Offsetting this, the next columns show the costs of the subsidiary incurred during related parties' transactions in the years 2007–2009, where interest expenses associated with deposits or loans from parent bank group entities constituted again around 90% of all expenses. The last three columns show the net income position of the subsidiaries to their parent bank groups for each of the years. We calculated the net income position as the difference between the expenses and income of the subsidiary that are related to the transactions with the parent group entities.

As deposit and loan transactions between the parent bank group and its subsidiaries were significant during the crisis, interest revenues and expenses related to them represent a substantial part of the income or losses of the subsidiaries. As an example, the SEB subsidiaries in the Baltic countries transferred income to the parent bank, which was related mainly to the loans received from it. The income transferred to the parent bank was equal to 1.5 and 2 of subsidiaries gross profits in the period 2007–2009. As a result, the expenses related to the loans are significant and reflect also the magnitude of the transactions with the parent bank group, which are shown in Table 7.

In most of the countries the existing regulations limit the possibility to grant loans to a related party on more favorable terms. In contrast, there are no regulations that provide limits on loans to subsidiaries at disadvantageous terms. As the terms of the related party loans were not disclosed by the subsidiaries it is possible that some of them were given by the parent bank on disadvantageous terms. Moreover, as deposit transactions are not covered by the current regulations their terms were also not reported in the annual statements. Again, the lack of regulation and disclosure might allow the parent banks to enforce less favorable terms on the deposits of subsidiaries. Hence, parent bank group members might have improved their profitability by receiving cheap deposits from some subsidiaries and lending capital at above market rates to other subsidiaries.

As the terms of all those transactions are not disclosed, it is very hard to assess the profitability of related party transactions between the parent bank and its subsidiaries. However, Table 10 shows that in many subsidiaries those transactions constitute a significant proportion of its profit/loss. Therefore, in our opinion, these transactions and their terms need to be more detailed to be disclosed in order to assess its relevance and economics justification. On the other hand the income flows to parent banks do not represent a significant proportion of subsidiaries equity. Hence, they do not present a serious threat to subsidiaries financial stability in the short term but may have a negative impact on its profitability in the long term.

One expense position, which was seldom disclosed separately in most annual statements of the subsidiaries, was the management fees for the administrative services that the parent bank provided to them. These fees are recorded as revenue on the parent bank's books and as fee expenses or overhead costs on the subsidiary's books. As the management fees are not disclosed separately across the subsidiaries it is difficult to assess their value and make any kind of comparison. The information that was provided, however, showed that the amounts charged by the parent banks were relatively small in comparison to the equity, yet could be a substantial cost. In 2009, for example, Citigroup received from its subsidiary in Poland over 41 million euro or 16% of the subsidiaries gross profit in fees for services related to maintenance of the information system and advisory support. In the year before, the parent bank charges were higher and amounted to over 64 euro million or 12% of the subsidiary's gross profit. As the amount fluctuated and no further explanations were provided those flows may also be transfers of income to parent banks from their subsidiaries.

These flows nevertheless do not constitute a serious threat to the stability of the subsidiary. In the case of the Citigroup subsidiaries the value of the transfers was equal to 5% of equity in 2008 and 4% in 2009. Should all the transfer be taken into account – dividends, income, and expenses including the fees from services provided by the parent bank – the amounts transferred to the parent bank could be substantial. While, at the moment we are not able to differentiate those amounts and are not able to compare them across the subsidiaries and multinational banks, closer attention should be paid to them.

Acquisitions and Disposals of Assets

Acquisitions and disposals of assets between bank holding companies allows asset transfers, but most importantly moves income from the parent bank to the subsidiary, or vice-versa. Table 11 presents selected transactions between the parent banks and their subsidiaries during the crisis. In the table we show only those transactions where the acquired or disposed asset was another bank subsidiary. In this period, however, the entities sold also nonbanking businesses, especially insurance companies, leasing companies but also stakes in nonfinancial companies.

The acquisition or disposal of assets in bank holding companies might be used to create a more transparent financial organization. However, in a crisis those transactions may also have different goals. First, when one

Table 11. Intra-Group Acquisitions of Banks Subsidiaries and Branches in Millions of Euro.

Year	Parent Bank	Acquirer	Vendor	Target	Shares	Deal Value
2010	OTP	Hungary		Romania	100%	
2010	ING	Poland		Poland		2.54
2010	Commerzbank	Poland	Germany	Poland	100%	2.54
2009	KBC	Belgium	Czech Republic	Slovakia		484
2009	Swedbank	Estonia		Lithuania	100%	
2008	Swedbank	Sweden	Estonia	Russia	85%	
2007	OTP	Hungary		Ukraine	100%	32.88
2007	Unicredit	Poland	Germany	Ukraine		84.28

Sources: Companies annual statements and Zephyr database.

entity buys assets from another it increases the liquidity of the last. Increasing the liquidity of the subsidiaries may have been the main motive justifying the acquisition of the insurance and pension fund business by the Swedish parent banks from their Baltic subsidiaries in the years 2008–2009. Those operations were however often very profitable and hence the disposal will have a negative impact on the Baltic subsidiaries performance in the future.

As the divested operations were profitable, a second explanation could be that those transactions were not aimed at providing liquidity to the subsidiaries but to protect the interests of the parent banks in case of their failure. In this scenario the transactions would not be in the interests of the subsidiaries and the host regulators. Moreover, a remaining question is how the additional liquidity stemming from the sell-off will be used by the subsidiary. The Polish subsidiary of Commerzbank, for example, sold its pension business to a third-party investor, but later used the funds to acquire a branch in Poland from the parent bank.

A disposal of assets by the subsidiary may be in the interest of the parent bank and the subsidiary at the same time. In 2008, for example, the Swedbank subsidiary in Estonia sold its majority ownership in the Russian subsidiary to the parent bank. The subsidiary received €91 million for the Russian subsidiary and reported a loss on this transaction of €2.1 million euro. The transaction, however, allowed the Estonian subsidiary to limit its exposure to an unstable market during the crisis and therefore it was in its interests. At the same time the parent bank was more likely to be able to assist the Russian subsidiary should any additional funding be needed as the crisis further evolved. Consequently, we may assume that this transaction was in the interest of all the entities involved including the host regulator.

While acquisitions and disposals were reported in the financial statements, the information explaining the rationality of these transaction was lacking. Yet, it may be assumed that they do not provide any significant danger to the stability of the parent bank or its subsidiaries as these transactions are often monitored by different regulatory institutions. Furthermore, even as parent banks would try to protect their investments by acquiring assets from failing subsidiaries, the interest of its debt holders were protected by law in most countries. In most of the countries regulations exist that would declare any unfavorable transfer of assets to parent bank from a failed subsidiary as not binding when they are found to be unfavorable for the creditors. Nevertheless, those transactions allow the parent banks to protect valuable assets from third-parties in case of failure, but it is unlikely they can be used to transfer assets prior to the failure of a subsidiary.

Other Methods of Income Transfer

In a recent paper, Pistor (2010) presents a hypothetical scenario of a host-home regulation conflict, where she explains that multinational banks may have established prior to the crisis leasing companies and other vehicles that are not subject to the host's banking regulations. These financial institutions could have been founded in the period when the host regulator tried to slow the credit market expansion in the boom period by imposing ceilings on the permissible credit volume, especially in foreign currency. As the newly established institutions were not subject to the new regulation they were able to provide further loans despite the measures of the host's regulators and contributed significantly to the credit boom, especially in the emerging CEE markets.

Till now very little has been revealed in the literature about the impact of these vehicles on the recent credit boom in foreign markets. It may be assumed, however, that these institutions were indeed used by the parent banks to transfer an uncontrolled amount of capital to the foreign markets in the form of loans in the past. As a consequence, it may also be assumed that the parent bank may easily change the direction of the flow of funds in those vehicles from the host market to the home market subsequently. Therefore, multinational banks may now contribute significantly to credit contraction in the foreign markets as they have to the credit booms in the past.

THE EUROPEAN BANK COORDINATION "VIENNA" INITIATIVE

The European Bank Coordination "Vienna" Initiative (EBCI) is an informal forum that was launched by the EBRD, the IMF, and the Austrian Ministry of Finance at the height of the systemic financial crisis in late 2008 (Nitsche, 2010). The ECBI also invited the European Investment Bank (EIB), the World Bank, the European Commission, and the European Central Bank, but only as observers. Moreover, the forum included the home and host country regulatory authorities as well the representatives of the largest banking groups operating in CEE countries (the EBRD region).

The main aim of the ECBI was to prevent a large-scale withdrawal of cross-border bank groups from the CEE. At the time of the crisis the EBRD was afraid that an uncoordinated withdrawal might have triggered a systemic bank crisis not only in the host country but in the region as a whole (EBRD, 2011). Therefore, the EBRD wanted to ensure that the parent bank groups would commit to maintain their exposures and recapitalize their subsidiaries if needed. By introducing the initiative, the EBRD wanted to avoid a home bias and ensure that national support packages of cross-border bank groups would benefit their subsidiaries in CEE countries. At the same time host country authorities were made responsible for appropriate macroeconomic policies and liquidity support in local currency irrespective of bank ownership.

In parallel, the EBRD, the EIB, and the World Bank/IFC started a coordination process among themselves in the framework of a Joint Action Plan in support of the banking systems and lending to the real economy in CEE Europe. The objective of this Plan was to support banking sector stability and lending to the real economy with a joint financing of up to 24.5 billion euro for the year 2009–2010, of which over 19 billion euro had been delivered by 2010 (European Commission, 2010d).

Therefore, the potential recapitalization of the subsidiaries under the EBCI was only a part of the overall balance of payments support to countries, especially to Bosnia and Herzegovina, Hungary, Latvia, Romania, and Serbia. Whereas, the role of the Joint Action Plan was to signal a clear commitment of international financial institutions to regional financial stability at a time when deteriorating conditions in Romania and Serbia put the CEE region at risk (Nitsche, 2010).

The economic situation in the region was very important for the stability of the financial system in OMS as some of the Western European banking groups had a large exposure to the CEE countries. This exposure may also explain their willingness to recapitalize their subsidiaries in CEE countries if needed. As Table 12 shows, in 2008 the CEE countries borrowed USD 1.3 trillion from Western European banks. The top lenders to the CEE region were Austrian banks with USD 246 billion, German banks with USD 182 billion, and Italian banks with USD 181 billion.

However, at the beginning of the crisis the most exposed banks from Western European countries relative to their own size measured by loans as a share of GDP were Austria, Belgium, and Sweden. As Table 13 shows, Austrian banks' claims on the CEE add up to 55% of Austria's GDP, while Belgium and Sweden have claims equivalent to 23% and 21% of their GDP, respectively. As a result it is not surprising that the Austrian Ministry of Finance was a leader of the EBCI at the beginning of the crisis, and was supported by the Swedish or Belgium authorities.

In 2008 Austria's banks were particularly exposed to the Czech Republic, Romania, Hungary, and Slovakia, while Sweden was primarily exposed to the Baltic countries. Belgium had almost half of its exposure in the region to the Czech Republic and a fifth to Poland. The BIS does not provide bilateral claims of Greece on CEE countries, but according to Weistroffer and Möbert (2010) about 39% of Greek cross-border lending is

Table 12. Western European Banks' Claims on Central and Eastern Europe in 2008 in Billions USD.

	Austria	Belgium	France	Germany	Italy	Netherlands	Sweden	Western Europe
Bulgaria	5.7	2	3.6	2.8	8.1	0.7	0	41.5
Czech Rep	65.1	56.7	38.6	12.7	19	6.2	0.2	205.7
Hungary	38.3	18.7	11.9	37.9	29.3	5.6	0.3	153.3
Poland	17.2	25.2	22.9	55.4	54.4	41.2	8.1	287.4
Romania	46.5	1.2	17.6	3.8	12.9	11	0.2	124.1
Slovakia	33.2	10.9	6.4	4.1	23.6	6.7	0.2	87.3
Estonia	0.3	0.1	0.1	1.1	0.4	0	32.7	40.2
Latvia	0.8	0	0.4	4.8	1.4	0	25.0	43.3
Lithuania	0.3	0.1	0.4	3.8	0.7	0	28.9	45.5
CEE	246.3	126.1	147.4	181.8	180.6	100.7	110.9	1307.5

Source: BIS Quarterly Review, December 2008.

Table 13. Western European Banks Claims on CEE as a Share of GDP of the Lending Country.

	Austria (%)	Belgium (%)	France (%)	Germany (%)	Italy (%)	Netherlands (%)	Sweden (%)
Bulgaria	1.3	0.4	0.1	0.1	0.3	0.1	0.0
Czech Rep	14.6	10.4	1.3	0.3	0.8	0.7	0.0
Hungary	8.6	3.4	0.4	1.0	1.2	0.6	0.1
Poland	3.9	4.6	0.7	1.4	2.2	4.5	1.6
Romania	10.4	0.2	0.6	0.1	0.5	1.2	0.0
Slovakia	7.4	2.0	0.2	0.1	0.9	0.7	0.0
Estonia	0.1	0.0	0.0	0.0	0.0	0.0	6.3
Latvia	0.2	0.0	0.0	0.1	0.1	0.0	4.8
Lithuania	0.1	0.0	0.0	0.1	0.0	0.0	5.6
CEE	55.3	23.0	4.8	4.6	7.3	10.9	21.4

Source: Hansen (2009) based on *BIS Quarterly Review*, December 2008.

aimed at CEE countries. The strongest links of Greek banks are with Romania (15%) and Bulgaria (10%). Consequently, a default of Greek public debt could possibility result in contagion to CEE countries, which could result in a spillover risk to Austria.

The Western European bank claims consist of loans, but also include equity, and other securities, as well as deposits. Consequently, it can be assumed that the Austrian banks as well other Western European banks were interested in stabilizing the macroeconomic situation in those CEE countries where they had large exposure. In the case of a macroeconomic crisis or default of countries like Romania or Bulgaria the potential losses for Austrian or Greek banks could have been much greater than the capital needed to prevent a failure of the subsidiaries in those host countries. For instance, the biggest subsidiary of an Austrian bank in Romania, the UniCredit Tiriac Bank, which is a member of UniCredit Group, only had equity equal to 802 million USD as of December 2010. Consequently, for European banks the promise to recapitalize their subsidiaries when needed in exchange for a guarantee of international packages stemming from EBRD, EIB, World Bank, and IMF to support the real economy was a lesser cost than a potential macroeconomic crisis in those countries.

Moreover, the EBRD (Nagy, 2011) recently called the EBCI a great success, but admitted that foreign banks tightened credit more than domestic and state-owned banks in the year 2008–2009. The perception of risk was the dominant factor and not balance sheet constraints in these decisions. According to Schildbach (2011) the reason for the decline of lending to private sector customers by foreign banks did not mean a pullback from host countries as a whole. The foreign banks only substituted private for public credit as they satisfied the increasing financing needs of the host governments at the cost of reduced availability of loans for households and companies. Moreover, as public debt has a lower risk weight the change in the balance sheet structure of foreign banks provided another incentive to reduce private lending.

Another explanation for the loan policy change of the foreign banks might be other different initiatives of the EBCI, which were undertaken since its creation in 2008. For example, in 2010, the EBCI decided to set up two working groups. One working group focused on the development of local currency markets and another on the role banks could play in the absorption of EU funds (EBCI, 2011). The aim of the second working group was to provide a mechanism to facilitate the absorption of EU funds by national authorities, while cross-border banks should have a larger involvement in the selection, prefinancing and cofinancing of structural funds projects in CEE countries.

Since 2007 the EU has made available to the NMS a total amount of 178 euro billion in EU structural funds over the period 2007–2013, or about 19% of their aggregate 2010 GDP. The EU structural funds require, however, national cofinancing to strengthen project ownership and sound management. The rate of cofinancing varies in the range of 50–85%, depending on the project and the stage of development of the NMS. The national cofinancing was often seen as a major problem and henceforth the absorption has been disappointingly slow in most countries, particularly in Romania and Bulgaria (EBCI, 2011). Consequently, the ECBI encouraged foreign banks to participate in the management and in the absorption of EU funds, and this can also explain the change in the balance sheet structure of the foreign banks in CEE.

Moreover, as we have shown in the previous sections of the chapter, despite the ECBI, some of the cross-border banks transferred assets out of CEE countries in the year 2008–2009. One explanation for the situation is that the ECBI is only important to those countries and cross-border banks with large exposure to the CEE region. Consequently, Austrian, Belgium, or Swedish banks reduced their exposure to the region, but did not withdraw funds or even supported their subsidiaries when needed in the CEE countries. In contrast, the United States or Dutch cross-border banks that did not have such an exposure to the region prior to the crisis decided to transfer assets out of the region regardless of the ECBI. It was feasible as the home authorities could discipline its own banks when it was vital to their own interest, but did not have any power to do the same with other cross-border banks.

Therefore, in our opinion the ECBI was more a success for the cross-border banks than for the international financial institutions as EBRD or IMF taking part in the ECBI. The ECBI provided stability to the CEE region through the Joint Plan, but it was in the vital interest of some of the cross–border banks and governments to prevent a major crisis in the region. It should be noted that the stress test for Austrian banks in 2009 revealed that a major crisis in the CEE region might result in losses equal to 10% or more of Austrian GDP (Hansen, 2009). As a result the prevention of the crisis was not only in the interest of the cross-border banks but also the Austrian government. At the same time cross-border banks coming from countries with lower exposure to the region benefited from the situation and transferred assets regardless of the ECBI. Henceforth, the question remains whether the ECBI is a good crisis management tool and should be used in crisis prevention in the future.

The issue is especially relevant in case of Greece, where cross-border banks again have a vital interest in preventing the default of the country. Moreover, as mentioned already above, the default of Greece might lead to a spillover to Romania and Bulgaria, and consequently also to Austria. Therefore, it is not surprising that the Vienna Initiative is put forward as a way to resolve the Greek crisis today.

CONCLUSIONS

In our chapter we document that the existing EU framework governing intra-group transactions of multinational banks does not sufficiently address the problems and risks countries face and that materialized in the global financial crisis. On one hand, domestic supervisors must safeguard the financial soundness of their banking system and therefore should prevent intra-group transactions that may jeopardize the solvency of foreign subsidiaries. On the other hand, we found that the existing regulations, including the disclosure requirements, are not able to identify and prevent those transactions.

As a result, during the crisis foreign bank subsidiaries engaged in transactions that might have jeopardized their own security. As the foreign bank subsidiaries have dominant positions in host countries banking sectors, especially in the NMS, they have created a serious risk to the soundness of the financial systems in those regions. Furthermore, we documented that the threats created by a single subsidiary might not only affect one country but also multiple several countries at the same time due to the network of its own subsidiaries.

In the chapter we show also that those transactions took place regardless of the European Bank Coordination "Vienna" Initiative, which aim was to prevent a large-scale withdrawal of cross-border bank groups from CEE countries. Henceforth, we question the ECBI as crisis management tool, while we attribute its weakness to different goals of multinational banks, governments, and authorities across Europe.

Consequently, this chapter seriously questions the soundness of the existing regulations and advocates especially for more detailed disclosure of all the transactions between the parent bank and its subsidiaries. Moreover, due to the gravity of the problems shown in the chapter, in our opinion, not only new transnational regulations needed but in addition a transnational supervisory organization enforcing them. Furthermore, we also argue that the governance of foreign subsidiaries should be changed as currently parent banks may easily instruct their subsidiaries to engage in certain transactions, which may be to their disadvantage and as a result make the host financial systems more vulnerable.

NOTES

1. In EU-10 countries which belong to the enlargement in 2004, five of them are from the CEE (Czech Republic, Hungary, Poland, Slovakia, and Slovenia), three of them are from the Baltic States (Estonia, Latvia, and Lithuania), and the remaining two are Cyprus and Malta. In 2007, the EU was enlarged to 27 member states, when Bulgaria and Romania joined. In the preparations before accession, all these countries had undertaken political and economic reforms, which included the liberalization of their financial systems.
2. See the statistics of ECB at http://www.ecb.int/stats/money/mfi/general/html/mfis_list_102.en.html
3. According to the authors' calculation, in 2009, around 71.2% of the total assets of CEE banking assets were owned by foreign banks.
4. The disagreement between Iceland, the United Kingdom, and the Netherlands began in 2008 when Landsbanki failed. The Icelandic government declared that it would not compensate depositors in the United Kingdom and the Netherlands with Icesave accounts, which have been offered by Landsbanki through branches in those countries.
5. According to the European Commission (2008), currently there's no regulation existing in the EU that expressly lays down a general prohibition on asset transferability between group's entities. The only prudential restriction is the largest

exposures regime, which limits institutions' exposures to 20% of the respective institution's own funds. However, the current EU regulation allows member states an option to partially of fully exempt intra-group exposures, what has been done in most of the countries in our study.

6. In this chapter nonexecutive directors are equal to supervisory board members in banks with two-tier boards. Moreover, we discuss mostly issues related to listed subsidiaries of multinational banks in the host countries. In non-listed banks we found that in almost all the cases the nonexecutive directors were related to the parent bank.

7. See Section 5 Large Exposures, Directive 2006/48/EC of the European Parliament and of the Council of 14 June 2006 relating to the taking up and pursuit of the business of credit institution, Official Journal L 177, 30/06/2006.

ACKNOWLEDGMENTS

We would like to thank Editors Bang Nam Jeon and Maria Pia Olivero for assistance. We also thank Iftekhar Hasan, Yawen Jiao, and the participants of the seminar at Lally School Management and Technology at the Rensselaer Polytechnic Institute and the Kozminski University for their valuable comments. Oskar Kowalewski work was supported by Polish National Science Centre (NCN) contract nr DEC-2012/07/B/HS4/03091.

REFERENCES

Allen, F., Bartilori, L., & Kowalewski, O. (2005). *The financial system of the EU 25 (long version)*. Working Paper No. 05–44, Wharton Financial Institutions Center, University of Pennsylvania.

Allen, F., & Gale, D. (2000). Financial contagion. *Journal of Political Economy, 108*(1), 1–33.

Allen, F., Hryckiewicz, A., Kowalewski, O., & Tumer-Alkan, G. (2010). *Transmission of bank liquidity shocks in loan and deposit markets: The role of interbank borrowing and market monitoring*. Working Paper 10–28, Wharton Financial Institutions Center, University of Pennsylvania.

Altman, T. (2006). *Cross-border banking in Central and Eastern Europe, issues and implications for supervisory and regulatory organization on the European level*. Working Paper No. 06–16, Wharton Financial Institutions Center, University of Pennsylvania.

Aydin, B. (2008). *Banking structure and credit growth in Central and Eastern European countries*. IMF Working Paper No. 08/215. International Monetary Fund, Washington, DC.

Basel Committee on Banking Supervision. (2010). *Principles for enhancing corporate governance*. Bank for International Settlements, Basel.

Berger, A. N. (2006). Obstacles to a global banking system: 'Old Europe' versus 'New Europe'. *Journal of Banking and Finance, 31*, 1955–1973.

Caprio, G., Laeven, L., & Levine, R. (2007). Governance and bank valuation. *Journal of Financial Intermediation, 16*, 584–617.

Cardenas, J., Graf, J. P., & O'Dogherty, P. (2003). *Foreign bank entry in emerging market economies: A host country perspective*. Committee on the Global Financial System (CGFS) Working Group Paper. Bank for International Settlements, Basel.

Cerutti, E., Dell'Ariccia, G., & Martinez Peria, M. S. (2007). How banks go abroad: Branches or Subsidiaries? *Journal of Banking and Finance, 31*, 1669–1692.

Clarke, G., Cull, R., Martinez Peria, M. S., & Sanchez, S. M. (2003). Foreign bank entry: Experience, implications for developing economies, and agenda for further research. *World Bank Research Observer, 8*(1), 25–29.

Committee on the Global Financial System. (2010). *Funding patterns and liquidity management of internationally active banks*. CGFS Paper No. 39. Bank for International Settlements, Basel.

Cottarelli, C., Dell's Ariccia, G., & Hollar, I. V. (2003). *Early birds, late risers, and sleeping beauties: Bank credit growth to the private sector in Central and Easter Europe and the Balkans*. IMF Working Paper No. 03/213. International Monetary Fund, Washington, DC.

DBB LAW. (2010). *Study on the feasibility of reducing obstacles to the transfer of assets within a cross border banking group during a financial crisis for european commission*. Demlin Broulard Barthelem. Retrieved from http://ec.europa.eu/internal_market/bank/docs/windingup/200908/final_report20091218_en.pdf

De Andres, P., & Vallelado, E. (2008). Corporate governance in banking: The role of the board of directors. *Journal of Banking and Finance, 32*, 2570–2580.

De Haas, R., & Van Lelyveld, I. (2006). Foreign banks and credit stability in central and eastern Europe: A panel data analysis. *Journal of Banking and Finance, 30*(7), 1927–1952.

De Haas, R., & Van Lelyveld, I. (2010). Internal capital markets and lending by multinational bank subsidiaries. *Journal of Financial Intermediation, 19*, 1–25.

Dermine, J. (2006). European banking integration: Don't put the cart before the horse. *Financial Markets, Institutions and Instruments, 15*(2), 57–106.

EBRD. (2011). *Vienna Initiative – Moving to a new phase*. European Bank for Reconstruction and Development, The Factsheet, May.

Eisenbeis, R. A., & Kaufman, G. G. (2005). Bank crisis resolution and foreign-owned banks. *Economic Review, Federal Reserve Bank of Atlanta, Q4*, 1–18.

Eisenbeis, R. A., & Kaufman, G. G. (2008). Cross-border banking and financial stability in the EU. *Journal of Financial Stability, 4*, 168–204.

Ekhlom, K. (2010). Dealing with cross-border banking without rolling back financial integration. *BIS Review, 82*, 15–24.

Erkens, D., Hung, M., & Matos, P. P. (2010). *Corporate Governance in the 2007–2008 Financial Crisis: Evidence from Financial Institutions Worldwide*. ECGI – Finance Working Paper No. 249/2009; CELS 2009 4th Annual Conference on Empirical Legal Studies Paper. Retrieved from http://ssrn.com/abstract=1397685

European Central Bank. (2010, September). *EU banking structure*. European Central Bank, Frankfurt am Main.

European Commission. (2008, November). *Commission services' report on 'asset transferability'*. Internal Market and Services DG, European Commission, Brussels.

European Commission. (2009). *European Financial Integration Report 2009, Commission Staff Working Document SEC(2009) 1702 final*. Brussels: European Commission.

European Commission. (2010a). *Corporate governance in financial institutions: Lessons to be drawn from the current financial crisis, best practices*. Commission Staff Working Document

COM (2010) 284 final, Accompanying document to the Green Paper, European Commission, Brussels.

European Commission. (2010b). *Green Paper. Corporate governance in financial institutions and remuneration policies*. Commission Staff Working Paper COM(2010) 284 final, European Commission, Brussels.

European Commission. (2010c). *European financial integration, commission staff working document*. SEC(2009) 1702 final, Bruessel.

European Commission. (2010d). *European bank co-ordination initiative – Full forum meeting*. IP/10/335, Bruessel.

Francis, B., Hasan, I., Song, L., & Yeung, B. (2009). *What determines information content in bank stock price? Global evidence*. Working Paper, Lally School of Management and Technology of Rensselaer Polytechnic Institute.

Goldberg, L. G., Sweeney, R. J., & Wihlborg, C. (2005). *From subsidiary to branch organization of international banks: New challenges and opportunities for regulation*. Presenting at Economics and Financial Institutions at CBS (LEFIC).

Habib, M. A., Johnsen, D. B., & Nail, N. Y. (1997). Spinoffs and information. *Journal of Financial Intermediation*, *6*, 153–176.

Hansen, F. Ø. (2009). *Euro area: Exposure to the crisis in central and eastern Europe*. Investment Research: General Markets, Danske Bank.

Herring, R. J. (2007). *Conflicts between home and host country prudential supervisors*. Working Paper No. 07–33, Wharton Financial Institutions Center, University of Pennsylvania.

Hryckiewicz, A., & Kowalewski, O. (2010). Economic determinates, financial crisis and entry modes of foreign banks into emerging markets. *Emerging Markets Review*, *11*(3), 205–228.

IMF. (2009). *World economic outlook*. Washington, DC: International Monetary Fund.

IMF. (2010). *Finland: Financial system stability assessment update*. IMF Country Report No. 10/275. International Monetary Fund, Washington, DC.

Kahn, C., & Winton, A. (2004). Moral hazard and optimal subsidiary structure for financial institutions. *Journal of Finance*, *59*(6), 2531–2575.

Kim, B., Prescott, J. E., & Kim, S. M. (2005). Differentiated governance of foreign subsidiaries in transnational corporations: An agency theory perspective. *Journal of International Management*, *11*, 43–66.

Krimminger, M. H. (2008). The resolution of cross-border banks: Issues for deposit insurers and proposals for cooperation. *Journal of Financial Stability*, *4*, 376–390.

Lavine, L., & Levine, R. (2008). Bank governance, regulation, and risk-taking. *Journal of Financial Economics*, *93*, 259–275.

Maechler, A. M., & Ong, L. L. (2009). *Foreign banks in the CESE countries: In for a penny, in for a pound?* IMF Working Paper No. 09/54. International Monetary Fund, Washington, DC.

Martinez Peria, M. S., Powell, A., & Hollar, I. V. (2002). *Banking on foreigners: the behavior of international bank lending to Latin America, 1985–2000*. Working Paper No. 2893, Washington DC: World Bank.

Masulis, R. W., Wang, C., & Xie, F. (2012). Globalizing the boardroom—The effects of foreign directors on corporate governance and firm performance. *Journal of Accounting and Economics*, *53*(3), 527–554.

Navaretti, G. B., Calzolari, G., Pozzolo, A. F., & Levi, M. (2010). *Multinational banking in Europe: Financial stability and regulatory implications. Lessons from the financial crises.*

Development Studies Working Paper No. 292, Centro Studi Luca D'Agliano, University of Milano, Milano, Italy.

Nagy, P. M. (2011). The Vienna Initiative in Southern-Eastern Europe: Record and Way Forward. *Conference Proceeding*, High Level EC-JVI Conference Vienna, 22 March.

Nestor Advisors. (2009). *Governance in Crisis: a comparative case study of six US investment banks*. NeAd Research Note 0109, London: Nestor Advisors Ltd.

Nitsche, W. (2010). *The Vienna Initiative/European Bank coordinational initiative: assessment and outlook*. Working Paper Series 2010(4). Austrian Federal Ministry of Finance, Australia.

Pathan, S. (2009). Strong boards, CEO power and bank risk-taking. *Journal of Banking and Finance*, *33*, 1340–1350.

Peek, J., & Rosengren, E. S. (1997). The international transmission of financial shocks: The case of Japan. *American Economic Review*, *87*, 495–505.

Peek, J., & Rosengren, E. S. (2000a). Collateral damage: effects of the Japanese bank crisis on real activity in the United States. *American Economic Review*, *90*(1), 30–45.

Peek, J., & Rosengren, E. S. (2000b). Implications of the globalization of the banking sector: the Latin American experience. *New England Economic Review, Federal Reserve Bank of Boston*, 45–62.

Pistor, K. (2010). *Host's dilemma: Rethinking EU banking regulation in light of the global crisis*. ECGI – Finance Working Paper No. 286/2010. Retrieved from http://ssrn.com/abstract=1631940

Popov, A. & Udell, G. F. (2010). *Cross-border banking and the international transmission of financial distress during the crisis of 2007–2008*. Working Paper Series 1203, European Central Bank.

Schildbach, J. (2011). *Home sweet home – International banking after the crisis*. DB EU Monitor 80, Deutsche Bank.

Uhde, A., & Heimeshoff, U. (2009). Consolidation in banking and financial stability in Europe. *Journal of Banking and Finance*, *33*, 1299–1311.

Upper, C., & Worms, A. (2002). *Estimating bilateral exposures in the German interbank market: Is there a danger of contagion?* Deutsche Bundesbank Discussion Paper No. 09/02.

Van Rijckeghem, C., & Weder, B. (2000). *Spillovers through banking centers: a panel data analysis*. Working Paper No. 00/88, Washington DC: International Monetary Fund.

Van Rijckeghem, C., & Weder, B. (2001). Sources of contagion: Finance or trade? *Journal of International Economics*, *54*(2), 293–308.

Weistroffer, C., & Möbert, J. (2010). *Monitoring cross-border exposure*. Deutsche Bank Research, November.

BANK CREDITOR STRUCTURE AND BANK RISK DURING LIQUIDITY CRISES: A SURVEY WITH POLICY IMPLICATIONS

Jungsoo Park, Hyun-Han Shin and Jeong Ho Suh

ABSTRACT

This chapter surveys papers and the related literature on the relationship between banks' creditor structure and bank risk during the period of liquidity crises. Departing from the conventional banking literature, which points to deteriorating asset quality to be the culprit for the amplified bank risk in the midst of financial crises, the studies in the aftermath of the global financial crisis look into the liability side of the bank balance sheet as a potential source for the augmented bank risk during the financial crisis when there is a liquidity contraction. Recent studies theorize and provide empirical evidence that banking institutions with a greater share of large lenders and an economy with high noncore bank

Global Banking, Financial Markets and Crises
International Finance Review, Volume 14, 433–447

ISSN: 1569-3767/doi:10.1108/S1569-3767(2013)0000014017

liabilities in the banking sector may experience heightened bank risk or country risk. We also search for policy implications from this survey.

Keywords: Bank risk; creditor structure; noncore liabilities; liquidity crisis; bank run; prudential regulations

JEL classifications: G01; G21; E44

INTRODUCTION

In September 2007, Northern Rock plc, the fifth largest mortgage bank in the United Kingdom, faced an old-fashioned bank run, fueled by the British government's announcement that it would guarantee all deposits within Northern Rock. However, following the announcement, approximately 4 percent of the bank's total deposits were withdrawn in a single day, which prompted an immediate and dramatic fall of its stock price by 31 percent. Despite the announcement made by the Bank of England to secure emergency liquidity for the bank, many individual depositors waited in lines outside the branch offices for the withdrawal of their money. Moreover, even though further efforts were made by Financial Supervisory Authority (FSA) and the Bank of England, a takeover arrangement by another bank was not materialized until after a long period of time.

This episode sheds a new light on the path to bank failure or systemic risk in the wake of liquidity crises. That is, unlike other bank runs initiated mainly by the depositors' concern on asset deterioration of the banks, the run on Northern Rock seems to show that the heavier reliance on large lenders can lead to higher probability of a bank run especially in the midst of liquidity shortage. In this regard, Shin (2009) and Liu and Mello (2009) explain that the Northern Rock episode may have resulted from large lenders who had deleveraging motives to preemptively hedge against their balance-sheet risk when a drain on market liquidity was foreseen. Shin (2009) and Liu and Mello (2009) are paying attention to the risks created by the creditor structure in a bank, which is fairly new to the literature on bank risk. This study provides a review on findings in various studies on bank risk during liquidity crisis periods in relations to banks' creditor structure.

Fig. 1 depicts how the composition of Northern Rock's liabilities changed from June 1998 to June 2007. While the proportion of retail funding kept falling throughout the period, that of noncore funding like securitized

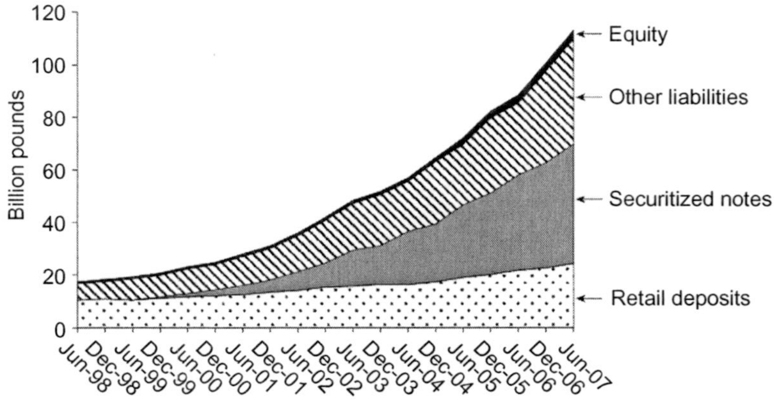

Fig. 1. Composition of Northern Rock's Liabilities (June 19998–June 2007). *Note*: This figure depicts how the composition of Northern Rock's liabilities has changed. While the proportion of retail funding continues to fall throughout the period, the proportion of nontraditional fundings like securitized notes has significantly increased. *Source*: Shin (2009, p. 105).

notes increased to a large extent during the same period. This data seems to lend some support to the aforementioned story.

Korea was a country significantly influenced by the global financial crisis of 2008–2009. Although the soundness of bank assets was not the cause of worry, the Korean banks faced risk due to severe contraction in market liquidity. Fig. 2 shows the trend of Korean banks' creditor structure during the period of 2002–2008. It is worth noting that the funding structure for Korean bank was severely biased toward deposits (as opposed to marketable securities) and the proportion of retail deposit out of the total deposits fell throughout the sample period. It would be interesting to see whether this change in the funding structure played an important role in triggering public concerns for Korean banks.

The chapter is organized as follows. Section titled "Literature Review on Bank Capital and Bank Risk" reviews the related literature on banks' capital structure and bank risk. First, studies relating to bank equity capital and bank risks are reviewed, and then a review on new theories on the relation between the creditor structure and bank risk is provided. In section titled "Empirical Studies on Link Between the Bank Credit Channel and Bank Risk", several empirical papers that test the hypothesized link between banks' creditor structure and bank risk are introduced

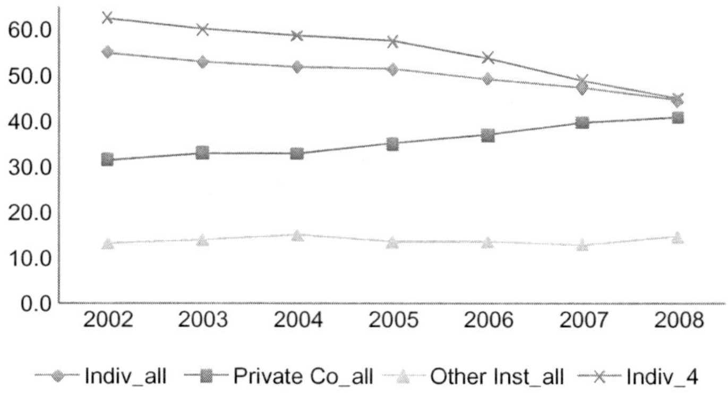

Fig. 2. Depositor Structure of Commercial Banks in Korea. *Note*: This figure shows that the proportion of retail funding in Korean commercial banks has continued to decrease since 2002. It is also observed that such pattern has been led by larger banks. Indiv_all: the proportion of deposits from individuals out of the total deposits in all commercial banks. PrivateCo_all: the proportion of deposits from private companies out of the total deposits in all commercial banks. OtherInt_all: the proportion of deposits from other institutions out of the total deposits in all commercial banks. Indiv_4: the proportion of deposits from individuals out of the total deposits in four major commercial banks (KB, Woori, Shinhan, Hana). *Source*: Korea Federation of Banks (Suh, Park, & Shin, 2010, Fig. 2).

and discussed in search of policy implications. Section titled "Policy Implications and Concluding Remarks" concludes with policy implications.

LITERATURE REVIEW ON BANK CAPITAL AND BANK RISK

Capital Structure, Regulations, and Bank Risk

Numerous studies in the conventional banking literature analyze the relationship between banks' capital structure and bank risk. Since the stable source of bank funding and the adequate level of capital were identified as important factors in reducing bank risk, many studies have concentrated on how institutions and regulations such as the deposit insurance system or equity capital standards can affect bank behavior and thus bank risk.

Sharpe (1978) argues that when the deposit insurance system is adopted, regulations on the equity capital ratio reduce the bank debt ratio, which eventually reduces bank risk. Furlong and Keely (1989) and Keely and Furlong (1990) suggest that because reduction in the debt ratio lowers the option value of deposit insurance, bank risk can be reduced using requirement on bank equity capital. Cebula (1999) finds that bank failure has a negative relationship with the equity capital ratio, real interest rate of 3-year maturity Government Bond, and real GDP growth rate, but has a positive relationship with the Federal Deposit Insurance payment level, the degree of bank competition, and real costs of deposits.

Some studies discuss how the institution of capital standards affect bank risk and also bank liquidity creation. Besanko and Kanatas (1996) discuss how capital standards affect bank risk considering the principal-agent problem between banks and their shareholders. In an agency problem framework, higher capital standards help reducing the risk of the bank's assets. However, with the bank issuance of equity to meet the new standards, bank insider effort weakens since their equity stake is reduced. Diamond and Rajan (2000) suggest equity capital can act as a buffer to protect depositors in times of distress. However, holding excessive equity capital can reduce liquidity creation and the flow of credit. According to Gorton and Winton (2000), during recessionary periods, regulators are inclined to increase capital standards in an effort to reduce the threat of bank failures. However, they should be aware that it could lead to reduction in market liquidity. Berger and Bouwman (2009) argue that the effect of capital standards on liquidity creation depends on bank size. They find that higher capital standard crowds out deposits and lowers liquidity creation at smaller banks, but it absorbs risk and increases liquidity creation at larger banks.

Bank Creditor Structure and Bank Risk

In the aftermath of 2008–2009 global financial crisis, studies on bank risk look deeper into the liability side and identify the creditor structure of banks as a new potential source of bank risk. Shin (2009) and Liu and Mello (2009) are the first to indicate that, in the age of securitization and complex capital markets, a bank run can occur on account of the bank's liability structure (more specifically, composition of creditors). They point out that Northern Rock failure is not so much due to deteriorating bank assets, but due to the bank's heavy reliance on nonretail deposits and short-term borrowings. The total asset size of Northern Rock increased from 17.4 billion pounds to 113.5 billion pounds during the period from June 1998 to June 2007, at an "unusually high" annual growth rate of 23 percent. However, the rapid growth of bank assets was not properly held up by stable or core funding sources like branch-based retail deposits. Instead, the bank financed most of its money through securitized notes, covered bonds, and nontraditional deposits such as interbank deposits and postal and telephone accounts. This specific funding behavior may have been an important source of failure in renewing their short-term borrowing, and eventually may have led to a bank run.

Inspired by recent cases of bank failure, Liu and Mello (2009) present a model to explain how financial institutions can proceed to a bank run through the credit channel. In their model, the creditors to a financial institution are divided into two categories: large lenders (or wholesale lenders) and small investors (e.g., retail depositors). When a liquidity shock strikes large lenders' portfolio, the large lenders might want to take their money back immediately. This potential channel of crisis spillovers may arise due to large lenders' prudent risk management where the assets of large lenders are often marked to market on a daily basis. This possibility causes small investors to panic and to rush into the financial institution. Under these circumstances, the borrower would attempt to adjust its asset portfolio, accelerating the liquidity shocks in the market. In this regard, Liu and Mello (2009) call large lenders to be a double-edged sword; "the presence of a large lender is an element of stability in good times, but it increases fragility in bad times." This new channel is distinctly different from the conventional channels such as asymmetric information on asset quality or financial contagion.

Bank wholesale funding may become a source of risk due to insufficient monitoring and inefficient liquidations of banks by short-term wholesale financiers. Huang and Ratnovski (2011) suggest that wholesale funds can be beneficially used in "traditional" banks, which hold mostly opaque and nontradable relationship loans. In contrast, these funds can create significant risks in "modern" banks that hold mostly arm's length assets with readily available, but noisy, public signals on their values. In their model, short-term wholesale financiers tend to withdraw based on negative public signals especially when these signals are costless but noisy on bank project quality. Under these circumstances, they jump into inefficient liquidation instead of costly monitoring.

Similar to Huang and Ratnovski (2011), Goldsmith–Pinkham and Yorulmazer (2010) show that both the run on Northern Rock and the subsequent bailout announcement had significant effects on the rest of the banking system. Furthermore, the effects were a rational response by investors to market news and reflected the characteristics of affected banks. In particular, the spillover effects can be explained by banks' funding characteristics given that the banks that relied on funding from wholesale markets were affected severely. This is a result consistent with the liquidity crunch in debt and interbank markets prior to the run on Northern Rock. Their results contribute to the discussion on the origins of bank failures by providing evidence that the liability side and funding characteristics of banks can be a leading source of bank failures and spillover effects.

Although noncore liabilities (or wholesale funding) are seen as an unstable source of bank funding, there is a systemic reason why banks expand loans through noncore liabilities, which eventually give rise to a build-up of financial vulnerability. Hahm, Shin, and Shin (2013) develop a model of credit supply to explain how banks expand lending through noncore liabilities during the times when perceived risks are low. When measured risks are low and core deposits are "sticky" and do not have a capacity to grow in line with credit supply, banks finance the expansion in credit using the noncore funding from the capital market without any substantial increase in risk.

EMPIRICAL STUDIES ON LINK BETWEEN THE BANK CREDIT CHANNEL AND BANK RISK

There have been a few empirical studies in the banking literature on how the structure of bank credit channels influences bank risk. First, there is a study that links bank risk with the creditor structure and the cost of funding. Craig and Dinger (2013) focus on the relationship between deposit market competition and bank risk to test whether the risk of bank assets is linked with its funding costs. Estimating a joint system of equations incorporating the interrelation among bank risk, deposit market competition, and wholesale funding costs on U.S. bank-level panel data, they report that the costs of retail and wholesale liabilities have a statistically robust and significant positive effect on the riskiness of bank assets. It is noteworthy that they integrated the wholesale market component in their analysis of the relationship between deposit market competition and bank risk. However, this study does not directly test the relationship between the bank risk and bank funding structure, nor deal with differentiating consequences in crisis and in normal periods.

While core liabilities in the bank creditor structure are an important source of bank stability, studies suggest that rapid growth in credits is usually accompanied by the accumulation of noncore liabilities in the boom period, which in turn raises chances of financial crisis. Hahm et al. (2013) test whether recent financial crises in emerging and developing economies are related to noncore liabilities of the banking sector, using random effects of panel probit analyses on a comprehensive country-level panel dataset. Noncore liabilities are defined in several ways by combining following variables: liabilities of banks to the foreign sector, liabilities to the nonbanking financial sector, and a gap between M3 and M2. They find strong evidence that noncore liabilities, especially the liabilities to the foreign sector, increase the chances of currency crisis and credit crisis. During normal period, the credit expands rapidly mainly through wholesale funding channels because the retail funding (or core deposit) is *sticky*. However, as the cycle turns, the decline in credit is accompanied by the sudden stop in capital flows leading to collapse of currency and stock market. Noncore liability ratio is shown to have a strong predictive power of crisis, in addition to the credit to GDP ratio.

When there is a rapid growth of credits compared to deposits, the banks resort to noncore liabilities to meet the excess demand as pointed out in Kilinc, Karasoy, and Yucel (2013). This fact implies a close relationship between credit growth and noncore bank liabilities. Using VAR and VECM framework based on Turkish time-series data, they provide empirical evidence that there is a close relationship between credit growth and noncore liabilities. Their study finds that increased demand for credit may induce an increase in noncore liabilities as suggested by Hahm et al. (2013).

During the global financial crisis of 2008–2009, financial markets in Korea were no exception in experiencing credit contraction in the credit market. Financial crisis severely influenced the Korean banks and the banking behavior of the public, as the market sensed the augmented vulnerability of banks. Capital market participants and bank depositors are concerned about bank risk in relation to creditor structure during a liquidity crisis. This is because they expect potential withdrawals from large depositors during a liquidity crisis when the proportion of bank deposits by major credit suppliers is large. Suh, Park, and Shin (2010) look into the Korean bank-level data to see how depositor structure might influence the bank risk during the liquidity crisis.[1] They provide an empirical study showing that the depositor structure of an individual bank may have a significant impact on bank risk when market liquidity dries up. More specifically, if the share of deposits by companies and institutions (opposed to those by individuals) among total deposits is high for a bank, the bank risk may be negatively influenced when market liquidity contracts. Here, we present their work in detail.

Their chapter use volatility (standard deviation) of stock price returns as a proxy for bank default risk as it is one of the most widely used and representative of market information.[2] One can argue that because volatility of stock price returns represents only the equity risk and variance of return on bank debt may not be reflected, it does not well represent the default risk of the bank as a whole. However, Aharony, Jones, and Swary (1980) and Smirlock (1984) show that the bank's default risk tends to move in the same direction with the volatility of stock price returns.

To appropriately capture the response of the depositors during the liquidity crisis, they use deposit growth of each bank as an alternative proxy for bank risk. This variable may not have been used as a proxy for bank risk in conventional studies. However, growth of deposit can be an important source of bank funding in times when the deposits are not fully insured and when funding through marketable securities dries up and, thus, reduction in deposit growth may imply heightened bank liquidity risk. Since it is reasonable to argue that during the financial crisis of 2008–2009, the risk for Korean banks was incurred not due to the deterioration of bank asset quality, but due to the difficulty in securing bank funding in the face of market liquidity crisis; it would be interesting to see how deposit growth changed.

They use an unbalanced quarterly bank-level panel data from 2004 to 2008 to estimate the following bank-specific fixed effects model.

$$Y_{it} = \alpha + \beta_1 \cdot \mathrm{rdepo}_{it} + \beta_2 \cdot \mathrm{rdepo}_{it} \cdot \mathrm{crisis}_{it} + \beta_3 \cdot \mathrm{crisis}_t + \gamma \cdot Z_{it} + \varepsilon_{it}$$

where Y_{it} is the dependent variable representing bank risk, rdepo_{it} represents depositor structure where it is defined as the proportion of deposits from large lenders (private companies and other institutions) out of the bank's total deposits. The variable crisis_t is a proxy variable for liquidity crisis. Z is a set of the variables to control for the bank's capital adequacy, liquidity, bank size, asset quality, loan structure, and leverage. The list of control variables include capital adequacy ratio (bis) stipulated by Bank for International Settlement, household loan share (hse), nonperforming loan ratio (npl), log of total assets (size), ROA (roa), loan-to-deposit ratio (ldr), deposit rate gap (int), and leverage (lev).[3]

They first assess the impact of depositor structure during liquidity crisis on the bank risk when it is measured by the bank's stock price volatility (sdr). Since stock price is needed, only the (10) listed banks are in the sample for this analysis. Four different proxies were used for crisis variable (crisis): crisis period dummy, CDS premium, 1-year yield spread, and 3-year yield spread.[4] Their basic results shown in Table 1 illustrate that the

Table 1. Impact of Depositor Structure During Liquidity Crisis on the Stock Price Volatility.

Liquidity Crisis Variable	(1) Crisis Dummy	(2) CDS	(3) SPREAD1	(4) SPREAD3
rdepo	0.009	−0.013	−0.001	−0.005
	(0.382)	(−0.606)	(−0.0240)	(−0.249)
rdepo × crisis	0.040*	0.020**	0.023*	0.022*
	(1.773)	(2.241)	(1.843)	(1.883)
crisis	0.001	0.000	0.006	0.005
	(0.0983)	(0.149)	(0.901)	(0.804)
bis	0.002***	0.001*	0.002**	0.001*
	(3.409)	(1.896)	(2.549)	(1.966)
hse	−0.001*	−0.000	−0.000	−0.000
	(−1.740)	(−1.172)	(−1.090)	(−1.106)
npl	0.007***	0.005***	0.005***	0.005***
	(4.240)	(3.252)	(3.588)	(3.422)
size	0.007	0.005	−0.005	−0.004
	(0.891)	(0.659)	(−0.724)	(−0.540)
roa	−0.002	−0.001	−0.001	−0.001
	(−1.408)	(−0.532)	(−0.473)	(−0.530)
ldr	−0.000	−0.000	−0.000	−0.000
	(−0.564)	(−0.334)	(−0.385)	(−0.456)
lev	−0.000	−0.000	0.000	−0.000
	(−0.355)	(−0.418)	(0.354)	(−0.008)
Observations	182	182	182	182
Adjusted R^2	0.537	0.639	0.642	0.647

Notes: Dependent variable is stock price volatility (sdr). The variable rdepo represents depositor structure, which is defined as the proportion of deposits from large lenders (private companies and other institutions) out of the bank's total deposits. Control variables are capital adequacy ratio (bis) stipulated by Bank for International Settlement, household loan share (hse), nonperforming loan ratio (npl), log of total assets (size), ROA (roa), loan-to-deposit ratio (ldr), deposit rate gap (int), and leverage (lev). Regressions are based on unbalanced quarterly panel data of Korean banks from 2004 to 2008. Four different proxies were used for crisis variable (crisis): crisis period dummy, CDS premium, 1-year yield spread, and 3-year yield spread. Numbers in the parentheses are t-statistics. All regressions include unreported estimates of bank-specific fixed effect dummies. ***$p<0.01$, **$p<0.05$, * $p<0.1$. This table is reconstructed from Tables 3 and 4 of Suh et al. (2010).

depositor structure does not influence the stock price volatility during normal times, but have significantly negative impact on stock price volatility during the liquidity crisis, as the interaction term between the rdepo and crisis is significantly positive. This implies that as the share of private companies and other institutions (wholesale deposits) in the total deposits increases, the bank risk measured in terms of stock price volatility augments during the liquidity crisis.

They check the robustness of their results by using deposit growth as the dependent variable. The market might respond to the heightened bank risk by avoiding the respective bank when depositing funds. Since the deposit variable is widely available, all (16) Korean commercial banks are included in the sample. The results provided in Table 2 show that the depositor structure influences the deposit growth positively during normal times, but have a significantly negative additional impact on deposit growth during the liquidity crisis, as the interaction term between the rdepo and crisis is significantly negative. This implies that as the share of private companies and other institutions (wholesale deposits) in the total deposits increases, the bank risk measured in terms of deposit growth increases during the period of a liquidity crisis.

In sum, their findings indicate that if a bank relies too much on funding from large lenders such as financial institutions, corporations, and major credit suppliers, it may lead to heightened bank risk during a liquidity crisis.

POLICY IMPLICATIONS AND CONCLUDING REMARKS

This chapter reviews the literature on bank risk with a specific focus on recent researches highlighting the relationship between bank creditor structure and bank risk during the period of a liquidity crisis. Departing from the conventional theoretical framework, which points to deteriorating asset quality to be the culprit for the amplified bank risk in the face of financial crisis, the studies in recent years look into the liability side of the bank balance sheet as a potential source for the augmented bank risk during the period of financial crisis leading to liquidity contraction. Recent studies including Suh et al. (2010) and Hahm et al. (2013) provided empirical supports to the newly developed hypothesis. Empirical evidence from using bank-level panel data in Korea indicates that if a bank relies too much on funding from large lenders such as financial institutions, corporations, and

Table 2. Impact of Depositor Structure During Liquidity Crisis on the Growth of Deposits.

Liquidity Crisis Variable	(1) Crisis Period Dummy	(2) CDS	(3) SPREAD1	(4) SPREAD3
rdepo	74.647***	78.829***	77.252***	79.785***
	(5.437)	(5.572)	(5.571)	(5.661)
rdepo × crisis	−23.922*	−10.120*	−17.474*	−17.056**
	(−1.653)	(−1.664)	(−1.969)	(−2.074)
crisis	10.161	0.042	6.828	7.014
	(1.306)	(1.266)	(1.417)	(1.571)
bis	0.893**	0.962**	0.981**	1.010**
	(1.993)	(2.139)	(2.202)	(2.257)
hse	0.040	0.018	−0.005	0.005
	(0.222)	(0.0969)	(−0.0294)	(0.0289)
npl	−1.301	−1.129	−0.982	−1.036
	(−1.206)	(−1.018)	(−0.903)	(−0.949)
size	12.958***	13.245***	15.290***	14.675***
	(2.805)	(2.876)	(3.180)	(3.081)
roa	1.603	1.528	1.256	1.329
	(1.291)	(1.228)	(1.010)	(1.071)
ldr	−0.031	−0.033	−0.036	−0.035
	(−0.636)	(−0.680)	(−0.757)	(−0.728)
lev	0.647***	0.632***	0.588***	0.610***
	(3.038)	(2.985)	(2.752)	(2.873)
int	1.590	1.457	1.688	1.793
	(0.488)	(0.447)	(0.516)	(0.549)
Observations	262	262	262	262
Adjusted R^2	0.515	0.517	0.522	0.522

Notes: Dependent variable is growth in deposits (DEP). The variable rdepo represents depositor structure, which is defined as the proportion of deposits from large lenders (private companies and other institutions) out of the bank's total deposits. Control variables are capital adequacy ratio (bis) stipulated by Bank for International Settlement, household loan share (hse), nonperforming loan ratio (npl), log of total assets (size), ROA (roa), loan-to-deposit ratio (ldr), deposit rate gap (int), and leverage (lev). Regressions are based on unbalanced quarterly panel data of Korean banks from 2004 to 2008. Four different proxies were used for crisis variable (crisis): crisis period dummy, CDS premium, 1-year yield spread, and 3-year yield spread. Numbers in the parentheses are *t*-statistics. All regressions include unreported estimates of bank-specific fixed effect dummies. ***$p<0.01$, **$p<0.05$, *$p<0.1$. This table is reconstructed from Table 6 of Suh et al. (2010).

major credit suppliers, it may lead to heightened bank risk during a liquidity crisis.

In the face of sudden contraction of market liquidity, bank risk can be significantly influenced not only by the degree of asset quality, but also by the liability structure. These new studies strongly suggest that regulations on liability structure should be seriously considered in revising and redesigning banking sector regulations to guard against worsening bank risk.

In recent years, regulations on liquidity have been strengthened somewhat reflecting these concerns about having sound liability structure. Since 2007, the Basel Committee has put into place a new liquidity standard called Net Stable Funding Ratio (NSFR), which is defined as a ratio of the available amount of stable funding to the required amount of stable funding. Overall, retail funding is regarded as more stable source of funding in this regulatory framework. Recent empirical studies have offered clear evidence that such regulations have good reasons to be instituted.

NOTES

1. Bank risk is usually divided into financial risk and operational risk. Financial risk is classified, depending on the source of risk, as credit risk, market risk, liquidity risk, and interest rate risk. However, since capital market participants are interested in default risk of bank the most, the bank risk is defined as more general risk such as insolvency risk or probability of default.
2. Volatility of stock price returns and systematic risk were used as the market measure proxies based on market information (Lepetit, Nys, Rous, & Tarazi, 2008). Many other kinds of proxy have been used for bank default risk. For example, the standard deviation of ROA (return on assets) or ROE (return on equity) are used as accounting measures (Lepetit et al., 2008). Credit risk measurement using the option pricing model such as the distance to default in the KMV model (1993) could also be used as a proxy. In addition, credit spreads of bonds issued by banks (Krishnan, Ritchken & Thompson, 2006) and the subordinated debt yield to maturity (Evanoff & Wall, 2001) are also used as a proxy for default risk.
3. Deposit rate gap (int) is derived from the gap between the average deposit rates of an individual bank and the average deposit rates of all commercial banks during the same period and leverage (lev) is calculated as an individual bank's total asset over its Tier I capital.
4. The crisis period dummy is one from 2008 3Q onward and zero otherwise. CDS premium is credit default swap premium for Korea. One-year (3-year) yield spread represents the yield spread between 1-year (3-year) bank notes and 1-year (3-year) Treasury notes in Korea.

ACKNOWLEDGMENT

Jungsoo Park acknowledges research fund support from National Research Foundation of Korea Grant funded by the Korean Government (NRF-2010-330-B00069).

REFERENCES

Aharony, J., Jones, C., & Swary, I. (1980). An analysis of risk and return characteristics of corporate bankruptcy using capital market data. *Journal of Finance, 35*, 1001–1016.

Berger, A. N., & Bouwman, C. H. S. (2009). Bank liquidity creation. *Review of Financial Studies, 22*(9), 3779–3837.

Besanko, D., & Kanatas, G. (1996). The regulation of bank capital: Do capital standards promote bank safety? *Journal of Financial Intermediation, 5*(2), 160–183.

Cebula, R. J. (1999). New evidence on determinants of bank failures in the US. *Applied Economics Letters, 6*(1), 45–47.

Craig, B. R., & Dinger, V. (2013). Deposit market competition, wholesale funding, and bank risk. *Journal of Banking and Finance, 37*, 3605–3622.

Diamond, D. W., & Rajan, R. G. (2000). A theory of bank capital. *Journal of Finance, 55*(6), 2431–2465.

Evanoff, D. D., & Wall, L. D. (2001). Sub-debt yield spreads as bank risk measures. *Journal of Financial Services Research, 20*, 121–145.

Furlong, F. T., & Keely, M. C. (1989). Capital regulation and bank risk-taking: A note. *Journal of Banking and Finance, 13*, 883–891.

Goldsmith-Pinkham, P., & Yorulmazer, T. (2010). Liquidity, bank runs, and bailouts: Spillover effects during the northern rock episode. *Journal of Financial Services Research, 37*(2–3), 83–98.

Gorton, G., & Winton, A. (2000). *Liquidity provision, bank capital, and the macroeconomy*. Available at SSRN: http://ssrn.com/abstract=253849

Hahm, J. H., Shin, H. S., & Shin, K. (2013). Noncore bank liabilities and financial vulnerability. *Journal of Money, Credit, and Banking, 45*(s1), 3–36.

Huang, R. R., & Ratnovski, L. (2011). The dark side of bank wholesale funding. *Journal of Financial Intermediation, 20*(2), 248–263.

Keely, M. C., & Furlong, F. T. (1990). A Re-examination of mean-variance analysis of bank capital regulation. *Journal of Banking and Finance, 14*, 69–84.

Kilinc, Z., Karasoy, H. G., & Yucel, E. (2013). *Non-core liabilities and credit growth*. Working Paper No. 1324, Research and Monetary Policy Department, Central Bank of the Republic of Turkey, Istanbul, Turkey.

KMV. (1993). *Credit monitor overview*. San Francisco, CA: KMV Corporation.

Krishnan, C. N. V., Ritchken, P. H., & Thompson, J. B. (2006). On credit-spread slopes and predicting bank risk. *Journal of Money, Credit and Banking, 38*(6), 1545–1574.

Lepetit, L., Nys, E., Rous, P., & Tarazi, A. (2008). Bank income structure and risk: An empirical analysis of european banks. *Journal of Banking and Finance, 32*, 1452–1467.

Liu, X., & Mello, A. S. (2009). The creditor channel of liquidity crises. Available at SSRN: http://ssrn.com/abstract=1320684

Sharpe, W. F. (1978). Bank capital adequacy, deposit insurance and security values. *Journal of Financial and Quantitative Analysis*, *13*(4), 701–718.

Shin, H. S. (2009). Reflections on Northern Rock: The bank run that heralded the global financial crisis. *Journal of Economic Perspectives*, *23*(1), 101–119.

Smirlock, M. (1984). An analysis of bank risk and deposit rate ceilings: Evidence from the capital markets. *Journal of Monetary Economics*, *13*, 195–210.

Suh, J. H., Park, J., & Shin, H. H. (2010). The impact of depositor structure on bank risk in liquidity crisis. *Journal of Money & Finance*, *24*(1), 99–129.

BANK MONITORING AND ACQUIRER RETURNS: EVIDENCE FROM THE U.S. SYNDICATED LOAN MARKET

Hae Jin Chung, Eunyoung Jang and Kwangwoo Park

ABSTRACT

This chapter examines the effect of creditors' monitoring role on the profitability of firm acquisitions. We use the shares retained by the lead arranger of a syndicated loan as a proxy for monitoring level. We find that acquirer announcement returns are positively related to the shares retained by the lead arranger. The effect of the lead arranger's shares on the acquirer's return becomes pronounced in cash acquisition deals, and when there exist financial covenants. Our results suggest that lead arrangers are important not only for monitoring loans but also for successful acquisitions by borrowers. An important policy implication of the main findings of this chapter on bank monitoring is that policy makers should

Global Banking, Financial Markets and Crises
International Finance Review, Volume 14, 449–475

ISSN: 1569-3767/doi:10.1108/S1569-3767(2013)0000014018

design financial covenants to improve the efficiency of monitoring activities by lead arranging banks in syndicated bank loan deals.

Keywords: Mergers and acquisitions; bank monitoring; syndicated loan; corporate governance

JEL classifications: G34; G35

INTRODUCTION

Theory in the banking literature suggests that banks' effective monitoring and screening activities result in certification and value-enhancement for borrower firms. Extant theoretical studies such as Diamond (1984) and Rajan and Winton (1995) argue that banks perform unique monitoring roles and show how firm–bank relationships affect the firm value and investment policy. Empirical evidence broadly confirms the notion that stock markets react positively to the announcements of new bank loan and renewal where there is wealth gained by the shareholders of borrowing firms (Billett, Flannery, & Garfinkel, 1995; James, Lummer, & McConnell, 1989).[1]

One might then question whether a good banking relationship can help borrower firms to make good corporate finance decisions and, as a result, see favorable market reactions. This chapter empirically examines the disciplining role of creditors in the corporate finance decision-making process in the United States. In particular, we use the syndicated loan structure to examine the effect of bank monitoring on the profitability of acquisitions. Mergers and acquisitions (M&As) are among the most important corporate finance decisions that a firm makes. Successful mergers can create substantial synergies, while misguided acquisitions can lead firms to misallocate important resources. In addition, as many studies have shown, acquisition decisions can create disparities between shareholders' and managers' interests because managers do not always make decisions that maximize shareholder value. This disparity causes agency problems, and lowers firm value. Therefore, if creditor monitoring mitigates the agency problems, acquisition decision of borrowing firms can increase firm value, benefiting shareholders. Creditors, especially banks, specialize in monitoring borrowers' financial activities and investment policies.

In examining the creditor's monitoring role and activities, we look at the syndicated loan structure, especially the shares retained by lead arrangers.

The majority of academic research on syndicated loan is based on the information asymmetry between lead arrangers and participants in a syndicate (Dennis & Mullineaux, 2000; Ivashina, 2009; Lee & Mullineaux, 2004; Lee, Kwak, Mullineaux, & Park, 2010; Sufi, 2007). Despite the importance of syndicated loans and the uniqueness of the syndication process, studies have not examined the effect of monitoring on firm governance, and little is known about how the structure of a syndicated loan addresses and mitigates moral hazard problems within the syndicate. In addition, while academics have shown considerable interest in the monitoring role of institutional investors in reducing agency problems between managers and shareholders, few studies have shown how creditors perform monitoring roles, so direct evidence that creditors monitor corporate decisions and therefore enhance firm value is lacking.[2] This chapter fills this gap by providing empirical evidence.

The remainder of the chapter is organized as follows. Section titled "Literature Review and Hypotheses Development" discusses the related literature and develops hypotheses. Section titled "Data and Variables" describes how the samples were constructed and discusses the variables we used. Section titled "Empirical Results" presents the methodology and empirical results. Finally, Section titled "Concluding Remarks" concludes the chapter.

LITERATURE REVIEW AND HYPOTHESES DEVELOPMENT

Agency Problems and the Monitoring Role of Creditors

It has been well documented that agency problems can be mitigated by the disciplining role of large or institutional shareholders. Shleifer and Vishny (1986) argue that large shareholders are expected to monitor management effectively using enough voting control to reduce the agency problem, that is, the conflicts of interests between shareholders and managers arising from dispersed ownership. For example, if shareholders could perfectly monitor and control managers' investment decisions, acquisitions that deliver managerial benefits but reduce shareholder wealth would not be allowed. Chen, Harford, and Li (2007) argue that institutional investors will monitor and that their monitoring activities will result in information advantages when monitoring benefits exceed costs. They find that only concentrated holdings by independent institutional investors are related to post-merger performance.

There are several forms that concentration can take, including large shareholders and large creditors, and these forms of concentrated ownership address the agency problem (Shleifer & Vishny, 1997). Large creditors like banks have many similarities to large shareholders. Since they have made a large investment in the firm, like the large shareholders, they need to see a return on their investments. Creditors, especially banks, specialize in monitoring borrowers' financial activities and investment policies. In general, the purpose of monitoring is to reduce a bank's credit risk by preventing borrowers from engaging in opportunistic behavior. Diamond (1984) presents one of the first models of monitoring by banks that use their informational advantages to monitor compliance with loan covenants. Rajan and Winton (1995) argue that both covenants and collaterals can be motivated as contractual devices that increase a lender's monitoring incentive. Garleanu and Zwiebel (2009) analyze the design and renegotiation of covenants in debt contracts and find that a covenant design is a key monitoring device for banks to obtain control rights in situations where creditor's interests are at risk. They also find that banks are likely to impose restrictive covenants to retain the right to collect additional information and to deter borrowers from excessive risk-taking.

Theories suggest that banks serve as a bridge between borrower firms and the capital market because of their information advantage and evaluation capabilities, and predict that the market will respond favorably when borrower firms announce bank loans. This theory is consistent with both the certification and the monitoring role of banks. James (1987) finds that a positive stock price response to the announcement of new bank credit agreements is greater than that to the announcement of private debt agreements. Billett et al. (1995) investigate whether the lenders' identity influences the market reaction to a loan announcement and find that lenders with a higher credit rating are associated with larger abnormal borrower returns, while there is no statistically significant difference between the stock price responses to bank and nonbank loans. Dahiya, Puri, and Saunders (2002) provide evidence that the market reacts negatively to the announcement of the sale of a borrower's loans by its lending bank, indicating that stock prices respond unfavorably to the news of a failure of lending relationship.

Among the studies on creditor control of borrowing firms, Chava and Roberts (2008) show how violations of financial covenants impact corporate investment policy. They find that covenant violations lead to declines in capital investment when creditors use the threat of accelerating the loan to intervene in management. Nini, Smith, and Sufi (2012) provide evidence that creditors play an active role in corporate governance. Other studies like Boyd and Prescott (1986), Diamond (1991), and Almazan and Suarez (2003) also show that banks perform governance activities related to a firm's investment policy.

The Syndicated Loan Market and Hypotheses

In this section, we describe the syndicated loan market structure based on Sufi (2007) and Ivashina (2009). As a result of growth in the syndicated loan market, syndicated lending has become not only a significant source of financing for firms but also one of the largest sources of underwriting revenue for lenders. In a syndicated loan, two or more lenders agree to make a joint loan to a borrower. Every syndicate member has a separate claim on the debtor, although there is a single loan agreement contract; the members are divided into two groups: lead arrangers and participant lenders. This distinction is important since each group has a different purpose for participating in the syndicated loan market, as well as a different role in syndication process.

In the syndication process, the lead arranger negotiates key terms, including loan amounts, fees, and covenants, with the borrower and signs a preliminary loan agreement ("mandate"). Once the preliminary loan agreement is signed, the lead arranger finds participants and prepares an "information memorandum" with detailed descriptions of the borrower and the proposed loan. After the participants agree to fund a portion of the loan, all parties sign the loan agreement. Each participant has a responsibility for his or her share of the loan, and the terms of the loan are identical among all syndicate members. During the life of the loan, the lead arranger monitors the firm, serves as a clearinghouse for interim cash flow, and enforces financial covenants for participants.

A lead arranger who sells part of a loan to other participants originates the syndicated loan. The structure of the syndicated loan is determined as a result of interaction between the lead arranger and the participants. Although the lead arranger retains only part of the loan, it acts as the agent for the loan, with a primary responsibility for *ex ante* due diligence and *ex post* monitoring of the borrower. In addition, participants depend on the information that the lead arranger collects, so there is information asymmetry problem between the lead arranger and the participants. Specifically, before the syndication, there is an adverse selection problem because the lead arranger has incentives to syndicate low-quality loans. After the syndication, there is a moral hazard problem because the lead arranger's incentive to monitor is reduced. Both problems are mitigated if the lead bank retains a larger fraction of the loan, as a larger share signals a high-quality loan and improves the alignment of incentives between the lead bank and the syndicate participants.

Several studies are related to how syndicated loans are structured, why loans are syndicated, and how syndicated loans are priced. Simons (1993) finds that the main reason for syndication is diversification. Dennis and Mullineaux (2000) observe that a larger proportion of the loan is syndicated if the borrower has more public information than if it has less information. Lee and Mullineaux (2004) show that syndicated loans have a more concentrated (with fewer lenders) structure when borrowing firms are more likely to default.

Sufi (2007) finds that the lead bank retains a larger share of the loan and forms a more concentrated syndicate when the borrower requires more intense monitoring and due diligence, empirical results that are consistent with moral hazard in monitoring. Ivashina (2009) finds that the cost that arises from information asymmetry between the lead bank and the participants of the lending syndicate accounts for approximately 4 percent of the total cost of credit. Gopalan, Nanda, and Yerramilli (2011) look at the consequences of shocks to lead arrangers' reputations from large-scale bankruptcy filings by their borrowers (Chapter 11), and find that the lead arranger retains a significantly larger fraction of the loans it arranges in the subsequent year.

These studies indicate that the lead arranger could lack the incentive to provide an optimal level of effort, so participants should consider moral hazard problems and require that the lead arranger hold a larger fraction of the loan in order to enhance incentives, especially if the borrowing firm requires considerable due diligence and monitoring. In addition, acquisitions have the potential for wide disparity between shareholders' and managers' interests, which can be mitigated by monitoring of lead arrangers. Finally, since a syndicated loan is a source of corporate financing, it is rational to consider that lead arrangers are particularly interested in cash M&A deals and in making an effort to monitor in those cases. Accordingly, we have the following two hypotheses:

Hypothesis 1. Lead arrangers of a loan syndicate have greater incentives to monitor the borrower if they retain higher proportion of the loan, leading to better investment decisions of the borrower. We expect that the acquirer's announcement returns are higher if higher proportion of the acquirer's loan is retained by the lead arrangers.

Hypothesis 2. Lead arrangers have greater incentives to monitor the acquisition if entire deal is paid in cash while having less of incentives if entire deal is paid in equity. Thus, acquirers' return should be higher for cash deals given the proportion of the loan held by the lead arrangers.

DATA AND VARIABLES

Data

We collect the acquisition data using the Securities Data Corporation's (SDC) U.S. M&As database. Our sample consists of the U.S. domestic acquisitions announced from 1993 to 2006. To be included in our sample, acquisitions must be complete, and all the acquirers, the target, and the firm that results from the acquisition should be available on both COMPUSTAT and Center for Research in Security Prices (CRSP) Daily Stock Price and Returns file. We drop the acquisition if the acquirer's initial stake of the target exceeds 50 percent or if its final stake is less than 100 percent. We also exclude acquisitions valued at less than either $1 million or 1 percent of the acquirer's market value of equity on the 11th trading day prior to the announcement date.

We also collect syndicated loan data using the LPC DealScan database, which contains comprehensive information on the terms of syndicated loan contracts. The sample we employ consists of syndicated loans issued from 1991 to 2006 that have data on the shares retained by the lead arranger. We match the syndicated loan data with COMPUSTAT using the DealScan–COMPUSTAT link data provided by Michael Roberts' personal website (Chava & Roberts, 2008). The unit of observation in DealScan is a loan, also known as a facility or a tranche. (A syndicated loan can be structured to have more than one loan tranche.) If a syndicated loan has multiple tranches, we use the largest tranche for the deal-level analysis because actual syndicated loan contract terms, including covenants and lenders, are determined at the deal level. To identify the lead arranger, we first look at "Lenders–Lead Arranger" if it is available; otherwise, the lead arranger is assumed to be the lender identified as a "Lead Role" in the "Lenders–All Lenders" data. Once we identify the lead arranger, we obtain the shares retained by the lead arranger at loan origination. For the loans with multiple lead arrangers, the lead share is the sum of the shares retained by the multiple lead banks. To analyze the effect of the acquirer's syndicated loan characteristics on acquisition performance, we look at the characteristics of the acquirer's loan with the largest lead share two-and-half years prior to the acquisition announcement date to avoid the effect of selection bias in case that banks make loans to the borrowers with better acquisition opportunities. Our final sample has 598 acquisition deals.

Table 1 shows summary statistics of the sample acquisitions by announcement year. The number of acquisitions per year increases until 1998's 95 acquisitions and then plummets significantly in the following years to a nadir of 12 acquisitions in 2005. The median relative deal size to acquirer market value is stable during the sample period, but the median absolute deal value fluctuates with the acquirer's firm size, which is measured by the market value of equity. The matched syndicated loans of acquirers have median lead share ranges in the 20–25 percent range, with some exceptional years. The amount of the largest facility in a loan package varies over the years, with a median of $150 million during the entire sample period. These trends in acquisitions and syndicated loan characteristics are similar to those reported in other studies, such as Masulis, Wang, and Xie (2007) and Ivashina (2009).

Variable Construction

Acquirer Return

We adopt 5-day cumulative abnormal returns (CARs) as a performance measure to evaluate the monitoring role of large creditors in acquisition. The 5-day CAR is the acquirer's abnormal announcement-period return during the window of two days before through two days after the initial acquisition announcement. Daily abnormal returns are computed using the market model, where the CRSP equal-weighted return is used as the market return. The parameter estimation period is from 210 days to 10 days prior to the acquisition announcement date.

Table 2 shows how the announcement abnormal returns differ according to the characteristics of the acquisition and the syndicated loan. The whole sample has 1.14 percent of the average 5-day CAR, which is significantly different from zero at the 1 percent level. All stock deals have an insignificant positive mean CAR, but all cash deals have a significant positive mean CAR of 1.15 percent. Acquisitions of subsidiary targets generate the highest average CAR of 1.84 percent, and the acquisitions of private firms

Table 1. Sample Distribution by Announcement Year.

Year	Number of Acquisitions	Lead Share (%)		Facility Amount ($mil)		Market Value of Equity ($mil)		Acquisition Deal Value ($mil)		Relative Size of the Acquisition	
		Mean	n	Mean	Median	Mean	Median	Mean	Median	Mean	Median
1993	21	33.74	25.00	111	85	583	260	72	46	0.21	0.17
1994	54	28.90	20.21	214	198	1,063	649	96	51	0.23	0.08
1995	82	28.76	25.58	366	125	1,167	546	103	32	0.21	0.10
1996	83	29.68	27.00	393	100	1,630	455	122	61	0.22	0.08
1997	92	36.39	35.00	193	100	1,345	533	131	40	0.38	0.10
1998	95	27.70	21.67	335	200	2,807	713	152	85	0.26	0.10
1999	41	24.93	20.00	548	275	3,534	946	188	108	0.35	0.11
2000	25	26.43	20.40	256	200	1,082	655	136	56	0.27	0.08
2001	17	23.73	20.00	346	225	3,481	2,123	195	45	0.09	0.05
2002	14	27.96	21.84	309	150	3,437	1,205	203	122	0.16	0.15
2003	19	27.68	18.67	261	225	1,917	952	159	115	0.13	0.11
2004	22	23.03	22.50	305	225	2,249	1,638	190	88	0.12	0.07
2005	12	28.17	25.00	241	150	3,272	1,163	116	80	0.23	0.05
2006	21	21.87	20.00	418	250	3,550	1,677	267	91	0.17	0.10
19937 – 2006	598(Total)	29.06	23.34	315	150	1,956	681	139	56	0.25	0.10

The sample consists of 598 completed U.S. mergers and acquisitions (listed in SDC) between 1993 and 2006. We look at the loan characteristics of the largest lead share during the two-and-half years prior to the M&A announcement date. Variable definitions are in the Appendix.

Table 2. Announcement Abnormal Returns.

	CAR (−2, +2)		
	Mean	Median	Obs
Whole sample	1.14***	0.53	598
Payment method			
All cash	1.15**	0.33	161
All stock	0.58	−0.56	93
Target ownership status			
Public	−0.59	−1.50	113
Private	1.23***	0.91	235
Subsidiary	1.84***	1.07	250
Lead share			
High (A)	1.89***	1.15	180
Middle	1.30***	0.56	240
Low (B)	0.18	0.33	178
Difference (A − B)	1.72**	0.82	
Financial covenant			
Yes	0.99***	0.40	442
No	1.57***	1.30	156
Collateral			
Yes	1.36***	0.84	370
No	0.44***	0.44	228
Rated			
Yes	0.32	−0.24	303
No	1.99***	1.63	295

The sample consists of 598 completed U.S. mergers and acquisitions (listed in SDC) between 1993 and 2006. We look at the loan characteristics of the largest lead share during the two and half year prior to the M&A announcement date. Variable definitions are in the Appendix. **, *** stand for statistical significance based on two-sided tests at the 5% and 1%, respectively.

have an average CAR of 1.23 percent; both of the means are significantly different from zero, while the mean CAR from the acquisitions of public firms is negative and insignificant. The same pattern is observed at the median CARs. These results coincide with those of Masulis et al. (2007).

We further divide the sample into three groups based on Lead share, the key explanatory variable in our analysis, and report the mean and median CARs. Because Lead share is a proxy for the lead arranger's level of monitoring, we expect that CAR increases as Lead share increases. In univariate analysis, acquisitions made by firms with high lead share loans show significantly higher CARs than do those made by firms with low lead share loans. Table 2 also shows that CAR varies with the loan characteristics, such as the existence of financial covenants, collateral, and ratings. As these loan characteristics are known to also determine the Lead share of the syndicated loan, we model these factors to predict Lead share in our analysis.

Determinants of Acquirer Returns

This chapter employs bidder and deal characteristics from those of Masulis et al. (2007) to explain acquirer returns. Our process for constructing each control variable and the argument on which sign we expect is from Masulis et al. (2007). The bidder characteristics that we employ for control are firm size, Tobin's Q, leverage, free cash flow, and stock price run-up. All of the variables except stock price run-up are the value at the end of the fiscal year prior to the acquisition announcement, while stock price run-up is estimated over the 200-day window from the announcement.

Firm size is expected to have a negative association with acquirer returns. Moeller, Schlingemann, and Stulz (2004) document that small firms have significantly higher abnormal announcement returns than large firms do. They interpret this evidence in light of the managerial hubris hypothesis by Roll (1986), as managerial hubris plays more of a role in the decisions of large firms. Tobin's Q is defined as the ratio of a bidder's market value of assets over its book value of assets. The effect of an acquirer's Tobin's Q on acquirer return has shown mixed results.[3] Leverage is defined as the sum of the book value of long-term debt and short-term debt, divided by the market value of total assets. Higher debt levels discourage managers from empire-building, since leverage decreases future free cash flows and limits managers' discretion. Free cash flow is operating income before depreciation, minus interest expense, minus income taxes, minus capital expenditures, scaled by the book value of total assets.

Jensen's (1986) free cash flow hypothesis predicts that high free cash flows are related to low acquirer returns since managers who have more free cash flows at hand are more likely than those who don't to waste their cash pursuing private benefit of control. However, higher free cash flows can be associated with higher acquirer returns if the cash flows are the result of improved firm performance. If high-quality managers improve firm performance, they may also make better acquisition deals. We expect free cash flows to have either a positive or a negative relationship with acquirer returns. The stock price run-up is defined as a bidder's buy-and-hold abnormal return over the 200-day window (from 210 to 11 days before announcement) from the market model to control for acquirer's prior stock performance. We use the CRSP value-weighted market index as the benchmark of the market model.

We also control for the deal characteristics, which include target ownership status, method of payment, relative deal size, whether the acquisition is a diversifying acquisition, and whether the acquisition is between two firms from the high-tech industry. Fuller, Netter, and Stegemoller (2002) examine acquirer returns for firms that made multiple acquisitions within a short time period and find that acquirers realize significantly positive abnormal returns when they are purchasing a private firm or subsidiary but significantly negative abnormal returns when they are purchasing a public firm. The authors interpret this result as a liquidity discount because bidders acquire a private firm or subsidiary in a relatively illiquid market. In line with this evidence, other studies, such as Moeller et al. (2004) and Masulis et al. (2007), show that acquisitions of subsidiary targets are the most profitable. Following these studies, we include indicator variables, Public, Private, and Subsidiary, for these three categories of target firms.

It is well known that equity payment for acquisitions is related to negative abnormal returns because there is an adverse selection problem in equity issuance (Myers & Majluf, 1984). Previous studies, such as Travlos (1987), Amihud, Lev, and Travlos (1990), and Servaes (1991), find that equity deals have significantly negative abnormal acquirer announcement returns, while cash deals do not. We construct two indicator variables, denoted as All-stock deal and All-cash deal, to capture the effect of the payment method.

There is evidence that the bidder announcement returns are positively related to deal size (Asquith, Bruner, & Mullins, 1983; Moeller et al., 2004), so we control for relative deal size. We also include an indicator variable, denoted as High tech, that equals 1 if both the acquirer and the target are in high-tech industries and 0 otherwise. We adopt the definition of the high-tech industry from Loughran and Ritter (2004).

We control for an indicator variable, denoted as Diversifying acquisition, that equals 1 if the bidder and the target are from different Fama-French 48-industry classifications and 0 otherwise. The empirical evidence of the relationship between diversification and firm value shows mixed results. Studies like Morck, Shleifer, and Vishny (1990) and Masulis et al. (2007) provide evidence that diversifying acquisitions destroy shareholder value. Especially, Masulis et al. (2007) find that anti-takeover provisions are related to a greater probability that a firm will make diversifying acquisitions, which have negative acquirer announcement returns. On the other hand, Villalonga (2004a, 2004b) reports no such value destruction from diversifying acquisitions. Campa and Kedia (2002) argue that it is

Table 3. Summary Statistics.

Variable	Mean	Std Dev	*Q*1	Median	*Q*3
CAR (−2, +2)	1.142	7.212	−2.912	0.531	4.419
Loan characteristics					
Lead share (%)	29.06	19.09	14.67	23.34	40.00
Facility amount ($mil)	315	549	55	150	300
Maturity (months)	51.40	19.78	36.00	59.00	60.00
Number of lenders	9.40	8.37	3	7	13
Collateral (dummy)	0.62	0.49	0	1	1
Financial covenants (dummy)	0.74	0.44	0	1	1
Performance pricing (dummy)	0.65	0.48	0	1	1
Purpose: corporate (dummy)	0.29	0.45	0	0	1
Purpose: acquisition (dummy)	0.17	0.38	0	0	0
Purpose: refinancing (dummy)	0.43	0.50	0	0	1
Purpose: backup line (dummy)	0.10	0.30	0	0	0
Purpose: other (dummy)	0.01	0.09	0	0	0
Bidder characteristics					
Assets ($mil)	1,757	3,865	215	583	1,682
Market value of equity ($mil)	1,956	4,237	250	681	1,975
Tobin's *Q*	1.75	0.82	1.22	1.52	1.97
Leverage	0.34	0.17	0.21	0.31	0.44
Free cash flow	0.01	0.10	−0.01	0.03	0.06
Stock price runup	0.14	0.80	−0.18	0.03	0.27
Rated (dummy)	0.51	0.50	0	1	1
Relationship (dummy)	0.44	0.50	0	0	1
Acquisition deal characteristics					
Public (dummy)	0.19	0.39	0	0	0
Private (dummy)	0.39	0.49	0	0	1
Subsidiary (dummy)	0.42	0.49	0	0	1
All cash (dummy)	0.27	0.44	0	0	1
All stock (dummy)	0.16	0.36	0	0	0
Deal value ($mil)	139	190	20	56	168
Relative deal size	0.25	0.41	0.04	0.10	0.24
Diversifying acquisition (dummy)	0.40	0.49	0	0	1
High tech (dummy)	0.13	0.34	0	0	0

The sample consists of 598 completed U.S. mergers and acquisitions (listed in SDC) between 1993 and 2006. We look at the loan characteristics of the largest lead share during the two-and-half years prior to the M&A announcement date. Variable definitions are in the appendix.

acquirers' self-selection, rather than diversification itself, that results in the lower firm value in diversifying acquisitions. Table 3 reports the summary statistics for these variables. Both the acquirer characteristics and the deal characteristics in our sample are similar to those in previous studies.

Determinants of Syndicated Loan Structure

Following previous studies that focus on the effect of information asymmetry and the monitoring role of lead banks on loan syndication, we consider factors that are related to syndicated loan structure. The lead banks and other participant banks take the loan and the borrower characteristics into account to determine the proportion of the loan the lead banks will retain. The lead banks try to minimize their holdings of a syndicated loan to diversify their risk, subject to their commitment to other participant banks to perform sufficient due diligence and monitoring.

One of the most influential determinants of the syndication structure is the degree of information asymmetry the borrower faces. Opaque firms require more due diligence and monitoring by the lead bank than transparent firms do, which requires that the lead bank hold more shares in order to ensure it is committed to perform its responsibilities. Dennis and Mullineaux (2000) observe that loans are more likely to be syndicated if the borrower has more public information than if it has less information. Similarly, Sufi (2007) classifies the information environment of the borrower based on whether the borrower is listed and files for SEC and whether it has third-party credit ratings. One of Sufi's (2007) main findings is that opaque firms are related to significantly more concentrated syndicates than transparent firms are. Since our sample firms are fully covered by CRSP, they are all listed. Therefore, we construct a measure of information asymmetry that is based on the availability of third-party credit ratings; that is, we consider a borrower to be transparent if it has the S&P senior debt rating and to be opaque if it lacks the rating. We include an indicator variable, denoted as Rated, that takes the value of 1 if the firms' S&P senior debt is rated and 0 otherwise. We also control firm size, which is defined as the log transformation of the total assets, as an additional proxy for information availability of the borrower.

Other loan characteristics are related to lead banks' monitoring intensity. Rajan and Winton (1995) argue that the banks have more incentives to monitor if there is long-term debt with covenants and that both collateral and covenants can increase the lender's monitoring incentive. Dennis and Mullinaux (2000) find that maturity and security are determinants of whether a loan is syndicated. As longer-term loans reduce duplicative monitoring costs, it leads to more syndication. Empirical evidence shows that secured loans bear higher default risk than unsecured loans do and that these loans are less likely to be syndicated. When secured loans are syndicated, they are likely to be small and to have a more concentrated structure (Lee & Mullineaux, 2004). Following these studies, we control for the lead banks' incentives to monitor using the loan maturity in months, and indicator variables for the existence of financial covenants and collateral.

Sufi (2007) measures the lead bank's information advantage by looking at whether the lead bank has a previous lending relationship with the borrower and finds that the lead bank's share is smaller when there is such a relationship. We include an indicator variable, denoted as Relationship, that equals 1 if the same lead bank has arranged other loan for the same borrower during the past three years and 0 otherwise. Performance pricing links the loan spread to the firm's financial indicators, such as the leverage and/or interest coverage ratio, by changing the spread automatically with the changes in financial indicators. Studies like Ivashina (2009) find that performance pricing can reduce the costs of information asymmetry. We control for performance pricing using an indicator variable that is equal to 1 if the loan has performance pricing and 0 otherwise. Finally, following Sufi (2007) and Ivashina (2009), we include additional loan characteristics in the form of multiple-tranche and loan purpose indicators.

Table 3 presents the summary statistics of each of the variables. The average percentage of the loan syndicate kept by the lead arranger (Lead share) is 29.6 percent. Most of the acquirers' loans are for the purpose of refinancing, followed by general corporate loans and acquisition loans. Seventy-four percent of the acquirers' loans have financial covenants, and 62 percent have collateral. These figures are higher than Ivashina's (2009) figures.

EMPIRICAL RESULTS

Methodology

To determine how lead arrangers' level of monitoring affects the acquirer's abnormal returns, we use the percentage held by the lead arranger, denoted as Lead share, as the proxy for the monitoring intensity of lead arrangers because the lead arranger is more concerned about the riskiness of a deal when it has a larger stake in it. However, the proportion of deals retained by lead arrangers sometimes grows (or shrinks) not because of its willingness to monitor but because of other factors, such as market condition or the lead arranger's nonordinary need for diversification. Therefore, we take a two-stage approach of first projecting the Lead share based on the factors that determine the monitoring intensity of lead banks and then running the main regression of CAR of acquirer using the projected value of Lead share from the first stage.

Syndicated Loan Structure Analysis

The first stage of our loan structure analysis adopts a variation of Sufi's (2007) model to determine Lead share related to bank monitoring. An analysis of Lead Amount, which is the dollar amount held by lead arrangers, is also conducted for a robustness check. For the analysis of Lead share, we use the Tobit regression instead of ordinary least squares (OLS) because the value of Lead share must lie between 0 and 100 percent. We consider the residuals from Sufi's (2007) model as a kind of measurement error caused by negotiation failures, limited rationality, unexpected pressure from the outside, the bank's internal conditions, and so on. The variables we employ in the analysis are described earlier.

We follow Sufi's (2007) methodology to control for the effect of loan size. We divide the sample into three groups based on loan amount and assign a dummy variable for both the large and the middle group. We include the log of the loan amount and its interaction with the Large group dummy and the Middle group dummy in the estimation to allow the coefficient on Loan amount to be different for each group. Loan amount and borrower firm size may proxy for information asymmetry, as large firms are generally transparent and they tend to take larger loans. The dummy Rated is also a measure of information availability of the borrower. Other explanatory variables include a Relationship dummy, which captures the existence of past interactions between the firm and the lead arranger; Maturity; and the existence of financial covenants and collaterals. Finally, we control for multiple tranches, term loan, and loan purpose. All regressions include year dummies, and standard errors are robust to heteroscedasticity.

Table 4 presents the results of the first-stage analysis that explains the syndicated loan structure. It shows that Lead share is higher when the information asymmetry is worse and when the loan lacks contractual devices to reduce the cost of information asymmetry. The coefficient on Rated is significantly negative, which suggests that information generated by rating agencies reduces the need for lead arrangers' monitoring. The presence of performance pricing and financial covenants also reduces the lead share significantly because they lower the cost of information asymmetry. Maturity has a significantly negative relationship with Lead share since

Table 4. Regression Analysis of Syndicate Structure.

Dependent Variable	(1) Lead Share (% Held by lead)	(2) Lead Amount (Amount held by lead ($mil))
Log (Loan amount)	−7.34***	46.62***
	(−6.84)	(5.82)
Log (Loan amount) × Middle	−0.24**	−1.62***
	(−2.15)	(−3.60)
Log (Loan amount) × Large	−0.17	−1.28**
	(−1.11)	(−2.06)
Log (Assets)	−2.12***	0.98
	(−2.63)	(0.15)
Maturity	−0.08**	−0.64**
	(−2.21)	(−2.10)
Rated	−3.49***	−2.03
	(−2.68)	(−0.29)
Financial covenant	−3.48**	−1.43
	(−2.15)	(−0.21)
Relationship	1.26	1.26
	(1.03)	(0.19)
Performance pricing	−3.42*	−4.61
	(−1.96)	(−0.45)
Collateral	0.25	4.74
	(0.17)	(0.44)
> 1 Tranche indicator	2.17*	11.86*
	(1.74)	(1.64)
Term loan	−1.16	35.58**
	(−0.54)	(2.10)
Purpose: corporate	2.92	11.57
	(0.49)	(0.82)
Purpose: acquisition	4.97	17.22
	(0.83)	(1.25)
Purpose: refinancing	3.35	10.58
	(0.56)	(0.86)
Purpose: backup line	7.30	26.17
	(1.15)	(1.14)
Constant	217.99***	−827.10***
	(9.07)	(−5.09)
Observations	598	598
Adj. R^2 (Pseudo R^2 for Column 1)	0.0932	0.0315

This table reports coefficient estimates from a Tobit regression in Column 1 and OLS regression in Column 2. Variable definitions are in the appendix. All regressions include year dummies, and standard errors are robust to heteroskedasticity. ***, ** and * indicate significance at the 1%, 5%, and 10% level, respectively.

longer maturity decreases the cost of information gathering. Larger firms and larger deals also have lower lead shares. The existence of a past relationship and collateral, however, shows positive and insignificant effects on Lead share. Overall, the key results are consistent with the findings from previous literature. The analysis with Lead amount shows similar results to those in Lead share analysis, with the exception of the relationship with firm size and with loan amount, and most of the coefficients are insignificant.

Acquirer Returns Analysis

The main results of our analysis of how the monitoring incentives of lead banks affect the acquisition announcement returns are presented in Table 5. The dependent variable is the 5-day CARs of the acquirer, and the variable of our interest is the predicted lead share we obtained from Table 4. Loan amount and its interaction with predicted lead shares are controlled. The control variables related to the characteristics of the acquisition deal and the bidder, which follow Masulis et al. (2007), are Tobin's *Q*, leverage ratios, free cash flow, stock price run-up, target ownership status, methods of payment, relative deal sizes, and dummy variables for diversifying acquisitions and high-tech industries. All regressions include year dummies, and the standard errors are robust to heteroscedasticity.

In each regression, the predicted lead share has a significantly positive coefficient, lending support to the hypothesis that the lead arranger's level of monitoring is related to acquirers' returns in general. The baseline result in Table 5 shows that the acquirer's 5-day CAR increases by 0.71 percent per percent increase in the predicted lead share. The loan amount has a significantly net positive effect on the acquirer's returns, even after taking its interaction with predicted lead share into account. We observe that the acquirer's size has a significantly negative effect on the acquirer's returns, which is consistent with findings of previous studies. Tobin's *Q* and leverage have insignificant effects and diversifying acquisitions have a negative but insignificant effect on the acquirer's returns. The payment methods of acquisition also have little effect. We observe that acquirer's returns are lower if the acquirer experiences positive stock price run-up prior to the announcement. The relative deal size has a significantly positive association with the acquirer's return, which is consistent with previous findings. Purchasing public firms has significantly negative effect on the acquirer's return, as shown in other studies. When the acquirer and the target firm

Table 5. Regression Analysis of Acquirer Returns.

	(1)	(2)	(3)	(4)
Lead share (predicted)	0.71**	0.70**	0.80**	0.75**
	(2.20)	(2.17)	(2.36)	(2.29)
Lead share (predicted) × Acquisition purpose		−0.01		
		(−0.41)		
Lead share (predicted) × All cash			0.07	
			(1.31)	
Lead share (predicted) × Financial covenant				0.06*
				(1.87)
Log (Loan amount)	2.42***	2.49***	2.52***	2.27***
	(2.99)	(3.10)	(3.05)	(2.77)
Lead share (predicted) × Log (Loan amount)	−0.03*	−0.03*	−0.04**	−0.04**
	(−1.87)	(−1.82)	(−2.08)	(−2.13)
Log (Assets)	−1.02**	−1.04***	−0.98**	−0.98**
	(−2.57)	(−2.61)	(−2.49)	(−2.38)
Tobin's Q	0.30	0.30	0.25	0.12
	(0.63)	(0.63)	(0.52)	(0.24)
Leverage	0.02	0.11	−0.12	−0.30
	(0.01)	(0.05)	(−0.05)	(−0.14)
Free cash flow	9.90***	9.96***	9.98***	9.35***
	(3.32)	(3.35)	(3.37)	(3.15)
Stock price run-up	−1.23***	−1.25***	−1.27***	−1.27***
	(−3.19)	(−3.20)	(−3.24)	(−3.41)
Public	−2.49***	−2.48***	−2.49***	−2.51***
	(−2.78)	(−2.76)	(−2.79)	(−2.82)
Private	−0.93	−0.91	−0.92	−0.97
	(−1.36)	(−1.31)	(−1.35)	(−1.42)
All cash	0.11	0.11	−1.81	0.00
	(0.16)	(0.17)	(−1.39)	(0.00)
All stock	0.19	0.15	0.19	0.08
	(0.20)	(0.16)	(0.20)	(0.08)
Relative deal size	2.06*	2.05*	2.03*	1.94*
	(1.75)	(1.75)	(1.76)	(1.67)
Diversifying acquisition	−0.09	−0.06	−0.07	−0.19
	(−0.15)	(−0.10)	(−0.12)	(−0.32)
High tech	0.16	0.20	0.17	0.19
	(0.18)	(0.22)	(0.18)	(0.21)

Table 5. *(Continued)*

	(1)	(2)	(3)	(4)
Constant	−24.65	−25.60	−26.67	−20.26
	(−1.35)	(−1.42)	(−1.44)	(−1.10)
Observations	598	598	598	598
Adj. R^2	0.0775	0.0764	0.0794	0.0815

The dependent variable is the acquirer's 5-day CAR. Variable definitions are in the appendix. All regressions include year dummies, and standard errors are heteroskedasticity robust. ***, **, and * indicate significance at the 1%, 5%, and 10% level, respectively.

are both in the high-tech industry, the fact of belonging to the same industry has an insignificant effect.

Table 5 also reports the results of analysis of whether the lead bank's level of monitoring has a different effect on the acquirer's return if the loan is made especially for acquisition, if the acquisition is a cash deal, or if the loan has financial covenants. We include the interaction term between the predicted lead share and the dummy for the loans made for acquisition purposes in the baseline analysis and find it has an insignificant effect. This result suggests that the effect of the lead bank's level of monitoring on acquisition does not differ based on the loan's purpose. In our examination of whether the lead arranger's monitoring incentives are stronger for cash deals than for equity deals, the interaction term between the predicted lead share and the dummy for an all-cash acquisition deal has a positive, but not significant, coefficient of 0.07. We investigate this issue further by running separate regressions for the deals with each payment method (Table 6). Finally, in order to determine the role of financial covenants in lead banks' monitoring levels, we include the interaction term between predicted lead share and the dummy for the existence of financial covenants. Table 5 shows that the interaction term has a positive and significant coefficient of 0.06, which we interpret as an indication that the monitoring of the lead arrangers is more effective and adds more value to the acquisition deal when the lead arrangers are equipped with a contractual device with which to control management.

How the monitoring incentives of lead banks have different effects on acquisition returns depending on the method of acquisition payment is reported in Table 6. Cash deals have a direct impact on the value of the debt outstanding, as they reduce the cash available to serve the debt payments, while equity deals dilute shareholders' value but preserve

Table 6. Regression Analysis of Acquirer Returns by Payment Methods.

	(1) Whole Sample	(2) All Cash	(3) All Stock
Lead share (predicted)	0.71**	1.17**	−0.50
	(2.20)	(2.16)	(−0.33)
Log (Loan amount)	2.42***	1.46	3.01
	(2.99)	(1.03)	(0.72)
Lead share (predicted) × Log (Loan amount)	−0.03*	−0.06**	0.03
	(−1.87)	(−2.04)	(0.41)
Log (Assets)	−1.02**	−0.26	−2.17
	(−2.57)	(−0.33)	(−1.57)
Tobin's Q	0.30	0.12	0.86
	(0.63)	(0.16)	(0.44)
Leverage	0.02	−0.34	4.75
	(0.01)	(−0.08)	(0.46)
Free cash flow	9.90***	13.31	−1.61
	(3.32)	(1.52)	(−0.21)
Stock price run-up	−1.23***	−0.02	−2.04
	(−3.19)	(−0.01)	(−1.41)
Public	−2.49***	−0.38	−8.53**
	(−2.78)	(−0.35)	(−2.20)
Private	−0.93	−1.36	−5.60*
	(−1.36)	(−0.96)	(−1.71)
All cash	0.11		
	(0.16)		
All stock	0.19		
	(0.20)		
Relative deal size	2.06*	5.83**	−0.09
	(1.75)	(2.23)	(−0.02)
Diversifying acquisition	−0.09	−0.75	2.73
	(−0.15)	(−0.77)	(1.43)
High tech	0.16	0.84	1.09
	(0.18)	(0.64)	(0.47)
Constant	−24.65	−22.97	−11.40
	(−1.35)	(−0.84)	(−0.12)
Observations	598	161	93
Adj. R^2	0.0775	0.136	0.187

The dependent variable is the acquirer's 5-day CAR. Variable definitions are in the appendix. All regressions include year dummies, and standard errors are heteroskedasticity robust. ***, **, and * indicate significance at the 1%, 5%, and 10% level, respectively.

debt value. Bharadwaj and Shivadasani (2003) examine how the source of financing for cash-tender offers affects the acquirers' returns and find that bank financing has a significantly more positive relationship with the acquirer's announcement return than does internal cash financing. We expect the effect of the lead share on the acquirer returns is stronger in cash deals and that it has less effect in all-equity deals. The results in Table 6 confirm this prediction. Table 6 shows that the predicted lead share has a significantly positive coefficient of 1.17 in the subsample regression of cash deals only, which is about 1.6 times greater than the coefficient of the whole sample regression, 0.71. The coefficient of the predicted lead share for all-equity deals is -0.50, which is not significantly different from 0.

CONCLUDING REMARKS

This chapter provides empirical evidence of the relationship between creditors' level of monitoring and acquirers' announcement abnormal returns. This chapter empirically examines the disciplining role of creditors in the corporate finance decision-making process in the United States. In particular, we use the syndicated loan structure to examine the effect of bank monitoring on the profitability of acquisitions. M&As are among the most important corporate finance decisions that a firm makes.

We explore the predicted value of the lead share to account for the factors that can affect both the abnormal returns and the lead shares. We first predict lead share by using the characteristics of the syndicated loans, and then we use the predicted value for the lead share as a proxy for the monitoring level. We find that the lead share has a significantly positive effect on the acquirer's returns, which means that the lead arranger's monitoring adds value to acquisitions. The effect of the lead share on the acquirer's returns becomes pronounced when acquisition deals are paid in cash and when loan contracts have financial covenants.

Our results indicate that lead arrangers are more interested in cash M&A deals, that they make an effort to monitor these deals, and that financial covenants improve the efficiency of monitoring activities. Our results further suggest that lead arrangers are important not only for monitoring loans but also for successful acquisitions by borrowers. These main findings of this chapter suggest an important policy implication that policy makers should design financial covenants to improve the efficiency of monitoring activities by the lead bank in syndicated bank loan deals.

NOTES

1. On the other hand, a few studies report that the impact of the termination (or reduction) of durable banking relationship on the borrower's returns is negative (Dahiya, Puri, & Saunders, 2002; Slovin, Sushka, & Polonchek, 1993).

2. One exception is the study by Jung, Minetti, and Yun (2012), which finds that the borrowers of loan syndicates underperform if the lead bank retains a larger share or if a loan syndicate has more concentrated structure, contrary to our findings that monitoring of the lead bank increases firm value.

3. For example, see Lang, Stulz, and Walking (1991), Servaes (1991), and Moeller et al. (2004).

REFERENCES

Almazan, A., & Suarez, J. (2003). Managerial compensation and the market reaction to bank loans. *Review of Financial Studies*, *16*, 237–261.

Amihud, Y., Lev, B., & Travlos, N. G. (1990). Corporate control and the choice of investment financing: The case of corporate acquisitions. *Journal of Finance*, *45*, 603–616.

Asquith, P., Bruner, R. F., & Mullins, D. W. (1983). The gains to bidding firms from merger. *Journal of Financial Economics*, *11*, 121–139.

Bharadwaj, A., & Shivdasani, A. (2003). Valuation effects of bank financing in acquisitions. *Journal of Financial Economics*, *67*, 113–148.

Billett, M. T., Flannery, M. J., & Garfinkel, J. A. (1995). The effect of lender identity on a borrowing firm's equity return. *Journal of Finance*, *50*, 699–718.

Boyd, J. H., & Prescott, E. C. (1986). Financial intermediary-coalitions. *Journal of Economic Theory*, *38*, 211–232.

Campa, J. M., & Kedia, S. (2002). Explaining the diversification discount. *Journal of Finance*, *57*, 1731–1762.

Chava, S., & Roberts, M. R. (2008). How does financing impact investment? The role of debt covenants. *Journal of Finance*, *63*, 2085–2121.

Chen, X., Harford, J., & Li, K. (2007). Monitoring: Which institutions matter?. *Journal of Financial Economics*, *86*, 279–305.

Dahiya, S., Puri, M., & Saunders, A. (2002). Bank borrowers and loan sales: New evidence on the uniqueness of bank loans. *Journal of Business*, *76*, 563–582.

Dennis, S. A., & Mullineaux, D. J. (2000). Syndicated loans. *Journal of Financial Intermediation*, *9*, 404–426.

Diamond, D. (1984). Financial intermediation and delegated monitoring. *Review of Economic Studies*, *51*, 393–414.

Diamond, D. (1991). Monitoring and reputation: The choice between bank loans and privately placed debt. *Journal of Political Economy*, *99*, 689–721.

Fuller, K., Netter, J., & Stegemoller, M. (2002). What do returns to acquiring firms tell us? Evidence from firms that make many acquisitions. *Journal of Finance*, *57*, 1763–1794.

Garleanu, N., & Zwiebel, J. (2009). Design and renegotiation of debt covenants. *Review of Financial Studies*, *22*, 749–781.

Gopalan, R., Nanda, V., & Yerramilli, V. (2011). Does poor performance damage the reputation of financial intermediaries? Evidence from the loan syndication market. *Journal of Finance*, *66*, 2083–2120.

Ivashina, V. (2009). Asymmetric information effects on loan spreads. *Journal of Financial Economics*, *92*, 300–319.

James, C. (1987). Some evidence on the uniqueness of bank loans. *Journal of Financial Economics*, *19*, 217–235.

Jensen, M. C. (1986). Agency costs of free cash flow, corporate finance, and takeovers. *American Economic Review*, *76*, 323–329.

Jung, D., Minetti R., & Yun, S. (2012). *The effect of monitoring on the ex post performance of borrowers*. Working Paper. Michigan State University.

Lang, L. H. P., Stulz, R. M., & Walkling, R. A. (1991). A test of the free cash flow hypothesis: The case of bidder returns. *Journal of Financial Economics*, *29*, 315–336.

Lee, S. W., & Mullineaux, D. J. (2004). Monitoring, financial distress, and the structure of commercial lending syndicates. *Financial Management*, *33*, 107–130.

Lee, S. W., Kwag, A., Mullineaux, D. J., & Park, K. (2010). Financial distress, information asymmetry, and syndicate structure: Evidence from Japanese borrowers. *Finance Research Letters*, *7*, 119–126.

Loughran, T., & Ritter, J. (2004). Why has IPO underpricing changed over time?. *Financial Management*, *33*, 5–37.

Lummer, S. L., & McConnell, J. J. (1989). Further evidence on the bank lending process and the capital-market response to bank loan agreements. *Journal of Financial Economics*, *25*, 99–122.

Masulis, R. W., Wang, C., & Xie, F. (2007). Corporate governance and acquirer returns. *The Journal of Finance*, *62*, 1851–1889.

Moeller, S. B., Schlingemann, F. P., & Stulz, R. M. (2004). Firm size and the gains from acquisitions. *Journal of Financial Economics*, *73*, 201–228.

Morck, R., Shleifer, A., & Vishny, R. W. (1990). Do managerial incentives drive bad acquisitions? *Journal of Finance*, *45*, 31–48.

Myers, M. C., & Majluf, N. S. (1984). Corporate financing and investment decisions when firms have information that investors do not have. *Journal of Financial Economics*, *13*, 187–221.

Nini, G., Smith, D. C., & Sufi, A. (2012). Creditor control rights, corporate governance, and firm value. *Review of Financial Studies*, *25*, 1713–1761.

Rajan, R., & Winton, A. (1995). Covenants and collateral as incentives to monitor. *Journal of Finance*, *50*, 1113–1146.

Roll, R. (1986). The hubris hypothesis of corporate takeovers. *Journal of Business*, *59*, 197–216.

Servaes, H. (1991). Tobin's *Q* and the gains from takeover. *Journal of Finance*, *46*, 409–419.

Shleifer, A., & Vishny, E. W. (1986). Large shareholders and corporate control. *Journal of Political Economy*, *94*, 461–88.

Shleifer, A., & Vishny, R. W. (1997). A survey of corporate governance. *Journal of Finance*, *52*, 737–783.

Simons, K. (1993). Why do banks syndicate loans? *New England Economic Review of the Federal Reserve Bank of Boston*, 45–52.

Slovin, M. J., Sushka, M. E., & Polonchek, J. A. (1993). The value of bank durability: Borrowers as bank stakeholders. *Journal of Finance*, *48*, 247–266.

Sufi, A. (2007). Information asymmetry and financing arrangements: Evidence from syndicated loans. *Journal of Finance*, *62*, 629–668.

Travlos, N. G. (1987). Corporate takeover bids, methods of payment, and bidding firms' stock returns. *Journal of Finance*, *52*, 943–963.

Villalonga, B. (2004a). Diversification discount or premium? New evidence from the business information tracking series. *Journal of Finance*, *59*, 479–506.

Villalonga, B. (2004b). Does diversification cause the "diversification discount?" *Financial Management*, *33*, 5–27.

APPENDIX: DEFINITIONS OF THE VARIABLES USED IN THE ESTIMATION

Variable	Definitions
Dependent variable	
CAR (−2, +2)	Five-day cumulative return (in percentage points) calculated using the market model. The market model parameters are estimated over the period (−210, −11) with the CRSP equally weighted return as the market index.
Syndicated loan characteristics	
Lead share	The share of the loan that is retained by lead arranger at loan origination. In the case of more than one lead arranger, the sum of the shares is taken (%).
Facility amount	Size of the largest facility within loan package that starts at the loan origination date.
Loan amount	Size of the loan package that starts at the loan origination date.
Maturity	Maturity of the largest facility within loan package that starts at the loan origination date (months).
Number of lenders	The total number of lenders on a loan facility.
Collateral	Dummy variable: 1 if the loan is secured, 0 otherwise.
Financial covenants	Dummy variable: 1 if the loan has financial covenants, 0 otherwise.
Performance pricing	Dummy variable: 1 if the loan has performance pricing, 0 otherwise.
Purpose: corporate	Dummy variable: 1 if the purpose of loan is corporate purpose, working capital, or capital expenditure, 0 otherwise.
Purpose: acquisition	Dummy variable: 1 if the purpose of loan is takeover, LBO, or LBO/LMO, 0 otherwise.
Purpose: refinancing	Dummy variable: 1 if the purpose of loan is debt repayment, or recapitalization, 0 otherwise.
Purpose: backup line	Dummy variable: 1 if the purpose of loan is commercial paper back up, of acquisition line, 0 otherwise.
Purpose: other	Dummy variable: 1 if the purpose of loan is other purpose.
1 > tranche indicator	Dummy variable: 1 if the loan has multiple tranche, 0 otherwise.
Term loan	Dummy variable: 1 if the loan includes term loan, 0 otherwise.
Firm characteristics (bidder characteristics, borrower characteristics)	
Assets	Book value of total assets [data6].
Market value of equity	Number of shares outstanding multiplied by the stock price at the 11th trading day prior to announcement date.
Tobin's *Q*	Market value of assets [data6−data60 + data25 × data199] over book value of assets [data6].
Free cash flow	Operating income before depreciation [data13] − interest expenses [data15] − income taxes [item16]− capital expenditures [data128], scaled by book value of total assets [data6].
Leverage	Book value of debts [data34 + data9] over market value of total assets [data6 − data60 + data25 × data199].

Appendix *(Continued)*

Variable	Definitions
Stock price runup	Bidder's buy-and-hold abnormal return (BHAR) during the period (−210, −11). The market index is the CRSP value-weighted return.
Relationship	Dummy variable: 1 if the lead bank was a lead bank of the firm in previous three years, 0 otherwise
Rated	Dummy variable: 1 if the firm's S&P senior debt is rated at close of the loan, 0 otherwise
M&A deal characteristics	
Public target	Dummy variable: 1 for public targets, 0 otherwise.
Private target	Dummy variable: 1 for private targets, 0 otherwise.
Subsidiary target	Dummy variable: 1 for subsidiary targets, 0 otherwise.
All-cash deal	Dummy variable: 1 for purely cash-financed deals, 0 otherwise
All-stock deal	Dummy variable: 1 for purely stock-financed deals, 0 otherwise
Relative deal size	Deal value (from SDC) over bidder market value of equity defined above.
Diversifying acquisition	Dummy variable:1 if bidder and target do not share a Fama-French industry, 0 otherwise
High tech	Dummy variable: 1 if bidder and target both from high-tech industries defined by Loughran and Ritter (2004), 0 otherwise.

SUBJECT INDEX